Footprint Croat

Jane Foster
4th edition

"It was still distant by half a mile or so, but the scent of myrtle and rosemary and thyme was as strong and soothing a delight as sunshine. Through this lovely invisible cloud we rode slowly into the harbor of Rab, and found ourselves in one of the most beautiful cities of the world."

Rebecca West, *Black Lamb and Grey Falcon* (1942)

❶ Grožnjan
A medieval walled hill town, colonized by artists, page 127.

❷ Poreč
Croatia's most visited seaside resort, noted for its Byzantine mosaics, page 117.

❸ Rovinj
A colourful fishing town much loved by artists, page 114.

❹ Brijuni National Park
Landscaped parkland on an island that was once Tito's private residence, page 108.

❺ Vrbnik
A small town perched on a cliff and renowned for its wine cellars, page 154.

❻ Plitvice Lakes National Park
A series of blue and emerald lakes connected by cascades and waterfalls, page 97.

❼ Rab Town
A medieval stone town with four elegant bell towers, page 169.

❽ Krka National Park
A series of waterfalls running through a steep-sided wooded canyon, page 224.

❾ Kornati National Park
A vast seascape of scattered islands that's best explored by yacht, page 189.

❿ Split
A city within the walls of an impressive Roman palace, page 198.

Croatia

See colour maps at back of book

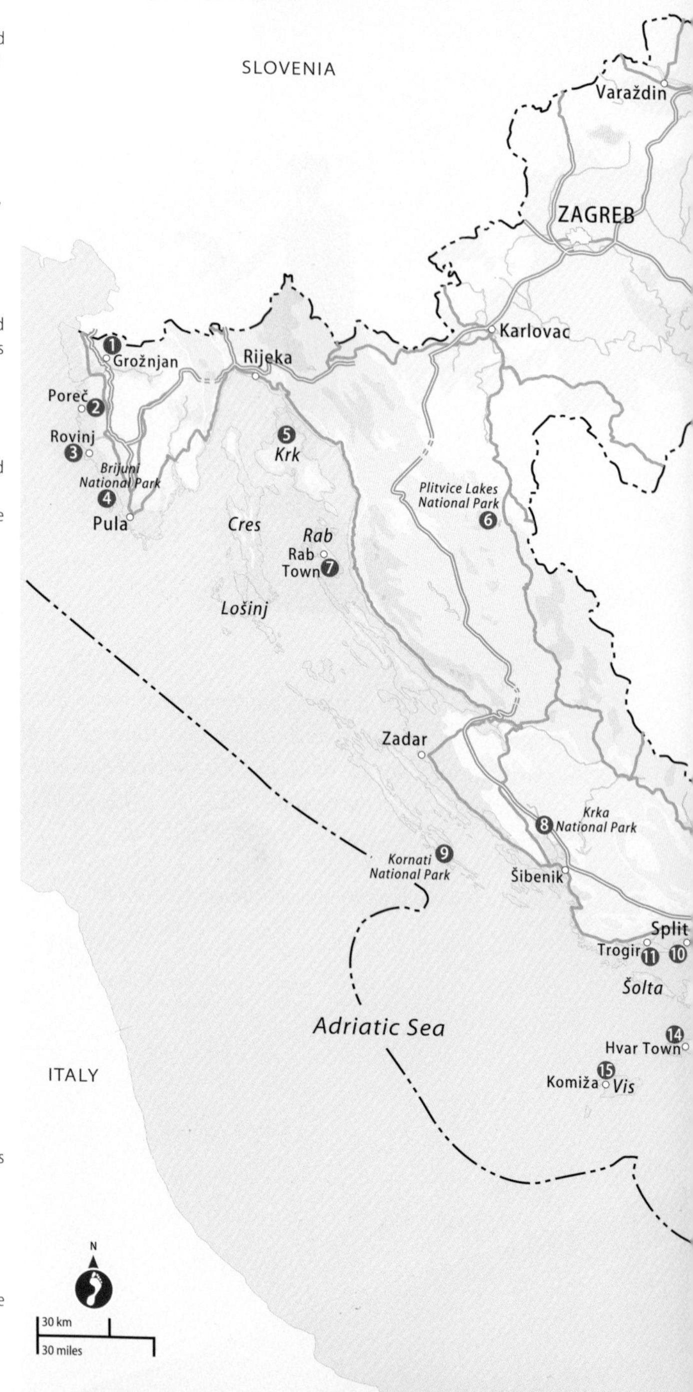

11 Trogir
A medieval city on a small island, accessed from the mainland by bridge, page 214.

12 Mount Biokovo
Climb to the top for stunning views west to Italy and east to Bosnia, page 235.

13 Zlatni Rat
The most photographed beach in Croatia, page 242.

14 Hvar Town
The island's most fashionable resort: yachts and late-night bars, page 249.

15 Komiža
An unspoilt fishing village on the island of Vis, page 264.

16 Korčula Town
A beautifully preserved medieval town on a small peninsula, page 296.

17 Orebić
A cheerful coastal village with a long sandy beach, close to the *Dingač* vineyards, page 291.

18 Mljet National Park
Two connected salt-water lakes surrounded by dense pine forest, page 310.

19 Lopud
A tiny car-free island with two small family-run hotels and a sand beach, close to Dubrovnik, page 282.

20 Dubrovnik
The 'Pearl of the Adriatic': a UNESCO-listed medieval walled city, page 272.

Rovinj

Its beauty and easy-going atmosphere have long made Rovinj popular with Croatian and Italian artists, writers, musicians and actors.

Contents

North Dalmatia

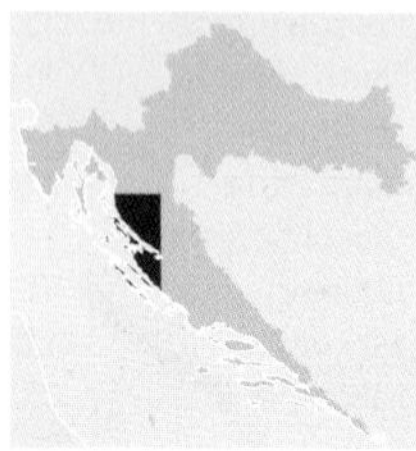

Central Dalmatia

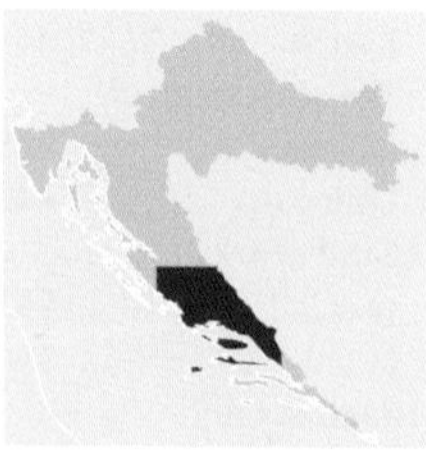

South Dalmatia

Background

Footnotes

Dubrovnik
One of the world's finest and best-preserved fortified cities; visit the historic sites or come for a sunbathe and a swim.

Plitvice Lakes National Park
Croatia's oldest national park, Plitvice is home to 16 emerald-green lakes connected by a series of spectacular waterfalls, stretching 8 km in length.

A foot in the door

Croatia is a country of rugged limestone mountains, crystal-clear water and over a thousand islands (48 of which are inhabited). Think blues and greens: sea and islands, lakes and pine forests, rivers and meadows. Justly proud of her natural and architectural heritage, Croatia ensures that any new buildings along the coast will only enhance its beauty. Stone predominates, be it in the rugged slopes that back the Dalmatian shores, in the dry-stone walls that criss-cross the islands, or in the traditional architecture. In many areas, local fishermen still sail heavy wooden fishing boats and read the weather in the cloud formations, and if you visit Pelješac you will see donkeys still being used during the harvest. In summer, the islands are scented with indigenous Mediterranean herbs such as rosemary and sage, and the stalls in the open-air markets are stacked with freshly picked tomatoes, peppers, peaches and figs. In winter, the air carries a bracing chill, the mountains are snow capped and locals drink stiff home-made liquor to keep warm.

Traces of the war are fading fast, with only the omnipresent red, white and blue flags bearing witness to the nationalist fervour that lead to the break up of former-Yugoslavia. A nation of natural athletes, today Croats display their colours with pride on the football pitch and tennis court, and, if you try to come up with the names of well-known Croats, the majority of them will probably be from the world of sport.

Visitors will be struck by the apparent impenetrability of the Croatia language, with its mysterious Slavic sounds, abundance of consonants and charming *hačeks*. Luckily for travellers, many Croats speak several foreign languages, including English, Italian and German. However, if you make the effort to learn a few new words, your trip will be all the more enjoyable.

Croatia today

Croatia has come a long way since the 1990s. Now firmly in line to be the next country to join the European Union, which it may enter as early as 2010, its politicians have made concerted efforts to recreate the nation's image and to gain international credibility by handing over war criminals to The Hague. The economy is fast being 'rationalized' with the privatization of state companies and the opening up of the property market to foreign buyers.

The country's economy lies largely in tourism, and current trends point towards a select, high-class range of accommodation and activities, very different from the package tourism of the 1970s.

Since 2004, Croatia has seen the opening of several chic design hotels with Wellness Centres, and a good selection of small, family-run hotels

Dubrovnik market
The open-air fruit and vegetable markets are animated, colourful affairs, well worth a look round to check out local seasonal produce.

offering personalized hospitality, and an ever-increasing number of agrotourism centres providing cosy rooms and home-made meals on working farms. The best restaurants purvey local dishes prepared with seasonal, organically produced ingredients and many of the wines are also organic.

Activities on offer include sailing, scuba-diving and sea kayaking along the coast, plus adventure sports such as rafting, canyoning and free climbing inland. During the summer, many towns organize cultural festivals, staging classical music, opera, theatre and dance below the stars. The largest of these, Dubrovnik and Split summer festivals, attract internationally renowned performers. And summer nightlife continues well into the small hours with open-air cocktail bars and waterside dance clubs.

Diocletian's Palace, Split

The south façade of the palace, which once rose directly from the sea, is now beside a coastal promenade lined with cafés and palm trees known to locals as the Riva.

1
2
4
5
7
8
10
11

3

6

9

12

1 *The coastal road from Rijeka to Dubrovnik winds its way high above the sea.* ▸▸ *See page 30.*

2 *Some of Croatia's finest wines come from the vineyards of southern Hvar, where the pace of life is slow and relaxed.* ▸▸ *See page 256.*

3 *Rab Town's four elegant bell towers line the crest of a narrow peninsula; climb to the top of one for a spectacular panorama over the town.* ▸▸ *See page 169.*

4 *Rovinj old town is a labyrinth of narrow cobbled streets flanked by densely packed medieval houses.* ▸▸ *See page 114.*

5 *Paklenica National Park is one of the best places for free climbing in Croatia.* ▸▸ *See page 186.*

6 *Some of the best shellfish, notably oysters and mussels, can be found in Ston on Pelješac Peninsula in South Dalmatia.* ▸▸ *See page 36.*

7 *Poreč town is a cluster of Venetian-style terracotta-roofed houses, and is Istria's most visited seaside resort.* ▸▸ *See page 117.*

8 *Unique to Carnival in Rijeka and the surrounding villages, Zvončari chase away the forces of evil and invite the coming of spring.* ▸▸ *See page 142.*

9 *The Arena in Pula is a first-century Roman amphitheatre; it is the sixth-largest building of its type in the world.* ▸▸ *See page 106.*

10 *A Venetian fortress crowns the highest peak in Hvar Town, and from the ramparts you have fantastic views out across the sea.* ▸▸ *See page 249.*

11 *With so many islands, the deep clean sea and the moderate winds, Croatia is a sailor's paradise.* ▸▸ *See page 23.*

12 *Krk is one of the most accessible of the Croatian islands.* ▸▸ *See page 151.*

Forza Roma

The Romans colonized the region 2000 years ago, building military camps and trading ports. Their finest surviving monuments are the imposing amphitheatre in Pula, where gladiators and early Christians once confronted lions, and Diocletian's Palace in Split, where subjects would fall to their knees upon the appearance of their former emperor. Today the Pula amphitheatre still arouses cheers from the public with rock concerts and an annual film festival while Diocletian's Palace is a labyrinth of medieval streets, packed with coffee bars and chic boutiques.

Within these walls

The coastal resorts of Poreč, Hvar and Korčula owe their appearance to the Venetians, who built them as ports of call for trade ships en route to the Black Sea. Although the harbours are now filled with fishing boats, water taxis and flashy yachts, the historic centres, surrounded by defensive walls, take you back through the centuries. The narrow, pedestrian-only flagstone streets open onto marble piazzas ringed by open-air cafés. The queen of all the walled cities is Dubrovnik, built not by Venice but by her own citizens.

The big blue

With 1778 km of mainland coast (5790 km counting the islands), finding a place to lie in the sun and swim in sapphire-blue sea isn't a problem. During the 20th century, when tourists first started to visit Croatia, it wasn't the cultural attractions that brought them to these shores, but the shores

Close to the seafront, Šibenik's main sight is the monumental Renaissance Cathedral of St Jacob, which is included on the UNESCO list of World Heritage Sites.

Natural beauty and lack of commercial development make the island of Mljet a wonderful escape for those in search of peace and tranquillity.

themselves. The golden shingle beach of Zlatni Rat on Brač and the curving sands of Baška on Krk, with their sunbeds and coloured umbrellas, are featured in all the glossy brochures, and indeed they are splendid. But better still are the undiscovered coves, backed by terraced vineyards and olive groves, where the rocky shoreline gives way to smooth white pebbles, and the only sound you'll hear will be the lapping of the sea.

Breaking the waves

Sailing along the coast aboard a yacht is probably the finest way to explore Croatia. A day at the mercy of the wind and waves is exhausting but experiencing the open sea, eating in the open air and slumbering to the gentle movements of the tide is guaranteed to replenish the body and soul. It also gives you unlimited freedom as you can anchor wherever you wish: in a sophisticated resort where you can feast on lobster and wine, or at an isolated island where you are guaranteed peace and solitude.

The rural way

For those who prefer terra firma, Croatia has excellent hiking paths. Some, such as Velika Paklenica canyon, lead into the rugged karst mountains, while others take you inland to meet the rapids and cascades of Krka and Plitvice waterfalls. Official routes are clearly marked, while many of the islands are criss-crossed by old donkey paths, running between villages through vineyards and olive groves; you may even find one that leads to a deserted bay.

Island of Korčula
Medieval Korčula Town is often referred to as a 'mini-Dubrovnik', terracotta-roofed houses perched above the sea on a peninsula fortified with walls and round towers.

Essentials

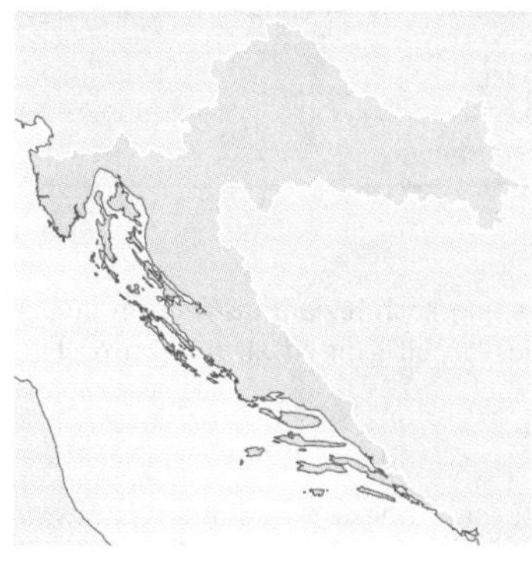

Footprint features

Planning your trip

Where to go

Croatia offers a wide variety of landscapes and each region has its own unique characteristics. However, for most people the real pull is the coast, and above all the islands.

One week

If you are short of time and planning to spend a week or less here it is best to concentrate on one area. Take either Istria, Central Dalmatia or South Dalmatia, and use a coastal town as a main regional base.

In Istria, the most popular region with the best tourist facilities, Pula, Poreč or Rovinj each warrant a visit. You could choose one of them as your base, and use it for making day trips to the islands of Brijuni National Park and the inland hill towns of Motovun and Grožnjan.

In Central Dalmatia, the monumental Roman city of Split is an ideal starting point for exploring the islands of Brač, Hvar and Vis, as well the nearby coastal towns of Trogir and Makarska and the inland village of Klis.

In South Dalmatia, the walled city of Dubrovnik will undoubtedly absorb two or three days of sightseeing, as well as serving as a launching pad for visiting the Elaphiti islands, Mljet National Park, the coastal resort of Cavtat and Trsteno Arboretum. ▸▸ *For planning a week's sailing, see opposite.*

Two weeks

If you have two weeks at your disposal, the number of options opens up considerably. To understand the country's complexity, spend some time in the capital, Zagreb, a city culturally and geographically closer to Vienna and Budapest than to the Venetian-influenced coastal region. Having visited the city's museums and churches, devote a couple of days to the rural villages and medieval castles of Zagorje, and the small baroque city of Varaždin.

From Zagreb, you could take the overnight train directly down to Split to visit Dalmatia, and follow the itineraries mentioned above. Alternatively, take a bus or train to Rijeka in the Kvarner region. Close by lie the restful seaside resorts of Opatija and Lovran, made up of elegant Vienna Secession-style hotels and villas. From Rijeka port there are direct boat lines to the islands of Rab, Cres and Lošinj, each of which offer unspoilt nature and endless opportunities for bathing, watersports and hiking. From Rijeka there are regular overnight ferries and daytime buses down the coast to Split and Dubrovnik in Dalmatia.

One month

North Dalmatia is in many ways less attractive than Central and South Dalmatia, but if you have three weeks or more in Croatia it may be worth a visit, particularly if you enjoy unspoilt nature parks. The chief city, Zadar, is renowned for its Romanesque churches. Close by, Kornati National Park is a haven of small uninhabited rocky islands, while a day hiking in Paklenica National Park will give you a taste of the mountains. The region's most interesting island is Pag, home to the delicious *paški sir* (sheep's cheese).

Finally, Slavonia, the easternmost region of Croatia, has little of great interest to holidaymakers, but if you want to get a complete picture of the country and its recent tragic history, the largely devastated town of Vukovar, sitting on the west bank of the

River Danube, illustrates better than anywhere else the suffering caused by the war for independence. Neighbouring Osijek is a more cheerful place to spend the night, and makes an ideal starting point for visiting Kopački Rit Nature Park.

Sailing itinerary

A week aboard a sailing boat gives you the freedom to explore the mainland coast and islands in direct contact with the sea. You can devise your own route, discover hidden coves with deserted beaches accessible only from the water, or moor up for a night in the harbour of a pretty fishing village or in one of Croatia's 50 sophisticated marinas. Croatia offers perfect training ground for inexperienced sailors as the islands run parallel to the mainland coast, affording easy line-of-sight navigation and island- hopping in protected waters.

The main centre for charter companies is Split in Central Dalmatia. If you charter a boat from Split you could spend a week exploring the region following this itinerary: **Day 1**: Set sail from Split to Maslinica on the island of Šolta (15 nm). **Day 2**: Maslinica to Vis Town on the island of Vis (22 nm). **Day 3**: Sail around Vis, from Vis Town to Komiža, stopping at Biševo en route (16 nm). **Day 4**: Komiža to Hvar Town on the island of Hvar (26 nm). **Day 5**: Hvar Town to Bol on the island of Brač (19 nm). **Day 6**: Bol to Milna on the island of Brač. **Day 7**: Early-morning departure from Milna to Split (12 nm).

There are countless other options, each region offering its own peculiarities. In South Dalmatia you could include Dubrovnik and the islands of Korčula, Mljet and the Elaphiti in your itinerary, while if you set sail from Pula in Istria you could also explore the islands of the Kvarner Gulf. Remember that Croatia has three national parks on the sea that can be visited by sailing boat: Brijuni (an archipelago of 14 green islets in Istria), Kornati (an archipelago of 89 arid rocky islands, islets and reefs in North Dalmatia) and Mljet (a large fertile island in South Dalmatia, much of which is covered with coniferous forest). In addition, Krka National Park (a series of waterfalls that cascade through a deep canyon in Central Dalmatia) can be approached by boat, sailing up the Šibenik Channel as far as Skradin.

When to go

Peak season runs from July to August, which is when most Germans and Italians take their summer holidays. On the upside, nightlife is at its most animated, with open-air cultural performances – the top events being the Summer Festivals in Dubrovnik and Split – and outdoor cocktail bars and dance clubs along the coast. On the downside, the beaches can be horribly crowded and restaurants and bars so busy you may have to queue for a table. Accommodation prices also rise steeply during this period, and availability may be scarce, so you should really book a place to stay in advance.

Mid-season (May to June and September to October) is probably the most rewarding time to visit. Throughout June and September the sea is warm enough to swim (hardier types will also manage in May and October) and the beaches reasonably peaceful. Hotels and restaurants are open but not overly busy, so you'll tend to get more personalized service. As temperatures are not unbearably hot, this is an ideal time for active land sports such as hiking and biking. Spring and autumn are also the best moments to catch local delicacies: wild asparagus and cherries in late April, and mushrooms, truffles and chestnuts in early October.

During low season, November to April, many restaurants and hotels on the islands close down completely. Although you can't be guaranteed good weather, if you do visit Croatia during this period you can be almost certain there will be few foreigners around.

The Adriatic coast is blessed with a Mediterranean climate. The summers are warm, dry and brilliantly sunny, with July temperatures averaging 25°C in Dubrovnik, while winters are mild and rainy, with January temperatures averaging 9°C. In contrast, inland Croatia has a continental climate, with hot summers – July temperatures average 24°C in Zagreb – and cold winters, temperatures averaging 0°C throughout January.

Activities and tours

With a rugged indented coastline, countless islands and a pleasant Mediterranean climate, Croatia is a great place for sunbathing and swimming. The water is crystal clear, has a classic emerald-blue colour and can reach temperatures of up to 27°C in summer. This also makes it a popular destination for watersports and diving. With so many islands, the deep clean sea and the moderate winds, Croatia is a sailor's paradise. A total of 50 fully equipped modern marinas line the coast all the way from Umag in the north to Dubrovnik in the south, while temporary mooring facilities are available along the seafront in most coastal towns and villages, and there are plenty of deserted bays, ideal for dropping anchor and bathing in total solitude. Croatia also offers some good cycling, hiking and climbing.

Beaches and bathing

Along the coast and on the islands, 117 beaches have been awarded the **Blue Flag**, www.blueflag.org, a European eco-label indicating high environmental standards as well as good sanitary and safety facilities. Beware of large modern hotels that claim to have a beach out front – in reality this is often no more than a concrete bathing area giving easy access into the water. The general rule with Croatian beaches is the more difficult it is to reach, the more worthwhile the journey; many of the most stunning beaches are accessible only by boat.

★ Head for ...

Baška (island of Krk) ▸▸ *p151* **Lopar** (island of Rab) ▸▸ *p167* **Makarska Rivijera** ▸▸ *p235* **Zlatni Rat** (island of Brač) ▸▸ *p242*

Birdwatching

Still relatively undeveloped, there are some excellent opportunities for spotting rare species in beautiful surroundings.

★ Head for ...

Lonjsko Polje Nature Park ▸▸ *p85* **Kopački Rit Nature Park** ▸▸ *p90* **Cres Town** ▸▸ *p158* **Paklenica National Park** ▸▸ *p186* **Biograd-na-Moru** ▸▸ *p188*

ⓘ **Eco-Centar Caput Insulae**, www.supovi.hr.

Cycling and mountain biking

Local tourist boards have begun designating bike routes, though there is plenty of scope for further development. Mountain bikes are generally available for rent in places suitable for cycling, either from agencies that specialize in hiring bikes, mopeds and boats, or from large hotels with extensive sporting facilities. Expect to pay around 20Kn for an hour or 100Kn for a day.

If you are planning on taking your own bicycle, it is worth noting that on overnight ferries from Italy to Croatia bikes travel free (you just pay the passenger ticket), but some local ferries between the mainland and the islands add a small surcharge for bikes.

★ Head for ...

Rovinj ▸▸ *p123* **Novigrad** ▸▸ *p124* **Labin** ▸▸ *p132* **Rab** ▸▸ *p172* **Hvar** ▸▸ *p248* **Mljet** ▸▸ *p270*

ⓘ **Skedaddle Tours**, T0191-265 1110, www.skedaddle.co.uk. Offer biking tours of rural and coastal Istria staying in agrotourism farmhouses.

Agencies specializing in adventure sports, including organized cycling tours, include: **Big Blue**, Podan Glavice 2, Bol, Island of Brač, T021-635614, www.big-blue-sport.hr; **Huck Finn**, Vukovarska 271, Zagreb, T01-618 3333, www.huck-finn.hr; **Marco Polo**, Mažuranić 25, Rovinj, T052- 816955, www.marcopolo.hr.

★ Top ten dive sites

1 **Baron Gautsch** (near Rovinj) A passenger ferry wreck from 1914; suitable for advanced divers only, depth 28-42 m.
2 **Lina** (island of Cres) A merchant shipwreck; suitable for advanced divers only, depth 22-55 m.
3 **Margarina** (island of Susak) An underwater reef and canyon with amphorae and a shipwreck; beginner to advanced levels, depth 5-40 m.
4 **Rasip** (Kornati islands) An underwater cliff with corals, sponges and schools of fish, excellent visibility up to 40 m; beginner to advanced levels, depth 3-65 m.
5 **Stambedar** (Pakleni otoci, near Hvar Town) A sea wall with red and violet gorgonians (type of coral); beginner to advanced levels, depth 5-45 m.
6 **Te Vega** (island of Sušac, between Korčula and Lastovo) A small sea lake entered through a 2-m-long tunnel; beginner to advanced levels, depth 5-35 m.
7 **Modra Spilja** (island of Biševo, close to the island of Vis) A sea cave; beginner to advanced levels, depth 3-40 m.
8 **S57** (Pelješac Peninsula) A well-preserved German torpedo shipwreck from 1944; suitable for advanced divers only, depth 25-39 m.
9 **Taranto** (Dubrovnik) A merchant shipwreck from 1943; suitable for advanced divers only, depth 23-55 m.
10 **Sv Andrija** (Elafiti islands, near Dubrovnik) A sea wall with red coral and a cave at a depth of 26 m; beginner to advanced levels, depth 3-78 m.

Diving

Along the coast you will find a total of 150 diving clubs offering lessons (with multilingual instructors), guided tours and rental equipment. To dive in Croatia, you need to hold a valid diver's card issued by the **Hrvatski Ronilački Savez** (Croatian Diving Federation). These can be obtained from all recognized Croatian diving clubs, are valid for one year as of the date of issue, and were priced at 100Kn (€15) in spring 2008. Expect to pay 2250Kn (€300) for a 1-week diving educational programme, or if you are already experienced, 330Kn (€45) for an organized group dive with a qualified guide (including equipment rental) or 220Kn (€30) for the same tour using your own equipment.

★ Head for ...
Rovinj ⏩ *p123* **Krk Town** ⏩ *p156* **Hvar** ⏩ *p248* **Vis** ⏩ *p261* **Dubrovnik** ⏩ *p284* **Korčula** ⏩ *p285*

ⓘ **Dive Tours**, Total Diving Solutions Ltd, 46 Watergate St, Chester CH1 2LA, T01244-401177, www.divetours.co.uk. Organize diving holidays throughout the world, with a base in Korčula, Croatia.
Hrvatski Ronilački Savez, Dalmatinska 12, Zagreb, T01-484 8765, www.diving-hrs.hr.
Pro Diving Croatia, Bulevar Oslobodjenja 23, Rijeka, T051-219111, www.diving.hr.

Hiking and climbing

Croatia's unspoilt nature, varied landscapes ranging from slopes supporting meadowland and forests ideal for gentle hiking to steep grey cliffs ideal for free climbing, plus a pleasant mild and reasonably dry climate through spring and autumn, make it a great place to explore on foot. The majority of mountains belong to the Dinaric range, and although none are over 2000 m, they require the same efforts from the climber as many much higher mountains thanks to their rugged rocky karst landscape and sparse population. There are a number of marked trails and *planinarski dom* (mountain refuges) offering simple food and accommodation.

★ Ten highest mountains

1 **Dinara**, Central Dalmatia, 1831 m.
2 **Kamesnica**, Central Dalmatia, 1809 m.
3 **Biokovo**, Central Dalmatia, 1762 m (peak Sv Jure).
4 **Velebit**, North Dalmatia, 1758 m (peak Vaganski Vrh).
5 **Lićka Pljesivica**, Lika, 1657 m (peak Ozeblin).
6 **Velika Kapela**, Gorski kotar, Kvarner, 1534 m (peak Bjelolasica).
7 **Risnjak**, Gorski kotar, Kvarner, 1528 m.
8 **Svilaja**, Central Dalmatia, 1508 m.
9 **Snježnik**, Gorski kotar, Kvarner, 1506 m.
10 **Učka**, Istria, 1400 m (peak Vojak).

★ Head for ...
Baška (island of Krk) ▸▸ *p156* **Paklenica National Park** ▸▸ *p186* **Makarska** (Biokovo Nature Park) ▸▸ *p233* **Bol** (island of Brač) ▸▸ *p241*

ⓘ **Hrvatski Planinarski Savez** (Croatian Hiking Association), Kozarčeva 22, Zagreb, T01-4824142, www.plsavez.hr. An umbrella group for some 170 local walking clubs, can supply maps and information about mountain huts throughout the country.
Biokovo Active Holidays, Kralja P Krešimira IV 7B, Makarska, T021-679655, www.biokovo.net. Organize 1-week and 2-week hiking and climbing tours, exploring Mt Biokovo and various other regions of Croatia.
Paklenica National Park, Tudjmana 14a, Starigrad Paklenica, T023-369202, www.paklenica.hr. Can arrange guided hiking tours of Velebit.

Naturism

Organized naturist bathing began on the island of Rab in the early 20th century, and the real naturist expansion started in the 1960s when the first naturist camps opened in Istria and Dalmatia, making Croatia the first country in Europe to commercialize naked bathing. An estimated 15% of all tourists to Croatia are naturists. Most are from Germany, Austria, the Netherlands, Italy and Slovenia (Croats themselves make up less than 5% of nudists here). During the 1990s, naturism decreased significantly, a trend that many put down to the influence of the Catholic Church in society. However, naturism is still strongly supported by official Croatian government bodies: during the presidential campaign of 2000, Stipe Mesić declared himself a naturist. And he won. There are about 30 official naturist resorts and beaches, marked 'FKK', as well as countless unofficial naturist beaches, usually found in more secluded areas.

★ Head for ...
Vrsar ▸▸ *p116* **Rovinj** ▸▸ *p123*

ⓘ **Croatia Naturally**, www.cronatur.com.
Dune Leisure, 2 Market Pl, Great Dunmow, Essex CM6 1AT, T0870-751 8866, www.awaywithdune.co.uk. Specialize in naturist holidays around the world, focusing on Dalmatia in Croatia.
Peng Travel, 86 Station Rd, Gidea Park, Romford, Essex RM2 6DB, T0845-345 8345 (in UK) or T01708-471832 (from outside the UK), www.pengtravel.co.uk. Specialize in naturist holidays around the world, focusing on the Rovinj area in Croatia.

Rafting

Of all the so-called extreme sports that have emerged over the last decade, whitewater rafting is probably the most accessible to complete beginners. The best rivers for rafting in Croatia are the Dobra and the Kupa in inland Croatia, the Zrmanja in North Dalmatia, and the Cetina in Central Dalmatia.

★ Head for ...
Karlovac ▸▸ *p95* **Zadar** ▸▸ *p176* **Omiš** ▸▸ *p232*

ⓘ **Active Holidays**, Knezova Kačića bb, Omiš, T021-863015, www.activeholidays-

croatia.com. Include rafting in their programmes.
Atlas, Vukovarska 19, Dubrovnik, T020-442222, www.atlas-croatia.com.
Generalturist, Praška 5, Zagreb, T01-481 0033, www.generalturist.com. Organize 1-day rafting trips and 1-week adventure trips which include rafting.
Huck Finn, Vukovarska 271, Zagreb, T01-618 3333, www.huck-finn.hr.

Sailing

There are over 140 charter companies in Croatia, operating tens of thousands of sailing boats and motorboats of all sizes. Most companies rent yachts on a weekly basis from 1700 Sat to 0900 the following Sat. When you charter a yacht this can be bareboat (meaning you are alone) or with a skipper (a qualified yachtsman who normally knows the area well). To go bareboat you, or one of the crew, must have a sailing licence and at least two years' sailing experience. The third alternative is to sail as part of a flotilla (a group of yachts, normally between 5 and 10, with people of mixed levels of sailing experience, lead by a qualified expert). Prices vary greatly depending on the size and type of yacht, as well as the season.
›› *See page 19 for planning your itinerary.*

★ Head for ...
Zadar ›› *p176* **Split** ›› *p198* **Omiš** ›› *p232*
Dubrovknik ›› *p272*

ⓘ **Activity Yachting**, South View, Boxham Lane, Sidlesham, West Sussex PO20 7QF, T01243-641304, www.activityyachting.com. Specialize in sailing in Croatia and Turkey, offer 1-week sailing instruction, as well as skippered charter, both bareboat (1 yacht) and flotilla sailing (groups of 5-10 yachts).
Adriatic Holidays Ltd, 1 Victoria St, Oxford OX2 6BT, T01865-516577, www.adriatic holidaysonline.com. Operate with charter companies in Croatia with bases all the way down the coast from Istria to South Dalmatia. Also offer a selection of luxury villas so you can opt for 1 week aboard, 1 week on land.
Adriatic Nautical Academy (ANA), T051-711814, www.sailing-ana.hr, run an annual sailing school, Mar to Oct, based at the ACI Marina in Jezera on the island of Murter, offering intensive courses at all levels with multi-lingual instructors. They also have a summer school in Cavtat near Dubrovnik.
Club Adriatic, www.charter.hr. An on-line charter service with special low-season offers and last-minute deals on over 1300 yachts.
Cosmos Yachting, T0800 376 9070, www.cosmosyachting.com. Specialize in bareboat and crewed yacht charters, with several bases in Croatia.
Nautilus Sailing, 87 High St, Edenbridge, Kent TN8 5AU, T01732-867445, www.nautilus-yachting.com. Specialize in sailing in various parts of the world, with yacht charter bases in Pula, Zadar, Biograd, Murter, Split and Dubrovnik in Croatia.
Sail Croatia, 160 Brompton Rd, London SW3 1HW, T0871-733 8686, www.sailcroatia.net. Charter sailing boats, with or without a skipper, from their base in Split, also offer sail-and-stay, combining time afloat with time on land (islands of Hvar and Brać).
Sailing Holidays Ltd, 105 Mount Pleasant Rd, London NW10 3EH, T020-8459 8787, www.sailingholidays.co.uk. Specialize in sailing in Greece and Croatia, organize flotilla holidays with itineraries concentrating on Central Dalmatia and the Kornati Islands.
Ultra Sailing, T021-398980, www.ultra-sailing.hr. Offer courses, Mar to Oct, in Milna on the island of Brač (Central Dalmatia).

Spectator sports

For a country of only 4 million, Croatia has scored outstanding success in international sporting events. Before the country's break-up in 1991, Yugoslavia was a force to be reckoned with in sports such as football, basketball, handball and water polo, all of which remain favourite team games in Croatia today.

Football (Nogomet)

As in most countries, football is the most popular spectator sport. During the late 1990s the Croatian national team was extremely strong, reaching the quarter-final in the European Championship 1996, and coming third in the World Cup in France in 1998. The team fared less well in the World Cup 2002 and the European Championship 2004. Of late, they secured a place at the World Cup 2006, impressively beating Sweden and Bulgaria to finish top of the

European qualifying Group 8, undefeated and with eight wins out of 10 matches. In 2007, they once again finished top of their group in the Euro 2008 qualifiers, knocking England out on the way. The current national team is made up mainly of youngsters (and that includes the coach, Slaven Bilić); the old stars of the late 1990s such as Davor Šuker and Zvonimir Boban having retired. New names to look out for include Brazilian-born striker, Eduardo da Silva.

Tennis (Tenis)

Croatia's best known sportsman is probably tennis player Goran Ivanišević (born in Split in 1971) who ranked second in the world in 1992 and won the much coveted Wimbledon tournament in summer 2001. It seems he has inspired a whole new generation of players, Croatia having taken the bronze in the Men's Doubles at the Athens 2004 Olympics, represented by Ivan Ljubičić and Mario Ančić. Croatia then went on to win the international Davis Cup in 2005, thanks to Ljubičić, Ančić, plus Ivo Karlović and Goran Ivanišević (who came out of retirement to make up the national team, though he did not play).

★ Head for ...

Umag ⏩ *p119* **Bol** ⏩ *p241*

ⓘ **Croatian Football Federation**, www.hns-cff.hr; **ATP Croatia Open**, www.croatiaopen.hr; **WTA Croatia Bol Ladies Open**, www.bolladies.hr.

Windsurfing

Croatia's top windsurfing locations are Bol on the island of Brač in Central Dalmatia and Viganj on Pelješac Peninsula in South Dalmatia, both of which catch the *maestral* (wind from the northwest) through summer. Further north, the coast is less suitable for windsurfing as the main wind is the *bura* (wind from the northeast), which blows mainly through winter. The windsurfing clubs work from early Apr to late Oct. Courses are normally arranged in blocks of 2-hr lessons: expect to pay €100 for 8 hours at beginner level or €150 for 10 hours at advanced level. If you just want to rent a board, expect to pay €15 for 1 hr or €45 for 1 day, including surf shoes, harness and wetsuits.

★ Head for ...

Bol ⏩ *p241*

ⓘ **Big Blue**, Podan Glavice 2, Bol, T021-635614, www.big-blue-sport.hr; **Orca Sport**, Račić 9, Bol, T021-740625, www.orca-sport.com. Both offer courses at all levels from beginner to advanced and rent equipment to experienced surfers.

Wine tasting

Several of the better vineyards have cellars open to the public for wine tasting and direct purchasing, while a number of chic wine 'boutiques' stocking the country's best wines can be found in the larger resorts. In Istria, the tourist board have set up a network of wine routes leading to countless vineyards, wine cellars and agrotourism centres where it is possible to sample and purchase the region's wines.

★ Head for ...

Čakovec ⏩ *p81* **Vrbnik** ⏩ *p154* **Hvar** ⏩ *p248* **Vis** ⏩ *p261* **Pelješac** ⏩ *p274*

ⓘ www.istra.com/vino, for maps and contact details.

Atlas, www.atlas-croatia.com. Run 1-day wine-tasting trips from Dubrovnik to Pelješac and Korčula, plus an 8-day Wine and Gourmet Tour, travelling from Zagreb to Dubrovnik by coach.

Responsible tourism

Fortunately Croatian tourism has not been commercialized to the extent of that in Greece and Spain, and most people who come here on holiday are interested in more than drinking cheap beer and lounging by a pool.

Package tourism to the region reached its peak during the 1970s and 1980s, when large state-owned resorts were constructed along the Adriatic coast. As the boom appeared unstoppable, many locals who had traditionally lived from wine-making and

How big is your footprint?

Beaches In spring it may be warm enough to sunbathe or even swim, but many beaches will be strewn with waste. This has not been dumped intentionally, but has been washed up by the sea currents, and is usually cleaned up by locals once the holiday season gets underway. Do not leave picnic litter on beaches, no matter what state they are in when you arrive.

Cars Try to avoid taking a car to the islands – if you really want to appreciate nature to its fullest, walk or cycle instead. Alternatively, use public transport, which is cheap and (relatively) efficient, and in any case gives you a chance to meet the locals.

Date shells Known in Croatian as *prstaci* (and in Italian as *datteri*), date shells are similar to mussels but have a more refined flavour. There is a national campaign against collecting and eating them, as they grow inside rocks along the coast, and can only be obtained by smashing open the rocks, which leads to the erosion of the coast. By law restaurants are not allowed to sell them; although they will not be listed on menus, they may be on offer, at a price. However, the environmental damage caused in collecting them far outweighs the pleasure of eating them.

Fires During summer, especially along the coast, when the vegetation is bone dry, there is a constant danger of forest fire. On no account at all throw away glowing cigarette stubs, and do not light fires anywhere except in purpose-built barbecues.

Hiking paths Leave paths as you find them. If you get lost do not tramp through other people's vineyards and olive groves unnecessarily.

National parks Entrance fees are payable to national parks. Although they may seem steep, this money goes towards the upkeep of the natural environment, and is therefore money well spent.

Rubbish Getting rid of rubbish on the islands is a major problem, and on some of the tinier, more remote islands, people are expected to take their litter back to the mainland by ferry when they leave. If there are no bins in sight, check whether this is the correct procedure.

the production of olive oil abandoned their fields and invested in building concrete seaside villas with rooms and apartments to let to foreign visitors. Easy money indeed, but in many families an entire generation consequently lost the know-how of cultivating grapes and olives. Fortunately, today things are changing, and with agrotourism slowly but surely catching on, Croatians are re-evaluating the small scale production of traditional local specialities: wine, various types of *rakija*, olive oil and cheeses.

The potential for agrotourism is enormous, though to date it's only really taken off in Istria, where the tourist board have laid down certain rules, requiring farms that register themselves under this category to be built of traditional materials (eg natural stone). Grants are also becoming available, through various European organizations, for the restoration of old farm buildings and diversification into agro-tourism and ecotourism.

Getting there

Air

Croatia's main airports are Zagreb (ZAG), Split (SPU) and Dubrovnik (DBV). Flights from most European capital cities land in **Zagreb Airport** ⓘ *T01-626 5222, www.zagreb-airport.hr*. There is no tourist office here, but the travel agency **Atlas** ⓘ *T01-456 2248, daily 0700-1830*, is located in the passenger terminal building. There are two banks, **Zagrebačka banka** ⓘ *T01-456 2414*, and **Privredna banka** ⓘ *T01-456 2032*, both of which are open daily 0900-2100 and are located in the landside transit area of the Passenger Terminal Building. The post office is next to the banks and works the same hours. Other facilities include a duty-free shop, a newsagents, and a bar and restaurant. All the major international rent-a-car companies have bases here (eg **Europcar** and **Hertz**). An airport bus makes regular runs between the airport and the city centre (see page 56 for further details). Taxis are also available – expect to pay 150-200Kn over the same route.

It's also possible to take flights from most European capital cities to **Split Airport** ⓘ *T021-203171, www.split-airport.hr*. There is no tourist office in the airport. In the passenger terminal area you will find **HVB-Splitska banka**, a bank open daily 0600-1300 and 1400-2100. Close by, the post office opens 0700-2100 daily in peak season, and Monday-Friday 0700-2000 and Saturday 0700-1700 the rest of the year. Other facilities include a duty-free shop, a newsagents, and a bar and restaurant. The international rent-a-car companies **Budget** and **Hertz** have bases here. An airport bus makes regular runs between the airport and the city centre (see page 198 for further details). Taxis are also readily available.

Many European capital cities also have direct flights to **Dubrovnik Airport** ⓘ *T020-773377, www.airport-dubrovnik.hr*. There is no tourist office here, but you will find the travel agency **Atlas** ⓘ *T020-773383*. Airport facilities include a bank, a post office, a duty-free shop, a bar and **Budget** and **Hertz** car hire offices. An airport bus makes regular runs between the airport and the city centre (see page 272 for further details). Taxis are also readily available.

Pula Airport (PUY) ⓘ *T052-530105, www.airport-pula.hr*, and **Zadar Airport** (ZAD) ⓘ *T023-205800, www.zadar-airport.hr*, also have flights to and from several European capitals throughout the year, though the number of destinations and frequency of flights is reduced in winter. **Rijeka Airport** (RJK) ⓘ *T051-842040, www.rijeka-airport.hr*, **Brač Airport** (BWK) ⓘ *T021-559715; www.airport-brac.hr*, and **Osijek Airport** (OSI) ⓘ *T031-514441, www.osijek-airport.hr*, all work in summer only, and offer restricted timetables to suit the mainsteam tourist traffic.

International flights to Croatia usually arrive in Zagreb, Split or Dubrovnik, though in summer there are also lines direct to Pula, Zadar, Rijeka and Bol on the island of Brač. Fares vary greatly from airline to airline and according to the time of year. To get the best deals avoid peak time travel (Monday mornings, Friday evenings and bank holidays) when tickets are at their most expensive. Generally, cheaper flights depart mid-morning or mid-afternoon. Check the following websites for cheap deals: www.bargain flights.com; www.travelmood.com; www.lastminute.co.uk; www.statravel.co.uk.

From the UK and the rest of Europe

Through winter, **Croatia Airlines** ⓘ *www.croatiaairlines.hr, T020-8563 0022*, offers direct flights from London Heathrow to Zagreb, Split and Dubrovnik. Flights cost from £150-260. It is advisable to book early during the summer months as availability is limited. Approximate flight time from London to Zagreb is 2½ hours. In summer,

Croatia Airlines

Dubrovnik, Brslaje 9, T020-413776.
Pula, Ulica Carrarina 8, T052-218909.
Rijeka, Jelačićev Trg 5, T051-330207.
Split, Obala Hrvatskog Narodnog Perporoda 9, T021-362997.
Zadar, Poljana Natka Nodila 7, T023-250101.
Zagreb, Zrinjevac 17, T01-481 9633.

there are additional flights from Heathrow to Pula, Zadar and Rijeka. Flight time is approximately two hours.

In addition, through summer flights are available from Manchester to Zagreb, Split, Dubrovnik and Pula, from Nottingham to Split and from Glasgow to Dubrovnik.

From the UK and the rest of Europe

From the UK, the cheapest way to get to Croatia is with **Wizz Air** ⓘ *www.wizz air.com*, which launched a service between Luton and Zagreb in 2006.

Alternatively, **Ryanair** ⓘ *www.ryanair.com*, offer bargain flights from London Stansted to Pula and Zadar, and from Dublin to Zadar. Or travel with **EasyJet** ⓘ *www.easyjet.com*, from London Stansted to Ljubljana in neighbouring Slovenia, then catch a train to Zagreb. Note that through summer, EasyJet also flies to Split from London Gatwick and Bristol. **Flybe** ⓘ *www.flybe.com*, offers summer flights from Birmingham to Split and Dubrovnik, and from Exeter to Dubrovnik. If you are based in Scotland, bear in mind that **Flyglobespan** ⓘ *www.flyglobespan.com*, fly direct from Edinburgh to Pula and Dubrovnik.

Croatia Airlines offer direct flights to Zagreb from Amsterdam, Bari, Berlin, Bologna, Brussels, Catania, Copenhagen, Dusseldorf, Frankfurt, Genoa, Gothenburg, Hamburg, Helsinki, Istanbul, Lisbon, Lyon, Munich, Oslo, Palermo, Paris, Prague, Rome, Sarajevo, Skopje, Stockholm, Turin, Vienna and Zurich.

The same company also offers direct flights to Split from Amsterdam, Bari, Berlin, Bologna, Brussels, Catania, Copenhagen, Dusseldorf, Frankfurt, Genoa, Gothenburg, Hamburg, Helsinki, Istanbul, Lisbon, Lyon, Munich, Oslo, Palermo, Paris, Prague, Rome, Sarajevo, Skopje, Stockholm, Turin, Vienna and Zurich; and to Dubrovnik from Amsterdam, Bari, Berlin, Bologna, Brussels, Catania, Copenhagen, Dusseldorf, Frankfurt, Genoa, Gothenburg, Hamburg, Helsinki, Lisbon, Lyon, Munich, Oslo, Palermo, Paris, Prague, Rome, Sarajevo, Skopje, Stockholm, Turin, Vienna and Zurich.

From North America, New Zealand and Australia

There are no direct flights from Australia, Canada, New Zealand or the US to Croatia.

For **Croatia Airlines** (sales agents) in the USA contact T01 973-884 3401, in Australia T61 3-9699 9355 and New Zealand T64 9-838 9897. The most common routes are via Rome, Frankfurt, Paris or London. Flight times and prices vary enormously depending on the route and availability.

Rail

Regular daily international trains run direct to Zagreb from Italy (Venice, 7½ hours), Slovenia (Ljubljana, 2½ hours), Austria (Vienna, 6½ hours), Hungary (Budapest, six hours), Germany (Munich, nine hours), Serbia (Belgrade, six hours) and Bosnia and Herzegovina (Sarajevo, nine hours).

From the UK

The cheapest and fastest route is London-Paris-Venice-Zagreb, taking the **Eurostar** through the Channel Tunnel. The entire journey takes about 39 hours and requires an overnight train. Depart from London at 1404, and change in Paris to arrive in Venice at 0939 the following morning, and finally depart from Venice at 2127 to arrive in Zagreb at 0418. Prices vary greatly depending on how far in advance you book – if you know the exact days you want to travel try to buy your ticket several weeks before you wish to depart.

For further details or information about alternative routes, contact **Rail Europe** ⓘ *1 Regent St, London SW1, T08448 484064, www.raileurope.co.uk*, or check out the excellent website www.seat61.com, which is dedicated to travelling without flying.

Inter Rail pass The Inter Rail pass offers unlimited second-class train travel in 30 countries throughout Europe. In the past, the entire area was been divided into eight zones, but this no longer applies. Inter Rail tickets are now either 'Global' (for all 30 participating countries) or 'One-Country' (for one participating country). If you are 26 or under, a Global Inter Rail pass for all 30 participants countries costs €399. If you are over 26, a Global pass for all countries costs €599. For further details check out the website, www.interrailnet.com.

The **Eurail pass**, intended for residents of non-European countries, is now valid in Croatia. For details see www.eaurail.com.

Road

Car

There are good road links to Croatia from the neighbouring countries of Slovenia, Hungary, Bosnia and Herzegovina, and Serbia and Montenegro. Visitors arriving from Italy or Austria will pass through Slovenia.

Bus

There are regular international buses to Croatia from major towns in Italy, Slovenia, Hungary, Austria, Germany, Bosnia and Herzegovina, Serbia and Montenegro, and the Former-Yugoslav Republic of Macedonia. Buses depart from Trieste (Italy) to Rijeka taking 2½ hours. Buses also depart from Trieste for Pula taking 3¾ hours.

Slightly less frequent services (once or twice a week) run from France, Belgium, the Netherlands, the UK, Switzerland, Slovakia and the Czech Republic. **Eurolines** ⓘ *T08717-818181, www.eurolines.com*, run a direct weekly service from London Victoria to Zagreb (journey time 31 to 38 hours, return ticket £163). The bus leaves London at 2100 and arrives in Zagreb at 0400 two days later, having passed through Paris and Frankfurt, where occasionally it is necessary to change. From Zagreb it continues south to Split in Central Dalmatia, stopping at Šibenik en route. If you're heading for Istria, you'll need to change in Zagreb. With two nights on the road, the journey is pretty exhausting and you'll probably need another day to recuperate. **Eurolines** agent in Croatia is the Rijeka-based company **Autotrans** ⓘ *www.autotrans.hr*.

Sea

Catamaran

Italy to Dalmatia During summer (roughly mid-June to late September), fast daytime catamarans run between Italy and Croatia. **SNAV** operate a daily catamaran service (taking passengers and vehicles), leaving Ancona at 1100 to arrive in Split at 1530, then departing from Split at 1700 to return to Ancona at 2130. Expect to pay €90 in high season or €60 in low season one way. The same company also operates a daily summer service from Pescara to Stari Grad (on Hvar). In addition, **Larivera Lines** run a catamaran service from Termoli to Korčula and Lastovo from mid-June to early September.

Ferry

Croatia is well connected to Italy by overnight ferry lines the year through, and by fast daytime catamarans during summer. Services have increased as tourism has picked up, and the number of companies operating and the routes covered could expand still further. Tickets can be purchased in the port of departure, though through summer and over Easter cabins may be fully booked.

Italy to Dalmatia The main route is Ancona-Split, though Ancona-Zadar, Bari-Dubrovnik and Pescara-Split are possible options. During high season, some services call en route at the more popular islands such as Hvar and Korčula a couple of times a week, though for exact information you should check with the companies (websites are not totally reliable as schedules are liable to last-minute alterations). **Jadrolinija** run regular overnight services Ancona-Split, Ancona-Zadar and Dubrovnik-Bari. **Blue Line** also cover the Ancona-Split line. During summer, both **Jadrolinija** and **Blue Line** sail Ancona-Split every evening, but through winter services are slightly reduced. **Azzurra Line** operate a Bari-Dubrovnik service several times weekly through summer only.

Exact times vary from day to day and season to season, but in general ferries leave Ancona at 2100 to arrive in Split at 0700, then depart from Split at 2100 to arrive in Ancona at 0700. Others leave Ancona at 2200 to arrive in Zadar at 0600, then leave Zadar at 2300 to return to Ancona at 0700. The ferry from Bari normally leaves at 2200 to arrive in Dubrovnik at 0600, and leaves Dubrovnik at 2300 to arrive in Bari at 0800.

Through high season, expect to pay around €100 for a return ticket without a cabin (many sleep rough on the deck), or €180 for a return ticket with a bed in a double cabin. A return ticket for a car is an extra €140 and bicycles travel free of charge.

Italy and Slovenia to Istria During summer it is possible to arrive in Istria by boat from either northern Italy or Slovenia. **Venezia Lines** operate catamaran services from Venice to Istria. From early April to early October, they run a line from Venice to Poreč and Rovinj, departing at 1700 from Venice to arrive in Poreč at 1930 and in Rovinj at 2030. In high season (July-August) tickets cost €53 (one-way) and €89 (return). From early June to early September, they also run from Venice to Pula, Rabac and Mali Lošinj. Through peak season **Emilia Romagna Lines** run catamarans from Cesenatico, Ravenna and Rimini (Italy) to Rovinj, Lošinj, Zadar and Hvar.

Ferry companies

Azzurra Line, Dubrovnik, Croatia, T020-313178, www.azzurraline.com.
Blue Line, Split, Croatia, T021-352533, www.blueline-ferries.com.
Emilia Romagna Lines, Italy, T39 0547-675157, www.emiliaromagnalines.com.
Jadrolinija, Rijeka, Croatia, T051-666111, www.jadrolinija.hr.
Larivera Lines, Termoli, Italy, T39 0875-82248, www.lariveralines.com.
SNAV, Split, Croatia, T021-322252, www.snav.it.
Tirrenia Navigazione, Italy, T39 081-8449297, www.tirrenia.it.
Venezia Lines, Italy, T39 041-242 4000 (call centre), www.venezialines.com.

Getting around

Air

If you plan a short stay, the fastest way to move quickly from city to city is obviously to fly. The airports, with the exception of Rijeka, are all close to the town centres adding little to the journey time. **Croatia Airlines** ⓣ *www.croatiaairlines.hr*, offers the following internal flights from the capital: Zagreb to Split (45 minutes); Zagreb to Dubrovnik (50 minutes); Zagreb to Pula (40 minutes); Zagreb to Zadar (50 minutes); Zagreb to Bol (Brač) (one hour). Prices vary greatly depending on season, time of day and availability.

Rail

All major Croatian cities, except Dubrovnik, are connected by rail. Train travel into more remote regions has been limited by topography, the rocky Dinaric Alps making it extremely difficult to build railways. The most useful long-distance routes covered by train are Zagreb-Osijek (3½ hours), Zagreb-Rijeka (four hours) and Zagreb-Split (5½ hours by day, eight hours by night), the latter being covered by both a *brzo* (fast) day train and an overnight service with comfortable sleeping cars.

For a one-way ticket, expect to pay: Zagreb-Osijek 113Kn; Zagreb-Rijeka 96Kn and Zagreb-Split 160Kn. A return ticket is sometimes, but not always, cheaper than two one-way tickets. For further information contact **Hrvatske Zeljeznice, HZ** (Croatian Railways) ⓣ *www.hznet.hr*.

The Global **Inter Rail pass** (see page 28) gives you free second-class train travel throughout Croatia and the other 29 participating European countries. There are no national discount rail passes.

Road

Croatia has an extensive road network with frequent bus services. In summer 2005 two new motorways opened, connecting Zagreb and Rijeka, and Zagreb and Split. Tolls are payable on the following roads: Zagreb-Rijeka, Zagreb-Split, Zagreb-Karlovac, Zagreb-Krapina, Varaždin-Čakovec and Zagreb-Slavonski Brod, as well as for passage through the Učka tunnel and over the Krk Bridge.

The coastal road from Rijeka to Dubrovnik offers truly stunning views over the sea, but is twisty and tiring, and gets notoriously slippery after rain. The inland road from Zagreb to Dalmatia, passing through Lika, is occasionally blocked by snow during winter, and Maslenica bridge (north of Zadar) and Krk bridge (from the mainland to the island of Krk) are apt to short closures when the *bura* (northeast) wind is very strong. On the islands, roads tend to be narrow and less well maintained.

Bus

Buses tend to be slightly faster and marginally more expensive than trains, though they are generally less comfortable. However, while train services are limited, by using the bus you can get from any major city to the most remote village, albeit having to change several times en route. There are numerous private companies, each operating on their own terms, so there's no such thing as an unlimited travel pass. Prices and quality of buses vary greatly from company to company, and a return ticket is sometimes, but not always, cheaper than two one-way tickets. Expect to pay 180Kn for a one-way ticket Zagreb-Split (between 4½ and seven hours depending on the route taken), or 140-180Kn for a one-way ticket Zagreb-Pula (four to five hours). For national information contact **Zagreb Bus Station** ⓘ *T060-313333, www.akz.hr.*

Car

Having a car obviously makes you more independent so you can plan your itinerary more freely. However, it also creates various problems that you would not encounter if using public transport. Medieval walled cities such as Split and Dubrovnik are traffic free so you'll have to park outside the walls – even then, finding a place can be difficult as the more central parking spots are reserved for residents with permits. Having a car can also make ferry transfers to the islands extremely problematic: during high season be prepared to sit in queues for hours on end to get a place on the boat (there is no reservation system for vehicles: you buy a ticket and then it is first come, first aboard).

Rules and regulations Croatians drive on the right. A national and international driving licence is required and you should also have a passport or identity card close at hand. If you are from outside the EU, and entering Croatia with your own vehicle, you will need a Green Card. Croatia has imposed zero alcohol tolerance on drivers, so be sure not to drink, and when on the road, headlights should be switched on at all times.

Speed limits Maximum speeds are 50 kph (30 mph) in towns; 80 kph (50 mph) out of town; and 130 kph (80 mph) on motorways. Heavy fines are imposed for exceeding these limits.

Motoring organizations **Hrvatska Autoclub** (Croatian Automobile Club) ⓘ *T987 (staffed by multi-lingual operators), www.hak.hr*, offers a 24-hour breakdown service.

Car hire Expect to pay in the region of €43 per day for a small car such as an Opel Corsa 1.2; €54 for a VW Golf 222.0 or €73 for an Opel Vectra. Payments can be made by credit card, and your credit card number will be taken in lieu of a deposit. Most companies require drivers to be 21 or over. Car hire companies include **Budget**, www.budget.hr; **Hertz**, www.hertz.hr; and **Sixt**, www.sixt.hr.

Petrol stations Normally open daily 0700-1800, and often until 2200 in summer. The larger cities and major international roads have 24-hour petrol stations.

Hitching

On the smaller islands where public transport is limited, it is quite normal for drivers to stop and offer a lift to someone who is walking, even if they are not thumbing a ride.

Sea

The Croatian Adriatic has 66 inhabited islands, many of which can be reached by **ferry**. There are regular connections between the mainland ports and the major islands: Rijeka serves Rab, Cres and Lošinj; Zadar serves Dugi Otok; Split serves Šolta, Brač, Hvar, Vis, Korčula and Lastovo; and Dubrovnik serves the Elafiti islands and Mljet. Prices are reasonable as the state-owned ferry company **Jadrolinija** has been subsidized by the government in an attempt to slow down depopulation of islands. Timetables are normally geared towards the islanders, enabling them to work or attend school on the mainland. In low season there may be only one boat per day, leaving the island in the early morning and returning in the early evening. This can be inconvenient for brief visits in the opposite direction, as visitors from the mainland have to take the evening ferry to the island, stay a couple of nights, and return home in the early morning.

As well as connecting the islands, **Jadrolinija** operates a twice-weekly overnight coastal service (with cabins available) running from Rijeka to Dubrovnik, stopping at Split, Stari Grad (island of Hvar), Korčula and Sobra (island of Mljet) en route.

Jadrolinija also runs a number of **catamaran** services between the mainland and the islands. On the upside these are much faster than ferries, while on the downside they are slightly more expensive, do not take cars and do not allow passengers on the deck.

Sample **high season prices** are: Rijeka-Split by ferry, one way, passenger €25, car €67; Split-Stari Grad (Hvar) by ferry, one way, passenger €4.30, car €29; Dubrovnik-Sobra (Mljet) by ferry, one way, passenger €4.30, car €29. There is no discount on return tickets.

Besides **Jadrolinija**, a number of smaller local companies run ferries and catamarans on certain routes. TKTK, **Mediteranska Plovidba,** based in Korčula Town on the island of Korčula in South Dalmatia, run a daily passenger service from Korčula Town to Orebić, and a summer service from Korčula Town to Drvenik on the mainland, just south of Makarska. **Rapska Plovidba,** based in Rab Town on the island of Rab in Kvarner, run regular daily ferry services from Mišnjak on the island of Rab to Jablanac on the mainland, and between Rab Town and Lun on the island of Pag.

Mia Tours run a catamaran and a hydrofoil from Zadar to several of the nearby islands of North Dalmatia. **Split Tours,** based in Split in Central Dalmatia, operate daily catamarans from Split to the island of Šolta, and summer-only catamaran services from Split to Komiža on the island of Vis, and from Zadar to Pula, stopping at Mali Lošinj en route. As of January 2008, they also run a twice daily ferry service from Valbiska on Krk to Lopar on Rab.

Ferry companies

Jadrolinija, Rijeka-based head office, T051-666111, www.jadrolinija.hr. UK agent **Via Mare**, T020-8206 3420. **Jadrolinija** offices along the coast and on the islands: Rijeka, T051-666100; Mali Lošinj, T051-231765; Zadar, T023-254800; Brbinj, T023-378713; Šibenik, T022-213468; Split, T021-338333; Supertar, T021-631357; Hvar Town, T021-741132; Stari Grad, T021-765048; Korčula Town, T020-715410; Vela Luka, T020-812015; Vis Town, T021-711032; Dubrovnik, T020-418000.

Other companies include:

Mediteranska Plovidba, based in Korčula Town, T020-711156, www.medplov.hr.

Mia Tours, based in Zadar, T023-254300, www.miatours.hr.

Rapska Plovidba, based in Rab Town, T051-724122, www.rapska-plovidba.hr.

Split Tours, based in Split, T021-352533, www.splittours.hr.

Sleeping

Along the coast, private accommodation, either in a rented room or apartment, is the best choice in terms of cost, facilities and insight into the way the locals live. However, if you feel like splashing out and being pampered here and there, the hotels listed in this guide have been selected for their authentic atmosphere and central location.

There aren't any central websites listing private accommodation but local tourist offices often have details and their websites are listed throughout the book.

Hotels

Croatian tourism dates back to the late 19th century when the region was under Austro-Hungary and so along the coast you'll find a number of Vienna Secession-style hotels built for the Central European aristocracy of the time, the best examples being in Opatija.

Hotel price codes explained

Accommodation price codes in this book are based on the cost per person for two people sharing a double room with an en suite bathroom during the high season with breakfast. Be aware that many hotels offer substantial discounts during low season. Here is an idea of what to expect at each level:

LL-L (over 800Kn) These are the top-notch hotels, only existing in Zagreb and Dubrovnik. They should offer all the pampering extras such as sauna and massage, business facilities (including internet), several bars and restaurants. Credit cards are always accepted and they will usually change foreign currency for you.

AL-A (600-800Kn) This category includes some of the best recently refurbished hotels, generally offering comfortable, tastefully furnished rooms with all mod cons (including internet). You can expect a generous breakfast and good dining facilities. Credit cards are always accepted.

B-D (300-600Kn) These are the average-priced hotels, which vary greatly in quality, but all rooms should have an en suite bathroom, TV and telephone, and most also have a minibar. Generally there is a hotel restaurant, but the standard of the food is not guaranteed. Credit cards are normally accepted.

E-G (under 300Kn) This category includes anything from small hotels offering B&B-type accommodation to youth hostels. At this level you may be sharing a bathroom and, although most supply towels, you might need to bring your own soap. Very few have restaurants, and credit cards are not always accepted.

During the tourist boom of the 1970s and 1980s, many of the older hotels were neglected in favour of large modern complexes, which sprang up in popular resorts such as Poreč, Rovinj, Bol, Hvar Town, Korčula Town and Dubrovnik. Although they tend to be vast and somewhat impersonal, these socialist-era hotels are equipped with excellent sports facilities, generally overlook the sea and are discreetly hidden by careful landscaping, a short walk from the centre of town. Over the last few years, some have been totally refurbished and have introduced chic minimalist design and Wellness Centres, bringing them into the luxury market.

The third, and most recent, breed of hotel are the small, private, family-run establishments, often in refurbished town houses, which have opened over the last decade and are now united under the **National Association of Small and Family Hotels** ⓘ *www.omh.hr*. For a comprehensive list, check out their website.

All hotels are officially graded by the Ministry of Tourism into five categories: five-star, luxury; four-star, de luxe; three-star, first class; two-star, moderate; and one-star, budget. Classified hotels are listed by the **Croatian National Tourist Board** ⓘ *www.croatia.hr*, under their respective regions.

When referring to price lists, you will find that some hotels list half-board and full-board only. Simple 'bed and breakfast' works out only very slightly cheaper than half-board, but is recommended as, by and large, hotel restaurants lack atmosphere, and the standard of the food unfortunately reflects the savings made in order to be able to offer cheap package deals. You are far better eating out in local restaurants.

Last but not least, if you are staying on the coast it is well worth asking for a room with a sea view (most of which have balconies); it may cost a little more, but makes all the difference when you wake up in the morning.

Private accommodation

Along the coast you will find a plethora of families offering *sobe* (rooms) and *apartmani* (apartments) for rent, usually with en suite bathrooms and simple self-catering facilities provided (see page 40). These can be in anything from quaint, old stone cottages with gardens to modern concrete-block three-storey houses with spacious balconies. Hosts are generally welcoming and hospitable, and many visitors find a place they like and then return each summer. Local tourist offices and travel agents have lists of recognized establishments and can arrange bookings for you. In busy areas, you'll also find people waiting for travellers at the ferry ports and bus stations, and offering rooms by word of mouth, but in this case you're not guaranteed to find the best standards.

Prices vary enormously depending on location, season and facilities provided, but you can expect to pay anything from 100-180Kn (€15-25) per person per day for a double room with an en suite bathroom, and anything from 300-900Kn (€42-126) per day for a four-person apartment with a kitchen and dining area. Note that there is normally a 30% surcharge for stays of less than three nights.

A British-based operator specializing in private accommodation in Croatia is **Croatian Villas Ltd** ⓘ *Wood Green Business Centre, 5 Clarendon Rd, Wood Green, London N22 6XJ, T020-8888 6655, www.croatianvillas.com*, who specialize in quality villas and apartments for holiday rentals in top Croatian resorts.

So-called **'Robinson Crusoe' style accommodation** started out on the Kornati islands, though it is gradually spreading to other isolated locations. As the term implies, this type of accommodation consists of a simple stone cottage, basically furnished and offering minimum modern comforts: gas lighting and water from a well. The beauty of these cottages lies in their detachment from the rest of the world – they are normally found on small unpopulated islands with no regular ferry links to the mainland, no shops and no cars. They are generally for rent on a weekly basis, and transport to them is arranged by the agencies responsible for letting them. Croatian agencies specializing in these cottages include **Kornat Turist** ⓘ *Hrvatskih vladara 2, Murter, T022-435854/5, www.kornatturist.hr*, and **Lori** ⓘ *Zdrače 2, Betina, T022-435631, www.touristagency-lori.hr.*

The British-based operator **Croatia for Travellers** ⓘ *63 Therberton St, London N1 0QY, T020-7226 4460, www.croatiafortravellers.co.uk*, can also book a cottage for you.

Another novel and highly popular form of accommodation is the **lighthouse**. Along the Croatian coast, there are now 11 carefully restored lighthouses with apartments to rent on a weekly basis. Nine of these are on islands (you will be taken there and brought back by boat), and three on peninsulas along the mainland coast. In Istria, these include Savudrija (Umag), Rt Zub (Novigrad), Sv Ivan (Rovinj) and Porer (Pula), while in Dalmatia there are Prišnjak (Murter), Sv Petar (Makarska), Palagruža (Vis), Pločica (Vela Luka), Sušac (Lastovo), Struga (Lastovo) and Sv Andrija (Elafiti). Most lighthouses have one or two apartments sleeping anything from two to eight people, and several are still home to a resident lighthouse keeper. However, you can be sure of extreme isolation and minimum contact with the outside world, as most of them are located on lonely islets far out to sea. Each apartment has electricity, running water, TV and a fully equipped kitchen. Bed linen and blankets are provided, but be sure to take a week's provisions as there will be no chance of shopping once you are there, unless you manage to make a special agreement with local fishermen or the lighthouse keeper.

Prices vary greatly depending on the size of the apartment, location and season, but as an indicator the cost of renting a four-person apartment in the lighthouse of Sv Ivan, near Rovinj, for one week, are as follows: July to August €949; June and September €749; and during the rest of the year €539. However, as this has become a hugely popular alternative, be sure to book several months in advance. For further details contact **Adriatica Net** ⓘ *Heinzelova 62a, Zagreb, T01-241 5611, www.adriatica.net (online booking service).*

Brodet

This is an old-fashioned dish originally invented by fishermen to use up the fish they had not sold by the end of the day. It is best made with a mixture of several types of fish, preferably from the Adriatic. If you are in Croatia ask the fishmonger's advice, otherwise consider including snapper, bream, perch, shark, mullet, as well as octopus and squid.

Ingredients

1 kg mixed fresh fish
1 onion
4 or 5 cloves of garlic
1 tbsp concentrated tomato puree or 2 ripe tomatoes
1 tbsp chopped parsley
10 cl water
10 cl dry white wine
3 tbsp vinegar
8 tbsp olive oil
Salt and freshly ground black pepper

Method

Clean and gut the fish, removing the scales and head but leaving the back bone. Dice the onion and fry in oil until translucent, add the chopped garlic and continue to fry to a light golden colour. Add the tomato and fish, and cook for five minutes. Add the water, wine and vinegar, salt and pepper. Cook for 30 minutes over a gentle flame (without a lid so the juice thickens) until the fish is falling freely from the bone. Do not stir – to stop the *brodet* sticking to the bottom of the pan, shake it occasionally with a sharp side to side rotating movement. Take off the heat, add the parsley and leave to stand for 5-10 minutes.

Eat warm, served with polenta, and use fresh crusty bread to mop up the juices.

Agrotourism

An increasingly popular option is so-called agrotourism: farmhouses offering overnight accommodation and home cooking. This is a great solution for families with young children, as exploring the farm and getting to know the farm animals is guaranteed to go down well with kids. To date, the idea has only really taken off in Istria, but the potential is enormous.

Most of these establishments are off-the-beaten track (you normally need a car to reach them) and offer bed and breakfast deals in simply furnished rooms with en suite bathrooms. Many also have a restaurant area, generally done out in rustic style, serving authentic local dishes (generally far superior to the food served in commercial restaurants), along with their own wine, cheese and olive oil. Some of the larger centres also offer a range of sporting activities such as horse riding and mountain biking.

Prices vary greatly depending on the type of room, the location and season, but expect to pay anything from 180-320Kn (€25-45) per person per day for a double room (with an en suite bathroom) with breakfast in August.

For a list of farms and rural homes offering overnight accommodation and meals throughout the country, visit www.seoski-turizam.net (in Croatian with some texts also in English), and in Istria check out www.istra.com/agroturizam.

Camping

The sunny, dry climate and unspoilt nature make Croatia an ideal place for camping. Of at least 130 registered campsites, about 90% are on the mainland coast or on the islands, many backed by pinewoods overlooking the sea. Most operate from early May to early October, are well run and offer basic facilities such as showers and toilets and a small bar, while the larger ones may include restaurants and extensive sports facilities, such as scuba-diving courses and mountain bike rentals. The most developed regions in terms of capacity and facilities provided are Istria and Kvarner, while Dalmatia is in many ways more attractive thanks to its rugged, untamed natural beauty. As in other European countries, camping outside of designated areas is prohibited.

For further information contact **Kamping Udruženje Hrvatske** (Croatian Camping Union) ⓘ *8 Marta 1, Poreč, T052-451324, www.camping.hr*. This excellent website lists all official campsites, complete with contact details, facilities and prices. Naturist campsites are also listed and marked 'FKK'.

Naturist camps

Naked bathing was first pioneered in Croatia in the early 20th century and Europe's first naturist campground opened here in 1953. Today there are 20 naturist campsites, almost all along the coast and on the islands, attracting visitors from Germany, Austria, the Netherlands, Italy and Slovenia, as well as other countries around the world. Europe's largest naturist camp, **Koversada**, is in Istria, and can provide accommodation for up to 7000 visitors.

For more information about naturism in Croatia, including a list of naturist camps accompanied by comments from people who have stayed at them, check out the **Croatia Naturally** website, www.cronatur.com. See also page 22.

Youth hostels

There are youth hostels in Pula, Rijeka, Punat and Krk (both on the island of Krk), Veli Lošinj (on the island of Lošinj), Zadar and Dubrovnik. The Zagreb hostel is currently undergoing renovation, but some rooms are still available to visitors. These provide basic but comfortable dormitory-style overnight accommodation (expect to pay around 100Kn per person per night), and some offer the option of half or full board.

For information about hostels contact **Hrvatski Ferijalni i Hostelski Savez** (Croatian Youth Hostel Association) ⓘ *Savska 5, 10000 Zagreb, T/F01-482 9294, www.hfhs.hr.*

Eating and drinking

Croatian cuisine can be divided into two main groups: Mediterranean along the coast and Continental in the inland regions. That said, each region has its own particular specialities reflecting its geography, history and culture. Croatia's highly complex past is clearly evident in its cooking, which displays the traces left by centuries of occupation by three foreign empires: the Venetians brought pasta and risotto to the coast; Austro-Hungary introduced paprika-flavoured goulash and strudel inland; and the Ottoman Turks bequeathed the region with *sarma* (stuffed sauerkraut rolls) and *baklava*.

Food

Dalmatia

Along the Dalmatian coast, simple, honest fish and seafood dishes top the menu. All ingredients are fresh and seasonal, so there's little attention paid to fussy preparation. The classic favourite is fresh fish, barbecued and served with olive oil and lemon, plus *blitva sa krumpirom* (swiss chard and potatoes with garlic and olive oil) as a side dish. Likewise, shellfish such as *kucice* (clams) and *škampi* (shrimps) are flashed over a hot flame with garlic, white wine and parsley, a method known as *na buzaru*, which cooks the flesh to a turn and produces a delicious rich sauce to mop up with bread. Worth mentioning here is that some of the best shellfish, notably *ostrige* (oysters) and *dagnje* (mussels), can be found in Ston on Pelješac Peninsula in South Dalmatia.

In summer, a popular and refreshing starter is *salata of hobotnice* (octopus salad) made from octopus, boiled potatoes, onion and parsley, dressed with olive oil

Dining out

Remember that fish (especially Class I white fish such as bass, bream and john dory) is sold by the kilogram and is expensive, while seafood risotto and pasta dishes are fairly economical. Therefore, you can pay almost as much for a portion of fresh fish in a cheap restaurant as you would for a portion of risotto in an expensive restaurant. The price coding used here is for a three-course meal with house wine.

Expensive (over 300Kn)
High-class restaurants with food, wine, service and setting that warrant inflated prices. Often either geared to business people (in Zagreb) or the yachting fraternity (along the coast).

Mid-range (150-300Kn)
Most restaurants fall into this category. However, if you choose large quantities of fresh fish in a mid-range restaurant you can easily exceed the 200Kn mark.

Cheap (under 150Kn)
At the upper end of this category, pizzerias and informal eateries serve fixed-menu lunch and dinner. At the bottom end (under 30Kn), small shops serve seriously cheap takeaway food such as sandwiches and pastries.

and vinegar. Venetian influence is apparent in the abundance of risottos, the most popular being *crni rižot* (black risotto) made from cuttlefish ink, as well as *rižot frutti di mare* (seafood risotto), normally combining mussels, clams and prawns, and *rižot sa škampima* (shrimp risotto) invariably served with a splash of cream at the end. Pasta dishes are also served with a variety of seafood sauces, though the pasta is often overcooked by Italian standards. Another classic Dalmatian dish is *brodet*, ahearty mixed fish stew made with onions and tomatoes, and normally served with polenta. On the island of Hvar a local version of *brodet* is *gregada*, made with onions, potatoes and fresh herbs but no tomato.

When it comes to meat dishes, locals rave about *dalmatinski pršut*, smoked dried ham on a par with Italian prosciutto. It's normally served as an appetizer on a platter together with *paški sir* (sheep's cheese from the island of Pag) and a few olives. Meats such as steak, sausages and home-made burgers are invariably prepared on a charcoal fire and served with chips and a side salad (lettuce, cucumber and tomato). Another classic Dalmatian dish, brought to the area by the Venetians, is *pasticada*, beef stewed in sweet wine and served with *njoki* (gnocchi).

Lamb has a cult following throughout the Balkans, and in Croatia you'll see many roadside restaurants serving *janjetina* – whole lamb roast on a spit – especially in inland Dalmatia. A special mention also needs to be given to the *peka*, a metal dome dating back to Illyrian times. Food is placed in a terracotta pot and covered entirely with a *peka*, which in turn is buried below white embers. Delicious casseroles of either octopus, veal or lamb can be prepared using this long, slow cooking method, though most restaurants that offer it stipulate that you should order a day in advance.

Desserts are limited, the standard offering being *palacinke* (pancakes), served either *sa orasima* (with walnuts), *sa marmeladom* (with jam) or *sa cokoladom* (with chocolate). In Dubrovnik, look out for *rožata*, similar to crème caramel.

If you visit the island of Vis, *pogaca* makes a perfect snack – similar to Italian *focaccia* (from which it takes its name), it consists of a light bread base filled with tomato, onion and anchovy; you can buy it in several local bakeries.

Istria

Besides the aforementioned, in Istria you can expect slightly more adventurous dishes with extra care given to presentation, probably due to Italian influence. Look out for the regional speciality, *tartufi* (truffles), usually served with pasta or steak, and risotto and pasta dishes *mare monti*, literally meaning 'sea and mountains', which combine shellfish and mushrooms. The best oysters and mussels are to be found in Limski Kanal, between Rovinj and Poreč. On the meat front, Istrians prepare delicious *srnetina* (venison) stew, normally served with *njoki* (gnocchi) or *fuži*, a local form of pasta. As in Dalmatia, rich casseroles can be prepared under a *peka*, but in Istria it's known as a *cirepnja*. Regarding side dishes, you'll find delicious, colourful salads combining mixed leaves such as *rukola* (rocket) and radicchio.

Inland Croatia

Moving inland, food is generally heavier, with lard or dripping used in place of olive oil for frying and roasting. The Zagreb area, and especially Zagorje, is known for *štrukli*, dumplings filled with curd cheese, which can either be boiled or baked. The most popular meats are roast turkey, duck or goose, classically served with *mlinci*, wafer thin pastries cooked in dripping. The best bread is made from maize flour rather than wheat, giving it a yellow colour and a heavier consistency.

In Slavonia, pork is used to make *kulen*, a delicious spicy salami often served as an appetizer. Hungarian influence is apparent in meat specialities such as *gulaš* (goulash) and *fiš paprikaš* (a rich stew made from river fish), both of which are generously seasoned with hot paprika.

In Lika, the inland area between Zagreb and Dalmatia, look out for *škripavac* cheese, roast lamb and hearty peasant dishes employing *kiseli kupus* (sauerkraut), *grah* (beans) and *krumpir* (potatoes).

Throughout the country you will come across Turkish-inspired dishes, which make tasty and filling snacks: *burek* (filo pastry filled with either minced meat and onions or curd cheese) and *cevapcici* (meat rissoles served in pitta bread with *ajvar* – a relish made from red peppers and aubergines). Also of Turkish origin are *sarma* (cabbage leaf rolls filled with minced meat and rice), better known as *arambašici* in Sinj, which are often eaten for special celebrations. Last but not least, *baklava* is a delicious syrup-drenched sweet made from filo pastry and ground walnuts.

Drink

Meeting friends for *kava* (coffee) is something of a morning ritual. Many bars open as early as 0600, and are busy all day. While most people prepare Turkish coffee at home, cafés and bars serve Italian-style espresso and cappuccino. If you ask for *čaj* (tea) you will automatically be given *šipak* (rosehip) served with lemon; if you want English-style tea ask for *indijski čaj sa mlijekom* (Indian tea with milk). Most cafés have tables outside, even in winter where possible, and there is no extra charge for sitting down.

Wine

Croatian wines are little known abroad as they are exported in relatively small quantities, though some of them, such as the highly esteemed *Dingač*, are excellent. By and large the north produces whites and the south reds, though there are some exceptions.

Among the whites, names to look out for are: *Pošip* and *Grk* (from the island of Korčula), *Vugava* (island of Vis), *Žlahtina* (island of Krk), *Malvazija* (Istria), *Graševina* and *Traminac* (Slavonia). Of the reds, be sure to try: *Dingač* (Pelješac Peninsula), *Plavac* (islands of Hvar and Vis), *Babič* (Primošten) and *Teran* (Istria). Dalmatia also produces a rich sweet wine known as *Prošek*, similar to sweet sherry.

To buy top wines at better prices, go direct to the producer. You will find vineyards open to the public on Pelješac Peninsula and the island of Hvar. On the island of Vis, some producers have opened small shops where you can sample wine and then buy bottles to take home. In Istria, the regional tourist board has drawn up a series of wine

How to prepare Turkish coffee

For each person you need:
1 coffee cup of water
1 teaspoon of sugar
2 teaspoons of ground coffee

Put the water and sugar in the *džezver* and heat till simmering. Take off the flame, stir in the coffee, put back on the flame and heat till just before simmering point. Take off the heat and allow to sit for 2-3 minutes before serving (so the coffee can start to settle). Pour and drink immediately without stirring.

routes with a list of producers who receive visitors, for an interactive map check out the website, www.istra.com/vino.

Lower-grade wines are bottled in one-litre bottles with a metal cap, while better wines come in 0.75 litre with a cork. Sometimes you will find the same label on both, but the 0.75-litre bottle will be more expensive and of much higher quality. Most bars serve wine by the glass, either by the *dec* (1 dl) or *dva deca* (2 dl). In Dalmatia, *bevanda* (half white wine, half water) is a refreshing summer drink.

Beer

Beer was introduced to Croatia under Austro-Hungary, when the Hapsburgs built the first breweries to supply their soldiers. Light-coloured lager, served well chilled, is the most common sort of beer, with popular brands being *Karlovačko*, *Kaltenburg*, *Laško Zlatorog* and *Ožujsko*. *Tomislav* is a stout (dark beer) brewed in Zagreb. When you buy beer by the bottle, you pay a small deposit, which you can get back upon return of the empties and display of the receipt. Imported draught *Guinness* is popular but tends to be about three times the price of local beer.

Spirits

Rakija, a distilled spirit usually made from a grape base, was introduced to the region by the Turks, and is normally drunk as an aperitif before eating, but can also be taken as a digestive at the end of a meal. The most popular types are: *loza* (made from grapes), *travarica* (flavoured with aromatic grasses), *šljivovica* (made from plums) and *pelinkovac* (flavoured with juniper berries and bitter herbs, similar to Italian *amaro*). In addition, there are various regional specialities such as *biska* (flavoured with mistletoe) in inland Istria and *rogoš* (flavoured with carob) on the island of Vis. Imported spirits such as whisky and gin are popular but expensive.

Eating out

For a full blown lunch or dinner, visit a *restoran* (restaurant), where you can expect formal service and a menu including a wide range of Croatian dishes. Most restaurants are open 1200-1500 and 1900-2300, and many, especially along the coast, have a large terrace for open-air dining through summer. For a simpler meal, try a *gostionica*, a place you can also go just to drink. There may not be a written menu, but many *gostionice* in Dalmatia serve *merenda* (a hearty cut-price brunch), offer daily specials chalked up on a board, and sometimes have a set **three-course** meal, which works out very cheap. Service will be less formal, but you can often land some excellent home cooking, and they tend to stay open all day, Monday to Saturday 0800-2300. The terms *konoba* (in Dalmatia) and *klet* (in Zagorje) were originally associated with places for making and storing wine, but the names are now used by many rustic-style restaurants serving local specialities. Some open in the evenings only and may stay open for late-night drinking. Most towns have a pizzeria, and some serve excellent pizza, comparable to the best in Italy. A few also offer a choice of substantial salads and a limited selection of pasta dishes.

For something sweet, call at a *slasticarnica*. Many are run by Albanians (who made up one of former-Yugoslavia's ethnic minorities) and they offer eastern goodies such as *baklava* (see above), along with a selection of *sladoled* (ice cream). Most work 0800-2000, and serve coffee, tea and fruit juices, but no alcohol.

If you are travelling in inland Istria, look out for agrotourism centres where you can expect quality local produce such as home-made cheese and wine, as well as unusual seasonal specialities such as *šparoge* (wild asparagus) in spring, and *tartufi* (truffles) and *gljive* (mushrooms) in autumn.

Eating in

If you opt for private accommodation you will be able to eat in occasionally, which is a great solution for longer stays and families with children, and gives you the added pleasure of shopping at the open-air markets. Along the coast, all apartments (and even some rooms) come with a small cooking space, including a fridge and hot-plates (but not always an oven) and a sink. Some larger apartments and houses also have a built-in barbecue on the terrace or in the garden, in which case you'll have great fun preparing fresh fish over charcoal, just as the locals do.

All cooking utensils and kitchen equipment such as pans, bowls, plates, glasses, cups and cutlery will be provided: if anything is missing ask your host and they will give you anything extra you require. Occasionally basics such as sugar, salt and pepper are provided – normally left by the people who were there before you.

You will probably also be supplied with a *džezver* – a small metal coffee pot with a handle, used for preparing Turkish-style coffee, which is usually drunk here rather than instant, filter or espresso coffee. Vacuum-packed ground coffee can be bought in packs of 100 or 250 g in general stores.

Entertainment

Nightlife along the coast is great through summer when opening hours are extended: open-air bars work till 0300 and open-air discos till 0500 at weekends. Holidaymakers are the main spenders, especially at the overpriced cocktail bars that have opened in fashionable resorts such as Dubrovnik, Hvar Town and Rovinj, but young locals also dress up and stay out late, particularly on Friday and Saturday nights. The most notorious late-night open-air parties are held on Zrče beach in Novalja on the island of Pag, on Sakarun beach near Božava on Dugi Otok, Pudarica beach near Rab Town on the island of Rab, on Girandella beach near Rabac and on Gradsko Kupalište beach in Poreč in Istria.

Winter tends to be a bit miserable: the police are quite strict about bars closing at 2300 Sunday to Thursday and 2400 Friday and Saturday, and most young Croatians are short of money so they either go out rarely or go out often but don't drink a lot. Young married couples with kids do not go out much – mainly because of financial problems. Of the older generation, 50 and over, it is normal for the man to go out drinking occasionally but for the wife to stay at home.

Cinema is quite popular, though most cinemas just show the current American box-office successes – the only really good place for alternative art films is **Kinoteka** in Zagreb. The open-air cinemas through summer are wonderful – the atmosphere is very romantic, even if the films are not always fantastic. Theatre and opera tend to be the domain of the middle-aged middle-class. The Summer Festivals in Dubrovnik and

Split are perfect for older holidaymakers, offering a range of open-air musical and theatrical performances – here again, the atmosphere can be more memorable than the spectacle itself. » *See also Spectator sports, page 23.*

Festivals and events

Festivals aren't celebrated with the same flamboyancy in Croatia as in some other European countries. The most striking thing is the number of Croatian flags that are hoisted up on national holidays – above churches and town halls, in shops windows and even hanging from people's balconies. Croatians celebrate Christmas and Easter at home with their families, so there's very little activity on the streets and most bars and restaurants are shut. However, midnight mass on 24 December is quite a big event, with churches probably seeing their biggest turn out of the year that night. New Year's Day is seen in with massive firework displays in most places. All Saints' Day is known as Day of the Dead in Croatia – people visit the family grave and fresh flowers are on sale in extraordinary quantities in the days leading up to 1 November.

Shopping

Croatia is hardly a shoppers' paradise, a state of affairs clearly illustrated by the number of organized shopping buses to Trieste in Italy and Graz in Austria. As manufacturing industries struggle to recover from the crisis of the 1990s, clothes and household goods are largely imported from Western Europe, and come with the predictable mark-up price.

However, the open-air fruit and vegetable markets are animated, colourful affairs, well worth a look round to check out local seasonal produce. If you opt for private accommodation with self-catering facilities you will find shopping for food gives closer insight into the way people live, and eat. There are very few large supermarkets in Croatia, the nearest thing being small general stores, where you can shop for basics. But remember that fresh bread is best bought from a *pekarna* (bakery), meat from a *mesnica* (butchers) and fruit, vegetables and fish from the open-air morning market.

What to buy

Top of the list, both during your stay and when it's time to go home, should be Croatian **wine** and **rakija** (see Eating and drinking, page 36). Each region makes its own wines, and even though they are all available in general stores throughout the country, it is worth tasting local wines while you travel from region to region. Better still, in some areas it's possible to visit cellars for wine-tasting sessions and then buy direct from the producer. On a slightly more sober note, Croatia produces some excellent **herbal teas**, available freshly dried on the open-air market, or in packages in the shops; the most popular varieties are *šipak* (rosehip), *menta* (mint) and *kamilica* (camomile).

Throughout Europe, **olive oil** varies greatly from country to country. Although Croatia is not big on preserving olives to eat, Istrian and Dalmatian farmers produce some excellent *maslinovo ulje* (olive oil); when selecting a bottle, be sure to choose *djevičansko* (virgin), which is slightly more expensive but has a fuller flavour. And if you like **truffles**, look out for *tartufi* (truffles) and truffle-based products in Istria.

Other ideas for gifts include **handmade lace** (the best being from the island of Pag), **lavender** (either dried or distilled, from the island of Hvar), and an original **Croatian tie** (in a presentation box complete with a brief history of the tie), see page 60. Look out for **Aromatic** ⓘ *www.aromatica.hr*, shops in Zagreb, Samobor, Pula, Rovinj and Split, stocking their range of scented soaps and cosmetics made from olive oil and wild herbs.

A-Z

Accident and emergency

Contact the relevant emergency service and your embassy or consulate (see page 43). Remember to get police/medical records for insurance claims. Ambulance T94; Fire T93; Police T92; Road assistance T987.

Children

Like all south Europeans, Croatians love children and give a lot of time and attention to them. They also let their kids stay up late, so through summer it's quite usual to turn up at a restaurant around 2200 for dinner with the little ones in tow.

Very few Croatian hotels go along with the idea of putting an extra bed for a young child in the parents' double room. Some hotels have rooms with 3 or 4 beds that are designed to accommodate a family, though there are no cheap rates for kids in this case. Likewise, few hotels offer babysitting facilities. If you have very young children, private accommodation is probably your best bet. This way you can agree directly with the person from whom you are renting on how best to arrange rooms and beds to suit your needs, and as you will probably also have a kitchen, you can prepare meals as and when you like.

Ask any Croatian child what their favourite food is and the reply will more than likely be pizza. This is a good starting point, and it's quite normal in pizzerias to ask for an extra plate then cut up the pizzas and share. Pasta dishes and barbecued meats also go down well with kids, though fish is obviously more tricky because of the bones. If you opt for self-catering, you'll find an endless range of yoghurts and biscuits, which make good snacks, as well as locally produced fruit juices.

Croatia Airlines and **Croatian Railways** both offer a 50% discount on tickets for children under the age of 12. Regarding buses, each bus company has its own rules, which can even vary depending on the route. Some offer free travel for children up to the age of 4, others offer a 50% discount up to the age of 6, and some a 20% discount up to the age of 12. For exact details, ask when buying tickets.

Children love the freedom of running around on beaches and splashing in the sea, but bear in mind that there's not much sand here. Most of the beaches are pebbly, so plastic sandals are recommended for those with sensitive feet. Sea urchins can be a stumbling block (literally): while local children have an inexplicable ability to pluck them off the rocks with their fingers, these black prickly monsters can seriously upset those who are not in the know. Once again, plastic sandals are the best solution.

Customs and duty free

You can bring into Croatia, free of duty, 200 cigarettes or 50 cigars, 5 litres of wine, 1 litre of spirits, 60 ml of perfume or 250 ml of toilet water. Valuable professional and technical equipment, such as expensive cameras and laptop computers, should be declared at the *carina* (customs) upon entry at the border – this way you can be sure to get them out again. Boats and yachts do not need to be reported, but you should have proof of ownership. Before launching a boat of over 3 m you should notify the harbour office, and you need a special permit for transporting boats on trailers of over 18 m. Pets need to have a recent vet's certificate. Foreign currency can be brought in and out of the country freely. When leaving Croatia, you can take up to 15,000Kn.

Disabled travellers

As a consequence of the increase in the number of physically disabled people after the war, Croatians have become more aware of the problems faced by those with mobility difficulties. In the past many public buildings such as airports, hotels, railway stations and bus stations did not make special provision for wheelchair access, but projects to rectify the situation are now underway, and in some cases are already complete. The problem of facilitating access onto ferries has yet to be resolved, but you will normally find a steward who is ready to help. The more expensive, modern hotels are generally better equipped – when choosing a place to stay ask exactly what provisions they have. It's often a good idea to request a ground floor room or a room close to the lift.

Useful organizations

Holiday Care, T0845-124 9971, www.holidaycare.org.uk. Basic information about facilities for disabled people in various countries and can help find a tour operator specializing in travel for people with mobility difficulties.
Savez Organizacija Invalida Hrvatske (Association of Organisations of Disabled People in Croatia), Savska Cesta 3, 10000 Zagreb, T01-482 9394. Publish guides for disabled travellers to Zagreb, Split, Pula, Rijeka, Varaždin and Koprivnica, available in both Croatian and English.

Drugs

Prohibitions are the same as for any other European country. Penalties for the possession, use or trafficking of illegal drugs (from marijuana to heroin) are strict, and convicted offenders can expect prison sentences and hefty fines.

Electricity

220 volts AC, 50Hz; plugs have 2 round pins (as in most of continental Europe).

Embassies and consulates

Australia, 14 Jindalee Cres, O'Malley Act 2606, Canberra, T61 2-6286 6988.
Austria, Heuberggasse 10, 1170 Vienna, T43 1-4859524.
Belgium (and Luxembourg), Ave Louise 425, 1050 Brussels, T32 2-639 2036.
Bosnia and Herzegovina, Mehmeda Spahe 16, 71000 Sarajevo, T387 33-251640.
Bulgaria, Veliko Trnovo 32, 1504 Sofia, T359 2-943 3225.
Canada, 229 Chapel St, Ottawa, Ontario K1N 7Y6, T1 613-562 7820.
Czech Republic, V Pruhledu 9, 16200 Prague 6, T42 02-3334 0479.
Denmark, Frederiksgade 19, 1265 Copenhagen, T45 33-919095.
France, 39 Ave Georges Mandel, 75116 Paris, T33 1-5370 0280.
Germany, Ahornstrasse 4, 10787 Berlin, T49 30-2191 5514.
Greece, Tzavela 4, Neo Psychico, 15451 Athens, T30 210-677 7059.
Hungary, Munkacsy Mihaly utca 15, 1065 Budapest, T36 1-354 1315.
Ireland, Adelaide Chambers, Peter St, Dublin 8, T353 1-476 7181.
Italy, Via Luigi Bodio 74/76, 00191 Roma, T39 06-3630 4630.
Japan, 3-3-10 Hiroo, Shibuya-ku, Tokyo 150-0012, T81 3-5469 3014.
FYROM, Mitropolit Teodosij Gologanov 44, 91000 Skopje, T389 2-324 8170.
Montenegro, Vlada Ćetkovića 2, Podgorica, T382 81-269760.
Netherlands, Amalistraat 16, NL-2514 JC The Hague, T31 70-362 3638.
New Zealand (Consulate), 291 Lincoln Rd, Henderson PO Box 83-200, Edmonton, Auckland, T64 9-836 5581.
Norway, Drammensveien 82, 0271 Oslo, T47 2-301 4050.
Romania, Dr Burghelea 1, Sector 2, Bucharest, T40 21-313 0457.
Serbia, Kneza Miloša 62, 11000 Belgrade, T381 11-361 0535.
Slovakia, Mišikova 21, Bratislava, T42 12-5443 3647.
Slovenia, Gruberjevo nabrežje 6, 1000 Ljubljana, T386 1-425 6220.
South Africa, 1160 Church St, 0083 Colbyn Pretoria, T27 12-342 1206.
Spain, c/Claudio Coello 78/2, 28001 Madrid, T34 91-577 6881.
Sweden, Birger Jarlsgatan 13/I, 11145 Stockholm, T46 8-678 8310.
Switzerland, Thunstrasse 45, 3005 Bern, T41 31-352 0275/9.
UK, 21 Conway St, London W1T 6BN, T44 20-7387 2022, http://uk.mfa.hr.
USA, 2343 Massachusetts Av NW, Washington DC, 20008-2853, T1 202-588 5899, www.croatiaemb.org.

Gay and lesbian

Homosexuality has been legal in Croatia since 1977, though it remains taboo among the older generation and is only now beginning to be accepted in the more alternative youth circles. In October 2005, in a government-sponsored bid for greater tolerance, 1200 Croatian gays and lesbians 'came out' by publishing their names in 3 of the country's newspapers under the heading "I don't want to hide anymore".

Croatia still has a long way to go before gays and lesbians can feel free to openly express themselves here, though Dubrovnik and Hvar Town are becoming increasingly popular destinations for well-heeled gay travellers. In fact, Dubrovnik now has a travel agency catering exclusively for gay holidays – see www.gay-dubrovnik.com.

The website, www.gaytimes.co.uk, has short country guides, including Croatia. For general information about tours for lesbian and gay travellers, check out the website of the **International Gay and Lesbian Travellers Association**, www.iglta.org.

Health

Basic precautions

Make sure you are up to date with the most basic vaccines such as tetanus, diphtheria and polio. It is still wise to be up to date with hepatitis A vaccine and typhoid even for this relatively safe destination. Tap water is safe to drink throughout the country.

▸▸ *See individual town and city directories for details of medical services.*

Most EU countries have a reciprocal healthcare agreement with Croatia, meaning that you pay a basic minimum for consultation and hospital treatment is free if you can show your European Health Insurance Card (EHIC), which has replaced the E111. Forms are available from the post office or from the Department of Health's website (www.dh.gov.uk). If your country doesn't have such an agreement, you will have to pay in accordance with listed prices. For minor complaints visit a *ljekarna* (pharmacy); most are open Mon to Fri 0800-1900 and Sat 0800-1400, and in larger cities they have a rota system whereby at least 1 should be open at night and weekends. For something more serious, visit the local doctor's surgery – most doctors speak some English. Outside surgery hours or in an emergency, go to *hitno pomoć* (casualty). Dial 94 for an ambulance. You can also check which clinics and hospitals are used by British diplomats for their own ailments.

Common complaints

Insect bites The insects you will come across here are more unpleasant than dangerous, unless you have a specific allergy. Mosquitoes are rarely a problem, except in the Osijek and Kopački Rit wetland area. To ward them off, buy insect repellent at a local pharmacy.

Sea sickness Even on short trips out to the islands, the movement of the sea can be unsettling. Try Kwells or other sea-sickness tablets.

Sea urchins Black spiky sea urchins are common along the rocky shorelines; if you step on one it can result in infection. To avoid the problem altogether, invest in a pair of plastic sandals for getting in and out of the water.

Snake bites The best way to protect yourself from snake bites is to be well dressed and to keep to marked roads and paths. Snakes only bite if they feel threatened, and very few here are poisonous. However, if you are bitten, you should immediately immobilize the bitten part and bind the arm or leg to slow down the circulation. If it is poisonous the bite will normally swell within 30 mins. Send someone for help at once.

Sun burn Avoid extensive exposure to the sun, wear a hat and sunglasses and use a high-protection factor suncream, especially during the hottest part of the day (1100-1500). Drink plenty of water to avoid dehydration.

Sexual health

The range of visible and invisible diseases is awesome. Unprotected sex can spread HIV, Hepatitis B and C, Gonorrhea (green discharge), chlamydia (may cause painful urination and later female infertility), painful recurrent herpes, syphilis and warts, to name a few. You can cut down the risk by using condoms, a femidom or avoiding sex altogether. Consider getting a sexual health check on your return home if you do have intercourse.

Insurance

Travel insurance is highly recommended and should cover theft or loss of possessions including passport and money, the cost of medical and dental treatment, cancellation of flights, delays in travel arrangements, accidents, missed departures, personal liability and legal expenses. Keep any relevant medical bills and police reports to substantiate your claim. Note that many policies exclude 'dangerous activities' or charge a higher premium for them. This may include scuba-diving, skiing and even trekking. Some companies will not cover people over 65 years old, or may charge high premiums. **Age Concern**, T01883-346964, www.ageconcern.org.uk, usually have the best deals for seniors. **Columbus Direct**, T0207-375 0011, www.columbusdirect.com, is one of the most competitive British companies.

STA Travel and other reputable student travel organizations also offer good-value policies. Young travellers from North America can try the **International Student Insurance Service** (ISIS), available through **STA Travel**, T1800-777 0112, www.statravel.com, or **Travel Guard**, T1800-826 1300, www.travelguard.com; **Access America**, T1800-284 8300, www. accessamerica.com; **Travel Insurance Services**, T1800-937138, www.travelinsure. com; and **Travel Assistance International**, T1800-821 2828, www.travelassistance.com.

Internet

Internet cafés are springing up all over the place. Even on the islands, if you ask around you'll often find a bar with a computer set up in a corner, though it may not be signed as an internet café from the outside. Well-established internet cafés are listed in this book in individual town directories. Expect to pay 10-15Kn per hour.

Language

The official language is Croatian. Most people working in tourism, as well as the majority of younger Croatians, speak good English, so you won't have much of a problem communicating unless you get off the beaten track. If you do make the effort to learn a few words and phrases, though, your efforts are likely to be rewarded with a smile of appreciation and probably a new-found respect. If you are serious about learning the language a self-study course is a good option, but better still, is a language course completed in the country itself.

Colloquial Croatian and Serbian: The Complete Course for Beginners, by Celia Hawkesworth (Routledge), is an easy-to-use, up-to-date book, which includes concise grammar notes, a useful vocabulary and pronunciation guide, and interactive exercises.

Zagreb University, Sveučilište u Zagrebu, University School of Croatian Language and Culture, Trg maršala Tita 14, 10000 Zagreb, T01-469 8103, www.unizg.hr, organizes Croatian language courses through Jun and Jul. Primarily intended for people of Croatian origin born outside the country, they are also open to anyone else who is interested in learning the language. The courses take place in the university 'Cvjetno Naselje' complex in Zagreb. Students are divided into small groups (maximum 12 participants per class) which cater for various levels from beginner to advanced. Besides the language lessons (Mon to Fri), the school organizes weekend cultural trips.

⏩ *See page 75 for private language schools also offering courses in Croatian for foreigners in Zagreb. See page 348 for a list of useful words and phrases.*

Local customs

Clothing

For business, like anywhere else, appearance counts and you should dress smartly. In all other situations you can get away with casual wear, though scanty clothing is frowned upon in churches – cover your legs and shoulders before entering, even if it's just for a quick peek at the interior. Very few restaurants or nightclubs demand a shirt and tie, but remember that Croatians, and especially Dalmatians, are quite style conscious, so you may receive some withering looks if you turn up in a smart restaurant in shorts and a grubby T-shirt.

Croatia is well known for its nudist beaches, which are marked 'FKK' (from the German, *Freie Kunst und Kulture*). In secluded bays it's also acceptable to bare all, but on crowded family beaches you should definitely wear swimming trunks or bikini bottoms. At beachside bars and eateries it's normally acceptable to sit at a table in a swimsuit, but never, ever topless.

Conduct

A formal greeting takes the form of a handshake – social kissing is reserved for friends and family. Croatians are generally friendly and hospitable, though they are not ones for false smiles: shop assistants can be a little dour and waiters and waitresses in overcrowded bars and restaurants are quite open about displaying exasperation.

People in Croatia like to discuss politics and religion, but following the war there remain a few thorny issues that should be treated with care. The extradition of war criminals is a matter of concern, as is the return of people who were displaced during the 1990s. Many Croats have heart-rending stories to tell, but remember that many families have mixed marriages somewhere down the line, so do not be too blatant about displaying personal views about who was right and who was wrong.

Eating

It's usual to 'clink' glasses when making a toast and you should look the person you're clinking with straight in the eyes so as not to seem evasive. Croatians often eat cheese at the beginning of a meal as an appetizer rather than at the end, so if you order everything at once the cheese will probably arrive first. In informal eateries along the coast, it is quite normal for people to eat barbecued fish with their hands, which is actually far more practical than struggling with a knife and fork.

Croatians are very proud and when they go out to eat it's a matter of 'no expense spared'. They therefore find it very odd when a table of foreigners divides up a bill proportionally according to who has eaten what – stinginess is regarded very badly here. Worse still, on some menus the basic cover charge is listed as *kruh* (bread). Occasionally foreign visitors dispute this tiny sum at the end of the meal, telling their waiter or waitress they never touched the bread. Such penny-pinching only serves to give foreigners a bad name, especially if they come from countries where the average monthly salary is several times than that of a Croatian.

Maps

An excellent source of maps is **Stanfords**, 12-14 Longacre, London WC2E 9LP, T0207-836 1321, www.stanfords.co.uk. As well as stocking maps of the country you will be able to acquire *Imray* and *British Admiralty* charts for sailing maps. There are also branches in Bristol and Manchester. The **Freytag & berndt** Croatia map 1:500 000 and Adriatic coast 1:250 000 are recommended.

Media

Speaking at a conference in Zagreb in early 2002, the Croatian President, Stipe Mesić, said that in the countries of the former Yugoslavia "the lack of media freedom in the 1980s was followed by government control of the media in the 1990s that disseminated intolerance and hatred".

His predecessor, Franjo Tudjman, was renowned for having made **HRT**, the state radio and television company and the primary news source for the majority of Croatians, a mere mouthpiece of the government. Television was certainly a major player in encouraging inter-ethnic hatred and violence during the war of independence, with many news reports being no more than nationalist propaganda. The post-war governments have made some attempt to encourage objective reporting and freedom of speech.

Newspapers

The most widely distributed dailies are *Večernji List*, *Vjesnik* and *Jutarnji List*, all from Zagreb, and *Slobodna Dalmacija* from Split. *Novi List* is a respected independent daily from Rijeka, and *La Voce del Popolo*, also from Rijeka, is an Italian-language daily published for the Italian minorities living in Croatia and Slovenia. You will also find British, American, Italian, German and Slovenian newspapers and magazines readily available in all the main tourist destinations.

Magazines

The most talked-about magazine is *Feral Tribune*, a Split-based satirical weekly, which has won more journalism awards than any other Croatian publication over the last decade, but has also incurred the most lawsuits (mainly during the Tudjman years). The former government's repeated attempts to close the magazine left it in financial crisis, at which point the Hungarian-born multi-millionaire George Soros stepped in and offered *Feral* considerable financial support in the interest of free press. *Globus* and *Nacional* are weekly magazines reviewing current national and international news and events, while *Klik* and *Nomad* are aimed at the late-teen and early-20s market, and concentrate on music, fashion and cultural trends.

Television and radio

Hrvatska radiotelevizija , www.hrt.hr, is the state-run national TV and radio company, which airs three channels: HRT1 shows mainly Croatian-made programmes including news, documentaries, educational, scientific and cultural transmissions; HRT2 broadcasts mainly foreign light entertainment and comedies plus regional news; and HRT3 concentrates on sports and music. In addition, there are many local TV channels, which vary greatly in quality, some being no more than mere advertising networks.

Foreign productions are shown in original version with subtitles. British comedies such as *Allo Allo*, *Only Fools and Horses*, and *Men Behaving Badly* have an astonishing cult -following here, as do David Attenborough BBC wildlife documentaries. However, over the last decade, cheap American films have started to hog a fair chunk of viewing time. All that said, most hotels have satellite TV so you can tune in to foreign channels.

Hrvatska Radio 2 (98.5 Mhz) broadcasts traffic news and nautical reports in English several times a day as well as brief news round-ups in English from the UK's Virgin Radio each hour on the hour.

Money

Currency

The official currency is the Kuna (Kn), which is divided into 100 lipa. The word kuna means 'pine marten' (there's a picture of one on the coins), and refers back to medieval times when the animals' pelts were used as a way of exchange. When the Kuna was reintroduced as a form of currency in May 1994 (replacing the Croatian Dinar, which itself had replaced the Yugoslav Dinar in December 1991) it aroused protests from local Serbs, Jews and Gypsies, as it was last used under the fascist Ustaše government that controlled Croatia during the Second World War from 1941 to 1945.

The Kuna is still not fully convertible so you can't buy it at your bank at home before arriving in Croatia, or sell it back when you return, though you can exchange small amounts at border points in neighbouring countries, eg the ferry port in Ancona and the train station in Trieste.

A limit of 15,000Kn can be taken out of the country. Before leaving Croatia, you can exchange unused Kune for foreign currency in a bank, but officially you need a receipt showing where you got the Kune from in the first place.

The euro is the most readily accepted foreign currency and can be changed easily in banks and bureaux de change. By law in shops, restaurants and hotels you should pay in Croatian Kuna.

Exchange

Credit cards and ATMs Most hotels, restaurants and shops now accept the major credit cards (American Express, Diners Club, MasterCard and Visa) though some of the smaller establishments take cash only. Until recently it was advisable to take plenty of cash when travelling to the islands, but now even the small towns in remote places, such as Komiža on the island of Vis, are equipped with an ATM. Don't rely on this completely, however, as some towns literally have one ATM and if this is out of service, or money runs out, and the bank is closed you will be caught short unless you have a reserve of cash. Make sure you know the correct procedure if you lose your card – it's normally easiest to call the 24-hour helpline of the issuer in your home country.

Traveller's cheques The safest way to carry money is in traveller's cheques, but with the rise in availability of ATMs and the ever-wider acceptance of credit cards, traveller's cheques are accepted less frequently and exchanged at less favourable rates.

Banks and bureaux de change Most towns and villages, even on the islands, have a *banka* (bank), which will generally be open Mon to Fri 0700-1900 and Sat 0700-1300. All the main towns have a *mjenjačnica* (bureaux de change), which is normally located close to the bus or train station. In smaller towns it is often possible to change money at the post office or the local travel agents. Larger hotels will also change money, though their rates are normally pretty bad.

Money transfers If you are stranded in a remote place and need money urgently, the easiest way to receive it is to have it wired via **Western Union**, www.western union.com, to the nearest post office. **Hrvatska Pošta** (Croatian Post) is an agent for Western Union and even the smallest post offices on the islands offer this service.

Cost of living

In spring 2008, the minimum monthly salary in Croatia was 2080Kn (approximately €282), a figure which had been fixed back in 2005. Given the fact that a recent survey showed that the monthly wage is barely enough to cover the costs of basic subsistence, everyday life for local people is obviously not easy. However, Croatians dress well and are extremely proud and generous, so from the outside it's difficult to realize how big the current economic crisis is.

Cost of travelling

Croatia is much more expensive than other former Eastern bloc countries such as the Czech Republic or Hungary. Some Western Europeans come here with the idea that it's a cheap option and then complain about the prices, not taking into consideration the high quality of locally produced food and the fact that most manufactured goods are imported from Western Europe in the first place.

Hotels and restaurants are reasonably cheaper by EU standards, though prices rise significantly through Jul and Aug with an influx of Italian and German tourists. Private rooms are the best source of low-cost, clean, comfortable accommodation – expect to pay anything between 200Kn and 600Kn for a double, depending on the place, time of year and furnishing. There are not many really top-class luxury hotels in Croatia – the rich and famous who turn up here are normally aboard a private yacht – the exception being in Dubrovnik and Hvar Town where you can expect to pay as much as 2000Kn for a double room. It is worth noting here that prices in Dubrovnik have escalated out of all proportion, so that even a cup of coffee now costs double what it would cost anywhere else in Croatia. In some fashionable resorts on the islands, such as Hvar Town on the island of Hvar, prices for everything are hiked up through Jul and Aug, but drop again in Sep.

Public transport – buses, trains and ferries – is very cheap by Western European standards. The exception is cabins on ferries and sleeping cars on the overnight trains, which cost around the same as a night in a lower to mid-range hotel, but are optional in any case.

Opening hours

Banks: Mon-Fri 0700-1900, Sat 0700-1300. Open-air markets: normally Mon-Sat 0700-1300, Sun 0700-1100. **General stores**: generally Mon-Fri 0700-2000 and in most towns at least one will be open Sun 0700-1100. **Clothes shops and bookshops**: normally Mon-Fri 0900-1300, 1700-1930, Sat 0900-1300. Shops may work extended hours in tourist areas during summer.

Post

In Zagreb, the main *pošta* (post office) next to the train station is open 24 hours. In other towns, most post offices work Mon-Fri 0700-2000 and Sat 0700-1300, while in villages on the islands you may find them open mornings only, Mon to Fri 0930-1200.

The postal service is run by **Hrvatska Pošta** and is pretty reliable. Airmail letters and postcards take about 5 days to reach EU countries and 2 weeks to get to the US, Canada and Australia. *Marke* (stamps) can be bought at post offices and newspaper kiosks. Larger post offices also have a facility whereby you can send and receive faxes.

Public holidays

1 Jan New Year's Day
6 Jan Epiphany
Mar/Apr Easter Sun and Mon
1 May May Day
22 Jun Anti-fascist Day
25 Jun Statehood Day
5 Aug National Thanksgiving Day
15 Aug Assumption Day
8 Oct Independence Day
1 Nov All Saints' Day
25 and 26 Dec Christmas

Various towns have local public holidays to celebrate their respective Saint's Day, eg **Sveti Vlaho** in Dubrovnik on **3 Feb**, **Sudamja** in Split on **6 May** and **Sveti Nikola** in Komiža on the island of Vis on **6 Dec**.

Religion

Historically, religion has always been the main defining factor between Croats and Serbs: the former adhering to the Roman Catholic faith, the latter to the Eastern Orthodox church. Religion therefore forms an important factor in ethnic identity – during the war many Croats underwent hasty baptisms, and the numbers attending church soared. Also during the 1990s, most Orthodox churches ceased to function, but today in larger cities such as Zagreb, Rijeka, Zadar and Dubrovnik, and in many smaller towns which once had a large Serb population, they are working once more. Many Croats (even tourist guides) refuse to enter them, though visitors are quite welcome and if the doors are open you can freely take a look inside.

Safety

Despite the negative image created by the war, Croatia has a lower crime rate than most other European countries. Foreigners do not appear to be singled out, though as in any other country, crimes such as pickpocketing are more likely to occur in crowded public spaces such as bus or train stations. The loss or theft of a passport should be reported immediately to the local police and your nearest embassy or consulate.

Rare cases of violent crime are usually targeted at specific persons or property as a result of organized criminal activity or actions prompted by ethnic tensions left over from the war for independence.

Although military action connected to the war ended in 1995, the problem of landmines, mostly along the former confrontation lines in eastern Slavonia and the Krajina, remains. De-mining is not complete: if you are passing through such areas, exercise caution and do not stray from known safe roads and paths.

Student travellers

If you are a full-time student, an **International Student Identity Card** (ISIC) will entitle you to reductions at youth hostels, museums and certain international train and air fares. They are available at student travel offices and travel agents around the world in over 100 countries; to find your nearest office, go to www.isic.org.

If you are already in Croatia, and have proof that you are a student, you can get an ISIC through the travel section of the **Hrvatski Ferijalni i Hostelski Savez** (Croatian Youth Hostel Association), Savska 5/1, 10000 Zagreb, T01-482 9294, www.hfhs.hr.

Telephone

Public payphones are blue and operate with a *telekarta* (phonecard) which can be bought at newspaper kiosks. As many payphones are on busy streets, which tend to be noisy, you may find it more comfortable to telephone from a cabin at the post office, where your call will be timed and you pay when finished. Cheap rates are in force Mon-Sat 1900-0700 and all day Sun.

To call Croatia from abroad, dial 00 from the UK, Ireland and New Zealand, 011 from the US and Canada, 0011 from Australia, all followed by 385, then the area code minus the first zero, then the number. To call abroad from Croatia dial 00 followed by the country code: UK 44; Ireland 353; Australia 61; New Zealand 64; US and Canada 1. International directory enquiries: 902. Local directory enquiries: 988.

Mobile phones are as popular in Croatia as anywhere else in Europe. System dialling codes are 091 and 098. If you are going to stay in the country for a longer period it may be worth subscribing to a Croatian 'pay as you go' network.

Time

Croatia is 1 hr ahead of GMT.

Tipping

Tips are not included on bills. At the end of a good meal at a restaurant it is customary to leave 10% extra if you are satisfied with the service, but it is not normal to tip waiters and waitresses in bars. There are no particular rules regarding taxis.

Tourist information

All the major cities and most smaller towns along the coast and on the islands have a *turistički ured* (tourist office). Their addresses and telephone numbers can be found in the relevant sections of this book. Opening hours vary depending on the time of year, with many of the smaller offices working mornings only through winter. All tourist offices provide information about local hotels, sports facilities as well as public transport, and most can also help you find self-catering accommodation. The larger tourist offices provide maps and sightseeing information. In addition, the telephone service **Croatian Angels**, T062-999999, provides tourist information for the entire country, and operates Apr to Oct.

Austria, Am Hof 13, 1010 Wien, T43 1-585 3884.
Belgium, Vieille Halle aux Bles 38, 1000 Brussels, T32 2-550188.
Czech Republic, Krakovská 25, 110 00 Praha 1, T420 2-2221 1812.
France, 48 Ave Victor Hugo, 75116 Paris, T33 1-4500 9955.
Germany, Rumfordstrasse 7, 80469 München, T49 89-223344.
Hungary, Magyar u 36, 1053 Budapest, T36 1-267 5588.
Italy, Via dell'Orca 48, 00186 Roma, T39 06-3211 0396; Piazzetta Pattari 1/3, 20122 Milano, T39 02-8645 4497.
Netherlands, Nijenburg 2F, 1081 GG Amsterdam, T31 20-661 6422.
Poland, Ul Koszykowa 54, 00 675 Warszawa, T48 22-828 5193.
Slovakia, Trenčianska 5, 821 09 Bratislava, T421 2-5556 2054.
Slovenia, Gosposvetska 2, 1000 Ljubljana, T386 1-230 7400.
Sweden, Kungsgatan 24, 11135 Stockholm, T46 8-5348 2080.
UK, 2 Lanchesters, 162-164 Fulham Palace Rd, London W6 9ER, T44 20-8563 7979.
USA, 350 Fifth Av, Suite 4003, 10118 New York, T1 212-279 8672.

Useful websites

www.cronatur.com Croatia Naturally (naturism)
www.gastronaut.hr Food and restaurants
www.hr Croatian homepage
www.hic.hr Croatian information centre
www.hina.hr Croatian news agency
www.mvp.hr Croatian Ministry of Foreign Affairs and EU Integration
www.seoski-turizam.net Agrotourism (farm holidays), in Croatian and some English
www.visit-croatia.co.uk Visit Croatia, general information for visitors from the UK

Tour operators

» *See page 20 for specialist tour operators.*

In the UK

Balkan Holidays, T0845-130 1114, www.balkanholidays.co.uk. Arrange holidays to the seaside resorts of Istria, Kvarner and Dalmatia.
Croatia for Travellers, 63 Therberton St, London N1 0QY, T020-7226 4460, www.croatiafortravellers.co.uk. Offer programmes for independent travellers island hopping in Dalmatia.
Explore, Nelson House, 55 Victoria Rd, Farnborough, Hampshire GU14 7PA, T0844 499 0902, www.explore.co.uk. Offer a selection of adventure tours, including hiking, cycling and boating.
Holiday Options, 0844 477 0451, www.holidayoptions.co.uk. Arrange holidays in numerous resorts along the coast.
Neilson, Locksview, Brighton Marina, Brighton BN2 5HA, T0870-333 3356, www.neilson.co.uk. Offer sail-and-stay holidays, based in Lumbarda on the island of Korčula, South Dalmatia.
Ramblers Holidays, T01707-331133, www.ramblersholidays.co.uk. Offer a 1-week sight-seeing break based in Dubrovnik, with trips to Cavtat and Čilipi.
Saga Holidays, T0800 096 0074, www.saga.co.uk/travel. Organize 7-day breaks for the 50-plus age group in Poreč in Istria, and Makarska and Dubrovnik in Dalmatia. Some of their Mediterranean cruises stop at Dubrovnik en route.
Thompson Holidays, T0871 231 4691, www.thompson-holidays.com. Arrange packages to numerous destinations along the coast.

Voyages Jules Verne, 21 Dorset Sq, London NW1 6QG, T020-7616 1000, www.vjv.co.uk. Offer several Croatia-based land holidays and cruises.

In the US

Remote Odysseys Worldwide, PO Box 579, Coeur d'Alene, ID 83816, T800 451 6034, www.rowinternational.com. Offer a **Jewels of the Adriatic** 11-day tour, from Venice to Dubrovnik by private yacht, combining sailing, walking, history, culture and wine tasting.

Smithsonian Journeys, PO Box 23293, Washington DC 20026-3293, T202-357 4700, www.smithsonianjourneys.org. Offer a 2-week **Pearls of Dalmatia** tour, departing from Zagreb and visiting Plitvice National Park, then travelling along to the Dalmatian Coast, calling at Dubrovnik, Hvar, Split, Zadar and Opatija.

Visa and immigration

EU, US, Canadian, Australian, New Zealand and Israeli passport holders can enter Croatia without a visa and stay for up to 90 days. South Africans, however, require a visa, which can be obtained at the Croatian Embassy in Pretoria. For further details, visit the Croatian government website, www.mvpei.hr (in Croatian and English), or contact the Croatian embassy in your country.

Foreigners are required to register with the local police within 24 hours of arrival. If you are staying in a hotel or renting a room, it is the owner's responsibility to do this for you. If you are staying with friends, they should by law register you, though in reality people are quite relaxed about this. However, theoretically failure to comply with this rule risks deportation.

Women travellers

Croatian society is basically patriarchal, and local men, like most south European males, will be quite open about expressing their interest in a woman. Advances are normally totally harmless – a few flattering comments then it's up to you to respond. If you are not impressed, ignore them and they will more than likely go away. Local women are quite head strong and don't stand any nonsense – act the same way and you'll be fine. However, some bars are frequented almost exclusively by men: these are best avoided by a woman travelling alone as her presence could be interpreted as an open invitation.

Working in Croatia

Unemployment rates in Croatia are around 11.8% (2007), so opportunities for foreign workers are obviously very limited. Anyone wishing to take on a full-time paid job must apply to the Croatian Embassy for an appropriate visa; to do this you should present a copy of the employment contract for the job you intend to take, plus details of the type of work you will be doing, in Croatian. The options are generally teaching a language or volunteer work.

Useful organizations

Eco-centre Caput Insulae, Beli 4, Beli, Island of Cres, T051-840525, www.supovi.hr. Take on volunteers to help with the upkeep of the centre (see page 159). Activities include maintaining ecotrails, repairing drystone walls and clearing ponds, as well as work in the interpretation centre. Cost includes accommodation in a shared, fully furnished house. Jun-Sep 1 week costs €149 (this includes accommodation) plus €5.50 per day for food. Oct-May 1 week costs €98.

Lancon, Kumičićeva 10, Zagreb 10000, T01-485 4985, www.lancon.hr. Run business English-language courses for companies in the Zagreb area, and are always on the look out for qualified TEFL teachers. Salaries (including healthcare and pension) are gauged on the candidate's educational background and teaching experience.

Plavi Svijet (Blue World), Kaštel 24, Veli Lošinj, Island of Lošinj, T051-204666, www.blue-world.org. This environmental organization takes on volunteers to help with the **Adriatic Dolphin Project** off the coast of Lošinj and Cres. The research team includes experts from Croatia, Italy, UK and Germany, who are currently studying 120 photo-identified bottle-nosed dolphins living in the surrounding waters. It's possible to join the team as an eco-volunteer for

12 days at their base in Veli Lošinj. Activities include observing the dolphins at sea (the group goes out daily by boat) and collecting and analyzing data in the office. Cost (currently €640-770 for 11 days) includes accommodation in a shared, fully furnished house. The organization also runs the **Lošinj Marine Education Centre**.

Inland Croatia

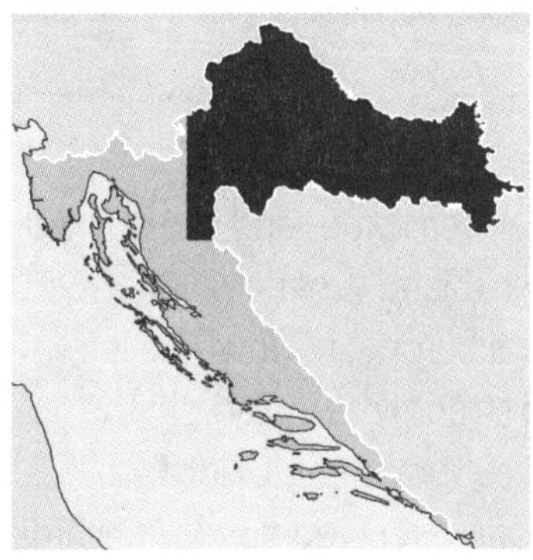

Footprint features

Introduction

Quite another world from the open seascapes and sun-soaked medieval stone towns of the coast, inland Croatia is flatter, damper and infinitely more Central European. Nowhere is the Hapsburgian influence felt so strongly as in Zagreb, the country's economic, political and cultural capital. Northwest from here, the rolling hills of Zagorje offer woodland, vineyards and rural villages, as well as several proud castles, monuments to the days when local peasants were held in the grip of a harsh feudal system.

North of Zagreb, close to the Hungarian border, Varaždin is noted for its well-preserved baroque old town, while northeast of the capital, the village of Hlebine is home to several galleries displaying the unusual works of Croatia's so-called Naïve artists.

Moving east, the flat, fertile plains of Slavonia extend all the way to the border with Serbia. The main town here is Osijek, built on the south bank of the River Drava and worth visiting to see Tvrda, a complex of 18th-century buildings erected by the Austrians to defend the region from the Turks. Close by, Kopački Rit Nature Park is a vast wetland supporting protected birds such as storks and herons.

South of Zagreb, on the road to Dalmatia, you will pass through Lika. In the past many Serbian families lived here and, having fled during the early 1990s, they are only now beginning to return. The main sight here is Plitvice National Park, a paradise of emerald-green lakes and thundering waterfalls set amid a dense forest, close to the border with Bosnia and Herzegovina.

★ Don't miss ...

1 Gornji Grad Follow winding cobbled streets through the loveliest part of Zagrebto the city's cathedral, page 60.

2 Zagorje Celebrate St Martin's Day northof the capital, for the ritual blessing of the region's young wine, page 76.

3 Trakoščan Pretend you are Sleeping Beauty at a fairytale castle overlooking a lake, page 77.

4 Varaždin Tour the 16th-century castle or enjoy classical music at the Varaždin Baroque Evenings, page 79.

5 Kopački Rit Nature Park Spot 260 Species of bird in this beautiful wetland habitat, page 90.

6 Plitvice Lakes National Park Explore the park's stunning lakes and waterfalls by boatand on foot, page 97.

Zagreb

→ *Phone code: 01. Colour map 1, B5. Population: 1 million.*

With most holidaymakers heading straight for the sea and sunshine of the coast, the Mitteleuropean-style capital, Zagreb, is often overlooked as a tourist destination. However, as Croatia's economic and administrative centre, and home to one in four Croats (including most of the country's politicians, businessmen and intellectuals), it's certainly worth devoting a few days to if you want to understand what (or who) makes the nation tick.

The city centre is composed of two main areas, the hilltop Gornji Grad (Upper Town) and the lower-lying Donji Grad (Lower Town), which meet at Trg Bana Jelačića, the main square. Medieval Gornji Grad, home to the cathedral and the Croatian Parliament, is reminiscent of old Prague, thanks to its romantic winding cobbled streets, red-tiled rooftops and church spires. In contrast, Donji Grad, where you'll find the museums, the National Theatre and the university, was laid out on a strict grid system during the 19th century and is made up of grandiose Hapsburgian buildings interspersed between a series of green squares linked by tree-lined boulevards. Beyond the city centre lie the standard suburbs of high-rise apartment blocks, constructed during the latter half of the 20th century.

Apart from peeling paint here and there, most of the buildings still manage to carry off their proud Austro-Hungarian image pretty well. Unfortunately, high living costs, low wages and mass unemployment are still a harsh reality for the people who live here, but as a visitor you can spend a pleasant enough few days exploring the city's museums (many of which are closed on Mondays but now stay open late on Thursday evenings), parks and churches. ▸▸ *For Sleeping, Eating and other listings, see pages 68-75.*

Ins and outs

Getting there

→ *Zagreb is 182 km from Rijeka, 365 km from Split and 581 km from Dubrovnik.*

Throughout the summer, **Croatia Airlines** operate regular international flights to and from Amsterdam, Bari, Berlin, Bologna, Brussels, Catania, Copenhagen, Dusseldorf, Frankfurt, Genoa, Gothenburg, Hamburg, Helsinki, Istanbul, Lisbon, London (Gatwick and Heathrow), Lyon, Munich, Oslo, Palermo, Paris, Prague, Rome, Sarajevo, Skopje, Stockholm, Turin, Vienna and Zurich. Internal flights link the capital with Brač (island of Bol), Dubrovnik, Pula, Split and Zadar. The number of destinations and the frequency of flights are reduced in winter. The airport is at Pleso, 17 km from the city centre; shuttle buses run to the city centre.

There are frequent bus connections with all the main Croatian cities and also daily international connections with Slovenia, Hungary, Serbia and Montenegro, Austria, Germany and Switzerland. The bus station ⓘ *Avenija M Držića 4*, is a 15-minute walk from the main square.

There are train connections to the major cities and some international connections. The train station ⓘ *Trg Kralja Tomislava 12*, is a 10-minute walk from the main square. ▸▸ *See Transport, page 73, for further details.*

Getting around

The city centre is compact and reasonably manageable on foot. An amusing (though rather unnecessary) funicular links Donji Grad to Gornji Grad, operating 0630-2100, tickets 4Kn. To reach more outlying sights you may need to rely on public transport. Regular tram and bus services operate through the day 0400-2345, with slightly less frequent services at night 2335-0345. Tickets cost 8Kn when bought from a kiosk,

24 hours in the city

Watch the city wake up over coffee and a croissant at **Mala Kavana**, seated at an outdoor table overlooking the main square, Trg Bana Jelačića. Five minutes away, stallholders at **Dolac** open-air market will be setting up their fruit and vegetable stands – certainly worth a peep.

Spend the morning in Gornji Grad, taking a look in the **cathedral** to see a 12th-century inscription in the little-known Glagolitic script, and visiting the **Church of St Mark's** with its much-photographed red-white-and-blue tile roof. Lovers of modern sculpture should also reserve an hour for the **Meštrović Atelier**.

Try to arrive at **Lotršćak Tower** just before noon for the firing of the cannon at 1200, then enjoy stunning panoramic views over the city rooftops from **Strossmayer Šetalište**. For an early lunch, stop at the nearby **Pod Gričkim Topom** for seafood risotto and a salad on the summer terrace, then take a short funicular ride down to Donji Grad.

Spend the afternoon in Donji Grad checking out the **Mimara Museum** and the **Arts and Crafts Museum**, pausing for tea at the Viennese-style **Kavana Palace**. If you tire of the sightseeing lark, get back in touch with nature amid the beautifully landscaped **Maksimir Park**, remembering to check out the zoo with its new *Homo sapiens* cage.

Whet your appetite with an early evening aperitif at an open-air café on **Tkalčićeva**, then head to the old-fashioned **Stari Fijaker** for dinner, where you're guaranteed to sample the best of traditional Zagrebian roast meat and game dishes.

Round off the evening in a club: the young and rebellious should head for either **Tvornica** or **Močvara**, while mature and/or glamorous types will feel infinitely more comfortable sipping cocktails at **Hemingway**.

or 10Kn when bought from the driver. You can find taxis in front of the bus and train stations, near the main square and in front of the larger hotels.

Tourist information

The main **Tourist Information Centre (TIC)** ⓘ *Trg Bana Jelačića 11, T01-481 4051, www.zagreb-touristinfo.hr, Mon-Fri 0830-2000, Sat 0900-1700, Sun 1000-1400*, is on the main square. Close to the train station, the **Zagreb Tourist Guide Association** TIC ⓘ *Trg Nikole Šubića Zrinskog 23, T01-481 7022, Mon-Fri 0900-1300*, offers guided city tours. There's also the **Zagreb County Tourist Office** ⓘ *Preradovićeva 42, T01-487 3665, www.tzzz.hr, Mon-Fri 0800-1600*. The centres are helpful and all the staff speak English. They can provide information about accommodation, events, public transport, etc, plus maps and promotional material. The TIC close to the train station deals specifically with organizing guided tours of the city.

Best time to visit

Being the capital, Zagreb is fairly animated the year through. Two major cultural events, the **Summer Festival**, with open-air classical music concerts and theatre in Gornji Grad, and the **Folk Festival**, with displays of regional costume, singing and dancing on the main square, both take place in July.

The city is notoriously cold and foggy through winter (there are even songs about it) and can be extremely hot in summer (when most Zagrebians pack up and head for the coast). It's probably best visited in spring or autumn, when the parks and gardens are at their prettiest and temperatures are ideal for exploring on foot and enjoying the open-air bars and cafés.

Zagreb

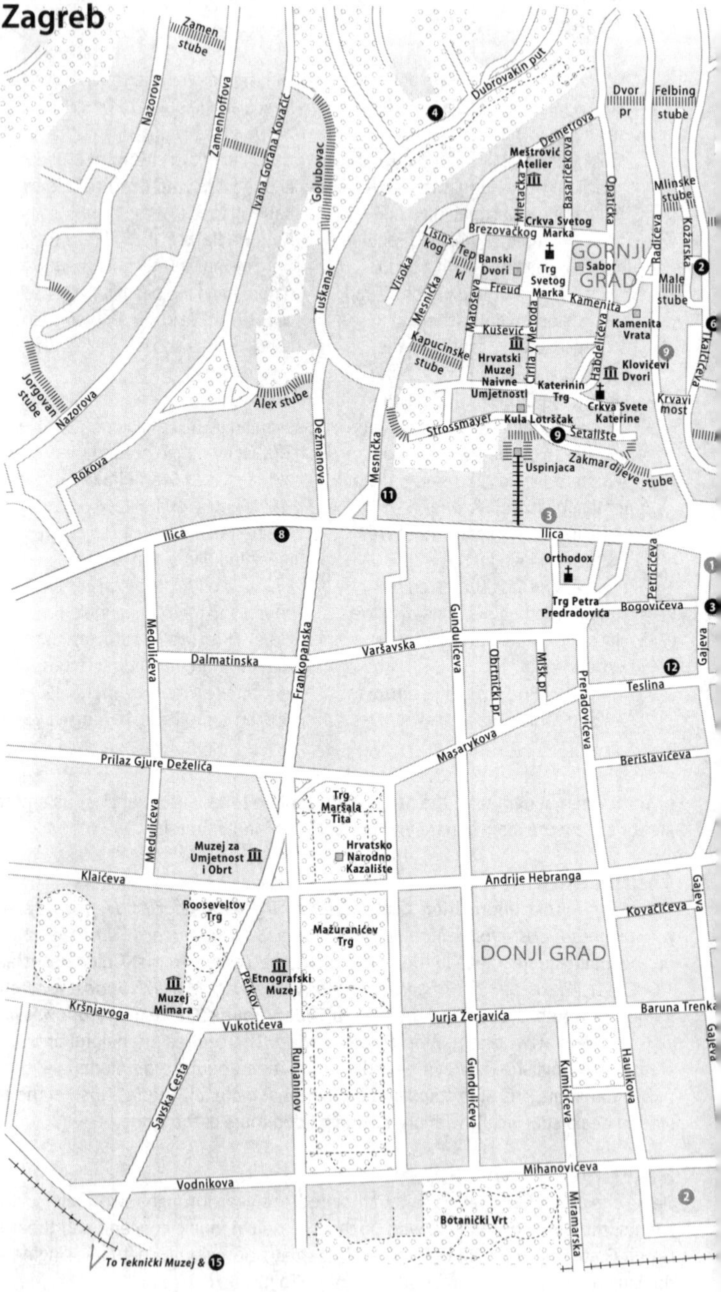

Zamen stube
Nazorova
Zamenhoffova
Ivana Gorana Kovačića
Golubovac
Dubrovakin put
Dvor pr
Felbing stube
Demetrova
Meštrović Atelier
Mletačka
Basaričekova
Opatička
Mlinske stube
Radićeva
Kožarska
Crkva Svetog Marka
Brezovačkog
Lisinskog
Tep kl
Visoka
Banski Dvori
Trg Svetog Marka
GORNJI GRAD
Sabor
Male stube
Freud
Kamenita
Kamenita Vrata
Tuškanac
Mesnička
Matoševa
Ćirila y Metoda
Kušević
Kapucinske stube
Hrvatski Muzej Naivne Umjetnosti
Habdelićeva
Klovićevi Dvori
Tkalčićeva
Katerinin Trg
Crkva Svete Katerine
Krvavi most
Jorgovan stube
Nazorova
Alex stube
Dežmanova
Strossmayer
Kula Lotrščak
Šetalište
Uspinjaca
Zakmardijeve stube
Rokova
Ilica
Orthodox
Petrićeva
Trg Petra Predradovića
Bogovićeva
Gundulićeva
Medulićeva
Frankopanska
Varšavska
Dalmatinska
Obrtnički pr
Mišk pr
Preradovićeva
Teslina
Gajeva
Masarykova
Prilaz Gjure Deželića
Berislavićeva
Trg Maršala Tita
Muzej za Umjetnost i Obrt
Hrvatsko Narodno Kazalište
Klaićeva
Andrije Hebranga
Rooseveltov Trg
Mažuranićev Trg
Kovačićeva
DONJI GRAD
Etnografski Muzej
Perkov
Muzej Mimara
Kršnjavoga
Vukotićeva
Jurja Žerjavića
Baruna Trenka
Runjaninov
Gundulićeva
Kumičićeva
Haulikova
Savska Cesta
Vodnikova
Mihanovićeva
Botanički Vrt
Miramarska
To Teknički Muzej & 15

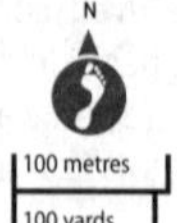

Sleeping
Carpe Diem **8**
Central **11**
Dubrovnik **1**
Fala **13**
Hostel Fulir **9**
Jadran **12**
Jagerhorn **3**
Palace **4**
Ravnice **6**
Regent Esplanade **2**
Sliško **10**
Vila Tina **7**
Youth Hostel **14**

Eating
Atlanta Café **2**
Baltazar **13**
Boban **3**
Dubravkin Put **4**
Ivica i Maritsa **6**
Kaptolska Klet **5**
Maškin i Lata **1**

Medvedgrad Pivnica **15**
Mimice **17**
Nova **8**
Paviljon **7**
Pod Gričkim Topom **9**
Stari Fijaker **11**
Vinodol **12**

Orientation

Finding your way around the city is not difficult. The basic urban layout is clear, with Gornji Grad and Donji Grad meeting at Trg Bana Jelačića, the main square.

Gornji Grad

The loveliest part of Zagreb is, undoubtedly, Gornji Grad (Upper Town). A two-hour stroll through peaceful cobbled streets will take you to the cathedral and several other notable churches, the Sabor (Croatian Parliament), and a handful of good museums.

Trg Bana Jelačića

Lying between Gornji Grad and Donji Grad, Trg Bana Jelačića, the main square, makes an ideal starting place for exploring Zagreb. A vast paved space, it's closed to cars but plays the role of the city centre's main tram intersection, making it an important public meeting place and providing the surrounding cafés with a steady influx of customers. Buildings lining the square date from 1827 onwards, and include several fine examples of Vienna Secessionist architecture. In the centre of the square stands a **bronze equestrian statue** of Ban Jelačić (19th-century Croatian viceroy, see page 325) created by the Viennese sculptor Antun Fernkorn and first erected in 1866. In 1945, Tito, who regarded Jelačić as a symbol of Croatian nationalism, renamed the square Trg Republika, and had the statue dismantled. In 1991, when the HDZ came to power, the square reverted to its former name and a campaign was launched for the return of the statue. Several months later, accompanied by a spectacular firework display, the new president, Franjo Tudjman, performed a triumphant re-inauguration ceremony, the Ban reassembled and back in his former position, having spent 44 years in pieces, hidden away in a cellar.

On the northern edge of the square **Dolac** ⓘ *Mon-Fri 0700-1600, Sat-Sun 0700-1200*, has been the city's main market since 1930. Arranged on two levels, it's a colourful and entertaining affair, with farmers from the surrounding countryside setting up stalls of fruit and vegetables on a raised piazza, while meats and dairy products are sold in an indoor area below. Behind the fruit and vegetable

The place where ties began

Around the world an estimated 600 million businessmen wake up each morning and put on a tie before setting off to work. What many of them probably don't realize is that the tie originates from Croatia.

During the early 17th century, Croatian soldiers began wearing narrow scarves, tied loosely around the neck. Those worn by officers were of coloured silk or fine cotton, while those worn by lower ranking soldiers were of a coarser material.

In 1635, when France entered the Thirty Year's War as an ally of Sweden and the protestant princes of Germany against the Hapsburgs, some 6000 foreign soldiers and knights came to Paris to give their support to King Louis XIII and Cardinal Richelieu. And among them were a group of Croatian mercenaries.

The chic French were immediately impressed by the Croatian soldiers' stylish neck ties, and by 1650 the new style 'à la croate' had arrived in the court of Louis XIV, who was well known for his love of ornamentation and grandeur.

The expression, 'à la croate', soon evolved into a new French word, which still exists today: *la cravate*. When the exiled English King Charles II (also noted for extravagant taste) returned home in 1660 he brought this new fashion accessory to Britain, and over the following decades the cravat came to symbolize the height of culture and elegance throughout Europe.

section, you'll find people selling handmade items such as lace, hats and jewellery, and to each side of the piazza a conglomeration of snack bars serving cheap eats.

Katedrala

ⓘ *Kaptol 31, daily 0800-2000.*

From Dolac, it's just a couple of minutes' walk to the Katedrala (cathedral). Much of the original structure, dating back to the 12th century, was destroyed by the Tartars in 1242. While reconstruction and extension work took place between the 13th and 16th centuries, this in turn was badly damaged by the 1880 earthquake, thus the neo-Gothic façade and twin steeples we see today were designed by an Austrian architect, Herman Bolle. Inside, the north wall bears an inscription of the Ten Commandments in 12th-century Glagolitic script (see page 127) and, nearby a touching relief by Ivan Meštrović portrays the late Archbishop Alojzije Stepinac kneeling before Christ, and marks the controversial bishop's final resting place. In front of the cathedral, a gilded statue of the Virgin, protected by four angels, stands on a high stone column. Like the Ban Jelačić statue, it is the work of Antun Fernkorn.

Tkalčićeva

From the cathedral, proceed along the street of Kaptol, then take the first left, followed by the first right, pass through a walled public garden and descend a short flight of steps to arrive on Tkalčićeva. Until 1898, when it was filled in, this street was a channel forming the boundary between Kaptol and Gradec, and was known as 'Potok' (The Brook). Today it's a pretty pedestrian zone lined with 19th-century town houses, most of which host popular street-level café-bars and informal restaurants with open-air seating: an amusing place for morning coffee, lunch or an early evening drink, perfect for people-watching.

Kamenita Vrata (Stone Gate)

From Tkalčićeva, a flight of steep wooden steps leads to the parallel street of Radićeva, where you'll find a number of small private galleries and gift shops. From here, it's five minutes to Kamenita Vrata, formerly one of four entrances into the walled town of Gradec.

In 1731, after a devastating fire had consumed the surrounding wooden buildings, a painting of the Virgin Mary was found in the ashes, remarkably undamaged. Kamenita Vrata was reconstructed and became regarded as a place of miracles. Today locals come here to pray and pay tribute to the Virgin: there's a delightful shrine adorned with flickering candles and the walls are hung with small plaques saying *Hvala* (thank you), so it obviously works. Close by, at Kamenita 9, stands a pharmacy dating back to the mid-14th century and still functioning today. On the wall, a memorial stone records that the grandson of the Italian poet Dante Alighieri worked here in 1399.

Trg Svetog Marka

Kamenita Ulica leads to Trg Svetog Marka, for centuries the centre of Zagrebian political, cultural and commercial life. A daily market used to be held here, and it was the main public meeting place until Trg Bana Jelačića took over the role during the 19th century. The centrepiece is **Crkva Svetog Marka** (St Mark's Church) ⓘ *daily 0800-2000*, erected in the 13th century as the parish church of Gradec. Its most remarkable feature is the steeply pitched roof, added during reconstruction in 1880 and decorated in red white and blue tiles depicting the coats of arms for Zagreb (on the right) and the Kingdom of Croatia, Dalmatia and Slavonia (on the left). Inside, the walls are frescoed with biblical scenes, painted by Jozo Kljaković between 1936 and 1938. During the Middle Ages, a pole of shame was erected in front of the church, where local lawbreakers were punished with a public whipping. One such 'offender', Matija Gubec, was less fortunate: having organized an unsuccessful peasant uprising in 1573, he was brought to Markov Trg and 'crowned with molten iron for his impertinence'. Local myth has it that a stone face carved on the corner building between Ćirolmetodska ulica and Kamenita ulica is a monument to him.

Facing the main entrance to the church stands the **Sabor** (Croatian Parliament), housed within a neoclassical building completed in 1910. On 25 June 1991, this was the very place where members of the Sabor voted in favour of national independence, thus marking the beginning of the end of the Socialist Federal Republic of Yugoslavia. On 7 October 1991 the building was hit by a bomb: the next day Croatia cut off all state and legal links with Belgrade. On the opposite side of the square stands a single-storey baroque building, **Banski Dvori** (Ban's Court Palace), where the Croatian viceroy resided from 1809 to 1918.

Meštrović Atelier

ⓘ *Mletačka 8, T01-485 1123, www.mdc.hr/mestrovic, Tue-Fri 1000-1800, Sat-Sun 1000-1400, 20Kn.*

A short walk north of the square will bring you to the charming Meštrović Atelier. During the 1920s, the Dalmatian sculptor Ivan Meštrović (see page) refurbished this 17th-century building to serve as a home and studio. Dividing his time between Zagreb and Split, he lived and worked here on and off until fleeing the country during the Second World War. When he died in 1962 it was turned into a memorial museum with a beautifully presented exhibition of his sculptures and drawings.

Hrvatski Muzej Naivne Umjetnosti (Croatian Naïve Art Museum)

ⓘ *Ćirila i metoda 3, T01-485 1911, www.hmnu.org, Tue-Fri 1000-1800, Sat-Sun 1000-1300, closed Mon, 20Kn.*

Returning to Trg Sv Marka, Ćirila i metoda, the street running south of the square, leads to this museum. You may not consider Croatian Naïve art (see pages 83 and 337) aesthetically pleasing, but it certainly is unusual. During the 1930s, a group of farmers from the village of Hlebine in Slavonia took up painting (with no previous tuition), and the canvasses on display here show what they produced. Several of them, most notably Ivan Generalić, went on to receive international recognition.

Crkva Svete Katerine (St Catherine's Church)

ⓘ *Katerinin Trg, daily 0800-2000.*
Ćirila i metoda leads to Katerinin Trg, overlooked by the baroque church. Built for the Jesuit order between 1620 and 1632, it was modelled on Giacomo da Vignola's Il Gesu in Rome. The vaulted ceilings are encrusted with sugary pink and white stuccowork, and there's a clever 18th-century illusionist fresco above the main altar.

Klovićevi Dvori

ⓘ *Jezuitski Trg 4, T01-485 1926, www.galerijaklovic.hr, Tue-Sun 1100-2000, 20Kn.*
Close by, most major international exhibitions are staged at Klovićevi Dvori, a 17th-century Jesuit College that was reconstructed in 1982 to form a large art gallery. There isn't a permanent collection. Temporary exhibitions have included Marc Chagall, '2000 years of Nigerian Art' and 'Jewels of Ottoman Art from the Topkapi Museum'. During the Zagreb Summer Festival, concerts are staged in the internal courtyard. The museum café makes an ideal stopping point for weary legs.

Strossmayer Šetalište (Strossmayer Promenade)

Returning to Ćirila i metoda then turning left, you will arrive on Strossmayer Šetalište, a pleasant walkway following the line of Gradec's former south-facing wall, offering stunning views over the city rooftops. Pride of place is taken by **Kula Lotrščak** (Lotrščak Tower) ⓘ *Strossmayer Šetalište 9, Tue-Sun 1100-1900, 10Kn*, part of the 13th-century fortification system. The tower now houses a gallery, and it is possible to climb to the top for dramatic views across the city to Novi Zagreb, on the south side of the River Sava. Each day at noon, a small (but extremely loud) cannon is fired from the top of the tower, in memory of the times when it was used to warn off the possibility of an Ottoman attack.

Opposite the tower stands the upper station of the **Uspinjača (funicular railway)** ⓘ *Strossmayer Šetalište, daily 0630-2100, 4Kn*, connecting Gornji Grad and Donji Grad. Built in 1891, it ran on steam until 1934 and makes an amusing way to descend 40 m (130 ft) to Tomićeva, just off Ilica. From here it's just a five-minute walk back to Trg Bana Jelačića, the main square.

Donji Grad

While Gornji Grad is made up of higgledy-piggledy cobbled streets which evolved spontaneously over the centuries, Donji Grad (Lower Town) was built on a formal grid during the late 19th century. The urban plan was drawn up by Milan Lenuci, who proposed a succession of adjoining squares with central gardens, laid out to form a 'U', now known as Lenuci's Green Horseshoe.

Trg Petra Predradovića

About five minutes southwest of Trg Bana Jelačića (and equally accessible from Ilica) is Trg Petra Predradovića, better known to locals as Cvijetni Trg (Flower Square), in reference to the flower sellers who used to set up stalls here. Alas, the stalls are no longer, but there are a couple of colourful kiosks vending fresh bouquets. At the north end of the square stands the Orthodox Church, still frequented by Zagreb's (seriously depleted) Serb community.

Trg Maršala Tita (Marshall Tito Square)

From Trg Petra Predradovića, the street of Preradovićeva leads south, and if you follow this then take the first right onto Masarykova, you arrive at the vast green Trg Maršala Tita (Marshall Tito Square). This is the first of a series of three squares that make up one side of Lenuci's Green Horseshoe. The centrepiece is the monumental neo-baroque **Hrvatsko Narodno Kazalište** (Croatian National Theatre) ⓘ *Trg Maršala*

Tita 15, T01-488 8488, www.hnk.hr, the theatre season runs Sep-Jun, designed by two Viennese architects, Hellmer and Fellner, in 1894. Construction work was completed in record time, so as to be ready for an official opening by Emperor Franz Josef on his state visit in 1895. In front of the theatre is the slightly neglected *Zdenac Života* (Well of Life) by Ivan Meštrović, dating from 1912.

Muzej za Umjetnost i Obrt (Arts and Crafts Museum)

ⓘ *Trg Maršala Tita 10, T01-488 2111, www.muo.hr. Tue-Wed and Fri-Sat 1000-1800, Thu 1000-2200, Sun 1000-1400, closed Mon, 30Kn.*

On the western side of the square stands the Arts and Crafts Museum, a pleasant purpose-built 19th-century structure designed by Herman Bolle. The interior is refreshingly light and airy, providing a visitor- friendly exhibition space for a vast collection of furniture, laid out in chronological order and illustrating how Croatian design has been influenced by Austrian and Italian tastes, from the baroque period up to the Modern Movement.

Muzej za Umjetnost i Obrt is probably the best museum in Zagreb, after the Meštrović Atelier.

Muzej Mimara (Mimara Museum)

ⓘ *Rooseveltov trg 4, T01-482 8100, Tue-Wed, Fri-Sat 1000-1700, Thu 1000-1900, Sun 1000-1400, closed Mon, 40Kn.*

Across the busy main road of Savska Cesta, Roosevelt Trg is dominated by this renowned museum, housed within a neo-Renaissance former grammar school building. This phenomenal private collection was donated to the city by Ante Topić-Mimara. No one is quite sure how Mimara amassed such a treasure trove of art works. Born in Dalmatia in 1898, he spent most of his life abroad, where he made his fortune, supposedly as a merchant. In 1973 he began transferring his collection to Zagreb and arranged for the founding of a museum, which opened in 1987, the year he died. On display are canvases attributed to Old Masters such as Raphael, Rembrandt and Rubens, as well as more modern paintings by Manet, Degas and Renoir (though whether all these pieces are genuine remains a matter of controversy). The collection also includes an astounding hoard of ancient Egyptian glassware, Chinese porcelain and Persian carpets – all well worth seeing but of little relevance to Croatian culture.

Tehnički Muzej (Technical Museum)

ⓘ *Savska Cesta 18, near Cibona Stadium, T01-484 4050, Tue-Fri 0900-1700, Sat-Sun 0900-1300, closed Mon, 15Kn.*

Further down Savska Cesta is the Tehnički Muzej, best visited in mid-afternoon when three highly enlightening 30-minute guided tours are on offer. While the ground floor displays a slightly mystifying selection of engines and turbines (appreciated almost exclusively by children and mechanical engineers), the star attraction is the Nikola Tesla demonstration, performed daily at 1530 in an area arranged to look like the early 20th-century scientist's laboratory. If you arrive a little earlier, there's a guided visit of a reconstructed mine at 1500, and then a planetarium visit at 1600.

Etnografski Muzej (EthnographicMuseum)

ⓘ *Mažuranićev trg 14, T01-482 6220, Tue-Thu 1000-1800, Fri-Sun 1000-1300, closed Mon, 15Kn (free Thu).*

Returning to Trg Maršala Tita, the next square in the Green Horseshoe series is Mažuranićev Trg, home to this museum. Worth a look in if you're interested in traditional folk costumes – the variety of colours, materials and styles on display illustrates the cultural diversity of Croatia's contrasting inland and coastal regions. The lace from the island of Pag and the gold embroidered scarves from Slavonia are particularly worth seeing. There's also a section devoted to artefacts from the South Pacific, Asia and Africa, collected by 19th-century Croatian explorers and travellers.

Tesla the inventor

Nikola Tesla was born in 1856 to a Serbian family in Smiljan, Croatia, and educated in Graz and Prague. Having completed his studies in 1881, he worked as electrical engineer for a telephone company in Budapest, before emigrating to the US in 1884. There he was briefly employed by Thomas Edison, but soon decided to work alone on research and inventions, and the two thus became archrivals.

In 1888, Tesla designed the first system of generating and transmitting alternating current, though the patent rights to this revolutionary invention were bought by the American scientist George Westinghouse. In 1891 he invented the Tesla coil, a transformer still used today in radios and television sets. In 1895, he designed the first hydroelectric power plant on the Niagara Falls. However, in the same year his laboratory was destroyed by fire, and he began a series of economic and mental ups and downs that were to taint his later years.

An eccentric loner, he lived almost exclusively in hotels. From 1897 to 1933 he resided at the luxury Waldorf-Astoria Hotel, where he entertained New York celebrities: 6ft 6in tall, dark and handsome, many women are said to have been intrigued by him, but he remained a lifelong bachelor.

In 1915 he was nominated for the Nobel Prize for physics, which he was to share with Thomas Edison, but he refused to divide it with his former employer so in the end neither of them received the award. On 10 July 1931, his 75th birthday, he was featured on the cover of *Time* magazine. However, by this time he had become totally solitary and had developed an unusual obsession with rescuing pigeons from Central Park. In 1933, due to financial problems, he moved from the Waldorf-Astoria to the far less glamorous Hotel New Yorker in Manhattan where he died in 1943. In 1956, the Tesla (T), a unit for measuring magnet flux density, was named after him.

Botanički Vrt (Botanical Gardens)

ⓘ *Trg M Marulića 9a, Jun-Aug Mon-Tue 0900-1430, Wed-Sun 0900-1900, Apr-May and Sep-Oct Mon-Tue 0900-1430, Wed-Sun 0900-1800, free.*

Founded in 1889 as research grounds for the Faculty of Botany at Zagreb University, the gardens are small but well kept, and offer a welcome retreat from the bustle of the city. The main section is an arboretum, arranged informally in the style of an English garden, beside two artificial ponds with stunning water lilies and an ornamental bridge.

Trg Kralja Tomislava

Five minutes from the gardens stands the **Glavni Kolodvor** (main train station). From 1919 to 1977 the Orient Express used to stop here. The James Bond film *From Russia with Love* (1963) features Sean Connery in Zagreb station, as one of the train's illustrious passengers, en route to Istanbul. Glavni Kolodvor overlooks Trg Kralja Tomislava, named after Tomislav (the first king of the medieval state of Croatia), and bears an equestrian statue of him. In the centre of the square stands the **Umjetnički Paviljon** (Art Pavilion) ⓘ *Trg Kralja Tomislava 22, T01-484 1070, www.umjetnicki-paviljon.hr, Mon-Sat 1100-1900, Sun 1000-1300, 20Kn*, originally built to celebrate '1000 years of Hungarian Culture' in Budapest in 1896, then dismantled and reassembled here, under the initiative of the Croatian artist Vlaho Bukovac (see page 337). Today it is used for temporary exhibitions.

Moderna Galerija (Modern Art Gallery)

ⓘ *Andrije Hebranga 1, T01-492 2368, Tue-Fri 1000-1800, Sat-Sun 1000-1300, 30Kn.* Exhibiting paintings, sculpture, posters, instillations and videos, this gallery traces 200 years of Croatian art, spanning the 19th and 20th centuries. Refreshingly colourful and modern.

Trg Nikole Šubića Zrinskog

You are now in the second set of three leafy squares that make up the remaining side of Lenuci's Green Horseshoe. Proceeding back towards the city centre, the next square is overlooked by the 19th-century Croatian Academy of Sciences and Arts (formerly named the Yugoslav Academy of Sciences and Arts) housing the **Strossmayerova Galerija Starih Majstora** (Strossmayer Gallery of Old Masters) ⓘ *Trg Nikole Šubića Zrinskog 11, T01-481 3344, www.mdc.hr/strossmayer, Tue 1000-1300, 1700-1900, Wed-Sun 1000-1300, closed Mon, 10Kn.* Founded by Bishop Strossmayer in 1884, the collection has expanded gradually over the last 120 years and now includes many notable canvases by Venetian Renaissance and baroque painters such as Bellini and Carpaccio, and Dutch masters Brueghel and Van Dyck. Worth a special mention is a small *Mary Magdalene* by El Greco.

Across the road, the **Arheoloski Muzej** (Archaeological Museum) ⓘ *Trg Nikole Šubića Zrinskog 19, T01-487 3101, www.amz.hr, Tue-Wed and Fri 1000-1700, Thu 1000-2000, Sat-Sun 1000-1300, 20Kn*, exhibits finds from prehistoric times up to the Tartar invasion. Pride of place is taken by the Vučedol Dove, a three-legged ceramic vessel in the form of a bird, dating back to the fourth millennium BC and found in Vukovar, Eastern Slavonia.

Around Zagreb

If you plan to stay more than three days in the Zagreb area, an excursion into the surrounding countryside will give you a clearer picture of what inland Croatia is all about. Zagrebians love walking and most would probably nominate **Mount Medvenica** as their favourite out-of-town trip. Cake lovers might opt for a leisurely afternoon in **Samobor** where the local delicacy is *kremšnita* (custard pie).

Another popular excursion is a drive through Zagorje, a region north of the capital, noted for its undulating hills, vineyards and *klets*. Here you can visit Tito's birthplace and Staro Selo (Old Village Farm Museum) at **Kumrovec**, plus the romantic castle of **Trakoščan**, and the imposing **Veliki Tabor** fortress which was restored in 2007.

Last but by no means least, architectural fanatics are advised to make a trip to the well-preserved baroque town and former capital, **Varaždin**. Those interested in modern art may be intrigued (or reviled) by the Hlebine Art Gallery, displaying works by local Naïve artists, at **Hlebine**. ▸▸ *For details of these destinations, see North of Zagreb, pages 76-83.*

Maksimir Park

ⓘ *Sunrise to sunset, 3 km east of the city centre, tram No 11 and No 12 (direction Dubrava) from Trg Bana Jelačića, the main square.*
East of the city centre lies the green expanse of Maksimir Park, animated by joggers, lovers and families with kids. Founded as a city garden by Archbishop Maximilian Vrhovac (after whom it is named) in 1784, Maksimir claims to be the first public park in southeast Europe. During the 19th century, Archbishop Juraj Haulik extended the park to its present 18 ha, and proposed the English-style landscaping with lawns, woods, tree-lined avenues, artificial lakes and romantic follies. The **zoo** ⓘ *T01-230 2198, www.zoo.hr, summer daily 0900-2000, winter daily 0900-1700, 30Kn*, was added in 1925. In 2005 a new and amusing addition was made: two cages labelled *Homo sapiens*, which visitors can enter to experience how it feels to be on view behind bars.

Savouries, sweets and shots

You'll find plenty of small traditional restaurants serving up excellent local dishes in Samobor and its surroundings. Look out for *cesnjofke* (garlic flavoured sausages) and *rudarska gredlica*, a concoction of egg, flour, oil, cheese and walnuts, known as *miner's pie* after the men who used to work the copper mines at Rude. If you have a sweet tooth, be sure to try *samoborska kremšnita*, a delicious custard pie made with flaky pastry. In May 2001, the people of Samobor were nominated for the *Guinness Book of Records*, having just knocked up the 'world's largest custard pie', weighing 1.1 tons. Last but not least, the local liquor, Bermet, and *muštarda* (mustard) make unusual presents to take home. They are both based on recipes brought here by the French between 1809 and 1813, when Samobor was part of Napoleon's Illyrian Provinces.

Opposite the park stands the **Dinamo Football Stadium**, home ground to the city football team and the main venue for international matches played in Croatia.

Mirogoj Cemetery

ⓘ *2 km northeast of city centre, daily 0800-2000, bus No 106 from Kaptol, opposite the cathedral.*

North of the city centre, Mirogoj Cemetery was designed by Herman Bolle in 1876. The west side of the cemetery is enclosed within a protective wall sheltering a neo-Renaissance arcade, while the monumental main entrance is crowned with a copper cupola. Over the decades citizens of varying religious and political persuasion have been laid to rest here, as can be seen by the stylistic range of tombs: the elongated pentagonal Muslim headstones, the Orthodox stones bearing Cyrillic script, the Jewish with the six-point star, Socialists the five-point red star and, of course, the majority, Catholics.

Medvednica Nature Park

ⓘ *Mon-Fri 0800-1600; Nature Park office, Bliznec bb, Zagreb, T01-458 6317, www.pp-medvednica.hr. Supply maps and information about mountain huts.*

Just north of Zagreb – in fact the city's suburbs extend on to the lower slopes – Medvednica Mountain has long been a popular hiking destination for the people of Zagreb, with the first organized walking groups setting out to scale its heights in the late 19th century. Still today it's a popular destination, especially on Sundays, when the early morning tram is literally heaving with hikers – many well past retirement age – setting out to climb to Sljeme, the 1033-m summit, many decked in appropriate walking gear and armed with a picnic lunch.

Medvednica was declared a nature park in 1981, with marked walking paths winding their way across the slopes, 64% of which are covered with deciduous and coniferous woods of oak, beech, chestnut and fir. The park is at its prettiest in spring, when the woodland paths are dense with wild flowers, and in autumn, when the trees take on golden and russet hues. In winter there are basic skiing facilities.

The highest peak, **Sljeme**, which can be reached by cable car, is crowned by a TV tower and a small chapel, and on a fine day it's possible to see Zagreb to the south, Zagorje to the north and the Slovenian Alps to the west from this fine vantage point.

Traces of prehistoric man have been found in **Veternica Cave** ⓘ *Apr-Nov, Sun 1000-1600, 25Kn*, on the mountain which was first mentioned as *Mons Ursi* (Bear Mountain) in 1209. Its present name is derived from the Croatian *medvjed*, meaning 'bear', and indeed the slopes were once populated by bears.

Medvednica is ideal for picnicking, with several designated areas equipped with wooden tables and benches, though cheap substantial food is also available at several mountain huts. Alternatively, if you can hold out till the homeward journey, there are a number of good traditional restaurants on the road between the park and the capital. ▸▸ *See Transport, page 74, for details of how to get there.*

Samobor

Close to the hills of the recently designated Žumberak i Samobor Gorje Prirodni Park, Samobor has a somewhat Alpine feel. Narrow cobbled streets meet at the large main square, Trg kralja Tomislava, surrounded by palatial 19th-century town houses and open-air cafés. Just off the square you'll find **Mala Venecija** (Little Venice), a pretty area built along the banks of Gradna Brook, traversed by a series of wooden bridges. Samobar provides well for Zagrebian's favourite pastimes – hiking and dining (see box, page 66) – so it's a popular weekend retreat. If you are arriving from the Slovenian border there is a lovely, reasonably priced, old-fashioned hotel, making it an ideal first-night base. There is a town **tourist office** ⓘ *Trg kralja Tomislava 5, T01-336 0044, www.tz-samobor.hr.*

The town dates back to 1270, when supporters of the Czech king, Otokar, built Stari Grad fortress on Tepec Hill. A settlement grew up below the fortress, expanding rapidly during the 16th century with the opening of copper mines in the nearby village of Rude, plus the arrival of Franciscan monks. Stari Grad was abandoned during the late 18th century and now lies derelict, though the remaining walls and defence tower are worth the uphill hike if you're a ruins fan. In 1797 fire destroyed much of the town below, hence most of today's buildings are post 18th century.

A five-minute walk from the main square stands Livadićev Dvor, dating back to 1764. Members of the Illyrian Movement (see page 325) used to meet here during the mid-19th century, and in 1949 the building was turned into the **Gradski Muzej** (Town Museum) ⓘ *Livadićev Dvor, Livadićeva 7, T01-336 1014, Tue-Fri 0900-1500, Sat-Sun 0900-1300, 10Kn*. Inside you'll find various exhibits relating to Samobor's past, ranging from a small archaeological collection to the history of the local mountaineering club.

Close by, in a 19th century manor, the **Muzej Marton** (Marton Museum) ⓘ *Jurjevska 7, T01-332 6426, www.muzej-marton.hr, Sat-Sun 1000-1300, 15Kn*, displays a private collection including furniture, paintings, glassware, porcelain and clocks, predominantly from Central Europe and all dating from the 18th and 19th centuries.

Leave the main square by Sv Ane, a winding pathway leading through wooded parkland up to **Anindol Šetalište** (Anindol Promenade) on **Tepec Hill**. From here there are wonderful views over the town and surrounding countryside. If you reach the top you'll come to the ruins of Stari Grad, and close by you'll find two small baroque chapels, **Kapelica Sv Ane** and **Kapela Sv Jurja**, joined together by a pilgrimage path known as **Križni Put** (Stations of the Cross).

Žumberak i Samobor Gorje Prirodni Park (Nature Park)

ⓘ *Nature Park Information Centre, Slani Dol 1, Samobor, T01-332 7660, www.pp-zumberak-samoborsko-gorje.hr. No public transport.*

The people of Samobor have long been known as keen hikers, with organized walks going back to the late 19th century. In 1999, the hills of Samobor Gorje and Žumberak were declared **Žumberak i Samobor Gorje Prirodni Park**. Displaying typical karst features such as caves and gorges, the region is covered with dense forests of beech and chestnut, interspersed with sub-Alpine meadows, isolated hamlets and a series of well-marked footpaths. You can pick up a hiking map at the nature park office in Slani Dol. Many of the **village churches** of the Žumberak region belong to a community of *Grkokatolici* (Greek Catholics), descendants of Orthodox Uskoks (see page 146) who were invited by the Hapsburgs to repopulate the region in the early 17th century, and were allowed to continue practising Orthodox rites on the condition that they acknowledged papal supremacy.

Gornji Grad *p59, map p58*

F Hostel Fulir, Radićeva 3a, T01-483 0882, www.fulir-hostel.com. Close to Zagreb's main square, this cosy 16-bed hostel is run by 2 young Croats who have lived in the US. There's a big 12-bunk dorm and a smaller 4-bed room, plus 2 shared bathrooms. Facilities include a kitchen, and a colourful common room with satellite TV, internet access, a small library and a DVD collection.

Donji Grad *p62, map p58*

AL Hotel Regent Esplanade, Mihanovićeva 1, opposite the train station, T01-456 6666, www.regenthotels.com. Built in 1925 for travellers on the Orient Express, the grandiose interior of this 220-room hotel has retained its old-fashioned charm, while renovations have provided modern facilities including a business centre, and massage, sauna and beauty salon.

A Hotel Dubrovnik, Gajeva 1, just off the main square, T01-487 3555, www.hotel-dubrovnik. hr. The most centrally located hotel in town is best known for its unfortunately garish mirrored-glass façade. However, its 266 rooms are modern and comfortable, and some offer views of the cathedral.

B Hotel Palace, Stross-mayerov Trg 10, between the train station and the main square, T01-492 0530, www.palace.hr. Overlooking a leafy square, this Secessionist building was converted to become the city's first hotel in 1907. There are 126 rooms, plus a pleasant street-level Viennese-style café.

C Central, Branimirova 3, T01-484 1122, www.hotel-central.hr. In a side street (with no view to speak of) just 100 m from the train station, this 76-room hotel was renovated in 2001 to provide smart functional rooms with en suite bathrooms, satellite TV, minibar, internet access and a/c.

D Jadran, Vlaška 50, T01-455 3777, www. hup-zagreb.hr. Excellently located, just a 5-min walk from the main square, this old building has been renovated to provide a tastefully furnished 48-room hotel with basic amenities but no extras.

D Jagerhorn, Ilica 14, 100 m west of the main square, T01-483 3877, F01-483 3446. Adjoining a well-known game restaurant of the same name, **Jagerhorn** is tucked away in a passageway off Ilica, and offers 13 simply furnished, cosy rooms.

D Vila Tina, Bukovačka Cesta 213, 20 mins from the main square, close to Maksimir Park, T01-244 5204, www.vilatina.hr. This delightful family-run hotel comprises 25 tastefully furnished rooms, adorned with extras such as fresh fruit and flowers. There's an excellent restaurant, plus a small indoor pool, solarium and sauna.

E Hotel Fala, II Trnjanske ledine 18, T01-611 1062, www.hotel-fala-zg.hr. A 15-min walk south of the train station brings you to this small family-run hotel. The 13 rooms all have TV and minibar. There's a cheerful breakfast room with a pine floor and blue details, and guests can use the internet in the reception.

E Hotel Sliško, Supilova 13, 200 m from the bus station, T/F01-618 4777, www.slisko.hr. This small hotel has 18 smartly furnished rooms, each with a private bathroom. There's a bar and breakfast room (but no restaurant) and ample parking space.

F Carpe Diem, Milana Sufflaya 3, T01-468 0199, www.hostel.com.hr. Opened in Jun 2007, this friendly, funky 16-bed hostel is in the Medveščak area, north of the Cathedral. There are 3 rooms totalling 16 beds, each decorated in a bright colour with old-fashioned furniture. Extras include a small garden and a communal living room with internet, refreshments and TV. Open all year.

F Ravnice, Ravnice 38d, www.ravnice-youth-hostel.hr, 20 mins from the main square, close to Maksimir Park, T01-233 2325. This clean and genuinely friendly hostel remains open all year and offers 30 beds, arranged in double and quadruple rooms with parquet floors and bright, cheerful colours. Facilities include a kitchen, laundry and internet.

G Youth Hostel, Petrinjska 77, T01-484 1261, www.hfhs.hr. Open throughout summer 2008, then closing for renovation during winter, this hostel will reopen with a new look in time for spring 2009. The location is perfect for backpackers, just a stone's throw from the train station. There are 210 beds arranged in single, double and triple rooms, and 6-bed dorms. There will also be a new restaurant.

Private accommodation

Evistas, Šenoina 28, T01-483 9554, www.evistas.hr. This agency can arrange short-term apartment rentals or rooms with local families.

Medvednica Nature Park *p66*

C **Tomislavov Dom**, Sljemenska cesta bb, T01-456 0400, www.hotel-tomislavovdom.com. Just a 5-min walk from the cable car, this mountain-top hotel set in pretty woodland offers 42 basic but comfortable rooms, plus a café, restaurant, a Wellness Centre with an indoor pool, gym and sauna, and conference facilities.

F **Hotel Zvonimir**, Slemenjska cesta 10, T01-458 0397, F01-4552185. Formerly known as **Hotel Hunjka**, this chalet-style building has 23 rooms and 2 suites, a restaurant, billiard room and internet. There's a large grassy area out front with picnic benches for hikers.

Samobor *p67*

E **Hotel Livadić**, Trg Kralja Tomislava 1, T01-336 5850, www.hotel-livadic.hr. Overlooking the main square, this romantic, family-run hotel occupies a building dating back to 1800. The 12 rooms are truly luxurious – wooden antique furniture, parquet flooring and oriental rugs – without being expensive. Well worth staying at.

F **Hotel Lavica**, Ferde Livadića 5, T/F01-336 8000, www.lavica-hotel.hr. Just off the main square, with 32 basic but comfortable rooms, each with en suite bathroom, TV and telephone. Facilities include a restaurant and a large congress hall.

Eating

Gornji Grad *p59, map p58*

All the restaurants listed here are open daily for lunch and dinner, unless otherwise stated.

TTT-TT **Baltazar**, Nova Ves 4, T01-466 6999. Located north of the cathedral, **Baltazar** specializes in classic Balkan dishes such as *ražnjić* (mixed grilled meat), *Ćevapčići* (kebabs) and *zapečeni grah* (oven-baked beans). In summer there are tables outside in a pretty courtyard. Closed Sun.

TTT-TT **Dubravkin Put**, Dubrovakin put bb, in Tuškanac Park, 10 mins from the main square, T01-483 4975. Considered by many to be the best fish restaurant in town, **Dubravkin Put** comprises a light and airy dining room decorated with colourful modern canvasses by Edo Murtić, plus outdoor seating on a leafy terrace. The house speciality is *brodet* (fish stew) prepared with fresh herbs.

TT **Atlanta Café Restaurant**, Tkalčićeva 65, T01-481 3848. One of the few restaurants in a street lined with busy cafés, **Atlanta** is fun and stylish. Inside, terracotta walls are hung with gilt-framed mirrors, and the menu features pastas, risottos and creative meat dishes.

TT **Ivica i Maritsa**, Tkalčićeva 70, T01-482 8999. On Tkalčićeva, behind Dolac market, this cosy eatery offers an old-fashioned interior, homely Croatian cooking and waiters dressed in folk costumes. Favourites include *rezanci sa tartufima* (pasta with truffles), *govedja pisanica sa umakom od zelenog papra* (fillet steak with green pepper sauce) and *Žumberačka pastrva* (Žumberak trout). The adjoing *slastičarna* (cake shop) comes under the same management.

TT **Kaptolska Klet**, Kaptol 5, T01-481 4838. Opposite the cathedral, this popular rustic eatery offers extensive seating both indoors and out. The menu features reasonably priced hearty local dishes like *purica sa mlincima* (turkey with savoury pastries) and *zagorski štrukli* (baked cheese dumplings).

TT **Pod Gričkim Topom**, Za kmardijeve stube 5, T01-483 3607. This small, homely restaurant has stunning views over the city rooftops. Dalmatian fish dishes predominate: try the *ligne na* žaru (barbecued squid).

Cafés

For informal café-bars, head for the pretty street of Tklačićeva, where you'll find a wide choice of laid-back studenty haunts.

Gallery Klovićevi Dvori museum café, Jezuitski trg 4. If you're doing a round of the museums in Gornji Grad this café offers a peaceful, cultural ambience.

Sunčani Sat, Tklačićeva 27, with tables and comfy wicker chairs outside, is as good as any.

Donji Grad *p62, map p58*

TTT **Paviljon**, Trg kralja Tomislava 22, T01-481 3066. Occupies the ground floor of the charming 19th-century Art Pavilion, close to the train station. Choose from delights such as grilled salmon on wild rice and crispy roast duck on red cabbage with figs. In summer it is possible to eat outside. Closed Sun.

¥¥¥-¥¥ **Mašklin i Lata**, Andrije Hebranga 11a, T01-481 8273. Fresh fish and Dalmatian specialties such as *pašticada* (beef stewed in prošek and prunes) are favourites at this highly regarded eatery, located between the train station and the main square.

¥¥ **Nova**, Ilica 72, T01-481 0059. On first floor level, this modern vegetarian restaurant has a slick minimilaist interior. The menu includes a good range of macrobiotic and vegan dishes, made mainly from organic and wholegrain ingredients. Closed Sun.

¥¥ **Stari Fijaker**, Mesnička 6, T01-483 3829. Located a 5-min walk along Ilica from the main square, **Stari Fijaker** serves up traditional Zagrebian fare such as roast meats and *zagorski štrukli* (baked cheese dumplings) in an old-fashioned dining room with wooden panelled walls and crisp white table linens.

¥¥ **Vinodol**, Nikole Tesle 10, T01-481 1341. A good choice for meat lovers, the specialities are lamb and veal prepared under a *peka*. There's outdoor seating on a large summer terrace, with whole lamb turning on a spit.

¥ **Medvedgrad Pivnica**, Božidara Adžije 16, T01-364 6546. A popular microbrewery, serving up generous portions of roast meats, goulash, and beans and sausage, with a range of salads. You'll find it close to the Zagreb stadium.

¥ **Mimice**, Jurišićeva 21, T01-481 4524. Just a couple of miles' walk east of the main square, this renowned eatery serves fried *srdele* (sardines) and *papaline* (sprats) daily till 2100. Delicious and economical.

¥ **Restoran Boban**, Gajeva 9, just off the main square, T01-481 1549. Owned by Zvonimir Boban (captain of the Croatian football team during the 1998 World Cup), this popular basement restaurant specializes in pasta dishes. Be prepared to queue.

Cafés

Of several cafés overlooking Trg Bana Jelačića, the main square, **Gradska Kavana**, at No 10, and **Mala Kavana**, at No 5, are the largest and most popular; both offer outdoor seating through summer.

Kavana Palace, ground floor of **Hotel Palace** at Strossmayerov trg 10, close to the station. Viennese-style interior and a summer terrace.

Medvednica Nature Park *p66*

¥¥¥-¥¥ **Okruglak**, Mlinovi 28, T01-467 4112. Expensive but worth it, this renowned eatery offers authentic Croatian cuisine, on the road from Zagreb to Medvednica. In a large, wooden beamed dining room, expect dishes such as *punjena pisanica Okrugljak* (pork fillet stuffed with cream cheese and prosciutto) and *biftek na rukoli* (rump steak with rocket). Through summer there are tables outside in the courtyard. Open all year.

¥¥ **Stari Puntijar**, Gračanka cesta 65, on the road between Zagreb and Medvednica, T01-467 5500. A charming restaurant well-known for 19th-century Zagreb dishes such as *podolac* (ox) medallions in cream and saffron, *zagorski štruki* (baked cheese dumplings), *orehnjača* (walnut loaf) and *makovnjača* (poppy seed cake).

Samobor *p67*

¥¥ **Pri Staroj Vuri**, Giznik 2, T01-336 0548. This highly regarded restaurant serves up all-but-forgotten local dishes, recorded in a cookery book by Canon Birling from 1812. It's close to the main square, in an 18th-century town house with a cosy dining room decorated with traditional folk objects and a collection of old clocks.

¥ **Kavana Livadić**, Trg Kralja Tomislava 1. The best place in town to try *samoborske kremšnita*, this old-fashioned café occupies the ground floor of **Hotel Livadić** (see Sleeping). Indoors it's furnished with beautiful antiques, and in summer there are tables outside in a pretty courtyard.

¥ **Krčma Izletište Anindol**, Sv Ane 71, T01-336 7020. This delightful old wooden building, on the path up to Anindol Šetalište, has been converted into a small restaurant specializing in barbecued meats. On a sunny day you can eat in the garden. Closed Mon.

¥ **Samoborska Pivnica**, Šmidhenova 3, T01-336 1623. Centrally located beer hall serving excellent ale plus good inexpensive local dishes.

Žumberak i Samobor Gorje Nature Park *p67*

¥¥-¥ **Krčma Florian**, Slani Dol, Samobor, T01-338 4083. A great spot to refuel after a day's hiking, this down-to-earth eatery serves up hearty dishes such as *grah s domaćom* *kobasicom* (beans and home-made sausage), *kiselo zelje s grahom i dimljenim mesom* (sauekraut with beans and smoked pork), and štrukli (cheese dumpling). It's open Mon-Fri 1630-2000, Sat-Sun 0800-2100.

Bars and clubs

Gornji Grad *p59, map p58*

Gjuro II, Medveščak 2, T01-468 3367, www.gjuro.hr. Tue-Sat 2100-0200. Young professionals with an alternative streak meet up here to drink, chat and dance. Wed is R'n'B night, Thu sees 80s classics, and Sat is devoted to commercial pop and house.

Saloon, Tuškanac 1a, T01-483 4903, www.saloon.hr. Tue-Sat 2200-0400. Still the place to be seen if you want to hit the gossip magazines, though tamer than it once was. In summer the crowds spill out onto an open-air terrace. Commercial disco predominates, along with Croatian techno.

Tolkein, Vraničanijeva 8, T01-4852050. A tiny bar hidden away in an old stone building in Gornji Grad, with a few tables outside when the sun shines.

Donji Grad *p62, map p58*

Aquarius, Aleja Mira bb, T01-364 0231, www.aquarius.hr. Closed Mon. Zagreb's top club for dance, commercial and techno, plus occasional concerts by popular Croatian bands. Overlooking Lake Jarun, 4 km from city centre.

BP Jazz Club, Nikole Tesle 7, T01-481 4444, www.bpclub.hr. A friendly jazz club located in a basement. Can get very crowded when there are live concerts.

Bulldog Pub, Bogovićeva 6, T01-481 7393. Very popular with both young Croatians and English-speaking visitors, this large pub is just 5 mins from the main square. Through summer tables spill onto the pedestrian area out front.

Gallery, Matije Ljubeka bb, T099-444 2444 (mob), www.gallery.hr. Overlooking Lake Jarun, 4km from the city centre, Gallery is close to Aquarius, which it now rivals in the 'cool' stakes. House and techno music predominate at weekends, though you'll also hear R'n'B during the week. Closed Sun.

Hemingway, Trg Maršal Tita 1, www.hemingway.hr. In a lovely old building opposite the Croatian National Theatre, this is one of several new (and very expensive) cocktail bars that make up the Hemingway chain. Popular with Zagrebian yuppies.

K Pivovari, Ilica 222, T01-375 1808. Within the Ožujsko brewery, where Croatia's best-selling beer is made, this late 19th-century beer hall serves a selection of local and imported ales, plus hearty platters of grilled meats and chips, at heavy wooden tables.

Močvara (The Swamp), Trnjanski Nasip bb, T01-615 9668, www.mochvara.hr. A very popular alternative youth club, located in a disused factory on the banks of the River Sava. Founded in 1999 by a cultural association that wanted a venue for off-beat Croatian and foreign music and drama. Mon-Thu 2000-0100, Fri-Sun 2200-0400.

Old Pharmacy, Andrije Hebranga 11a, T01-492 1912. A peaceful pub with a collection of English-language newspapers, TV and a non-smoking side room.

Pivnica Medvedgrad, Savska 56, T01-617 7110, www.pivninca-medvedgrad.hr. The best choice in town for a beer, this spacious microbrewery serves 4 of its own brews. There's an adjoining dining hall (see Eating) if you feel peckish.

Škola, Bogovičeva 7, T01-482 8196, www.skolaloungebar.com. Occupying a former school (after which it is named) this ultra-cool lounge bar is done out in 1970s retro style. Downstairs there's ambient music and cocktails, while up top the old canteen is now a chic restaurant. You'll find it one block south of the main square. Closed Sun.

Tvornica (The Factory), Šubićeva 2, T01-465 5007, www.tvornica-kulture.hr. Another alternative venue, attracting some of Europe's top DJs as well as staging rock concerts and theatre. Open day and night, located close to the bus station. Fri-Sat 0900-0400, closes earlier in the week.

Entertainment

Cinemas

Broadway Tkalča, in the Centar Kaptol complex at Nova Ves 11, in Gornji Grad behind the cathedral. The city's largest cinema, with 3 screens, T01-466 7686, www.broadway-kina.com.

Classical music

Hrvatski Glazbeni Zavod (Croatian Music Institute), Gundulićeva 6, T01-483 0822. Chamber music recitals and occasional performances of Dalmatian *klapa* (page 343).

Koncertna Dvorana Vatroslav Lisinski (Vatroslav Lisinski Concert Hall), Trg Stjepana Radića 4, T01-612 1166, www.lisinski.hr. A modern complex, home to the Zagreb Philharmonic Orchestra. It also hosts occasional musicals and jazz concerts.

Theatre

Hrvatsko Narodno Kazalište (National Theatre), Trg Maršala Tita 15, T01-488 8488, www.hnk.hr. Classical and contemporary drama, opera and ballet, Sep-Jun.

Komedija, Kaptol 9, T01-481 4566, www.komedija.hr. A small theatre in Gornji Grad, close to the cathedral, staging operettas and Croatian musicals.

Festivals and events

Zagreb *p56, map p58*

Jul Folklore Festival. A 5-day celebration of music and dance with performers from Croatia and other southeast European countries dressed in traditional folk costumes. Main events take place on Trg Bana Jelačića and in the Gallery Klovićevi Dvori courtyard in Gornji Grad. For information, go to www.msf.hr.

Jul-Aug Zagreb Summer Evenings, mid-Jul to mid-Aug, www.kdz.hr. Evening musical performances by Croatian and foreign orchestras and soloists. Main events are staged in the cathedral, St Catherine's Church and the Gallery Klovićevi Dvori courtyard in Gornji Grad.

Samobor *p67*

Feb-Mar Fašnik. 2 weeks of bawdy carnival celebrations, climaxing with the lighting of a bonfire, a firework display and the burning of Prince Fašnik. Locals suitably dress in masks and costume.

Shopping

Zagreb *p56, map p58*

Algoritam, Gajeva 1, just off the main square, T01-481 8672. The best bookshop for foreign-language publications, including novels, travel guides and maps.

Aromatica, Vlaška 7, T01-481 1584, www.aromatica.hr. Sell soaps, shampoos and massage oils scented with herbal extracts.

Croata, Kaptol 13, close to the cathedral in Gornji Grad, T01-481 4600, www.croata.hr. Sell original Croatian ties in presentation boxes with a history of the tie included.

Dolac, the open-air market, just off the main square. The best place for fresh fruit and vegetables. There is also a smal crafts section.

Galerija Bil Ani, Radićeva 37, parallel to Tkalčićeva in Gornji Grad, T01-485 2345. Throughout Croatia you'll find souvenir shops selling handmade miniature ceramic replicas of traditional Dalmatian, Istrian, Slavonian and Zagrebian houses. This gallery was the first to start producing them.

Gharani Štrok Boutique, Dežmanov Prolaz 5, T01-484 6152. You might be surprised to see this top-design house (much loved by the likes of Madonna and Kate Moss) in Croatia, but Vanya Štrok is in fact Croatian. It opened in May 2005 and promises to stock clothes, shoes, jewellery and items from the interiors line.

Tourist Information Centre, Trg Bana Jelačića 11, T01-481 4051. As well as picking up maps and leaflets, buy a *litsitarsko srce* (gingerbread heart with icing) and *paška čipka* (handmade lace from the island of Pag).

Vinoteka Bornstein, Kaptol 19, close to the cathedral in Gornji Grad, T01-481 2363. A beautiful vaulted brick cellar stocked with quality Croatian wines, olive oils and truffle products: ideal as presents to take home.

Samobor *p67*

Aromatica, Perkovićeva 14, T01-332 4123, www.aromatica.hr. Stock their own line of scented herbal soaps and beauty products.

Podrum Obitelj Filipec, Stražnička 1a, 20 m off the main square. T01-336 4835. Family-run wine cellar. The best place to buy *Bermet* (local vermouth liquor) and *muštarda* (spicy grape mustard), typical Samobor souvenirs.

Activities and tours

Fitness centres

Mladost Sports Park, Jarunska 5, T01-365 8541. Mon-Fri 1100-1500 and 1800-2000, Sat 1300-1700, Sun 1000-1400. Vast sports complex with an indoor Olympic pool, 16 tennis courts and a fitness centre.

Sheraton Hotel fitness centre, Kneza Borne 2, T01-455 2655. Mon-Fri 0700-2200, Sat Sun 0900-2200. The hotel fitness club, swimming pool, solarium, sauna and massage facilities are open to non-residents at 70Kn per day.

Ice skating

Ice-skating Rink, Paviljon 40, Zagrebački Velesajam, inside the Trade Fair Centre complex in Novi Zagreb, T01-655 4357. Fri 1930-2100; Sat 1700-1830 and 1930-2100; Sun 1030-1200, 1700-1830 and 1930-2100. 15Kn.

Spectator sports

Dinamo Stadium, Maksimirska 128, T01-238 6111. The Croatian national football team, and the Zagreb city football team, Dinamo, play here. Tickets 30-150Kn.
Dražen Petrović Basketball Centre, Savska 30, T01-484 3333. The Zagreb basketball team, Cibona, play here. Tickets 20-80 Kn.

Tennis

Maksimir Tennis Club, Ravnice 1, close to Maksimir Park, T01-291 0055. Mon-Fri 1000-1800, Sat 1000-1500. The centre comprises 4 indoor and 22 outdoor tennis courts, plus a bowling alley and table tennis.

Tour operators

Atlas, Zrinjevac 17, T01-487 3064, www.atlas-croatia.com. Organize a variety of cultural and sporting excursions, primarily in Dalmatia, plus yacht charters from Split and Dubrovnik.
Generalturist, Praška 5, T01-481 0033, www.generalturist.com. One of the largest Croatian travel agencies, specializing in tailor-made trips both with and without guides, pilgrimage tours and yacht charters.
Globtour Zagreb, Zrinjevac 1-1, T01-481 0020, www.globtour.hr. Offer guided tours in Zagreb and the surrounding area.
Kompas zagreb, N Tesle 12, T01-488 2500, www.kompas.hr. Arrange hotel bookings and trips, primarily in Zagreb.

Žumberak i Samobor Gorje Nature Park *p67*

Eco Selo Žumberak (Žumberak Eco Village), Krovljak bb, Kalje, T01-338 7472. Located within the nature park, 18 km east of Samobor, this small mountainside sports centre offers pony trekking, hiking, waterfall tours and simple overnight accommodation. Open all year.

Transport

Zagreb *p56, map p58*

Air

Through summer, there are regular flights to and from **Amsterdam**, **Bari**, **Berlin**, **Bologna**, **Brussels**, **Catania**, **Copenhagen**, **Dusseldorf**, **Frankfurt**, **Genoa**, **Gothenburg**, **Hamburg**, **Helsinki**, **Istanbul**, **Lisbon**, **London** (Gatwick and Heathrow), **Lyon**, **Munich**, **Oslo**, **Palermo**, **Paris**, **Prague**, **Rome**, **Sarajevo**, **Skopje**, **Stockholm**, **Turin**, **Vienna** and **Zurich**. Internal flights link the capital with **Brač** (island of Bol), **Dubrovnik**, **Pula**, **Split** and **Zadar**. The number of destinations and the frequency of flights are reduced in winter. Sample prices for Zagreb: London Heathrow with **Croatia Airlines**, departing daily through Aug varies from £197 return to special (off-season) economy return at £68.

Zagreb Airport, Pleso bb, T01-626 5222 (information), T01-456 2229 (lost and found), www.zagreb-airport.hr. It is 17 km from the city centre. A shuttle bus, T01-633 1999, runs from the airport to Zagreb bus station every 30 mins 0700-2000, and from Zagreb bus station to the airport 0430-2000. The journey takes about 25 mins and a one-way ticket costs 30Kn. Expect to pay 150-200Kn by taxi.

Airlines offices

Adria Airways, Praška 9, T01-481 0011. **Aeroflot**, Varšavska 13, T01-487 2055. **Air Canada**, Krsnjavoga 1 (Hotel Opera), T01-482 2033. **Air France**, Kršnjavoga 1, **Hotel Opera**, T01-483 7100. **Austrian Airlines**, Zagreb Airport, T01-626 5900. **Avioimpex**, Savska 1, T01-482 9439. **Bosna Air**, Zagreb Airport, T01- 456 2672. **British Airways**, Kneza Borne 2, Hotel Sheraton, T01-455 3336. **CSA**, Trg Nikole Šubića Zrinskog 17, T01-487 3301. **Croatia Airlines**, Zrinjevac 7, T01-481 9633. **Delta**, Trg N Šubića Zrinjskog 14, T01-487 8760. **KLM-Northwest**, Langov Trg 2, T01-487 8600. **LOT**, Trg Bana Jelačića 2, T01-483 7500. **Lufthansa**, Zagreb Airport, T01-456 2187. **Malaysia Airlines**, Strossmajerov Trg 7/1, T01-481 0777.

Malev (Hungarian Airlines), Kršnjavoga 1, Hotel Opera, T01-483 6935. **Turkish Airlines**, Zagreb Airport, T01-456 2008.

Bus and tram

For all information about buses to and from Zagreb, T060-313333, www.akz.hr. The bus station is at Avenija M Držića 4, a 15-min walk from the main square. 24-hr left luggage costs 10Kn per item per hr.

Internal services include about 26 buses daily to **Rijeka** in Kvarner (3 hrs); 18 buses to **Pula** in Istria (4-5 hrs); 12 to **Osijek** in Slavonia (4 hrs); 22 to **Zadar** in North Dalmatia (3½-5 hrs); 30 to **Split** in Central Dalmatia (4½-7 hrs); and 6 to **Dubrovnik** in South Dalmatia (10½ hrs). There are also daily international bus lines to **Ljubljana** (Slovenia); **Barcs** and **Nagykanisza** (Hungary); **Belgrade** (Serbia and Montenegro); **Graz** (Austria); **Munich**, **Stuttgart**, **Frankfurt**, **Dortmund**, **Cologne**, and **Dusseldorf** (Germany) and **Zurich** (Switzerland).

Car

Expect to pay €43 per day for a small car such as a Fiat Uno, €73 per day for a large car such as an Opal Vectra.
Budget, T01-626 5854, www.budget.hr, at the airport and city centre at Kneza Borne 2, T01-455 4943; **Hertz**, www.hertz.hr, T01-456 2635, at the airport and in the city centre at Vukatinovićeva 4, T01-484 6777; **Sixt**, T01-621 9900, www.sixt.hr, at the airport.

Taxi

Radio Taxi, T01-668 2505/668 2558. 24-hr service, usually arrive within 5-10 mins.

Train

National train information T060-333444, www.hznet.hr. Left luggage costs 10Kn per item per hr, open 24 hrs.

Long distance Internal services include 5 trains daily to and from **Rijeka** in Kvarner (about 3½ hrs), 4 trains daily to **Split** in Dalmatia (5½ hrs by day, 8½ hrs by night) and 4 trains daily to **Osijek** in Slavonia (4 hrs). Daily international trains run direct to and from **Budapest** (Hungary), **Belgrade** (Serbia), **Munich** (Germany), Sarajevo (Bosnia and Herzegovina)**Vienna** (Austria) and **Venice** (Italy).

Medvednica Nature Park *p66*

Take **tram** No 14 from the city centre, all the way to the terminal stop, Mihaljevac. From there, take tram No 15 to its terminal stop, Dolje. From Dolje a **funicular** runs hourly 0800-2000, bringing you close to **Sljeme**, in 23 mins. Return ticket 17Kn. If you're driving, head out of the city centre north along Medveščak, passing through the village of Gračani to arrive at the funicular.

Samobor *p67*

Bus

Bus station, Gajeva bb, T01-336 6634. 50 buses daily to **Zagreb**, 40 mins, one-way ticket 22Kn. You need private transport to reach **Žumberak i Samobor Gorje Nature Park**.

Directory

Zagreb *p56, map p58*

Cultural centres

British Council, Ilica 12, T01-489 9500, www.britishcouncil.hr. Mon-Fri 0900-1700 (Library Mon and Fri 1100-1700; Tue-Thu 1330-1930). **French Cultural Institute**, Preradovićeva 35, T01-485 5222. Mon-Fri 0900-1700. **Goethe Institute** (German), Ulica Grada Vukovara 64, T01-619 5000. Mon-Thu 0830-1700, Fri 0830-1530. **Italian Cultural Institute**, Preobraženska 4, T01-483 0208. Mon-Thu 1000-1600, Fri 0900-1400.

Embassies

Australia, Centar Kaptol, Nova Ves 11 III Kat, T01-489 1200; **Austria**, Jabukovac 39, T01-488 1050; **Belgium**, Pantovčak 125b, T01-457 8901; **Bosnia and Herzegovina**, Torbarova 9, T01-468 3761; **Canada**, Prilaz Djure Deželića 4, T01-488 1200; **Czech Republic**, Savska cesta 41, T01-617 7246; **Denmark**, Trg N Šubića Žrinskog 10, T01-492 4540; **France**, A Hebranga 2, T01- 489 3600; **Germany**, Ulica grada Vukovara 64, T01-630 0100; **Hungary**, Pantovčak 255-257, T01-489 0900; **Italy**, Medulićeva 22, T01-484 6386; **Japan**, Boskovićeva 2, T01-487 0650; **Macedonia**, Kralja Zvonimira 6/1, T01-462 0261; Montenegro, Trg N Šubića Žrinskog 1/IV, T01-457 3362, **Netherlands**, Medveščak 56, T01-464 2200; **Norway**, Petrinjska 9, T01-492 2829; **Poland**, Krležin Gvozd 3, T01-489 9444; **Slovakia**, Prilaz

Djure Deželića 10, T01-487 7070; **Slovenia**, Alagovićeva 30, T01-631 1000; **Spain**, Tuškanac 21a, T01-484 8950; **Sweden**, Frankopanska 22, T01-492 5100; **Switzerland**, Bogovićeva 3, T01-487 8800; **UK**, Ivana Lučića 4, T01-600 9100; **US**, Thomas Jeffersona 2, T01-661 2200; **Serbia**, Pantovčak 245, T01-457 9067.

Emergencies

Ambulance: T94; **Fire**: T93; **Police**: T92.

Internet

Ergonet, Centar Kaptol, Badalićeva 26c, T01-368 9400, www.ergonet.hr. Mon-Fri 0800-2200, Sat 0900-2200. The following are in Donji Grad; **Charlie Net**, Gajeva 4, T01-488 0233, Mon-Sat 0800-2200, Sun 1100-2100; **Cyber Café Sublink**, Teslina 12, T01-481 1329, www.su blink.hr, Mon-Sat 0900-2200, Sun 1500-2200; **Iskoninternet**, Preradovićeva 5, T01-481 1758, Mon-Sat 0900- 2300, Sun 1200-2300; and **Net Kulturni Klub Mama**, Preradovićeva 18, T01-485 6400, Mon-Sat 1000-2200, Sun 1600-2200 .

Language schools

Berlitz, Amruševa 10, T01-481 2116, www.berlitz.hr. **Škola za strane jezike**, Varsavska 14, 10000 Zagreb, T01-483 0570, www.sova.hr.

Laundry

Petecin, Kaptol 11, T01-481 4802; **Predom**, Draškovićeva 31, T01-461 2900.

Libraries

City Library, Trg Ante Starčevića 6, T01-457 2344, www.kgz.hr, Mon-Fri 0800-2000, Sat 0800-1400; **National Public Library**, Hrvatske bratske zajednice bb, T01-616 4111, www.nsk.hr, Mon-Fri 0800-2100, Sat 0800-1500. See also Cultural centres above.

Medical services

Hospitals Ignjata Djordjica 26, T01-460 0911, for emergencies. Draškovićeva 19, T01-461 0011, for casualty. **Pharmacies** Marked by a glowing green cross, 24-hr pharmacies are at Trg Bana Jelačića 2, T01-481 6159, and Ilica 301, T01-375 0321.

Post office

Main post office, Branimirova 4, next to the train station, open 24 hrs; **Central post office**, Jurišićeva 4, close to the main square, Mon-Fri 0700-2100, Sat 0800-1800, Sun 0800-1400.

Telephone

If you prefer to telephone from a peaceful phone booth, go to the main post office (see above). Otherwise, if you don't mind the traffic noise, you'll find countless blue phone kiosks dotted around the city.

North of Zagreb

Northwest of Zagreb, beyond Medvednica Nature Park, lies the rural area of Zagorje. The scenery is calm and enchanting: rolling hillsides are planted with vineyards and orchards, and narrow country roads meander through a succession of villages of red-brick cottages and open-sided wooden barns filled with maize. Zagorjians are renowned for their drinking habits, and there is a local song that says "There is no man from Zagorje who can produce as much wine as his friends can drink", or words to that effect. Indeed, St Martin's Day on 11 November is a big event throughout the region, when the ritual blessing of the season's young wine is accompanied by copious festivities until the early hours.

Public transport is slow and sporadic, but if you have a car and are prepared to devote an entire day to Zagorje, you can visit a modern sculpture gallery in Klanjec, an open-air ethnological museum in Kumrovec, the medieval hilltop castles of Veliki Tabor and Trakoščan, and an unusual museum dedicated to prehistoric man in Krapina.

Close to the Hungarian border and easily reached by public transport from Zagreb, the neighbouring provincial towns of Varaždin and Čakovec are both presided over by 16th-century castles, open to the public as museums. Close by, Koprivnica and Hlebine are worth the trek for their well-arranged galleries displaying paintings by local Naïve artists. ▸▸ *For Sleeping, Eating and other listings, see pages 83-86.*

Zagorje ▸▸ *pp83-86.*

Klanjec → *Phone code: 049. Colour map 1, A5. 55 km northwest of Zagreb.*

This picturesque small town sits on the east bank of the River Sutla, which forms the natural border with Slovenia. The main reason for coming here is to visit the Augustinčić Gallery. Klanjec also produced a noted poet, Antun Mihanović (1796-1861), who wrote the words to *Lijepa Naša* (the Croatian national anthem). Some 3 km north of Klanjec, on the road to Kumrovec, you will pass the Lijepa Naša Monument, recording that it was this particular stretch of countryside that inspired Mihanović. There is a town **tourist office** ⓘ *Trg A Mihanovića 2, T049-550235.*

Augustinčić Gallery ⓘ *Trg A Mihanovića 10, T049-550343, Apr-Sep daily 0900-1700, Oct-Mar Tue-Sun 0900-1500, 20Kn*, is devoted to the works of this local born 20th-century sculptor, Antun Augustinčić. Born in Klanjec in 1900, he studied fine art in Paris, then became student to another noted Croatian sculptor, Ivan Meštrović. During the Tito years he was made the official state artist: works from that time, such as the *Heroic Worker*, one of many works on show here, portray the appropriate socialist ideals of the period. Later the *Pieta* and *Carrying the Wounded* became favourite themes – his best known sculpture is *Peace*, erected in front of the United Nations building in New York in 1954. In 1970, Augustinčić donated his works to the state. When he died in 1979, he was buried next to his wife in the garden surrounding the gallery, below one of his most moving pieces, *Carrying the Wounded*.

Kumrovec → *Phone code: 049. Colour map 1, A5. 40 km from Zagreb, 6 km from Klanjec.*

The sleepy village of Kumrovec, like Klanjec, sits on the east bank of the River Sutla. It was here that the late President Josip Broz Tito was born in 1892, and his home and several houses in the old quarter surrounding it have been turned into an open-air ethnological museum, known as Staro Selo (Old Village).

Consisting of about 20 carefully restored 19th- and 20th-century thatched cottages and wooden farm buildings, **Staro Selo** ⓘ *T049-553107, www.mdc.hr,*

Apr-Sep 0900-1900, Oct-Mar 0900-1600, 20Kn, is set amid orchards and with a stream flowing through animated by ducks. The quarter offers a lifelike reconstruction of 19th-century Zagorje rural life. Tito's childhood home, which was the first brick house in the village, built in 1860, was turned into a small memorial museum in 1953. The furniture inside is just as it would have been when Tito was a child, and there's a small room displaying letters and gifts sent to the Yugoslav leader by foreign allies. In the garden stands an imposing bronze statue (an occassional target for local vandals) of the man himself, created by Antun Augustinčić from neighbouring Klanjec in 1948.

Reconstruction of the surrounding building started in 1977, so that today you can see a blacksmith's shop, a potter's studio, a candlemaker's workshop and a kitchen, where demonstrations are laid on by respective craftsmen at weekends.

Veliki Tabor → *Phone code: 049. Colour map 1, A5. 15 km north of Kumrovec.*

ⓘ *Desinić, T049-343963, www.veliki-tabor.hr. May-Sep daily 1000-1800, Oct-Apr daily 1000-1500, 20Kn.*

Sitting on a hill close to the small village of **Desinić** the lofty ochre-coloured castle of Veliki Tabor is quite impressive seen from a distance. Closer inspection reveals a medieval structure with high-pitched terracotta roofs, which has been carefully restored and was reopened in autumn 2007. Close by, an informal farm restaurant serves delicious, reasonably priced local goodies.

Although some people believe that Veliki Tabor stands on the site of a second-century Roman fortress, the main pentagonal form of the castle dates back to the 12th century when it was the property of the Counts of Celje (in present-day Slovenia). In the 16th century the castle passed to the Ratkaj family, who added four semicircular side towers as protection against the Turks and enhanced the internal courtyard with three levels of open-arched galleries. During the Second World War, Franciscan nuns used the building as an orphanage to host 80 children who had lost their families, after which the castle became state property.

The custodians of Veliki Tabor are happy to recount a love story connected to the castle, which may or may not be true. According to hearsay, during the 15th century, Freidrich, the son of Count Herman II Celjski, who resided in the castle at the time, fell in love with a pretty peasant girl, named Veronika, from the nearby village of Desinić. Deeming the fair maiden unworthy of his son, the count prohibited the affair, upon which the two young lovers ran away together. Count Herman sent his soldiers in hot pursuit: Freidrich was captured and locked up in a tower in the castle and Veronika was tried for witchcraft – she had, after all, enchanted the young man. When judges found Veronika innocent, the enraged count had her drowned and her body bricked up in a wall in the castle. Strangely, during renovation work in 1982, a woman's skull was found here. It is now on show in the castle chapel on the first floor and is said to be the last trace of the unfortunate Veronika.

Trakoščan → *Phone code: 042. Colour map 1, A5.*

ⓘ *40 km south of Varaždin and 36 km north of Veliki Tabor, T042-796422, www.trakoscan.hr. Apr-Oct daily 0900-1800, Nov-Mar daily 0900-1600, 30Kn.*

Dvor Trakoščan (Trakoščan Castle) is one of the most visited castles in Croatia and probably the most popular sight in Zagorje. A white fairy-tale fortress complete with turrets and a drawbridge, it stands on a small hill overlooking a small lake, and is undoubtedly at its most magical at night, when it is floodlit.

The first castle on this site was built in the 13th century as an observation point above the road between Ptuj (in present-day Slovenia) and the Bednja Valley. It then passed on to various feudal lords, until being presented to the Drašković family, as a way of thanks for their dedication to defending the region against the Ottoman Turks, in the late 16th century. Over the following 200 years various defence towers and a

Tito

The seventh of 15 children, Josip Broz was born on 7 May, 1892, in Kumrovec (then part of Austria-Hungary) to a Slovenian mother and a Croatian blacksmith father. Although he only attended school between the age of 7 and 12, he was to become one of the 20th century's most extraordinary world leaders.

During the First World War he served with the Austrian army in Russia and was wounded and taken prisoner – a turn of events he used to his advantage, learning Russian and discovering the ideals of the Bolshevik movement. He returned to his homeland (by this time the Kingdom of the Serbs, Croats, and Slovenes) in 1920 and joined the Communist Party. After a series of arrests and a six-year stint in prison (the Communist Party was outlawed here at that time) he adopted the pseudonym of Tito and went to work for the Balkan sector of Comintern in Moscow. In 1937 he returned home and became Secretary General of the Yugoslavian Communist Party.

When Germany attacked Yugoslavia in 1941, Tito formed the Partisan resistance movement, fighting the German Nazis and their allies, the Croatian Ustaše, as well another anti-fascist group, the pro-royalist Serbian Chetniks, who were initially backed by the British. In 1944, however, the allied forces switched their backing to the Partisans and, at the end of the Second World War, Tito set up the new Yugoslav government, based on Communist ideology.

After a series of disagreements over foreign policy, Tito broke with Stalin in 1948 and began to govern Yugoslavia along socialist lines, decentralizing the economy and setting up workers' self-management organizations. This gained him considerable favours from the West, which began giving Yugoslavia massive loans. When Stalin died in 1953, Tito forged good relations with Kruschev, making Yugoslavia a 'midway country' between the Communist USSR and the capitalist west. In the 1960s he founded the Non-Alligned Nations together with leaders of African and Asian countries.

Undoubtedly a colourful character, he went through four wives and had a marked penchant for Scotch whisky, Cuban cigars and fast cars – the collection he left behind includes a 1960 Rolls Royce Phantom and several Mercedes limousines. His circle of glamorous friends included Elizabeth Taylor and Richard Burton, who played Tito in *The Fifth Offensive*, a 1972 production based on a true story from the Second World War.

At 1505 on 4 May 1980, sirens sounded throughout Yugoslavia. Tito was dead. The entire country came to a standstill. His funeral, in Belgrade, was attended by representatives from over 125 countries. On 4 May 2000, his death was openly commemorated in Croatia for the first time since 1991; 10,000 people gathered in Kumrovec to celebrate the great man who, on his deathbed, prophetically described himself as the last of the Yugoslavs.

drawbridge were added, until the castle fell into disuse (the Turks long since gone) and abandon. However, in the mid-19th century the Romanticist movement became fashionable among Central European aristocracy, and Vice-Marshall Juraj Drašković had the building restructured in neo-Gothic style and turned into a sumptuous country residence. He also landscaped the surrounding parkland, and created an artificial lake surrounded by a mixed forest of beech and fir, by damming up the River Bednja. Following the events of the Second World War, the Drašković family moved to Austria in 1944 and the property was nationalized and opened to the public in 1953.

On the first floor you can visit the luxurious wooden-panelled living quarters, complete with late 19th-century furniture and solemn family portraits, while the bedrooms, mainly furnished in baroque style, are on the second floor. There is also an arms collection on display, consisting of rifles, pistols and Turkish weapons from between the 15th and 19th centuries. The grounds are especially pretty in spring and autumn. In summer a floating café operates on the lake, and it is also possible to rent boats for rowing.

Krapina → *Phone code: 049. Colour map 1, A5. Population: 4647. 57 km north of Zagreb.*

Nestled in a valley, sits the peaceful market town of Krapina. It's known throughout the country as the home of the *Krapinksi Ćovjek* (Krapina man), a tribe of Neanderthals, who lived here some 30,000 years ago, the remains of which were dug up by a Croatian archaeologist in 1899. The settlement itself was first recorded as a castle, no longer in existence, during the 12th century, and since then it's been the administrative and cultural centre of rural Zagorje. During the 17th century, a Franciscan Monastery and the baroque Church of St Catherine were built, giving Krapina the airs of a sedate and prosperous provincial town.

Krapina's second most noted citizen is Ljudevit Gaj, who was born here in 1809 and founded the Illyrian Movement in 1835, campaigning for the union of the South Slavs (Croats and Serbs) as an alternative to Austro-Hungarian hegemony. Aided by Ban Jelačić, the Croatian Viceroy at the time, Gaj secured the recognition of Serbo-Croatian as the nation's official language, and helped bring an end to the feudal system. You can see a monument to him, by the Dalmatian sculptor Ivan Rendić, on the main square.

A short walk west of the centre, the **Muzej Evolucije** (Museum of Evolution) ⓘ *Šetalište V Sluge, T049-371491, Apr-Sep 0900-1700, Oct-Mar 0900-1500, 20Kn*, records the work of Dragutin Gorjanović-Kramberger, who discovered the *Krapinksi Ćovjek* in a nearby cave on Hušnjakovo Hill. From the museum, a path leads through woods to the cave in question, where you can see life-size sculptures of these prehistoric people and the animals that would have lived at that time. The actual bones of the 20-odd Neanderthals that were discovered here are now kept in the Croatian Museum of Natural Sciences in Zagreb.

Varaždin » *pp83-86. Colour map 1, A6.*

→ *Phone code: 042. Population: 49,075. 77 km northeast of Zagreb.*

Varaždin, with its 18th-century baroque churches and town houses, makes a manageable day trip from the capital. Stari Grad, a well-preserved 16th-century castle surrounded by grassy ramparts, now housing a museum, is the main attraction. The best time to visit is autumn, when the trees take on russet hues complementing the pink and ochre façades. If you're lucky, you'll also catch the renowned **Varaždin Baroque Evenings** music festival, staged late September to early October. There's a town **tourist office** ⓘ *Ivana Padovca 3, T042-201005, www.tourism-varazdin.hr.*

Background

The town evolved from its most beautiful and best-loved monument, the castle, which was first mentioned in 1181, in a document sealed by King Bela III of Hungary. In 1209, King Andreas II of Hungary and Croatia declared Varaždin a 'Free Royal City' (33 years before Zagreb was granted a similar honour, as locals proudly point out), and from that date onwards citizens were free to choose their own city governor. The Tartars besieged the town in 1242, plundering and burning much of it, but the townsfolk were undeterred and soon rebuilt it into an important trade centre, albeit amid ongoing conflicts between the local noble families.

During the Hapsburg era, Varaždin became an important military stronghold in the battle against Ottoman expansion. The town was enclosed within a sturdy fortification system and, though the Turks never succeeded in capturing it, they frequently plundered the surroundings.

In the 17th century, in reply to the emergence of a budding Protestant movement, Rome sent in Jesuit monks to revive and reinforce the Catholic faith in the region. It was the Jesuits who brought baroque architecture to Varaždin, for which the town is now noted.

The city became the capital of Croatia in 1756 – a short-lived period of joy which came to an abrupt end when more than half of the town (including the government building) was destroyed by fire in 1776. According to records, the fire was started by a young man who was smoking, tripped over a sow and dropped his cigarette in a haystack. After the disaster, smoking was banned and the poor culprit was whipped 12 times in his native village of Sračinec, and 12 times more in front of Varaždin Town Hall.

Although an unfortunate event, the fire brought about a major period of development, and during the 18th century the town was rebuilt in baroque style, as seen today. In 1997 Varaždin became the seat of a diocese.

Sights

Start a tour of the town from Trg Kralja Tomislava, the main square. The most impressive building here is undoubtedly the 15th-century **Gradska Vijećnica** (Town Hall) ① *Trg Kralja Tomislava 3*, which has been the seat of the town council since 1523, making it one of the oldest buildings of its type in Europe. The slightly incongruous clock tower was added in 1793. If you're here in summer (early May to mid-October) on a Saturday morning between 1000 and 1200, you can see the *Purgari* (Varaždin guards), dressed in blue military uniforms dating back to 1750, keeping watch outside the main door.

Officially taking on the title of cathedral in 1997, when Varaždin became the seat of a diocese, **Katedrala** (Cathedral of the Assumption) ⓘ *Pavlinska ulica, just off Trg Kralja Tomislava, daily 0800-1200, 1600-1800*, was the first baroque building in town. It dates back to the mid-17th century, when the style was brought here by Jesuit monks, who, besides erecting the church, also constructed the neighbouring three-storey monastery and former grammar school building, now used as the Bishop's residence. Inside the cathedral, the richly gilded main altar fills the central nave and bears paintings of the Virgin. The space is said to have exceptional acoustic qualities, and during the **Varaždin Baroque Evenings** music festival, concerts are held here.

Founded in 1954 and occupying the ground floor of **Dvor Herzer** (Herzer Palace), the slightly quirky **Entomološki Odjel** (Entomological Museum) ⓘ *Franjevački trg 6, T042-210474, May-Sep Tue-Sun 1000-1800, Oct-Apr Tue-Fri 1000-1500, Sat-Sun 1000-1300, 20Kn*, is worth a look in for its beautifully presented collection of butterflies and drawings of insects. (At the time of writing it was temporarily closed for renovation.)

Just a five-minute walk from the centre stands Varaždin's top attraction, an impressive **castle** ⓘ *Strossmayerovo Šetalište 7, T042-658754, Apr-Sep Tue-Sun 1000-1800, Oct-Mar Tue-Fri 1000-1700, Sat-Sun 1000-1300, 20Kn*, surrounded by lofty fortifications and ringed by a moat (now unfortunately empty). There's been a castle on the site for over 800 years, but the building's present appearance dates largely from the 16th century, when the existing structure was heavily reinforced against the possibility of a Turkish attack. The main entrance is an imposing gatehouse with a central tower and a wooden drawbridge, which leads into an internal courtyard ringed with three levels of open-arched galleries, designed by the Italian architect Domenico dell'Allio in the 1560s. In 1925 the castle was given to the town and turned into a **museum**. It now houses a splendid collection of period furniture, with individual rooms devoted to particular epochs, following on one from another in chronological order. Just outside the main entrance is **Sermaš**, a pleasant café with a summer terrace, ideal for coffee or a beer either before or after your visit.

Most guided tours of Varaždin begin from the **Gradsko Groblje** (City Cemetery) ⓘ *Hallerova Aleja, 400 m from the castle*, partly because of its exceptional landscaping, and partly because there's a large car park nearby. Founded in 1773, the cemetery that you see today was laid out in 1905 by Herman Haller. Haller had studied various cemeteries in Europe, and wanted to create a place of rest for the dead that would not put off the living, but actually attract them. The result is a romantic garden filled with trees and shrubs, and immense hedges trimmed and shaped around ornate memorial stones.

Čakovec and around » pp83-86. Colour map 1, A6.

→ Phone code: 040. Population: 30,455. 82 km northeast of Zagreb.

Čakovec is a proud though rather uninspiring provincial town, centring on Trg Kralja Tomislava, the main square, a pleasant pedestrian area surrounded by two-storey pastel-coloured baroque town houses with steep-sloping tile roofs. Throughout the rest of the country, Čakovec is known for its castle, textile industry and hard-working citizens. A world away from the *fjaka* (easy-going laziness combined with an appreciation of all things good in life) of Dalmatia, this is a region where people actually claim to enjoy work, some holding down full-time jobs plus participating in out-of-hours voluntary activities.

On the main road to Hungary, it is hardly a big tourist destination. However, the castle, *medjimurska pita* (a delicious pie made of poppy seeds, cream cheese and walnuts, unique to the area) and the region's excellent white wines make it worth a half-day visit. Čakovec lies just 15 km northeast of its neighbour and arch-rival,

 Varaždin, so the two can be comfortably combined as a day trip from the capital. There's a town **tourist office**① *Ivana Padovca 3, To42-201005, www.tourism-cakovec.hr.*

Background

There's been a castle here for centuries, though things didn't really take off until 1547, when Nikola Šubić Zrinski became owner of the area. As Zrinski's major preoccupation was protecting the Hapsburg territories from the Turks, he rebuilt the existing *castrum* into an impressive Renaissance fortress with strong defensive walls and a moat, intended to oversee the permanently unstable border with the Ottoman Empire to the southeast.

A settlement of simple wooden craftsmen's houses grew up around the castle, gaining the status of free market town in 1579. During the 17th century, when the Zrinskis were one of most powerful Croatian noble families, Čakovec saw a period of significant economic and cultural development.

In the 19th century, Čakovec became an important traffic intersection point for the new railways linking Slovenia, Hungary and the Adriatic ports. Mills and distilleries were set up here, and by the early 20th century the town had developed into a small but prosperous industrial centre.

Sights

In the centre of town, on the main square, first-time visitors to Čakovec are invariably struck by this extraordinary red brick and white stucco Secessionist building, the **Dom Sindikata** (Trade Union Hall) ① *Trg Kralja Tomislava*. It was erected in 1904, by the Hungarian architect Odon Horvath, and was originally intended as a meeting place for local tradesmen.

Located on the edge of town, set amid carefully tended parkland, stands the **castle complex**. A generous section of the old 16th-century walls, complete with three semicircular bastions, is still standing, though the original Renaissance castle, built by the Zrinskis, was devastated by an earthquake in 1738. The 'New Castle', as it stands today, is a four-storey baroque structure, based on a quadrangular ground plan with an inner courtyard, built by the Czech Counts of Althan during the 18th century. From 1855 to 1870 part of the complex was used as a sugar factory, and during the Second World War the northern wing was badly damaged. However, post-war restoration work saw the castle return to its former glory, and the **Muzej Medjimurja** (Museum of Medjimurje) ① *Trg Republike 5, To40-313499, Tue-Fri 1000-1500, Sat-Sun 1000-1300, 15Kn*, opened here in 1954. Inside, you'll find an Ethnographic Department, with a fine display of local costumes on the first floor and an Archaeological Department and Art Gallery, with a collection of paintings by 20th-century artists who were born, lived or worked in the region, on the second floor. The ground floor is devoted to heavy stone pieces, tombstones and sculpture, from the first to 20th centuries.

Wine tasting

A pleasant drive 20 km northwest of town, through undulating countryside planted with vineyards, brings you to the sleepy village of Štrigova, close to the Slovenian border. Here the **Lovrec** family run a small high-quality **vineyard** ① *Sv Urban 133, Štrigova, To40-830171, open daily for wine tasting, but better to telephone first to arrange a time*, producing a variety of award-winning white wines: Chardonnay, Pinot, Rizling, Graševina, Sauvignon and Trminac. In an authentic wooden outbuilding, complete with rustic furnishing, you can take part in an amusing and informative wine-tasting session (available in Croatian, Slovenian, English and German). Expect to sample six different wines, ranging from dry to sweet, accompanied by home-made bread, local cheese and salami. At the end, it is possible to buy wine to take home.

Koprivnica and around » pp83-86. Colour map 2, A2.

→ Phone code: 048. Population: 24,809. 98 km northeast of Zagreb; 70 km southeast of Varaždin.

Koprivnica is a provincial town on the left bank of a small river of the same name in the Podravina region. The main attraction is a number of small museums and galleries, both in Koprivnica and neighbouring Hlebine, displaying works by local artists who have been working in naïve style, characterized by rural landscapes and scenes from peasant life painted in vivid colours on glass, since the 1930s. There's a town **tourist office** ⓘ *Trg Bana Jelečić 7, T048-621433*.

Koprivnica was fortified against the Turks in the 16th century, though little of the old walls can be seen today. There are a number of notable baroque buildings, such as the 17th-century **Franciscan monastery** and **Church of St Anthony of Padua**, but the main sight is undoubtedly the **Koprivnica Gallery** ⓘ *Zrinski Trg 9, T048-622564, May-Sep daily 1000-1300 and 1800-2000, Oct-Apr daily 1000-1300 and 1700-1900, free*, housing a collection of Naïve paintings and sculpture. During the 20th century the town expanded with the founding of the Podravka food-processing factory, which today employs several thousand people and is one of the few Croatian companies to be floated on the world stock market. While in the area, be sure to try local culinary specialities such as *prge* (dried smoked cheese) and *gorički gulas* (a variation of Hungarian goulash).

Hlebine → *Phone code: 048. Colour map 2, A2. 13 km east of Koprivnica.*

The true birthplace of Croatian Naïve art is the rural village of Hlebine. The so-called Hlebine School was founded here in 1930 when Professor Krsto Hegedušić met the untutored peasant-painter Ivan Generalić and was highly impressed by his work. Hegedušić gave much encouragement to Generalić and another peasant-painter Franjo Mraz, and the pair went on to hold several exhibitions in Zagreb and Sofia (Bulgaria) between 1931 and 1935. Generalić, Mraz and a third artist, Mirko Virko Virius, became known as the first generation of Croatian Naïve art painters. After the Second World War, Ivan Generalić himself began teaching more local peasants to paint, and the second generation of Croatian Naïve artists evolved: Franjo Filipović, Dragan Gazi, Josip Generalić (Ivan's son), Mijo Kovačić, Ivan Večenaj, Stjepan Večenaj and Martin Mehkek. The best place for a general overview of their work is the **Hlebine Art Gallery** ⓘ *Trg Ivana Generalića 15, T048-836075, Mon-Fri 1000-1600, Sat 1000-1400, Sun closed, 10Kn*. Also well worth a visit are **Stara Kuća Ivana Generalića** (former home of Ivan Generalić) and the **Galerija Josip Generalić** (Josip Generalić Gallery) ⓘ *Gajeva 75, T048-836430, www.galerija-josip-generalic.hr, visits by appointment*, both of which are owned and managed by the Generalić family.

Sleeping

Trakoščan *p77*

E **Hotel Coning**, Trakoščan 5, T042-796224, www.coning-turizam.hr. Just across the road from the castle, this modern hotel complex comprises 80 guest rooms, a restaurant, 2 tennis courts and has bikes for hire.

Varaždin *p79, map p80*

If you arrive in the morning you can probably exhaust the town's sights in a single day. However, the **Varaždin Baroque Evenings** music festival may give you reason to prolong your stay. In which case you may need accommodation.

D **Hotel Turist**, Aleja K Zvonimira 1, close to the bus station, T042-395395, www.hotel-turist.hr. Varaždin's principal hotel, with 100 rooms. It is a modern, rather impersonal establishment, but comfortable enough and well equipped with extras such as a fitness centre, and kennels for 4-legged visitors.

D **Hotel Varaždin**, Kolodvorska 19, T042-290720, www.hotelvarazdin.com. Opposite the train station, this hotel offers

27 basic but comfortable rooms, each with an en suite bathroom with a massage shower. The interior is shiny and new, as it opened in summer 2007, while the hotel restaurant occupies a restored brick vaulted cellar.

E **Pansion Maltar**, Prešernova 1, T042-311 100, www.maltar.hr. A slightly cheaper and more homely option than the nearby **Hotel Turist**. All rooms have a TV and minibar, and road-weary travellers will welcome the laundry service.

Čakovec and around *p81*

D **Hotel Park**, Zrinsko Frankopanska bb, T040-311255, www.hotel-park.info. Centrally located 1960s building with 98 comfortable rooms, a restaurant and café. Renovated in 2003.

E **Hotel Aurora**, Franje Punčeca 2, T040-310700, www.hotelaurora-ck.com. A small hotel offering 10 cosy guest rooms, and a bar where they serve breakfast with outdoor tables on a pleasant terrace. Additional facilities include a small gym, sauna and massage. Open all year.

Koprivnica and around *p83*

E **Hotel Podravina**, Hrvatske Državnosti 9, T048-621025, www.hotel-podravina.hr. This centrally located, 4-storey, modern white hotel offers 105 basic but comfortable rooms, each with an en suite bathroom, TV and minibar, plus a large restaurant with a summer terrace.

F **Agroturizam Tara**, Teofila Hana 8, Starigrad, 3 km from Koprivnica, T048-634 091. This friendly bed and breakfast has 7 double rooms. It's very popular so try to book at least a week in advance. The owner occasionally prepares dinner for guests, otherwise **Restoran Podravska Klet** (see Eating) is just down the road.

Eating

Klanjec *p76*

ΨΨ **Zelenjak**, Rizvica 1, 3 km north of Klanjec, close to the Lijepa Naša monument on the road to Kumrovec, T049-550747, www.zelenjak.com. This popular restaurant and café is housed in a traditional Zagorje building with a glass conservatory overlooking the garden. Its main claim to fame is that it did the catering for one of Tito's parties, attended by Richard Nixon, Jacqueline Kennedy, Richard Burton and Elizabeth Taylor during the 1960s. There are also 7 double rooms upstairs (**E**).

Kumrovec *p76*

ΨΨ-Ψ **Zagorska Klet**, within Staro Selo complex, T049-553107. Unashamedly set up for the tourists who visit Staro Selo, this small eatery nontheless does good basic Zagorje fare such as *zagorski štrukli* (baked cheese dumplings) and *kobasice* (sausages). It's also possible to come here just for a drink. Open Sat-Sun 1000-1900.

Veliki Tabor *p77*

Ψ **Grešna Gorica**, Desinić, T049-343001, www.gresna-gorica.com. This homely rustic eatery serves up typical Zagorje dishes such as *zagorski štrukli* (baked cheese dumplings) and *pura s mlincima* (turkey with savoury pastries). Everything is made from local produce supplied by neighbouring farms. From the garden there's a good view of Veliki Tabor.

Varaždin *p79, map p80*

ΨΨΨ **Royal**, Uska ulica 5, T042-213477. The most expensive restaurant in town and highly regarded. Red carpets and wooden-panelled walls set a formal atmosphere in the dining room, while the chef takes similar care in turning out elegantly presented dishes. The house speciality is *Filesteak Royal* (fillet steak with Madeira sauce), and there's a wide choice of good Croatian wines.

ΨΨ **Restoran Zlatna Guska**, J Habdelića 4, T042-213393. Set in a vaulted cellar space, it's relaxed during the day and romantic at night. They do delicious chicken and mushroom filled pancakes, and there's a help-yourself salad bar and excellent house wine.

ΨΨ-Ψ **Pivnica Raj**, Gundulića 11, T042-213 146. Close by, this is a microbrewery serving up *Knaput* beer and barbecued meat dishes. Most Fri and Sat nights there's live *tamburaška* music.

For an explanation of the sleeping and eating price codes used in this guide, see inside the front cover. Other relevant information is found in Essentials, pages 32-40.

Čakovec and around *p81*

¥¥¥ Mala Hiža, Mačkovec 107, 5 km north of Čakovec, on the main road to Mursko Središće, T040-341101. One of the best places to eat in the area. Antique furniture and an open fireplace set a homely atmosphere in the dining room. Guests tuck into large platters of roast meats, along with local specialities such as fresh curd cheese and boiled ham. There's live music on Fri and Sat evenings.

¥¥-¥ Pilka Pivnica, Josip Kozarca 15, T040-395899. A cheaper option in the centre of town, this popular microbrewery serves excellent beer, plus pizzas and a selection of local fare if you feel peckish.

Koprivnica and around *p83*

¥¥ Pivnica Kraluš, Zrinski Trg 10, T048-622302. Next door to the Koprivnica Gallery, this large beer hall serves local specialities such as *punjena puritina sa svježem sirom* (turkey stuffed with curd cheese), *govedeg kuhanog jezika s prgama sira* (tongue with *prge* cheese) and *pivski kobasica* (beer sausage). There are tables outside in summer.

¥¥ Restoran Podravska Klet, Starogradska cesta, Starigrad, T048-634069. This highly regarded eatery is 3 km from Koprivnica, in a thatched cottage with a homely, old-fashioned dining room. Top dishes include *gorički gulaš* (a local version of Hungarian goulash) and *telaći kotletis vrganjima* (veal cutlets with mushrooms). There is live folk music Fri and Sat nights till 0200.

Festivals and events

Krapina *p79*

Sep Kajkavian Festival, celebrating Zagorje folk music.

Varaždin *p79, map p80*

Sep-Oct Since 1971, **Varaždin Baroque Evenings** (www.vbv.hr) have attracted international musicians and are hailed as being one of the country's most important cultural events. Each evening, for 2 weeks between late Sep and early Oct, baroque music concerts are held in the cathedral and the **Varaždin theatre auditorium**.

Čakovec and around *p81*

Feb-Mar Fašnik, traditional carnival celebrations are held the weekend before Shrove Tue, with locals disguised in bizarre costumes and masks.

Jul Ćakovačko Ljeto is the Summer Festival, with theatrical performances and concerts in the castle courtyard.

Koprivnica and around *p83*

Jul Podravski Motivi, 2nd weekend of Jul, is a celebration of local arts and crafts, folk customs, Naïve art and regional cuisine.

Transport

Zagorje *p76*

There is no public transport to Trakošćan, so you really need a car.

Bus

Krapina bus station T049-315018.

4 buses daily to **Kumrovec** from Zagreb (1½ hrs). From there it's a 20-min walk to Staro Selo. There are 8 buses daily from Zagreb to **Desinić** (1 hr 50 mins). From there it is a 30-min walk to the castle. There are 8 buses daily from Zagreb to **Krapina** (1½ hrs).

Train

Krapina train station T049-371012. There are 10 trains daily from Zagreb to **Krapina** (1½ hrs).

Varaždin *p79, map p80*

Bus

Bus station T060-333555. 26 buses daily to **Zagreb** (about 2 hrs).

Train

Train station, T 060-333444. 14 trains daily to **Zagreb** (about 2 hrs).

Čakovec and around *p81*

You need private transport to reach **Vinska Kuća Lovrec**, on the edge of Štrigova.

Bus

Bus station, T040-313947. 14 buses daily to **Zagreb** (2 hrs 20 mins).

Train

Train station, T040-384333.

8 trains daily to **Zagreb** (about 2 hrs or 3½ hrs (local)). 1-way ticket. 1 train daily to **Budapest** in Hungary (5 hrs).

Koprivnica and around *p83*

Bus

Bus station, T048-621282. From **Zagreb**, there are 7 buses (2½ hrs) daily to Koprivnica. From **Varaždin** there are 10 buses (1 hr) daily to Koprivnica (¾ hr). From Koprivnica to **Hlebine** there are 6 buses (Mon-Fri), 2 buses (Sat).

Train

Koprivnica train station, T048-621122.

From **Varaždin** there are 9 trains daily to Koprivnica (45 mins). From **Zagreb**, there are 15 trains daily to Koprivnica (1 hr 20 mins).

East of Zagreb

Seldom visited by tourists, other than those arriving from Serbia, the flat fertile plains of Slavonia spent several centuries under the Turks until they were reclaimed by the Hapsburgs. Up until the Second World War a sizeable German minority lived here and, still today, there are many Hungarian families. The region is known throughout Croatia for its excellent kulen *(spicy salami) and* fiš paprikaš *(fish stew flavoured with paprika).* ▸▸ *For Sleeping, Eating and other listings, see pages 93-96.*

Lonjsko Polje Nature Park

→ *Phone code: 044. Colour map 2, B1/2, C1/2. 82 km southeast of Zagreb.*

In the village of Čigoć lies the main entrance to Lonjsko Polje Nature Park, occupying a flood plain on the east bank of the River Sava, between the provincial towns of Sisak and Nova Gradiška. This vast area of wetland and oak woods is best known for its storks, which come here to nest between April and October, then spend the rest of the year in South Africa. Čigoć is also noted for its lovely Posavina-style wooden houses, complete with finely carved balconies and thatched roofs.

The **nature park information centre** ⓘ *Čigoć 26 in Čigoć, T044-715115, daily 0800-1600, 25Kn* , is located in a traditional wooden house on the west side of the park, close to the main entrance, and can supply maps and information. The **nature park head office** ⓘ *Trg Kralja Petra Svačića bb, Jasenovac (on the border with Bosnia), T044-672080, www.pp-lonjsko-polje.hr, all year Mon-Fri 0800-1600*, can supply maps of the park and basic information. If you call in at Jasenovac, look out for the giant concrete tulip, which is a memorial monument to the Serbs, Jews and gypsies killed in the town's infamous Ustaše concentration camp during the Second World War. ▸▸ *See Transport, page 95, for details.*

Declared a nature park in 1990, Lonjsko Polje is one of largest wetlands in Europe, displaying a landscape typical of large parts of Central Europe 150 years ago, before the advent of modern land-drainage systems. Each year come spring, as the surrounding rivers swell, the oak woods and meadows of the river basin flood providing a perfect natural habitat for some 240 bird species. While the best known visitors to the park are storks – some 600 couples, the highest concentration of storks in Europe – other endangered species such as herons, egrets, cormorants and eagles can also be spotted. The marshy meadows, woods of ash, willow and poplar, host more than 10,000 ducks through winter. Other indigenous species include the spotted Turopolje pig, which feeds on freshwater mussels and acorns, the semi-wild Posavac horse, wild boar, deer, otters, beavers and wild cats.

Požega

→ *Phone code: 034. Colour map 2, C3. Population: 20,943. 175 km southeast of Zagreb and 67 km west of Osijek.*

Požega is slightly off the beaten track and of little interest to tourists, but worth a brief mention for its charming baroque main square, **Trg Sv Trojstvo**, which is where you'll find the town **tourist office** ⓘ *Trg Sv Trojstvo 1, T034-274900, www.pozega-tz.hr*.

The oldest building on the square is **Crkva Sv Duha** (Church of the Holy Spirit), founded by Franciscan monks in 1280 (when Požega came under the Ottomans – 1537-1688 – it was used as a mosque). The adjoining Franciscan monastery was built during the 18th century, and the Church of the Holy Spirit was restored following a fire in 1842. Also overlooking the square, the Gothic **Crkva Sv Lovre** (Church of St Lawrence) dates back to 1300, and was taken over by the Jesuits, who in turn also built themselves a monastery here, in the 18th century. At the west end of the square lurks the **Gradski Muzej** (Civic Museum) housing a modest collection of archaeological finds, Romanesque reliefs and 18th-century baroque paintings. Most of the other buildings surrounding Trg Sv Trojstvo are elegant baroque town houses decorated with stucco-work, while a plague column in the centre dates from 1749. One block north from here, on Trg Sv Terezije, the late baroque **Sv Terezija** (St Theresa's) was built in 1763 and was one of a number of Croatian churches to be promoted to the status of cathedral in 1997. In the park in front of the cathedral stands a monument to Luka Ibrišimović Sokol, a Franciscan monk who was instrumental in liberating Požega from the Turks.

Slavonski Brod

➔ *Phone code: 035. Colour map 2, C4. Population: 58,642. 197 km southeast of Zagreb and 47 km southwest of Osijek.*

On the north bank of the River Sava, which forms the natural border with Bosnia, you'll pass by Slavonski Brod if driving along the main road (E70) from Zagreb to eastern Slavonia. It's by no means a tourist destination, but makes a decent stopping place for lunch, and you might also check out the 18th-century fortress and take a riverside stroll to the Franciscan Monastery. There's a town **tourist office** ⓘ *Trg Pobjede 30, T035-445765.*

The settlement was originally founded by the Romans as Marsonia. The Ottoman Turks occupied the area from 1526 to 1691, after which it was incorporated into the Military Border. The spectacular star-shaped **Brodska Tvrdjava** (Brod Fortress) complete with bastions and moats, designed to protect Slavonia from the Ottoman forces across the river, could accommodate 4000 soldiers. Construction work, carried out largely by local peasants under forced labour, was completed in 1741. It ceased to function as a military base in 1860. Today there are plans to restore some of the buildings and you can walk a circuit of the ramparts to get an idea of the scale of the place.

Just east of the fortress, **Trg I B Mažuranić** functions as the main square, with a number of open-air cafés offering views of the river. From here, a 10-minute walk along the riverside promenade will bring you to the 18th-century baroque **Franjevački Samostan** (Franciscan Monastery) centring on a fine cloistered courtyard.

During the 19th century the town developed in the area between the fortress and the monastery and soon became an important craft and trading centre due to its position on the river. The Tito years saw Slavonski Brod further industrialized and the modern high-rise suburbs were constructed to house workers. During the war for independence, the town was badly shelled. Its sister town, Bosanski Brod, lies just across the river and is now part of the Republika Srpska, the Serb-dominated area of Bosnia and Herzegovina.

Đakovo and around

» pp93-96. Colour map 2, C5.

➔ *Phone code: 031. Population: 20,912. 38 km southwest of Osijek.*

Đakovo is a small provincial town best known for its towering red-brick cathedral and quality white wines produced in the surrounding vineyards, which were originally owned by the Bishop. It is also home to a Lipizzaner stud farm – you can call by in the morning to see the horses in their stables, and at weekends they lay on occasional dressage performances for pre-arranged group visits. There's a town **tourist office** ⓘ *Kralja Tomislava 3, T031-812319, www.tz-djakovo.hr.*

Background

Đakovo was first mentioned as a Bishop's See in 1244, with far-reaching influence extending over most of Slavonia and Bosnia. By the 14th century, the town had developed in two distinct parts. **Castrum Dyaco**, consisting of the Bishop's Palace and the cathedral, protected by defensive walls (a 40-m-long stretch of the medieval wall still stands today), and **Civitas Dyaco**, with a local secular community. However, in 1536 Đakovo was conquered and largely destroyed by the Turks, who then rebuilt it as a Muslim centre with three mosques, one of which is still standing today, albeit as a Catholic church. The Turks were finally pushed out in 1687, and Đakovo resumed its role as the seat of a Bishop and grew into a prosperous market town.

Sights

Today the old town centres on the pedestrian **Ulica Hrvatskih Velikana**, known to locals as the Korzo, lined with 18th-century town houses with steep-pitched tile roofs, many of which host cafés and shops at street level.

The imposing red-brick, neo-Gothic **Katedrala** (cathedral) ⓘ *Strossmayerov Trg, daily 0800-1200, 1500-1900*, was commissioned by Bishop Josip Juraj Strossmayer in 1866, and the design work carried out by two Viennese architects, Karl Rosner and Friedrich Schmidt. The façade is flanked by two 84-m bell towers, and the interior decorated with late 19th-century Romantic religious frescoes by Alexander and Ljudevit Seitz, in a style reminiscent of the British pre-Raphaelites.

A 10-minute walk north of the cathedral, along the Korzo, will bring you to the small, charming, white **Crkva Svi Sveti** (Church of All Saints) ⓘ *normally closed, but if you ask at the tourist office they can have it opened on request*, It started out as Hagipasha's Mosque, based on a square ground plan with a dome. When the Turks left Đakovo, the minaret was pulled down and it was converted into a small Catholic church. The classicist façade was added in the 19th century.

From the cathedral, walk for 15 minutes east along Ulica Matije Gupca, then turn right on Ulica A Senoe to reach the small but welcoming **Državna Ergela Lipicanaca** (State Lipizzaner Stud Farm) ⓘ *Ulica A Senoe 45, T031-813286, www.ergela-djakovo.hr, Mon-Fri 0800-1400, Sat-Sun group visits by arrangement, 20Kn*. Founded by the Hapsburgs in 1506 for the breeding of high-quality horses for the Court of Vienna, it is one of several farms in Central Europe that still produce Lipizzaners for the Spanish Riding School of Vienna. Brown at birth, the horses later turn white, and are renowned for their intelligence and ability to learn complex semi-acrobatic movements with an able rider. Queen Elizabeth II visited the Đakovo stud in 1972 and a team of four Lipizzaners from here took part in the opening ceremony of the Olympic Games in Munich in 1972.

If you're interested in the sculptor Ivan Meštrović a visit to the village of **Vrpolje**, 10 km south of Đakovo, is well worthwhile. Although Meštrović is always considered a Dalmatian (his family were from Otavice in Dalmatia and he grew up there), he was by chance born here in Vrpolje in 1883, when his parents were visiting Slavonia for the summer harvest. The small **Spomen Galerija** (Memorial Gallery) ⓘ *Trg Ivana Meštrocića 1, T035-439075, Mon-Fri 0700-1400, Sat 0700-1200, 10Kn*, contains about 30 works by Meštrović, donated to the village by the artist himself.

Osijek and around » *pp93-96.*

Colour map 2, B5.

→ *Phone code: 031. 280 km from Zagreb; 30 km from the Hungarian border; 20 km from the Serbian border.*

Osijek is the largest town in Slavonia and an important road and rail intersection point. Strung along the south bank of the River Drava, the three distinct parts of town are interspersed by tree-lined avenues and green parks, giving it an airy and relaxed feel.

You can probably cover the main sights, notably the 18th-century Tvrdja complex, in a day, after which you might visit the nearby Kopački Rit Nature Park. There's a town **tourist office** ⓘ *Županijska 2, T031-203755, www.tzosijek.hr.*

Background

The town was founded by the Romans as the fortified military camp of Mursa in the first century AD, in the area that is now Tvrdja, and was last mentioned in 591, after which it was destroyed by invading Goths and Huns and sank into oblivion. By the 12th century a new settlement had grown up in the area that is now Gornji Grad: it was a market town and river port, owned by a Cistercian Abbey and known by the Hungarian name of Eszek. However, the medieval town was ransacked by the Turkish leader Sultan Suleiman II the Magnificent in 1526, and an important Ottoman administrative centre, complete with mosques, built in its place. The Turks linked Osijek to Darda in the north with an 8-km-long wooden bridge, which ran across the River Drava and the Baranja marshes.

In 1687, the Hapsburgs pushed the Turks out of the area, and set the town up as one of the principal army barracks on the Slavonian Miltary Border, based in the purpose-built Tvrdja fortress complex. Almost a century later, in 1786, the three town boroughs of Tvrdja, Gornji Grad and Donji Grad were united, and Osijek became the administrative centre of the wealthy agricultural region of Slavonia.

In the 20th century, industries such as food processing, chemicals, agricultural machinery, textiles and footwear grew up here, mainly due to the town's location on a transport crossroads between Zagreb and Belgrade, and Hungary and Bosnia and Herzegovina. During the war for independence Osijek came under siege for several months in 1991 and 1992, lying dangerously close to the front line after the Serbs took Vukovar, just 35 km to the southeast. The theatre and the old rooftops of Tvrdja were hit several times, though subsequent restoration work has repaired the worst of the damage.

Sights

Osijek can be divided into Gornji Grad (Upper Town), the main commercial centre, Donji Grad (Lower Town), a residential area, and Tvrdja, a picturesque 18th-century quarter originally built by as a military barracks. The reference to 'upper town' means 'up the river', not 'up the hill'. Of these, Gornji Grad and Tvrdja are of prime interest to sightseers. One of the nicest aspects of Osijek is its relation to the river. A pleasant 2-km waterside walkway, known to locals as the *promenada*, leads along the south bank from Gornji Grad to Tvrdja, while a pedestrian suspension bridge

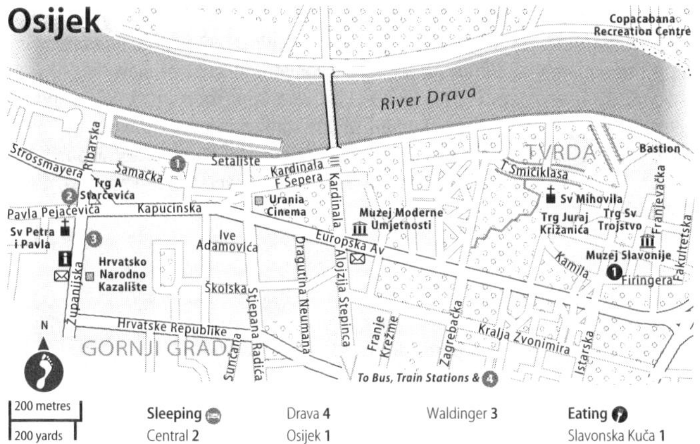

 connects Gornji Grad to Copacabana, the 'town beach', where bathing is possible through summer.

Gornji Grad's main sight, the red-brick, neo-Gothic church **Crkva Sv Petra i Pavla** (Church of St Peter and Paul) ⓘ *Trg A Starčevića, daily 0800-1200, 1600-1900*, was erected in 1894 to designs by the German architect Fritz Langenberg. Apparently the people of Osijek wanted something to rival the cathedral in neighbouring Đakovo, and today locals call this the *Katedrala* (cathedral), though officially it is not one. The interior is adorned with stained-glass windows, and frescoes painted by the Croatian artist Mirko Racki during the 1930s.

The building of the **Hrvatsko Narodno Kazalište** (Croatian National Theatre) ⓘ *Županijska 9, T031-220700*, by the local architect Carlo Klausner in 1866, was an important landmark in Osijek's cultural development. In November 1991, during the war, it was hit by a grenade, and the auditorium and part of the stage were consequently destroyed by fire. Restoration of the theatre was carried out by the fast-food chain McDonalds, on the condition that they could occupy part of the building at street level. It reopened in December 1994.

The pleasant, leafy **Europska Avenija** is lined with some of Croatia's finest art nouveau buildings, including a succession of three-storey town houses designed by local architects for wealthy merchants between 1903 and 1906, a post office, and the charming **Urania Cinema**, added by the Osijek-born architect Victor Axmann in 1912. Incidentally, the Urania is still working, being one of only two cinemas in town.

Tracing Croatian art from the 18th century up to the present day, the **Galerija Likovni Umjetnosti** (Visual Arts Gallery)ⓘ *Europska Avenija 9, T031-251280, Tue-Fri 1000-1800, Sat-Sun 1000-1300, 10Kn*, houses a horde of painting and sculptures from baroque portraits of local nobility up to 20th-century abstract canvasses. It also hosts occasional temporary exhibitions dedicated to one particular artist or movement.

Tvrdja is especially lovely at night, when the cobbled streets are lamplit and a number of popular bars and cafés, plus a handful of excellent little restaurants (see Eating), attract the local student community. Osijek town council has put forward Tvrdja as a candidate for the UNESCO World Heritage list, and there are plans to restore many of the old buildings and turn them over to educational and cultural institutions. Work on Tvrdja began in 1712, when the Austrians set about constructing a large army barracks surrounded by eight bastions linked by defensive walls (now only partly visible). Besides military and public buildings, civilian town houses were erected within the complex, along with several fine churches and monasteries, which cared for the centre's spiritual welfare as well as providing schools and a printing press. Today Tvrdja is something of an open-air museum, looking now much as it would have done in the 18th century. The complex centres on a main square, Trg Sv Trojstvo, lined by ochre-coloured baroque buildings with steep-pitched tile roofs, overlooking a plague monument erected in 1729 and flanked by two identical marble fountains from 1761. Also on the square you'll find the **Muzej Slavonije** (Museum of Slavonia) ⓘ *Trg Sv Trojstvo 6, T031-250730, Tue-Fri 0900-1400, Sat-Sun 1000-1300, 15Kn*, housing a collection of stone finds from Roman Mursa, and staging temporary exhibitions devoted to local history. Close by, the **Crkva Sv Mihovila** (Church of St Michael) ⓘ *Trg Juraj Križanica, daily 0800-1200, 1600-1900*, with twin towers topped by onion domes, was built in baroque style by the Jesuits in 1748 on the site of the former Kasim Pasha Mosque.

Kopački Rit Nature Park → *Phone code: 031. Colour map 2, B5. 12 km northeast of Osijek.*

ⓘ *Visits to the park are by appointment only as part of a guided tour, 20Kn. The main entrance to the park is at Kopačevo, 3 km from Bilje.*

Kopački Rit Nature Park is a vast expanse of marshland prized for its wealth of rare birds. Lying between the River Drava and the River Danube, the park is part of

Casualties of war

Some people say the war started and ended in Vukovar. When Croatia claimed independence, Serbs from the surrounding villages were adamant that they would rather remain part of Yugoslavia. A group of Croatian activists (among them members of Tudjman's HDZ ruling party) provoked the situation by firing three rockets at the Serb-populated village of Borovo Selo. Tensions escalated and the situation soon got out of control. By 1 August 1991 Vukovar lay under siege, surrounded by Yugoslav army reinforcements and Serb irregulars. On 19 November 1991, the town fell, by this time devastated, buildings lying in rubble, the streets lined with corpses and 264 people killed in the hospital. Of those who remained, the women and children were spared, but many men disappeared and have never been found, though several bodies have been identified in a mass grave at nearby Ovćara.

Vukovar officially came back under Croatian administration in January 1998 and a lengthy reconstruction programme was initiated in the hope that former residents, both Croats and Serbs, would return. The process of rebuilding and reintegration is slow and will take many years to complete. Today there are two football teams, two radio stations; two separate communities that live side by side but ignore one another. At the nursery school, two separate playgroups are held under one roof, one for Croats, one for Serbs. And at the secondary school, Croatian and Serbian teenagers alternate morning and afternoon classes so as not to be in the same room at the same time. Reconciliation looks a long way off. Nowhere else in the country are the physical and psychological traumas caused by the war so apparent.

Baranja, a region of flat, fertile agricultural land, which until the war for independence hosted a mixed farming community of Croats, Serbs and Hungarians. It was taken by the Serb military at the beginning of the war in 1991, was designated a UN-protected zone from 1992 to 1996, and then came under UN transitional administration until it was incorporated into Croatia in January 1998. Guided visits to the park can be given by boat or on foot – access to certain areas is still restricted as the park was heavily mined during the war.

Said to be one of the largest and most beautiful wetlands in Europe, the park's waters, flora and fauna attract experts and scientists from far afield, as well as curious day trippers. Around 260 bird species nest here, including geese, duck, heron, stork, coot, gull, tern, kingfisher and woodpecker, and in spring and autumn many other migratory species use the area as a temporary shelter. The waters are abundant in fish – which is why so many birds are attracted to the park – including pike, tench, bream, carp, catfish and perch, while the surrounding oak woods host deer, wild boar, wild cats, pine martens, stone martens and weasels. Some of the willow-lined ponds are home to otters. Park headquarters is the **nature park tourist information centre** ⓘ *Petefi Šandora 5, Bilje, T031-750855, www.kopacki-rit.com, daily 0800-1600, 20Kn.*

Vukovar

» *pp93-96. Colour map 2, B6.*

→ *Phone code: 032. Population: 30,126. 303 km east of Zagreb and 35 km southeast of Osijek.*

On the west bank of the River Danube, which forms a natural border with Serbia, Vukovar was once a prosperous market town famed for its elegant 18th-century baroque architecture. Since 1991, it has become better known as an image of the suffering and devastation caused by the war for independence. Many who fled at this time remain in other parts of Croatia or abroad. An eerie silence pervades in a town still divided between Croats and Serbs. There's a town **tourist office** ⓘ *JJ Strossmayera 15, T032-442889, www.turizamvukovar.hr.*

Background

People lived in the area as long ago as the Bronze Age: the renowned Vučedol Dove, a three-legged vessel in the form of a bird from around 2000 BC (now in Zagreb Archaeological Museum), was found at Vučedol, an archaeological site 5 km from Vukovar.

The town itself grew up at the confluence of the River Vuka and the River Danube. It became a free royal town in 1231 and the chief settlement of the *upanija* (country) of Vukovo, an area of rich arable farmland dotted with noble fortresses and villages of serfs. In 1526, after Vukovar fell to the Ottoman Turks lead by Sultan Suleiman the Magnificent, mosques and public baths were built, and the town had a population of around 3000, until the Turks were finally driven out in 1687. In 1736, a German nobleman, Philipp Karl zu Eltz (1665-1743), bought the Lordship of Vukovar, which covered 23 villages and some 31,000 serfs, and from then on the Eltz family played a crucial role in the town's development. Most of the population were employed in farming, notably the production of cereals and wine, but craftsmen's guilds also sprung up, and goods were exported along the River Danube by steamship. At the end of the Second World War, the Eltz family lost their property and returned to Germany, as did many other German settlers in the region, but following the declaration of Croatian independence in 1991, Jakob Graf zu Eltz moved back to Croatia and now sits as a member of parliament in Zagreb.

During the Tito years the area surrounding Vukovar was rapidly industrialized: the **Borovo** factory produced rubber goods such as footwear and tyres; **Vuteks** manufactured textiles and **Vupik** was a larger producer of wheat, maize, sugar beet, wine, livestock and milk. The standard of living was high, and by 1991 Vukovar had a population of almost 45,000, of which 44% were Croats, 37% Serbs, and the remainder members of various minorities such as Hungarian, Slovaks and Ruthenians. The war of independence tragically changed the fortunes of Vukovar (see box, page 91).

Sights

Gradski Muzej (Town Museum) ⓘ *Županska 2, T032-441270, www.muzej-vukovar.hr, Mon-Fri 0800-1500, 10Kn*, suffered the same fate as the rest of Vukovar – the baroque **Dvorac Eltz** (Eltz Manor), in which it was housed, was shelled and badly damaged. Built in 1751 by the Eltz family, the manor is now under restoration and the ground floor has already reopened. Many of the original exhibits were looted or destroyed, but a new collection is gradually being built up, largely with donations from abroad. The museum also stages temporary art exhibitions.

On raised ground a short distance southeast of the centre stands the three-storey **Franjevački Samostan** (Franciscan Monastery) ⓘ *T032-442641*, centring on a charming 18th-century cloistered courtyard. The complex includes the monastery church and a museum housing a collection of religious paintings, both of which were damaged during the war but have now been restored. You can visit the complex upon request; for information enquire at the tourist office, or call the monastery directly.

Sleeping

Lonjsko Polje Nature Park *p86*
Several small agrotourism centres, offering locally produced organic food and overnight accommodation (**E**) , have popped up in the area. The 2 listed in Eating, below, are happy to receive visitors, but call first so they can have a meal and/or a room ready for you.

Požega *p86*
E **Hotel Grgin Dol**, Grgin dol 20, T034-273222. A 5-min walk east of the main square, **Grgin Dol** offers 18 comfortable rooms, each complete with en suite bathroom, TV and minibar. There's a hotel bar and an excellent restaurant. Pets welcome.

Slavonski Brod *p86*
E **Hotel Central**, Petra Krešimira IV 45, T035-492030, www.hotelcentralsb.hr. Located in the town centre, this small family-run hotel opened in spring 2008. It offers 15 comfortable rooms, all with LCD-TV, mini-bar, safe and Wi-Fi, plus a small restaurant.

Đakovo and around *p87*
E **Hotel Blaža**, Dr Ante Starčevića 158, Đakovo, T031-816760; F031-816764. A post- modern building with 20 rooms, each with satellite TV and telephone. Facilities include a restaurant, conference room and open-air pool.

Osijek and around *p88, map p89*
C **Hotel Osijek**, Šamačka 4, T031-230333, www.hotelosijek.hr. This colossal high-rise concrete block stands just a 5-min walk from the main square, overlooking the river. The 147 rooms are functional, if somewhat impersonal, and each has a TV, bathroom and minibar. There's also a hotel bar and restaurant. Pets welcome.
C **Waldinger Hotel**, Županijska 8, T031-250450, www.waldinger.hr. This elegant Secessionist building, dating from 1904, is in the centre, just a few doors down from the tourist office. The 14 rooms and 2 suites each have satellite TV, minibar, safe deposit, and internet connection, and most also have jacuzzi. Facilities include a fitness studio and sauna.
D **Hotel Central**, Trg A Starčevića 2, T031-283399, www.hotel-central-os.hr. Located in a prime position on the main square, this 19th-century hotel was completely renovated in 2004. The 39 rooms have satellite TV, minibar and internet connection, and there's a plush Viennese-style café and a restaurant, plus bikes for hire.
E **Hotel Drava**, I.F.Gundulica 25a, T031-250500, www.hotel-drava.com. Opened in 2007, this small, stylish, family-run hotel is close to the train station. There are 11 well-equipped guest rooms all with en suite bathrooms and internet access, plus a pleasant ground floor café where a buffet breakfast is served.

Kopački Rit Nature Park *p90*
Several families offer bed and breakfast style accommodation (**E**) in Bilje, 3 km from the park. Try either the Sklepić family at Dubrovačka 30, Bilje, T031-750243, or the Galić family at Ritska 1, Bilje, T031-750393. Both have 2 double bedrooms and serve up hearty breakfasts with home-made local salami and cheeses, and can also arrange fishing trips by boat.

Vukovar *p91*
C **Hotel Lav**, JJ Strossmayera 18, T032-445100, www.hotel-lav.hr. Reopened after reconstruction in 2005, this hotel dates back to 1840, and has the unenviable record of having been destroyed 3 times by war. There are 38 rooms and 4 suites, all with satellite TV, minibar, a/c and internet connection.
E **Hotel Dunav**, Trg Republike 1, T032-441 285, F032-441762. Part of this hotel was damaged during the war, though miraculously most of it kept working. It's a functional 8-storey 1970s concrete block, with 38 basic rooms, a bar and restaurant. Plans to renovate a further 22 rooms have yet to be fullfilled.

Eating

Lonjsko Polje Nature Park *p86*
¶¶ **Obitelj Ravlić**, Mužilovčica 72, Mužilovčica, village next to Čigoć, T044-710151. This traditional wooden house was restored by the Ravlić family and done out with old-fashioned furniture. There is a taverna, a small private ethnological museum and several rooms available for overnight stays.

🍴 **Stara Hiža**, čigoć 44, Čigoć, T044-715321. This friendly family-run farmstead occupies one of the traditional wooden houses in Čigoć. If you come for lunch or dinner, expect hearty fish-based dishes such as *riblji paprikaš* (fish stew with paprika). They have 6 Posavac horses for riding, as well as a boat and bikes for hire. The 2 guest rooms are done out with old-fashioned furniture.

Slavonski Brod *p87*

🍴 **Slavonski Podrum**, Andrije Štampa 1, T035-444856. A 15-min walk east of the fortress, close to the Franciscan Monastery, this highly popular restaurant occupies a charming 18th-century building with a beamed dining room. The house speciality is *teletina ispod peke* (veal prepared under a *peka*).

Đakovo and around *p87*

🍴 **Croatia Turist**, Petra Preradovića 25, T031-813391. Just 200 m from the cathedral, this is good a place to try *slavonski kulen* (sausages and salami flavoured with paprika), ham and game dishes. Be sure to order a bottle of local white wine: the *Riesling* or *Graševina* are both recommended. The dining room is vast and somewhat impersonal, but in summer there are tables outside on the terrace.

Osijek and around *p88, map p89*

🍴 **Restoran Muller**, Trg Jure Križanića 9, T031-204770. In a restored Baroque building in the romantic Tvrdja area, this refined restaurant serves a selection of Slavonian, Dalmatian and international dishes – try the *biftek u crnom vinu i š ampinjonima* (beef in red wine with mushrooms).

🍴 **Slavonska Kuća**, Kamila Firingera 26, T031-208277. Within the Tvrdja complex, this cosy, rustic eatery specializes in traditional local dishes. Try the *riblja kobasica*, a type of sausage made from smoked fish, as an unusual starter, followed by the house speciality *riblji paprikaš* (fish stew with paprika), which comes to the table in a large bowl with a ladle.

Kopački Rit Nature Park *p90*

🍴 **Restoran Kod Varge**, Kralaja Zvonimira 37a, Bilje, T031-750031. Just outside the park in Bilje, **Kod Varge** is known for tasty fish dishes and home-made sausage. The house speciality is *šaran s kajmakom i krumpirom* (carp with sour cream and potatoes).

🍴 **Restoran Komoran**, Podunavlje, Bilje, T031-753099. Located within the park, this highly regarded restaurant is housed in a traditional hunting lodge. The dining room is decorated with hunting and fishing equipment and trophies, and favourite dishes are *sakadaški fiš paprikaš* (hearty fish stew prepared with paprika) and *ražnjići od divljaći* (wild boar and venison kebabs).

Vukovar *p91*

🍴 **Tri Vrske**, Parobrodska 3, T032-441788. Accessed across a footbridge, this charming informal riverside restaurant is one of the few places that managed to keep functioning during the war. Freshwater fish tops the menu, with local dishes such as *riblji paprikaš* (fish stew with paprika) and smoked carp highly recommended.

Bars and clubs

Osijek and around *p88, map p89*

The main concentration of bars (and cafés) is found along the riverside promenade and in the trendy student area of Tvrdja.

Tufna, Kuhačeva 10, T032-215020, www.tufna.hr. Currently regarded as Osijek's trendiest club, you'll find Tufna in the Tvrdja area of town. Spread over 2 floors, it plays 70s and 80s hits, R'n'B and House music, and arranges occasional themed party evenings.

Festivals and events

Požega *p86*

12 Mar Grgurevo (Feast of St Gregory). A display of cannons and mortars on the main square commemorates a local victory over the Turks in 1688.

Sep Music Festival Zlatne Zice Slavonije (Golden Strings of Slavonia). Folk festival featuring Slavonian *tambura* music and traditional regional costumes.

Slavonski Brod *p87*

Mid-Jun Brodsko Kolo. The oldest and largest folk dance festival in Croatia, dates back over 30 years.

Đakovo and around *p87*
Jul Dakovački Vezovi (Dakovo Embroidery), 1st week of Jul. This is one of the largest folk festivals in Croatia, presenting traditional costumes, folk music and folk dancing from the regions of Slavonia and Baranja.

Osijek and around *p88, map p89*
May Croatian Tambura Music Festival. A folk music festival, attended by groups from throughout the country.
Jun-Aug Osijek Summer Nights. Open-air cultural events.

Activities and tours

Osijek and around *p88, map p89*
Across the river from town, the waterside Copacabana recreation centre offers a large open-air pool, a sand beach and a number of pleasant bars and cafés.
Hobby Tours, Kapučinska 23, T031-201070. Organize guided tours of Osijek, Kopački Rit and Dakovo, as well as wine-tasting sessions at local vineyards.

Transport

Lonjsko Polje Nature Park *p86*
Car
Public transport facilities in the area are poor, so you really need a car.

Požega *p86*
Bus
Požega bus station, Industrijska 2, T034-273133. There are 4 buses daily from **Zagreb** (2½ hrs) and 6 buses daily from **Slavonski Brod** (1 hr).

Train
Požega train station stands close to the bus station, T034-273911. There is 1 train daily from **Zagreb** (3½ hrs).

Slavonski Brod *p87*
Bus
Slavonski Brod bus station, Trg Hrvatskog Proljeća, T035-444300.

There are 14 buses daily from **Zagreb** (2 hrs 20 mins) and 6 buses daily from **Požega** (1 hr).

Car
If you are planning on driving to Slavonski Brod from Zagreb, remember that the main road (E70) incurs a 68Kn toll for this stretch.

Train
Slavonski Brod train station stands opposite the bus station, T035-441082. There are 15 trains daily from **Zagreb** (2 hrs 10 mins).

Đakovo and around *p87*
Bus
Bus station, T060-302030. There are 6 buses daily to **Zagreb** (3 hrs 20 mins) and 20 buses daily to **Osijek** (40 mins).

Osijek and around *p88, map p89*
Air
Osijek Airport, T031-514400, 7 km from town. The only flights are internal to Split and Dubrovnik. There are no flights in winter.

Bus
The bus station is a 10-min walk from the centre at Bartula Kašića bb, T060-334466.

There are 12 buses daily to **Zagreb** (4 hrs); 20 daily to **Dakovo** (40 mins); and 20 daily to **Vukovar** (45 mins). An international bus departs from Osijek for **Pecs** in Hungary, Mon-Sat (3 hrs).

Buses leave for Bilje every hour; you have to walk the final 3 km to the park entrance.

Car
Hertz, Gundulićeva 32, T031-200422, www.hertz.hr.

Taxi
There is a taxi rank in front of the train station, Trg Ružičke, T031-200100 (day), T031-372555 (night).

Train
The train station is a 10-min walk from the centre, next to the bus station, at Trg Ružičke, T060-333444.

There are 6 trains daily to **Zagreb** (4 hrs), 1 to Rijeka (7½ hrs), and 2 international trains daily for **Pecs** in Hungary (3 hrs).

Vukovar *p91*
Bus
The bus station is a 10-min walk from the centre at Olajnic bb, T060-332233.

There are 20 buses daily to **Osijek** (¾ hrs) and 5 to **Zagreb** (4½ hrs). 4 daily international buses also depart from Vukovar for **Belgrade** in Serbia, and there are 2 buses weekly to **Berlin** and **Hamburg** in Germany.

Directory

Osijek and around *p88, map p89*
Consulates There is only 1 consulate in Osijek. **Hungarian**, S Radića 15, T031-250150. **Internet** VIP Internet Café, L Jager 24; **Internet Klub Ukrik**, Sunčana 18, www.ukrik.hr. **Medical services** Osijek **Hospital**, J Huttlera 4, T031-511511; casualty, T031-506920. **Pharmacies**: **Ljekarna Centar**, Trg A Starcevica 7, T031-205722, works regular hours and also covers nights shifts; **Ljekarna Park**, Park Kralja P Kresimira IV 6, T031-208323, works regular hours and also covers Sat and Sun afternoons. **Post offices** Županijska 8, Mon-Fri 0700-2000, Sat 0700-1400.

Vukovar *p91*
Consulate Serbia , Vukovarske Brigade 2, T032-441016. **Medical services** Hospital: Županijska 37, T032-452111. **Post office** M Pijade 4, Mon-Fri 0700-2000, Sat 0700-1400.

South of Zagreb

Southwest of Zagreb, the provincial town of Karlovac is probably best known today for its beer, Karlovačko pivo, *though during the 16th century it was an important military base marking the border between Austro-Hungary and the Turkish empire. Moving further south, on the inland road to Dalmatia, you will come Plitvice Lakes National Park, worth a stop for its spectacular waterfalls.* ►► *For Sleeping, Eating and other listings, see pages 99-100.*

Karlovac

►► *pp99-100. Colour map 1, B5.*

→ *Phone code: 047. Population: 59,395. 55 km from Zagreb.*

Karlovac sits on a major road junction between Zagreb, with Rijeka to the west and Split to the south. It's not a town you'd specially set out to visit, but you're bound to pass through en route from the capital to either the Kvarner region or Dalmatia, and it's a great place to stretch your legs, with tree-lined promenades following the old town walls, and a pleasant riverside path leading to a small castle hotel. There's a **tourist office** ⓘ *Ulica Petra Zrinskog 3, T047-615115, www.karlovac-touristinfo.hr.*

Background

Founded by the Hapsburgs in 1579 as a military base, for some time Karlovac marked the southern border of the Austro-Hungarian Empire. As a defence post against Ottoman expansion, the settlement was built to a sturdy Renaissance plan based on a six-point star with bastions and a moat, which was filled with water from the nearby rivers, the Korana and the Kupa. During the late 17th century, as the Turks were pushed further south and the settlement no longer served as a military base, it developed into a provincial town filled with baroque architecture.

Sights

Today, the main square, **Trg Bana Jelačića**, is overlooked by the late 17th-century baroque **Sv Trojstvo** (Holy Trinity Church), while café life centres on the **Korzo**, a pedestrian street lined with cafés and shops. Although the walls were demolished during the 19th century, the basic star plan can still be clearly seen in aerial views. The moats have been turned into a 2.5-km string of promenades lined by horse chestnut trees, with the loveliest part being the former Maria Valeria Promenade, renamed after the late President, Franjo Tudman.

Close to the main square, housed within the baroque Frankopan Palace, the **Gradski Muzej** (Town Museum) ⓘ *Strossmayerov Trg 7, T047-615980, Tue-Fri 0800-1500, Sat-Sun 1000-1200, 10Kn (Wed free)*, displays archaeological finds such as clay figures from an Illyrian shrine, scale models showing the development of the town, period furniture, traditional folk costumes, and local craftwork such as pottery, woodwork and basketry.

Managed by the Town Museum, the **Galerija Vjekoslav Karas** (Vjekoslav Karas Gallery) ⓘ *Ljudevita Šestica 3, T047-412381, Tue and Thu 0800-1500, Wed and Fri 0800-1500 and 1700-1900, Sat-Sun 1000-1200, 10Kn (Wed free)*, opened in 1976. It is named after the local artist Vjekoslav Karas (1821-1858) and highlights Croatian painters from late 19th and early 20th centuries.

East of town, a pleasant 30-minute stroll along the banks of the River Kupa brings you to the **Stari Grad Dubovac** (Dubovac Castle) ⓘ *Zagrad 10, T047-615980, Tue-Fri 0800-1500, Sat-Sun 1000-1200, 10Kn*, complete with three towers and a triangular courtyard, built by the Frankopan family from the island of Krk in the 13th century. The dungeon and the 13th-century defence tower are open to the public. A brochure, available in English and Croatian, is available at the entrance. It is managed by the City Museum.

Foginovo Kupalište (Foginovo bathing area), on the bank of the River Korana, is known as the 'town beach', complete with a diving platform, an area set aside for beach volleyball, and a number of waterside bars and cafés. It's just a 10-minute walk from the centre, and bathing is possible from mid-June to early September.

Plitvice Lakes National Park » pp99-100.

Colour map 1, C6.

→ *Phone code: 053. 128 km from Zagreb and 73 km from Karlovac.*

Travelling south on the road for Dalmatia, the remote Plitvice Lakes are Croatia's most popular inland destination. As the country's oldest national park, Plitvice is home to 16 emerald-green lakes connected by a series of spectacular waterfalls, stretching 8 km in length. The surrounding slopes are covered with dense forests of beech and fir, and visitors can explore the area following a series of marked paths and wooden bridges. If you enjoy walking you'll want to spend a couple of days here – there are several good hotels within the park and private accommodation is available in nearby villages. Approximately 30 buses, on the route between Zagreb and Dalmatia, pass Plitvice NP daily.

Ins and outs

The **national park tourist information centre** ⓘ *Entrance 2, Plitvička Jezera, T053-751014/5, www.np-plitvicka-jezera.hr, park open daily Jun-Aug 0700-2000, Apr-May and Sep-Oct 0800-1800, Nov-Mar 0900-1600, Apr-Oct 110Kn, Nov-Mar 70Kn*, sells the tickets which include free use of national park buses and boats. The local **tourist office** ⓘ *Trg Sv Jurja 6, Korenica, T053-776798, summer only*, is south of the park. » *See Transport, page 100, for details.*

Sights

Making up part of a spectacular karst landscape, the lakes and falls of Plitvice developed over the last 10,000 years, and the process is continuing today. Such features are formed when limestone rock, consisting largely of calcium carbonate ($CaCO_3$), dissolves in water, which then becomes super-saturated and deposits the $CaCO_3$ in the form of microcrystals. In the case of Plitvice, the deposits have built up to make rapids and travertine barriers that form the waterfalls. It's beautiful the year through, though bear in mind that the area is often covered by snow November to March, and the lakes may well be frozen from December to January.

The lakes here are rich in trout (though fishing is prohibited within the park), while the surrounding forests are home to foxes and badgers, as well as the seldom sighted lynx, wolf and bear. Birdwatchers should look out for woodpeckers and herons, plus rare species such as grey eagles and peregrine falcons. Owls are plentiful, though rarely seen in daylight hours.

The best way to explore the lakes is to begin at Entrance 2 (close to the national park office and the village of Plitvička Jezera) then take the national park bus to **Labudovac Falls**, where the water from **Proščansko Jezero**, the highest of the lakes (639 m above sea level) begins a spectacular journey, cascading down through a succession of smaller basins to reach the park's largest lake, **Jezero Kozjak**.

Plitvice Lakes National Park

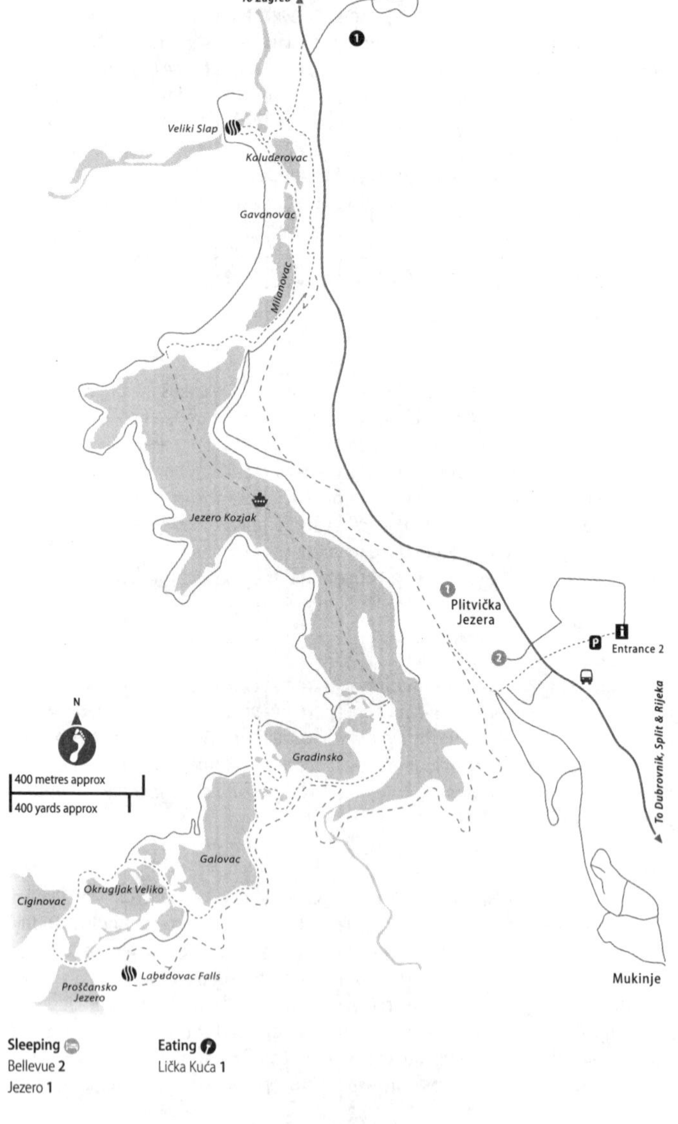

The stretch from Labudovac Falls to Jezero Kozjak is comfortably completed on foot, after which you can ride a national park boat the length of the lake, then follow a series of wooden bridges and walkways over and around a number of smaller pools to arrive at the park's largest and most spectacular waterfall, **Veliki Slap**, where water thunders down to the lowest lake, **Kaluderovac** (503 m). You are now just a 10-minute walk from Entrance 1, where you might stop for refreshments at **Lička Kuća** (see Eating), and then take a national park bus back to your starting point. This entire circuit takes about four hours (excluding time for eating). A map and information about alternative routes are available from the national park office. Each year on the first Saturday in June, the Plitvice Marathon takes place, starting and ending at Entrance 2.

Sleeping

Karlovac *p96*
The tourist office website includes a list of families offering private accommodation.
C Hotel Korana Srakovčić, Perivoj Josipa Vrbanića 8, T047-609090, www.hotelkorana.hr. Set in parkland close to the River Korana, 5-min by car from the city centre, this small, high-class hotel has 15 rooms and 3 suites. Extras include a Wellness Centre with sauna, massage, gym and indoor pool. Adventure sports such as rafting on the River Dobra and canoeing on the River Korana can be arranged upon request.
E Hotel Carlstadt, A Vraniczanya 1, T/F047-611111, www.carlstadt.hr. In the city centre, just a couple of blocks back from the river, this grey, 4-storey corner building has 37 rooms with satellite TV, telephone and minibar. Facilities include a restaurant, casino and laundry, plus internet available at reception.

Plitvice Lakes National Park *p97, map p98*
D Hotel Jezero, Plitvička Jezera bb, close to Entrance 2, T053-751400, www.np-plitvicka-jezera.hr. The most luxurious hotel in the park is a large mountain lodge built on high ground overlooking the lakes. The 210 rooms and 7 suites are panelled in natural pine and have matching wooden furniture. Facilities include tennis courts, a fitness centre and sauna, and a bowling alley. It usually stays open all year.
E Hotel Bellevue, Plitvička Jezera bb, close to Entrance 2, T053-751700, www.np-plitvicka-jezera.hr. This slightly cheaper option offers 81 basic rooms, including 6 singles, with en suite bathrooms but few extras. Popular with excursion groups. Open May-Oct.
Both the national park office and local tourist office can help you find private accommodation.

Eating

Karlovac *p96*
¥¥¥-¥¥ Kvaka, Žorovica bb, T047-416616. On the banks of the River Kupa, along the tree-lined waterside path to Dubovac, Kvaka is best known for its fresh water fish such as *pastrva* (trout), though it also serves sea fish, barbecued meats and a small selection of vegetarian dishes. Open all year.
¥¥¥-¥ Restoran Lovački Rog, Pojatno bb, T047-637675, www.lovacki-rog.hr. Lovački Rog means the 'Hunter's Horn', and this restaurant specializes in game, along with barbecued meats and fish. 2 km north of Karlovac on the old road to Zagreb, it occupies a wooden pavilion with an open-air terrace surrounded by oak trees.

Plitvice Lakes National Park *p97, map p98*
¥¥ Lička Kuća, opposite Entrance 1, T053-751024. This large, highly regarded restaurant is done out in rustic style with heavy wooden tables and benches. The menu features traditional Lika dishes such as *lička juha* (soup made from lamb's innards and vegetables) and *teletina ispod peke* (veal prepared under a *peka*). Closed Nov-Apr.

For an explanation of the sleeping and eating price codes used in this guide, see inside the front cover. Other relevant information is found in Essentials, pages 32-40.

❂ Festivals and events

Karlovac *p96*
23 Jun Ivanski Krijes, St John's Day Bonfire. Festivities, organized by the tourist office, take place on the banks of the River Kupa.

Transport

Karlovac *p96*
Bus
Karlovac bus station, T060-338833. The daily buses from **Zagreb** to **Split** stop in Karlovac, as do those from **Zagreb** to **Rijeka** (50 mins).

Car
If you are planning to drive from **Zagreb** to Karlovac on the main road (E65), remember that there's a 16Kn toll.

Train
4 daily trains from **Zagreb** to **Split** pass through Karlovac (30 mins). The 12 daily local trains from Zagreb to Karlovac are slow (1 hr) due to numerous stops in small stations. Karlovac train station, T060-333444.

Plitvice Lakes National Park *p97, map p98*
Bus
The 30 buses daily running from **Zagreb** to **Dalmatia** all pass through the village of Plitvička Jezera, but make sure the driver knows you want to get off there (2½ hrs from Zagreb).

Istria

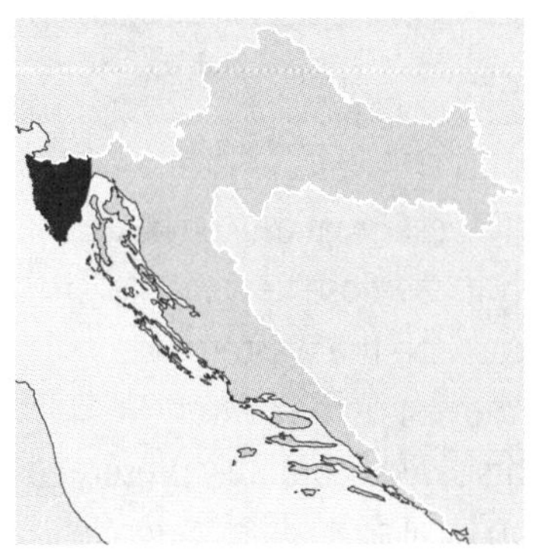

Footprint features

Introduction

A large, triangular peninsula in northwest Croatia, Istria has an identity all of its own. Historically it has close ties with Italy and, still today, many towns, especially on the western side, are bilingual. It's notably ahead of the rest of the country regarding current trends: restaurants serve beautifully presented creative cuisine, farmhouses dish up local specialities and offer overnight accommodation (agrotourism), and the tourist board has set up a series of bike paths and wine roads.

Lying on the tip of the peninsula, the region's principal city and port is Pula, with a first-century Roman forum as the main square and an ancient amphitheatre dominating the skyline. Close by are the islands of Brijuni National Park, which once served as the summer residence of the late President Tito.

Croatia's most popular seaside resorts lie on the Istrian west coast: Poreč, home to a splendid sixth-century basilica decorated with stunning golden Byzantine mosaics, and neighbouring Rovinj, made up of ochre- and russet-coloured houses clustered around a pretty fishing harbour, crowned by a hilltop church. Besides its cultural wealth, this area is renowned for nudist resorts, with the largest one in Europe, Koversada, lying in Vrsar, between Poreč and Rovinj.

Moving inland to the Srce Istre (Heart of Istria), narrow country roads meander through a gently rolling landscape of woodland and vineyards.

Less visited than the west coast, the eastern side of Istria faces onto the Kvarner Gulf. The main resort is Rabac, a modern settlement with a decent pebble beach and several good fish restaurants. It's not the sort of place where you'd want to spend very long, but combined with neighbouring hilltop Labin, a former mining town, it offers a seaside-inland experience all in one. Nearby Brestova serves as the mainland port for ferries to the island of Cres (see Kvarner).

★ Don't miss ...

1 Pula Attend a night time concert at the Roman Arena – an unforgettable setting for opera, rock, jazz and pop, page 106.
2 Brijuni National Park Spend a leisurely day checking out the Tito Exhibition and the safari park, then take time off to walk and swim, page 108.
3 Euphrasius Basilica See the glittering religious mosaics in Poreč, page 118.
4 Villa Angelo d'Oro Splash out on a night in this unforgettable luxury hotel in Rovinj, page 119.
5 Grožnjan Visit the crafts workshops and artists' studios in this isolated hill town, page 127.
6 Buzet Order a dish prepared with locally unearthed truffles – undoubtedly an acquired taste, but this is the perfect place to try them, page 128.

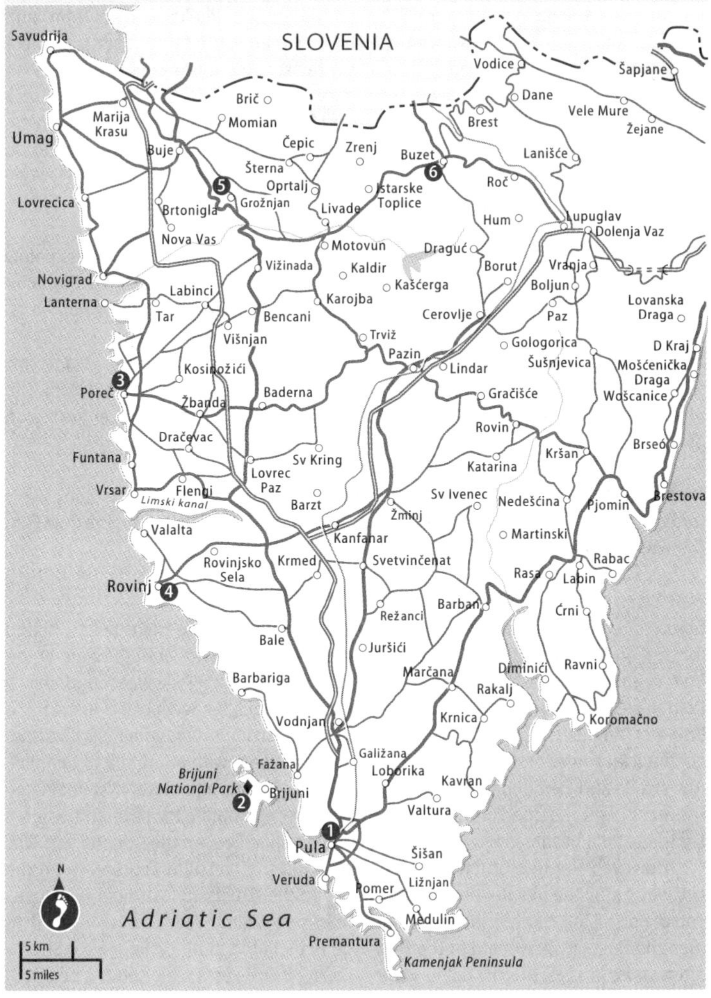

Pula and around

→ Phone code: 052. Colour map 1, C1. Population: 58,594.

Pula is something of an enigma. Here magnificent ancient Roman ruins stand side by side with a declining industrial port, in a city that is Istria's administrative and economic centre. Somewhat surprisingly, it's also one of the top places in Croatia for small, high-class, family-run hotels and chic seafood restaurants serving beautifully presented creative cuisine. With two well-equipped marinas, one directly in front of the city centre and the other at Veruda, it's a popular destination for yachters, as well as sightseers who come to visit the monumental first-century Roman amphitheatre and the nearby Brijuni National Park, and holidaymakers on package deals, who normally sleep in the large seaside hotels south of the centre at Verudela and Medulin. ▸▸ For Sleeping, Eating and other listings, see pages 110-114.

Ins and outs

Getting there Pula is 193 km from Zagreb, 98 km from Rijeka, 448 km from Split and 664 km from Dubrovnik. Through summer there are regular flights to most European capitals. The airport is 12 km northeast of Pula city centre. There is no airport bus connection, but taxis are readily available. The **bus station** ⓘ *Trg 1 Istarska Brigade*, is 1 km northeast of the centre. There are daily connections with the major cities in Croatia and Trieste, Italy. The **train station** ⓘ *Kolodvorska bb*, is 1 km north of centre. Services only cover the Istria Region. ▸▸ See Transport, page 113, for further details.

Getting around The historic centre is quite compact and the sights described below can comfortably be visited on foot. Verudela Peninsula, where many of the large commercial hotels and several good restaurants are located, is served by bus No 7.

Tourist information The **tourist office** ⓘ *Forum 3, T052-219197, www.pulainfo.hr, summer daily 0800-2200, winter daily 0900-1900*, is in the heart of the old town. The **official tourist office** ⓘ *Pionirksa 1, T051-452797, www.istra.com*, for the entire region of Istria is in Poreč.

Best time to visit Being Istria's economic and cultural centre, Pula is fairly lively throughout the year, though the most popular time to visit is July, when the **Pula Film Festival** and the **Istra Etno Jazz Festival** both take place.

Background

Some time during the fifth century BC, the Illyrian tribe of the Histri built a hilltop fortress on the present-day site of Kaštel. However, it was not until the time of the Roman general and statesman Julius Caesar (100-44 BC) that Pula was founded as a Roman colony, *Colonia Julia Pollentia Herculanea*. During the reign of the first Roman Emperor, Augustus (63 BC-AD 14), it developed into an important administrative and commercial centre of about 5000 inhabitants, complete with a forum and temples, town walls and 12 monumental gates, and a water supply and sewer system. In 539 the region was absorbed into the Byzantine Empire, and during the sixth and seventh centuries Pula became the main base of the Byzantine fleet on the Adriatic.

However, the tide of fortune was reversed in the late 13th century, when the city was hit by the plague: people were dying on the streets so fast that the corpses could not all be buried, inspiring the Italian poet Dante Alighieri (1265-1321) to mention Pula city graveyard in the *Divine Comedy* in the ninth cycle of *Hell*. Shortly afterwards, in 1331, the city fell to Venice. Losing its role as a major port, a period of decline set in, and by the time the Venetians left, in 1797, the population stood at only 600.

Under the Hapsburgs from 1813 to 1918, Pula was made the chief base and arsenal of the Imperial Austrian Navy, and thus entered its second golden age. The small city of fading antique splendour was transformed into an industrial port with a prosperous middle class, though apparently it did little to impress the Irish novelist James Joyce, who worked here briefly in 1904, teaching English

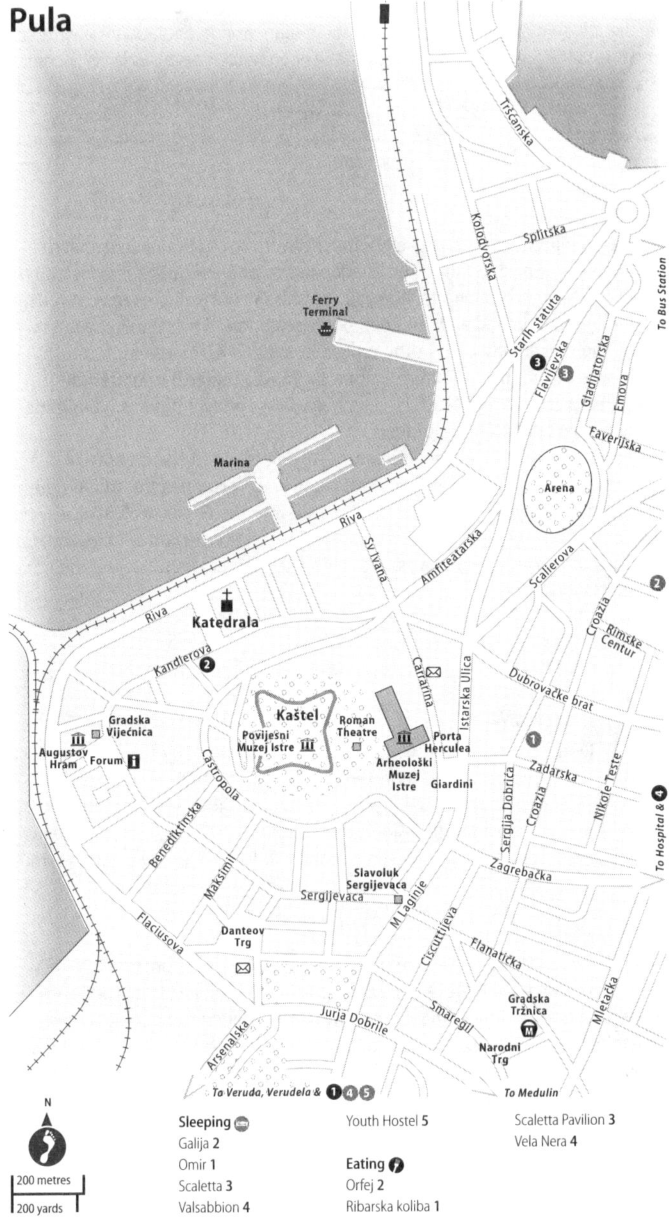

 to Austrian naval officers: he referred to Pula as a "godforsaken nest" and "Siberia upon sea".

Under Italy in the run up to the Second World War, Mussolini came here in person to make a speech in the theatre and, as the war drew to a close, the city was badly damaged by Anglo-American bombing.

During the Yugoslav years Pula lived through a period of intense industrial development, with the shipyard becoming a major source of employment. The Pula Film Festival was born in the 1950s, regularly attended by Tito and his celebrity friends such as Sofia Loren, Elizabeth Taylor and Richard Burton. Today, although it's a popular sightseeing destination thanks to its Roman monuments, unemployment is high and it is still struggling to recover from the economic and social damage caused by the war.

Sights

Forum

The vast paved piazza has been the city's most important public meeting space since Roman times. It's closed to traffic and overlooked by popular open-air cafés and the city tourist office, and on the north side you can still see the well-preserved **Augustov Hram** (Temple of Augustus) with an open portico supported by six tall columns with Corinthian capitals. It was built in the early first century AD to celebrate the cult of Augustus, who founded the Roman Empire in 27 BC. Under Byzantine rule it was converted into a church and later used as a granary. Today it houses a **lapidarium**, displaying pieces of Roman sculpture.

In Roman times, next to the Temple of Augustus stood the **Temple of Diana**, dedicated to the goddess of hunting. It has long since disappeared, though during the 13th century the back wall was incorporated into the **Gradska Viječnica** (Town Hall) ⓘ *Augustov Hram, T052-218603, Jun-Sep daily 0900-1300 and 1800-2100, Oct-May by appointment*, which was later renovated to gain its present appearance with a Renaissance façade.

Katedrala (Cathedral)

ⓘ *Obala Maršala Tita, Jun-Sep daily 0900-1200 and 1800-2100, Oct-May open for mass only.*

From the north end of the Forum, Kandlerova ulica leads to the cathedral, with a 17th-century Renaissance façade concealing a three-nave early Christian basilica, built on the foundations of a Roman temple during the fifth century. In front of the cathedral, the free-standing bell tower was built in the late 17th century, partly from stone blocks taken from the Arena (Roman amphitheatre). The complex was badly damaged by bombing during the Second World War, but was fully restored in 1946.

Arena

ⓘ *Flavijevska ulica, May-Sep daily 0800-2100, Oct-Apr daily 0900-1500, 20Kn.*

Continue to the end of Kandlerova ulica then take Amfiteatarska ulica to arrive in front of the Arena, a first-century Roman amphitheatre. Designed to host gladiator fights and able to accommodate 22,000 spectators, way beyond the city population of that time, it is the sixth-largest building of its type in the world (after the Colosseum in Rome, and the amphitheatres in Verona, Catania, Capua and Arles). The outer walls

Today the Arena is used for open-air concerts: performers have included Jamiroquai, Anastacia and Marilyn Manson. The annual Pula Film Festival is also held here.

are remarkably well preserved, though through the centuries stones from the inside have been carried off for use on other buildings. Originally the interior would have been encircled by tiers of stone seats, the central floor would have been covered with sand, and a *velarium* (large awning) would have been used as a temporary roof structure, to shelter spectators from the sun and rain.

The Arena fell into disuse in the sixth century, when gladiator games were forbidden. During the 16th century the Venetians planned to transfer it, stone by stone, to Venice, though fortunately a local senator, Gabriele Emo, protested and the project was abandoned. The building was restored in the early 19th century by General Marmont under Napoleon's Illyrian provinces. The underground halls house a musty and rather disappointing display of wooden oil presses and amphorae.

Arheološki Muzej Istre (Archaeological Museum of Istria)

ⓘ *Carrarina 3, T052-218603, Jun-Sep Mon-Sat 0900-2000, Oct-May Mon-Fri 0900-1500, 12Kn.*

From the Arena, retrace your steps along Amfiteaterska ulica, then take the first left to arrive on Carrarina ulica. Here, the second-century **Porta Gemina** (Twin Gate) is one of two surviving gates (originally there were 12) that led into the Roman walled town. Today it serves as the main entrance to the Archaeological Museum of Istria, housing an extensive but rather uninspiring display of local finds. The ground floor is dedicated to heavy stone pieces such as Roman gravestones and sarcophagi, and medieval stone altars from early Christian churches. On the first floor you'll find the prehistoric collection, including early daggers, axes, bracelets and pendants, and necklaces made of amber beads. Directly behind the museum, a path leads to the remains of a small semicircular second-century Roman theatre, which is still used for small open-air concerts through summer. A few doors down from the museum, still on Carrarina ulica, stands **Porta Herculea** (Hercules Gate), a simple arch in the only surviving section of the original city walls from the first century BC.

Slavoluk Sergijevaca (Triumphal Arch of the Sergi)

Continue along Carrarina ulica and across Giardini to reach the Triumphal Arch of the Sergi, built in the first century BC to honour the local Sergi family for their role at the Battle of Actium, fought between the Roman fleet of Octavian and the Roman-Egyptian fleet of Mark Antony and Cleopatra in 31 BC. The Sergis were on the side of Octavian, who was victorious and consequently went on to become the first Roman emperor under the name of Augustus. Next to the arch and marked with a small plaque stands the house where the Irish author James Joyce (1882-1941) lived briefly during a spell in Istria. West of the arch, **Ulica Sergijevaca** is the city's main street in Roman times and today a pedestrian area lined with Pula's highest concentration of clothes shops. East of the arch, Flanatička leads to Narodni Trg, where the daily market is held.

Gradska Tržnica (Main Market)

ⓘ *Narodni Trg, Mon-Sat 0700-1330, Sun 0700-1200.*

Built as a covered market in 1903, this iron and glass structure was revolutionary in its time. The daily fish and meat market is still held inside, while fruit and vegetable stands are set up outside, in the shade of a fine row of chestnut trees.

Kaštel (Venetian fortress)

For the best views over the city, climb any one of several steep flights of steps off Ulica Sergijevaca to arrive on Ulica Castropola, leading up to the hilltop Kaštel. The present fortress was built by the Venetians in 1630 and later renovated by the Austrians in 1840. Today it houses the rather disappointing **Povijesni Muzej Istre** (Historical Museum of Istria) ⓘ *Kaštel, T052-211740, Jun-Sep daily 0800-2000,*

 Oct-May daily 0800-1500, 10Kn. In summer, the central courtyard is used for open-air cultural events including the **Pula Film Festival** and the **Istra Etno Jazz Festival**.

Beaches

The nearest beaches to the city centre are at **Veruda** and **Verudela**, 3 km south of the centre, where most big modern hotels are located. However, the most stunning beaches are on **Kamenjak Peninsula**, on the very southern tip of Istria, within Donji Kamenjak Nature Park. Some 9.5 km long and 1.5 km wide, Kamenjak is ringed by an indented 30-km coastline, with countless coves and secluded beaches. It's also a popular spot for windsurfing. Nine buses leave Pula daily for the small village of Premantura, on Kamenjak.

North of Pula » *pp110-114. Colour map 1, C1.*

Vodnjan (Dignano) → *Phone code: 052. Population: 3406.*

Just 10 km north of Pula, on the main road to Rijeka, Vodnjan makes a good half-day trip from Pula. It warrants a visit for two reasons: a church containing an unusual collection of mummified saints and an excellent little restaurant where you can try authentic local cuisine. The town itself is worth an amble, with charming medieval buildings tightly packed onto a hillside, surrounded by vineyards and olive groves. There is a **tourist office** ⓘ *Narodni trg 2, T052-511700, www.istria-vodnjan.com.*

The baroque **Crkva Svetog Blaža** (Church of St Blaise) ⓘ *Trg Zagreb bb, Jun-Sep daily 0900-1900, winter by appointment*, was built in the 18th century on the site of a Romanesque basilica, while the 65-m bell tower was added in 1882. Inside, in glass cases hidden by a curtain behind the main altar, lie the extraordinary mummified bodies of three saints: St Leon Bembo, St Giovanni Olini and St Nicolas Bursa. Although their skin and nails have dried, giving them the quality of weathered wood, experts are unable to explain why they never decomposed, and they are said to be among the best-preserved human relics in Europe. What's more, ailing believers who have prayed to them have been cured and have left votive offerings (such as wedding rings) as a way of thanks.

Svetvinčenat (Sanvincenzo) → *Phone code: 052. Colour map 1, C1.*

On the regional road between Vodnjan and Pazin, 26 km north of Pula, the tiny hill town of Svetvinčenat is named after its oldest building, the **Crkva Sv Vinčenata** (Church of St Vincent). Standing in the grounds of the town cemetery, the interior of this 12th-century Romanesque structure is adorned with three layers of wall paintings from different periods, the most valuable being the Romanesque frescoes attributed to Master Ognobenus Trivisanus. In the centre of town, the Renaissance main square, known as Placa, is overlooked by the **medieval castle**, a quadrangular stone structure with corner towers, now used to stage open-air cultural events, notably the **Festival of Dance and Non-Verbal Theatre** ⓘ *www.dancefestivalcroatia.com*, through summer. There's a local **tourist office** ⓘ *Svetvinčenat 20, T052-560349, www.svetvincenat.hr*.

Brijuni National Park » *pp110-114. Colour map 1, C1.*

Brijuni went down in history as Tito's summer residence: between 1949 and 1979 the charismatic Yugoslav president used it for entertaining countless world leaders, as well as glamorous friends such as Richard Burton and Elizabeth Taylor. After Tito died, the Brijuni archipelago, made up of 14 islands and islets, was made a national park, and the largest island, Veli Brijun, opened to the public. This low-lying island, with its beautifully tended parkland, herds of deer and strutting peacocks, makes a good day

Non-Aligned Nations

Founded during the Cold War by Josip Broz Tito of Yugoslavia, Gamal Abdel Nasser of Egypt and Jawaharlal Nehru of India, the Non-Aligned Nations was an association of countries that declined to take the side of either of the two world super powers of that time, the Capitalist USA and the Communist USSR. Many of the countries that joined the alliance were former colonies that had recently freed themselves from foreign domination and were against forming new ties with any big power. Key issues were politics, defence and economics and, although the organization was made up of members of vastly differing political persuasions, it formed an important buffer between the Communist East and Capitalist West. Today, the organization has 114 members, including Indonesia, Egypt, Ghana, Guinea, Cuba and Libya.

trip from Pula. If you stay for any longer, in one of the hotels, then you'll have the place to yourself for walking, bathing, playing tennis and golf. It's a place for total relaxation.

Ins and outs

The only way to visit the island is as part of an organized group. National park boats leave from Fažana (10 km northwest of Pula), ferrying visitors back and forth to the island. Reserve in advance (T052-521880, Monday-Friday 0700-1500). Tickets cost 110-190Kn (depending on the time of year) which includes the boat ride and a tour of the grounds. The tour is conducted by a professional guide. It is possible to stay overnight (see Sleeping, page 110); the hotels are in need of refurbishment, but provide space for 320 guests, who have the island all to themselves as no one lives here.

The national park **tourist office** ① *T052-525888, www.brijuni.hr*, is in Fažana opposite the quay. ▸▸ *See Transport, page 113, for further details.*

Background

Ancient ruins and archaeological finds show that the Romans used to summer here, though the islands were later abandoned for centuries due to an infestation of malaria-carrying mosquitoes. Finally, in 1893 Brijuni was bought by Paul Kupelweiser, an Austrian industrial magnate who employed the German scientist Robert Koch (founder of modern medical bacteriology, 1843-1910) to purge the place of the disease. Kupelweiser then set about creating a prestigious health resort: he laid out the parkland, tree-lined avenues and exotic planting, had fresh water and electricity brought to the island and built a heated seawater swimming pool. Brijuni fast became a haven for Vienna's nobility and high society, with elite guests including Archduke Franz Ferdinand and the German writer Thomas Mann. In the 1920s, under Italian rule, a casino, polo club and tennis courts were built. Brijuni fared badly during the Second World War, so that by the time Tito made it his official summer residence it was in need of extensive renovation: the war-ravaged hotels were rebuilt, the old villas restored, and the neighbouring island of Vanga planted with orchards, tangerine groves and vineyards. More recently, the golf course, dating back to 1922, has been upgraded from 9-hole to 18-hole.

Sights

Today a **museum** (renovated in spring 2008) houses a photography exhibition *Tito on Brijuni* showing the great man enjoying his summer retreat with friends and colleagues, and the signing of a pact marking the birth of the Non-Aligned Nations, which took place here in 1956.

Visitors can also see the **safari park**, with zebras, antelopes, llamas and elephants, many of which were given to Tito as presents, such as two Indian elephants, Sony and Lenka, a gift from Indira Ghandi. Brijuni is a lovely place to walk, but other options are to rent a bike or an electric buggy, and it's even possible to hire (at a price) Tito's 1953 **Cadillac**.

Tito's former favourite residence, the sumptuous **Bijela Vila** (White Villa), now serves as the setting for important state functions and international meetings between the Croatian president and his foreign counterparts.

Sleeping

Pula and around *p104, map p105*

Many of Pula's hotels and restaurants are located in Medulin, which started out as a fishing village 11 km from the city centre, but has now been incorporated into the suburbs thanks to urban sprawl along the coast.

C **Hotel Scaletta**, Flavijevska 26, T052-541025, www.hotel-scaletta.com. Close to the Arena, this 12-room family-run hotel occupies a tastefully refurbished old town house. Rooms are decorated in sunny shades of ochre and green, and come with spanking new bathrooms. Open all year.

C **Valsabbion**, Pješčana uvala IX/26, 4 km from city centre, Medulin, T052-218033, www.valsabbion.hr. With sea views, this small luxury hotel boasts 10 cheerful guest rooms adorned with pine furniture and primary coloured fabrics, plus fresh fruit and flowers. There's a swimming pool on the top floor, and beauty treatments are also available.

D **Galija Hotel**, Epulonova 3, T052-383 802, www.hotel-galija-pula.com. This small family-run hotel occupies a modern building in the centre of town. There are 20 comfortable rooms and a restaurant, plus sauna and massage.

D **Omir**, Sergija Dobrića 6, T052-218186, F052-213944. Another small, family-run hotel close to the Arena, with 14 plain but comfortable guest rooms. Pets welcome. Open all year.

D **Porer Lighthouse**, Islet of Porer, 20 km from Pula, 2 km from Premantura Bay. Book through **Adriatica Net**, Heinzelova 62a, Zagreb, T01-2415611, www.adriatica.net. Built on a tiny islet of bare rock in 1833, this lighthouse has been converted into 2 apartments, each sleeping 4. Daily trips to the village on the mainland can be arranged with the lighthouse keeper.

G **Youth Hostel**, Valsaline 4, Veruda. T052-391133, www.hfsh.hr. 192-bed youth hostel in a bay with its own beach. To get there, take bus No 7 for Verudela and get off at Ulica Veruda, then follow a signed path through a field. Open all year.

Private accommodation

The following agencies can help you find private accommodation:

Activa Travel, Scalierova 1, T052-215497, www.activa-istra.com; **Arena Turist**, Smareglina 3, T052-529 400, www.arena tursit.hr; and **Uniline**, Dobričeva 16/II, T052-390039, www.uniline.hr.

For a list of families offering agrotourism (farmhouse meals and accommodation), go to www.istra.com/agroturizam.

Vodnjan *p108*

C **Stancija Negricani**, Marcana, T052-391084, www.stancijanegricani.com. Lying 6km from Vodnjan, this old stone famhouse is set in extensive grounds with a pool in the garden. The 9 guest rooms are furnished with antiques, and have internet connection, satellite TV and modern en suite bathrooms. There is a large restaurant with exposed stone walls serving home-made local specialities – guests can visit the kitchen to watch the food being prepared. Local activities include hiking, biking and horse riding. Open all year.

Brijuni National Park *p108*

A **Hotel Neptun-Istra**, T052-525807, www.brijuni.hr. A large, 1970s-style hotel with 66 rooms and 22 suites, with views over the harbour on Veli Brijuni. Guests can leave their cars in the guarded parking area in Fažana and have unlimited ferry travel to and from the island. There's a restaurant serving fish and meat dishes, plus a café for coffee and cakes.

Svetvinčenat *p108*
D **Stancija 1904**, Smoljanci 2-3, Svetvinčenat, T052-560022, www.stancija.com. In the rural village of Smoljanci, 3 km west of Svetvinčenat, this peaceful agro-tourism venture occupies a beautifully restored stone farmhouse sleeping up to 8, while the 2 adjoining apartments sleep 2 and 4. It's set in lovely gardens with a covered terrace area for barbecues and a small playground for kids. Open all year.

Eating

Pula and around *p104, map p105*
TTT **Vela Nera**, Pješčana uvala bb, Medulin, T052-219209, www.velanera.hr. Voted the best restaurant in Croatia on several occasions, **Vela Nera** occupies a modern concrete and glass pavilion with a large terrace overlooking Marina Veruda. The house speciality is *rižoto Vela Nera* (risotto prepared with shrimps, peaches and champagne) but they also do excellent pasta dishes with lobster and truffles, and fresh fish.
TTT-TT **Restaurant Scaletta**, Flavijevska 26, T052-541599. Taking up the ground floor of **Hotel Scaletta** (see Sleeping), this highly regarded restaurant serves sophisticated dishes such as ravioli filled with shrimps, and breaded fillet mignon with dates and croquettes. Closed Sun in winter.
TTT-TT **Valsabbion**, Pješčana uvala IX/26, Medulin, T052-218033, www.valsabbion.com. Voted Istria's top restaurant several times over the last few years, this was one of the first Croatian restaurants to specialize in 'slow food' (a concept which began in Italy in the 1990s as a reaction against fast food and globalization – it means making the most of local seasonal produce, giving extreme care to preparation, and then eating the food in a relaxed, unhurried manner). The menu changes daily depending on fresh produce, but you can expect beautifully presented dishes such as tagliatelli with pine nuts, and frogfish in vine leaves.
TT **Gina**, Stoja 23, T052-387943. In the suburb of Stoja, a 20-min walk from the centre, this small restaurant has an elegant brick-and-stone interior, an open fire and wooden beamed ceilings. House specialities include ravioli with crab filling, and lavender ice cream with hot fig sauce.
TT **Ribarska koliba**, Verudela bb, T052-222966. With a terrace built over the water affording views across the bay to Verudela Marina, the walls of this seafood restaurant are hung with photos of well-known people who have eaten here, including the late Yugoslav President, Tito.
TT-T **Scaletta Pavilion**, Flavijevska 26, T052-541599. Across the street from **Hotel Scaletta** (see Sleeping) but under the same management, this wood and glass pavilion offers good pizzas, salads, and grilled meat and fish dishes. Closed Sun in winter.
T **Orfej**, Kandlerova 1, T052-214405. Just off the Forum, this small pizzeria is friendly and reasonably priced.

Cafés
Cvajner, Forum 2, T052-853465. This trendy but unpretentious café has open-air seating on the Forum square through summer. Inside are frescoes uncovered during restoration, modern furniture and contemporary art.

Vodnjan *p108*
TTT-TT **Vodnjanka**, Istarska bb, Vodnjan, T052-511435. In summer, guests can sit out on the open-air terrace, moving indoors to the cosy dining room, complete with beamed ceilings and an open fire through winter. Seasonal specialities are on offer year round: quiches and omelettes made from wild asparagus in spring, and snails with polenta in the last week of Aug. It closes each Sun in winter.

Brijuni National Park *p108*
Other than the hotel restaurants, there is nowhere to eat on Veli Brijuni. The alternative is to eat in Fažana.
TT-T **Feral**, Trg Stare Škole 1, on the quay in Fažana, T052-520040. Value-for-money pasta dishes, plus barbecued fish and meat, served up on a summer terrace with sea views.

Bars and clubs

Pula and around *p104, map p105*
Bounty Pub, Veronska 8. A buzzing English-style pub close to the covered market.
Imperial, Fucane 72, Medulin, www.disco-imperial.com. 10 km from the city centre, this is one of the largest nightclubs in Croatia (up to 2000 people). Open all year.

Rock Club Uljanik, Dobrilina 2, www.club uljanik.hr. A thriving venue for alternative rock concerts, in a disused building overlooking the shipyard, close to the city centre.
Uliks, Trg Portarata 1. A popular little bar looking onto the Triumphal Arch of the Sergi. It's next door to the house where James Joyce once lived, hence the life-size sculpture of the writer himself sitting outside.

Entertainment

Pula and around *p104, map p105*
Cinema
Kino Kaštel, summer-only open-air cinema in the grounds of Kaštel.
Gradsko Kino, Giardini 1, T052-212336. Centrally located, it's Pula's only cinema.

Theatre
Istarsko Narodno Kazaliste (Istrian National Theatre), Laginjina 5, T052-222380, www.ink.hr.

Festivals and events

Pula and around *p104, map p105*
Late Jul Pula Film Festival, www.pula filmfestival.hr. Founded in 1954, this 5-day competitive festival is held in the Roman Arena and at Kaštel, and features films from both Croatia and other European countries.
Late Jul Seasplash Reggae Festival, www.seasplash.net. 4-day reggae festival on the beach at Veli Vrh near Pula, with free camping included in the price of the ticket.
Aug Histria Festival, www.histriafestival. com. Live concerts in the Roman Arena, starring international musicians from the worlds of rock and classical music.

Svetvinčenat *p108*
Late Jul Festival of Dance and Nonverbal Theatre, www.svetvincenat.hr. Held over 6 days, again within the castle walls.

Shopping

Pula and around *p104, map p105*
Aromatica, Laginjina 4, close to the Arch of the Sergi, T052-382180. Stocks natural soaps and cosmetic products made from olive oil and scented with wild herbs.
Main Market, Narodni Trg. Meat and fish for sale within a steel and glass pavilion, fruit and vegetables at stalls on the square. Mon-Sat 0700-1330, Sun 0700-1200.
Zigante Tartufi, Smareglina 7, close to the covered market, www.zigantetartufi.com. Stock an excellent range of truffles and truffle products from the Mirna Valley, plus Istrian olive oil and wines.

Activities and tours

Pula and around *p104, map p105*
Diving
Indie, Ližnjan 186a, T052-573658, Banjole, www.divingindie.com.

Golf
There is an 18-hole golf course (www.golf klub-pula.com) on the island of Veli Brijun, within Brijuni National Park. See page 108.

Sailing
ACI Marina, Riva 1, T052-219142, www.aci-club.hr. Located directly in front of the city centre, within sight of the Roman Arena. 213 berths, open all year.
Tehnomont Marina Veruda, Cesta prekomrskih brigada 12, Veruda Bay, T052-224034, www.marveruda.hr. Has 630 berths.

The following charter companies are based in Pula: **Euromarine**, contact Svetice 15, Zagreb, T01-232 5234, www.euromarine.hr; **Pivatus**, T052-212155, www.pivatus.hr; **RR Nautika**, contact Vlaška 28, Zagreb, T01-462 8620, www.rrnautika.hr; **SM Mediteran**, T052-223873, www.sm-mediteran.com.

Tour operators
Activa Travel, Scalierova 1, T052-215497, www.activa-istra.com. Agrotourism in Istria, as well as cultural sightseeing packages, wine tasting and golf on Brijuni.
Atlas, Ulica Starih Statuta 1, T052-393 040, www.atlas-croatia.com. Various services throughout the country, including guided tours.
Generalturist, Carrarina 4, T052-218487, www.generalturist.com. Tailor-made trips both with and without guides throughout the country.
Uniline, Dobrićeva 16/II, T052-390039, www.uniline.hr. Accommodation plus excursions throughout Istria.

Brijuni National Park *p108*
The national park lays on facilities for **horse riding** and **cycling**. There are also 4 **tennis courts** (floodlit at night), and an 18-hole **golf course** built by the Austrians in 1922.

Transport

Pula and around *p104, map p105*
Air
Through summer, **Croatia Airlines** operate regular international flights to and from **Amsterdam**, **Berlin**, **Brussels**, **Dusseldorf**, **Frankfurt**, **Gothenburg**, **Hamburg**, **Helsinki**, **London** (Gatwick and Heathrow), **Lisbon**, **Munich**, **Oslo**, **Paris**, **Prague**, **Rome**, **Sarajevo**, **Skopje**, **Stockholm**, **Vienna** and **Zurich**. Internal flights link **Pula** with **Dubrovnik**, **Osijek**, **Split**, **Zadar** and **Zagreb**. The number of destinations and the frequency of flights are reduced in winter. Pula airport, T052-530105, www.airport-pula.hr.

Airlines offices Croatia Airlines, Carrarina 8, T052-218909.

Bus
Pula bus station, T060-304090. Left luggage costs 10Kn per item, open daily 0430-2400. Internal services include about 18 buses daily to **Zagreb** (4-5 hrs); 22 to **Rijeka** in Kvarner (2½ hrs); 3 to **Zadar** in North Dalmatia (7 hrs); 3 to **Split** in Central Dalmatia (10½ hrs); and 1 to **Dubrovnik** in South Dalmatia (14 hrs). There are also 4 international buses daily to **Trieste** (Italy) and 1 to Padova (Italy) stopping at Venice en route.

Car
Budget Cararrina 4, T052-218252, www.budget.hr; **Hertz** in Hotel Histria, Verudela bb, T052-210868, www.hertz.hr.

Ferry
Split Tours, www.splittours.hr, from mid-Jul to mid-Sep, operate a 5-times weekly service from **Pula** to Zadar (North Dalmatia), stopping on the island of Lošinj (Kvarner) en route. **Venezia Lines**, call centre T0039 041-242 4000, www.venezialines.com, operate a 3-times-weekly catamaran line, running between **Venice** (Italy) and Pula, mid-Jun to mid-Sep.

Taxi
Taxis are usually available at the bus station. The most central taxi rank is at Giardini, between the Arena and the Triumphal Arch of the Sergi, or call T052-223228.

Train
Pula train station, T052-541982. National train information, T060-333444, www.hznet.hr. Internal services cover the Istria region only, with regular daily trains from **Pula** to **Buzet**, stopping in **Vodnjan**, **Kanfanar**, **Pazin** and **Lupoglav** en route. From **Lupoglav**, **Croatian Railways** run a connecting bus to **Rijeka**.

Vodnjan *p108*
Bus
10 buses daily from **Pula** to Vodnjan (20 mins).

Train
Train station, Ulica Željeznička, is a 10-min walk from the centre. 8 trains daily from Pula to **Vodnjan** (15 mins).

Svetvinčenat *p108*
Bus
19 buses daily from Pula to **Svetvinčenat** (45 mins).

Brijuni National Park *p108*
Bus
There are 16 buses daily from Pula to **Fažana** (20 mins).

Ferry
Veli Brijuni is served by national park passenger boats from Fažana on the mainland, journey time 15 mins. The price of the ticket is included in the national park entrance fee.

Directory

Pula and around *p104, map p105*
Emergencies Ambulance: T94; **Fire**: T93; **Police**: T92. **Internet** MMC Luka **Multimedia Centre**, Istarska 30, www.mmcluka.hr, with art and photography exhibitions. **Medical services** Hospital: Zagrebačka 30, T052- 376000 (24-hr casualty). **Pharmacies**: marked by a glowing green cross. The centrally located pharmacy at Giardini 15, T052-222551, non-stop 24 hrs.

Post offices Danteov Trg 4, Mon-Fri 0700-2000, Sat 0700-1400; Čirilmetodske Družbe 1, Mon-Fri 0700-2000, Sat 0700-1400. **Telephones** If you prefer to telephone from a peaceful phone booth, rather than calling on the street, go to the post office (see above). Otherwise, you'll find numerous phone kiosks dotted round town.

West coast

The most-visited resorts here are Poreč and Rovinj, both well worth seeing, though they do get extremely crowded in peak season. They are separated by Limski Kanal, a spectacular 12-km long, steep-sided sea channel renowned for its excellent restaurants serving locally produced oysters and mussels. North of Poreč, the commercial resorts of Novigrad and Umag are noted respectively for big international sailing and tennis events. ▸▸ *For Sleeping, Eating and other listings, see pages 119-126.*

Rovinj (Rovigno) ▸▸ *pp119-126. Colour map 1, C1.*

→ *Phone code: 052. Population: 13,467. 35 km northwest of Pula.*

On the west coast, Rovinj is composed of densely packed medieval town houses, built into a hillside and crowned by a church and elegant bell tower. Down below, Venetian-style coloured façades curve their way around a pretty fishing harbour, rimmed with open-air cafés, restaurants and ice cream parlours. Out to sea lie a scattering of 14 small islands, while south of town, the green expanse of Zlatni Rt Park has tree-lined avenues and an indented shoreline with several pebble coves for bathing. The town's beauty and easy-going atmosphere have long made it popular with Croatian and Italian artists, writers, musicians and actors.

Ins and outs

Getting there There are regular daily buses from Pula and a daily fast ferry service (foot passengers only) during the summer (originating from Venice, Italy, stopping en route at Poreč. ▸▸ *See Transport, page 124, for further details.*

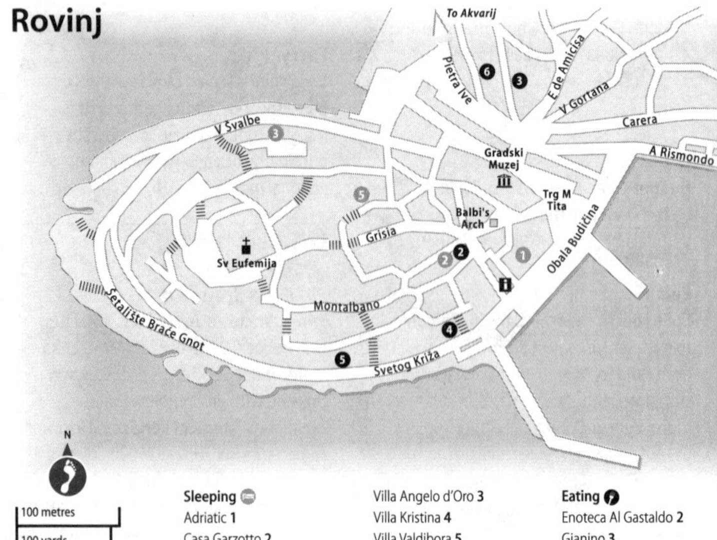

Getting around The historic centre is a small compact area, closed to traffic and easily manageable on foot. However, the rough cobbled streets and steep uphill climb make high-heeled shoes impractical. There's a local **tourist office** ⓘ *Obala P Budičina 12, T052-811566, www.tzgrovinj.hr.*

Background

Rovinj started out as a small village founded on an island by the Romans. During the Middle Ages it was fortified with double walls and seven gates, and in 1283 it fell to Venice. Although it was placed under a Venetian governor, who imposed heavy trade taxes, citizens retained a certain amount of communal freedom and enjoyed relative prosperity. During the 16th century, the number of inhabitants increased as refugees fleeing the Turks arrived from Dalmatia, Bosnia, Albania and Greece, and in the late 17th century a bridge was built connecting the island to the mainland, and the town expanded along the coast. In 1763, the narrow channel separating the island from the coast was filled in and thus Rovinj became a peninsula.

With the demise of Venice, the town entered a more difficult period under Austria: while Trieste in Italy became the Hapsburg's main trade port, and Pula their main military port and shipyard, Rovinj was seriously neglected, causing many families to leave and seek work in Pula. However, in 1872 the tobacco factory opened: still today it's the largest producer of Croatian cigarettes, and a warm, sweet smell of cured tobacco hangs in the air. A railway linking Rovinj with Kanfanar was built in 1876, but unfortunately closed in 1966 as it was considered unprofitable. Since the 1960s Rovinj has lived primarily from tourism, winning the prize for the 'best-kept resort' on several occasions. The town is still home to a sizeable Italian majority, who have their own schools and cultural associations, and it is not unusual to hear Italian spoken.

Sights

The main square, **Trg M Tita**, opens out on one side on to the harbour. The principal building here is the 17th-century Town Hall, which now houses the **Gradski Muzej** (City Museum) ⓘ *Trg M Tita 11, T052-816720, www.muzej-rovinj.com, Jun-Sep Tue-Sun 0900-1500, 1900-2200, Oct-May Tue-Sat 0900-1500, 15Kn*, which exhibits a collection of archaeological finds, Old Master paintings from between the 15th and 19th centuries, and contemporary works by Croatian painters and sculptors, many originating from Rovinj itself.

Gostionica Toni **6**
Puntulina **5**
Veli Jože **4**

Standing next to the Town Museum, the baroque **Balbi's Arch** was built in 1680 on the site of a former town gate. The outer side of the arch is crowned by a stone relief of the head of a Turk, while the inner side bears the head of a Venetian. The architrave bears two coats of arms of the Balbi family and the Lion of St Mark's.

From Trg M Tita, a labyrinth of steep, narrow cobbled streets run up to the hilltop church of **Sv Eufemija** (St Euphemia) ⓘ *Oct-Apr daily 1000-1200, 1600-1900, May-Sep daily 1000-1900*. The building gained its baroque appearance in 1736, though there had been a church here (originally dedicated to St George) for centuries. The 61-m Venetian bell tower, topped by a gleaming bronze weather vane of St Euphemia, was erected in 1677. Euphemia, who lived in the region that is now northwest Turkey, was thrown to the lions in 304, during one of Emperor Diocletian's anti-Christian purges. According to legend, her remains were placed in a sixth-century marble sarcophagus, which floated out to sea from Constantinople and was washed ashore in Rovinj in AD 800. The sarcophagus in question is now kept within the church, bearing Euphemia's bones, covered by a finely embroidered gold cloth.

Dating back to 1891, the **Akvarij** (Aquarium) ⓘ *Obala G Paliage 5, T052-804712, summer daily 0900-2100, winter by appointment, 15Kn*, is one of the oldest in Europe. Marine species such as octopuses, poisonous scorpion fish and large turtles are on display, plus other underwater creatures such as sponges and sea anemones.

Kuća Batana (Batana House) ⓘ *Obala Pina Budicina 2, T052-812593, www.batana.org, Jun-Sep daily 1000-1300, 1900-2200; Oct-May Tue-Sun 1000-1300, 1500-1700, entrance free, explanatory guide 15 Kn*, is on the seafront promenade, overlooking the harbour. This eco-museum is named after the batana, a traditional local fishing boat. Telling the story of Rovinj's centuries-old fishing community, it occupies two floors of a 17th-century building.

Zlatni Rt (Punta Currente), laid out between 1890 and 1910 by Georg Huetteroth, is a vast expanse of parkland planted with avenues of holm oaks, alpine pines, cedar and cypresses, and criss-crossed by footpaths leading down to a series of pebble coves ideal for bathing. Other places for a dip are the islands of **Sv Katarina** (St Catherine) and **Crveni Otok** (Red Island), both of which have pleasant rocky coastlines offering easy access to the water and, in peak season, boats from the harbour leave every half an hour.

Vrsar (Orsera) and around

» pp119-126. Colour map 1, C1.

→ *Phone code: 052. Population: 1872. Between Poreč (10 km) and Rovinj (25 km).*

The fishing village of Vrsar is backed by gently undulating hills covered with pinewoods and vineyards. During the Middle Ages, stone cottages were built around the hilltop castle and church and the entire complex fortified; it was not until the 19th century that the town expanded outside the walls and down to the bay. The Venetians exploited the area's quarries and stone from here was used to construct several palaces overlooking Venice's Grand Canal; still today the nearby Montraker quarry is an important element, attracting contemporary artists and providing quality material for an annual sculpture summer school. In 1960, Europe's largest naturist resort, Koversada, opened here, and in the years that followed several large modern hotels were built along the coast. There's a local **tourist office** ⓘ *Rade Končara 46, T052-441746, www.istra.com/vrsar.*

Sights

Built in the 12th century as the summer residence of the Bishop of Poreč, the hilltop **Kaštel** (Castle) ⓘ *opening times variable*, was continually reconstructed and extended over the centuries. A document from 1577 decrees, 'They [the peasants of Vrsar] are obliged to carry the Bishop's luggage without any charge whenever the Bishop comes to the castle or leaves it'. In 1778 it became Venetian state property. After serving as an exhibition space for several years, it has been renovated and divided into luxury private apartments.

Due to its resemblance to the Norwegian fjords, Limski Kanal was used as the set for some parts of two films about Vikings: The Vikings *(USA, 1958), starring Kirk Douglas and Tony Curtis, and* The Long Ships *(UK/Yugoslavia, 1963).*

Standing next to the Kaštel, the 19th-century **Church of St Martin** ⓘ *daily 1000-1200, 1600-1900*, is best known for its prominent (some would say obtrusive) free-standing bell tower, added in 1991. The interior was decorated with religious frescoes by Antonio Macchi, from Rovinj, in 1946. Through summer, classical music concerts are held here each Thursday evening. From behind the church, there are spectacular views over the town and sea below.

On a hill above the sea, just north of town on the road to Poreč, **Dušan Džamonja Sculpture Park** ⓘ *Jun-Sep Tue-Sun 0900-1100, 1800-2100*, displays over 20 large abstract sculptures in metal and stone, created by Dušan Džamonja. Born in what is now the Former Yugoslav Republic of Macedonia in 1928, he graduated from the Academy of Fine Arts in Zagreb. He now has two homes, one is Brussels and one in Vrsar, and has works displayed in various galleries around the world, including the Museum of Modern Art in New York and the Tate Gallery in London.

Limski Kanal (Lim Fjord)

Just 3 km south of Vrsar, the mouth of Limski Kanal is a 12-km-long flooded canyon, edged in part by dramatic limestone cliffs rising 120 m above the water, and in part by green slopes covered with woods of holm oak, ash and pines. Underwater springs give the seawater a low salt content, making it ideal for farming oysters and mussels, and several excellent fish restaurants have opened here, taking advantage of both the locally produced shellfish and the spectacular setting.

The Vrsar-based agency **R-Tour** ⓘ *T052-441046*, organize full-day excursions by boat from Vrsar, including a visit of Rovinj, a ride up Limski Kanal and a meal at one of the restaurants.

Poreč (Parenzo)

» pp119-126. Colour map 1, C1.

→ *Phone code: 052. Population: 10,448. 45 km northwest of Pula.*

Backed by a low-lying, fertile plain planted with vineyards and olive groves, Poreč is Istria's most-visited seaside resort. The old town itself is quite tiny, a cluster of Venetian-style terracotta-roofed houses lying compact on a small peninsula, though the interior of its main attraction, the sixth-century **Euphrasius Basilica**, is decorated with golden Byzantine mosaics so stunning to have earned it a place on the UNESCO list of World Heritage Sites. Café life centres on the seafront promenade overlooking

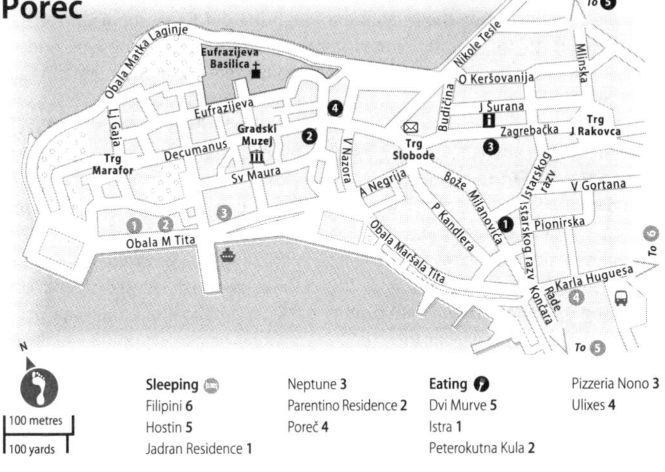

 the harbour, filled with fishing boats and water taxis, which shuttle holidaymakers back and forth to beaches on the nearby islet of **Sv Nikola** (St Nicholas). South of the centre, Plava Laguna and Zelena Laguna make up a 6-km stretch of modern hotel complexes, cleverly hidden by landscaping and dense pinewoods.

Ins and outs

There are daily buses from Pula and a summer ferry service from Trieste to Brijuni National Park stopping en route here. The old town is closed to traffic and can comfortably be explored on foot in an hour or so. There's a city **tourist office** ⓘ *Zagrebačka 9, T052-451293, www.to-porec.com*. The **official tourist office** ⓘ *Pionirksa 1, T051-452797, www.istra.com*, for the entire region of Istria is also in Poreč.

Background

Founded as a Roman *castrum* (military camp) in the second century BC, Poreč was later granted the status of a municipality, to become *Colonia Julia Parentium* in the first century BC. The layout of the old town still follows the original Roman plan, though most of the present buildings date from between the 13th and 18th centuries. The settlement became the seat of a diocese in the late third century AD, the first Bishop of Poreč being the martyr St Mauro, who like so many early Christians met a bloody end during the reign of Emperor Diocletian.

Following the collapse of the Western Roman Empire, Poreč passed successively under the Ostrogoths, the Byzantine Empire, the Franks and the Aquilean patriarch. In 1267, it was the first of the cities on the Istrian coast to come under the Venetian Republic. Despite its rather grand past, it gradually sank into decline, mainly due to several severe outbreaks of the plague, which decimated the population between the 14th and 17th centuries, so that by 1646 there were only about 100 inhabitants. During the second half of the 17th century, Venice repopulated the city and its surroundings with settlers from Dalmatia, Albania and the Greek island of Crete.

After the fall of the Venetian Republic, along with the rest of Istria, it came under Austria. In 1844, the steamship society Austrian Lloyd from Trieste set up a line for day trippers to Poreč, and in 1845 the first tourist guide to the city was published. During the 1970s it became Istria's principal resort, following the construction of several vast hotel complexes along the coast.

Sights

Laid out by the Romans in the first century BC, **Decumanus** is a wide, paved street that still forms the main thoroughfare through the old town, running the length of the peninsula to Trg Marafor. Today it's lined with fine Romanesque and Gothic town houses, several of which have been converted into boutiques and cafés at street level.

Housed within the 18th-century baroque Sinčić Palace, **Gradski Muzej** (City Museum) ⓘ *Decumanus 9, T052-431585, May-Sep daily 1000-1300, 1800-2000, Oct-Apr Mon-Sat 1000-1300, 10Kn*, displays Roman stone and ceramic finds on the ground floor, and 18th-century furniture and portraits belonging to the Carli family on the first and second levels.

Halfway down Decumanus, a narrow side street leads to **Eufrazijeva Basilica** (Euphrasius Basilica) ⓘ *Eufrazijeva bb, daily 0700-2000*, a well-signed complex consisting of a magnificent sixth-century basilica, a delightful atrium, an octagonal baptistery, a 16th-century bell tower and the bishop's palace. The interior of the church is decorated with stunning golden mosaics above, behind and around the main apse, making it one of the most important Byzantine monuments on the Adriatic, comparable to San Vitale in Ravenna. Above the altar, the central mosaic depicts the Virgin and Child, with the first Bishop of Poreč, St Mauro, to their right, and Bishop Euphrasius, who was responsible for the mosaic project, on their left. In front of the apse stands a 13th-century ciborium supported by four marble columns. The former bishop's palace now houses the **Basilica Museum** ⓘ *daily 1000-1700, 10Kn*, displaying a modest collection of paintings, sculpture, embroidered vestments and crucifixes.

Lying on the tip of the peninsula, **Trg Marafor** was once the site of a small Roman forum. The ruins of two Roman temples, dedicated to Mars and Neptune, can still be seen today. The best beaches are on **Otok Sv Nikola** (St Nicholas' Island), which can be reached by regular taxi boats, leaving the harbour every half an hour through peak season.

North of Poreč

» *pp119-126. Colour map 1, C1.*

Novigrad (Cittanova)

→ *Phone code: 052. Population: 2629. 41 km northwest of Pazin.*

The ancient town of Novigrad is now a busy package resort with the standard selection of large hotels, seaside restaurants, cafés and ice cream parlours. The old town as it stands today was developed under Venice in the 13th century, when it was fortified and used as a port for shipping oak from Motovun Forest. Much of the original medieval architecture was destroyed during a Turkish attack in 1687 and new buildings were reconstructed in Venetian-Gothic style. Everyday life centres on **Veliki Trg**, the main square, overlooked by an 18th-century Venetian **loggia** and the baroque **Crkva Sv Pelagija** (Church of St Pelagius), known by locals as the *Katedrala* (Cathedral), constructed on the site of an 11th-century Romanesque **crypt** and presided over by a free-standing bell tower.

Muzej Lapidarijium (Lapidarium Museum) ⓘ *Veliki trg 8a, T052-726582, www.muzej-lapidarium.hr, Jun-Sep Tue-Sun 1000-1300, 1800-2200, Oct-May Tue-Sun 1000-1300, 1700-1900, 10Kn,* is on the main square. This recently-opened museum displays ancient Roman tombstones and Byzantine stone carvings, and also stages temporary art exhibitions.

Rather unappealling concrete **bathing areas** sprawl in front of the large hotels southeast of town. There is a local **tourist office** ⓘ *Porporella 1, T052-757075, www.novigrad-cittanova.hr.*

Umag (Umago)

→ *Phone code: 052. Colour map 1, C1. Population: 7769. On the west coast, 83 km northwest of Pula.*

Several times over the last few years Umag has won a national competition for the best-kept and best-equipped resort on the mainland. Indeed, today it is well geared to the more commercial brand of tourism, with a string of vast modern hotels overlooking concrete bathing areas north of the centre. However, the compact old town, built on a peninsula next to a large semicircular bay, is worth a look for its narrow medieval streets and pretty squares. Umag hits the news each summer when it hosts the international **ATP Croatia Open** tennis tournament. There is a town **tourist office** ⓘ *Trgovačka 6, T052-741363, www.tz-umag.hr.*

There are no decent beaches in Umag, so many visitors make do with the man-made concrete bathing areas in front of the larger hotels. You're better off renting a bike (see Activities and tours, below) and peddling 5 km up the coast to **Savudrija**, where you'll find a rocky stretch of coast interspersed with pebble beaches and backed by pinewoods.

Sleeping

Rovinj *p114, map p114*

L **Villa Angelo d'Oro**, V Švalbe 38-42, T052-840502, www.rovinj.at. This small, luxury hotel is hidden away in the old town, 1 block back from the seafront, in the beautifully restored 17th-century

Bishop's Palace. The 24 guest rooms are each individually furnished with antiques, and breakfast is served on a delightful rooftop garden terrace. Extras include a jacuzzi, sauna and solarium, plus a hotel boat at the guests' disposal.

A **Villa Valdibora**, Chiurca Silvana 8, Rovinj, T052-845040, www.valdibora.com. In Rovinj's old town, this 17th-century villa has four 4-person apartments with tile floors, wooden beamed ceilings and well-equipped kitchenettes. Open all year.

B **Casa Garzotto**, Via Garzotto 8, T052-811884, www.casa-garzotto.com. In the old town, this small boutique hotel has 4 apartments, all with wooden floors, antique furniture and kitchenettes. 2 also have open fires. Buffet breakfast is served in the ground floor bar. Extras include free bike hire, plus sauna and hydro-massage shower in winter. Open all year.

C **Adriatic**, P Budicin 2, T052-802500, www.maistra.hr. Bang in the centre, just off the main square and close to the harbour, this old-fashioned hotel has 27 basic but comfortable rooms. Through summer, breakfast is served on an open-air terrace out front.

D **St Ivan Lighthouse**, Otok Sv Ivan na Pučini, organized through **Adriatica Net**, Heinzelova 62a, Zagreb, T01-241 5611, www.adriatica.net. On a tiny islet just 4 km from Rovinj, this lighthouse which was built in 1853 has been renovated to form 2 apartments, each sleeping 4.

E **Vila Kristina**, Luja Adamovića 16, T052-815537, www.kis-rovinj.com. In a modern building just a 10-min walk from the old town and a 5-min walk from the marina, this friendly, family-run B&B has 12 simple but clean and comfortable rooms with a/c, satellite TV, balcony and bathroom.

Private accommodation

The following agencies can help you find private accommodation: **Anetta Tours**, Carrera 59, T052-840414; **Marco Polo**, Ivana Mažuranića 21, T052-816955, www.marcopolo.hr; and **Uniline**, Francesca Sponge Uspera 8, T052-815199, www.uniline.hr.

For a list of families offering agrotourism (farmhouse meals and accommodation), check out www.istra.com/agroturizam.

Vrsar and around *p116*

Koversada Naturist Settlement, T052-441 761, www.maistra.hr. Located 1.5 km south of Vrsar, close to the mouth of Limski Kanal, **Koversada** is Europe's largest nudist colony. A complex of pavilions and a campsite stretch 5 km along the coast, providing space for 6000, and facilities including 2 supermarkets, 10 restaurants, pizzerias and snack bars, bathing areas, sports facilities and a post office. Pets welcome. Open mid-May to mid-Sep.

Private accommodation

Vrsar-based agency, **Bovi**, Jadranska 18, T052-441590, www.bovi.hr.

Poreč *p117, map p117*

The majority of Poreč's hotels are found within the modern complexes of Zelena Laguna and Plava Laguna, south of town. However, the hotels listed here are small-scale and centrally located.

C **Hotel Hostin**, Rade Končara 4, T052-408800, www.hostin.hr. Close to the bus station and just a 10-min walk from the old town, facilities in this smart, modern, 39-room hotel include a pool, sauna and jacuzzi. Open all year.

C **Hotel Neptune**, Obala M Tita 15, T052-465000, www.valamar.com. Fully renovated in 2001, this early 20th-century hotel offers 143 smart and comfortable guest rooms, and a bar and restaurant overlooking the seafront promenade in the old town. Open Mar-Nov.

C **Parentino Residence**, Obala M Tita 18, T052-465000, www.valamar.com. Managed by **Hotel Neptune**, the **Parentino** offers 14 rooms in an ochre-coloured early 20th-century building with a sunny terrace with view of the harbour. Open May-Oct.

D **Hotel Poreč**, Rade Končara 1, T/F052-451811, www.hotelporec.com. Comfortable mid-range hotel, conveniently located next to the bus station. 54 basic rooms, internet corner in reception. Open all year.

D **Jadran Residence**, Obala M Tita 24, T052-465000, www.valamar.com. Managed by **Hotel Neptune**, the **Jadran** offers 22 rooms with views of the seafront promenade, plus a ground-floor restaurant. Open May-Oct.

E **Filipini Hotel**, Filipini bb, T052-463200, www.istra.com/filipini. 5 km from Poreč, set in a garden surrounded by woodland, vineyards and olive groves, this small hotel has 4 rooms and 4 spacious apartments, all furnished in minimalist style with some traditional elements, a restaurant with a terrace out front, 2 tennis courts, and bicycles to hire.

Private accommodation

The following agencies can help you find private accommodation: **Adriatic Istra**, Trg Slobode 2a, T052-452633, www.adriatic-istra.com (also excursions to Plitvice, Brijuni and Lim Fjord); **Arlen**, Vukovarska 26, T052-434819, www.arlen.hr; **Di-Tours**, Prvomajska 2, T052-432100, www.di-tours.hr; and **Lucky Travel**, Bračka 39, T052-434050, www.last-minute-croatia.com.

For a list of families offering agrotourism (farmhouse meals and accommodation), check out, www.istra.com/agroturizam.

Novigrad *p119*

AL **Hotel Nautika**, Sv Antona 15, T052-600400, www.nautikahotels.com. In Novigrad's new marina, the plush Nautika has 38 rooms and 4 suites, all with LCD-TV, mosaic-tile bathrooms, and balconies with views onto the sea and the old town. There's also a luxurious Wellness Centre and the sophisticated Navigare restaurant. It stays open all year.

D **Hotel Cittar**, Prolaz Venecija 5, T052-757 737, www.cittar.hr. This modern, family-run hotel is in the centre, next to a remaining section of the old town wall. Has14 rooms, each with a TV, telephone and minibar.

D **Makin Hotel**, Šaini 2a, T052-757714, www.istra.com/makin. This small, family-run hotel has 15 rooms with wooden floors, and the homely Taverna Sergio with an open fire and a beamed-ceiling, plus outdoor tables in a leafy garden. It's 1 km from the centre and just a few mins' walk from the beach.

D **Rt Zub Lighthouse**, Lanterna Peninsula. Contact **Adriatica Net**, Heinzelova 62a, Zagreb, T01-2415611, www.adriatica.net. On a peninsula between 2 pleasant bays with beaches, 13 km south of Novigrad, this lighthouse dating back to 1872 has been converted to form 1 large apartment sleeping 8. Shops and restaurants are close at hand.

Umag *p119*

B **Hotel Kristal**, Obala J B Tita 9, T052-700000, www.hotel-kristal.com. This large, modern, pink hotel commands a prime position, on the tip of the peninsula, in the old town. There are 80 rooms and 4 suites, facilities include an indoor seawater pool, Thai massage and a casino.

Private accommodation

D **Svjetionik Savudrija**, Savudrija. Contact **Adriatica Net**, Heinzelova 62a, Zagreb, T01-241 5611, www.adriatica.net. 9 km north of Umag, this mainland lighthouse, built in 1818, has been converted to form 2 apartments, each sleeping 4. A boat is at guests' disposal. Pets welcome.

Eating

Rovinj *p114, map p114*

₶₶₶-₶₶ **Enoteca Al Gastaldo**, Iza Kasarne 14, T052-814109. With an open log fire, walls stacked with wine bottles, and candlelight, this is a great place to come on a cold winter night. Try the spaghetti with either truffles or crab, accompanied by a delicious fresh salad of rocket and radicchio, then round off with a glass of local *rakija*.

₶₶₶-₶₶ **Puntulina**, Sv Križa 43, T052-813186. In the old town, with an open-air terrace overlooking the sea, this small but elegant eatery and wine bar serves delicious seafood dishes such as squid with polenta cakes and sea bass baked in a salt crust. Open Mar-Nov.

₶₶₶-₶₶ **Restaurant Gianino**, A Ferri 38, T052-813402. In a narrow side street, just back from the harbour, **Gianino** has long been popular with the yachting fraternity. House specialities include *tagliatelli mare-monti* (pasta with shrimps and mushrooms), rigatoni with lobster and sole with truffles. Open Apr-Oct Tue-Sun; Nov-Mar Fri-Sun.

₶₶ **Gostionica Toni**, Driovier 3, Rovinj, T052-815303. For good, down-to-earth, Istrian home cooking, the house specialities at this informal, centrally located eatery are *brodet od sipe s palentom* (cuttlefish stew with polenta) and *njoki s dagnjama i rokulom* (gnocchi with mussels and rocket). Besides the standard menu, they also have daily specials on a board. Closed Wed.

₶₶ **Veli Jože**, Sv Križa 1, T052-816337. This highly popular, informal eatery serves old-fashioned local dishes such as *bakalar in bianco* (a salty pâté made from dried cod) and roast lamb with potatoes. Open Apr-Nov.

¥ **Vieccia Batana**, Trg M Tita 8. The oldest and most atmospheric café in town stands on the main square, close to the harbour. Perfect for morning coffee.

Vrsar and around *p116*

¥¥¥ **Restoran Fjord**, Limski Kanal, Sv Lovreč, T052-448222. With a vast open-air terrace overlooking the fjord, this popular restaurant serves up pasta dishes, fresh lobster, oven-baked fish, and steak with mushrooms.

¥¥¥ **Viking**, Limski Kanal, T052-448223. Ranked among the Top 10 Istrian restaurants, this large establishment is best known for fresh oysters, pasta with shrimps and mushrooms and barbecued fish dishes.

¥¥¥-¥¥ **Restoran Trošt**, Obala M Tita 19, T052-445197. This large, highly regarded restaurant is on the seafront, with a lovely summer terrace over the marina. Favourite dishes are pasta with asparagus, truffles and smoked ham, pasta with lobster, oven-baked fish and steaks.

¥¥ **Vrsaranka**, Sv Martin 1, on the edge of town, on the road to Poreč, T052-441197. House specialities at this large restaurant include pasta with truffles and large platters of either mixed fish or mixed meats for 2.

Poreč *p117, map p117*

The main concentration of cafés is found on the sunny seafront promenade, Obala M Tita.

¥¥¥-¥¥ **Dvi Murve**, Grožnjanska 17, outside the centre of Vranići, just north of Poreč, T052-434115. This highly regarded *konoba* serves ups specialities such as beefsteak *Dvi Murve* (steak with cream, mushroom and ham sauce), and *brancin u soli* (sea bass baked in a salt crust). The ample summer terrace is shaded by 2 mulberry trees, after which the establishment is named.

¥¥¥-¥¥ **Istra**, B Milanovića 30, between the bus station and the main square, Trg Slobode. T052-434636. Popular with locals and visitors alike, the house specialities here are *jastog sa rezancima* (pasta with lobster), and fish prepared under a *peka*. Closed mid-Jan to mid-Mar.

¥¥¥-¥¥ **Peterokutna Kula**, Decumanus 1, in the old town, T052-451378. Set in a 15th-century pentagonal tower, cleverly converted to form dining spaces on various levels, **Peterokutna Kula** serves up all that is best in Istria: fish, seafood, steak and truffles.

¥¥ **Ulixes**, Decumanus 2, in the old town, T052-451132. This tiny rustic *konoba*, with a centuries-old stone-and-brick interior, offers a good choice of local wines, seafood dishes, salads and platters of *pršut* (smoked ham) and *sir* (cheese).

¥ **Pizzeria Nono**, Zagrebačka 4, opposite the Poreč town tourist office, T052-453088. Busy with locals the year through, **Nono** serves up delicious pizzas baked in a brick oven, plus pasta and gnocchi dishes, steaks and colourful salads.

Novigrad *p119*

¥¥¥-¥¥ **Damir and Ornella**, Zidine 5, T052-758134. Despite its tiny dining room seating only 28, this friendly, family-run fish restaurant is definitely worth checking out. It's in the old town, close to the main square, and serves up delicious raw fish (sushi style), shrimps and lobster.

¥¥¥-¥¥ **Mandrač**, Mandrač 6, T052-757120. Considered by many to be the best restaurant in town, **Mandrač** is renowned for excellent tagliatelli with lobster, and barbecued fish and meat dishes. The ample summer terrace looks onto the harbour.

Umag *p119*

¥¥¥-¥¥ **Buščina,** Buščina 18, Marija na Krasu, T052-732088. 5km north of Umag, on the road to the Slovenian border, this authentic *konoba* is built of stone with a romantic summer terrace. House specialities include gnocchi and *fuži* (Istrian pasta), *biftek a tartufima* (steak with truffles) and lamb prepared under a *peka*. Open all year.

¥¥¥-¥¥ **Restoran Allegro**, Obala J B Tita 9, T052-700000. Housed within the **Hotel Kristal** (see Sleeping), this restaurant is popular with non-residents who are attracted by refined dishes – shrimps with artichoke mousse, and duck breast in basil sauce – served on a terrace with views of the sea.

¥¥¥-¥¥ **Restoran Badi**, Lovrečića bb, 6 km from Umag, T052-756293, www.restaurant-badi.com. Popular with Italian day trippers who drive over 2 borders especially to savour its excellent fish and seafood – house specialities include *rižoto škampima* (scampi risotto) and the *frijata od šparoga* (asparagus omelette). Closed Wed and Feb.

Bars and clubs

Rovinj *p114, map p114*
Bethlehem, Vodnjanska 1. This friendly pub has good rock music and a young crowd.
Valentino, Sv Križa 28. Extremely popular bar in the old town, with good music and several tables outside.
Zanzi Bar, Obala Pino Budicin. Ultra chic, very expensive and verging on the pretentious, with outdoor seating on a covered terrace, cocktails and cigars.

Poreč *p117, map p117*
Colonia Iulia Parentium, Gradsko kupališe (City beach), 1 km south of the centre. Poreč's most popular club is in a small bay. Music is predominantly house, with guest DJs from all over Europe, plus occasional live concerts. Open daily 2000 onwards, Jun-Sep.
Comitium, Trg Marafora 15, a small, seductive cocktail bar in the old town, with tables outside through summer.
Lapidarij, Svetog Maura 10. A romantic option in the evening, in the old town, where you'll find an unusual baroque bar space, plus tables outside in a large courtyard through summer.

Festivals and events

Rovinj *p114, map p114*
Late Apr Chioggia-Rovinj-Chioggia and **Pesaro-Rovinj-Pesaro**. Open sailing regattas.
Jul-Aug Rovinj Nights, Church of St Euphemia and the Franciscan Monastery. Classical music concerts.
Early Aug Grisia. Open-air art exhibition.
16 Sep Feast of St Euphemia.

Vrsar and around *p116*
Jul-Aug Summer concerts, hilltop Church of St Martin. Classical music concerts held Thu evenings.
Aug-Sep International Sculpture School. Held each summer since 1991 at Montraker Quarry, on a peninsula close to the centre. Works remain property of the town. Contact the tourist office for details.

Poreč *p117, map p117*
Jul-Aug Classical Music Festival, www.concertsinbazilika.com. Sacral and secular music in the Basilica of St Euphrasius. **Jazz Festival**, www.jazzinlap.com. Held in the courtyard of the Town Museum.
21 Nov Festival of St Mauro.

Novigrad *p119*
Late May Venice-Novigrad-Venice. Open sailing regatta.
Early Jun Rimini-Novigrad-Rimini; Caorle-Novigrad-Caorle. Open sailing regattas.
Late Jul Music Nights Novigrad. Founded in 1995 by the Croatian jazz musician Boško Petrović, in recent years this festival has attracted international performers such as the Temptations, Dan Gilespie, Scott Henderson and Hiram Bullock. Open-air evening concerts take place on Veliki Trg, the main square.
28 Aug Festival of St Pelagius.

Umag *p119*
May Feast of St Pelegrin, last Sun of the month.
Late Jul ATP Croatia Open. International tennis tournament.
Jul-Aug Summer Festival. Classical music concerts in the 18th-century baroque Church of the Assumption of the Blessed Virgin Mary, plus contemporary art exhibitions in a number of small galleries.

Activities and tours

Rovinj *p114, map p114*

Cycling
A marked bike path runs along the coast south of town from the ACI Marina, passing through Zlatni Rt, Rt Kuvi, Veštar and Cisterna to arrive in Sv Damijan. A map, *Bike Track Rovinj*, is available from the tourist office. See also www.istria-bike.com.

Diving
Croatia's top diving site, recommended for advanced divers only, is the *Baron Gausch* wreck, just off the Rovinj coast.
DSC Rovinj, based in Rijeka at Šetalište XIII divizije 28, T052-219111, www.diver.hr. Diving school here from early Apr to mid-Nov.
Diving Center Valdaliso, Hotel Valdaliso, T052-815992, www.scuba-valdaliso.de.
Nadi Scuba, J Dobrile 11, T052-813290, www.scuba.hr.

Sailing

ACI Marina, T052-813133, www.aci.club.hr. 380 berths, open all year.
Waypoint International, T052-815670, www.waypoint-int.com. Charter company.

Tour operators

Marco Polo, Ivana Mažuranića 25, T052-816955, www.marco polo.hr. Organize activities such as cycling, paragliding, free-climbing and scuba-diving.
Uniline, Francesca Sponge Uspera 8, T052-815199, www.uniline.hr. Organize excursions in the surrounding area.

Vrsar and around *p116*

Cycling

Vrsar is the starting point for 3 well-marked bike routes: a short trail (5 km) taking you to the Dušan Džamonja Sculpture Park, a circular trail (18 km) passing alongside Limski Kanal, and a long trail (27 km). Contact the tourist office for details and a map, or check www.istria-bike.com.

Diving

Adriatic Master Dive Center, Brionska 11, T052-441784, www.scuba.at.
Starfish Diving Centre, AC Porto Sole, T052-442119, www.starfish.hr.

Sailing

Marina Vrsar, Obala M Tita 1a, T052-441052, www.montraker.hr. 220 berths, open all year.

Poreč *p117, map p117*

Cycling

Poreč is the starting point for 2 well-marked bike routes, 1 north to Tar (45-km round route) and the other south to Funtana (47 km). Ask at the tourist office for details and a map or check the website, www.istria-bike.com.
Vetura, Trg J Rakovca 2, T052-434700, www.vetura-rentacar.hr. It is possible to rent bikes from here. Expect to pay 80Kn for a whole day or 50Kn for a ½ day.

Diving

Plava Laguna, Partizanska 5, T098-367619 (mob), www.plava-laguna-diving.hr.
Zelena Laguna, Zelena Laguna bb, T052-410594, www.diving-porec.hr.

Sailing

Marina Parentium, in the tourist complex of Zelena Laguna, T052-452210. Has 200 berths, open all year.

Tour Operators

Atlas, Eufrazije 63, T052-434933, www.atlas-croatia.com; **Be Tours**, 43 Istarske Divizije 25, T052-432310, www.be-tours.com; **Generalturist**, Obala bb, T052-451188, www.generalturist.com.

Novigrad *p119*

Cycling

6 marked bike paths lead from Novigrad through the surrounding vineyards and old stone villages to inland Grožnjan (see page 127) and Buje (see page 128). It is possible to rent bikes (and mopeds) from **Hotel Maestral**, T052-757557, and the tourist office can supply a map of suggested routes. See also www.istria-bike.com.

Sailing

Marina Novigrad, T052-757330, www.marinanovigrad.com.

Umag *p119*

Sailing

ACI Marina, T052-741066. Has 518 berths, open all year.

Tennis

Each Jul the **ATP Croatia Open** tennis tournament (www.croatiaopen.hr) is staged in the Stella Maris sports complex at **Savudriska Cesta bb**, north of town. There are 18 courts, which visitors are welcome to use. Expect to pay 40Kn per hr, T052-741704.

Transport

Rovinj *p114, map p114*

Bus

The bus station is at Trg na Lokvi bb, T060-302010. There are 12 buses daily to **Pula** (1 hr) and 6 to **Poreč** (1½ hrs).

To reach Italy, an early morning service runs from Pula to **Padova**, stopping at **Rovinj**, **Trieste** and **Venice** en route, while a slightly later morning bus runs from Pula to **Trieste**, stopping in Rovinj, and **Poreč** en route.

Funny about fungus

The truffle is a subterranean European fungus, generally found in damp soils on or near the roots of oak trees. It can be white, brown or black, and although it grows approximately 30 cm below the soil, its scent is so strong that dogs and pigs can be trained to detect it. Fetching prices of up to €5000 per kg, the truffle is among the most expensive foodstuffs in the world: it is used in foie gras, and can also be eaten grated on pasta or steak, or made into rich creamy sauce. Undoubtedly an acquired taste, past aficionados include Winston Churchill and Marilyn Monroe.

In Istria, about 500 registered truffle-hunters have a legal right to dig for this gnarled, tuberous fungus. However, each year between October and December an estimated 3000 people and three times as many dogs (usually a cross between a retriever and a hound) wander through Istria's forests and meadows searching for this prestigious delicacy, making it one of region's top sources of income and main reasons why many people come here.

The largest truffle in the world, listed in the *Guinness Book of Records*, was unearthed in the Mirna Valley, Istria, on 2 November 1999. It was found by Giancarlo Zigante and his dog, Diana, and weighed 1.31 kg and measured 19.5 cm x 12.4 cm x 13.5 cm. Zigante decided not to sell it but prepared a dinner for 100 guests, and had the original cast in bronze. He now runs Zigante Tartufi, a small chain of shops specializing in truffles and truffle-based products, which you can visit in Buzet, Buje and Pula.

Car
Uni Rent, Ante Starčevića 25, T052-841040, www.uni-rent.net.

Ferry
Emilia Romagna Lines, call centre T0039 899-656501, www.emiliaromagnalines.it, run a catamaran between **Cesenatico** and **Ravenna** (Italy), and Rovinj, Jul-Sep.

Venezia Lines, www.venezialines.com, operate a daily fast ferry (foot passengers only) between **Venice** and Rovinj, stopping at **Poreč** en route, late Apr to early Oct.

Taxi
There are normally several taxis available at the bus station, or you can call T052-811100.

Vrsar and around *p116*

Bus
Poreč bus station, T052-432153.

There are 12 buses daily from **Poreč** (20 mins) and 4 from **Rovinj** (25 mins).

Poreč *p117, map p117*

Bus
The bus station is at Rade Končara 1, a 5-min walk from the old town, T052-432153. There are 12 buses daily to **Pula** (1½ hrs) and 6 to **Rovinj** (45 mins). To reach Italy, a morning service runs from **Pula** to **Trieste**, stopping in **Rovinj** and **Poreč** en route.

Car
Budget, Obala bb, T052-451188, www.budget.hr; **Hertz**, Aldo Negri 1, T052-091-3108691, www.hertz.hr.

Ferry
Venezia Lines operate a daily fast ferry service (foot passengers only) between **Venice** (Italy) and Rovinj, stopping at **Poreč** en route, late Apr to early Oct.

Novigrad *p119*

Bus
Bus station, T052-757660. There are 8 buses daily from **Poreč** (30 mins) and **Umag** (20 mins). 3 buses run daily from **Pula**.

Umag *p119*

Bus
Bus station, T060-381381. There are 8 buses from **Poreč** (45 mins) and **Novigrad** (20 mins), and 4 buses daily from **Pula** (2 hrs 25 mins).

Directory

Rovinj *p114, map p114*
Medical services A 24-hr tourist first-aid centre operates in the casualty department of Rovinj doctors' surgery at Istarska ulica bb, T052-813004. **Pharmacies**: Gradska Ljekarna at Matteo Benussia, T052-813589. **Post offices** M Benussia 4, Mon-Fri 0700-2000, Sat 0700-1400.

Poreč *p117, map p117*
Internet Internet-Centar-Cybermac, Mira Grahalića 1, T052-427075, www.cybermac.hr. **Medical services** Hitna Pomoc, Dom Zdravlja, M Gioseffija 2, T052-451611, emergency treatment. 2 central **pharmacies** take turns to work extended hours: **Centralna Ljekarna**, M Gioseffija 2, T052-434950; **Gradska Ljekarna**, Trg Slobode 12, T052- 432362. **Post offices** Vukovarska 17, Mon-Fri 0700-2000, Sat 0700-1400.

Inland Istria

Frequently overlooked by tourists but much loved by Croatians, inland Istria is sometimes compared to Tuscany, thanks to its undulating green landscapes and medieval walled hill towns. This is the country's top area for agrotoursim (farms offering meals and overnight accommodation) and is at it prettiest in spring or autumn.

Many rural villages lie semi-abandoned, though it's fast becoming fashionable to have a restored stone holiday cottage in the area. The romantic fortified hilltop towns of Motovun and Grožnjan have established themselves as alternative cultural centres, the former with an annual festival of avant-garde film, the latter with its community of artists and craftsmen plus an annual music summer school. Buzet and its surrounding villages are much prized for rustic eateries serving dishes with locally found truffles.

▸▸ *For Sleeping, Eating and other listings, see pages 129-131.*

Pazin and around

➔ *Phone code: 052. Colour map 1, C2. Population: 9227. 35 km north of Pula and 32 km east of Poreč.*

Located in the centre of Istria, Pazin is the region's largest inland town and a major road and rail intersection point. Although it dates back to the ninth century, it's hardly a charming place, with a dreary industrial suburb and little of interest, other than the castle. However, the one place that does warrant a visit is the nearby medieval **Church of St Mary**, in Beram, decorated with a memorable cycle of 15th-century frescoes. For more information, contact the **tourist office** ⓘ *Franine i Jurine 14, T052-622460, www.tzpazin.hr.*

Perched above the gorge and entered across a drawbridge, the medieval **Kaštel** (castle) ⓘ *Trg Istarskog razvoda 1, T052-624351, Apr-Oct Tue-Sun 1000-1800, Nov- Mar Tue-Thu 1000-1500, Fri 1200-1700, Sat-Sun 1100-1700, 15Kn*, was founded in the ninth century. However, its present appearance, with four wings grouped around a large interior courtyard, dates from between the 14th and 16th centuries. Inside you'll find the **Ethnographic Museum of Istria** ⓘ *T052-622220, www.emi.hr*, displaying traditional Istrian folk costumes, farming and fishing tools, musical instruments and an old-fashioned kitchen. The adjoining **Town Museum** shows local archaeological finds from prehistoric times up to the Middle Ages, plus a collection of church bells.

The sleepy hilltop village of **Beram** is 7 km west of Pazin, just off the main road to Poreč. Although there is no direct bus from Pazin to Beram, the two settlements are connected by a hiking path marked with red-and-white circles. From the village of Beram, a 1-km track leads to a wood, where you'll find the cemetery church of **Sv Marija na Škriljinah** (St Mary's Church) ⓘ *the church is kept locked, but you can find the key in Beram; contact Mrs Sonja Šestan, T052-622903, house number 38, at least 30 mins before you plan to visit.* The interior is totally covered by a cycle of extraordinary frescoes, dated 1474 and executed by Vincent of Kastav and his pupils.

Glagolitic script

Invented by St Cyril (827-869) from Thessaloniki (Greece), the Glagolitic script was the forerunner to Cyrillic, today used in Russia, Serbia and Montenegro, Bulgaria and Ukraine.

Cyril devised the 38-letter Glagolitic alphabet (based on Greek characters) upon the request of the Moravian leader to the Byzantine Emperor, who wanted a form of writing that would more closely represent the sounds of the Slavic languages. Cyril and his brother St Methodius (826-884) then proceeded to translate books of the New Testament and develop a Slavonic liturgy, earning themselves the title of the 'Apostles of the Slavs'. At the time, Pope Nicholas I was against the use of the vernacular in church services, but it was later approved by his successor, Adrian II.

The script was used in many churches along the Croatian Adriatic coast right until the 19th century, though it met resistance from certain members of the clergy who favoured Latin as a way of forging closer ties with Rome. However, Croatian secular literature was traditionally written in Latin script, as the majority of the elite were educated at universities in Italy or Austro-Hungary.

Biblical scenes are portrayed against a backdrop of Istrian countryside, giving an amusing interpretation of the New Testament, as well as a record of how people lived here during the 15th century. There's also a small informal eatery in Beram, should you visit around dinnertime.

Motovun (Montona)

→ *Phone code: 052. Colour map 1, B1. Population: 531. Altitude: 277 m. 25 km northeast of Poreč.*

This well-preserved fortified hill town on the road to Buzet is frequently included on tours of inland Istria as a model example of local architecture. There are no outstanding buildings, but the complex as a whole is exceptionally pretty, with medieval stone houses and a Venetian loggia surrounded by defensive walls, towers and town gates. It is possible to walk a complete circuit of the ramparts, offering sweeping views of the oak forests and vineyards of the Mirna Valley. The informal summer **Film Festival** (www.motovunfilmfestival.com) is very 'in', and probably Croatia's most enjoyable cultural event; more than 70 films are shown in five venues, attracting 40,000 cinema buffs from all over Europe. The **tourist office** ⓘ *Trg Josefa Ressela 1, T052-617480*, can provide further information.

Grožnjan (Grisignana)

→ *Phone code: 052. Colour map 1, C1. Population: 185. 26 km northeast of Poreč and 8 km southeast of Buje.*

This charming medieval hill town was all but abandoned until the mid-1960s, when it was rediscovered by painters, potters and sculptors, and proclaimed a 'Town of Artists'. They restored the crumbling medieval buildings, converting them into studios, workshops and galleries. Today it's a truly lovely place to visit, with partly preserved 14th-century town walls hugging a warren of narrow winding cobbled streets and old stone cottages. There's a local **tourist office** ⓘ *Umberta Gorjana 3, T052-776131, www.tz-groznjan.hr*.

Look out for the **Venetian loggia** adjoining the town gate, the baroque **Church of Saints Mary, Vitus** and **Modest** with a free-standing bell tower on the main square, and the tiny 16th-century **Chapel of Saints Cosmas and Damian**, decorated with frescoes by Ivan Lovrenčić in 1990, in front of the town gate. There are some well-marked footpaths lead to the surrounding villages making good walks.

Each year **Jeunesses Musicales Croatia**, an international federation of young musicians, meets here for a summer school run by well-known European and Japanese professors, such as Geoffry Wharton, violin concertmaster of the Cologne Philharmonic Orchestra, and the world-renowned trombonist Branimir Slokar. Each day, the old streets are filled with the sounds of brass, woodwind and stringed instruments of varying tones and pitches, and come evening live performances are staged beneath the stars as part of the 'Jazz is Back' festival.

Buzet → *Phone code: 052. Colour map 1, B2. Population: 1721.*

Overlooking the fertile Mirna Valley, close to the Slovenian border in northern Istria, the fortified hilltop settlement of Buzet is frequently referred to as the 'Town of Truffles'. Indeed, many people visit the region specifically to indulge in this peculiar smelling earthy delicacy: you'll find countless small restaurants on the country roads between Buzet, Motovun and Pazin, several of which are listed under Eating, below.

Although the town itself can be traced back to Roman times, when it was known as *Pinguentum*, it owes its present appearance to the centuries spent under Venice (1421-1797), when it gained the town walls and gates, two of which have been preserved – the main gate from 1547 and the northern gate from 1592 – and the parish church on the main square. For a better picture of how locals once lived, call at the **Gradski Muzej** (Town Musuem) ⓘ *Trg Rasporski Kapetana 1, T052-622792, Mon-Fri 1100-1500, 10Kn*, displaying a collection of antique farm tools, kitchen utensils and traditional folk costumes, along with a space devoted to temporary exhibitions of Croatian and foreign artists. There is a **tourist office** ⓘ *Trg Fontana 7, T052-662343, www.tz-buzet.hr.*

Buje (Buie)

→ *Phone code: 052. Colour map 1, B1. Population: 3001. 8 km northwest of Grožnjan.*

The medieval hill town of Buje makes a pleasant outing for its sleepy cobbled streets, romantic old buildings and stunning views over the surrounding countryside, coupled with a number of informal eateries serving locally produced food and wine. Formerly referred to as the 'Watchtower of Istria' due to its elevated position overlooking two important transit routes – situated where the road from Pula to Trieste intersects with that from Umag to Buzet – it was founded by the Romans as *Bullea*. The historic centre, protected by defensive walls and a series of towers – of which two remain, one square, the other pentagonal – date from the period spent under Venice (1412-1797).

On the main square stands a **16th-century loggia** with a frescoed façade and the 18th-century baroque **Church of St Servelus**, constructed on the site of a 13th-century **Romanesque-Gothic church**: on the outer wall note a Roman *stele* (burial monument) featuring the busts of two men, said to be the Valeri brothers. Also worth seeing is the **Gradski Muzej** (Town Museum) ⓘ *Trg Slobode 4, T052-772023, summer Tue, Thu and Sat 0900-1300, Mon, Wed and Fri 1600-1900, winter on request, 10Kn*, housing a collection of local arts and crafts, plus the reconstruction of several rooms from a traditional Istrian house. There is also a **tourist office** ⓘ *Istarska 2, T052-773353, www.tzg-buje.hr.*

Glagolitic Alley » *pp129-131. Colour map 1, B2.*

→ *Phone code: 052.*

Glagolitic Alley was built in 1977 to record the historic importance of the Glagolitic script in this region. Lying between Roč and Hum, it stretches 7 km and includes 11 monuments celebrating important events and people associated with this all-but-forgotten form of writing (see box, page 127).

Roč

Despite its size (population 146), during the Middle Ages this unassuming little town was an important economic, cultural and religious centre, and many Glagolitic codices, manuscripts and Gospels, today found in museums in Zagreb and Vienna, were created here. The 16th-century **town walls** are still visible in part, as is the town gate, with a guard's room on the upper floor. The centre is dominated by the parish **Church of St Bartholomew**, which is of no great significance, but to its left stands the priest's home, where you can ask for the keys to two smaller churches: the adjacent **Church of St Anthony**, bearing a Glagolitic alphabet from the 12th century carved into a votive cross on the right-hand wall, and the **Church of St Roč**, next to the town gate, where you can see fragments of 14th-century frescoes and Glagolitic carvings.

The monuments

In Roč, at the junction for Hum, you can see the **Pillar of the Čakav Parliament**, a reference to Croatian self-rule and the *Čakav* dialect (one of three variants of the Croatian language, see page 342). The second monument shows the **Three-legged Table before Two Cypresses**, with the trees symbolizing the apostles of the Slavs, St Cyril and St Methodius. Monument three is dedicated to the **Assembly of Kliment of Ohrid** – Kliment was a pupil of Cyril and Methodius, and he founded the first Slav university near Lake Ohrid. The fourth monument, in front of the village church in Brnobici, is a **lapidarium** displaying Glagolitic inscriptions from various regions of former Yugoslavia. Monument five portrays **Mount Učka** partly hidden by clouds – in the Middle Ages it was regarded as the Croatian equivalent of Mount Olympus in Greece. The sixth monument is the **Grgur Ninski Observation Point**, featuring a block of stone engraved with the Glagolitic, Latin and Cyrillic alphabets. Monument seven represents the **Istarski Razvod**, the historic document defining Istria's borders, while monument eight is dedicated to **Croatian Protestants and Heretics**. The ninth monument is a huge stone block recording the first Glagolitic missal, dating from 1483. Monument ten, at the entrance to Hum, is devoted to **Resistance and Freedom** over the centuries, with three stone blocks representing the three historic periods of Antiquity, the Middle Ages and the Modern Age. The eleventh and final monument is the copper town gate of Hum, decorated with 12 medallions, each representing a month of the year and typical activities that take place at that time.

Hum

Claiming to be the smallest town in the world (population 17), Hum was once a strategically important border station between the Venetian and Hapsburg territories. Today there are only about a dozen old stone houses intact, but weekly mass is still held in the parish church and there are annual elections for a mayor. However, most people come here specifically to eat at the renowned **Humska Konoba**. Besides eating here, you can also ask for the key to the tiny Romanesque **Church of St Jerome**, decorated with 12th-century frescoes, standing in the grounds of the cemetery on the edge of town.

Sleeping

Motovun *p127*

D **Hotel Kastel**, Trg Andrea Antico 7, T052-681607, www.hotel-kastel-motovun.hr. Occupying an 18th-century building just outside the town walls, this peaceful old-fashioned hotel has 29 rooms and a restaurant with open-air dining in the garden through summer. Pets welcome.

Buje *p128*

C **Hotel San Rocco**, Srednja ulica 2, Brtonigla, T052-725000, www.san-rocco.hr. In the small village of Brtonigla, 6 km from Buje, this small family-run hotel occupies a beautifully restored old stone farmhouse.
The 12 well-equipped guest rooms are individually furnished in a classical style,

and most have wooden beamed ceilings. The highly regarded hotel restaurant serves local specialities in a dining room with exposed stone walls, wooden floors and wooden beamed ceilings. There is also an outdoor pool in the garden out front, and a sauna. Open all year.

D **La Parenzana**, Volpia 3, T/F052-777460, www.parenzana.com.hr. Just 3 km outside Buje, this beautifully restored old stone farmhouse has 16 comfortable guest rooms furnished with antiques and a large dining room with an open fire and summer terrace. Everything on the menu, including the wine, is organically produced on local farms. It is close to the disused Parenzana railway line, now a popular cycling route.

Eating

Pazin and around *p126*

ΨΨ **Agroturizam Ograde**, Lindarski katun 60, T052-693035, www.agroturizam-ograde.hr. 10 km south of Pazin, this agrotourism centre has a wooden-beamed, flagstone-floored *konoba* serving local specialities such as home-made sausages, cheeses and seasonal mushroom and asparagus dishes. They also have several rooms for overnight stays.

ΨΨ **Konoba Vela Vrata**, Beram 41, T052-622801. In tiny Beram, following a visit to St Mary's Church, you might stop for a meal at this small *konoba*. The menu features typical Istrian goodies such as pršut (prosciutto), home-made pasta, sausages and truffle dishes.

Motovun *p127*

ΨΨΨ-ΨΨ **Pod Voltom**, Trg Josefa Ressela 6, T052-681923. On the main square in Motovun's old town, close to the tourist office, this homely eatery has an exposed brick interior with an open fire. Its known for *fuži* (Istrian pasta) with truffles, steak with truffles, and local game dishes. Closed Wed.

ΨΨΨ-ΨΨ **Restaurant Mcotić**, Zadrugarska 19, T052-681758. Located in New Motovun, below the old town, this popular restaurant serves up delicious pasta, steak and truffle dishes on a vast summer terrace.

Buzet *p128*

ΨΨ **Mlini**, Milinić 54, Buzet. T052-669057. In Buzet itself, this tiny *konoba* with several tables both indoors and out, serves a range of local dishes, the speciality is trout in truffle sauce.

ΨΨ **Restoran Vrh**, Vrh 2, 10 km southwest of Buzet, off the main road to Motovun, T052-667123. This friendly eatery serves up meat and truffle dishes, many accompanied by *fuži*, a local variant of pasta. Closed Mon.

ΨΨ **Toklarija**, Sovinjsko Polje, T052-663031. This tiny but highly regarded *gostiona* is 8 km southwest of Buzet, off the main road to Motovun. Look out for home-made ravioli with prosciutto and cheese, ravioli with wild asparagus, rabbit, and mushroom and truffle dishes. Closed Tue. No credit cards.

Buje *p128*

ΨΨΨ-ΨΨ **Astarea**, Ronkova 9, Brtonigla, T052-774384. In Brtonigla, 6 km southwest of Buje, this rustic, family-run eatery serves up delicious seafood, including such delights as *jakovske kapice* (scallops), *brancin s kumpirima i lignjom pod pekom* (sea bass with potato and squid cooked under a *peka*), and excellent *štrudla od jabuka* (apple pie).

ΨΨΨ-ΨΨ **Igor**, Kaštel 120e, Kaštel Buje, T052-777131. Close to the Slovenian border, 5km north of Buje, this is great spot for the uninitiated to sample truffles. House specialities, prepared in the 'slow food' vein, include gnocchi filled with truffles and scampi, spaghetti with scampi and cognac, and steak with truffles. Closed Tue.

ΨΨΨ-ΨΨ **Malo Selo**, Fratrija bb, Fratrija-Buje, T052-777332. In Fratrija, 4 km from Buje, this typical Istrian *konoba*, built from stone and wood, is known for serving up tasty dishes made from seasonal delicacies such as *šparoge* (asparagus), *gljive* (mushroom) and *tartufi* (truffles). There's an open-plan cooking space, so you can watch the chef at work. Closed Wed.

ΨΨ **Pod Voltom**, A Bibić bb, T052-772232. In the heart of the old town, this small restaurant serves up pasta, meat and truffle dishes on a summer terrace offering fantastic views over the surrounding countryside.

Glagolitic Alley *p128*

ΨΨ **Humska Konoba**, Hum 2, T052-660005. A tiny, old-fashioned *konoba* serving typical home-made Istrian dishes such as *fuži* (a type of pasta) with truffles, roast meats and *biska*, a local liquor made from mistletoe. Nov-May Sat-Sun, Jun-Oct daily.

Ročka Konoba, Roč, T052-666451. A small *konoba* serving typical Istrian dishes such as *gulaš sa njokima* (goulash with gnocchi) along with home-made wine by the carafe. In summer it's possible to eat outside on the terrace. Closed Mon.

Festivals and events

Motovun *p127*

Late Jun Motovun Film Festival, www.motovunfilmfestival.com. 5-day international festival of avant-garde cinema, founded in 1999. The festival organizers have also set up the Motovun Film School, offering a series of 5- to 10-day workshops.

Grožnjan *p127*

Jun-Sep Jeunesse Musicales Croatia (JMC), contact Hrvatska Glazbena Mladež, Trg Stjepana Radića 4, Zagreb, T01-611 1600, www.hgm.hr. International summer school of music, modern dance and theatre.

Shopping

Buzet *p128*

Zigante Tartufi, Trg Fontana, www.zigantetartufi.com. Stock an excellent range of truffles and truffle products from the Mirna Valley, plus Istrian olive oil and wines. There are other branches in: Buje at JB Tita 12; Livade at Livade 7; Grožnjan at U Gorjan 5; and Motovun at Gradiziol 8.

Activities and tours

Buzet *p128*

Truffle gathering

Activa Travel Istra, based at Scalierova 1, Pula, T052-215497, www.activa-istra.com. 1-day truffle-gathering tours Oct- Nov. Participants should dress appropriately for a 3-hr (8-km) walk through Motovun Forest, which concludes with dinner at a local farm.

Transport

Pazin and around *p126*

Bus

Bus station, T052-624437. There are 10 buses daily from **Pula** to Pazin (1 hr), 5 from **Poreč** (1¼ hr) and 4 from **Rovinj** (1 hr 20 mins). There is no direct bus to Beram, so you need a car or to take a taxi. Alternatively, take any bus running from Pazin to either Poreč or Motovun, get off at Podberam and walk 15 mins uphill to Beram.

Train

Train station, T052-624310. There are 8 trains daily from **Pula** to Pazin (1 hr).

Motovun *p127*

Bus

For further information, contact the respective bus stations – there is no bus station in Motovun itself. 5 buses leave daily from **Pazin** (45 mins), 2 daily go from **Pula** (2 hrs) and 1 from **Poreč** (45 mins).

Grožnjan *p127*

Bus

Buses running between **Pazin** and **Buje** pass on the main road below Grožnjan – get off at the junction and walk the final 2 km up an unsurfaced track.

Buzet *p128*

Bus

There are 2 buses (2½ hrs) daily from **Pula**.

Train

There are 4 trains (2 hrs) daily from **Pula**.

Buje *p128*

Bus

For information contact the respective bus stations – there is no bus station in Buje itself. There are 5 buses daily from **Pula**, 7 from **Poreč** and 3 from **Rovinj**.

Glagolitic Alley *p128*

There is no public transport along the Glagolitic Alley, so be prepared to walk.

Bus and train

Buses from **Buzet** to **Rijeka** (1 hr) stop on the main road just below Roč (20 mins), which is also served by 4 trains daily from Pula (1¾ hrs). There are no buses to **Hum**, but the trains from Pula stop at Hum station (1½ hrs), which is confusingly located 5 km from Hum itself, close to the village of **Erkovići**.

East coast

The east coast offers few surprises and is far less rich in cultural sights and beaches than the west. The most interesting part, to the north, officially falls within the Kvarner region (see page 136), though geographically it is part of the Istrian Peninsula.

▸▸ *For Sleeping, Eating and other listings, see pages 133-134.*

Labin (Albona) ▸▸ *pp133-134. Colour map 1, C2.*

→ *Phone code: 052. Population: 7904.*

Labin, 40 km northeast of Pula, can be visited in conjunction with its seaside neighbour, Rabac. Today's town is divided into two distinct parts: old Labin, the original hilltop settlement, and the newer Podlabin, founded in the early 20th century as a housing estate for local coal miners and now surrounded by modern residential development. Many houses in the old town have remained derelict since walls started cracking due to subsidence in the 1960s, though people are gradually buying them up to restore as holiday cottages. The bus station is in Podlabin, so first impressions are daunting, but a 15-minute walk brings you to the old town, a compact nucleus of stone buildings, walled by the Venetians in the 15th century.

Ins and outs

The main **tourist office** ⓘ *Aldo Negri 20 in Labin, T052-855560, www.rabac-labin.com*, covers both Labin and Rabac. Through summer there is also a small **tourist information point** ⓘ *Titov Trg 10*, T052-852399, on the main square in Labin, just outside the town walls.

Background

The Illyrians, who were particularly partial to hilltop sites, founded the settlement around 2000 BC and called it *Alvona*. Like the rest of Istria, it then passed to the Romans. The Venetians arrived in 1422, leaving a hallmark loggia overlooking Titov Trg, the main square, which was used for court verdicts, the annual election of a mayor, and reading out the news. They also fortified Labin with walls and a gate, now known as Uskoška Vrata (Uskok Gate), after a failed attempt by 800 Uskoks to raid the town in 1599. Organized coal mining began in the area in 1785, to supply fuel to Rijeka, and increased under Austria during the 19th century. During the Mussolini period, Labin's miners went down in history on 2 March 1921 when they proclaimed the *Republica Albonessi* (Republic of Labin) as an independent workers' state, which held out for 34 days, until the Italian army was sent in. After the Second World War, when Istria became part of Yugoslavia, a lot of Italians left the area, and a wave of Bosnian migrants arrived in their place to work the mines. During the 1960s many houses in the old town were abandoned due to subsidence caused by mining, but fortunately a number of artists moved in to save the old houses, carrying out restoration work and opening several small ateliers. The last mine closed in 1999 – although there are still seams of underlying coal, it has a high sulphur content (up to 12%) making it unacceptable by modern environmental standards (sulphur burns to form sulphur dioxide, which becomes diluted in the atmosphere and returns to earth as acid rain).

Sights

Standing next to the **Church of the Birth of the Blessed Virgin Mary**, easily identified by its 17th-century façade with a winged Lion of St Marks and a rose window, the **Gradski**

Muzej (Town Museum) ⓘ *Trg 1 Maja, T052-852477, May-Oct Mon-Fri 1000-1300, 1700-1900, Sat 1000-1300, Nov-Apr on request, 15Kn*, contains a modest collection of Roman stones, amphorae, wooden farming tools and local folk costumes. However, the undisputed highlight is the mock coal mine: visitors don hard hats and walk through dimly lit tunnels, stooping under beams to get some idea of how difficult life was for local miners. It's an amusing experience and children will love it.

Just north of Labin, on the main road to Rijeka, the **Forma Viva Sculpture Park** ⓘ *Dubrova bb, free*, displays over 70 pieces of modern sculpture, created by artists from all over the world who have attended the Dubrova Mediterranean Sculptors' Symposium, held here each summer for over 30 years.

Rabac → *Phone code: 052. Colour map 1, C2. Population: 1472.*

Built into the slopes overlooking a narrow bay, 4 km below the hilltop settlement of Labin, Rabac is the most popular resort on the east coast of Istria. Since the 1960s, this small fishing village has seen the construction of 14 large hotels and a plethora of holiday apartments, and can now accommodate up to 10,000 guests at a time. There's little of cultural interest, the main attraction being a decent pebble beach in the centre, a second beach called **Girandella** renowned for parties just a short distance out of town, and a number of good fish restaurants. The main beach is on the northern side of the bay where it is possible to rent sunbeds and umbrellas. Girandella is 1.5 km north of the centre and can be reached on foot following the coastal promenade. The **tourist office** in Labin covers both Rabac and Labin.

Sleeping

Labin *p132*

Private accommodation

There are no hotels in Labin, though a number of stone cottages have been restored to provide holiday homes in the old town. **Veritas**, Sv Katarine 4, T052-852 758, www.istra-veritas.hr, can help you find private accommodation.

Rabac *p133*

A **Hotel Villa Annette**, Raška 24, Rabac, T052-884222, www.villaannette.hr. Overlooking Rabac Bay, this modern villa is set in a garden with a large outdoor pool. The 12 spacious rooms and suites have cream leather armchairs with splashes of vibrant red added by cushions and paintings. Each suite has a terrace with a sea view and a kitchenette. The hotel restaurant serves up local 'slow food' specialities and they also offer a 'slow food' weekend package. Open all year.

C **Hotel Amfora**, Rabac bb, T052-872222, www.hotel-amfora.hr. The only hotel in the centre of Rabac, the **Amfora** is 30 m from the sea. Originally built in the 1970s, it was renovated in 2003 and has 52 basic rooms and a restaurant.

D **Hotel Villa Calussovo**, Ripenda, Kras 18, Labin, T052-851188, www.villa-calussovo.com. Set amid pasture land, this renovated farmhouse offers 12 guest rooms, all simply furnished with wooden floors and exposed stonewalls, plus a ground floor restaurant with a covered summer terrace serving Istrian specialities. It stands on a hillside near the village of Ripenda, between Rabac und Labin.

Private accommodation

Contact either **Kvarner expree**, Obala m Tita 53, T052-872225, www.kvarner-express.hr, or **Top Adriatic Tours**, Rabac bb, T052-880468, www.top adriatic.hr, agencies which can help you find private accommodation.

Eating

Labin *p132*

ΨΨΨ-ΨΨ **Restaurant Dubrova**, Dubrova bb, T052-885054. This highly regarded restaurant is on the main road between Pula and Rijeka, on the edge of the Forma Viva Sculpture Park. With tastefully furnished dining rooms on 2 floors, 1 with an open fire, and a couple of open-air terraces, it can seat over 200. The menu features delicacies such as Italian- and French-style truffle dishes, fresh fish and steak. The pizza makes a cheaper alternative.

ΨΨΨ-ΨΨ Due Fratelli, Montozi 6, Labin, T052-853577. On the winding country road leading down from Labin to Rabac, you'll find this highly regarded eatery on a corner to the left. It's known for serving excellent fresh seafood – most of which the owner, who is also a fisherman, catches himself.

Rabac *p133*

ΨΨΨ Nostromo, Obala M Tita 7, T052-872601, www.nostromo.hr. Located 1 block back from the seafront, **Nostromo** is considered the best restaurant in town. It's a little pricier than the others, but worth it. The house specialities are sea bass fillets with truffle sauce, frogfish carpaccio, and frogfish in wine with polenta. They also have 6 rooms and 2 suites for overnight accommodation (**D**). Open all year.

ΨΨ Rapčanka, Obala M Tita 31, T052-872784. Arranged on 2 floors, with a classic fish restaurant in a beamed dining room on the upper level and a pizzeria with a large brick oven downstairs, **Rapčanka** has been on the go since the 1970s. The house specialities are *fuižna pastirski način* (pasta with wild asparagus, mushrooms and ham) and *grdobina na partlonski* (fish prepared with wine and shellfish). Closed Dec-Feb.

ΨΨ-Ψ Restoran Zelen Draga, Plominska 17, T052-872988. Opposite the bus stop for Labin, this unassuming modern restaurant knocks up delicious *frigne lignje* (fried squid), *špinat* (spinach) and *fuži sa istarskom slaninom* (pasta with Istrian bacon). Ask to try the excellent home-made *travarica* at the end of your meal. Open all year.

Festivals and events

Rabac *p133*

Girandella beach hosts several festivals of house and techno music.

Late Jul **Rabac Summer Festival**, www.rabacfestival.com. The best known festival, featuring rock and electronic music on stages in Dubrova Park in Labin and on Girandello beach in Rabac.

Activities and tours

Rabac *p133*

Cycling

A network of local bike paths centre on Labin and Rabac. It is possible to rent mountain bikes from **Hotel Neptune**, Rabac bb, T052-862520.

Transport

Labin *p132*

Bus

Bus station, T052-855220. From here 7 buses daily run between **Pula** and **Rijeka**, stopping in Labin en route. From Pula the journey takes 1 hr, from Rijeka 1½ hrs.

Rabac *p133*

Bus

Rabac is not served by regional buses. However, a local service connects it to **Labin**, with 14 buses daily. It is also possible to walk from Labin down to Rabac, following a well-marked 4-km footpath.

Car

Budget, Obala M Tita bb, T052-872357, www.budget.hr.

Directory

Labin *p132*

Medical services Pharmacy Ljekarna, T052-855509. **Post offices** Trg 2 Ožujka bb, Mon-Fri 0700-2000, Sat 0800-1200. Titov Trg bb, Mon-Fri 0800-1500.

Rabac *p133*

Bank There is a bank with an ATM. **Medical services** There is no **pharmacy** in Rabac, the nearest one is in Labin.

Kvarner

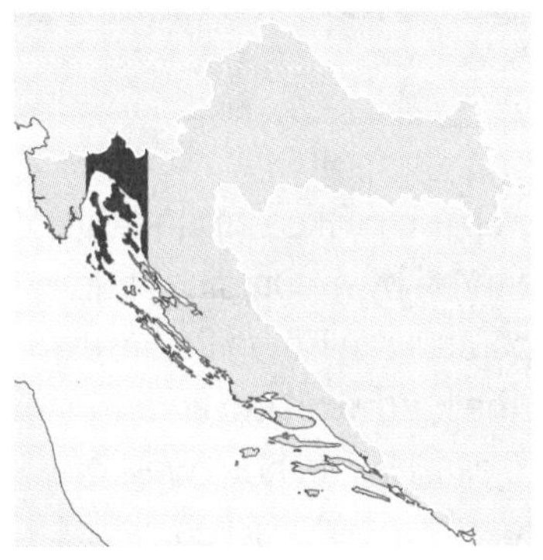

Footprint features

Introduction

The seaside resorts nearest to Zagreb are packed around the Kvarner Gulf, a large deep bay sheltered by mountains of up to 1500 m. The Kvarner region separates the Istrian Peninsula from Dalmatia and its chief city is the hard-working and slightly austere industrial port of Rijeka. Half an hour west of Rijeka is Opatija, Croatia's oldest coastal resort. Packed with grandiose, Austro-Hungarian-style hotels, it attracts an elderly clientele of middle-class Europeans.

Kvarner also has its share of islands. The largest and easiest to reach is Krk – linked to the mainland by bridge – which has a string of rather uninspiring package resorts along the west coast, a pretty monastery on the islet of Košljun and a stunning sand beach on the southeast coast at Baška.

Slightly more upmarket, the island of Rab is best known for Rab Town, a romantic medieval settlement built on a walled peninsula with four bell towers creating a distinctive skyline. There is no shortage of good beaches here, especially Lopar Peninsula to the north which offers long stretches of sand and pebbles.

West of Rab, Cres is a long, thin island of scanty pastures, dry stonewalls and more sheep than people. With few memorable cultural monuments, it remains firmly off the beaten track, but for those who enjoy hiking and wildlife, the pine forests of the Tramuntana offer blissful walks and great opportunities for birdwatching.

South of Cres, and linked to it by a bridge, the island of Lošinj attracts tourists to the pretty town of Mali Lošinj, renowned for a string of 19th-century villas, each set amid a garden filled with exotic plants. The sister town of Veli Lošinj is smaller, quieter and undeniably more authentic.

Returning to the mainland, east of Rijekja soar the rugged heights of Gorski Kotar, part of which is contained within Risnjak National Park, offering well-marked hiking paths, dense pine forests and bracing mountain air.

★ Don't miss ...

1 **Rijeka** Enjoy a drink overlooking the city at the hilltop bar in Trsat, page 142.
2 **Lungomare** Walk the 12-km coastal promenade between the fishing villages of Volosko and Lovran, passing through Opatija, Croatia's oldest seaside resort, page 144.
3 **Vrbnik** Try Žlahtina wine on the island of Krk, page 154.
4 **Tramuntane** Forest Look out for griffon vultures on the island of Cres, page 159.
5 **Rab Town** Explore the architectural treasures of this medieval town, page 169.
6 **Kandarola** Beach Skinny dip on the island of Rab, page 170.

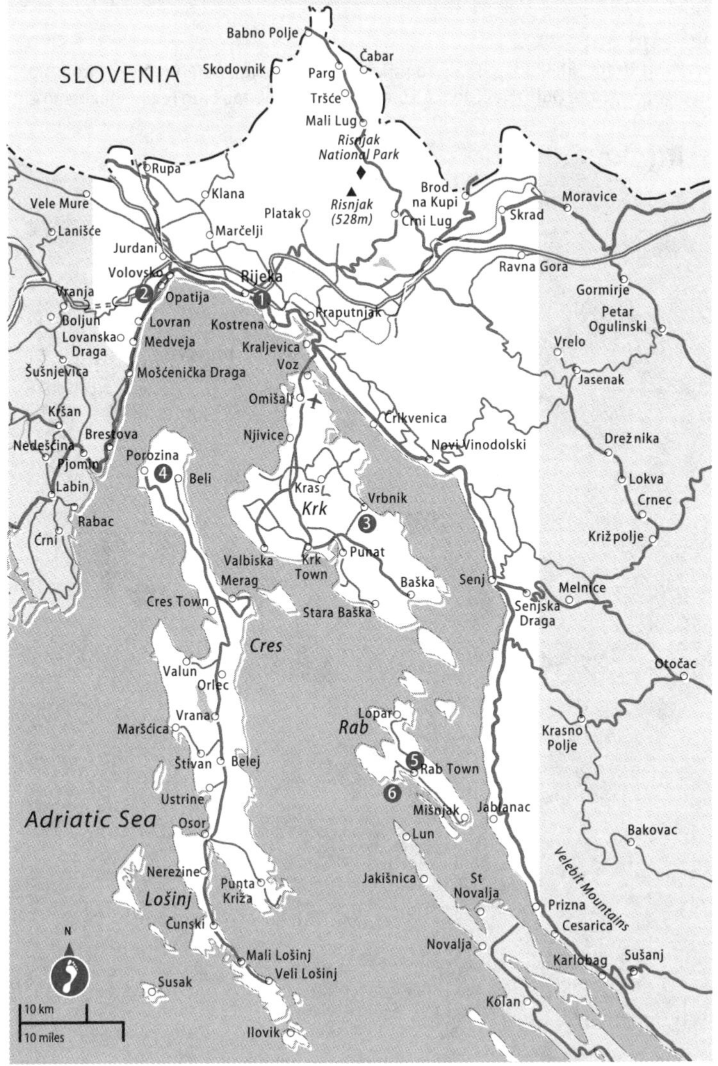

Rijeka and around

→ *Phone code: 051. Colour map 1, C3. Population: 143,800.*

Overlooking the Kvarner Gulf, Rijeka is Croatia's largest port, with a shipyard, massive dry dock facilities, refineries and other heavy industries. Architecturally, the centre is remarkably similar to Trieste in Italy, with a grid of grandiose 18th-century Austro-Hungarian buildings on the seafront, and a sprawling suburb of high-rise apartment blocks from the 1960s. The main public meeting place is the Korzo, a pedestrian street a couple of blocks back from the port, lined with shops and open-air cafés. There are few memorable sights here, other than the lovely hilltop castle and pilgrimage church of Trsat, and the city has only four hotels, as most visitors to the area stay in the nearby seaside resort of Opatija. Rijeka receives national television coverage each year for the staging of Croatia's largest Carnival. ▸▸ *For Sleeping, Eating and other listings, see pages 147-151.*

Ins and outs

Getting there Rijeka is 98 km from Pula; 182 km from Zagreb; 350 km from Split, and 566 km from Dubrovnik. In the summer, **Croatia Airlines** run regular flights to and

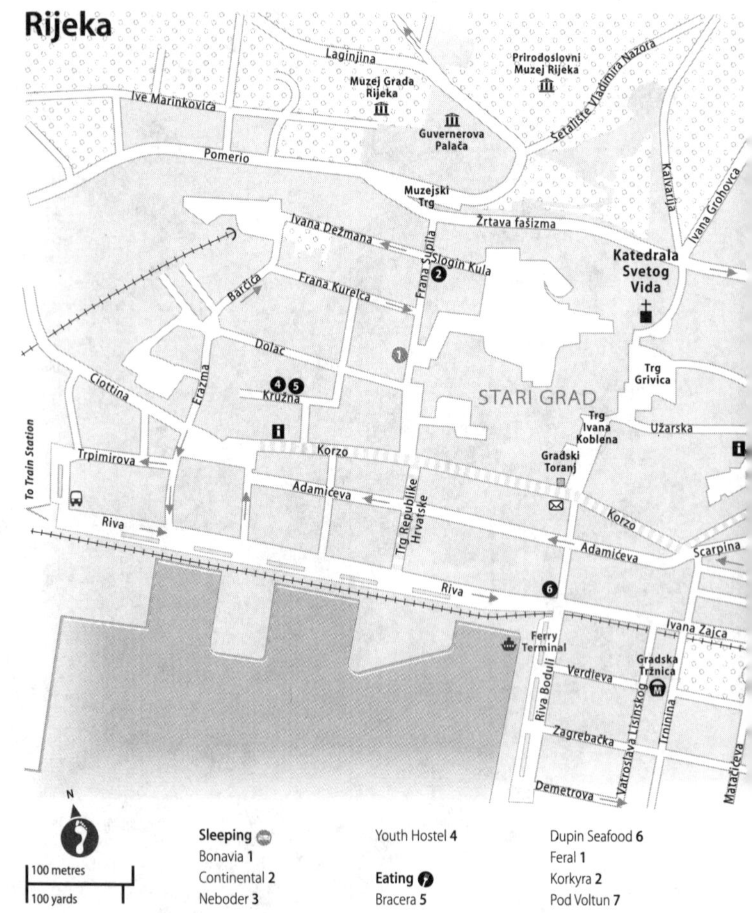

from London Heathrow. The **airport**, which now operates all year, is at Omišalj on the island of Krk, 26 km from Rijeka city centre. An **Autotrolej airport bus** ⓘ *2hr 20 mins before flight departures, takes 30 mins, €30*, leaves from Jelačić Square, in the city centre. The **city port** is on the Riva, a 10-minute walk south of the city centre. **Jadrolinija** run a coastal ferry from Rijeka to Dubrovnik, plus services to the islands of Cres, Unije, Susak, Lošinj, Rab and Pag. The **bus station** ⓘ *Žabica 1*, is a five-minute walk west of the city centre. The **train station** ⓘ *Krešimirova 5*, is a 10-minute walk west of the city centre. » *See Transport, page 150, for further details.*

Getting around The centre can be explored entirely on foot. It's possible to walk up to Trsat, using the pilgrimage path, though bus No 1 will also get you there. If you're staying in Opatija and visiting Rijeka, the two town centres are connected by bus No 32 which runs every 20 minutes. In addition, there's a double-decker sightseeing bus, with a guide, which runs several times daily between Rijeka and Opatija. Tickets cost 70Kn and are available from tourist information centres in both towns.

Tourist information There's a new walk-in **tourist information centre** ⓘ *Korzo 33, T051-335882, Mon-Fri 0800-2000, Sat 0800-1400*, and the **city tourist board office** ⓘ *Užarska 14, T051-315710, www.tz-rijeka.hr.*

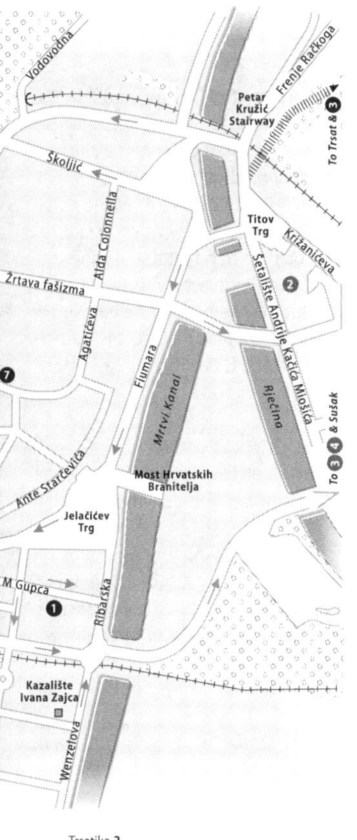

Trsatika **3**
Zlatna Školjka **4**

Best time to visit Like all the coastal towns, Rijeka is at its busiest from June to September. However, the town's Carnival celebrations (in late February or early March, depending when Easter falls) also pull in the crowds, notably on the Sunday before Shrove Tuesday, when the **International Carnival Parade** takes place.

Background

Founded as the Roman *Tarsatica*, Rijeka only really began to develop in 1466, when it came under Austrian rule. It fast became a major trading centre, with iron, oil, wood, wool, cattle and leather passing through the port by the 16th century. In 1723 it was awarded the status of a free port and, during the latter half of the 18th century, it expanded, spreading beyond the old town walls when a large strip of land was reclaimed from the sea, extending the seafront by several hundred metres. In 1779 it passed to Hungary and so, while other coastal towns came under Venice and were filled with Venetian-style architecture, Rijeka's buildings were being designed by architects from Budapest.

The world's first self-propelled torpedoes were produced here in 1866, though they are now on display in Split, Maritime Museum (see page 207), not in Rijeka. In the 1960s Rijeka became Yugoslavia's largest port, with a thriving shipyard and new heavy industries offering large-scale employment. Families moved in from rural areas of the country to find work here and the modern high-rise suburbs came into being. During the Croatian war of independence Rijeka was noted for its tolerance and many non-Croats were able to remain here safely. Today it is Croatia's largest seaport, but due to a national economic crisis, traditional industries such as shipbuilding, oil refining, paper milling and engine building are only just managing to continue functioning.

Sights

Korzo

A couple of blocks inland from the Riva (seafront), this main pedestrian thoroughfare follows the line given by the architect Arthur Gnamb at the end of the 18th century, when the city extended beyond the medieval city walls. Today, lined with clothes shops and open-air cafés, it is Rijeka's main shopping street and public meeting space. The name Korzo comes directly from the Italian, Corso.

Half way down the Korzo, the **Gradski Toranj** (City Tower) forms an arched entrance into the **Stari Grad** (Old Town), which was once walled. The lower section of the tower dates back to the 13th century, while the upper level was rebuilt in baroque style and decorated with the busts of two Austrian emperors and the Hapsburg coat of arms featuring the double-headed eagle in the 17th century. The clocks were added in 1784.

Katedrala Svetog Vida (St Vitus Cathedral)

ⓘ *Trg Grivica 11, daily 0800-1200, 1600-1900.*

From the City Tower, walk straight across the Stari Grad (Old Town), through Trg Ivana Koblena and Grivica, to arrive at the cathedral. Work on this baroque rotunda (a building with a circular ground plan), built on the site of an even older church, began in 1638 and was completed in 1744. It was designed by the Jesuit architect Giacomo Briano, and is said to have been inspired by the church of Santa Maria della Salute in Venice. Inside, above the main altar, stands a 13th-century wooden Gothic crucifix, which was also kept in the former church. Local myth has it that during the 13th century one Petar Lončarić was playing cards here with two friends. He was losing, and out of anger threw a rock at the crucifix, hitting the body of Christ, which immediately began to bleed. The unfortunate gambler was swallowed up by the ground and the crucifix consequently proclaimed miraculous. Events from this story are depicted on the cathedral's bronze doors, added in the 1990s.

Guvernerova Palača (Governor's Palace) and around

A five-minute walk northeast of the Stari Grad (Old Town), on the hillside facing down towards the port, stands the Governor's Palace, built in neo-Renaissance style in 1896 to designs by the Budapest architect, Alajos Haussmann. This is where the Hungarian governor used to reside: the building clearly conveys the grandeur of authority, and D'Annunzio obviously thought so too, as he chose this as his base during his one-year bid to rule the city. The building now houses the **Povijesni i Pomorski Muzej** (History and Marine Museum) ⓘ *Guvernerova Palača, Muzejski trg 1/1, T051-213578, www.ppmhp.hr, Tue-Fri 0900-2000, Sat 0900-1300, 10Kn*. The second floor is devoted to local shipping, with a display of model ships, navigational instruments, anchors, charts and old photos.

Muzej Grada Rijeka (Rijeka City Museum) ⓘ *Muzejski trg 1/1, T051-336711, www.muzej-rijeka.hr, Mon-Fri 1000-1300 and 1600-1900, Sat 1000-1300, 10Kn*. In the gardens of the Governor's Palace, and linked to it by an arcade, stands a modern pavilion built in 1976 to accommodate the Rijeka City Museum. Inside is a display of ancient stone finds, periodically supplemented by temporary exhibitions relating to the region's history.

Prirodoslovni Muzej Rijeka (Natural History Museum) ⓘ *Lorenzov prolaz 1, off Šetalište Vladimira Nazora, T051-553669, www.prirodoslovni.com, Mon-Sat*

Taken by a poet

After the First World War, Italy and Yugoslavia both put forward claims to Rijeka, firing a dispute that was to last for the following three decades. In 1915, at the Treaty of London, the city had been promised to Yugoslavia but, at the Paris Peace Conference, Italy claimed it on the grounds that Italian-speaking inhabitants formed a majority of the population. Meanwhile, Gabriele D'Annunzio (1863-1938), an Italian soldier, Romantic poet and outspoken supporter of Fascism, took control of the city in September 1919, along with a gang of some 300 legionaries. The situation became increasingly embarrassing for Rome, and over Christmas 1920 the Italian navy bombed the city from the sea in a successful bid to force out D'Annunzio. Rijeka was consequently established as a free city, a status it was to enjoy for only one year, as Italian troops, this time under the command of Benito Mussolini, occupied the city once again in 1922. In 1924 the Treaty of Rome awarded Rijeka to Italy, but declared the eastern suburb of Sušak, south of the River Rječina where the Slav majority resided, as part of Yugoslavia. After the Second World War, an Allied peace treaty with Italy handed Rijeka back to Yugoslavia in 1947, whereupon a large segment of the Italian population left the city.

0900-1900, Sun 0900-1500, 10Kn. Close by, an impressive late 19th-century villa houses the Natural History Museum, with a display of rocks and fossils illustrating the geological history of the Adriatic and an aquarium dedicated to the marine life of the same area. A multimedia presentation allows visitors to experience the depths of the sea through video, and three tanks display various fish, invertebrates, algae and marine flowering plants.

East of the Old Town

The elegant **Most hrvatskih branitelja** (Memorial bridge to Croatian soldiers) crosses the Mrtvi Kanal (Dead Canal) east of the town centre. Built in 2002, its minimalist design features clean lines in metal and glass; at night, thanks to subtle lighting effects, it appears to float on the water. While most Croatian towns commissioned heroic sculptures to honour local soldiers who fell during the war for independence, Rijeka chose to build this pedestrian bridge instead, symbolizing the city's high regard for tolerance. It was designed by Studio 3LHD from Zagreb and has won various international architectural awards.

South of the Old Town

Gradska Tržnica (Main Market) ⓘ *between Trninina and Vatroslava Lisinskog, daily 0600-1400*, close to the port, is a market complex made up of three pavilions. Stalls selling fresh fruit and vegetables are within two identical stone, steel and glass pavilions, designed by Isidor Vauching and completed in 1881. A third pavilion, designed by Karlo Pergoli in Liberty style, opened to the public in 1914. It houses the fish market and is decorated with stone carvings of fish and shells, by the Venetian sculptor Urbano Bottasso.

Kazalište Ivana Zajca (Ivan Zajc Theatre) ⓘ *Verdijeva bb, T051-355900*, stands across the square from the market complex. It was built by Fellner and Helmer, two architects from Vienna, who also designed the Croatian National Theatre in Zagreb. It was completed in 1885. Lovers of **Gustav Klimt** will be interested to know that some of Klimt's early work can be seen here – together with Franz Matsch; he painted three of the six oval frescoes on the theatre ceiling. The building is not generally open to the

Zvončari

Unique to Carnival in Rijeka and the surrounding villages, *Zvončari* are young men dressed in bizarre costumes consisting of a sheepskin slung over the shoulders, a mask of a grotesque animal head with horns, and a large iron bell tied around the waist. During the afternoons and evenings, in the week preceding Shrove Tuesday, they go from village to village and house to house in large groups acting roguishly and making a din with their bells. Traditionally, locals offer them *fritule* (similar to small doughnuts) and wine, then see them on their way. Their purpose is to chase away the forces of evil and invite the coming of spring and new life.

public other than for performances, but if you telephone first you can arrange to see the frescoes. In the garden in front of the theatre stands Belizar Bahorić's statue of the Rijeka-born composer Ivan Zajc.

Pilgrimage path to Trsat

Up on the hill (139 m), above the town, stand the Church of Our Lady of Trsat and Trsat Castle. The most rewarding way to arrive in Trsat is to follow the pilgrimage path (although bus No 1 will get you there too), which starts from Titov Trg on the left bank of the River Rječina. A baroque gateway topped with a relief of the Virgin marks the beginning of the **Petar Kružić Stairway**, named after the Uskok captain from Klis, who had the lower part of the stairway built in 1531. A steep but worthwhile climb of over 500 steps brings you up through the dramatic **Rječina Gorge**. At the top, turn left and follow the busy road of Šetalište Joakima Rakovca uphill until you arrive at Frankopanski Trg, home to the 15th-century church and Franciscan Monastery complex.

Gospa Trsat (Church of our Lady of Trsat) ⓘ *Frankopanski Trg, T051-452900, daily 0700-1900*, was built by the wealthy Frankopan family to commemorate the 'Miracle of Trsat', when angels were said to have carried the house of the Virgin Mary from Nazareth and delivered it on this spot in 1291. As the story goes, it remained here for three years and was then moved (by the angels again) to Loreto, near Ancona in Italy. Inside the church, above the altar, an icon of the Virgin Mary, sent as a present from Pope Urban V in 1367 to console the people of Trsat for the loss of the holy house, is hung with offerings from pilgrims such as pearl necklaces and trinkets. Next to the church, the baroque cloister of the Franciscan Monastery leads to the **Chapel of Votive Gifts**, displaying an extraordinary collection of offerings brought here by pilgrims, including a painted wooden sculpture of the Virgin and Child, countless religious portraits and even discarded crutches, proof of the Virgin's miraculous healing powers. There's a decent restaurant, **Trsatika** (see Eating, page 148), nearby.

A five-minute walk from Frankopanski Trg, **Trsat** (Trsat Castle) ⓘ *Ulica Zrinskog, T051-217714, Jun-Sep daily 0900-2200, Oct-May daily 0900-1700*, was built in the Middle Ages by the Frankopans on the foundations of a Roman observation point. In 1826 the remains of the castle were bought by Laval Nugent (1777-1862), an eccentric Irishman who had served as Field Marshall in the Austrian army. He had it restored in romantic style, and added a Classical Greek temple with four Doric columns brought in from Pula, intended as the family mausoleum.

The former dungeon now displays an exhibition of photos tracing Trsat's history, and from early April to late October the castle hosts an open-air café, offering views over the city and across the Kvarner Bay to the islands of Cres and Krk. On summer evenings, **outdoor theatrical events**, concerts and fashion shows are held here.

Risnjak National Park » pp147-151. Colour map 1, B3.

→ *Phone code: 051. 30 km northeast of Rijeka.*

The forested heights of Risnjak National Park make a pleasant contrast to Kvarner's seascapes, and in summer the air is cool and through winter the craggy peaks are snow covered. This is the most densely forested region in the country and two-thirds of the park is covered with beech and fir, which fare well up to an altitude of 1200 m.

Ins and outs

The park can be visited as an excursion from the coast or en route from Rijeka to Zagreb. Information and maps are available from the **park administration building** ① *adjacent to Motel Risnjak, Bijela Vodica 48, Crni Lug, T051-836133, www.risnjak.hr, entrance 30Kn.* » See Transport, page 151, for details.

Sights

Just north of Rijeka, the limestone mountains of **Gorski Kotor** form a natural boundary between Croatia and Slovenia. In 1953, an area of 64 sq km was declared a national park to protect the indigenous forests and mountain meadows. The highest peak, **Veliki Risnjak** (1528 m), is a rugged rocky mass unable to support plant life.

The Risnjak forests form a natural habitat for the lynx, after which the park is named (lynx in Croatian is *ris*). However, the last indigenous lynx were shot in the mid-19th century, while those that now live here were brought from the mountains of neighbouring Slovenia in 1974. Other wild animals here include the brown bear, wildcat, roe deer, red deer and chamois, plus the seldom-sighted wolf and wild boar. Risnjak is home to over 50 bird species, including the capercaillie, the largest type of European grouse.

The best place to start exploring the park is the picturesque little village of **Crni Lug** (726 m), where you might also decide to stay a night or two. Here, just a few minutes west of the park administration building, you'll find the beginning of the **Poučna Staza Leska** (Leska Educational Trail), a 4.5-km circular route with information points in both Croatian and English. Also from Crni Lug, a well-marked hiking path leads to the peak of Veliki Risnjak. Allow three hours each way, wear substantial walking boots and take plenty of water.

Opatija » pp147-151. Colour map 1, C2.

→ *Phone code: 051. Population: 7850. 15 km west of Rijeka.*

This is Croatia's longest-standing tourist resort with its old-fashioned hotels and an ageing clientele – through winter and spring at least half the guests are over 60. The seafront hotels, built largely in Viennese Secessionist style, offer neat gardens and sunny terraces where you can drink coffee and watch the world go by during the day, and through summer dinner is also served outside, often accompanied by live music. Several have sophisticated Wellness Centres.

Opatija owes much of its success to its wonderful microclimate, recommended for convalescence and people suffering from stress. Mount Učka shelters the coast from the cold *bura* wind, so that winters are mild and summers never unreasonably hot.

Ins and outs

There are regular buses from Rijeka and Pula. Opatija is a small place and it's easy to get around on foot. The main street, Šetalište Maršala Tita, runs parallel to the coast for the length of the resort, and you can walk from one end to the other in half an hour. There's a local **tourist office** ① *Vladimira Nazora 3, T051-271710, www.opatija-tourism.hr.* » See Transport, page 151, for further details.

Background

Opatija was named after a Benedictine Abbey (*opatija* means 'abbey' in Croatian) that was built here in the 15th century, though all that remains of it today is the reconstructed chapel of Sveti Jakov (St James), on the seafront. The settlement that grew up around the abbey was no more than a sleepy fishing village until 1844 when a wealthy Rijeka businessman, Iginio Scarpa, bought a piece of land close to the church and built a villa there. He named it Villa Angiolina, after his wife, and used it for entertaining the Central European elite of that time, including the Hapsburgs.

In 1882, with the opening of a railway linking Rijeka to Budapest and Vienna, the Society of Southern Railways bought Villa Angiolina and built the Hotel Kvarner next door, thus establishing the area as a winter health resort. They also initiated the building of the 12-km-long coastal promenade, Šetalište Franza Josefa. By the early 20th century, Opatija had become one of Europe's most elegant and fashionable seaside destinations, with a string of villas and hotels built in extravagant Viennese Secessionist style. Illustrious visitors included royalty and artists: Emperor Franz Josef, Wilhelm II of Germany and Prussia, Ferdinand I of Bulgaria, Carol I of Romania, Oscar II of Sweden, and the Italian opera composer Giacomo Puccini, the Irish novelist James Joyce, the Russian novelist Anton Chekhov and the American dancer Isadora Duncan.

Sights

Lungomare ⓘ *Šetalište Franza Josefa*, a 12-km coastal footpath, lined with century-old oaks and cypress trees, runs from **Volosko** to Lovran, passing through the seaside towns of Opatija, Ičići and Ika en route. Construction began in 1885, coinciding with the opening of Opatija's first hotels. It makes a lovely walk, with plenty of places to stop for a drink or a snack on the way.

Villa Angiolina ⓘ *Park Prvi Maj, between Šetalište Maršala Tita and the seafront, Tue-Sun from sunrise to sunset, free*, is still standing and in excellent condition, although at present its future as a tourist attraction is uncertain. The grounds were landscaped by the Viennese architect Carl Schubert at the end of the 19th century, and planted with exotic trees and shrubs, grown from seeds brought home from East Asia, India, Australia and North and South America by local sailors. The **Botanički Vrt** (Botanical Garden) centres on colourful flowerbeds and borders laid out with geometric precision, backed by fragrant camellias and magnolia trees, and dense clusters of bamboo grasses and palms.

There aren't real beaches in Opatija, though the concrete **bathing areas** along the seafront allow you to dip in and out of the sea. However, there are some pleasant pebble beaches south of Opatija at **Medveja** (10 km) and **Moščenićka Draga** (16 km) (see page 145).

Lovran

›› *pp147-151. Colour map 1, C2.*

→ *Phone code: 051. Population: 3241. 21 km from Rijeka and 8 km from Opatija.*

Lovran is the oldest settlement on the eastern slope of the surging rocky mass of Mount Uka (1396 m). Many people prefer it to Opatija, and indeed it is more authentic, with a medieval centre, a busy little harbour and a number of unpretentious fish restaurants. On the edge of town, set amid lush gardens overlooking the seafront promenade, stand a row of elegant late 19th-century villas, several of which have been converted into luxury holiday apartments. There's a town **tourist office** ⓘ *Šetalište Maršala Tita 63, T051-291740, www.tz-lovran.hr.*

Background

Lovran takes its names from sweet bay (*lovor* in Croatian), an aromatic shrub that grows in abundance here. The old town, which used to be walled, is made up of narrow, winding cobbled streets and 15th- and 16th-century cottages, many bearing the year they were built engraved in stone above the doorway.

During the late 19th century, Opatija's success as a seaside resort was extended along the coast with the building of the 8-km seaside promenade to Lovran. In no time at all, wealthy businessmen began constructing summer residences in Lovran, in the then fashionable Viennese Secessionist style. Tourism began developing around the same time, and escalated with the opening of the Hotel Bristol in 1917. Today Lovran offers some of the most luxurious accommodation in Croatia.

The Lovran hinterland is noted for its cherry orchards and chestnut trees, and the town organizes a number of annual gastro festivals (see Festivals and events, page 149).

On the main square in the old town, **Crkva Sv Juraj** (Church of St George) is dedicated to the Lovran's patron saint. It dates back to the 12th century, though the Renaissance façade was added in the 15th century. The ochre-coloured bell tower was originally free standing, but was joined to the church when a baroque chapel was constructed between the two elements during the 17th century.

Opposite the Church of St George, the doorway of the medieval **Gradska Vijecnica** (Town Hall) is topped by a 19th-century coloured wooden relief of St George spearing the Dragon. A few doors down, the entrance of another building is mounted with the much-photographed Mustakon – a bizarre, grotesque, coloured wooden relief of a bearded man, intended to frighten away bad luck and evil forces.

Around Lovran

Lovran is at the foot of Mount Učka. From town, 12 marked paths lead up to the highest point, **Vojak** (1396 m), where there's a stone tower from 1911 offering panoramic views over the Kvarner Bay. The lower slopes are covered with Mediterranean vegetation, which gives way to pines and mixed deciduous trees as you ascend, degenerating to spindly beech trees on the upper levels. There are plans to build a funicular cable car up to the summit, but nothing has materialized as yet. Lovran Tourist Office (see above) can supply a good map of the hiking paths.

Just a 15-minute walk along the coastal path from Lovran, **Ika** is an unspoilt fishing village built around a small cove with a pebble beach. It's a great place to stop for a drink or a snack if you're hiking from Lovran to Opatija.

The best place for bathing is at **Medveja**, 2 km south of Lovran, where a 1-km pebble beach stretches round a pleasant bay. **Mošćenice**, 8 km south of Lovran, is a small medieval fortified town built on a cliff above the sea, offering marvellous views over the Kvarner Bay. From here, a pleasant 2-km footpath leads down to **Mošćenička Draga**, with one of the region's finest bathing areas, a 2-km curving stretch of pebble beach, very popular with families. There's a town **tourist office** ⓘ *Aleja Slatina, Mošćenička Draga, T0517-39166, www.tz-moscenicka.hr.* Through summer a regular shuttle boat service runs three times daily from Opatija to Mošćenička Draga, stopping at Lovran and Medveja en route.

The coast south of Rijeka » *pp147-151. Colour map 1, C3.*

Before reaching Senj, the first place of any real cultural interest driving southeast of Rijeka on the coastal road for Dalmatia, you pass through the rather run-down seaside resorts of **Crikvenica** (37 km) and **Novi Vinodolski** (46 km). Both towns became popular vacation centres in the late 19th century under Austro-Hungary but today they offer little more than concrete bathing areas and large modern hotels catering for groups on cheap package holidays.

Uskoks

During the 16th century, as the Ottoman Empire expanded westwards, groups of Slavs abandoned the eastern inland areas and fled towards the coast. One particular group, which settled in Klis (Central Dalmatia) in 1532, became known as the Uskoks (a name probably derived from *uskočiti* meaning 'to jump into' in Croatian). They defended Klis fortress for five years until it too fell to the Turks, then migrated north along the coast, finally settling in Senj in 1537.

The Hapsburgs, seeing them as hardened fighters ready to confront further Turkish expansion, allowed them to remain in the area as irregular soldiers, but offered them very limited financial support. Forced partly by poverty and partly by a latent loathing of the Turks, the Uskoks turned to piracy, carrying out grizzly raids on Ottoman ships. Despite being men of no seafaring experience, they designed shallow galleys, with 10 oarsmen each side, which were notoriously speedy and particularly hard to catch.

The Austrians turned a blind eye to their antics, delighted to have an extra hand on their side, and even profited from them, allowing them to sell their captured goods in the international market in Trieste. The church also gave the gruesome pirates its blessing, celebrating the Uskoks as Catholic freedom fighters and taking a one-tenth cut of their loot, which was paid to the Franciscan and Dominican monasteries in Senj.

However, the Uskoks became embroiled in the ongoing struggle between the three great powers when they began raiding Venetian galleys on the pretext that they had Turkish merchandise aboard. By this time the Uskok's fame had spread far and wide, and many foreign villains had joined their forces; when a party of Uskoks were hanged in Venice, nine of them were English, and one a member of a British noble family. The saga culminated with the Uskok War, fought between Venice and Austria from 1615 to 1617. The Uskok's boats were consequently burnt, and they were forced to resettle inland, notably in the Žumberak hills between Karlovac and Zagreb.

Ins and outs

Senj is located at an important road junction, so you will pass through it if travelling from Rijeka to Plitvice National Park, or from Zagreb to the island of Rab. There's a town **tourist office** ⓘ *Stara Cesta 2, T053-881068, www.tz-senj.hr.* » *See Transport, page 150, for further details.*

Senj → *Phone code: 053. Colour map 1, C3. Population: 5531. 63 km southeast of Rijeka.*

Senj, built around a cove, is watched over by a hilltop castle once occupied by Uskok pirates (see box, page 146) and today has a museum dedicated to them. Something of a backwater until the 16th century, the town became notorious as the headquarters of the fearsome Uskoks, who instated themselves as its military guardians from 1527 to 1617. However, the Uskoks' excessive exploits on the high seas eventually saw them deported inland, and Senj was absorbed into the *Vojska Krajina* (Military Border), a buffer zone between Ottoman territories to the southeast and Hapsburg lands to the north, set up by the Austrians. When the inland area of Lika was liberated from the Turks in 1689, Senj developed into a small but busy port town. South from here, between the mainland coast and the island of Rab, is the island of **Goli Otok**, which was turned into an infamous political prison at the end of the Second World War.

Located on a hilltop 82 m above town, the **Nehaj Castle** (from *nehaj* meaning 'fear not') ⓘ *T053-885277, Jul-Aug daily 1000-2100, May-Jun and Sep-Oct daily*

1000-1800, Nov-Apr by appointment, 15Kn, was built in 1558 by Captain Ivan Lenović of Senj, in order to defend the town against the Turks. Based on a square ground plan, this three-storey structure afforded views over the Kvarner Bay and the surrounding mountains, and was defended by 11 cannons. The Uskoks set up their main base in the castle and after they were relocated inland in 1617 the Austrian navy was installed here. It was restored in 1977 and now houses an enlightening Uskok Museum, displaying a well-presented collection of costumes and weaponry, with texts in both Croatian and English.

Sleeping

Rijeka *p138, map p138*
Very few tourists stay overnight in Rijeka usually using the seaside resort town of Opatija, 15 km away, as a base for exploring the city.

A Hotel Bonavia, Dolac 4, 1 block back from the Korzo, T051-357100, www.bonavia.hr. This smart luxury hotel is in the city centre, a 10-min walk from the ferry port. The high-rise exterior conceals 114 plush rooms and 7 even plusher suites, a restaurant, jazz bar and fitness centre. There's even a hotel limousine and chauffeur service.

E Hotel Continental, Šetalište Andrije Kačića-Miošića 1, across the river from the centre, just south of Titov Trg, T051-372008, www.jadran-hoteli.hr. Built in 1888, the **Continental** is at the foot of the pilgrimage path up to Trsat. The 38 rooms and 4 suites are extremely basic. There's a restaurant and café, and a pleasant summer terrace shaded by chestnut trees.

E Neboder, Strossmayerova 1, T051-373538, www.jadran-hoteli.hr. A modern, high-rise building offering 54 rooms and a restaurant, in Sušak, just across the river from the centre of Rijeka.

F Rijeka Youth Hostel, Šetalište XIII divizije 23, T051-406420, www.hfhs.hr. Just a 15-min walk from the centre, this brand new hostel occupies a refurbished 19th-century villa and offers 61 beds, a restaurant, TV room and internet. It opened in Feb 2006.

Risnjak National Park *p143*

E Hotel Risnjak, Lujzinska 36, Delnice, T051-508160, www.hotel-risnjak.hr. On the go since the 1930s, this hotel reopened in 2004 after total renovation. There are 20 rooms, a restaurant and café, plus a small Wellness Centre. They offer 3-day and 7-day adventure packages including hiking, rafting and caving.

E Motel Lovački Dom, Japelniski vrh 2, Delnice, T051-812440. The large restaurant here specializes in game, notably venison. Has 8 guest rooms upstairs. Open all year.

E Motel Risnjak, Bijela Vodica 48, Crni Lug, T051-836133, F051-836116. Adjoining the national park office, this friendly 9-room hotel stays open all year and has an excellent restaurant serving local specialities such as venison stew and *škripavac* cheese.

Opatija *p143*
There are no budget hotels in Opatija, but the tourist office can help you find private accommodation.

B Grand Hotel Kvarner-Amalia, Park 1 Maja 4, T051-271233, www.liburnia.hr. Next to the botanical garden and **Villa Angiolina**, this ochre-coloured neoclassical building first opened its doors to guests in 1884. There's a lovely café terrace beside the gardens overlooking the sea. Facilities include indoor and outdoor pools filled with seawater, sauna and massage. 58 rooms and suites.

D Villa Ariston, Maršala Tita 179, T051-271 379, www.villa-ariston.net. This late 19th-century villa, set in a lovely garden running down to the seafront promenade, attained its present appearance during the 1920s when it was renovated by Carl Seidl. Today it has 8 luxury guest rooms and 2 suites, each with parquet flooring and antique furniture. There's an excellent restaurant on the ground floor, and many non-residents come here to eat.

E Belvedere, I Kaline 7, T051-271044, www.liburnia.hr. Looking out over the seaside promenade a couple of kilometres from the town centre, the **Belvedere** offers cheap accommodation with 95 rooms, a small indoor pool filled with heated sea-water, a restaurant, beauty treatments and massage.

Lovran *p144*

L **Villa Astra Hotel**, Viktora Cara Emina 11, T051-294400, www.lovranske-vile.com. This restored Venitian-Gothic villa, set in a garden with palms, has been turned into a boutique hotel with 6 guest rooms, an up-market restaurant, an outdoor pool, sauna, massage and a Wellness Centre.

AL **Villa Eugenia Hotel**, Maršala Tita 34, T051-294800, www.villa-eugenia.com. Dating from 1910, this Secessionist villa is set in a garden with views of the sea. It has 15 rooms, a café, sauna and jacuzzi, and a conference room.

A **Lovranske Vile**, Poljanska 27, Ičići, T051-704276, www.lovranske-vile.com. Beautifully furnished apartments in 2 Secessionist villas, **Villa Adela** and **Villa San Giovanni**. Through summer, rentals run on a weekly basis and it is essential to book well in advance. During the rest of the year it is possible to rent for shorter stays.

C **Hotel Bristol**, Šetalište Maršala Tita 27, T051-291022, www.liburnia.hr. This 6-storey hotel was built in 1917. It's on the seafront and is backed by parkland. There are 101 rooms, most with a sea view and balcony, a restaurant, a terrace and a private beach.

C **Hotel Lovran**, Šetalište Maršala Tita 19/2, T051-291222, www.hotel-lovran.hr. 2 early 20th-century villas, joined by a new reception area and café. There are 50 rooms and 3 suites, and it's set in a lush park overlooking the sea, close to the centre.

Around Lovran *p145*

D **Ika Hotel**, Primorska 16, Ika, T051-291777, www.hotel-ika.hr. Between Opatija and Lovran, on the seaside promenade, this small, family-run hotel has 17 rooms and a restaurant with a large terrace looking over the water, plus a small beach out front.

Eating

Rijeka *p138, map p138*

ΨΨΨ-ΨΨ **Feral**, M Gupca 6, T051-212274. Highly regarded fish restaurant up a side road close to the theatre. House specialities are *crni rižot* (black risotto prepared with cuttlefish ink) and *fuži sa šparogama i škampima* (pasta with asparagus and shrimps).

ΨΨΨ-ΨΨ **Zlatna Školjka**, Kružna 12a, in a side street off the Korzo, T051-213782. Serves creative seafood dishes in a sedate pastel-coloured dining room with exposed stone and woodwork and a curious combination of modern furniture and antiques. Closed on Sun.

ΨΨ **Korkyra**, Slogin Kula 5, behind **Hotel Bonavia**, T051-339528. The interior of this *konoba* is hung with fishing nets decorated with shells. There's a wide choice of meat and fish dishes, and the house speciality is *njoki od krumpira* (gnocchi).

ΨΨ **Trsatika**, J Rakovca 33, Trsat, T051-217 455. High up on Trsat, below the pilgrimage church, this popular restaurant has a large summer terrace offering fantastic views over Rijeka. Favourite dishes include *gulaš* (goulash) and *škampi na buzaru* (shrimps prepared with onion and tomato). Pizza makes a cheap option. Closed Wed.

ΨΨ-Ψ **Pod Voltun**, Pod voltun 15, T051-330806. This informal *konoba* is popular with locals for *merenda* (early lunch) and serves hearty home cooking with favourites including *brudet* (fish stew) and *bakalar* (salted cod).

Ψ **Bracera**, Kružna 12, T051-322498. Rijeka's favourite pizzeria is opposite the more upmarket fish restaurant, **Zlatna Školjka**.

Ψ **Dupin Seafood**, Riva 6, T051-333070. In a side street between the ferry port and the Korzo, **Dupin** cooks up cheap and tasty take-away seafood snacks.

Cafés

The city's most popular cafés are concentrated along the Korso.

Hemingway, Korzo 28 (part of the chain). Built in 1819, it has a ground floor café serving coffee and cocktails, plus a beautifully frescoed lounge-bar upstairs.

Opium Budha Bar, Riva 12a, T051-336397. On the seafront close to the ferry port, this mildly pretentious but very popular bar has a seductive lounge with outdoor tables over-looking the water. Open till late at weekends.

Trsat. There's a lovely summer café inside the castle complex offering fantastic views over the Kvarner Bay. Open 1 Apr-30 Oct.

Opatija *p143*

The best restaurants are mostly 4 km along the coast in **Volosko**, a small town built around a pretty fishing harbour, walkable along the coastal promenade. The eateries of Opatija are made up mostly of large hotels offering ½- or full-board.

ƟƟƟ Bevanda, Zert 8, Opatija, T051-718353. This long-standing favourite, renowned for excellent seafood, recently relocated from Volosko to Opatija. Expect quality fresh fish such as *orada* (gilt-head bream), *zubatac* (dentrix) and *brancin* (bass). Those who prefer meat could opt for beef stroganoff.
ƟƟƟ Le Mandrać, Obala F Supila 10, Volosko, T051-701357, www.lemandrac.com. Opened in 2004 and already regarded as one of Croatia's best restaurants, **Le Madrač** is housed in a minimalist glass conservatory with ambient music, candles and a sea view. There's a special 'slow food' menu consisting of 9 courses including delicacies such as foie gras, truffles and oysters.
ƟƟƟ-ƟƟ Plavi Podrum, Supilova Obala 4, Volosko, T051-701223. This classic seafood restaurant has a formal dining room and outdoor tables. It's noted for excellent fresh fish and an outstanding wine list.

Lovran *p144*
ƟƟƟ Najade, Šetalište Maršala Tita 69, T051-291866. This highly regarded restaurant has long been popular with rich Croatians, who come here to eat fresh fish on a terrace overlooking the sea. It's close to the harbour, and the owner reputedly gets first choice of the night's catch when the fishermen come in.
ƟƟƟ-ƟƟ Kvarner, Šetalište Maršala Tita 65, T051-291118. Close to the tourist office, Kvarner is easily recognized by its ample terrace with blue awnings overlooking the sea. The house speciality is *punjene lignje* (stuffed squid), but there's also a reasonable choice of meat dishes.
ƟƟ-Ɵ Konoba Lovranska Draga, Cesta za Lovranska Draga 34, T051-292720. Located on the road to Lovranska Draga, on the hill 2 km above Lovran, this friendly *konoba* serves up hearty home-made dishes such as *kobasica* (sausages), *fuži* (a local type of pasta), *njoki* (gnocchi) and *divljac* (game).

Around Lovran *p145*
ƟƟ Dopolavoro, Učka 6, Ičići, T051-299641. On the old road up Mount Učka, at an altitude of 1000 m, Dopolavoro's front terrace affords great views down onto Kvarner Bay. Come here for hearty local meat dishes such as venison, wild boar and lamb, as well as seasonal specialities including wild mushrooms, asparagus and truffles.

The coast south of Rijeka *p145*
E Garni Hotel Art, Obala kralja Zvonimira 15, T053-884377, www.coning-turizam.hr. Located on the main coastal highway, in the centre of Senj, the **Garni** offers 24 basic rooms with telephone and satellite TV.

Bars and clubs

Rijeka *p138, map p138*
Palach, Kružna 6, T051-215063. In a side street off the Korzo, **Palach** has been hosting live concerts for over 20 years and, as the birthplace of many new bands, has built up a cult following. It's named after Jan Palach, the Czech philosophy student who burnt himself to death in Prague in 1968 out of protest against Soviet occupation. Stays open until late and there's also an internet centre.

Opatija *p143*
Hemingway, Zert 2. One of a new chain of trendy cocktail bars, with tables looking out over the sea. They stock select cigars at the bar.

Entertainment

Rijeka *p138, map p138*
Cinema
Croatia, Krešimirova 2, T051-335219; and **Teatro Fenice**, Dolac 13, T051-335225.

Theatre and classical music
Hrvatsko Narodno Kazalište Ivana Zajca (Croatian National Theatre Ivan Zajc), Verdijeve bb, T051-355900, www.hnk-zajc.hr. Stages ballet and opera, and dramas in both Croatian and Italian. The Symphony Orchestra of the Rijeka Philharmonic perform here, with a particular emphasis on 20th-century music.

Festivals and events

Rijeka *p138, map p138*
Feb-Mar Riječki Karneval (Rijeka Carnival), www.ri-karneval.com.hr. Rijeka stages Croatia's largest Carnival celebrations. The main event is the **International Carnival Parade**, held the Sun before **Shrove Tue** and attracting over 100,000 spectators and several thousand participants in costumes and masks, notably the bizarre Zvončari, see also page 142.

Opatija *p143*
May-Aug Opatija Summer Stage. Cultural events staged in the open-air theatre.
Jul Opatija Week Galijola. A 4-day international sailing regatta.

Lovran *p144*
Feb-Mar Karneval (Carnival). The week leading up to Shrove Tue sees riotous celebrations in Lovran.

There are 3 annual gastronomic festivals, during which the town's restaurants prepare dishes based on seasonal delicacies:
Apr Dani Šparoga (Asparagus Festival).
Jun Dani Trešanja (Cherry Festival).
Late Sep to early Oct Marunada (Chestnut Festival).

Shopping

Rijeka *p138, map p138*
A popular (though rather gimmicky) souvenir from Rijeka is *morčići* gold jewellery – earrings, pendants and brooches featuring the head of a dark man swathed in a white turban. Apparently they date back to the 16th century, but first became fashionable in 1845 after the Austrian Empress Maria-Anna, wife of Ferdinand I, ordered a pair of *morčići* earrings. Since 1991 they have been adopted as a symbol of Rijeka. They are available from **Mala Galerija**, Užarska 25, T051-335403.

Activities and tours

Rijeka *p138, map p138*
Tour operators
Generalturist, Trg brigade Hrvatske vojske 8a, T051-214590, www.generalturist.com. One of the largest Croatian travel agencies, **Generalturist** specializes in tailor-made trips both with and without guides, pilgrimage tours and yacht charters.

Opatija *p143*
Sailing
ACI Marina, between Opatija and Ičići, T051-704004. Has 300 berths, open all year. The **ACI** headquarters are at Maršala Tita 151, T051-271288, www.aci-club.hr.
Katarina Line, T051-603400, www.katarina-line.hr, 1-week cruises aboard vintage sailing ships, departing from Opatija each Sat, May-Oct. Organize accommodation and excursions.

Tour operators
Da Riva, Maršala Tita 170, T051-272990, www.da-riva.hr. Minibus excursions to Risnjak National Park for groups of 6-8 people, with the possibility of a pick-up point in Rijeka.

Transport

Rijeka *p138, map p138*
Air
Through summer, there are regular flights to and from London Heathrow. Through winter there are no flights, but **Croatia Airlines** operate a daily bus connecting Rijeka to Zagreb airport. Rijeka airport, T051-842132, www.rijeka-airport.hr.

Airline offices Croatia Airlines, Jelačićev trg 5, T051-330207.

Bus
For information about buses to and from Rijeka, T060-302010. Left luggage 0530-1030, 10Kn per piece per day.

Internal services include 26 buses daily to **Zagreb** (3 hrs); 17 to **Pula** in Istria (2½ hrs); 11 to **Zadar** in North Dalmatia (4½ hrs); 12 to **Split** in Central Dalmatia (8 hrs) and 5 to **Dubrovnik** in South Dalmatia (12 hrs). Also regular international bus lines to **Trieste** (Italy), **Ljubljana** (Slovenia), **Berlin** (Germany) and **Sarajevo** (Bosnia and Herzegovina).

Car
Budget, Trg Republike Hrvatske 8a, T051-214742, www.budget.hr; **Dollar & Thrifty**, Riva 22, T051-325900, www.subrosa.hr; **Hertz**, Riva 6, T051-311098, www.hertz.hr.

Ferry
Jadrolinija, T051-211444, run a twice-weekly overnight coastal service between Rijeka and **Dubrovnik** in South Dalmatia, stopping at **Split**, **Stari Grad** (island of Hvar), **Korčula** and **Sobra** (island of Mljet) en route. The same company run daily catamaran services to **Rab Town** (island of Rab) and Novalja (island of Pag), and to Cres Town (island of Cres), Unije, Susak and Mali Lošinj (island of Lošinj) .

Taxi
There are taxi ranks at both the train station, T051-332893, and bus station, T051-335138.

Train
Rijeka train station, T051-213333. Left luggage 0900-2100, 10Kn per piece per day.

Internal services include 5 trains daily to **Zagreb** (3½ hrs) and 1 train to **Osijek** (7½ hrs). Daily international trains run direct to **Budapest** (Hungary) and **Ljubljana** (Slovenia).

Risnjak National Park *p143*
The best way to reach Risnjak is by car, as public transport is limited.

There are several **buses** and **trains** daily to **Delnice** (50 mins), and from here it's just 12 km to **Crni Lug**, a route covered twice daily by a school bus during term time (call the national park administration building). Alternatively, contact the Opatija- based agency, **Da Riva**, Maršala Tita 170, T051-272 990, www.da-riva. hr, as they can organize minibus excursions to the national park.

Opatija *p143*
Bus
Opatija is linked to **Rijeka** by local bus No 32 which runs every 20 mins takes 30 mins. There is also a double decker tourist bus, with a guide, running several times daily between Opatija and Rijeka.

Intercity buses travelling between **Rijeka** and **Pula** also stop here taking 2 hrs to get from Pula to Opatija.

Lovran *p144*
Bus
Hourly buses running between Rijeka and Pula pass through Lovran.

Senj *p146*
Bus
The bus station is at Ulica Kralja Zvonimira 8, T053-881235. All buses running along the coast south from **Rijeka** to **Dalmatia** stop at Senj (1½ hrs).

Directory

Rijeka *p138, map p138*
Consulates Austria, Stipana Konzula Istranina 2, T051-338554. **Denmark**, Splitska 2, T051-212522. **Hungary**, Riva Boduli 1/IV, T051-213494. **Italy**, Riva 16, T051-355200. **Netherlands**, Veslarska 1b, T051-213126. **Norway**, Žrtava fašizma 2/II, T051-335827. **Sweden**, Riva 16, T051-212287. **Serbia** , Erazma Barčića 9, T051-337420/1. **Emergencies** Ambulance: 94; **Fire**: 93; **Police**: 92. **Internet** Internet Club Cont, Šetalište A. Kačića Miošića 1, T051-371630, www.internet-cont.com; **Jan, MMC Palach**, Kružna 6, T051-215063, www.mmc.hr (see Bars and clubs). **Medical services** Rijeka **Hospital**, Krešimirova 42, beyond the train station, T051-658111 (24-hr casualty). **Pharmacies**: are marked by a glowing green cross. **Ljekarna Centar**, Jadranski Trg 1 (T051-213101) and Ljekarna Korzo, Korzo 22 (T051-211036) are open 24 hrs. **Post offices** The main post office is at Korzo 13, and is open Mon-Sat 0700-2100, Sun 0700-1400. **Telephones** If you prefer to telephone from a peaceful phone booth, rather than calling on the street, go to one of the post offices. Otherwise, you'll find phone kiosks in town.

Island of Krk (Veglia)

→ *Phone code: 051. Colour map 1, C3. Population: 16,402.*

Linked to the mainland by a 1430-m bridge, and home to Rijeka Airport, Krk is one of the most accessible of all the Croatian islands. It also happens to be the largest (38 km long and 20 km wide) and one of the most populous. While the northwest part of the island is low lying, fertile and fairly developed, the southeast part is mountainous and in places quite barren. It's certainly not the most beautiful island on the Adriatic, but its accessibility and wealth of tourist facilities make it very popular. The chief centre is Krk Town, which dates back to Roman times with a 12th-century seafront castle and a cathedral. The best beaches are found in Baška, Malinska and Omišalj, though unfortunately the latter two are spoilt by the nearby petrochemical industry. Punat, with its vast marina, is a haven for yachters, while Vrbnik is known for its excellent white wine, Vrbnička Žlahtina. ▸▸ *For Sleeping, Eating and other listings, see pages 154-157.*

Ins and outs

Getting there Rijeka Airport is at Omišalj, close to the northern tip of the island of Krk. The airport works in summer only, when **Croatia Airlines** run regular flights to and from Zagreb and London Heathrow. If you're thinking of driving to Krk, remember that there's a 30Kn toll for crossing the bridge, and that in winter, when the *bura* (northeast wind) is exceptionally strong, it is occasionally closed. Through summer there are 12 buses daily from Rijeka to Baška on Krk, stopping at Krk Town and Punat en route. The service is slightly reduced in winter. The year through, regular ferries operate between Valbiska on the southeast coast of Krk and Merag on the island of Cres taking about 30 minutes. » *See Transport, page 156, for further details.*

Getting around The main road runs the length of the island from the bridge in the north down to Baška in the southeast. Towns on this road – Omišalj, Njivice, Krk Town and Punat – are connected by regular local buses. Towns off the main road are served by less frequent buses.

Tourist information

Krk Island has a general **tourist information centre** ⓘ *Trg Sv Kvirana 1, T051-221359, www.krk.hr, open Apr-Oct*, in Krk Town.

Background

First settled by the Illyrian tribe of the Liburni, the island was later taken by the Romans, who established the municipality of *Curicum* on the site of present-day Krk Town. During the 12th century the Frankopan family came on the scene. Originally from Vrbnik, they built a castle in Krk Town and gradually expanded their large hereditary estates to the mainland. At the height of their power they possessed territory equal to half of today's Croatia, which they defended boldly against Venice and the Turks. Krk was the last Croatian island to fall to Venice, when Count Ivan Frankopan was deceived and taken prisoner in 1480.

Krk was connected to the mainland in 1980 with the opening of a monumental bridge, incorporating two reinforced concrete arches and carrying 20 pipelines for water and oil.

Krk Town → *Phone code: 051. Colour map 1, C3. Population: 3364. 25 km south of Krk Bridge.*

Krk Town is, and always has been, the island's economic and administrative centre While the old town is a compact cluster of terracotta-roofed houses built close up to the seafront, development has extended the settlement well beyond its former walls, not least to provide modern hotels for mass tourism. Krk Town has a **tourist office** ⓘ *Vela placa 1/1, T051-222414, www.tz-krk.hr.*

Few traces remain of the Roman municipality of *Curicum* which once stood here, though it was certainly a place of some importance, complete with a thermal baths decorated with mosaics, fragments of which can be see in a side chapel in the **Katedrala Uznesenja** (Cathedral of Our Lady of the Assumption) ⓘ *Trg Sv Kvirina, daily 1000-1300, 1700-1900*. Taking on its present form during the 12th century, the cathedral was built on the site of an early Christian basilica, which grew up over the first-century baths. Ancient stone columns, topped with finely carved capitals, were incorporated into the structure, and a Gothic chapel dedicated to the Frankopans was added in the 15th century.

Adjoining the cathedral stands the **Crkva Sv Kvirina** (Church of St Quirinus) ⓘ *Trg Sv Kvirina, daily 1000-1300, 1700-1900*, a 12th-century Romanesque church built of white stone and dedicated to the town's patron saint. It's actually split into two levels, with a lower crypt area where prisoners sentenced to death attended a final mass before execution. The adjoining 18th-century bell tower really belongs to the cathedral, but was built here due to lack of space on the square.

The Church of St Quirinus houses the **Riznica** (Treasury) ⓘ *T051-221341, summer Mon-Sat 1000-1300, 15Kn*, containing works of religious art including a stunning silver-plated altarpiece depicting *Virgin Mary in Glory* (1477) made in Venice as a gift for the cathedral, upon the request of Ivan Frankopan.

On the seafront, behind the cathedral, stands the **Frankopanski Kaštel** (Frankopan Castle) ⓘ *Kamplin Trg, open only for cultural events during the summer festival*, a sturdy, square structure with corner towers, from 1191. Besides building the castle, this powerful local family was responsible for the construction of the 12th-century town walls, part of which can still be seen today.

There are no real beaches here, concrete **bathing areas** substituting the long stretches of unspoilt shoreline you might be dreaming of, but will only find in **Baška**, on the southeast tip of the island.

Punat and the Islet of Košljun → *Phone code: 051. Colour map 1, C3.*

On the southwest coast, Punat lies in a wide, sheltered bay called Puntarska Draga, home to the largest marina on the Adriatic. People holidaying on the island flock to Punat on day trips to visit the nearby **Islet of Košljun** with its 15th-century Franciscan Monastery. Krk's most beautiful (and most isolated) beach, **Stara Baška**, is just 8 km southeast of Punta: it is not served by public transport, so you need a car or bike to get there. There's a Punat **tourist office** ⓘ *Obala 72, T051-854860, www.tzpunat.hr.*

Planted with dense woodland, this islet was first settled by Benedictine monks in the 11th century. The Franciscans took their place in the 15th century, building the

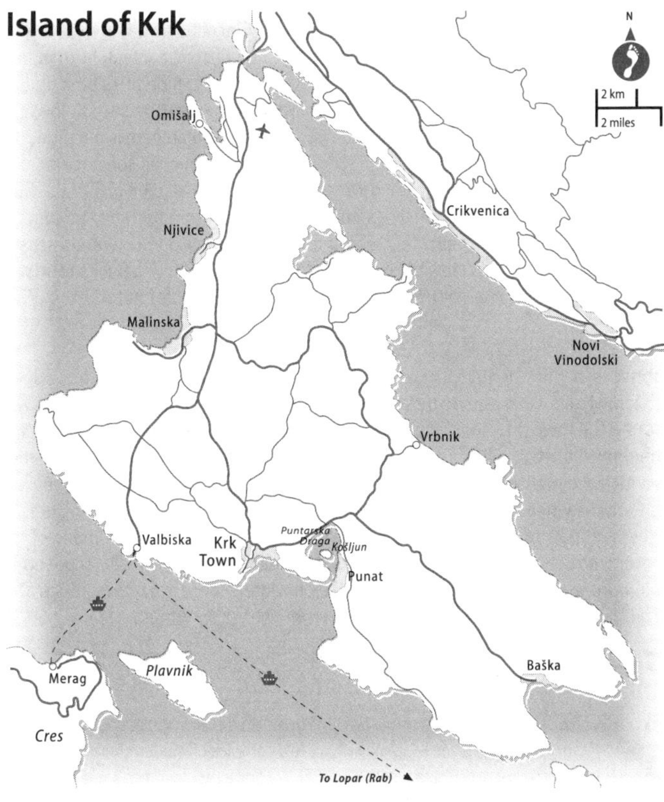

Franjevački Samostan (Franciscan Monastery) ⓘ *T051-854017, Mon-Sat 0830-1200, 1500-1700, Sun 1030-1200, 20Kn.* Inside, a museum display includes paintings, model ships, and a collection of folk costumes, with a set of ladies' scarves from the island of Krk, each one discreetly indicating which village the wearer came from and whether she was married, unmarried or widowed.

Košljun was home to one of the first European financial institutions, the so-called **Košljunska Posujilnica** (Košljun Lending House), which was set up to protect the poor from usurers, and functioned between the 17th and 19th centuries. During the **Krk Summer Festival** (mid-July to late August), classical music concerts are held here in a lovely cloistered courtyard.

Baška → *Phone code: 051. Colour map 1, C3. Population: 901. 19 km southeast of Krk Town and 43 km from Krk Bridge.*

Thanks to its spectacular beach, Baška is the oldest and best-known resort on the island. What was once a compact little fishing village now straggles almost 3 km along the coast, due to the restaurants, apartment blocks and the vast **Hotel Corinthia** complex, which have sprung up over the last 30 years. Behind town is a fertile plain of cultivated fields, and behind that a band of rugged limestone hills.

On the cultural front, the Romanesque **Crkva Sv Lucije** (Church of St Lucy) ⓘ *Jul-Aug daily 0900-1100, 1700-2200, Sep-Jun daily 1600-2000*, is 2 km inland in the tiny village of Jurandvor. It was here that the renowned **Bašćanska Ploča** (Baška Tablet) was discovered, set in the church floor, in 1851. This white limestone slab, 2 m wide and 1 m high, was engraved with 13 lines (about 100 words) in Glagolitic characters (see page 127) some time in the late 11th century. It records, in Old Slavonic language, the donation of land (probably the site the church is built on) from the early Croatian King, Zvonimir, to the local parish. Although it is not the oldest surviving Glagolitic text, it is regarded as the most important due to its graphic style, language and historic content. In 1934, despite strong resistance from the people of Jurandvor, who tried to hide the slab in the village school, the original was transferred to Zagreb, where it can now be seen in the Croatian Academy of Arts and Sciences. What you will see in the church here is a replica.

Directly in front of town, the 2-km stretch of pebble beach is spectacular and one of Croatia's loveliest beaches. The downside is that it can also be one of the busiest, with the tourist office ambitiously estimating space for 5000 bathers at a time. If you prefer something more peaceful, take a taxi boat to any one of the succession of small, secluded bays (accessible only from the sea) west of town. Baška **tourist office** ⓘ *Kralja Zvonimira 114, T051-856544*, can provide further information.

Vrbnik → *Phone code: 051. Colour map 1, C3. Population: 944. 37 km from Krk Bridge.*

Vrbnik is a tiny, tightly packed medieval settlement standing on the edge of a limestone cliff, 48 m above the sea. Off the beaten track, it is worth going for a wander around the town and specifically for the wine cellars. Below the town there's a small sheltered harbour, while the plain behind town is planted with the vineyards that produce the highly esteemed *Vrbnička Žlahtina*, a dry white wine which you should certainly try while here. First mentioned in 1100, Vrbnik was fortified during the Middle Ages, and part of the town walls can still be seen today, hugging a maze of narrow winding streets and old stone buildings. Northeast facing, it is fully exposed to the cold *bura* wind and can be extremely gusty in winter. There is a **tourist office** ⓘ *Placa Vrbičkog statuta 4, T/F051-857479, www.vrbnik.net/tz*, in Vrbnik.

Sleeping

Krk Town *p152*

AL Kado Resort and Spa, Brzac 85, Malinska, T051-862084, www.apartmani-krk.net. In Brzac on the west coast, south of Malinska, this complex of modern buildings has 13 apartments sleeping 2-4 people, perfect for families with young children. The interiors are all of stone, wood and terracotta, with subtle lighting and bedrooms with giant flowers painted on the walls behind the beds. Facilities include a *konoba*, a large outdoor pool, a children's pool, massage and yoga.

C Hotel Bor, Šetalište Dražica 5, T/F051-220200, www.hotelbor.hr. A 5-min walk along the seafront from the old town, this hotel dates back to 1920 and was renovated in 2002. There are 18 double rooms, 4 suites, and a restaurant.

C Hotel Marina, Obala hrvatske mornarice 6, T051-655766, www.hotelikrk.hr. This old white building is close to the cathedral, overlooking the seafront. There are 18 simple but comfortable guest rooms, several with balconies, and a café and restaurant with tables outside in summer. Pets welcome.

D Pansion Maritim, Braće Linardić 10, T051-221454, www.maritim-krk.com. Close to the old town and the beach, this modern building houses a friendly, family-run hotel. The 13 rooms are basic but spacious, with wooden floors and balconies. The ground floor restaurant serves Mediterranean cuisine on an arcaded terrace.

E Hotel Adria, Obala 40, Malinska, T051-859131, www.hotel-adria.com.hr. On the seafront, this hotel offers 37 basic but comfortable rooms. Rooms with a balcony and sea view are a little more expensive but worth it. Downstairs there's a pleasant restaurant terrace with views of the harbour.

F Youth hostel, OH Krk, Dinka Vitezića 32, T051-220212. This late 18th-century building once housed the island's first hotel. It reopened in 2001 as a 60-bed youth hostel with a restaurant. Open all year.

Punat and the Islet of Košljun *p153*

G Youth Hostel, Novi Put 8, T051-854037. Prices at this centrally located hostel depend on the room type. There are 90 beds and a restaurant. ½- and full-board are available. Open Jun-Sep.

Baška *p154*

B Hotel Zvonimir, T051-656810, www.hotelibaska.hr. With views of the promenade and beach, this hotel has 70 rooms and 15 suites, most with a balcony and sea view.

C Hotel Tamaris, Emila Geistlicha bb, T051-864200, www.baska-tamaris.com. Overlooking Baška's fine pebble beach, this hotel has 15 rooms and 15 apartments all simply but smartly furnished. The hotel restaurant serves Mediterranean cuisine on a large terrace.

Private accommodation

The following agencies can help you find private accommodation in Baška: **Šiloturist**, S Radića 26, T051-860171, www.siloturist.hr; **Splendido**, Kralja Zvonimira 148, T051-856 116, www.splendido.hr.

Vrbnik *p154*

E Hotel Argentum, Supec 68, T051-857370, www.hotel-argentum.com. This 10-room modern hotel is a short walk from the old town. It may not be very inspiring from the outside, but it has a good restaurant with a large terrace looking out to sea, and it makes an ideal base if you want to spend a couple of days here. Pets welcome.

Eating

Krk Town *p152*

¥¥ Konoba Šime, Antuna Mahnića 1, T051-220042. One block in from the Riva, on the left as you pass through Mala Vrata, this typical *konoba* is noted for good pasta dishes. Closed mid-Dec to mid-Jan.

¥¥-¥ Bracera, Kvarnerska 1, Malinska, T051-858700. This friendly eatery is run by an owner-chef who also catches the seafood on offer. Food is prepared over an open-fire in the old-fashioned dining room, which has a wooden beamed ceiling hung with fishing nets and old fishing tools, plus heavy wooden tables and benches.

Punat and the Islet of Košljun *p153*

¥¥ Marina, Puntica 9, T051-654380. Based in the marina with a view over the bay and the Islet of Košljun, this highly regarded restaurant serves up local specialities such as *ražnjić od morskih plodova* (seafood kebabs) and *janjeća jetrica i palenta* (lamb's liver with polenta). Closed 15 Jan-30 Jan.

Baška *p154*

¥¥¥-¥¥ Ribar, Palada bb, T051-856461. Just 20 m from the quay, this informal restaurant has a long-standing reputation for excellent seafood. If you've already had your fill of fish, try the *Baška Ploče*, a generous mixed-meat platter for 2. Open May-Oct.

¥¥-¥ **Cicibela**, Emila Geistlicha bb, T051-856013. This cosy restaurant is known for its discreet waiters and romantic evening atmosphere. There's a good selection of fish and seafood dishes, with pizza providing a cheaper option. Open Apr-Nov.

Vrbnik *p154*

¥¥¥-¥¥ **Nada**, Ulica Glavača 22, T051-857065, www.nada-vrbnik.hr. Close to the harbour, **Nada** doubles as a restaurant, where you can eat fresh fish and seafood on a wonderful terrace with views out to sea, and a *konoba* (wine cellar), where you can sample the excellent *Žlahtina Nada* along with nibbles such as *ovči sir* (sheep's cheese) and *pršut* (smoked ham). Reservations recommended. It's possible to buy bottles of wine and *rakija* in presentation boxes to take home. By prior agreement, you can also visit their main wine cellars (Zagrada 4, below the town walls) for a guided tour, a video presentation and wine tasting.

Bars and clubs

Krk Town *p152*

Jungle, Krk bb, T051-221503. Popular disco and cocktail bar in the centre of town. Open daily until 0500 in the high season.

Volsonis, Vela Placa 8, T051-880249. In the old town, in the basement of **Galerija Stanić**, this unusual cocktail bar is set amid Roman excavations, with exposed stonework and a sacrificial altar. Open daily from 1800, with live jazz on Tue evenings through summer.

Festivals and events

Krk Town *p152*

Mid-Jul to late Aug Summer Festival. Classical music, opera, ballet and drama in the cathedral and the Frankopan Castle in Krk Town, and in the Franciscan Monastery on the Islet of Košljun close to Punat.

Mid-Aug Volsonis Jazz Garden Festival. A 1-week open-air jazz festival held within the walls of the Frankopan Castle.

Punat and the Islet of Košljun *p153*

Late May Croatia Cup. A 4-day sailing regatta.

Mid-Jul to late Aug Summer Festival. See Krk Town, above.

Activities and tours

Krk Town *p152*

Diving

Dive Sport, Dunat bb, T051-867303, www.dive sport.de. Located in a bay between Krk Town and Punat.

Punat and the Islet of Košljun *p153*

Sailing

Marina Punat, Puntica 7, T051-654111, www.marina-punat.hr. 830 berths and a dry dock with space for 300 boats. Open all year.

The following charter companies are based here: **Daranji**, T01-3737160, www.daranji-sailing.hr; **Koro Charter**, T051-654155, www.korocharter.hr (motorboats only).

Baška *p154*

Diving

Rare Bird, Kricon 12, T051-856536, www.rare-bird.org; **Squatina Diving Centre**, Zarok 88a, T051-856034, www.squatinadiving.com.

Hiking

There are 14 well-marked hiking paths that criss-cross their way over the surrounding countryside. Hiking maps are available from the town tourist office.

Transport

Krk Town *p152*

Bus

Krk Town bus station (Rijeka office), T060-302010, www.autotrans.hr.

Long distance In summer there are 12 buses daily from **Rijeka** on the mainland to **Krk Town** (1 hr 40 mins). 7 of these continue across the island to **Baška**, stopping at **Punat** en route. Krk Town to Punat takes 10 mins. Punat to Baška takes 30 mins. Through winter the service is slightly reduced.

Ferry

Jadrolinija, www.jadrolinija.hr, run regular ferries (10 times daily in winter; 14 times daily in summer) from Valbiska to Merag on the island of Cres. **Split Tours**, www.splittours.hr, run a twice-daily ferry from Valbiska to Lopar on the island of Rab.

Punat and the Islet of Košljun *p153*
Bus
In summer there are 7 buses daily from **Rijeka** on the mainland to Baška, stopping at **Krk Town** and **Punat** (1 hr 50 mins) en route. In winter the service is slightly reduced.

Ferry
In summer, regular taxi boats run from the seafront to the **Islet of Košljun** (30Kn return).

Baška *p154*
Bus
For bus times contact the Rijeka office, T060-302010, www.autotrans.hr.

Through summer there are 7 buses daily from **Rijeka** on the mainland to Baška (2 hrs 20 mins), stopping at **Krk Town** and **Punat** en route. Krk Town to Baška takes 40 mins. In winter the service is slightly reduced.

Vrbnik *p154*
Bus
Contact the Rijeka office, T060-302010. There are 2 buses daily to **Krk Town** (30 mins).

Directory

Krk Town *p152*
Banks There are 2 banks in town. **Internet** Monkey Internet Centar, Ribarska 1, T051- 220039. **Medical services** Dom zdravlja, Vinogradska bb, T051-221224. **Pharmacies**: Ljekarna, Ljekarna, T051-221133. **Post offices** Bodulska bb, Mon-Fri 0700-2000, Sat 0700-1400.

Baška *p154*
Banks There is 1 bank. **Internet** Primaturist, T051-856971. **Medical services** Dom zdravlja, T051-856815. **Pharmacies**: Ljekarna, T051-856 900. **Post offices** Zdenka Čermakova bb, Mon-Fri 0700-1900, Sat 0700-1400.

Vrbnik *p154*
Banks There is 1 in town. **Medical services** Varoš bb, T051-857010. There is no pharmacy. **Post offices** Varoš 21, Mon-Fri 0800-1500.

Island of Cres (Cherso)

→ *Phone code: 051. Colour map 1/3, C2/A1. Population: 2959.*

Sparsely populated and little explored by the average tourist, this long, skinny, mountainous island is joined to a second island, Lošinj, by a bridge. The northern end is covered by a dense deciduous forest of beech and oak, known as the Tramunatana, which gradually gives way to meagre pastures and barren landscapes in the south. More for those in search of unspoilt nature, rather than culture, Cres offers good opportunities for hiking and birdwatching (the rare Eurasion griffon vulture nests here), but little in the way of art and architecture. The islanders live primarily from sheep farming: Creška janjetina *(Cres lamb) is especially tasty thanks to the clean pastures, rich in wild herbs such as* kadulja *(sage). In the middle of the island, Vransko Jezero (Lake Vrana) is an unusual natural phenomenom. This 6-km-long freshwater lake is 74 m deep and its bottom lies 61 m below sea level. A godsend for the islanders, it supplies drinking water to both Cres and Lošinj and is also used to irrigate the surrounding olive groves.* ▸▸ *For Sleeping, Eating and other listings, see pages 161-163.*

Ins and outs

Getting there Buses leave daily from Rijeka to Mali Lošinj, stopping at towns en route. In summer, a daily catamaran service runs between Rijeka and Cres Town. The year through, regular ferries operate between Rijeka and Mali Lošinj stopping at Cres Town en route, and between Brestova on the mainland (in Istria) and Porozina on Cres (30 minutes), and between Valbiska on the island of Krk and Merag on Cres (30 minutes). ▸▸ *See Transport, page 162, for further details.*

Getting around A main road runs the length of the island, from Porozina on the northern tip all the way to Osor in the south, where there is a bridge to Lošinj. Towns on this road, such as Cres Town and Osor, are connected by regular local buses. However, smaller villages off the main road are very poorly served by public transport.

Tourist information The island's main **tourist office** ⓘ *Conc 10, T051-571535, www.tzg-cres.hr*, is in Cres Town. In Valun there's a small **seasonal tourist office** ⓘ *T051-571161*. For information about Osor, contact the **Mali Lošinj tourist office** ⓘ *T051-231884*.

Background

Ancient sources record the islands of Cres and Lošinj under a common name, the *Apsyrtides*, connecting them with the Greek myth of Jason and the Golden Fleece. According to legend, the fleece was kept in the possession of King Aeetes, but when his daughter, Medea, fell in love with Jason, she agreed to help him steal it in return for eternal fidelity. Mission accomplished, the lovers set sail together with Medea's younger brother, Apsyrtos. When the King appeared in hot pursuit, Medea killed her brother, scattering his remains on the sea so as to slow down their father, who stopped to pick up the pieces. From Apsyrtos' body came into being the Apsyrtides, Cres and Lošinj.

Mythology aside, it seems Cres was originally settled by the Illyrian tribe of the Liburni around 1600 BC. No one is quite sure who dug the channel between Cres and Lošinj. Some historians attribute it to the Liburni, while others claim it was the work of the Romans, who arrived some time in the first century BC and developed *Apsoros* (present-day Osor), overlooking the channel, into a major trading centre.

Under Venice from 1409 to 1797, Cres was considerably wealthier and more developed than neighbouring Lošinj, but the tables were turned during the 19th century under the Hapsburgs, when Lošinj became an important shipping centre, while Cres fell into relative obscurity. At the end of the First World War the Treaty of Versailles awarded both Cres and Lošinj to Italy, and it was only in 1947 that they were reunited with Yugoslavia.

Cres Town and around

▸▸ *pp161-163. Colour map 1, C2.*

➔ *Phone code: 051. Population: 2333.*

Located on the north side of a sheltered bay on the west coast, the island's chief settlement is made up of pastel-coloured houses giving on to a broad seafront promenade, which cuts its way around a deep triangular harbour filled with small fishing boats. Backed by terraces of olive groves, it's a pleasant enough place with a down-to-earth atmosphere and decent choice of restaurants serving standard seafood and wine.

Sights

During the 16th century it was fortified with town walls, five towers and several gates, most of which were pulled down in the early 20th century, though three gates, **Gradska Vrata** (Town Gate), **Mala Vrata** (Little Gate) and **Vrata Sv Mikule** (St Michel's Gate), and one round tower can still be seen. Within these limits, the old town is made up of a maze of winding streets opening out onto small squares. Traditionally homes were built on two levels: the ground floor would be used as either a *butiga* by artisans or a *konoba* by farmers, and the family living quarters would be upstairs.

The seafront promenade leads west of town to a stretch of coast offering a series of small secluded **coves** ideal for sunbathing and swimming.

Valun and around

Valun, 13 km south of Cres Town (5 km off the main road), is a peaceful fishing village with pastel-coloured cottages built around a small harbour on the edge of Valun Bay, with a population of 62. A path on the seafront leads to blissful pebble beaches each side of the bay, and if you come outside peak season you may well have the place to yourself. The main sight here is the **Valunska Ploča** (Valun Tablet), a stone bearing an 11th-century inscription in both Glagolitic (see page 127) and Latin scripts, on display in the parish Church of St Mary. **Konoba Toš** is a small eatery with a vine-covered terrace overlooking the bay that is popular with yachters, who put down anchor here to indulge in the house specialities, *škampi* (shrimps) and Cres lamb.

Perched on a cliff, 387 m above the sea, 5 km south of Valun and with a population of 24, **Lubenice** is worth a visit for its romantic crumbling charm and spectacular views. Made up of medieval stone cottages built around a square and a 15th-century parish church, the village is semi-abandoned, but comes to life each year in summer when the **Lubenice Music Evenings** are held here (see Festivals and events, page 162). Only three buses a week run from Lubenice to Cres Town.

Beli and around → *Phone code: 051.*

Colour map 1, C2. 20 km north of Cres Town.

Beli stands on a hill, 130 m above a tiny harbour and pleasant pebble beach, on the northeast coast. Isolated and semi-abandoned with a population of 35, this cluster of old stone cottages is popular with hikers and nature lovers, who use it as a base for exploring the surrounding forests of the **Tramuntane**.

Before setting off to walk through the Tramuntane, be sure to call at the well-run **Eco-center Caput Insulae** ① *T051-840525, www.supovi.hr, daily 0900-1900, from mid-Feb to mid-Nov they run 1-day educational programmes.* There's an informative exhibition, **Biodiversity of the Archipelago of Cres and Lošinj**, and a reserve for injured Eurasian griffon vultures. It's also possible to pick up an illustrated

Islands of Cres & Lošinj

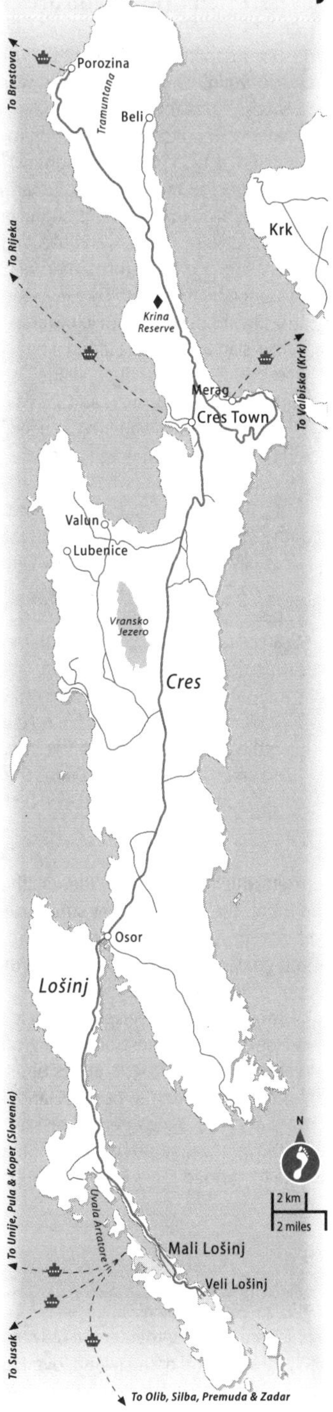

Eurasian griffon vultures

The Eurasian griffon vulture is one of the world's largest flying birds, with a wingspan of up to 2.8 m, a body weight of up to 15 kg, a maximum speed of 120 kph and eyesight nine times better than that of a human. It feeds on animal carcasses but never attacks living animals, and has long been respected by the farmers of Cres as it prevents disease by eating the bodies of dead sheep. However, as the island has seen a gradual but continual trend of depopulation, so the number of farmers and sheep has declined, and the griffon has been left with little in the way of food.

During the 1980s, when the number of griffon vultures had dropped to less than 50, the Eco-centre Caput Insulae established several feeding sites, where they deposit carcasses of slaughtered sheep and rescue injured birds so they can be taken to the centre and treated.

Their numbers have since risen, and there are now about 70 couples nesting in colonies on the vertical cliffs on the northeast side of the island. The female lays one egg per year, and during the two-month period of incubation both parents sit on the egg. After hatching, the chick grows in the nest for four months, then spends another couple of months learning to fly with its parents, after which it leaves for several years roving, travelling as far afield as Greece, Israel and Spain. At the age of five, the griffon returns to the cliff where it was born, finds a mate and builds a nest, and then lives in the vicinity of its birthplace for up to 60 years.

However, modern-day life remains a constant threat to these spectacular birds. They occasionally chance upon carcasses of vermin that have been intentionally poisoned, they have been known to fly into electric cables, and young birds may even lose control of their wings and fall into the sea if disturbed by tourists during the summer season.

The Nature Conservation Act has declared the Eurasian griffon vulture a protected species. The killing or disturbing of griffon vultures, and the stealing of their eggs or chicks, are offences liable to a penalty of up to 40,000Kn. The public display of stuffed griffon vultures is also illegal.

booklet, which will help you identify the trees and plants in the surrounding forests. From here, the most popular short walk is a 5-km eco-educative trail known as the *Tramuntana 1*, which takes you past 10 stations of natural and cultural significance. As you go, look out for birds such as the golden eagle, snake eagle, honey buzzard and, of course, the griffon vulture.

Almost 200 bird species are found on Cres, of which 90 breed here, making the island one of the richest ornithological areas on the Adriatic. The **Kruna Reserve**, between Beli and Merag, protects birds of prey such as the golden eagle, short-toed eagle, peregrine, honey buzzard and griffon vulture. Besides birds of prey, other species such as the eagle owl reside here. Visits to the ornithological reserve are restricted, but those interested in birdwatching can contact the **Eco-Centar Caput Insulae** for guided tours in small groups.

Osor

» *pp161-163. Colour map 3, A1.*

→ *Phone code: 051. Population: 73.*

Osor is a compact settlement of old stone buildings, located on a small peninsula on the southwest end of the island, overlooking **Kavuada**, an 11-m-wide and 100-m-long sea channel (now traversed by a swing bridge) separating Cres from Lošinj. It is the oldest, and was once the most important, settlement on either of the islands. Today Osor is often referred to as an open-air museum. Indeed, part of the ancient walls still exist, though the early settlement was largely destroyed by the Saracens in 841.

There's no tourist office in Osor, but for information you can contact the **Mali Lošinj tourist office** ⓘ *T051-231884, www.tz-malilosinj.hr.*

Background

Founded by the Illyrian tribe of the Liburnians and named *Apsoros* by the Greeks, Osor lived its golden age under Roman rule, when it became a municipality and prosperous trading centre with a population of several thousand. On the ancient land-sea Amber Route between the Baltic and the Aegean, it developed into an important transit point for merchants shipping amber from the north and silk and spices from the east. At that time ships sailed only with 'fair winds' (with the wind behind the vessel) and, as the winds in this area frequently change direction, ships kept close to the shores and were often forced to seek refuge in sheltered bays and inlets. Kavuada provided safe passage and shortened considerably the journey from the North Adriatic to Dalmatia.

During the 15th century, as ships became larger and navigational techniques more advanced, captains were able to sail their vessels more on the open sea. Kavuada consequently lost the bulk of its traffic and Osor fell into a period of decline from which it never recovered. Bouts of malaria and a plague epidemic only made matters worse and, under Venice, Osor lost its role as the island's administrative centre, which passed to Cres Town.

Sights

The most notable monuments date from the 15th century and are concentrated on the main square, once the site of the Roman forum. On the south side of the square, the 15th-century Renaissance **Crkva Uznesenja** (Church of the Assumption) features a trefoil façade bearing an early-Renaissance portal topped with a statue of the *Mother of God*, attributed to Juraj Dalmatinac. Inside, a baroque altar displays the relics of St Gaudencius, who was Bishop of Osor during the 11th century and is said to have banished all the snakes from the island. He died in Rome, but his body was miraculously transported back to Osor in a casket washed up by the sea. (The local Bishopric was founded in the sixth century but ceased to exist in 1828.)

On the opposite side of the square stands the 15th-century **Gradska Vijećnica** (Town Hall), a two-storey building with a large semi-circular arch on the ground floor leading into an open-fronted space that once functioned as the loggia. Today it houses a **lapidarium** with early-Christian and Venetian stone carvings. On the first floor, where local patricians used to meet, is a small archaeological collection, with scale models of ancient Osor and first- and second-century Roman gravestones. In a side street just off the square, the rather insignificant **Biskupova Palača** (Bishop's Palace) houses another lapidarium with more stone carvings from early Croatian churches. In summer it also hosts exhibitions of contemporary painting and sculpture. The closest **beach** is a few hundred metres north of the village in **Bijar Bay**.

Sleeping

Cres Town and around *p158*

D **Hotel Kimen**, Melin I broj 16, T051-571305, www.hotel-kimen.com. Refurbished in spring 2008, a 2-km walk along the coast from the centre, is the town's only hotel. There are 212 basic but comfortable rooms with balcony, shower, TV and telephone.

Private accommodation

The following agency can help you find private accommodation, organize hiking and culinary tours of the island: **Cresanka**, Varozina 25, Cres Town, T051-750604, www.cresanka.hr.

Beli and around *p159*
D **Pansion and Restoran Tramunata**, T/F051-840519, www.diving-beli.com. Close to the eco-centre, this friendly *pansion* has 8 double rooms and a small restaurant serving hearty home-cooked meals. The diving centre is also based here. Open all year.

Eating

Cres Town and around *p158*
Ⲯ **Belona**, Šetalište 20 Aprila 24, T051-571 203. The unrivalled favourite with locals and well-informed visitors, this small old-fashioned eatery is known for oven-baked *arbun* (sea bream), pasta with lobster, and oven-baked lamb with potatoes, all of which come with generous portions of home-made bread. In warm weather it's possible to eat outside on the terrace. Open all year.
Ⲯ **Riva**, Creskih kapetana 13, T051-571107. With a large terrace overlooking the harbour, this small fish restaurant serves up delicious octopus salad, barbecued scampi, and oven-baked fish with potatoes. Also serves house wine, *Malvazija*, by the carafe. Open Apr-Oct.

Valun and around *p159*
Ⲯ **Konoba Hibernicia**, Lubenice 17, Lubenice, T051-840422. This much-loved little *konoba* serves local lamb dishes such as *njoki s janjećim gulašom* (lamb goulash with gnocchi) along with home-made bread at outdoor wooden tables and benches. Open daily Apr-Oct.

Osor *p160*
Ⲯ **Konoba Livio**, Osor 30, Osor, T051-237 242. In Osor, this friendly *konoba* has an old-fashioned stone interior with chairs made from wooden wine barrels, plus a charming leafy terrace where they serve local meat and fish dishes. Open May-Oct.

Festivals and events

Cres Town and around *p158*
End Jun EMS European Championship. A 1-week sailing regatta that takes place during the last week of Jun.

Valun and around *p159*
Jul-Aug Lubenice Music Evenings. On Fri evenings, open-air classical music concerts, performed by renowned Croatian and foreign musicians, take place on the central square. Ask at the Cres Town tourist office for details.

Osor *p160*
Jul-Aug Osorske Večeri (Osor Musical Evenings). Classical music concerts have been held in the Church of the Assumption on the main square each summer since 1976.

Activities and tours

Cres Town and around *p158*
Sailing
Cres ACI Marina, Jadranska obala 22, T051-571622, www.aci-club.hr. Has 473 berths, open all year. The marina also has 8 comfortable apartments.

Beli and around *p159*
Diving
Diving Club Beli, Pansion Tramunata, T051-840519, www.diving-beli.com.

Transport

Cres Town and around *p158*
Bus
For Cres Town contact the Rijeka office, T060-302010, www.autotrans.hr.

There are 8 buses daily that cover the route from Cres Town to **Mali Lošinj** (1 hr) passing through **Osor** en route, 6 buses daily from **Rijeka** to **Mali Lošinj**, stopping at Cres Town (2½ hrs) and **Osor** en route.

Ferry
Jadrolinija, Rijeka office, T051-211444, www.jadrolonija, run regular ferries between **Brestova** on the mainland and **Porozina** (population 20) on Cres, with 19 crossings daily in summer and 15 in winter. The same company also operates a service between **Valbiska** on the island of Krk and **Merag** (population 3) on Cres, with 14 crossings daily in summer and 10 in winter. In addition, they run a daily year-round catamaran service between **Rijeka** and Malim Lošinj, stopping at Cres Town en route.

Taxi
It's often possible to find a taxi at the bus station, otherwise call T098-947 5592.

Beli and around *p159*

Bus

During the school summer break there are only 2 buses a week from **Cres Town** to Beli (30 mins). During term time a school bus covers the route, but you should check at the Cres Town tourist office for full details.

Osor *p160*

Bus

6 buses daily from Rijeka to Mali Lošinj pass through **Cres Town** and Osor en route. In addition, 2 local buses cover the same route between **Cres Town** and **Mali Lošinj**, also stopping in Osor. Cres Town to Osor takes 40 mins, Osor to Mali Lošinj takes 20 mins.

Directory

Cres Town and around *p158*

Banks There is a bank in town. **Medical services** Turion 26, T051-571116. Pharmacies: Trg Frane Petrića 4, T051-571243. **Post offices** Cons 3, Mon-Fri 0700-1900, Sat 0700-1400.

Beli and around *p159*

Post offices Beli 66, Mon-Fri 0930-1200.

Island of Lošinj (Lussino)

➔ *Phone code: 051. Colour map 3, A1. Population: 8388.*

Smaller but much more densely populated and certainly more touristy than neighbouring Cres, Lošinj is known for its mild climate, lush vegetation and the long-established resort of Mali Lošinj. ▸▸ *For Sleeping, Eating and other listings, see pages 165-167.*

Ins and outs

Getting there There are three buses daily from Rijeka to Mali Lošinj and Veli Lošinj which stop at Cres Town and Osor on the island of Cres on the way. A local service covers the same route from Cres Town to Mali Lošinj and Veli Lošinj five times daily. A twice-daily catamarn runs from Rijeka to Mali Lošinj, stopping at the islands of Cres, Unije and Susak en route. Through summer, an additional ferry service from Zadar to Pula stops at Unije, Mali Lošinj and Silba en route. ▸▸ *See Transport, page 166, for further details.*

Getting around Buses arriving in Mali Lošinj from the north then continue the 4-km stretch to Veli Lošinj, linking the towns eight times daily.

Tourist information The **tourist office** ⓘ *Riva Lošinjskih Kapetana 29, T051-231884, www.tz-malilosinj.hr*, is on the seafront at Mali Lošinj.

Background

In ancient times, known together with Cres as *Apsyrtides*, Lošinj seems to have remained unpopulated until the Middle Ages. The first settlers from the mainland were mentioned in 1280, and in 1389 they made an agreement for self-rule with the people of Osor on Cres, who owned Lošinj. The name Lošinj, probably derived from the Croatian *loš* meaning poor or weak, appeared around the same time. Under Venice (1409-1797), Lošinj was neglected in favour of neighbouring Cres, the island's golden age finally dawning under the Hapsburgs when it developed into an important seafaring and shipbuilding centre. Shipping declined in the late 19th century, only to be superseded by tourism. With their mild Mediterranean climates, lush vegetation and crystal clean sea, both Mali Lošinj and Veli Lošinj were proclaimed health resorts in 1892. The demise of Austro-Hungary in 1918 saw the island awarded to Italy. During and after the Second World War, when the political future looked uncertain, many Italians left: the population declined dramatically, plummeting from 9738 in 1910 to 5449 just after the war. Lošinj was reunited with Yugoslavia in 1947.

Mali Lošinj and around » pp165-167.

Colour map 3, A1.

→ *Phone code: 051. Population: 6296.*

Lying at the end of a sheltered, elongated bay on the southwest coast of the island of Lošinj, Mali Lošinj is the largest settlement on all the Croatian islands. Despite its name (*mali* means small, *veli* large), it's far bigger than neighbouring Veli Lošinj. Everyday life focuses on the harbour, skirted by a seafront promenade lined with cream, ochre and russet façades, many housing street-level cafés with open-air seating under colourful awnings through summer. The town's loveliest houses, set in lush gardens filled with Mediterranean planting, were built by retired sea captains during the 19th century. Through peak season the place is packed with visitors, most of whom sleep in the large, modern hotels on Čikat Peninsula, joined to the centre by a coastal path which meanders its way between the turquoise blue sea and scented pinewoods.

Background

During the 15th century the Church of St Martin was built overlooking the large sheltered bay. A small village grew up around it, and three centuries later the locals set up a shipping company: the village became a town and by 1870 the port of Mali Lošinj was second only to Trieste on the Adriatic in terms of registered tonnage handled per annum, and Lošinj ship owners accounted for 170 cargo ships. However, the late 19th century saw the advent of the steamship; Lošinj's wind-powered vessels could no longer compete, shipping declined and many families emigrated. Around the same time, a study of the local climate, emphasizing its health-giving properties, was published in Vienna by Ambroz Haračić, a nature-loving professor at the Naval Academy in Lošinj. Convinced a sojourn in such a place could only do them good, ailing Austrians began to visit Lošinj. The first villas and hotels were built on Čikat Peninsula, and it soon became a fashionable winter health resort. The same Haračić initiated a 10-year reforestation scheme, planting the area behind town with dense pinewoods. Since then Mali Lošinj has never really looked back. Today it lives primarily from tourism, though there is still a shipyard producing small motorboats.

Sights

There is little here of great cultural note, but if you're interested in art be sure to catch the **Umjetničke Zbirke** ① *Vladimira Gortana 35, T051-231173, summer Mon-Sat 0900-1200, 1900-2100, winter Mon-Sat 1000-1200, 10Kn*, combining two private art collections donated to the town. That of the local art historian, Andro Vid Mihičić (1896-1992), is refreshingly modern, featuring 87 works of Croatian 20th-century painting and sculpture. The other collection, formerly belonging to the Italian Piperata family, consists of 27 paintings, mainly romantic landscapes produced between the 16th and 18th centuries by Venetian artists, along with several works by Dutch and French painters.

The best place for swimming is **Čikat**, where a coastal path west of town leads past a series of concrete bathing areas and pebble beaches, backed by villas, hotels and summer cafés.

Island of Susak → *Colour map 3, A1. 10 km west of Mali Lošinj.*

The tiny island of Susak attracts up to 700 visitors daily in peak season. In contrast to the other islands of the Adriatic, it's made up of compact sand forming a small hill (98 m) on a limestone base. Clumps of reeds protect the island from erosion, and the locals cultivate terraces of vines, producing small quantities of surprisingly good white wine. In Italian the island is called *Sansego*, probably from the Greek *sansegus*, meaning oregano, which also grows here in abundance. Susak's real oddity is the unusual costume paraded by its womenfolk (today only for special occasions): a multi-coloured embroidered miniskirt worn well above the knee, over crimson woollen stockings and six layers of lace petticoats, so it sticks out like a ballerina's tutu. The island's population peaked at almost 2000 in 1936, but after the Second World War many families emigrated to the US. Houses are gradually being sold off as holiday cottages, and a handful of bars and restaurants work from late-April to mid-September.

The only settlement, also called **Susak**, is in two parts: the hilltop **Gornji Selo** (Upper Village), which grew up around an 11th-century Benedictine monastery (no longer standing), and **Donji Selo** (Lower Village) on the east coast, which serves as the island's port. From Donji Selo, 120 steps lead up to the **Crkva Sv Nikole** (Church of St Nicholas) built in 1770, the year the monastery closed. Inside, *Veli Bog* is a 12th-century crucifix that was reputedly washed up on the island by the sea; local superstition predicts catastrophe should it ever leave the church.

Veli Lošinj

→ Phone code: 051. Colour map 3, A1. Population: 917. 4 km southeast of Mali Lošinj.

Veli Lošinj is a compact, little fishing town of pastel-coloured houses built around a narrow bay. It's quieter and more authentic than its neighbour, but still has a few things worth seeing, a modest selection of decent fish restaurants and an unusual dolphin research centre.

Set back from the harbour, the **Fortress Tower** ⓘ *summer daily 0900-1200, 1900-2100*, was built by the Venetians in 1445 to protect the village from pirate attacks. It is now a small museum, the showpiece being a copy of a bronze life-size statue of an athlete found in the sea in 1999, which some scholars attribute to the renowned fourth-century BC Greek sculptor Lysippus.

During the late 19th century, when the island was making its name as a popular winter destination for members of the Austrian aristocracy, Karl Stephan von Hapsburg had a mansion built on the edge of town. He called it **Seewarte** (*Morska Straža* in Croatian) and had the surrounding parkland planted with exotic trees, such as magnolia and eucalyptus, and evergreen firs, pines and cypresses. Today the building houses a sanatorium for the treatment of respiratory diseases.

Sleeping

Mali Lošinj and around *p164*

A Villa Diana, Čikat uvala bb, T051-232055, www.losinj-hotels.com. With view of Čikat Bay, 2 km west of town, this villa provides 8 luxury en suite rooms with modern furnishing. Residents and non-residents frequent the excellent restaurant, which has an open-air terrace shaded by pine trees.

B Hotel Apoksiomen, Riva Lošinjskih Kapetana 1, T051-520820, www.apoksiomen.com. In the old town, overlooking the seafront promenade, this smart hotel has 25 rooms, each with a marble bathroom, a/c, satellite TV, internet, minibar and safe deposit.

B Hotel Manora, Nerezine, T051-237460, www.manora-losinj.hr, 25 km north of Mali Lošinj, at the foot of Mount Osoršćica, just a 10-min walk from a small fishing harbour. This family-run hotel has 22 double rooms with wooden floors and modern minimalist furniture, an excellent restaurant serving local specialities, and a garden with a small pool. They also offer fishing trips.

B Villa Favorita, Sunčana uvala bb, T051-520640, www.villafavorita.hr. With view of the sea and backed by pinewoods, this yellow Secessionist building has been restored to form a small luxury hotel with 8 double rooms, a restaurant, sauna, massage and an outdoor pool filled with seawater set in a carefully nurtured garden.

E Hotel Alhambra, Čikat uvala bb, T051-232 022, www.losinj-hotels.hr. Also overlooking Čikat Bay, 3 km west of town, this old pink villa offers 29 peaceful rooms with simple modern furnishing. In summer you'll find the restaurant on a terrace shaded by palms. Pets welcome.

Private accommodation

Cappelli, Kadin bb in Mali Lošinj, T051-231 582, www.cappelli-tourist.hr. This agency specializes in accommodation on the islands of Lošinj and Cres.

Veli Lošinj *p165*

E **Pansion Saturn**, Obala Maršala Tita bb, T051-236102. Overlooking Veli Lošinj's tiny bay, this red-fronted building has 9 rooms, each with a bathroom, plus a ground-floor bar with a pleasant waterfront terrace.

F **Youth Hostel**, OH Zlatokrila, Kaciol, T051-236312. Set in a lovely villa with a terrace and a garden dominated by tall palm trees, the Veli Lošinj youth hostel has 60 beds and is open Jun-Sep.

Eating

Mali Lošinj and around *p164*

ΨΨΨ-ΨΨ **Corrado**, Sv Marije 1, Mali Lošinj, T051-232487. This is the best place to try traditional Lošinj fare such as *gulaš od junjetine* (lamb goulash). The owner is a cook and fisherman, so you can also expect top-class seafood dishes: stuffed squid and scampi with pasta. See also **Villa Diana** in Sleeping, above.

ΨΨ **Artatore**, Artatore 132, Uvala Artatore, 7 km north of Mali Lošinj, T051-232932. This restaurant is especially popular with yachters, who moor up in front of the terrace overlooking the bay. The owner does the cooking himself and his top dishes are *škampi rižot* (shrimp risotto), *jastog s rezancima* (lobster with pasta) and *ribe nažaru* (barbecued fish).

ΨΨ **Pizzeria Draga**, Braće Vidulića 77, T051-231132. This friendly, bustling restaurant offers a range of pasta dishes and salads at lunchtime, and in the evenings adds a vast choice of delicious brick-oven baked pizzas to the menu. There's a large covered terrace area so you can eat out even if it rains. Closed mid-Jan to mid-Feb.

Veli Lošinj *p165*

ΨΨ **Bora Bora**, Rovenska 3, T051-867544. In Rovenska Bay near Veli Lošinj, funky **Bora Bar** is run by an Italian-born owner-chef who is married to a Croatian. Expect modern Mediterranean cuisine using local produce, with an emphasis on seafood and truffles, plus fresh home-made pasta. Popular with sailing types, there are water and electricity connections for boats out front, as well as Wi-Fi. Open May-Oct.

ΨΨ **Marina**, Obala Maršala Tita 38, T051-236 178. With dining on a seafront terrace, this restaurant specializes in tasty spaghetti with lobster, barbecued meat and fish dishes. Open Mar-Nov.

Festivals and events

Mali Lošinj and around *p164*

1 Jan International underwater spear fishing contest.
Early Aug Lošinj regatta.

Activities and tours

Mali Lošinj and around *p164*

Diving

DSC Lošinj, based in Rijeka at Šetalište XIII divizije 28, T051-219111, www.diver.hr. Organize a diving school here from early Apr to mid-Nov.

Veli Lošinj *p165*

For eco-volunteer work at the **Adriatic Dolphin Project**, see Essentials, page 51.

Transport

Mali Lošinj and around *p164*

Bus

Autotrans can supply bus times, Rijeka office, T060-302010, www.autotrans.hr.

6 buses run daily from **Rijeka** to Mali Lošinj (3½ hrs), passing through **Cres Town** and **Osor** en route. In addition, 2 local buses daily cover the route from **Cres Town** to Mali Lošinj (1 hr).

Car

Hertz, Kadin bb, T051-231582.

Ferry

Jadrolinija, T051-231765, run a twice-daily catamaran from Rijeka to Mali Lošinj, stopping at Cres, Unije and Susak en route (3 hrs 45 min). The same company also run a twice-weekly ferry service from **Zadar** to Mali Lošinj (5 hrs 20 mins), stopping at **Olib**, **Silba** and **Premuda** en route. The boat leaves Zadar early morning to arrive in Mali Lošinj early afternoon, then returns to Zadar for the late evening the same day. **Split Tours**, www.splittours.hr, operate a daily summer service from **Pula** to **Zadar**, stopping at **Unije**, **Mali Lošinj** and **Silba** en route.

Taxi
T051-231102.

Island of Susak *p164*

Ferry
Through summer it's possible to take a day trip to the island, with boats leaving each morning from Mali Lošinj harbour.

Veli Lošinj *p165*

Bus
Autotrans can supply bus times, Rijeka office, T060-302010, www.autotrans.hr. 8 buses cover the route from Cres Town to Mali Lošinj and Veli Lošinj each day. It's also possible to walk from Mali Lošinj to Veli Lošinj. 6 buses run daily from **Rijeka** to Mali Lošinj and Veli Lošinj, passing through **Cres Town** and **Osor** en route.

Directory

Mali Lošinj and around *p164*

Banks There are several in town. **Medical services** Dom zdravlja, T051-231824. **Pharmacies**: Ljekarna, T051-231661. **Post offices** Vladimir Gortana 4, Mon-Fri 0700-2000, Sat 0700-1400.

Veli Lošinj *p165*

Banks There is a bank in town. **Medical services** T051-236180. **Pharmacies**: The nearest is in Mali Lošinj. **Post offices** Obala M Tita 33, Mon-Fri 0700-2000, Sat 0700-1400.

Island of Rab

→ *Phone code: 051. Colour map 3, A1/2. Population: 9480. 20 km south of the island of Krk.*

Rab is probably the most beautiful of all the Kvarner islands. While the windswept northeast side is rocky and barren with steep cliffs plummeting down to the sea, the sheltered southwest part is gently undulating and covered with dense, green pinewoods. The main reason for coming here is to explore the medieval Rab Town, an architectural treasure perched on a walled peninsula, rising high above the sea. There are also some blissful stretches of sandy beach on the northern coast, so you can combine sightseeing with swimming and sunbathing, not to mention the excellent fish restaurants. Rab is a particularly popular destination for Germans and Hungarians, being one of the easiest islands to access from Central Europe.
▸▸ *For Sleeping, Eating and other listings, see pages 171-172.*

Ins and outs

Getting there Two buses daily run direct from Rijeka to Rab Town (the ferry crossing is included in the price of the ticket). In addition, **Imperial** ⓘ *T051-667790, www.imperial.hr, Mar-Oct, €19*, offer a bus transfer from Rijeka airport (on the island of Krk) direct to Rab Town (reservations should be made at least 5 days in advance). There is also a daily catamaran from Rijeka to Rab Town, but the most frequent ferry service from the mainland runs from Jablanac (3 km off main coastal road) to Mišnjak (8 km from Rab Town) several times daily. From the neighbouring islands, there is a once-daily ferry service from Lun on Pag to Rab Town and a twice-daily ferry from Valbiska on Krk to Lopar (13km from Rab Town). ▸▸ *See Transport, page 172, for further details.*

Getting around Through summer a local bus runs every 30 minutes from Rab Town to Lopar; the service is slightly reduced in winter. In summer, taxi boats transport visitors from Rab Town to nearby beaches along the coast. Alternatively, you can rent a motorboat and explore the island's shoreline independently.

Tourist information The **tourist office** ⓘ *Trg Municipium Arbe 8, T051-771111, www.tzg-rab.hr*, is in the old town.

Background

The Romans occupied the island in the second century BC and called it *Arba*, a name probably derived from the Illyrian *Arb* (meaning dark, green, forested). Their main settlement, on the site of Rab Town, was proclaimed a *municipium* (a self-governing municipality) in 10 BC, and later passed under Byzantine rule.

During the Middle Ages, Rab enjoyed a period of freedom and prosperity, earned through the production of silk. The town was fortified in the 13th century and many fine churches were constructed. However, it fell to Venice in 1409 and, despite becoming a major trading point between East and West and the port to a large merchant fleet, began to slump into economic decline. The islanders were obliged to pay the Doge an annual tax of ten pounds of silk and five pounds of gold, and the local fleet was restricted to preventing competitive trade.

During the 15th century, Rab was ravaged by two successive outbreaks of the plague. In Kaldanac, you can still see abandoned houses, with doorways and windows bricked up in an attempt to curtail the spread of the disease. Although the local population was decimated, the church seems to have fared pretty well out of the fear aroused by such misery. When Alberto Fortis visited the island in the 18th century, he found a community of only 3000 peasants and fishermen contributing to the stipends of 60 priests. There were also three monasteries and three convents.

In 1808, Napoleon put an end to Venetian rule and also dissolved several religious institutions. After a short period under the French, the island became part of the Austro-Hungarian Empire. During the years prior to the First World War, Rab became a favourite winter retreat for wealthy Viennese. The first hotel, the **Imperial**,

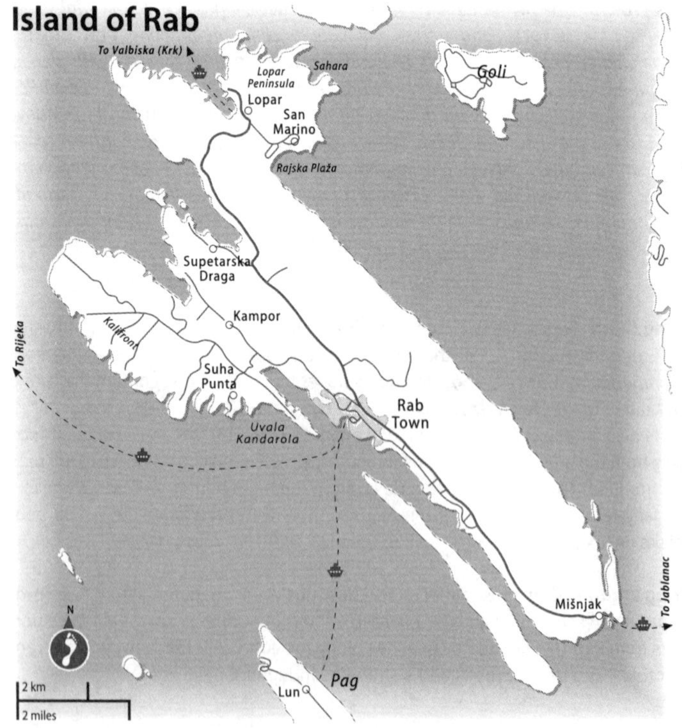

was built, and the green expanse of Komrčar Park was laid out. At the same time, the island was one of the first places in Europe to advocate nudism, an activity much publicized following a visit by the British king, Edward VIII, and his American fiancée, Wallace Simpson, in summer 1936. The couple apparently swam naked at Kandarola, which has remained a popular nudist beach to this day.

During the Yugoslav years, Rab Town expanded east of the port, and a number of large hotel complexes were built. Today Rab is a popular tourist resort, particularly with yachters, who moor up in the large marina next to the town port.

Rab Town » *pp171-172. Colour map 3, A2.*

→ *Phone code: 051. Population: 554 in the Old Town.*

With four elegant bell towers lining the crest of a narrow peninsula, viewed from the sea the night-time silhouette of Rab Town is poetically compared to a giant sailing boat with four slender masts. The old town is compact and well preserved, and can be divided into two parts: the medieval stone cottages of **Kaldanac** – on the tip of the peninsula, where the early Roman settlement was located – and **Varoš**, which takes up the land end of the peninsula and is made of narrow paved streets lined with elegant 15th- to 17th-century Gothic and Renaissance buildings, many with ornate balconies, finely carved windows and doorways topped with family coats of arms. Through summer, the old town sees a constant influx of visitors.

Sights

The compact old town is closed to traffic and can be explored in an hour's leisurely stroll. The layout is simple: three longitudinal streets running parallel to the waterfront promenade and linked together by a series of steep alleyways. The lower street is known as **Donja Ulica**; the middle street, **Srednja Ulica**; and the upper street, **Gornja Ulica**. While the main cultural monuments are on Gornja Ulica, you'll find standard tourist haunts such as ice cream parlours and night-time bars on Srednja Ulica, where local street artists set up their easels through peak season.

The large paved square, **Trg Municipium Arbe**, opens out onto the seafront, halfway along the peninsula. It's rimmed with a number of popular open-air cafés and the tourist office is also located here. The main monument is the **Knežev Dvor** (Rector's Palace), built between the 13th and 16th centuries, with a tall square tower and a stately balcony supported by three lions' heads sculpted in stone above the main entrance. The ground floor houses a cosmetics shop selling locally made natural products.

Standing on the highest point of the peninsula, the 12th-century Romanesque basilica, **Crkva Svete Marije Velike** (Church of St Mary the Great) ⓘ *at the end of Ivana Rabljanina, daily 0800-1200, 1700-2000*, was blessed by Pope Alexandar III in 1177, who happened to be passing through on his way from Zadar to Rome. Slightly squat in appearance, the façade is made up of alternating bands of pink and white stone, and decorated with two rows of six Romanesque blind arches to each side of the main portal. Above the portal, a *Pieta* featuring the Virgin holding the body of Christ was completed by the Dalmatian sculptor Petar Trogiranin in 1514. Inside, above the main altar, six slender marble columns support an ancient ciborium, which was restored in the 15th century. In front of the church, a pleasant terrace offers views over the sea. St Mary's was a cathedral until the bishopric was shut down in 1828, though locals still refer to it as the *Katedrala*.

A short distance from the Church of St Mary the Great, the free-standing, 13th-century **Veli Zvonik** (Great Bell Tower) ⓘ *Ivana Rabljanina, summer daily 1000-1300, 1900-2200, 15Kn*, is the tallest (25 m) and most beautiful of Rab's four *campanili*. You can climb to the top for spectacular views over the town and the surrounding seascapes.

A Benedictine convent for the daughters of patrician families was founded here in 1020. **Crkva Sveti Andrije** (St Andrew's Church) ⓘ *Ivana Rabljanina, rarely open*, dedicated to St Andrew, was restructured during the Renaissance, but the bell tower, dating from 1181 (making it the oldest in town) has retained its Romanesque appearance.

Rab's second Benedictine convent, **Crkva Sv Justina** (St Justine's Church), intended for nuns from non-noble families, was consecrated in 1578. When the French dissolved it in 1808, the nuns were relocated to St Andrew's. The convent church now houses the small **Muzej Sakralne Umjetnosti** (Museum of Sacral Art) ⓘ *Gornja Ulica, T051-771111, summer daily 0900-1200, 1930-2200, 15Kn*, displaying, among other things, an ornately decorated 13th-century silver-plated box containing the skull of St Christopher (the town's patron saint), a 15th-century Tuscan Renaissance terracotta *Our Lady with the Child*, and a mid-14th-century polyptych by Paolo Veneziano. The church bell tower, topped with an onion dome, dates from 1672.

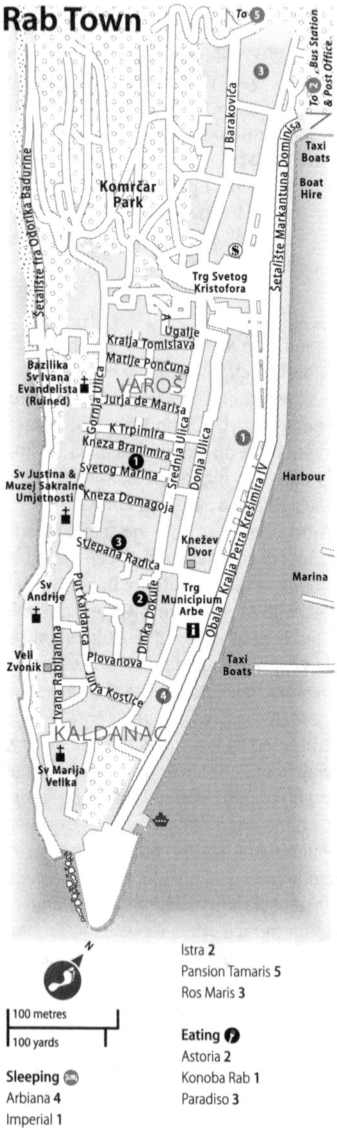

Probably originating from the early Christian era, **Bazilika Sv Ivana Evandeliste** (Basilica of St John the Evangelist) ⓘ *Gornja Ulica, summer daily 1000-1300, 1900-2200, 15Kn*, now in ruins, was abandoned in the early 19th century. Today, all that remains is the 12th-century bell tower, which was restored in 1933 and stands 20 m high, offering a spectacular panorama over town.

Landscaped in the 1890s by Pradvoje Belija, the 16-ha **Komrčar Park** is planted with Aleppo pine, holm oak, spruce and cypress trees. A series of paths lead through the woodland to a pleasant coastal promenade with a series of rocky coves interspersed by concrete bathing areas and steps down to the sea.

Rab Town

100 metres
100 yards

Sleeping
Arbiana 4
Imperial 1
Istra 2
Pansion Tamaris 5
Ros Maris 3

Eating
Astoria 2
Konoba Rab 1
Paradiso 3

The beaches » pp171-172.

Colour map 3, A2.

The most central places to swim and sunbathe are on the west side of **Komrčar Park.** Through summer, taxi boats shuttle visitors to and from Frkanj Peninsula, close to the tourist village of **Suha Punta**, west of Rab Town, where there are plenty of secluded rocky coves backed by pinewoods, as well as the renowned nudist beach of **Kandarola**. However, Rab's best beaches are on **Lopar Peninsula** on the northern tip of the island.

Lopar Peninsula

On the northern tip of the island, the sparsely populated Lopar Peninsula boasts some of Croatia's sandiest beaches.

There are two rather uninspiring little villages here: **Lopar** on the west coast (the departure point for summer ferries to the island of Krk) and **San Marino** on the east, which claims to be the birthplace of an early Christian stonecutter, Marinus, who fled religious persecution and settled on Mount Titano in Italy, where he founded the city state of San Marino in AD 301. Next to San Marino is Rab's largest and most popular family beach, **Rajska Plaža** (Paradise Beach), a 1.5-km stretch of sand backed by pinewoods and a string of seasonal restaurants and cafés. A 15-minute walk north of Rajska Plaža is the nudist beach of **Stolac**, while an even more remote nudist beach, **Sahara**, is found in the peninsula's northernmost bay.

Sleeping

Island of Rab *p167, map p170*

A **Arbiana**, Obala Petra Krešimira 12, T051-775900, www.arbianahotel.com. Standing on the harbour front, this building dates back to 1924. Now a lovely boutique hotel, it has 28 rooms with sumptuous furnishing and sweeping curtains. Known for its friendly staff and personal service, it also has a highly-regarded restaurant. Open May-Oct.

A **Hotel Ros Maris**, Obala kralja Petra Krešimira IV, Rab Town, T051-778899, www.rosmaris.com. Now the most luxurious hotel in town, the former **International** reopened as the **Ros Maris** in 2004, with 126 rooms, plus 20 suites with jacuzzi, and a spa and Wellness Centre. It stays open all year.

C **Imperial**, Palit bb, Rab Town, T051-724 522, www.imperial.hr. Rab Town's oldest hotel, dating back to the early 1900s, sits on the edge of the old town, amid the greenery of Komrčar Park. The 134 rooms are smart and modern. Has a restaurant, 3 tennis courts and a hotel beach just 100 m away.

D **Hotel Istra**, Rab Town, T051-724134, www.hotel-istra.hr. With views of the harbour, between the bus station and the old town, this 103-room hotel offers simple but comfortable accommodation, plus a ground-floor café with a terrace on the seafront.

E **Pansion Tamaris**, Palit 285, T051-724925, www.tamaris-rab.com. Overlooking the sea in St Euphemius Bay in Palit, this friendly little hotel has just 14 rooms plus a restaurant serving excellent seafood on a pleasant terrace. You can walk through Komrčar Park to be in Rab Town in just a few minutes, and there are regular taxi boats from the jetty to the beaches on Frkanj peninsula.

Private accommodation

Katurbo, M Dominisa 5, T051-724495, www.katurbo.hr. This agency can help you find private accommodation in Rab Town and Lopar.

The website, www.otokrab.hr, also has a good selection of rooms and apartments across the island (see **Zlatni Zalaz**, below).

Eating

Island of Rab *p167, map p170*

ŸŸŸ **Astoria**, Dinka Dokule 2, Rab Town, T051-774844. On the first floor of Residence Astoria, this sophisticated restaurant has a lovely candle-lit terrace overlooking Rab's main square and the harbour. The menu features traditional local meat and fish dishes using organic ingredients and fresh herbs. Open Apr-Oct.

ŸŸŸ-ŸŸ **Konoba Rab**, Kneza Branimira 3, Rab Town, T051-725666. In a side street running between Srednja Ulica and Gornja Ulica, this *konoba* serves up meat and fish prepared either on a barbeque or under a *peka*. The dining room is warm and inviting with exposed stonewalls hung with knick-knacks. Open Feb-Nov.

ŸŸŸ-ŸŸ **Zlatni Zalaz**, Supertarska Draga 379, about 10 km northwest of Rab Town, T051-775150, F051-775465. This highly regarded restaurant serves some of the best food on the island. The house speciality is *janjeći but s jabukama* (leg of lamb with apple) but there's also a good choice of fish dishes. Located in a bay overlooking a pebble beach and backed by pinewoods, the terrace is divine. There are also 14 rooms and 4 apartments to rent. Closed Nov-Mar.

ŸŸ **Restoran Paradiso**, Stjepana Radića 1, Rab Town, T051-771109. In the heart of the old town, this romantic restaurant is hidden away in a courtyard garden in a 13th-century stone building. They serve tasty Croatian cuisine and excellent wines.

Bars and clubs

Island of Rab *p167, map p170*
San Antonio Club, Trg Municipium Arba 4, T051-724145, www.sanantonio-club.com. During the day San Antonio works as a café, livening up into a cocktail bar and club (with occasional live music) after dark.
Santos Beach Club, Pudarica Beach, 10 km from Rab Town. This long-standing and much-loved beach bar serves cocktails and holds parties. In summer, an hourly shuttle bus operates between Rab Town and Pudarica the night through. It's run by the same people who manage **San Antonio Club** in Rab Town.

Festivals and events

Island of Rab *p167, map p170*
25-27 Jul **Rab Tournament**. Dating back to 1364, this medieval tournament records the defence of the town by knights with crossbows. Since 1995 it has been celebrated by a crossbow contest, with competitors in period costume.
Jun-Aug **Rapske Glazbene Večeri** (Rab Musical Evenings). Classical music performances by Croatian and international musicians, staged on Thu evenings in the Church of the Holy Cross in the old town.

Activities and tours

Island of Rab *p167, map p170*

Cycling
There are a series of bike paths on the relatively flat peninsula of Kalifront, close to Kampor, northeast of Rab Town. You can rent mountain bikes from the agency **Katurbo**, M Dominisa 5, Banjol (the modern part of Rab Town east of the harbour), T051-724495, www.katurbo.hr.

Boating
The best way to discover the most idyllic hidden beaches is by boat. You can rent small motorboats in Rab Town from **Kristofor**, Mali Palit 70, T051-725543, www.kristofor.hr.

Diving
Aqua Sport, Supetarska Draga 331, T051-776145, www.aquasport.hr. Open all year.
Moby Dick, Lopar 493, T051-775577, www.mobydick-diving.com. Open Apr to Nov.

Sailing
ACI Marina, Rab Town, T051-724023, www.aci-club.hr. 140 berths, open mid-Mar to end-Oct.
ACI Marina, Supetarska Draga, on the island's northwest coast, 7 km from Rab Town, T051-776268, www.aci-club.hr. 270 berths, open all year.

Transport

Island of Rab *p167, map p170*

Bus
Bus station, T051-724189. On the island, regular local buses run between Rab Town and Lopar Peninsula (30 mins).

There are 2 daily from Rab Town to **Rijeka** (3 hrs 25 mins).

Ferry
Jadrolinija, Rijeka office, T051-211444, www.jadrolinija.hr, run a regular daily ferry service from **Mišnjak** on the island of Rab to **Jablanac** on the mainland (22 daily through summer, reduced gradually to 9 daily in winter, 15 mins), plus a once-daily ferry between Rab Town and **Lun** on the island of Pag (35 mins). The same company also run a daily ferry direct to Rab Town from **Rijeka** on the mainland. As of Jan 2008, **Split Tours**, www.splittours.hr, run a twice-daily ferry from Valbiska on the island of Krk to Lopar.

Taxi
It's often possible to find a taxi at the bus station otherwise call T051-724955.

Directory

Island of Rab *p167, map p170*
Banks There is a bank with an ATM behind the bus station close to the post office, and on Trg Sv Kristofora at the entrance to the old town. **Medical services** Dom zdravlja, T051-724094. **Pharmacies**: In the shopping centre behind the bus station, T051-724121. **Post offices** Behind the bus station at Mali Palit 67, Mon-Fri 0700-2000, Sat 0700-1400.

North Dalmatia

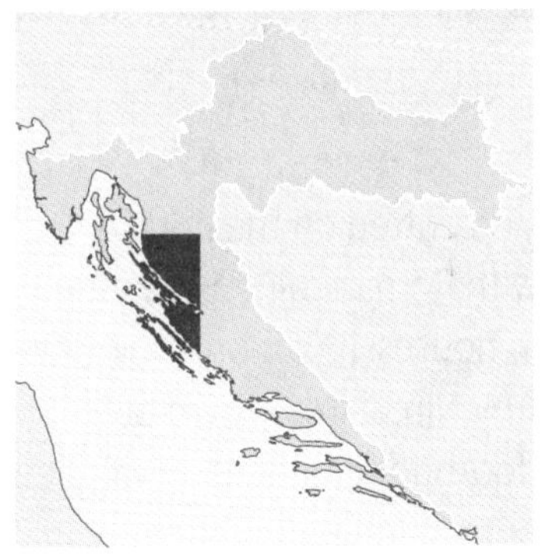

Footprint features

Introduction

North Dalmatia, south of Kvarner, is centred on the port of Zadar, its historic centre packed with Roman ruins, Byzantine churches and Venetian-style town houses. It was once the capital of all Dalmatia and, in nearby Nin, a small town built on an island accessed by a stone footbridge, the medieval Croatian royal family held their court.

The most interesting island in the region is Pag, renowned for delicious salty *paški sir* (sheep's cheese) and a long tradition of lacemaking. Its chief settlement, Pag Town, is a perfect model of Renaissance urban planning, having been designed entirely by one architect, Juraj Dalmatinac. On the northern tip of Pag, Novalje has fine pebble beaches and one of the hottest night-clubbing scenes in Croatia.

However, North Dalmatia's main attraction, especially for yachters, has to be Kornati National Park, a unique seascape of almost 90 scattered islands and islets. Dry, rocky and practically devoid of vegetation, the islands are uninhabited. If you don't have your own boat, it's possible to visit them on an organized day trip, while the more adventurous might even consider renting a Robinson Crusoe-style cottage here. No electricity or running water: just sea, rocks and solitude.

If you prefer terra firma and the sweet smell of meadows and pinewoods you can retreat to Paklenica National Park on the seaward slopes of the rugged Velebit mountain chain – an area criss-crossed by well-marked hiking paths and much loved by free climbers.

★ Don't miss ...

1 Church of St Donatus Attend a classical music concert on a summer evening in this ninth-century church in Zadar, page 178.
2 Gold and Silver of Zadar Admire the collection of reliquaries in Zadar's treasury, featuring the arms and legs of various saints, encased in minutely detailed gold plating, page 179.
3 Nin Make a pilgrimage to the tiny, perfectly proportioned ninth-century Church of the Holy Cross, page 185.
4 Island of Pag Buy delicious paški sir (sheep's cheese) direct from a local producer, page 185.
5 Paklenica National Park Pack a picnic, put on your boots and hike up a karst canyon for stunning views over the sea and islands, page 187.
6 Kornati National Park Spend a day on a boat, sailing between uninhabited 'moonscape' islands, page 189.

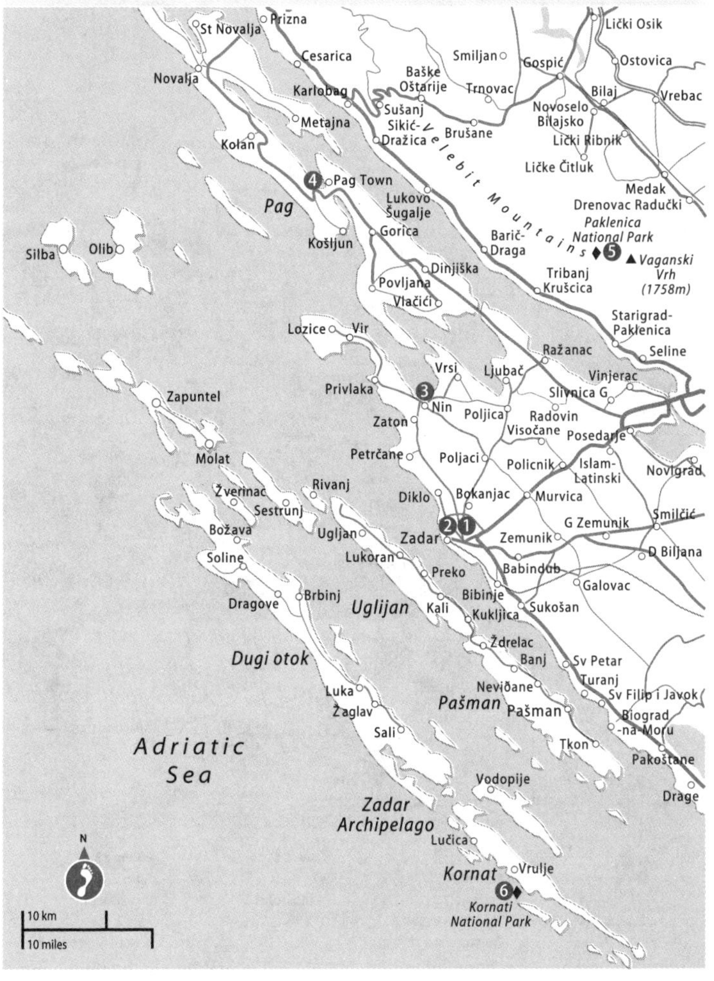

Zadar ➔ *Phone code: 023. Colour map 3, B2. Population: 72,718.*

Sitting compact on a rectangular peninsula, accessible only to pedestrians, the historic centre of Zadar is renowned throughout Croatia for its beautiful medieval churches, the most impressive being St Donat, which stands on the site of the ancient Roman forum. Close by, in the St Mary's Convent complex, the Gold and Silver of Zadar exhibition is a stunning collection of minutely detailed Byzantine reliquaries. The narrow cobbled streets are lined with fine Venetian-style town houses, many converted into shops and cafés at ground level, giving the old town the buzz of a modern-day urban centre. The surrounding modern suburbs are dispersed and more difficult to negotiate: most of the hotels, restaurants and sports facilities lie 5 km along the coast at Puntamika. Before leaving, be sure to try Maraschino, *a cherry-flavoured liquor made in Zadar since 1821.*

During the war of independence, backed by the Serb-held Krajina territory, the city was repeatedly shelled, and electricity and water supplies cut off for some time. Zadar became a hotbed of Croatian nationalism, a sentiment that pervades to this day, despite its long history as a sophisticated multi-ethnic urban centre. ➤➤ *For Sleeping, Eating and other listings, see pages 180-184.*

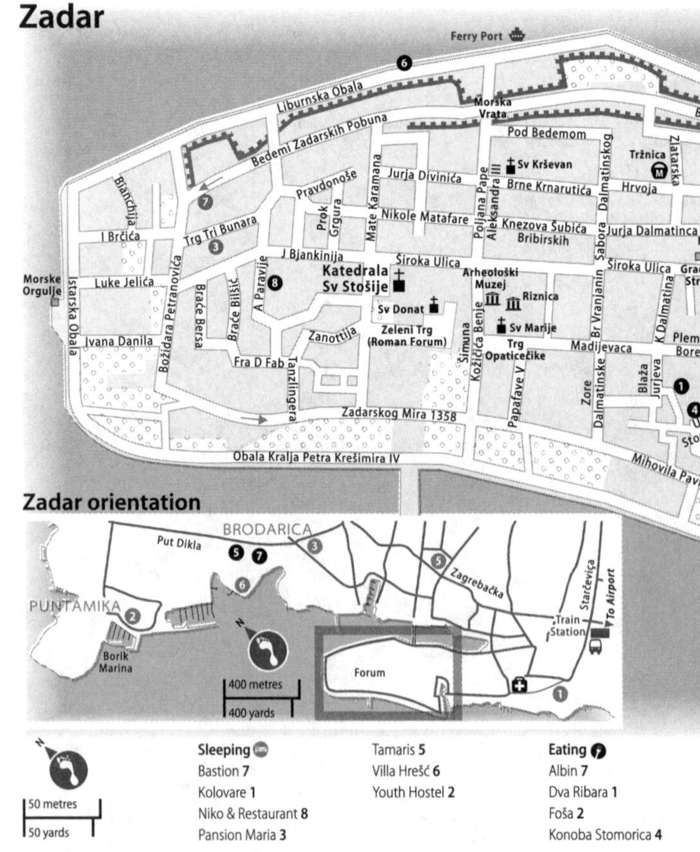

Ins and outs

Getting there Zadar is 190 km from Zagreb, 190 km from Rijeka, 288 km from Pula, 160 km from Split and 376 km from Dubrovnik. Through summer, **Croatia Airlines** run regular flights to and from most European capitals. The airport is at Zemunik, 7 km from the city centre. A **Liburnija** airport bus leaves Zadar bus station 60 minutes before each flight, ticket 25Kn. For bus departure information, T023-343700.

The **bus station** ⓘ *Starčevića 1*, is a 15-minute walk from the old town and the **train station** ⓘ Starčevića 3, is next to the bus station. There is left luggage at the railway station (0600-2200), 20Kn per piece per day.

The city port is on Liburnska Obala, immediately outside the old town walls, accessed through the Sea Gate. **Jadrolinija** run an overnight ferry to Ancona, Italy, plus local services to the surrounding islands. » *See Transport, page 183, for further details.*

Getting around The old town, compact on a peninsula closed to traffic, can easily be explored on foot. However, most of the large hotels and many of the sports facilities are at Puntamika, 5 km northwest of the centre. Puntamika can be reached by bus No 5 and No 8, both of which depart from outside the main bus station and stop en route close to the footbridge near the old town.

Tourist information There's a city **tourist office** ⓘ *Ilije Smiljanića bb, T023-212212, www.tzzadar.hr*, a regional **tourist office** ⓘ *Leopolda Mandića 1, T023-315107, www.zadar.hr*, as well as a walk-in **tourist information centre** ⓘ *M Klaića 5, Narodni trg, T023-316166*, overlooking the main square.

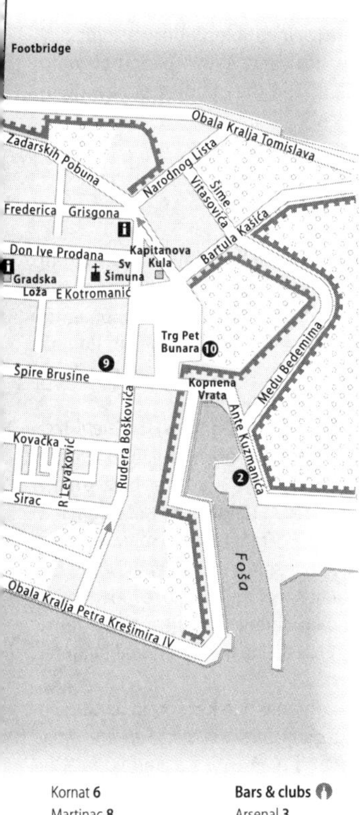

Kornat **6**
Martinac **8**
Na po Ure **9**
Pizzeria Pet Bunara **10**
Roko **5**

Bars & clubs
Arsenal **3**

Best time to visit Like most cities along the coast, Zadar is at its most animated in summer, when you'll find open-air restaurants and cafés, plus a variety of outdoor cultural events in the old town.

Background

First mentioned in a Greek document from the fourth century BC as a settlement founded by the Illyrian tribe of the Liburnians, Zadar was later taken by the Romans, who called it Jadera and developed it into a port and fortified market town with a forum, theatre and public baths.

Following the fall of the Western Roman Empire in the fifth century, Zadar became the capital of the Byzantine *thema* (province) of Dalmatia: within the ancient walls a medieval town developed, with churches decorated with frescoes and mosaics, and workshops where goldsmiths crafted ornately detailed objects for religious ritual use.

In 1105 Zadar came under the Hungarian king, Koloman, and around the same time Venice, which wanted the city for its sheltered port, began a series of repeated attempts to conquer it. Upon the request of the blind Venetian Doge, Enrico Dandolo, when the Fourth Crusades set off for Constantinople in

1202, they stopped at Zadar and after a five-day siege captured and ransacked the city, an act for which Dandolo was later excommunicated by Pope Innocent III. However, Venice continued to dispute Zadar with Hungary and, in 1409, finally obtained permanent possession of the city.

By this time Zadar was the largest urban centre in Dalmatia and possessed the strongest naval fleet on the East Adriatic. So as to retain control, the Venetians rapidly curtailed all political and economic rights of its citizens. In the early 16th century, when the Ottoman Turks conquered the Zadar hinterland, the city was fortified with a system of sturdy defensive walls, and became an important stronghold for ensuring the safe passage of Venetian merchant ships up and down the Adriatic. During the 17th century, refugees from the Turkish occupied territories of Bosnia and Albania arrived in the area, and still today several villages outside Zadar have retained a local dialect heavily influenced by the Albanian language.

After the fall of Venice in 1797, Zadar came under Austria (and remained so until the Second World War except for a brief period of French rule (1805-1813). During the 19th century the city walls were largely demolished, and new public buildings such as an army barracks and post office were erected. **Hotel Bristol**, later renamed **Hotel Zagreb**, opened in 1902, hailing the birth of tourism.

At the end of the First World War, the 1920 Treaty of Rapallo awarded the city to Italy; unfortunate timing, given Mussolini's rise to power in 1922. Thus when Italian fascists occupied Dalmatia in 1941, they chose Zadar as their headquarters. After Italian capitulation in September 1943, the Italian forces left, the Germans moved in, and the Allies began a brutal bombing campaign, so that by the time the Yugoslav *partizani* arrived in 1945, two-thirds of the city centre lay in rubble. Zadar was officially reunited with the rest of Yugoslavia in 1947. The Tito years saw a period of rapid reconstruction coupled with industrial development, and the building of new high-rise residential suburbs and modern tourist facilities.

Sights

Now known as Zeleni Trg, the **Roman Forum** measures 95 m by 45 m and dates from between the first century BC and the third century AD. In Roman times it served as the main market place and public meeting space; still today the city's top monuments, floodlit at night, are found here. On the northwest corner stands an ancient Roman column used as a 'pole of shame' from the Middle Ages up until 1840, where criminals were chained and exposed to public scorn and ridicule.

Standing in the centre of the Forum, **Sv Donat** (Church of St Donatus) ⓘ *Zeleni Trg, Jul-Aug daily 0900-2200, May-Jun and Sep-Oct daily 0900-1300, 1600-1900, closed Nov-Apr, 6Kn*, is an imposing ninth-century rotonda; it's Zadar's best-known monument and the largest Byzantine building in Croatia. Standing 27 m high, it's a robust cylindrical structure flanked by three circular apses. Fragments of Roman stones have been incorporated into the sturdy outer walls, and inside a *matroneum* (womens' gallery) is supported by six pilasters and two Roman columns, and capped by a central dome. St Donat ceased to function as a church during the early 19th century. Today it stands empty, but due to its excellent acoustics it hosts the annual summer festival of medieval, Renaissance and baroque music.

Next to Sv Donat stands the 12th-century late-Romanesque **Katedrala Sv Stošije** (Cathedral of St Anastasia) ⓘ *Zeleni Trg, Jul-Aug daily 0800-2000, Sep-Jun daily 0800-1200, 1700-2000*, built on a rectangular ground plan with a splendid façade bearing three doors, a series of blind arches and two central rose windows, the lower one Romanesque and upper one Gothic. Inside, you'll find a simple stone altar and finely carved wooden choir stalls from the 15th century. At the end of the left aisle, a smaller altar displays a ninth-century stone casket containing the remains of

St Anastasia, to whom the cathedral is dedicated. Work on the **bell tower** began in the 15th century, though the upper three floors weren't completed until 1892 to drawings by the English architect TG Jackson. If you have a head for heights it's well worth climbing to the top of the bell tower for spectacular views over the city.

Housed in a modern concrete building close to the Forum, the **Arheološki Muzej** (Archaeological Museum) ⓘ *Trg Opaticečike 1, on the east side of Zeleni Trg, T023-250516, summer daily 0900-1300, 1800-2100, winter Mon-Sat 0900-1300, 1700-1900, 10Kn*, traces local history from the Stone Age to the late Middle Ages. The ground floor is devoted to finds from between the seventh and 12th centuries, and includes several fine examples of medieval stone carving. The first floor examines North Dalmatia under the Romans, while the second floor is given over to the Palaeolithic, Neolithic, Copper, Bronze and Iron Ages.

Close by, the early-Romanesque **Crkva Sv Marije** (Church of St Mary) ⓘ *Trg Opaticečike, Jul-Aug daily 0800-2000, Sep-Jun daily 0800-1200, 1700-2000*, dates back to 1066, though the present Renaissance façade was added in the 16th century and the interior stucco work completed in 1744. The Romanesque **bell tower**, often referred to as Koloman's Tower after the 12th-century Hungaro-Croatian king, was built between 1105 and 1111. The complex was badly damaged during the Second World War and reconstruction only completed in 1972.

Standing next door to the Church of St Mary, **Riznica** (Treasury) ⓘ *Trg Opatice Čike, T023-250496, summer Mon-Sat 1000-1300, 1800-1930, Sun 1000-1300, winter Mon-Sat 1000-1230, 1800-1930, Sun 1000-1230, 30Kn*, houses a stunning collection known as **Zlato i Srebro Zadra** (Gold and Silver of Zadar), curated by the Benedictine nuns who live in the neighbouring Convent of St Mary. The first floor displays a horde of sumptuous reliquaries – arms and legs of various saints, encased in minutely detailed gold plating – and gold and silver processional crosses. On the second floor you'll find an equally well-displayed collection of religious paintings – look out for three panels from a 15th-century polyptych by the Venetian artist Vittore Carpaccio (1455-1526) and a striking *Assumption of the Virgin* from 1520 by Lorenzo Luzzo. Before leaving, be sure not to miss the adjoining ground floor chapel, **Crkvica Sv Nedjeljica**, behind the ticket office by the main entrance.

North of the Forum, along the street of Pape Aleksandra, is the 12th-century Romanesque **Sv Krševan** (Church of St Chrysogonus) ⓘ *Jul-Aug for evening concerts*. Strangely, the most beautiful part of the building is the exterior decoration of the apses at the back of the church, with a series of Romanesque blind arches. The church is rarely open, but if you have the chance to go inside you'll see statues of the city's four patron saints, Chrysogonus, Zoilus, Simeon and Anastasia, on the main altar.

Following Pape Aleksandra beyond the Church of St Chrysogonus you will come to the **Morska Vrata** (Sea Gate), also known as Vrata Sv Krševana (Gate of St Chrysogonus), leading out to the **ferry port**. Originally a Roman arch, it was reconstructed by the Venetian architect Michele Sanmichele in 1560. On the landward side is a plaque commemorating the 1171 visit of Pope Alexander III, after whom the street is named. On the seaward side the gate bears a chiselled relief of the Lion of St Mark's (emblem of Venice), plus a memorial stone honouring local sailors who fought at the Battle of Lepanto (see page 255) in 1571.

On the tip of the old town peninsula, the **Morske orgulje** (Sea Organ) is an extraordinary instrument with 35 pipes forming whistles that are played by the sea. The notes produced depend on the size of the waves, creating ever changing sounds created by the sea's energy. It was designed by Nikola Bašić and installed in 2005.

Tržnica, the open-air fruit and vegetable market, is east of the Sea Gate. From here, just outside the town walls, you will find a modern **footbridge**, spanning the channel and joining the peninsula to the newer part of town to the north.

Two blocks south of the market is **Narodni Trg**, which took over the role of the Forum as the city's main square in the 16th century. On the west side stands the **Gradska Straža** (City Guardhouse) from 1562 with an imposing 18th-century clock tower. On the opposite side of the square, the **Gradska Loža** ⓘ *Mon-Fri 0900-1200, 1700-2000, Sat 0900-1300*, is a Renaissance loggia designed by Michele Sanmichele in 1565. The open-sided front has been glazed and the interior now houses an exhibition centre.

East of Narodni Trg stands the 17th-century **Sv Šimuna** (Church of St Simeon) ⓘ *Trg Šime Budinića, Mon-Sat 0800-1200 and 1500-1700, Sun for mass 0830.* Inside, on the high altar, the main attraction is a magnificent 14th-century silver casket weighing 250 kg and containing the mummified body of St Simeon, one of the city's four patron saints, which is opened and displayed to the public on 8 October, St Simeon's Day.

East of St Simeon's Church, just within the town walls, **Trg Pet Bunara** is named after five identical wells, still complete with pulleys, which supplied fresh drinking water to the entire population until the late 19th century. On the edge of the square stands the pentagonal **Kapitanova Kula** (Captain's Tower) ⓘ *Trg Pet Bunara bb*, which is currently closed for restoration. It is a 16th-century lookout post built to observe the comings and goings of boats in the nearby channel, and has been renovated to provide a four-level gallery space with a heady spiral staircase leading all the way up to the roof terrace.

South of Trg Pet Bunara stands the monumental **Kopnena Vrata** (Land Gate), which, as its name suggests, was built as the main landside entrance to the city. Based on a classical Roman triumphal arch, it was designed by the Italian Renaissance architect Michele Sanmichele in 1543. The main central arch is topped by a proud Venetian Lion of St Mark's, and flanked to each side by a smaller arch.

Sleeping

Zadar *p176, map p176*

Unfortunately most hotels and restaurants are situated in the Borik complex at Puntamika, 5 km northwest of the centre. Summer 2008 will see the opening of Hotel Bastion, the first and only hotel in the old town.

A **Hotel Bastion**, Bedemi zadarskih pobuna 13, T023-250724, www.hotel-bastion.hr. This stylish 4-star boutique hotel has 23 rooms and 5 suites, a video conference room, small Wellness Centre and restaurant.

C **Hotel Kolovare**, B Peričića 14a, T023-203200, www.hotel-kolovare.com. Zadar's most central hotel, the 235-room **Kolovare** is a 5-min walk from the bus and train stations. It's smart and modern, with a bar, restaurant, sauna, swimming pool and beach.

D **Villa Hrešć**, Obala kneza Trpimira 28, T023-337570, www.villa-hresc.hr. This villa has been renovated to form a modern, luxurious establishment with 6 apartments and 2 rooms. It's on the coast, offering a view of the old town across the water. Facilities include an upmarket restaurant and a garden with a pool.

D **Hotel Niko**, Obala Kneza Domagoja 9, Puntamika-Borik, T023-337880, www.hotel-niko.hr. Elegantly furnished with reproduction antiques, plush red carpets and sweeping curtains, the 12 rooms all have a/c, minibar and satellite TV. Downstairs, on a waterside terrace, is the excellent **Restaurant Niko** (see Eating).

E **Pansion Maria**, Put Petrića 24, just north of the old town, on the road to Borik, T/F023-334244, www.pansionmaria.hr. This small family-run B&B occupies a 3-storey modern building. There are 11 doubles and 2 triples, all with en suite showers.

E **Tamaris**, Zagrebačka 5, T/F023-318700, www.tamaris-zadar.com.hr. On the edge of town, this small modern hotel offers 9 doubles, 2 singles and 1 apartment, all with en suite bathroom and TV. The adjoining restaurant is popular with business people, and is reputed to serve excellent lamb.

F **Youth Hostel**, Obala kneza Trpimira 78, Borik, T023-331145, www.hfhs.hr. This friendly hostel is 5 km from the centre, overlooking the marina in Borik. Take either bus No 5 or No 8 from the bus station. Open all year: 35 beds in winter, 290 in summer.

Private accommodation

Interalfa, Matice dalmatinske 6, T023-315704, www.interalfa.hr. Can arrange private accommodation on the islands of the Zadar archipelago.

Terra Travel Agency, Matije Gupca 2a, T023-337294, www.terratravel.hr. Can arrange private accommodation in the Zadar area and on the neighbouring islands.

Eating

Zadar *p176, map p176*

ƒƒƒ **Kornat**, Liburnska obala 6, T023-254501. On the seafront promenade, close to the ferry port, Kornat is said by many to be the best restaurant in town. It has a stylish modern interior, and serves Croatian dishes spiced up with a dash of Italian flair: look out for tuna carpaccio with rocket, and gnocchi with gorgonzola and pine nuts.

ƒƒƒ-ƒƒ **Foša**, Foša 2, T023-314421. Close to the Land Gate, just outside the city walls, this is probably the best centrally located fish restaurant. Pasta, risotto, seafood and steak are served on a lovely terrace looking out onto a small harbour.

ƒƒ **Albin**, Put Dikla 47, T023-331137. This long-standing favourite has been serving up fresh fish for 30 years. What's on offer depends on the night's catch, but the *riblja juha* (fish soup) wins endless praise. They also have several rooms to rent. It is 2 km from the old town, on the road to Puntamika.

ƒƒ **Dva Ribara**, Blaža Jurjeva 1, T023-213445. Most people come here to eat pizza, but it's also possible to order pasta, risotto, fish and meat dishes. You'll find it in the old town, with a small terrace for outdoor dining in warm weather.

ƒƒ **Martinac**, A Paravije 7, no phone. Home cooking with a creative twist, served in a courtyard garden on sunny days. Look out for veal in tuna and caper sauce. It is in the old town, in a side street close to the cathedral.

ƒƒ **Na po Ure**, Špire Brusine 8, T023-312004. This small *konoba* has an exposed stone interior and serves delicious dishes such as *morki pas* (shark) and *pašticada* (beef stewed in *prošek* and prunes). You'll find it in the old town, on the main street as you enter from Kopnena Vrata (Land Gate).

ƒƒ **Niko**, Obala Kneza Domagoja 9, Puntamika-Borik, T023-337880. Regarded by many as one of the best restaurants in town, Niko has been serving Mediterranean cusine, with an emphasis on seafood, since 1963.

ƒƒ **Pizzeria Pet Bunara**, Ulica obitelji Stratico 1, T023-224010. In the old town, close to Trg Pet Bunara, this restaurant takes pride in using fresh seasonal ingredients to create tasty pizzas, pasta dishes and salads, plus a limited selection of meat and fish dishes.

ƒƒ **Roko**, Put Dikla 54, Brodarica, T023-331000. On the road from the old town to Borik, this restaurant is owned by a fisherman and serves up delicious spaghetti with shrimps, and fresh lobster, on a large summer terrace.

ƒ **Konoba Stomorica**, Ulica Stomorica 12, T023-315946. In the heart of the old town, this tiny *konoba*, frequented by local fishermen, serves *girice* (small fried fish) and *pržene lignje* (fried squid), with house wine on tap.

Cafés

Forum, Široka bb. Pleasant café with a shady terrace overlooking the Roman Forum and the Church of Sveti Donat.

Kavana Sv Lovre, Narodni Trg bb. Occupying a former church next to Gradska Straža (City Guardhouse) this is an ideal place to stop while sightseeing in the old town.

Riva, Zadarskog Mira 1358. A great spot to have coffee on the seafront promenade in the old town.

Bars and clubs

Zadar *p176, map p176*

Arsenal, Trg Tri Bunar 1, www.arsenalzadar.com. In the vast 18th-century Venetian arsenal, this arts and entertainment centre includes a bar, a gallery for exhibitions, a

For an explanation of the sleeping and eating price codes used in this guide, see inside the front cover. Other relevant information is found in Essentials, pages 32-40.

wine shop and a tourist information area. Open daily 0700-0300.

Barbarella's Disco, Petrcane, www.thegardenzadar.com. In the grounds of **Hotel Pinja** in Petrcane, 12km northwest of Zadar, Barbarella's is managed by the same people who run the **Garden Club** (see below). Set on a peninsula, backed by pinewoods and giving onto the sea, it combines an open-air dance floor and a waterside cocktail bar.

Forum, Marka Marulića bb, T023-214556. Zadar's most central nightclub, located just outside the city walls. Plays commercial house music.

The Garden Club, Bedemi zadarskih pobuna, T023-254509, www.thegardenzadar.com. In a garden above the city walls, on the edge of the old town, Zadar's coolest club closed some years ago. It has now been revived by 2 members of the British band UB40, and is a romantic hideaway for cocktails and cool music.

Gotham Multimedia Center, M Oreškovića 1, Borik, T023-200289, www.gotham.hr. A large modern complex combining a café (daily 1800-2400), disco (winter Thu-Sat, summer daily, 2400-0600) and cinema, a 10-min walk north of the old town, via the footbridge.

Entertainment

Zadar *p176, map p176*

Cinema

Gotham Multimedia Center, M Oreškovića 1, Borik, T023-200289, www.gotham.hr.

Pobjeda, Kraljskog Dalmatina 1a, T023-214362.

Theatre

Hrvastsko Narodno Kazalište, HNK (Croatian National Theatre), Široka ulica 8, T023-314552.

Festivals and events

Zadar *p176, map p176*

Jun-Jul Zadar Snova (Zadar Dreams). Alternative open-air theatre festival.

Jul The Garden Festival. Held on the first weekend in July, this 3-day, open-air music festival is staged at **Barbarella's Disco** in Petrcane. It was launched by Zadar's Garden Club (www.thegardenzadar.com) in 2006 and the summer 2008 line-up includes many top European DJs including the UK's Mr Scruff.

Jul-Aug Glazbene veceri u Sv Donatu (Musical Evenings in St Donat's). Concert office, Trg P Zoranica 1, T023-315807, www.kuz.hr. Medieval, Renaissance and baroque music concerts staged inside the churches of St Donat, St Chrysogonus, St Michael, St Simeon and also the Franciscan Monastery. Held annually since 1960. Over the same period, **Zadarsko Kazalšno Ljeto** (Zadar Theatre Summer) perform open-air theatre in historic sites around town. Organized by HNK (see Theatre above).

Shopping

Zadar *p176, map p176*

Bibich, Put Nina 60, T023-325801. The Bibič family produce their own high-quality wines and herb-flavoured *rakija*, which you can taste and buy here. The shop is between the old town and Borik, and is open Mon-Sat 0800-1200 and 1600-2000.

Pet Bunara, Ulica obitelji Stratico 1, T023-224010, www.petbunara.hr. In the old town, close to Trg Pet Bunara, this shop stocks organic wines, extra virgin olive oil, and locally produced honey. The adjoining restaurant is under the same management (see Eating, above).

Tržnica, open-air fruit and vegetable market in the old town. Open daily 0700-1400.

Vinoteka Arsenal, Trg Tri Bunar 1, www.arsenalzadar.com. Inside the arsenal complex, this wine shop stocks wines from Croatia, Australia, Spain, France, Portugal, Chile and Argentina, as well as virgin olive oil from South Dalmatia.

Activities and tours

Zadar *p176, map p176*

Cycling

Super Nova, Obala kneza Branimira 2a, on the seafront, across the footbridge from the old town, T023-311010. Rents bikes on a daily basis, which may be a good option if you're staying outside the centre at Puntamika.

Diving

Zadar Sub, Dubrovačka 20a, T023-214848, www.zadarsub.hr. Run a diving centre at Sali on the island of Dugi Otok.

Sailing

Borik Marina, Kneza Domogoja bb, T023-333036, www.marinaborik.hr, 200 berths.; **Tankerkomerc Marina**, Ivana Meštrovića 2, T023-332700, 300 berths; **Marina Zadar Charter**, Ivana Meštrovića 2, T023-204880, www.zadar-charter.com, a charter company based in Tankomerc Marina.

Tennis

Tennis Club Zadar, Sutomiška 1, between the old town and Borik, T023-332022.

Tour operators

Generalturist, Obala Kneza Branimira 1, T023-318997, www.generalturist.com. One of the of largest Croatian travel agencies, **Generalturist** specialize in tailor-made trips both with and without guides.
Kompas, Natka Nodila 9, T023-254304, www.kompas-travel.com. Can arrange excursions and villas to rent in the area.
Terra Travel Agency, Matije Gupca 2a, T023-337294, www.terratravel.hr. Arranges private accommodation in the Zadar area and excursions to the nearby national parks.

Transport

Zadar *p176, map p176*

Air

Zadar Airport, T023-205800, www.zadar-airport.hr. Through summer, there are regular flights to and from **Amsterdam**, **Berlin**, **Brussels**, **Copenhagen**, **Dusseldorf**, **Frankfurt**, **Gothenburg**, **Hamburg**, **Helsinki**, **Lisbon**, **London** (Gatwick and Heathrow), **Munich**, **Oslo**, **Paris**, **Prague**, **Rome**, **Skopje**, **Stockholm**, **Vienna**, **Zagreb** and **Zurich**. The number of destinations and the frequency of flights are reduced in winter.

Airlines offices Croatia Airlines, Poljana Natka Nodila 7, T023-250101.

Bus

For all information about buses to and from Zadar, T023-211555, www.liburnija-zadar.hr.

Internal services include 22 buses daily to **Zagreb** (3½-5 hrs); 11 to **Rijeka** in Kvarner (4½ hrs); 3 to **Pula** (7 hrs) and 16 to **Split** (3½ hrs).

There are also daily international bus lines to **Ljubljana** (Slovenia), **Trieste** (Italy), **Munich** (Germany). Buses depart several times a week for various other destinations in Germany, Austria, Switzerland and the Netherlands.

Car

Dollar & Thrifty, Hotel Kolovare, B Peričića 14, T023-315733, www.subrosa.hr; **Zadar**, Liburnska obala 3, T023-251700, www.rentacarzadar.com.

Ferry

Schedules vary from day to day and season to season, so check times with the relevant ticket office.

Jadrolinija, T023-254800, www.jadrolinija.hr, run overnight ferries to **Ancona** (Italy) several times per week, 8 hrs. Days and times vary from month to month, check at the ticket office for details. **Mia Tours**, Vrata Sv Krševana (Sea Gate), T023-254300, www.miatours.hr, run a hydrofoil service to Sali and Zaglav on Dugi Otok. **Split Tours**, T021-352533, www.splittours.hr, operate a ferry mid-Jun to mid-Sep from **Pula** to Zadar, stopping at **Unije**, **Mali Lošinj** and **Silba** en route (no cars taken to Unije or Silba). Tickets can be bought in Zadar from **Jadrolinija** agent, Poljana Natka Nodila, T023-251052. **Jadrolinija** also runs daily ferry services connecting Zadar to the nearby islands of **Ugljan**, **Dugi Otok**, **Olib**, **Iž**, **Rava**, **Premuda**, **Mali Lošinj**, **Sestrunj**, **Molat** and **Ist**.

Taxi

Liburnska obala, in front of the ferry port, T023-251400.

Train

Zadar train station, T023-212555.

National train information, T060-333444, www.hznet.hr.

There are 3 trains daily from Zadar to Knin, from where it is possible to take connecting trains to **Zagreb** and **Split**, though this may involve a long wait.

Directory

Zadar *p176, map p176*

Emergencies Ambulance: 94; **Fire**: 93; Police: 92. **Internet** Acme, M Matafara 2a, T023-250708 and **Libar**, Stjepana Radića 11b, T023-301135 are both in the old town and are open daily throughout the summer. **Medical services** General Hospital Zadar, at Bože Peričića 5, between the old town and the bus station, T023-315677. **Pharmacies**: are marked by a glowing green cross. **Ljekarna Donat**, T023-251342, Braće Vranjanina 14, usually open 24 hrs. If closed, there will be a notice on the door saying which pharmacy to go to. **Post offices** The main post office is at Kralja S Držislava 1, Mon-Sat 0700-2100. **Telephones** If you prefer to telephone from a peaceful phone booth, rather than calling on the street, go to one of the post offices (see above). Otherwise, you'll find numerous phone kiosks around town.

Around Zadar

The hinterland to Zadar is a rather unappealing low-lying plain, so most people prefer to make day trips to the islands rather than venturing inland. However, there is one nearby mainland destination worth a visit: Nin, the birthplace of the Croatian state, which can be traced back to medieval times. » *For Sleeping, Eating and other listings, see pages 189-194.*

Nin » *pp189-194. Colour map 3, B2.*

→ *Phone code: 023. Population: 4603.*

Backed by a flat, fertile hinterland, the old town of Nin is wonderful, sitting compact on a small island (500 m by 500 m) jutting out into a lagoon and joined to the mainland by a 70-m-long pedestrian stone bridge which brings you directly to the town gate, built between the 15th and 18th centuries. The medieval churches are Nin's main attraction, the best known being the tiny but perfectly proportioned ninth-century Church of the Holy Cross. Today there are minimum tourist facilities. Most visitors arrive from Zadar, or stay in the purpose-built package resort of Zaton, 2 km to the south, where there are some decent stretches of sand and pebble beach and warm, shallow water for bathing.

Ins and outs

On the regional road to the small island of Vir, 17 km north of Zadar, Nin can comfortably be visited as a half-day trip from Zadar. There are no street names in the old town, but being small and compact all the sights are easily explored in a couple of hours. The **tourist office** ⓘ *Trg Braće Radića 3, T023-264280, www.nin.hr*, is just before the footbridge leading to the old town. » *See Transport, page 193, for further details.*

Background

Built on what was originally a peninsula, Nin was first settled by the Illyrians and later developed into a relatively prosperous town, known as Aenona, under the Romans. Between the ninth and 12th centuries it became the first political, religious and cultural centre of feudal Croatia: seven Croatian kings were crowned here, and Nin was the seat of a bishop, whose jurisdiction stretched over the entire Croatian territory of that time.

In 1328 the town came under Venice, and a canal was dug, converting the peninsula into an island joined to the mainland by a bridge. From the 16th century onwards, constant fighting between Venice and the Turks, coupled with several serious outbreaks of malaria, gradually depleted the population and Nin declined into relative obscurity.

Sights

From the town gate, a central thoroughfare runs the length of the island. Halfway along it stands the 18th-century **Crkva Sv Anzelma** (Church of St Anselmo) ⓘ *daily 0900-1200, 10Kn*, with a neighbouring treasury. Inside you'll find a small but precious collection of gold and silver religious objects, such as the ninth-century casket of St Marcela, ornately crafted jewellery and several finely decorated reliquaries. Close by stands a statue of Grgur Ninski, the notorious ninth-century Bishop of Nin, created by Ivan Meštrović (1883-1962), identical to the one in Split, only smaller.

Just off the main street, to the right of the Church of St Anselmo, is the tiny, ninth-century, whitewashed **Crkva Sv Križa** (Church of the Holy Cross). It is based on the plan of a Greek cross and topped by a central dome. A perfect example of Dalmatian pre-Romanesque architecture, the British architect Thomas Graham Jackson, who visited Nin in 1887, hailed it "the smallest cathedral in the Christian world". It's normally kept locked: the interior is quite bare, but if you'd like to see inside try asking for the key at the Archaeological Museum.

The small **Arheološki Muzej** (Archaeological Museum) ⓘ *T023-264160, Jul-Aug Mon-Sat 1000-2200, May-Jun and Sep Mon-Sat 0800-1200 and 1700-2000, Oct-Apr Mon-Sat on request 0800-1400, 10Kn*, is well laid out and the collection concentrates on local Roman finds, though pride of place is taken by an early Croatian baptismal font carved from block marble, incorporating a slender pedestal supporting a finely decorated hexagonal bowl. The piece on show here is a copy, with the original now kept in the Archaeological Museum in Split.

On the road to Zadar, the tiny 11th-century **Crkva Sv Nikole** (Church of St Nicholas) is perched on a small hill at Prahulje, 1 km from Nin. It is built on a clover-leaf plan and once held the tombs of several early Croatian kings, now on show in Zadar Archaeological Museum. The octagonal watchtower was added in the 16th century, as a defence post against the Ottoman Turks. Unfortunately it's seldom open, but merits inspection from the outside if you are interested in medieval architecture.

Island of Pag » *pp189-194. Colour map 3, A2.*

→ *Phone code: 023 and 053. Population: 7685. The island is 63 km long.*

Long and skinny, rocky and uncultivated, Pag's sparse pastures, scented with wild sage, support sheep farming with twice as many sheep on the island as people. The island is known throughout the country for its excellent *paški sir* (Pag cheese, made from sheep's milk) and succulent *janjetina* (roast lamb). Several fertile valleys are given over to vineyards, producing two local dry white wines, the golden-coloured *Žutica* and the light, crisp *Gegić*. The chief settlement is the picturesque 15th-century **Pag Town**, with a long tradition of salt production and lace making, while the main tourist destination is **Novalja**, a seaside resort with some decent pebble beaches and several late-night dance clubs, which have earned it the slightly exaggerated reputation of being Croatia's Ibiza.

Ins and outs

Getting there Pag is joined to the mainland by a 300-m-long road bridge on its southeast tip. There are six buses daily from Zadar and two from Rijeka, both arriving in the Pag Town. There are regular ferries from Prizna on the mainland to Žigljen on Pag, plus a once-daily ferry service from Rab Town on the neighbouring island of Rab to Lun on the north tip of Pag. » *See Transport, page 193, for further information.*

Getting around A scenic regional road runs the length of the island, joining all the main settlements. A local bus service between Pag Town and Novalja runs twice daily. Alternatively you can hire a bike.

Tourist information There are tourist offices in **Pag Town** ⓘ *Ulica od Spitala bb, T/F023-611301, www.pag-tourism.hr*, and **Novalja** ⓘ *T053-661404, www.tz-novalja.hr.*

Pag Town → *Phone code: 023. Colour map 3, A2. Population: 2701.*

Located at the southeast end of Pag Bay, at the mouth of a narrow channel leading to a shallow salt lake, Pag Town has been the island's chief economic and administrative centre since its founding in the 15th century. Although there are no notable beaches here, and the surrounding landscape is somewhat dreary, the old town is a gem of Renaissance architecture, as well as the best place to buy locally produced sheep's cheese and handmade lace.

The original settlement, now abandoned, is 3 km south of present-day Pag Town. Granted the status of a free royal town in 1244 by King Bela IV, it quickly became a prosperous trading centre, its wealth based on the production of salt, and indeed a vast expanse of salt pans, overlooked by the 12th-century Crkva Sv Marije (Church of St Mary), can still be seen there today. The island came under Venice in 1403, and in 1443, as the danger of a Turkish invasion looked ever more likely, plans were drawn up for a new fortified centre. The renowned architect and sculptor Juraj Dalmatinac (also responsible for Šibenik Cathedral) masterminded the project, which took several decades to build. A grid of narrow streets, centring on a main square with a cathedral and Rector's Palace, were to be enclosed by sturdy walls and 10 towers.

Today the complex remains well intact, though the walls have mostly gone. On the main square, **Trg Kralja Petra Krešimira IV**, you can see the 15th-century parish church of **Sv Marije** (St Mary) which, although it was never awarded the status of cathedral, remains a proud monument based on the form of a three-nave Romanesque basilica, with a fine façade featuring a Renaissance rose window above an elegant Gothic portal. Café life centres on the main square, while much of the post-1960s tourist development such as hotels, apartments and restaurants lie west of town, overlooking a family beach, with shallow water suitable for kids.

Novalja → *Phone code: 053. Colour map 3, A2. Population: 2078. 20 km northwest of Pag Town.*

In a sheltered cove backed by pinewoods, Novalja is Pag's largest and busiest resort. Pristine-clear emerald seawater and a number of bays with fine pebble beaches make it the best place for sunbathing on the island, while sports and late-night dance clubs compensate in part for its lack of cultural attractions. The one sight you might check out is the 1024-m-long underground **Roman aqueduct**. Visitors are offered raincoats and crash helmets with lamps at the entrance to this dark underground tunnel where, even in mid-summer, temperatures do not rise above 15°C. Some 3 km north of Novalja, the peaceful fishing village of **Stara Novalja** is hidden away at the end of a 5-km-long channel, happily protected from the prevailing winds, and backed by vine-covered slopes. The most popular bathing areas are the pebble beaches of **Zrće** and **Straško**, a short distance south of Novalja.

Paklenica National Park » pp189-194.

Colour map 3, A2/3.

→ *Phone code: 023. 42 km north of Zadar.*

Lying on the southeast slopes of the **Velebit** mountain chain (which itself is 145 km long and a designated nature park), the Paklenica National Park covers 100 sq km and runs for 20 km along the Riviera, combining coastal and mountain scenery, making it a haven for hikers and free-climbers. The lower levels are covered with beech forests, which gradually give way to pines, dramatic rocky outcrops, mountain meadows and scree slopes.

Ins and outs

The best starting point for exploring Paklenica National Park is the seaside town of Starigrad Paklenica, overlooking the narrow Velebitski Kanal (Velebit Channel). The **national park office** ⓘ *Tudjmana 14a, Starigrad Paklenica, T023-369202, www.paklenica.hr, entry to park Apr-Oct 40Kn, Nov-Mar 30Kn*, is at the entrance to the park and can supply visitors with maps of the walking paths and information about mountain refuges. ▸▸ *See Transport, page 193, for further details.*

Exploring the park

The most popular walking route leads up the impressive karst canyon of **Velika Paklenica**, which is 10 km long and up to 400 m deep, and runs from the highest peaks down to the sea. The path starts about 4 km inland from the park entrance at Starigrad Paklenica. Passing a couple of mountain refuges a stiff climb will bring you to the 1757-m peak of **Vaganski Vrh**, the highest point on southern Velebit, offering stunning views over the sea and islands. This walk requires an entire day, and you should only set out armed with good hiking boots and a plentiful supply of water. Alternatively, a little way up the gorge, a secondary path branches off to the right, leading to **Anića Kuk**, a bizarre 721-m vertical rock form and a popular training ground for free-climbers since the 1930s. From here the path continues, passing through a dense forest, and eventually arrives at a height of 550 m, where you will find **Manita Peć**, a 500-m-long illuminated cave, filled with stalactites and stalagmites, which can be visited as part of a guided tour (ask at the national park office for details). A final stretch of path brings you to the 800 m peak of **Vidakov Kuk**. The gorge is home to birds of prey such as peregrine vultures and sparrowhawks, while bears and wild boars are occasionally sighted in the more remote areas of Velebit.

Dugi Otok and the Zadar Archipelago

▸▸ *pp189-194. Colour map 3, B2/3.*

→ *Phone code: 023. Population: 1820.*

Dugi Otok, translating literally as 'Long Island', is the largest of a scattering of islands and islets that make up the Zadar Archipelago. Running 43 km from northwest to southeast, and never wider than 4.6 km, it's a rugged, sparsely populated place, which seems to have passed through the centuries with few notable events. The island's villages lie along the northeast coast, looking back towards the mainland, while the southwest side, opening on to the sea, is made up of steep cliffs and a series of small inlets. A scenic road runs the length of the island from **Veli Rat** in the northwest, passing through Božava, Brbinj and Zaglav, to arrive in the chief settlement, **Sali**, in the southeast. The main attractions are at the extremities of the island: **Telašćica Nature Park** on the southern tip, and **Sakarun Bay** in the north. However, tourist facilities are minimal and public transport limited, so you really need a car to get around.

Between Dugi Otok and Zadar are the similarly long and skinny, but not quite as rugged or dramatic islands of **Ugljan** and **Pašman**, which are joined together by a bridge and are connected to Zadar and Biograd-na-Moru by regular ferry services. Now almost a suburb of Zadar, many locals have summer houses here, although there is little of cultural or recreational interest to the passing traveller.

Ins and outs

Getting there Throughout the year, regular ferries operate from Zadar to Brbinj, and from Zadar to Sali and Zaglav. If you're thinking of taking a car to Dugi Otok, remember that the ferry for Brbinj carries vehicles, but that the boat for Sali and Zaglav is for foot passengers only, and that the only petrol station on the island is in Zaglav.

 The island's only **tourist office** ⓘ *Obala Petra Lorinija bb,T023-377094, www.dugiotok.hr*, is in Sali. » See Transport, page 193, for further details.

Getting around The main road runs the length of the island from Veli Rat to Sali. Buses are few and far between: a local bus meets incoming ferries at Brbinj, taking passengers to Božava and Veli Rat on the northern end of the island; likewise, another local bus connects Sali, Zaglav and Luka to correspond with incoming and outgoing ferries on the southern end of the island. But, for now, Veli Rat and Sali are only connected by a once-weekly bus, leaving the northern and southern ends of Dugi Otok somewhat divorced from one another.

Exploring the island

The best place for swimming and sunbathing, plus occasional all-night beach parties, is **Sakarun** (also known as Saharun), a white-sand beach in a large, sheltered bay backed by pine woods between Božava and Veli Rat on the northern tip of the island. Dugi Otok's most developed resort is **Božava** (population 127), an old stone fishing village built around a pretty harbour with a quay where yachts can moor up. On the edge of the village, overlooking the sea, is a modern hotel complex with eating and sports facilities. West from here, **Veli Rat** (population 83) is a sleepy seaside village which dates back to Roman times.

Dugi Otok's largest settlement is **Sali** (population 769), which takes its name, first mentioned in 1105, from the former saltpans. Built around a sheltered bay, it also has a long history of fishing, though today the locals are gradually moving towards tourism, with the main attraction being **Telašćica Nature Park** ⓘ *www.telescica.hr*, 3 km to the south. A natural extension of the Kornati, Telašćica is an 8.6-km-long bay surrounded by pinewoods and steep-sided cliffs of up to 166 m, with countless secluded coves ideal for bathing. Close by, a 2-km-long saltwater lake, **Jezero Mira**, contains water several degrees warmer than the sea and is said to have therapeutic properties. Most people arrive in Telašćica by boat, either private yacht or as part of an organized excursion to the Kornati, but it's also possible to walk through the olive groves from Sali.

Biograd-na-Moru

» pp189-194. Colour map 3, B3.

→ *Phone code: 023. Population: 5259.*

Overlooking the Pašman Channel, 20 km southeast of Zadar, the package resort of Biograd offers little of cultural interest, though its proximity to the Kornati Islands make it an important landmark for yachters, with two marinas and several charter companies hiring sailing boats on a weekly basis. There's a **tourist office** ⓘ *Trg hrvatskih velikana 2, T023-383123, www.tzg-biograd.hr.*

Historically, Biograd's greatest moment passed in 1102, when the Hungarian king, Koloman, was crowned King of Croatia and Dalmatia here, following the *Pacta Conventa*, an agreement between Croatian nobles and the Hungarian state. Sadly nothing of the medieval town remains, having been devastated by the Venetians in 1125. Although it was later rebuilt, it was destroyed once again by the townspeople themselves as they retreated from the Turks in 1646. Today it's a fairly unremarkable place, made up largely of the standard concrete-block summer houses that were built along the coast during the tourist boom of the 1970s.

Behind Biograd, **Vransko Jezero** ⓘ *www.vransko-jezero.hr*, is Croatia's largest lake; one of the country's few colonies of herons can be spotted in the ornithological reserve on the northwest shore. Last but not least, you will pass through Biograd if planning to visit the islands of Pašman and Ugljan: a regular **Jadrolinija** ferry service connects the town to Tkon on Pašman, which in turn is connected to Ugljan by a bridge.

Kornati National Park » pp189-194.

Colour map 3, B2/3.

Parallel to the mainland coast mid-way between Zadar and Šibenik, Kornati National Park covers an area 35 km long and 13 km wide, containing 89 islands, islets and reefs. Declared a national park in 1980 due to its wealth of underwater life and its unique natural beauty, the area is made up of crystal-clear blue sea and a scattering of eerie 'moonscape' islands supporting scanty vegetation.

Having no fresh water sources and little fertile land, the Kornati passed through the centuries with minimum human intervention. During the 17th century, noble families from Zadar, with the blessing of the Venetians, used the islands for sheep rearing, employing serfs from Murter as shepherds. Later the Murterini bought rights to 90% of the Kornati, and continued to use them for seasonal farming: grazing sheep, cultivating olives, grapes and figs and keeping bees (there are few wild animals here other than lizards). They also built some 300 simple stone cottages, mainly in sheltered coves, which they used as temporary homes when fishing or tending the land. Today many of these cottages, still without running water and electricity, have been turned over to tourism, and are available for rent through the summer months, often with a small boat included, as 'Robinson Crusoe' retreats (see Sleeping, below).

The largest island, **Kornat**, is 25 km long and up to 2.4 km wide. Travelling along the west coast by boat you'll pass a series of dramatic cliffs plummeting 100 m down to the sea, punctuated by small coves, many with pleasant sheltered beaches and, here and there, an informal summer restaurant serving fresh fish at tables by the water's edge.

Ins and outs

Although the Kornati are best explored by private sailing boat, they can also be visited as part of an organized day trip, arranged by private agencies operating from Zadar, Biograd-na-Moru, Murter, Vodice and Šibenik (see respective sections for details). The entrance fee to the park will be included in the price of the trip if you arrive as part of a group. If you're travelling by private boat, you should pay at any one of a number of kiosks scattered through the park from June to September (80Kn per person), or you can buy a reduced rate ticket from outside the park (50Kn per person), either at the national park head office in Murter, which operates the year through, or from marinas in Betina, Biograd-na-More, Murter, Primošten, Punat and Zadar. **Kornati National Park office** ⓘ *Butina 2, T022-435740, www.kornati.hr*, is based in Murter (see page 226).

Sleeping

Pag Town *p186*

C **Hotel Pagus**, Ante Starčevića 1, T023-492050, www.coning-turizam.hr. This modern, 3-storey hotel is close to the centre of Pag Town, and looks out onto the beach. It has 117 comfortable rooms as well as a new Wellness Centre and Spa Cissa, offering massage, sauna, beauty therapies, indoor and outdoor pool with jacuzzi.

E **Hotel Restoran Biser**, A G Matoša 8, T023 611333, www.hotel-biser.com. A 15-min walk west of the centre, this modern building conceals 20 comfortable rooms, each with a bathroom, TV and balcony, plus a large, highly regarded restaurant and great views back over town. Pets are welcome.

E **Hotel Tony**, Dubrovačka 39, T/F023-611370, www.hotel-tony.com. 1 km from Pag Town, this modern concrete building has 20 rooms, a large restaurant, Wi-Fi and a beach at the front.

Private accommodation

Maricom, S Radića 8, T023-612266, www.pag-tourist-service.hr. An agency which can help you find rooms and apartments to rent in Pag Town.

Novalja *p186*

A **Hotel Boškinac**, Novaljska Polje bb, T053-663500, www.boskinac.com. A small, luxury hotel in a stone building with 7 rooms and 4 apartments, plus a high-class restaurant with an open fire and a leafy terrace. The interior features natural materials combined with modern design and vivid colours.

C **Hotel Loža**, Trg Loža 1, Novalja, T053-663380, www.turno.hr. Bang in the centre of town, this unassuming but comfortable modern hotel has 35 rooms, each with satellite TV and a minibar. There's also a ground-floor restaurant and café with a summer terrace overlooking the seafront.

Private accommodation

The following Novalja-based agencies can help you find private accommodation: **Navalija Kompas**, Slatinska bb, T053-661 215, www.navalija-kompas.hr; **Sunturist**, Krančevićeva bb, T053-661211, www.sun turist.com.

Paklenica National Park *p186*

D **Hotel Vicko**, Joze Dokoze 20, Starigrad Paklenica, T/F023-369304, www.hotel-vicko.hr. A comfortable, modern hotel with 23 rooms and a pleasant restaurant with a summer terrace shaded by pine trees. Pets welcome.

F **Rajna**, Tudjmana 105, Starigrad Paklenica, T023-369130, www.hotel-rajna.com. Popular with Croatian and foreign climbers and walkers thanks to its location close to the national park entrance, **Rajna** has 10 guest rooms (most with balconies) and a highly regarded restaurant serving up a range of fish and meat dishes. The house speciality is *rižots morskim plodovima* (seafood risotto).

Dugi Otok and the Zadar Archipelago *p187*

C **Agava Apartments**, Božava, T023-291291, www.hoteli-bozava.hr. Set in pine woods, this complex comprises 18 apartments each with a double room, living room, bathroom, kitchenette and a balcony with sea views. Guests can use the **Hotel Lavanda** facilities.

D **Hotel Lavanda**, Božava, T023-291291, www.hoteli-bozava.hr. This refurbished modern building, overlooking the sea and backed by pinewoods, has 80 double rooms each with a balcony and sea view. Facilities include a restaurant, outdoor pool, fitness centre, sauna massage and mooring for boats.

D **Veli Rat Lighthouse**, contact **Adriatica Net**, Selska 34, Zagreb, T01-241 5611, www.adriatica.net. 3 km from the small village of Veli Rat, this 19th-century lighthouse provides 2 apartments, sleeping 3 and 4. Accessible by car, it is close to a decent pebble beach and is backed by pine trees.

E **Hotel Sali**, Sali, T023-377049, www.hotel-sali.hr. A complex comprising 4 pavilions with a total of 52 rooms, a restaurant and a scuba-diving centre, overlooking the sea and backed by pinewoods. Open Apr-Oct.

E **Pansion Roko**, Zaglav 28, T023-377182, www.pansion-roko.hr. In the small village of Zaglav, this modern white building offers 5 basic rooms, each with a bathroom, TV and balcony with a sea view. There's also a 4-bed apartment with a kitchen. The ground floor restaurant serves up local seafood specialities.

Private accommodation

Marlin Tours, R K Jeretova 3, T023-305 920, www.marlin-tours.hr. A Zadar-based agency that can help you find private accommodation on the island.

Biograd-na-Moru *p188*

C **Hotel Adriatic**, Tina Ujevica 7, Biograd, T023-383556, www.ilirijabiograd.com. This 6-storey building is close to the old town and overlooks a pebble beach with fine views to the islands. Renovated to form a smart design hotel, it has 100 rooms and 5 suites furnished in slick minimalist style. Facilities

For an explanation of the sleeping and eating price codes used in this guide, see inside the front cover. Other relevant information is found in Essentials, pages 32-40.

include an outdoor pool and whirlpool, plus the **Lavender Bed Bar**, which serves cocktails at canopied beds to a background of chill-out music. Open all year.

E **Hotel Bolero**, Meštrovića 1, T023-386888, www.hotel-bolero.hr. This modern building, renovated in 2002, has 76 rooms, a restaurant, sauna and internet café. Open all year.

E **Hotel Medusa**, A Šenoe 24, T023-383331, www.hotelmeduza.com. A small, family-run hotel occupying a modern 3-storey building with 15 rooms and 1 suite, all with satellite TV and a/c. Also has a restaurant. Open all year.

Private accommodation

Val Tours, Trg hrvatskih velikana 1a, T023-386479, www.val-tours.hr. An agency that can help you find accommodation in town, plus Robinson Crusoe cottages on the island of Pašman.

Kornati National Park *p189*

Camping within the park is strictly forbidden. The following Murter-based agencies both have a selection of Robinson Crusoe type accommodation: simply furnished cottages with gas lighting and water from a well, no cars, no shops, and probably no neighbours: **Kornat Turist**, Hrvatskih vladara 2, T022-435854/5, www.kornatturist.hr; **Lori**, Zdrače 2, Betina, T022-435631, www.tourist agency-lori.hr.

Eating

Nin *p184*

ŸŸ **Konoba Branimir**, Višeslavov trg 2, T023-264866. Directly opposite the Church of Holy Cross, this stone building houses a traditional Dalmatian *konoba* serving carefully prepared local meat and fish dishes.

Pag Town *p186*

ŸŸŸ-ŸŸ **Hotel Restoran Biser**, see Sleeping. This highly regarded restaurant serves delicious *paška janjetina ispod peke* (Pag lamb prepared under a *peka*) and offers great views of town.

ŸŸ **Na Tale**, S Radića 2, T023-611194. Close to the harbour, with outdoor tables and sea views, this small restaurant specializes in barbecued fish and Pag lamb, which you might round off with *palačinke* (pancakes). Pizzas are also available.

Novalja *p186*

ŸŸ **Antonio**, Obala Petra Krešimira 4, T053-661280. On a waterside terrace looking out over Novalja bay, close to the main square, this family-run eatery serves up tasty pizza and pasta dishes, as well as local specialities such as Novaljski brodet sa palentom (Novalja fish stew with polenta). Open all year.

ŸŸ **Moby Dick**, Obala Petra Krešimira IV bb, T053-662488. Located on the seafront promenade, **Moby Dick** serves Dalmatian seafood dishes, barbecued fish and meat, plus pizzas, on a large open-air terrace.

ŸŸ **Steffani**, Petra Krešimira IV 28, T053-661697. In the centre of Novalja, **Steffani** is popular with both locals and visitors who come here to savour fresh seafood and lamb, along with local specialities such as snails and dried octopus. Pizza makes a cheap option.

ŸŸ **Sveta Marija**, Stara Novalja bb, T053-661 655. Popular with yachters, **Sveta Marija** serves up *paški sir* (sheep's cheese), *janjetina* (roast lamb), fresh fish and local wine at tables on a summer terrace overlooking the sea in Stara Novalja, about 1.5 km from Novalja. They also have 5 doubles rooms and 6 apartments upstairs (**E**).

Dugi Otok and the Zadar Archipelago *p187*

ŸŸ **Restoran Kornat**, Sali, T023-377049. In the centre of Sali, this large restaurant serves traditional Dalmatian meat and fish dishes, and good choice of wines on an open-air terrace, May-Oct.

ŸŸ **Restoran Roko**, Zaglav, T023-377182. A small restaurant in Zaglav where the owner-cook serves barbecued fish and meat dishes prepared under a *peka*, May-Oct.

Biograd-na-Moru *p188*

ŸŸ **Restoran Guste**, Obala Kralja Petra Krešimira IV bb, T023-383025. A range of reasonably priced fish and seafood dishes are served at simple wooden tables and benches on a summer terrace looking out to sea.

Ÿ **Pizzeria Andrija**, Trg hrvatskih velikana 2, T023-385172. Centrally located, close to the bus station, **Andrija** serves pizzas from a brick oven, pasta dishes and colourful salads on a large open-air terrace.

Kornati National Park *p189*

The restaurants listed here are all found on the west coast of the largest island, **Kornat**.

Restoran Beban, Uvala Gujka (Gujak Cove),T098-553 1588 (mob). One of the few restaurants in the area to offer *janjetina* (roast lamb), as well as *brodet* (fish stew), seafood and barbecued fish, from mid-Apr to early Oct.

Restoran Darko-Strižnja, Uvala Strižnja (Strižnja Cove), T091-250 3233 (mob). Close to **Restoran Quattro**, **Darko-Strižnja** serves up seafood risotto and pasta dishes, *brodet* (fish stew), seafood and barbecued fish, from early May to early Oct.

Restoran Opat, Uvala Opata (Opat Cove), T091-473 2550. This highly regarded eatery serves delicious seafood specialities such as fish pâté, salted anchovies and tuna carpaccio, plus locally-grown olives preserved in seawater, and cake made from carob.

Restoran Quattro, Uvala Strižnja (Strižnja Cove), T022-435187. A decent range of Dalmatian meat and fish dishes, from Easter to late Oct.

Restoran Solana, Uvala Šipnate (Šipnata Cove), T022-435433. A tiny eatery with seating for just 30 people and a menu including seafood risotto, barbecued fish, steaks and pancakes. Early Jun to mid-Sep.

Bars and club

Novalja *p186*

A new law passed in 2007 means that bars and clubs on Zrće beach can stay open 24-hours a day, non-stop.

Aquarius Club, Zrće Beach, www.aquarius.hr. Through summer, Zagreb's hottest club moves from the capital to the island of Pag for open-air drinking and dancing by the sea, with regular live concerts given by popular Croatian musicians.

Kalypso, Zrče Beach, www.kalypso.com.hr. Bathing, badminton and beach volleyball by day; music, dancing and cocktails by night.

Papaya, Zrće beach, www.papaya.com.hr. A beach complex with water slides, a bar and a restaurant. Resident and international guest DJs generate a party mood, daily after 2000.

Biograd-na-Moru *p188*

Carpy More, Bana Josipa Jelačića, Biograd, T023-386119. Situated in the old town, this large bar has exposed stonewalls and rustic wooden furniture. Hosts live music each Thu evening.

Shopping

Pag Town *p186*

Lacemaking school, next to the church, on the main square, T023-611017. Founded in 1906, the school has opened a gallery with items made of Pag lace. Summer 0900-1200, 2000-2200.

Paška Sirana, Splitska bb, T023-600810, www.paskasirana.hr. The best place to buy *paški sir*, a hard, salty cheese similar to the Italian *pecorino*.

Activities and tours

Novalja *p186*

Diving

Connex Diving, Kunera bb, T917-213234, www.connexdiving.eu.

Paklenica National Park *p186*

Tour operators

The national park can organize ½-day and full-day **guided tours** of the park (400Kn and 800Kn respectively). These should be arranged 1 week in advance and include special **birdwatching tours**, in the company of a qualified ornithologist, for groups of 5-10 people, ½ day or full day (prices as above). Birdwatchers must bring their own binoculars and cameras.

Regular organized visits to **Manita Peć cave** leave the national park office at Starigrad Paklenica at 1000 and return at 1300 on the following days: Apr, Sat; May and Oct, Wed and Sat; Jun and Sep, Mon, Wed and Sat; Jul and Aug daily. 15Kn plus the standard national park entrance fee.

Dugi Otok and the Zadar Archipelago *p187*

Diving

Kornati Diver, Zaglav, T023-377167, www.kornati-diver.com.

Sailing
Although there are no marinas on the island, **Telašćica Bay** is a popular sheltered place to put down anchor. Zaglav is the only place (and the nearest to the Kornati), for petrol.

Biograd-na-Moru *p188*

Birdwatching
For visits to the ornithological reserve on Vransko Jezero contact the nature park office, Kralja Petra Svačića 2, Biograd, T023-383181, www.vransko-jezero.hr.

Diving
Albamaris, T023-385435, www.albamaris.hr; **Bougainville Diving**, T023-385900, www.bougainville.nl.

Sailing
Marina Kornati, Šetalište kneza Branimra 1, T023-383800, www.marinakornati.com. 600 berths, open all year.
Marina Šangulin, Kraljice Jelene 3, T023-385020, www.sangulin.hr. 200 berths, open all year.

The following charter companies are based in Biograd: **Full Team**, Ivana Mazuranića 7, T023-384502, www.full-team.com; **Gomar**, Splitska 21, T023-384508, www.gomar.hr; and **Šangulin**, Kraljice Jelene 3, T023-383738, www.sangulin.hr.

Tour operators
Val Tours, Trg hrvatskih velikana 1a, T023-386479, www.val-tours.hr. Offer day trips to the nearby Kornati and Paklenica national parks, 1-day rafting trips on the River Zrmanja, plus a 7-day birdwatching package.

Kornati National Park *p189*

Diving
Within the park, diving is restricted to organized groups. The following local clubs can arrange dives here: **Aquanaut**, Murter, T022-434988, www.divingmurter.com; **Bougainville Diving**, Biograd-na-Moru, T023-385900, www.bougainville.nl; **Moana**, Jezera, T022-438160, www.moana.pl; **Najada**, Murter, T022-436020, www.najada.com; and **Zadar Sub**, Zadar, T023-214848 www.zadarsub.hr.

Sailing
Setting down anchor around the Kornati is restricted to 16 designated coves.
ACI Marina, Piškera, within the national park, T091-470 0091 (mob), www.aci-club.hr, Apr-Nov, 150 berths. Facilities include water and power supplies, restaurant, telephone, toilets and showers, and a grocery. The nearest gas station is in Zaglav on Dugi Otok (19.5 km).
ACI Marina, Žut, just outside the national park, to the northeast, T022-786 0278, and T099-470028 (mob), www.aci-club.hr. Apr-Nov, 120 berths. Facilities include water and power supplies, restaurant, telephone, toilets and showers, and a grocery shop. The nearest gas station is in Zaglav on Dugi Otok (13 km).

Transport

Nin *p184*

Bus
There are hourly buses from **Zadar** (0600-2000).

Pag Town *p186*

Bus
There are 2 buses daily from **Rijeka**, which use the Prizna-Žigljen 20-min ferry crossing and then drive south along the island to Pag Town. 6 buses depart daily from **Zadar**, crossing Pag Bridge then driving 20 km to Pag Town.

Novalja *p186*

Bus
There are 2 buses daily from **Pag Town**.

Ferry
Jadrolinija, Zadar office, T023-254800, run regular ferries (12 daily in winter, 20 in summer) from **Prizna** on the mainland to **Žigljen** on Pag. From **Žigljen**, it is 5 km to Novalja.
Rapska Plovidba, Rab office, T051-724122, run a twice-daily ferry from **Rab Town**, on the island of Rab, to **Lun**, which is on a peninsula 20 km northwest of Novalja.

Paklenica National Park *p186*

Bus
All buses running along the coastal road from **Zadar** to **Rijeka** stop in Starigrad Paklenica.

Dugi Otok and the Zadar Archipelago *p187*

Ferry

Jadrolinija, Zadar office, T023-254800, operate a ferry service from **Zadar** to **Brbinj**, with 2 crossings daily through winter and 4 in summer. They also run a boat (foot passengers only) from Zadar to Zaglav, calling en route at Sali, departing 4 times daily in winter and 6 times daily in summer.

Biograd-na-Moru *p188*

Bus

All buses covering the coastal stretch from **Zadar** to **Šibenik** stop in Biograd.

Kornati National Park *p189*

Ferry

There are no ferries to the Kornati. The only way to arrive is as part of an organized tour group or by private boat. See page 189.

Central Dalmatia

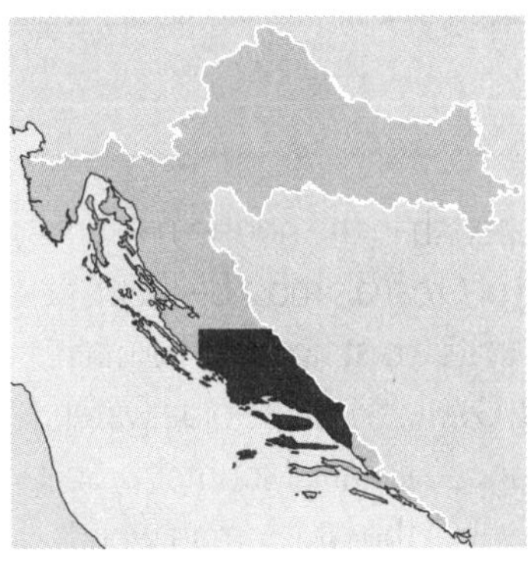

Footprint features

Introduction

More mountainous and less developed than the northern regions, Central Dalmatia is home to several of Croatia's most beautiful medieval coastal towns (and some of its worst hotels). The main cultural and economic pulse is Split. Overlooking the blue waters of the Adriatic and backed by the rugged Dinaric Mountains, Split is one of the most extraordinary towns of the late Roman world. With a busy port and regular ferry and catamaran services, it's a perfect point of arrival if you're coming from Italy and a good launching pad if you intend to explore the surrounding islands.

The nearest and probably the least appealing island is Brač. Its best-known resort, Bol, heaves with tourists during July and August, each one eager to find a space on the undeniably stunning Zlatni Rat beach. Outside peak season, however, it's well worth the trip and can be combined with a hike up to Vidove Gora, the highest peak on all the Adriatic islands.

For many people the most beautiful island is Hvar. Its capital, Hvar Town, now has the unenviable honour of being Croatia's hippest resort. Built around a small harbour and backed by a hilltop fortress, the old town is made up of winding cobbled streets, which converge on a vast piazza. The rest of the island falls away into a wilderness of lavender fields and vineyards.

Further out to sea, Vis is Croatia's most distant inhabited island and a place that, for now at least, has been spared commercial tourism. Its two main settlements, Vis Town and Komiža, are popular with yachters and offer a selection of authentic fish restaurants and wine cellars.

Back on the mainland, north of Split, is the little medieval town of Trogir and, further north still, Dalmatia's second-largest city, Šibenik, with its magnificent 15th-century cathedral. Nearby, Krka National Park conceals a series of dramatic waterfalls and steep wooded slopes. South of Split, the Makarska Rivijera offers a string of decent pebble beaches and is a good starting point for hiking up Mount Biokovo in spring and autumn.

★ Don't miss ...

1 Diocletian's Palace Spend a day exploring Split's Roman past, page 201.
2 Galerija Meštrović See the works of Croatia's greatest modern sculptor, page 208.
3 Krka National Park Bathe in river pools as spectacular waterfalls thunder through a steep-sided, wooded valley near Šibenik, page 224.
4 Zlatni Rat Soak up the sun on this beautiful beach on the island of Brač, page 242.
5 Hvar Town Stay a night on the island of Hvar in Dalmatia's most fashionable resort, page 249.
6 Modra Spilja Catch a boat to the stunning 'Blue Cave' on the islet of Biševo, near Vis, page 264.

Split

→ *Phone code: 021. Colour map 3, C5. Population: 188,694.*

Split is Croatia's second largest city, after Zagreb, and the main point of arrival for visitors to Dalmatia. Unfortunately, in the past Split was regarded as a transit centre rather than a destination in itself, and consequently suffers from a dearth of good hotels and restaurants. However, if you do decide to stay, you'll undoubtedly be impressed by the extraordinary mix of the old and the new: magnificent ancient buildings, romantic cobbled back streets, lively open-air seaside cafés and a vibrant nightlife.

Outside the historic centre there are some lovely coastal paths, each side of town, so you can explore the whole place on foot. A 15-minute walk from the centre rises Marjan Hill – a nature reserve planted with pine forests, palms, agaves and cacti – offering a wonderful panorama over the city rooftops, the sea and the surrounding islands. You'll find a number of well-equipped marinas, where countless charter companies hire out yachts for those who wish to explore the region in the best way possible, by sailing boat.

›› *For Sleeping, Eating and other listings, see pages 208-213.*

Ins and outs

Getting there Split is 365 km from Zagreb, 448 km from Pula, 350 km from Rijeka and 216 km from Dubrovnik. Through summer there are regular flights from most European capitals. The airport is at Kaštela, 25 km from the city centre. The **airport bus** ⓘ *T021-203305, 30Kn*, leaves 1½ hours before each flight. The city **port** ⓘ *Obala kneza domogoja*, is a 10-minute walk from the palace walls. **Jadrolinija** and **Blue Line** run regular overnight ferries to Ancona (Italy), departing daily at 2100 through summer. The twice-weekly **Jadrolinija** coastal ferry from Rijeka to Dubrovnik stops at Split en route **Jadrolinija** and **SEM** operate ferry and catamaran services to the islands of Šolta, Brač, Hvar, Vis, Korčula and Lastovo. The **bus station** ⓘ *Obala kneza domogoja 12*, is next to the train station. There are regular services to the major cities in Croatia and to nearby European cities. The **train station** ⓘ *Obala kneza Domogoja 10*, is a five-minute

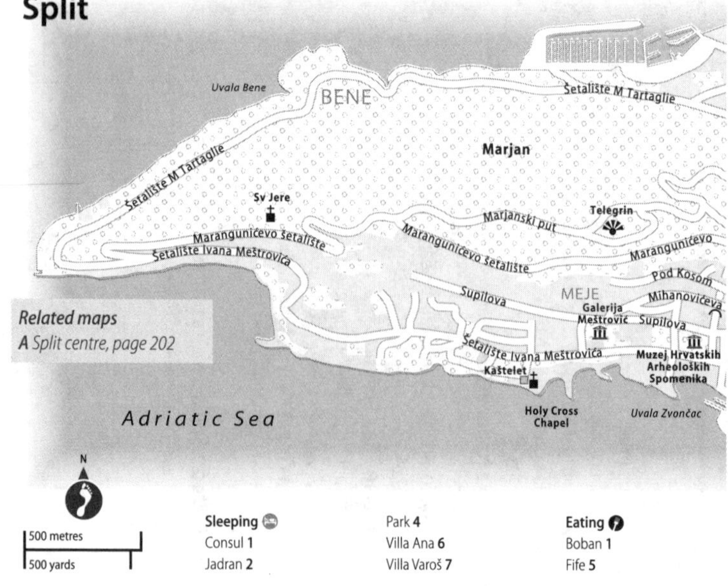

Related maps
A Split centre, page 202

walk from the city centre, in front of the port. There are services to Zagreb, Knin and Šibenik. »» *See Transport, page 212, for further details.*

Getting around The historic centre, where the city's main sights are found, is contained within the walls of Diocletian's Palace which is closed to traffic. A pleasant 20-minute stroll along the seafront will bring you to the Museum of Croatian Archaeological Monuments and the Meštrović Gallery. Alternatively, bus No 12 from Sv Frane (Church of St Francis) opposite Trg Republike, at the end of the Riva, runs every 40 minutes along Šetalište Ivana Meštrovića to Bene recreation centre at the end of Marjan Peninsula, passing both the Meštrović Gallery and the Museum of Croatian Archaeological Monuments en route.

Tourist information The main **tourist office** ⓘ *Peristil, T021-345606, www.visitsplit.com*, is in Crkvica Sv Roka (the former chapel of St Rocco). The **Tourist Guide Service** ⓘ *T021-346267, www.guides.hr*, for guided tours, is also on Peristil. The **Turistički Biro** ⓘ *Obala Hrvatskog narodnog preporoda 12, T021-347100*, on the seafront, is the place to go to find out about private accommodation.

Best time to visit Being a busy port town, Split sees people coming and going throughout the year. The major cultural event, the **Split Summer Festival**, takes place from mid-July to mid-August. During this period the city becomes extremely crowded, with tourists from all over the world coming to see Split itself, and passing through on their way to the islands.

The climate remains reasonably mild through winter. Temperatures very rarely fall below freezing, and it's quite feasible to drink morning coffee on the seafront in January, even though the surrounding mountains are often snow-covered between December and March. Having said this, Split is probably best visited in spring or autumn, when temperatures are neither too hot nor too chilly, and most tourist attractions and facilities are working.

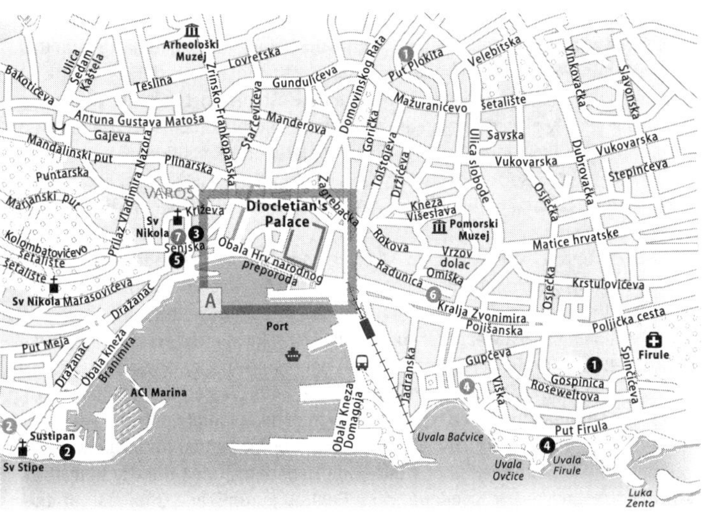

Jugo **2**
Konoba Varoš **3**
Šumica **4**

Arriving at night

Both the airport and bus station are perfectly safe if you arrive late at night. All incoming Croatia Airlines flights are met by an airport bus, which will transport passengers to the city centre. Charter companies with incoming flights usually arrange their own bus transfers. All reputable hotels have someone on duty through the night – book ahead and let them know that you are arriving late. In summer, bars in the centre and along the seafront remain open till at least 0200, so you'll still find the city reasonably animated if you arrive late. All ferry and catamaran services to Split arrive during the day or early evening.

Background

According to the 10th-century Byzantine Emperor, Constantine VII, the name Split is a contraction of *Spalatum*, from *palatium*, meaning 'Palace'. However, contemporary scholars believe that the name is more likely to have derived from the Greek name for the area, *Aspalathos*, after broom, the flowering shrub that colours the surrounding hills yellow in spring time.

Although this second theory suggests the Greeks may have had a settlement here, the founding of Split is generally recognized as 295, the year Roman Emperor Diocletian ordered the building of a vast palace in his native Dalmatia. He chose this site due to its undeniable splendour, and its proximity to Salona, the largest Roman settlement in Dalmatia at the time and his presumed birthplace. In 305, when the palace was completed, the emperor resigned from his position in Nikomedia (present day Izmir, in Turkey) and retired to his beloved homeland, where he lived the life of a near god – which indeed he believed himself to be – until his death in 313.

Over the following decades, various Roman rulers used the palace as a retreat, and the penultimate Western Roman Emperor, Julius Nepos, lived here after having been overthrown in 475. However, by the late sixth century the palace had been abandoned.

Life returned in 615, when refugees from Salona – which had been sacked by tribes of Avars and Slavs – found shelter within the palace walls, and divided up the vast imperial apartments and underground substructure into modest living quarters. They brought with them the bones of their saint, Duje (Domnius), the former Bishop of Salona, and ironically placed them in the late emperor's mausoleum – Diocletian had violently opposed Christianity and had himself ordered the execution of the bishop. By the 11th century the settlement had spread beyond the ancient walls, and during the 14th century, an urban conglomeration west of the palace was fortified, thus doubling the city area.

Split came under Venice from 1420 to 1797, a period of increased trade – as a gateway to the Balkan interior Split became one of the Adriatic's main trading ports – coupled with the ever-growing fear of an Ottoman invasion. The trade boom led to economic wellbeing and a wealth of cultural activity – local architects, notably Juraj Dalmatinac, endowed the city with beautiful Venetian-Gothic palaces, and writers, such as the poet Marko Marulic, began producing sophisticated Croatian-language literature. The Ottoman threat led the construction of an elaborate defence system – in the 17th century the entire city was surrounded by polygonal fortifications with projecting bastions. With the fall of Venice, the Hapsburgs ruled the city from 1813 to 1918, and connected it overland with Central Europe and the rest of the Austro-Hungarian Empire by the construction of the Split-Zagreb-Vienna railway line.

After the First World War, Split entered the Kingdom of Serbs, Croats and Slovenes (later renamed the Kingdom of Yugoslavia). As Zadar, formerly Dalmatia's official capital, had been awarded to Italy, Split took over as the region's economic and administrative centre. This period was also important creatively, with the sculptor Ivan Meštrović, painter Emanuel Vidović and poet Tin Uljevic all representing Split on the Yugoslav cultural scene.

The Second World War saw Split under occupation, first by Italy, then Germany, and the Allies caused further destruction through bombing raids aimed at 'liberation'. German occupation ended when Partisan units entered Split in October 1944, and in 1945 Federal Yugoslavia was born. The post-war years, under Tito, saw increased industrialization, with the expansion of the shipyards and the cement factory. This brought about an influx of workers from other parts of the country, which in turn led to the building of high-rise apartment blocks in the suburbs.

During the war of independence Split was attacked only once – in 1991 the Yugoslav Navy (who had their main base here) briefly shelled the city from the sea, but there were no serious consequences. However, economically and socially the city suffered from the complete collapse of the manufacturing and tourist industries, the exodus of many educated citizens, the arrival of countless refugees and inevitable political corruption. More than a decade later, unemployment remains a major problem, though factories are gradually reopening and tourism is back on its feet.

Diocletian's Palace and the historic centre

▸▸ *pp208-213.*

The heart of the city lies within the massive walls of the palace, a splendid third-century structure combining the qualities of an imperial villa and a Roman garrison. Rectangular in plan, this monumental edifice measures approximately 215 m by 180 m, with walls 2 m thick and 25 m high. Each of the four outer walls bears a gate: **Zlatna Vrata** (Golden Gate), **Željezna Vrata** (Iron Gate), **Srebrena Vrata** (Silver Gate) and **Mjedna Vrata** (Bronze Gate). Originally, there were two main streets: the Decumanus, a transversal street running east-west from Srebrena Vrata to Vrata, and the Cardo, a longitudinal street running from the main entrance, Zlatna Vrata. Both streets were colonnaded, and intersected at the central public meeting space, Peristil. On the east side of Peristil lay the mausoleum, and on the west, Jupiter's Temple. Diocletian's imperial apartments were located on the south side of the palace, overlooking the sea, while the servants' and soldiers' quarters overlooked the main land entrance. The stone used to build the palace came from the nearby quarries of Brač and Trogir, while the architects themselves may well have originated from the east – the names *Filotas* and *Zotikos* have been found, engraved in Greek within the palace walls.

In 1979 the complex was listed as a UNESCO World Heritage Site. Excavation and restoration work is still being carried out.

From the early Middle Ages onwards, new buildings were erected within the palace, so that the original Roman layout has been largely obscured. The first detailed plans and drawings of how it must have once looked were published in 1764, by the Scottish neoclassical architect, Robert Adam, in *The Ruins of the Palace of the Emperor Diocletian at Spalato in Dalmatia*. Adam, who is generally regarded as the greatest British architect of the 18th century, was fascinated by the scale and quality of Diocletian's building projects, and stayed in Split for five weeks in 1757 to investigate the palace. By asking permission to enter people's houses and inspecting their walls, he managed to trace the original Roman structure through the medieval buildings. No easy task – the Venetian governor of the time suspected the Scot of spying and nearly had him deported. Fortunately Adam completed his research, and the space and symmetry of Diocletian's Palace is said to have inspired some of his greatest buildings, which in turn became models for neoclassical architects throughout Europe.

Podrum (Underground chambers)

ⓘ *Between Obala Hrvatskog narodnog preporoda and Peristil, daily 0600-2300.*

The south façade of the palace, which once rose directly from the sea, is now beside the coastal promenade lined with cafés and palm trees, officially called Obala Hrvatskog narodnog preporoda, but better known to locals as the **Riva** (seafront). From here **Mjedna Vrata** (Bronze Gate) – where Roman ships would once have docked – leads into the Podrum. According to the Byzantine Emperor Constantine VII (905-959), Diocletian used this vast space as a prison, "in which he cruelly confined the saints whom he tormented". Today, most of this labyrinth of vaulted underground halls remains closed except for special events such as craft fairs and concerts. However, through daylight hours the main passageway, lined with stalls selling handmade souvenirs, is kept open and leads directly onto Peristil.

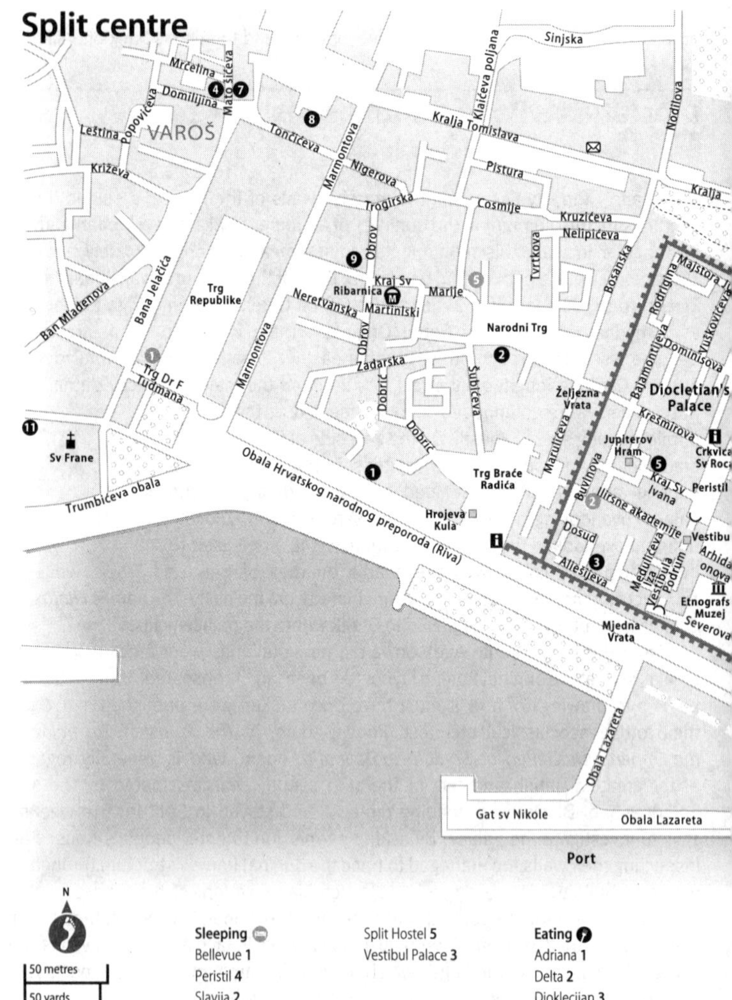

Peristil (Peristyle)

From Roman times up to the present day, this spacious central courtyard has been the main public meeting place within the palace walls. It is here that Diocletian would have made his public appearances – probably flanked by a guard, and dressed in an elaborately decorated silk toga – and his subjects would have kneeled or even prostrated themselves before him.

Each year from mid-July to mid-August, Peristil becomes an impressive open-air stage, hosting classical music and opera as part of the Split Summer Festival.

The two longer sides of the square are lined with marble columns, topped by Corinthian capitals and richly ornamented cornices linked by arches. On the east side stands Diocletian's mausoleum (now the cathedral), guarded by a black granite Egyptian sphinx dating back to 1500 BC. On the west side, the Roman arches have been incorporated into the late 15th-century Grisogono-Cipci Palace, now housing **Luxor Café**. Some architectural critics have compared this particular building to Andrea Palladio's 16th-century Palazzo di Giustizia (Palace of Justice) in Vicenza, and it could be that the Italian architect was influenced by sketches of Peristil, known to be in his possession.

At the south end of the square, immediately above the podrum exit, four columns mark the monumental arched gateway to the **Vestibule**, a domed space that served as the main entrance into Diocletian's private living quarters. To each side of the gate lies a 16th-century chapel: one now houses a small art gallery, and the other the Tourist Guide Service. At the opposite end of Peristil stands the small Renaissance **Crkvica Sv Roka** (Chapel of St Rocco) from 1516, now the Tourist Information Centre.

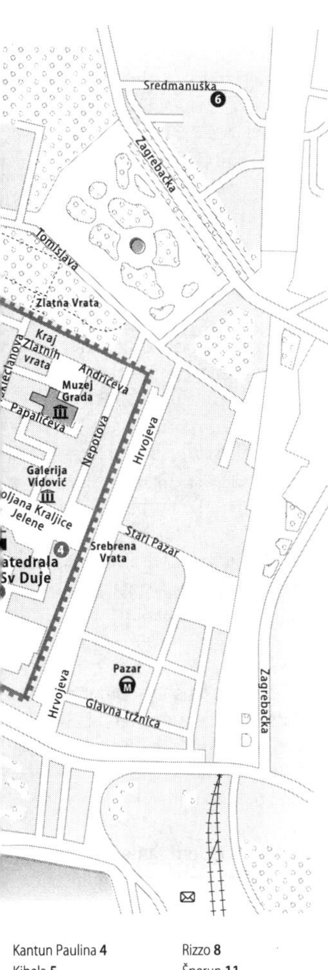

Kantun Paulina **4**
Kibela **5**
Kod Jose **6**
Pizzeria Galija **7**
Rizzo **8**
Šperun **11**
Zlatna Ribica **9**

Etnografski Muzej (Ethnographic Museum)

Severova 1, T021-344133, www.etnografski-muzej-split.hr. Jun Mon-Fri 0900-1400 and 1700-2000, Sat 0900-1300; Jul-Aug Mon-Fri 0900-2100, Sat 0900-1300; Sep-May Mon-Fri 0900-1400, Sat 0900-1300, 10Kn.

Pass through the Vestibule to reach this beautiful refurbished building displaying traditional Dalmatian folk costumes, jewellery and antique furniture on two floors.

Katedrala Sveti Duje (Cathedral of St Domnius)

ⓘ *Peristil, cathedral Jul-Aug daily 0800-2000, Sep-Jun daily 0800-1200 and 1630-1900, bell tower daily, May-Sep daily 0900-1900, Oct-Apr daily 0900-1200, 5Kn.*

Diocletian's **mausoleum**, an octagonal structure surrounded by 24 columns, now forms the main body of Split's cathedral. Before the third century, to prevent the spread of disease, dead bodies (no matter how illustrious) were disposed of outside city walls. However,

A sportsman from Split

"The trouble with me is that every match I play against five opponents: umpire, crowd, ball boys, court, and myself."
Goran Ivanišević

One of the best-loved bad boys of tennis (known for shouting and swearing at umpires, insulting linesmen and lineswomen, smashing rackets and kicking the net), Ivanišević was born in Split on 13 September 1971. He started playing at the age of seven (and also claims to have broken his first racket the same year) at Firule Tennis Club above Bačvice Bay.

A natural sportsman, he turned professional at 17. His powerful left-handed serve and aggressive style saw him scale the ranks to be rated ninth best player in the world by 1990. Around this time, his sister was diagnosed with cancer, from which she has since recovered, inspiring Goran to put extra energy into the game to raise money for her medical treatment. By 1992, the year he carried the Croatian flag at the Olympics in Barcelona, from which he brought home bronze medals from both the singles and doubles, he was ranked second in the world. But the victory he most wanted, and the one he always failed to grab, was the Wimbledon Cup. He reached the final in 1992 and lost to Andre Agassi, and reached it again in 1994 and 1998, losing both times to Pete Sampras. By 2001, almost considered a has-been, he received a wild card to play once more at the Lawn Tennis Championship. Referred to as a "one-shot wonder" by the BBC commentator and former Wimbledon champion John McEnroe at the beginning of the tournament, and rated as a 125/1 outsider by the bookies, he stunned fans and colleagues by knocking out rival after rival, to make it to the final, versus Pat Rafter. As usual, neither his mother nor girlfriend was among the spectators (apparently they make him nervous), but his firmest supporter, his father, was there to watch him play from start to finish. He made it through 6-3, 3-6, 6-3, 2-6, 9-7, and in a moving speech dedicated his win to a dear friend, the late Dražen Petrović, the NBA basketball player from Šibenik who was tragically killed in a car crash in Germany in 1993.

Back in his hometown of Split, the ships in the harbour blasted their sirens and children let off firecrackers, and the following night more than 100,000 people gathered to give him a massive welcome home party on the seafront, with music and dancing into the early hours. In autumn 2005 he was called out of semi-retirement to join the four-man Croatian team (along with Ivan Ljubičić, Mario Ančić and Ivo Karlović) for the Davis Cup finals against Slovakia.

Diocletian had raised the Emperor's status to that of divine, so as an 'immortal' he was to be an exception. Upon his death, he was laid to rest here, though his body later mysteriously disappeared. During the seventh century, refugees from Salona converted the mausoleum into an early Christian church, ironically dedicating it to Sv Duje, after Bishop Domnius of Salona, who Diocletian had had beheaded in 304 for sowing the seeds of Christianity.

In 1214, local sculptor Andrije Buvina carved the wooden cathedral **doors** (now kept behind glass screens in the main entrance). They are quite magnificent, ornamented with reliefs portraying 28 scenes from the life of Christ.

The interior space is round in plan: eight columns with Corinthian capitals support a central dome (symbolizing the Emperor's divine nature), which would originally have been decorated with golden mosaics. To the left as you enter, stands a 13th-century hexagonal **Romanesque stone pulpit**, with richly carved decoration.

To ach side of the main altar is a Gothic chapel. To the left is **Kapela Sv Staša** (Chapel of St Anastasius), executed by Juraj Dalmatinac in 1448 and dedicated to the martyr and the co-protector of Split, a clothmerchant from Aquileia, near present-day Venice. St Anastasius moved to Salona in Dalmatia and painted a cross on the door of his shop. As Christianity was outlawed at that time (AD 304), he was arrested and drowned, thrown into the River Jadro, a millstone around his neck. **Kapela Sv Dujma** (Chapel of St Domnius) stands to the right, completed by Bonino of Milan in 1427 and dedicated to the equally unfortunate Bishop Domnius.

In front of the main entrance, the elegant 60-m Romanesque-Gothic **bell tower** was constructed in stages between the 12th and 16th centuries, but then collapsed at the end of the 19th century and had to be rebuilt in 1908. If you have a good head for heights, climb to the top for a bird's-eye view of the palace layout.

Jupiterov Hram (Jupiter's Temple)

ⓘ *May-Oct daily 0800-1800, 5Kn.*

Leaving Peristil by the dark, narrow passageway of Kraj Sv Ivana you come to Jupiter's Temple, which would originally have stood in its own courtyard, directly facing Diocletian's mausoleum across the Peristil. Jupiter was the ruler of the Gods, and Diocletian proclaimed himself Jupiter's earthly representative to Rome.

During the Middle Ages the temple was converted into a baptistery. Inside, beneath a beautifully coffered barrel vault, an 11th-century baptismal font is carved with a stone relief showing a medieval ruler, possibly the Croatian King Zvonimir, seated on a throne.

Pazar

ⓘ *Mon-Sat 0700-1300, Sun 0700-1100.*

East of Peristil stands Srebrena Vrata (Silver Gate), leading onto Pazar, the colourful open-air fruit and vegetable **market**, held daily just outside the palace walls. It's well worth a look to size up the season's fresh produce: broccoli, spinach, wild asparagus and strawberries in spring; tomatoes, red peppers, peaches and melons in summer; grapes, pomegranates and walnuts in autumn; and cabbages, potatoes and oranges in winter. Thankfully the supermarket culture has yet to reach Dalmatia, and the only way to shop is to buy local seasonal produce, which means that while choice may be limited, quality is assured.

Galerija Vidović (Vidović Gallery)

ⓘ *Poljana Kraljice Jelene bb, T021-360155. Jun-Sep Tue-Fri 0900-2100, Sat-Sun 1000-1300; Oct-May Tue-Fri 0900-1600, Sat-Sun 1000-1300, 10Kn.*

Opened in spring 2007, this long-awaited gallery displays bold oil paintings of local sights by Split's best-known painter, Emanuel Vidović (1870-1953). He donated these works to the city when he died.

Muzej Grada (City Museum)

ⓘ *Papalićeva 1, T021-344917, www.mdc.hr. Jun-Oct daily 0900-1200, 1700-2000; Nov-May Tue-Fri 1000-1700, Sat-Sun 1000-1200, 15Kn.*

The 15th-century Papalić Palace, designed by Juraj Dalmatinac, is one of the city's finest examples of Venetian-Gothic architecture, with typical elements of a courtyard and ground-floor loggia, and an outer staircase leading up to the first floor. Inside there's a collection of medieval weaponry, and the dining room on the first floor is furnished just as it would have been when the Papalić family lived here, giving a good picture of 15th-century aristocratic lifestyle.

Zlatna Vrata (Golden Gate)

This, the largest and most monumental of the four palace gates, originally opened onto the road to the nearby Roman settlement of Salona (see page 216). It was walled

Diocletian the builder

Diocletian initiated a number of extraordinarily grandiose building projects. His best-known surviving monument is probably the Terme di Diocleziano (Diocletian Baths) in Rome. In 298, almost a century after Caracalla had given the Eternal City his gargantuan baths, Diocletian, who was at that time based in Nicomedia, decided to outshine his imperial predecessor by commissioning Rome's largest and most luxurious bathing establishment. Between 300 and 305, 10,000 Christian prisoners were used as forced labour to construct this massive edifice, comprising mosaic floors and marble façades, and covering 13 ha. It was designed to accommodate 3000 bathers, and included hot baths, steam baths and cold baths, plus dressing rooms, gymnasiums, meeting rooms, libraries and gardens.

In the draft introduction to *The Ruins of the Palace of the Emperor Diocletian at Spalato in Dalmatia*, the 18th-century Scottish neoclassical architect Robert Adam explains that he was particularly fascinated by Diocletian, "Not only from his Baths at Rome, but from the accounts of his extraordinary expenses bestowed on building, at Nicomedia, Milan, Palmyra and many other places of his Empire".

And Lactantius, a professor of literature appointed by Diocletian in Nicomedia, writes of the Emperor's extravagance in building, "Diocletian had a limitless passion for building, which led to an equally limitless scouring of the provinces to raise workers, craftsmen, wagons, and whatever is necessary for building operations. Here he built basilicas, there a circus, a mint, an arms factory, here he built a house for his wife, there one for his daughter."

up during the 14th century, and only uncovered again during the 19th. Just outside the gate stands a colossal bronze statue of Grgur Ninski (Bishop Gregory of Nin) by Ivan Meštrović. The ninth-century Bishop infuriated Rome by campaigning for the use of the Slav language in the Croatian Church, as opposed to Latin. The statue of him was created in 1929 and placed on Peristil (where its proportions must have been daunting) to mark the 1000th anniversary of the Split Synod. Under Italian occupation in 1941, the statue was seen as a symbol of Croatian nationalism and promptly removed. It was re-erected here in 1957. Touch the big toe on the left foot of the bronze statue of Grgur Ninski; it is considered a good luck charm, and has been worn gold by hopeful passers-by.

West of the palace walls

During the 13th and the 14th centuries, the town spread outside the Roman walls. A second centre developed west of the palace, and was in turn fortified in the 14th century. From then on, Peristil remained the focus of ecclesiastic activity, while Narodni Trg became the city's municipal centre.

From Peristil, Krešmirova leads to **eljezna Vrata** (Iron Gate) in the western wall of the palace, linking the 'old' and 'new' parts of the historic centre. Beyond the gate, **Narodni Trg** (People's Square) is better known to locals as *Pjaca*, from the Italian, 'piazza'. Paved with gleaming white marble, this is contemporary Split's main square, and you'll find a number of open-air cafés here, where you can happily sit and watch the world go by.

In the middle of the square stands the former Town Hall, constructed under Venice in 1443, and easily recognized by its three pointed Gothic arches.

From Narodni Trg, Šubićeva leads south to **Trg Braće Radića** (Radic Brothers' Square), better known to locals as **Voćni Trg** (Fruit Square) after the open-air market that used to be held here. In the centre of the square stands a statue of the local poet Marko Marulić (1450-1524), completed by Ivan Meštrović in 1924. **Hrvojeva Kula** (Hrvoje's Tower), an octagonal tower, now housing the tiny **AS Café**, is the remains of a 15th-century Venetian citadel, closing the square from the seafront.

West of Narodni Trg, at the **Ribarnica** (Fish Market) ⓘ *Kraj Sv Marije, Mon-Sat 0700-1300, Sun 0700-1100*, you'll find a daily selection of fresh fish and seafood.

West of the centre, built into the hill leading up to Marjan **Varoš** is a labyrinth of winding cobbled streets and traditional Dalmatian stone cottages, dating back to the 17th century. The oldest church in Varoš is the tiny 12th-century **Romanesque Sv Nikola** (St Nicholas), hidden away in the side street of Stagnja.

Outside the historic centre

» *pp208-213*

Arheološki Muzej (Archaeological Museum)

ⓘ *Zrinjsko-Frankopanska 25, T021-329340, www.mdc.hr. Mon-Fri 0900-1400, 1600-2000; Sat 0900-1400, 20Kn.*

A 10-minute walk north of the palace walls is the Archaeological Museum, founded in 1820, and in its present location since 1921. You'll find a well-displayed collection of Roman artefacts from Salona – jewellery, ceramics, glassware and coins – plus a few Greek pieces from Issa, on the island of Vis. Heavier stone objects such as sarcophagi are on show outdoors in the arcaded courtyard and leafy gardens.

Pomorski Muzej (Maritime Museum)

ⓘ *Glagoljaška 18, T021-347346, www.hpms.hr. Mon-Wed and Fri 0900-1430, Thu 1700-2030, Sat 0900-1300, 15Kn.*

A 10-minute walk east of the palace walls, past the old stone cottages of Radunica, brings you to Gripe Fortress, built by the Venitians as part of the 17th-century city fortification system against the possibility of an Ottoman invasion. Inside lies the Maritime Museum, entertaining enough even for those who know little about shipping. There are two distinct sections, one dedicated to naval war and the other to naval trading. You'll see scale models of ships, sailing equipment and a fine collection of early 20th-century naval paintings by Alexander Kircher. Of particular note are the world's first torpedoes, made in Rijeka in 1866, designed by a Croat, Ivan Blaž Lupis, and manufactured by an Englishman, Robert Whitehead.

Marjan

West of the historic centre, a 15-minute uphill hike through Varoš brings you to **Vidilica Café**, where an ample terrace offers panoramic views over the city. From here you can begin to explore Marjan, a nature reserve planted with Aleppo pines, holm oak, cypresses and Mediterranean shrubs such as rosemary and broom, located on a compact peninsula, 3.5 km long. From Vidilica, a path along the south side of Marjan leads to the 13th-century Romanesque church of **Sv Nikola** (St Nicholas) and, further on, to the 15th-century church of **Sv Jere** (St Jerome), built on the remains of an ancient temple.

Nearby is a cave carved into the cliffs. Each year in April the Marjan Cup free-climbing contest is held here.

The highest peak, **Telegrin**, 178 m, offers panoramic views of Trogir and Čiovo to the west, Kozjak, Mosor, Kaštela Bay, Solin and Klis to the north, as well as the islands of Šolta, Brač, Hvar and Vis to the south. At the western tip of Marjan, **Bene** is a recreation area with a family beach and sports facilities.

Sustipan

The gardens of Sustipan, planted with elegant cypress trees and dotted with park benches, offer memorable views out to sea, and over the ACI Marina back to town.

A Benedictine monastery was established here in the 11th century, only to be abandoned 300 years later. The foundations of the early medieval church of **Sv Stipe** (St Stephen) can still be seen; in 1814 a second church was constructed, with fragments from the earlier structure built into the new walls. The centrepiece to the gardens is a curious neoclassical pavilion, erected by the French in the 19th century, when Split spent a brief period under Napoleon's Illyrian Provinces.

Muzej Hrvatskih Arheoloških Spomenika (Museum of Croatian Archaeological Monuments)

ⓘ Šetalište Ivana Meštrovića bb, T021-358420, www.mhas-split.hr. Mon-Fri 0930-1600, Sat 0930-1300, 10Kn.

Two kilometres west of town, overlooking the sea and sheltered to the north by Marjan Hill, you'll find the upmarket residential area of Meje. Here you'll find the museum, a modern three-storey building opened in 1975, displaying early Croatian religious art from between the seventh and 12th centuries. Unfortunately only one floor is now in use, many exhibits having been lent to other museums abroad. However, well worth seeing are the fine stone carvings decorated with plaitwork design, reminiscent of the geometric patterns typical of Celtic art. In the garden stand several *stećci*, monolithic stone tombs dating back to the cult of the Bogomils, an anti-imperial sect that developed in the Balkans during the 10th century.

Galerija Meštrović (Meštrović Gallery)

ⓘ Šetalište Ivana Meštrovića 46, T021-340800, www.mdc.hr. May-Sep Tue-Sun 0900-2100; Oct-Apr Tue-Sat 0900-1600, Sun 0900-1800, 15Kn.

Close by is one of Split's most delightful cultural institutions: the Meštrović Gallery. Croatian sculptor Ivan Meštrović designed this monumental villa in the early 1930s, and used it as his summer residence and studio until fleeing the country during the Second World War. On display in the villa and the garden are almost 200 sculptures and reliefs, in wood, marble, stone and bronze, created between the begining of the century and 1946. The entrance ticket is also valid for the **Holy Cross Chapel** within Kaštelet, a 17th-century complex bought by Meštrović in 1932, situated 100 m down the road at Šetalište Ivana Meštrovića 39. Here you can see a cycle of New Testament bas-relief wood carvings, considered by many to be Meštrović's finest work.

Beaches

Locals generally prefer to go to the islands. However, the main city beach at **Bačvica** is clean and functional (if not very romantic); it is possible to rent a sunbed and umbrella, and there are showers and a plethora of (rather noisy) bars. **Bene**, on the tip of Marjan Peninsula, offers a number of small, secluded rocky coves backed by pine trees; there are also showers and a pleasant bar for refreshments.

Sleeping

Due to the lack of good central hotels and restaurants, finding a place to eat and sleep in high season can be quite a challenge. Book a room as far in advance as possible.

The following agency can arrange private accommodation in Split and the surrounding area: **Turisički Biro**, Obala Hrvatskog narodnog preporoda 12, T021-342544.

Diocletian's Palace and the historic centre *p201, map p202*

L Hotel Vestibul Palace, Iza Vestibula 4, 21000 Split, T021-329329, www.vestibulpalace.com. This luxury boutique hotel opened in summer 2005. Located within the palace walls, just off Peristil, it has 5 rooms and 2 suites, a bar and a restaurant. The ancient Roman stone and brickwork have been exposed and played off against

minimalist design details. The Villa Dobrić annex, opened in spring 2007, provides a further 2 suites and 2 rooms.
B **Hotel Peristil**, Poljana Kraljice Jelena 5, T021-329070, www.hotelperistil.com. Within the palace walls, next to Srebrena Vrata, this small hotel has 12 rooms and a restaurant. Great location, helpful staff, plus a lovely terrace out front where breakfast is served through summer.
D **Hotel Slavija**, Buvinova 2, T021-323840, www.hotelslavija.com. Within the walls of Diocletian's Palace, this small hotel was fully renovated in 2004. The 25 rooms are basic but comfortable and the location fantastic, if you don't mind the noise from surrounding bars.
F **Split Hostel**, Narodni Trg 8, T021-342787, www.splithostel.com. Tucked away in a narrow side street just off the main square, this friendly 24-bed hostel is an ideal solution for backpackers. The mixed dorms have 6-10 bunks and immaculate bathrooms, there's free Wi-Fi and a small terrace out front. Open all year.

Outside the historic centre

p207, map p198

A **Hotel Park**, Hatzeov Perivoj 3, looking out over Bačvice Bay, a 10-min walk east of the palace walls, T021-406400, www.hotelpark-split.hr. In a 1920s building with a garden and palm-lined terrace, this hotel's 54 rooms are smart and modern following extensive renovation work completed in 2001. Facilities include a restaurant, a meeting room, sauna and massage.
C **Hotel Consul**, Trščanska 34, just off Domovinskog Rata, a 10-min walk from the centre, T021-340130, www.hotel-consul.net. Situated in a leafy side street in a quiet residential area, this 23-room hotel is modern and comfortable. It's some distance from the sea, but there's a pretty terrace out front.
C **Hotel Bellevue**, Bana Josipa Jelačića 2, overlooking Trg Republike, T021-345644, www.hotel-bellevue-split.hr. In a 19th-century building, this hotel is gradually being renovated, though staying open while work takes place. It's central and reasonably comfortable, and has a pleasant old-fashioned café.
C **Hotel Jadran**, Sustipanjska Put 23, overlooking Uvala Zvončac, a 15-min walk west of the centre, T021-398622, www.hoteljadran.hr. A pleasant but basic 1970s hotel with sea views, close to the gardens of Sveti Stipan. In summer, guests have the use of an outdoor swimming pool, gym and sauna.
D **Villa Ana**, Vrh Lučac 16, T021-482715, www.villaana-split.hr. This tiny hotel occupies an old stone building in the Radunica area, just a short walk from the port and the old town. The 5 spacious rooms have wooden floors and new bathrooms, plus a/c, satellite TV and a minibar. The staff are extremely helpful and serve a decent buffet breakfast.
E **Villa Varoš**, Miljenko Smoje 1, T021-483469, www.villavaros.hr. In Varoš, this small family-run hotel occupies a traditional Dalmatian stone building with green wooden window shutters. There are 8 basic but comfortable rooms, plus one apartment with a terrace and jacuzzi. Breakfast is served at the nearby **Konoba Pizzeria Leut**, looking out over the fishing boats of Matejuška.

Eating

Diocletian's Palace and the historic centre *p201, map p202*

Dioklecijan (**Tri Volta**), Dosud 9, no phone. Known affectionately as **Tri Volta**, after the 3 arches on the terrace that form part of the palace walls, this bar is popular with local fishermen. You can get *merenda* here the year through: early morning helpings of hearty dishes such as *gulaš* (goulash) and *tripice* (tripe). During summer the menu is refined and extended to cater for tourists.
Kibela, Kraj Sv Ivana 5, in front of Jupiter's Temple, T021-346205. Hidden away in a narrow passageway off Peristil, this small family-run bar serves up simple *merenda* at lunchtime. During winter, the house speciality is *fažol sa kobasicom* (beans and sausage).

Cafés

Café Bellevue, Trg Repubike. Old-fashioned café with summer terrace.
Luxor, Peristil. Ideal stopping place while sightseeing, right in front of the cathedral. They even put cushions out so you can sit on the steps if all the tables are occupied.
Teak Caffe, Majstora Jurja 11, close to Zlatna Vrata. Currently 'in' with locals, the smart

interior comprises rough stone walls and polished woodwork, and there are several tables outside in summer.

Outside the historic centre

p207, map p198

¥¥¥ **Restaurant Boban**, Hektoroviceva 49, off Spiničićeva, a couple of blocks back from Luka Zenta (Zenta Bay), T021-543300, www.restaurant-boban.com. Dating back to the 1970s, **Boban** is often cited as the best restaurant in town. In summer, excellent fresh seafood dishes are served up on a leafy terrace. In winter, the rather kitsch dining room – black and silver chrome furnishing with violet table linens – comes into use.

¥¥¥ **Šumica**, Put Firula 6, T021-389897. Set in pinewoods overlooking Bačvice Bay, **Šumica** pulls in the black-BMW crowd. The house speciality is tagliatelli with salmon and scampi, and popular meat dishes include barbecued steak, beef stroganoff and veal escalopes. Indoors the atmosphere tends to be over formal, but outdoor tables below the pine trees offer a blissful sea breeze.

¥¥ **Adriana**, Obala Hrvatskog narodnog preporoda 6, T021-344079. A large and boisterous restaurant in the centre, with an ample terrace overlooking the seafront. Popular dishes include *rižot fruta di mare* (seafood risotto), *pohani sir* (cheese fried in breadcrumbs), *frigane lignje* (fried squid) and *ražnjiči* (kebabs). It gets very crowded in summer, and the music is often rather loud.

¥¥ **Kod Jose**, Sredmanuška 4, just outside the palace walls, close to Zlatna Vrata, T021-347397. Highly recommended, this typical Dalmatian *konoba* combines rough stone walls, heavy wooden tables and candlelight. Top dishes are the risottos and fresh fish – the choice changes daily so you'll need to ask to see what is on offer. The waiters deserve a special mention for their discretion.

¥¥ **Konoba Varoš**, Ban Mladenova 7, between the centre and Marjan, T021-396138. Less atmospheric than **Kod Jose**, though some believe the food to be better here. The walls are decorated with seascapes and paintings of ships, and the ceiling hung with fishing nets.

¥¥ **Restoran Jugo**, close to **Hotel Jadran**, between the gardens of Sveti Stipan and the ACI Marina, T021-398900. Worth the 15-min walk from the centre for its summer terrace with views of the marina, with a fantastic view of the city behind. Serves up passable Dalmatian dishes and pizza.

¥¥ **Šperun**, Šperun 3, T021-346999. In a side street between the Riva and **Varoš**, this cosy but rather sophisticated restaurant offers typical Dalmatian dishes such as *brodet* (fish stew), *bakalar* (dried cod) and *crni rižot* (risotto prepared in cuttlefish ink).

¥ **Delta**, Narodni Trg 3 (main square). Bakery selling *pita sa sirom* (cheese in filo pastry), croissants, cakes and pastries.

¥ **Fife**, Trumbićeva obala 11, T021-345223. Overlooking Matejuška, where fishermen from Varoš keep their boats, this eatery is truly local and down-to-earth. The menu changes daily: look out for *juha* (soup), *crni rižot* (risotto prepared with cuttlefish ink) and *palačinke* (pancakes).

¥ **Kantun Paulina**, Matosica 1, opposite **Galija Pizzeria**. The place to come for take-away *ćevapčići*, a Bosnian meat speciality similar to kebabs.

¥ **Pizzeria Galija**, Tončićeva 12, T021-347 932. Close to the fish market, **Galija** reputedly does the best pizzas in town, plus pasta dishes and salads. The informal atmosphere and set up – wooden tables and benches, draught beer and wine by the glass – make it popular with locals. The owner, Željko Jerkov, is an Olympic-gold-medal-winning basketball player.

¥ **Rizzo**, Tončićeva 6. Excellent sandwich bar, hidden away between the fish market and **Pizzeria Galija**. Oven-warm bread buns are filled with cheese, salami, tuna and salad of your choice.

¥ **Zlatna Ribica**, Kraj Sv Marije 8, next to the fish market. A simple bar working Mon-Fri until 2000 and Sat until 1400, this is the place to eat *girice* (small fried fish) or *frigane ligne* (fried squid), accompanied by a glass of *bevanda* (half white wine, half water).

Bars and clubs

Diocletian's Palace and the historic centre *p201, map p202*

Galerija Plavac, Trg braće Radića (Voćni Trg). Bar staging temporary exhibitions by local artists and occasional live music, tables indoors and outside in a small internal courtyard.

Ghetto Club, Dosud 10. The alternative crowd meet here for drinks, occasional exhibitions and performances. Throughout the summer, tables spill outside onto a delightful candlelit courtyard.
Fluid, Dosud 1. A tiny, cosy, stone-walled late night drinking den, popular with locals and visitors alike.
Puls 2, Buvinina 1, opposite Prenočište Slavija. Probably still the most 'in' bar for the mainstream 16-25 age group. Industrial interior with thumping techno music, crowded summer terrace outside with cushions so you can sit on the stone steps.

Outside the historic centre

p207, map p198

Discovery, Kupalište Bačvice. A big, new club occupying an underground space below the Bačvice seafront cafés. Closed Jun-Sep.
Jungle, Uvala Zvončac, close to ACI marina, west of the palace walls. Popular bar with loud music and a terrace open until 0300 in summer.
Metropolis, Matice Hrvatska 1, T021-305110. Decent mix of commercial, techno and rock, with occasional live concerts.
Ovčice, 5-min walk east of Kupalište Bačvice, east of the city centre, www.ovcice.hr. Pleasant terrace café with sea views, open until 0100. In summer you can hire an umbrella and sunbed on the pebble beach during the day.
Pivnica Klara, Kavanjinova 5, 10-min walk north of the palace walls. Good place for a beer, especially in summer when there are tables under the trees in the walled garden.
Tropic Club Equador, Kupalište Bačvice (bb), T021-323574. A 1st-floor café with great sea views. Pricey cocktails, Caribbean music and fake palms – undeniably pretentious but fun.

Entertainment

Cinemas

Kino Bačvice, open-air summer cinema under the pine trees, in a garden above Bačvice Bay.

The following cinemas are open all year: **Central**, Trg Gaje Bulata bb, T021-343813; **Karaman**, Ilićev prilaz 3, T021-345833; **Marjan**, Trg Republike 1, T021-347838; **Tesla**, Kralja Tomislava 15, T021-344633.

Theatre and classical music

Hrvastsko Narodno Kazalište, HNK (Croatian National Theatre), Trg Gaje Bulata 1, T021-344399, www.hnk-split.hr. Responsible for organizing the **Summer Festival**.

Festivals and events

Feb-Mar Karnivale (Carnival), on Shrove Tue. When locals dress up in *maskera* (masks) and an evening procession culminates with the burning of Krnjo (an effigy made to resemble a contemporary political figure) on the Riva (seafront), thus relieving citizens of the past year's sins.
7 May Sudamje (Feast of St Domnius), celebrates the patron saint of Split, whose bones go on display for a week in the cathedral. It's a local public holiday. Stands sell handmade wooden objects and basketry.
Jul-Aug Split Summer Festival, founded in 1954. Hosts opera, theatre and dance at open-air venues within the walls of Diocletian's Roman Palace. The highlight is *Aida* on Peristil. For information go to www.splitsko-ljeto.hr.
Mid-Sep Splitska Luda Noč (Split Mad Night). A night of live music on the Riva – a binge of eating, drinking and dancing bring the summer season to its official end.

Shopping

Algoritum, Bajamontijeva 2, close to Srebrena Vrata, between Peristil and Narodni Trg, T021-348030. The best book-shop for foreign-language publications, including novels, travel guides and maps.
Aromatica, Dobrić 12, T021-344061. Delicious smelling soaps, shampoos and massage oils made from local aromatic herbs.
Croata, Mihovilova Širina 7, overlooking Trg Brace Radica (Vocni trg), T021-346336, www.croata. hr. Sells original Croatian ties in presentation boxes, with a history of the tie.
Pazar, colourful open-air market just outside the palace walls, with stalls selling fruit and vegetables, plus clothes and leather goods.
Vinoteka Bouquet, Obala hrvatskog narodnog preporoda 3, on the seafront, T021-348031. A tiny shop well-stocked with the best Croatian wines, truffle and olive oil products.

Vinoteka Sv Martin, Majstora Jurja 17, close to Zlatna Vrata, T021-343430. Another tiny store filled with quality Croatian wines, olive oils and truffle conserves, plus natural soaps and cosmetic oils from Dalmatia.

Activities and tours

Diving

Akvatorij, T091-3132120, www.scuba.diving.hr. Have their summer diving base in Primošten.

Issa, T021-713651, www.scuba-diving.hr. Run this centre in Komiža on the island of Vis.

Hiking and climbing

Croatian Mountaineering Association Mosor, Marmontova 2, T021-431131. Sun morning walking trips up to the peak of Mosor (1339 m) and free-climbing on Marjan.

Sailing

ACI Marina, Uvala Baluni bb, T021-398548, www.aci-club.hr. 1 km southwest of city centre, near Sustipan Peninsula. 360 berths, open all year.

Sailing School, Ultra Sailing, T021-398980, www.ultra-sailing.hr. A sailing school offering 1-week courses, Mar-Oct.

Charter companies based in the Split ACI marina include: **Croatia Yacht Charter**, T021-474464, www.croatia-yacht-charter.com; **Euromarine**, T01-323101, www.euromarine.hr; Nautika Centar Nava, T021-407700, www.navaboats.com; **Pivatus Yachting**, T021-321300, www.pivatus.hr; **Ultra Sailing**, T021-398980, www.ultra-sailing.hr.

Tennis

Tennis Club Split, Put Firule, close to Bačvice Bay, T021-389576. Visitors welcome, 50Kn per hr daytime, 100Kn per hr evening (floodlit). Wimbledon 2001 champion, Goran Ivanišević, learnt to play here (see box, page 204).

Tour operators

Atlas, Nepotova 4, T021-343055, www.atlas-croatia.com. Organize 1-day excursions to Dubrovnik, Šibenik and Krka, Salona (Solin), Plitvice National Park, Bol, Hvar and Biševo, plus rafting trips on the River Cetina, near Omiš.

Generalturist, Obala Lazareta 3, T021-345183, www.generalturist.com. One of the largest Croatian travel agencies, specializing in tailor-made trips both with and without guides, pilgrimage tours and yacht charters.

Transport

Air

Split Airport, Kaštela, T021-203171 (information), T021-203218 (lost and found), www.split-airport.hr. Airport bus service, T021-203305.

Through summer, there are regular flights to and from **Amsterdam**, **Bari**, **Berlin**, **Bologna**, **Brussels**, **Catania**, **Dubrovnik**, **Dusseldorf**, **Frankfurt**, **Genoa**, **Gothenburg**, **Hamburg**, **Helsinki**, **Istanbul**, **Lisbon**, **London** (Gatwick and Heathrow), **Ljubljana**, **Lyon**, **Manchester**, **Milan**, **Munich**, **Oslo**, **Palermo**, **Paris**, **Prague**, **Pula**, **Rome**, Sarajevo, **Skopje**, **Turin**, **Warsaw**, **Vienna**, **Zagreb** and **Zurich**. The number of destinations and the frequency of flights are reduced in winter.

Airlines offices Adria Airways, Obala kneza Domagoja bb, T021-338445. **British Airways**, Split Airport, T021-203132. **Croatia Airlines**, Obala hrvatskog narodnog preporoda 9, T021-362997. **ČSA**, Dominisova 10, T021-343422. **Lufthansa**, Obala Lazareta 3, T021-345183, Malev, Split airport, T021-895274.

Bus

UK via **Paris** (France). For all information about buses to and from Split, T060-327327, www.ak-split.hr. Left luggage until 2200, 30Kn per piece per day.

Local Buses serve the city suburbs and surrounding towns of **Trogir** (40 mins), **Salona** (Solin) (30 mins), **Klis** (35 mins) and **Omiš** (40 mins), all of which make pleasant day trips from Split.

Long distance Internal services include about 30 buses daily to **Zagreb** (4½-7 hrs); 14 to **Zadar** in North Dalmatia (3½ hrs); 12 buses daily to **Rijeka** in Kvarner (8 hrs); and 12 to **Dubrovnik** in South Dalmatia (4 hrs). There are also daily international bus lines to **Ljubljana** (Slovenia), **Trieste** (Italy) and **Munich** and **Stuttgart** (Germany). Buses depart once a week for **Vienna** (Austria), and for **London**.

Car

Budget, www.budget.hr, at the airport, T021-203151, and in the centre at Trubičeva Obala 2, T021-399214; **Dollar Thrifty**, at the airport, T021-895329, and in the centre at Trubičeva Obala 2, T021-399000; **Hertz**, www. hertz.hr, at the airport, T021-895230, and in the centre at Tomica stine 9, T021-360455.

Ferry

Jadrolinija run a twice-weekly overnight coastal service between **Rijeka** and **Dubrovnik**, stopping at **Split**, **Stari Grad** (island of Hvar), **Korčula** and **Sobra** (island of Mljet) en route. **Jadrolinija** also run daily ferry services connecting Split to the islands on **Mljet**, **Brač**, **Hvar**, **Vis**, **Korčula** and **Lastovo** the year through. Schedules vary from day to day and season to season, so you need to check times with their ticket office.

In peak season (Jul-Aug) **Split Tours** run a daily catamaran service connecting Split to Komiža on the island of **Vis**.

Jadrolinija and **Blue Line** both run overnight ferries to **Ancona** (Italy), departing from Split at 2100 and arriving in Ancona at 0700 the following day. The same vessels depart 2100 from Ancona to arrive in Split at 0700. Through summer these services operate almost every day, in winter they are reduced slightly. **SNAV**, an Italian company, run a daily high-speed catamaran service between **Split** and **Ancona** (Italy) from Jun to Sep. The catamaran departs from Split at 1700 and arrives in Ancona at 2130. The same vessel departs from Ancona at 1100 and arrives in Split at 1530.

Ferry companies Jadrolinjia, T021-338 333; **Blue Line** T021-338292; **SNAV Croatia Jet** ; T021-322252; **Split Tours**, T021-352533.

Taxi

The 2 main taxi ranks are at either end of the Riva (Obala hrvatskog narodnog preporoda), in front of the market and in front of **Hotel Bellevue**. **Radio taxi**, T970.

Train

Split train station, T021-338535; national train information, T060-333444, www.hznet.hr. Left luggage 0700-2200, 30Kn per piece per day.

5 trains daily to and from **Zagreb** (5½ hrs by day, 8½ hrs by night); 5 trains daily to **Knin** (2 hrs) and 3 trains daily to **Šibenik** (3½ hrs, change at Perković).

Directory

Consulates Denmark, Supilova 10, T021-358488; **Finland**, Trubičeva Obala 5, T021-345275; **Germany**, Svačićeva 4, T021-409 347; **Italy**, Obala hrvatskog narodnog preporoda 10/II, T021-348155; **Netherlands**, Mažuranićevo Šetalište 1, T021-312399; **Slovenia**, Spinčićeva 25, T021-389224; **Spain**, Kavanjinova 1, T021-343377; **Sweden**, Gat Sv. Duje 4, T021-338234; **UK**, Obala hrvatskog narodnog preporoda 10/III, T021-346007. **Emergencies** Ambulance: 94. **Fire**: 93. Police: 92. **Internet** Cyber Club Mriža, Križićeva 3, close to the theatre, T021-321 320. Mon-Sat 0900-2200. 5Kn per 15min. **Libraries** British Consulate, Obala hrvatskog narodnog preporoda 10, T021-346007. **City Library Marko Marulić**, Tolstojeva 32, T021-343913. **Medical services** Hospital Firule, Spinčićeva 1, a 15-min walk east of the centre, T021-556 111 (24-hr casualty). **Pharmacies**: marked by a glowing green cross. **Dobri** at Gunduliceva 52, T021-348074, and **Lučac** at Pupačićeva 4, T021-533188, alternate as non-stop 24-hr pharmacies. **Post offices** The main post office is at Obala kneza Domogoja, near the bus station and ferry port, and is open daily 0700-2000. The central post office is at Kralja Tomislava, north of the palace walls, and is open Mon-Fri 0700-2000 and Sat 0700-1300. **Telephones** If you prefer to telephone from a peaceful phone booth, rather than calling on the street, go to one of the post offices (see above). Otherwise, you'll find phone kiosks on the seafront.

Around Split

If you are based in Split, several nearby towns and villages make pleasant half-day trips. The star of them all has to be Trogir, along the coast west of Split, with its magnificent medieval cathedral. Alternatively, Omiš is beautifully situated southeast along the coast, at the mouth of the River Cetina. Moving inland, east of Split you'll find the remains of the ancient Roman settlement of Salona, while to the northeast stands the hilltop fortress of Klis and further inland still is Sinj, renowned for its annual horse riding event celebrating victory over the Turks. ▸▸ *For Sleeping, Eating and other listings, see pages 220-221.*

Trogir ▸▸ *pp220-221. Colour map 3, C5.*

→ *Phone code: 021. Population: 12,995. 27 km west of Split.*

Medieval Trogir, just off the main coastal road, sits compact on a small island, connected to the mainland by one bridge and tied to the outlying island of Čiovo by a second. It's a quiet, lonely place in the winter, but swarms with visitors on warm summer evenings. Once protected by city walls, a labyrinth of narrow cobbled streets twists its way between the medieval town houses bringing you out on to a splendid main square, overlooked by a monumental Romanesque cathedral. In 1997, Trogir was listed a UNESCO World Heritage Site. It is well worth a visit.

The south-facing seafront promenade is lined with cafés and restaurants, and there are also a couple of good, reasonably priced hotels. Just across the narrow Trogir Channel, on the island of Čiovo, a well-equipped marina makes a base for several companies chartering yachts.

Ins and outs

There are regular buses running from Split to Trogir. The town itself is small enough to get around by foot. There's a **tourist office** ⓘ *Trg Ivana Pavla II 1, T021-881412, www.trogir-online.com.* ▸▸ *See Transport, page 221, for further details.*

Background

Trogir was founded in the third century BC by Greeks colonists from Issa (on the island of Vis) who named it Tragurion. From AD 78 Tragurium flourished as a Roman port, and after the fall of the Western Roman Empire, it became part of Byzantium. Thanks to its island location, it was saved from a similar fate to nearby Salona, which was devastated by rampaging Avar and Slav tribes during the seventh century, but in 1123 it was almost completely demolished by the Saracens. However, successful trade relations throughout the Mediterranean had brought the citizens of Trogir a certain affluence, and they soon rebuilt their city, adding to it a splendid Romanesque cathedral, built from fine local stone, described by Rebecca West in *Black Lamb and Grey Falcon*, as "the colour of rich crumbling shortbread". In 1242, when King Bela IV found temporary refuge here as he fled the Tatars, he would have seen the almost completed cathedral, minus the bell tower, which was added later. Over the following centuries Trogir became one of the most important cultural centres in Dalmatia. In June 1420, after a bloody battle, the city was taken by Venice – a conquest that met continual resistance from the people of Trogir who, having been born into an independent city with its own glorious past, resented being governed by outsiders. The Venetians took tough measures, sending in specially imported language teachers to instruct the nobles, and forcing local families to change their names to Venetian equivalents – Čubranović, for example, became Cipriani. However, Trogir remained a hive of artistic activity, with renowned architects and sculptors such as Nikola Firentinac and Andrija Aleši living and working here during the second half of the 15th century. The Venetians, ever fearful of the possibility of a Turkish invasion, reinforced the city walls, adding St Mark's Tower and Kamerlengo Fortress. The Turks never succeeded in taking Trogir, but the devastation they caused in the surrounding hinterland led the city into economic decline during the 17th century. Upon the fall of Venice in 1797, Trogir passed to Austria, and then spent a brief period under Napoleon's Illyrian Provinces. This too met with local opposition, and the French condemned several of the town leaders to death after a failed uprising. After a final phase under Austria, Trogir entered the Kingdom of Yugoslavia in 1918.

In 1932, an unfortunate affair led Trogir and the rest of Yugoslavia into a diplomatic scuffle with Italy. Apparently a relief of the Venetian Lion, hung in the town loggia in Trogir, had been badly disfigured in an act of 'anti-Italian' vandalism. Mussolini, who was rising to power in Italy and coveted this particular part of the Dalmatian coast, caught wind of the affair and took umbrage. Anti-Yugoslav demonstrations were held in Italy and Mussolini announced chillingly, "The lions of Trogir are destroyed, but in their destruction they stand stronger than ever as a living symbol and a certain promise." The Yugoslav Government was obliged to deliver a formal apology. Nine years later, with the outbreak of the Second World War, Trogir was occupied by Italian soldiers. Under Tito, the economy picked up in the 1970s and most of the population worked in shipbuilding and tourism. Today the small shipyard lies all but abandoned, but tourism has taken off once more with several cosy little family-run hotels in the old town making it a pleasant place to stop over for a night or two.

Sights

The city walls were constructed under Venice during the 15th century. However, the main entrance into Trogir, the **Kopnena Vrata** (Land Gate), was rebuilt in late Renaissance style during the 17th century. Above the arch stands a statue of **Sv Ivan Trogirski** (St John of Trogir, also often referred to by the Italian version of his name, Giovanni Orsini), a 12th-century bishop and one of the city's two patron saints.

Muzej Grada Trogira (City Museum) ⓘ *Gradska Vrata 4, T021-881406, Jun-Sep daily 0900-2100, Oct-May by appointment, 10Kn*, just inside the walls, close to the Land Gate, is a rather dull city museum housed within the baroque Garagnin-Fanfogna Palace. There's a small lapidarium on the ground floor displaying various Greek and Roman finds, while the first floor is given over to 18th-century furniture and a collection of city documents.

Katedrala Sveti Lovrijenac (Cathedral of St Lawrence) ⓘ *Trg Ivana Pavla II, May-Oct daily 0800-1900, Nov-Apr daily 0800-1200 and 1500-1800*, a triple-nave Romanesque basilica, is undoubtedly Trogir's most remarkable building, and one of the most perfect examples of medieval architecture in the country. Work began in 1213, and the main core of the building was completed in 1250, well before the arrival of the Venetians.

The main portal, sheltered within a spacious vestibule edged by a marble banquette, is adorned with elaborately detailed Romanesque sculpture by Master Radovan. The great door is flanked by a pair of burly lions that form pedestals for figures of Adam and Eve. Around the portal, scenes from the Bible are mixed with references to everyday peasant life, in an extraordinary orgy of saints, apostles, animals and grotesques. Still within the vestibule, to the left of the portal, is a baptistery dating from 1467, the most important preserved work by Andrija Aleši (who also completed the delightful Baptistery of Šibenik Cathedral). Inside, above the altar, check out the relief of *St Jerolim and the Cave.*

The cathedral itself is dimly lit, the main sight being the **Kapela Sv Ivana** (Chapel of St John) to the left of the main aisle. Considered one of the most beautiful Renaissance monuments in Dalmatia, it was built in 1480 by Nikolo Firentinac (who also worked on Šibenik Cathedral). Below a barrel-vaulted ceiling, statues of Mary, Christ, the saints and the apostles watch over a sarcophagus, on which lies the figure of St John of Trogir (Giovanni Orsini). The building of the elegant **bell tower** ⓘ *Jun-Sep daily 0900-1200 and 1600-1900, 5Kn*, began in the early 15th century, and took place in successive stages – the first two storeys are Gothic, while the third and final level, in Renaissance style, was completed in 1610. You can climb to the top for stunning views across the ancient rooftops.

Čipiko Palace ⓘ *Trg Ivana Pavla II*, opposite the main entrance to the cathedral, was once the home of the Čipikos, Trogir's leading noble family during the 15th century. It's of special note for the delicately carved Venetian-Gothic triple window with pointed arches, completed by Adrija Aleši in 1457. Within the main entrance (which is usually open) stands a giant wooden cockerel, a trophy taken from the prow of a Turkish ship at the Battle of Lepanto (see box, page 255) in 1571. Seven Dalmatian cities were each ordered to send a galleon to fight in this decisive battle, where the Turkish navy suffered a defeat it never fully recovered from. The Trogir crew was captained by Alviz Čipiko.

Across the square, the 15th-century **Loža** (Loggia) would originally have been used as a court. The stone table where judges once sat is still there, and behind it there's a wall relief, appropriately portraying *Justice* by Nikola Firentinac from 1471. In contrast, the back wall bears a 1950s modernist equestrian relief by Ivan Meštrović, portraying *Ban Berislavić*, a native of Trogir who became Ban of Croatia and Bishop of Zagreb, and eventually died in battle against the Turks in 1520. Close by stands the town **clock tower**, once part of the small Renaissance church of St Sebastian.

Behind the loggia stands the Benedictine **Samostan Sv Nikole** (Convent of St Nicholas) ⓘ *Gradska ulica 2, T021-881631, Jun-Sep daily 0800-1300 and 1500-1900, Oct-May by appointment, 10Kn*, founded in 1064 but rebuilt during the 16th century. The nuns here look after a collection known as the **Zbirka Umjetnin Kairos**, with the centrepiece being a remarkable third-century BC Greek marble relief of Kairos, the god of opportunity. There's also an ancient Greek inscription built into the cloister walls.

Kaštel Kamerlengo (Kamerlengo Fortress) ⓘ *Jun-Sep Mon-Sat 0900-2000, 10Kn*, perched on the southwest corner of the island, overlooking the sea, is an impressive fortress built by the Venetians as part of the improved city fortification system in 1430. On summer evenings, the internal courtyard becomes an open-air cinema. Just north of the fortress stands **Kula Sv Marka** (St Mark's Tower), built at the same time.

Before the sea level dropped, this small neoclassical gazebo, **Marmontov Paviljon** (Marmont's Pavilion), used to rise directly from the water, on the western tip of the island, close to the fortress. It dates from the period spent under Napoleon's Illyrian Provinces. Napoleon's right-hand man in Dalmatia, General Marmont, loved the place and used to play cards here and watch the sunset.

Salona ⊛⊜ » *pp220-221. Colour map 3, C5.*

→ *Phone code: 021. 6 km inland from Split.*

At the foot of **Kozjak Mountain**, Salona is the most important archaeological sight in Croatia. As the largest Roman settlement on the Dalmatian coast, during the third century it is said to have had a population approaching 60,000. Today the site is rather poorly maintained, due to lack of funds, and most of the important finds are in the Archaeological Museum in Split. However, with a bit of imagination you can visualize how it must once have looked as a prosperous Roman settlement, backed by rugged mountains and facing out towards the sea. In some ways it's the very lack of upkeep and 'sanitization' that give it this special atmosphere of having been abandoned. The modern town of Solin, which has grown up southeast of ancient Salona, is of little interest, being no more than a suburb of Split.

Ins and outs

Tusculum ⓘ *T021-212900, at the entrance to the archaeological site*, serves as a small information centre where you can pick up a plan of the site and buy postcards. The **Salona site** ⓘ *Jun-Sep Mon-Fri 0700-1900, Sat 0900-1900, Sun 0900-1300, Oct-May Mon-Sat 0900-1500, 20Kn*. There's a **tourist office** ⓘ *Kralja Zvonimita 69, T021-210048, www.solin-info.com*, in Solin town.

Background

Salona was probably founded by Greek colonists from Issa (on the island of Vis) in the fourth century BC, later becoming a Greek-Illyrian settlement. The Greek geographer and historian, Strabon (63 BC to AD 24), mentions Salona as the harbour of the Illyrian Delmata tribe. In the first century BC, it was conquered by the Romans, and went on to become their most important base in Dalmatia. Public buildings were erected, with a forum serving as the centre of the region's public, political and religious life, and a large *terme* (baths). During the third century, under Diocletian (who was probably born here, though he governed from Nicomedia, present-day Izmir in Turkey) Salona expanded further. An influx of immigrants arrived from the east, bringing with them various oriental religions. Findings on the site prove that Isis (the goddess of fertility and motherhood, originating from Egypt and later adopted by the Greeks); Cybele (the goddess of nature and fertility, originating from Asia Minor and later becoming the Roman 'Great Mother of the Gods') and Mithras (the Persian god of light) were all worshipped here.

Christianity arrived in mid-third century through Bishop Verantius, who came from Rome with the mission of spreading the religion throughout Dalmatia. However, in 304 Diocletian ordered the execution of all Christian bishops, and Domnius, the first Bishop of Salona, along with other Christian leaders of the time, probably met his end in the amphitheatre. Less than a decade later, the Edict of Milan, passed in 313, legalized Christianity. A powerful Christian community rapidly developed in Salona, and in the early fifth century Salona's bishop became the Metropolitan of the province of Dalmatia. Many churches were built on the Salona site, and the centre moved from the Forum to what is now Manastirine, where a basilica was built over the site of Domnius' grave. In the sixth century Salona became part of the Byzantine Empire under Justinian (the son of Slavonian peasants, born near present-day Skopje in Macedonia). Salona was destroyed by Avars and Slavs in 614, and the surviving inhabitants fled for shelter within the walls of Diocletian's Palace, where they founded Split.

Since then, ancient Salona has lain in ruins. Much of what remained was deliberately destroyed in the 17th century by Venetian generals, to prevent the Turks, who had already captured nearby Klis, from taking refuge here. And in the 18th century, British historian Edward Gibbon wrote, "A miserable village still preserves the name of Salona; but so late as the 16th century the remains of a theatre, and a confused prospect of broken arches and marble columns, continued to attest to its ancient splendour."

The site, by this time overgrown with vineyards and olive trees, was excavated during the late 19th century by Father Frane Bulić (1846-1934) from Split, and most of the finds were transferred to the Archaeological Museum in his hometown.

Sights

On the road between Split and Salona, you will pass the **Roman aqueduct** to your right. Built by Diocletian during the third century, it was 9 km long and conducted water from the spring of the River Jadro on the slopes of Mosor, all the way down to the palace. It was renovated in 1879 and is still partly in use today.

Tusculum (Father Frane Bulić Memorial Museum) ⓘ *Put Starina bb, Manastirine, left of the main entrance, T021-212900, Mon-Fri 0900-1400*, is a two-storey house commissioned by Father Frane Bulić in 1898 as a base for archaeologists working on the site. Various stone finds such as inscriptions and statues were built into the façade. On the ground floor there's a memorial room to Bulić, displaying his furniture and documenting his work. The garden features a charming pathway flanked by columns and capitals of various styles found on the site, now overgrown with climbing roses and honeysuckle.

Manastirine, immediately south of the entrance, is the place where the early Christians buried their martyrs, notably Bishop Domnius. It subsequently became a place of worship, and countless sarcophagi were placed around the Bishop's tomb. In the early fifth century a triple-nave basilica, measuring 48 m by 21 m was built over the site. The foundations, sections of the crumbling walls and several sarcophagi can still be seen today. In 1934, Bulić was buried to the west of the site, in an area surrounded by cypresses.

Built into a hillside in the northwest corner of the site stands Salona's most impressive building, an elliptical **amphitheatre** from the late second century. It was designed to seat 18,000 spectators, and **gladiators** and wild animals, and later Christians, would have fought here. In the sixth century, Byzantine Emperor Justinian banned gladiator fights, and it was probably used instead for religious and defensive purposes.

Klis

▸▸ *pp220-221. Colour map 3, C5.*

→ *Phone code: 021. Population: 2557.*

Just 9 km inland from Split, the sleepy village of Klis nestles on the south-facing slopes between the mountains of Kozjak (779 m) and Mosor (1339 m). Historically it's known for its medieval hilltop fortress, once the site of many gruelling battles; today it is an all-but-abandoned monument offering romantic views over the sea at sunset. Locally, Klis is also esteemed for its down-to-earth restaurants serving *janjetina* – you can't miss them, each one has a whole lamb turning on a spit by the roadside.

Today many of the original families from Klis have moved to Split but keep weekend cottages here, while the elderly people who have remained run small-holdings with goats, chickens and orchards. Klis is divided into three distinct parts: **Klis-Varoš**, below the fortress; **Klis-Grlo**, behind the fortress, separated from Klis-Varoš by a tunnel; and **Klis-Megdan**, by the main entrance to the fortress. In Klis-Megdan you'll find the **tourist office** ⓘ *Megdan 57, T021-240578*.

Tvrdjava (Fortress)

ⓘ *Summer daily 0900-1900, winter Tue-Sun 1000-1600, 10Kn.*

The Tvrdjava, set on rocky mass 340 m above sea level, was probably first settled in the first century BC by the Illyrian tribe of the Delmata, who were particularly fond of hard-to-reach hilltop sites. During the ninth century, it became a seat of the medieval Croatian Kings, and subsequently passed to the Hapsburgs. On the borders between Austro-Hungary, Venetian Dalmatia and the rapidly expanding Ottoman Empire, and overlooking a mountain pass traversed by lucrative trade routes leading from the coast inland to Bosnia, this was a vital strategic base. The Hapsburgs thus established a garrison here, under the command of Captain Peter Kružić. His army was made up primarily of Uskoks (see page 146), a notorious Slav people who had fled the Turks in the east and obtained permission to stay in the Hapsburg territories, without being subjected to taxes, on the condition that they provided military service. During the early 16th century, the Ottoman Turks, who had already taken nearby Sinj, laid siege upon Klis several times, but Kružić and his men held them off.

Finally in 1537 the Uskoks were defeated: details of the events are recorded in heroic ballads, concluding with Kružić being captured, having his throat slit and his head mounted on a pole. The Turks thus established *Klisko-lički sandjak* (Klis-Lika county), stretching from Bosnia in the east to Skradin (near Šibenik) and Klis in the west. This turn of events spread terror along the coast – the fear of falling under Ottoman dominance became an ongoing preoccupation. In 1648, the fortress was eventually captured by the Venetians, and a village grew up below its ramparts. Built into the south face of a rocky mass and barely discernable as a man-made structure from a distance, the present day aspect of the stone fortress dates from restructuring work carried out by the Venetians in the 17th century. The grassy ramparts offer spectacular views down to the sea and an impressive sunset over the islands. The oldest remaining building is a former Turkish mosque, though the Venetians pulled down the minaret and promptly converted it into a church.

Sinj

» *pp220-221. Colour map 3, B5.*

→ *Phone code: 021. Population: 25,373. 34 km inland from Split.*

Set in a broad valley, close to the River Cetina, Sinj is a provincial market town with a sizeable Croatian Army base. There's nothing much to see here, but the spectacular **Sinjksa Alka** – a medieval riding tournament – assures the town national media coverage at least once a year. It's also a popular pilgrimage centre, thanks to a supposedly miraculous painting of the Virgin. More information is available at the **tourist office** ⓘ *Vrlička 41, T021-826352, www.sinj.hr.*

Background

Sinj came under various local noble families until being captured by the Ottoman Turks in 1513. The *raja* (non-muslims) fared pretty badly at the time, and there are countless stories of the atrocities suffered by the local population. The town was finally liberated by the Venetian army in 1686.

The most prominent event in Sinj's history dates back to the early 18th century. On 7 August 1715, a massive Turkish offensive, led by Mehmed Paša and comprising several thousand soldiers, hit the town for a second time. A local contingent of just 700 men managed to hold off the army for over a week, finally seeing the complete withdrawal of the Turks on Assumption Day, 15 August. The event is now celebrated by the annual **Sinjska Alka**. Sinj's main period of expansion occurred under the Hapsburgs during the 19th century.

Sights

The miraculous *Sinjska Gospa* (Our Lady of Sinj), a painting of the Virgin Mary by an unknown 16th-century Venetian artist, takes pride of place inside the parish church, **Crkva Gospa Sinjska** (Church of Our Lady of Sinj) ⓘ *Šetalište Alojzije Stepanica 1, daily 0630-1200, 1700-1900 (for mass)*, which is part of the Franciscan monastery complex. The painting formerly belonged to the Franciscans in Rama, Bosnia, during which time it became apparent that it was able to perform miracles. It was transferred to the monastery in Sinj in 1687, and its reputation was only boosted by the Ottoman defeat of 1715 – apparently local women had prayed to the Virgin and the Sinj victory was in part attributed to the magical powers of the painting. As a way of thanks, the town's military officers had a golden crown made to adorn the *Sinjska Gospa*, which was put in place by the Archbishop of Split in 1716. Today this is one of Croatia's best-known pilgrimage sites. Each year on Assumption Day, 15 August, the

Kružić and his men have not been forgotten: the local football team is called NK Uskok, in tribute to their struggle against the Turks.

painting is ceremoniously paraded around town, and thousands of people from all over the country walk, some for miles and some barefoot, to pay their respects to the Virgin.

Sleeping

Trogir *p214*

C Hotel Pašike, Sinjska bb, T021-885185, www.hotelpasike.com. This small hotel in the old town has 14 rooms with antique furniture and modern en suite bathrooms, plus one apartment with a hydro-massage tub. On the ground floor, Konoba Pašike serves barbecued Dalmatian meat and fish dishes at outdoor tables, with occasional live music.

C Hotel Tragos, Budislavičeva 3, T021-884 729, www.tragos.hr. In an 18th-century Baroque palace in the old town, Tragos has 12 simply furnished, modern rooms, decorated in warm creams and yellows. In the courtyard garden, **Restaurant Tragos** serves Dalmatian favourites such as *pasticada* (beef stewed in sweet wine) and *brudet* (fish stewed in a tomato and onion).

D Hotel Fontana, Obrov 1, T021-885744, www.fontana-commerce.htnet.hr. Overlooking Trogir Channel, this old building has been tastefully modernized to accommodate 13 guest rooms (several with jacuzzis) plus a suite. The same management run the popular **Restaurant Fontana** (see Eating).

D Villa Sikaa Hotel, Obala kralja Zvonimira 13, T021-881223, www.vila-sikaa-r.com. This small family-run hotel occupies an 18th-century villa looking out over Trogir Channel with a view back to the old town. The 8 rooms and 2 suites have wooden floors and newly tiled bathrooms.

E Concordia, Obala bana Berislavića 22, T021-885400, www.concordia-hotel.net. 14 comfortable rooms, close to **Hotel Fontana**, in an 18th-century town house looking out over Trogir Channel.

Sinj *p219*

E Hotel Alkar, Vrlička bb, T021-824474, www.hotel-alkar.hr. Modern 3-storey white concrete hotel with 50 comfortable rooms, close to the tourist office. To stay here the weekend of the **Alka**, book well in advance.

Eating

Trogir *p214*

ΨΨΨ Restaurant Fontana, Obrov 1, T021-884811. This highly esteemed restaurant has tables outside on a waterfront terrace through summer. The fish and seafood dishes can be pricey, pizza makes a cheap option.

ΨΨ Čelica, Čiovo bridge, T021-882344. This old wooden car ferry, anchored by Čiovo bridge, has been converted to form an unusual restaurant. The owner catches and cooks the seafood, his speciality is *riblja juha* (fish soup).

ΨΨ Škrapa, Augustina Kazotića, T021-885313. Popular with both locals and visitors, **Škrapa** serves up large platters of delicious *frigne ligne* (fried squid) and *ribice* (small fried fish). It's informal and fun, with heavy wooden tables and benches both indoors and out.

Klis *p218*

ΨΨ Restaurant Perlica, Grlo 3, T021-240004. Although there are 3 restaurants serving up *janjetina* (roast lamb) in Klis Grlo, this is possibly the best – people drive for miles to eat here. Open day and night, Feb-Dec.

Sinj *p219*

ΨΨ Konoba Ispod Ure, Istarska 2, T021-822 229. Located in the centre of town, this restaurant serves a wide choice of Croatian dishes, including the local speciality, *arambašići* (cabbage leaves stuffed with minced meat and rice), elsewhere known as *sarma*.

Bars and clubs

Trogir *p214*

F1, large techno-orientated nightclub, 5 km northwest of town, along the coast. Fri and Sat open until 0500.

Intermezzo Cyber Café Bar, Ribarska 3. Popular café on the seafront, large summer terrace, open daily until 0300. Internet.

For an explanation of the sleeping and eating price codes used in this guide, see inside the front cover. Other relevant information is found in Essentials, pages 32-40.

Festivals and events

Trogir *p214*

Jul-Aug Trogir Summer Festival. Features classical and folk music concerts, staged in the cathedral and Kamerlengo Fortress, and at various open-air venues around town.

Salona *p216*

Jul Ethnoambient Salona, www.ethnoambient.net. A 3-day open-air event in late Jul, attracts musicians from as far afield as Scotland, Portugal and Greece.

Sinj *p219*

Aug Sinjska Alka, www.alka.hr, 1st Sun in Aug. Commemorates the 1715 victory over the Turks. It's an entertaining affair, with whole roast lamb on spits, a brass band, competitors in traditional costume (blue uniforms with silver buttons and tall fur hats) and around 15,000 spectators. The competition, which has taken place for almost 300 years, starts at 1500 and involves *alkari* (mounted knights) riding at full gallop carrying 3-m-long jousts, with the goal of spearing an *alka* (small metal ring) suspended at a height of 3.32 m. The winner, who becomes a local hero for 12 months, gets a cash prize, a silver shield and sword.

15 Aug Assumption Day. Religious pilgrims flock to town, some ailing and in hope of a miraculous cure, to pay their respects to the *Sinjksa Gospe*.

Activities and tours

Trogir *p214*

Diving

Diving Medena, Seget Donji (4km from Trogir), T021-800223, www.diving-medena.com.hr.

Sailing

ACI Marina, Čiovo, T021-881544, www.aci-club.hr. Across the bridge, a 10-min walk from the centre of Trogir. 180 berths, open all year.

Charter companies based here include: **Blue Yacht Charter**, T021-796273, www.blue-yachts.com; **Dalmatia Charter**, T021-797239, www.dalmatiacharter.com.

Transport

Trogir *p214*

Air

Split airport is located just 2 km from Trogir.

Bus

Trogir bus station, T021-881405. A regular local bus service runs from Split to Trogir every 30 mins, 0600-2200 (40 mins).

Coaches running along the coast between **Split** and **Šibenik** also stop here.

Salona *p216*

Bus

Buses leave from Trg Gaje Bulata (opposite the National Theatre) in **Split**, every 20 mins, 0700-2200, for Salona (30 mins).

Klis *p218*

Bus

18 daily buses depart from **Split** for **Sinj** (35 mins), passing through Klis-Varoš en route. There is also a less frequent service from Split to Klis-Megdan.

Sinj *p219*

Bus

18 buses daily from **Split** (1 hr). Buses taking the inland route Split-**Zagreb**, also pass through Sinj.

Šibenik and around

→ *Phone code: 022. Colour map 3, B4. Population: 51,553. 300 km from Zagreb, 403 km from Pula, 300 km from Rijeka, 74 km from Zadar, 75 km from Split, and 291 km from Dubrovnik.*

In a protected channel, at the mouth of the River Krka, the medieval part of Šibenik is a warren of steep, winding alleyways and terracotta-roofed houses, built into a hillside below the remains of a Venetian fortress. Close to the seafront, the city's main sight is the monumental Renaissance Cathedral of St Jacob, which is included on the UNESCO list of World Heritage Sites.

From the small harbour, local ferries enter the open sea through a narrow channel, stopping at the peaceful islands of Zlarin and Prvić, before continuing to the nearby mainland resort of Vodice. On the edge of town, disused factories and sprawling modern suburbs reveal a period of 20th-century industrial development followed by economic collapse caused by the war. Šibenik is not well geared towards tourists – most visitors to the area stay in Vodice – but you can happily devote half a day to the historic centre, and it makes a good starting point for a visit to Krka National Park.

▸▸ *For Sleeping, Eating and other listings, see pages 228-232.*

Ins and outs

Getting there There are good bus and train links with the main cities in Croatia and from surrounding countries. The bus station is at Draga 14, on the seafront, a five-minute walk from the city centre. Left luggage 0630-2100, 15Kn per piece per day. The train station is at Milete bb, south of the bus station, a 10-minute walk from the city centre. There's no left luggage. ▸▸ *See Transport, page 232, for further details.*

Getting around The historic centre occupies a small area, concentrated on the hillside below the fortress. It can only be explored on foot, as the winding cobbled alleyways are too narrow to allow traffic – be sure to wear comfortable walking shoes.

Tourist information There's a walk-in **city tourist information centre** ⓘ *Obala Dr F Tudjmana 5, T022-214411, www.sibenik-tourism.hr*, and a **county tourist office** ⓘ *Fra N Ružića bb, T022-212346.*

Best time to visit As it's not really a tourist destination, life in Šibenik continues at its own pace the year through, with little seasonal variation. If you're planning on visiting Krka National Park, the woods are at their most beautiful in spring and autumn, when the river is also quite swollen, making the waterfalls all the more impressive. However, one of the greatest pleasures at Krka is swimming, which is only possible in mid- summer as the water is icy cold the rest of the year.

Background

Unlike other major cities along the east Adriatic coast – such as Zadar, Trogir and Split – which were established by Greeks and Romans, Šibenik was founded by Slavs. It was first documented in a Royal Charter issued by the Croatian king, Petar Krešimir IV, in 1066. In 1298, it gained the status of town, and was described as a settlement of triangular plan, with a hilltop fortress (present-day Sv Ana) overlooking a quarter of tightly packed stone houses built into a hillside (present-day Gradina).

In 1412, following three years of strong local resistance, Šibenik fell to Venice. Over the following three centuries, lucrative trade, conducted between the Ottoman-held hinterland and the Venetian port, brought material wealth coupled with a surge of creative activity. Inspired by the beauty of the cathedral in nearby Trogir (see page 215), the people of Šibenik set about building a similar yet even grander monument, and the Cathedral of St Jacob, sponsored by local citizens of all social classes, was erected. Not so well documented but even more innovative for its time, the local scientist Faust Vrančić (1551-1617) published *Machinae Novea* several decades later, in which he anticipated the invention of the parachute.

During the 20th century, under Yugoslavia, Šibenik expanded into a busy industrial centre, with a large aluminium factory, metal works and a shipyard, drawing workers from all corners of the country. The war of the 1990s saw the city in a complex situation, as its mixed population of Croats and Serbs were driven to internal conflict. The result, a decade later, is a situation of social and economic depression, industrial collapse and high unemployment.

The city

» *pp228-232.*

Katedrala Sv Jakova (Cathedral of St Jacob)

ⓘ *Trg Republike Hrvatske, daily 0900-1900.*

Built between 1431 and 1536, this splendid cathedral was constructed in several stages. The result, a mix of late Gothic and Renaissance styles, is a three-aisle basilica based on the plan of a Latin cross, with a trefoil façade and cupola. The project was initiated by Venetian architects, who worked here for 10 years. They were responsible for the ornate Gothic portals – the main door portraying *The Last Judgement*, surrounded by the Apostles and crowned by a portrait of Christ, and the side door, the *Entrance to Paradise*, guarded on either side by a lion, one carrying Adam and the other Eve. In 1441, Juraj Dalmatinac, a Dalmatian from Zadar, who had trained as an architect in Venice, took over. He proposed a far grander edifice, a three-aisle basilica topped by an octagonal cupola, introducing the newly emerging Renaissance style. He also created one of the building's best-loved features – a frieze running around the outer walls, made up of 74 faces, some moustachioed, some turbaned, said to be those citizens too stingy to contribute to the cost of the building. Sadly, Dalmatinac died in 1473, before his masterpiece was completed. The final works were conducted by one of his pupils, Nikola Fiorentinac, who oversaw the mounting of the cupola and the construction of the vaulted roof, employing a unique system of interlocking monolithic stone slabs cut to shape.

The baptistery was designed by Dalmatinac but completed by another of his pupils, Andrija Aleši, an Albanian from Durres. It is to the right of the main altar, and is accessed by a short flight of stone steps. It is an enchanting space, with decorative stonework carved fine as lace. The final stone of the building was laid in 1536, and in 1555 it was dedicated to St Jacob.

In front of the cathedral, opposite the main portal, stands a bronze statue of Dalmatinac, by the 20th-century sculptor, Ivan Meštrović.

Šibenski Muzej (Šibenik Museum)

ⓘ *Gradska Vrata 3, T022-213880, www.muzej-sibenik.hr. Daily 1000-1300 and 1800-2000, free.*

Immediately behind the cathedral stands the late Renaissance **Kneževa Palača** (Rector's Palace), built in Venetian times as the residence of the city governor. Today it houses a small display of archaeological finds from Šibenik and the surrounding area and a number of 15th-century religious icons. It also hosts temporary exhibitions.

Gradska Vijecnica (Old Town Hall)

ⓘ *Trg Republike Hrvatske 1.*

Opposite the cathedral stands the Old Loggia, which served as the seat of the town council under Venice. It was built between 1533 and 1542, to a design by the Venetian Mannerist architect, Michele Sanmichele. Badly damaged during the Second World

War, it was subsequently restored, and the ground level now houses a restaurant, with tables outside in the arched portico through summer.

Tvrdava Sv Ana (St Anne's Fortress)

Perched on the hilltop above Gradina, the medieval quarter of town, this fortress merits a visit for the spectacular view it offers over the terracotta rooftops and out across the sea. Orientated towards the west, it's particularly evocative at sunset. It's the city's oldest defensive structure, though what you see today – little more than crumbling ramparts – dates back to the 16th century. From the cathedral follow any one of the steep winding streets up through the medieval quarter, to arrive at the hilltop fortress.

Beaches

Locals recommend going to the nearby islands of **Zlarin** and **Prvić**, where the water is crystal clear and perfect for swimming. Otherwise, the beaches in front of the **Hotel Solaris** complex, 3 km south of town, are probably the best.

Krka National Park

» *pp228-232. Colour map 3, B4.*

Ins and outs

→ *Phone code: 022. Population: 3986. 16 km north of Šibenik.*

There's a **National Park office** ⓘ *Trg Republike Hrvatske 2, Šibenik, T021-201777, www.npkrka.hr, Jun-Sep daily 0800-2000, 80Kn, Mar-May and Oct daily 0900-1700, 65Kn, Nov-Feb daily 0900-1500, 25Kn*. National park boats leave from Skradin for Skradinski Buk on the hour, departing for the return journey on the half hour (25 minutes). The cost of the boat ride is included in the entrance ticket.

Skradin

The picturesque small town of Skradin is at the point where the Krka River enters a long sea channel. Backed by dense woodland and directly on the waterfront, Skradin's old stone houses and two church spires (one Roman Catholic, the other Orthodox) appear the epitome of peace and harmony. However, less than a decade ago this was the front line between the Croat-dominated municipality of Šibenik and the Serb-controlled area of Krajina. Many families fled, though thankfully the town suffered little structural damage. Over the last couple of years Skradin has re-established itself as a popular tourist destination, with an excellent marina and a number of good fish restaurants overlooking the harbour. The main reason for coming here though is to catch a boat up to the Krka National Park. The town **tourist office** ⓘ *Trg Male Gospe 3, T022-771329, www.skradin.hr*, can provide more information.

Skradin was founded as *Scardona* by the Romans in the third century BC, but met the fate of other early settlements when tribes of Avars and Slavs rampaged along the east Adriatic coast during the seventh century. In 1522 it was conquered by the Turks, who held onto it until 1684, when it passed to Venice. Tourism began here during the 1960s, when the Krka Falls area became a popular place for camping. Since the national park was established in 1985, camping has been prohibited, but a regular boat now shuttles day trippers upriver from Skradin, 4.5 km to the park's main entrance a Skradinski buk.

Vinarija Bedrica ⓘ *Fra Luje Maruna 14, T022-771095, Jun-Sep daily 1800-2200*, in the centre of town, is a family-run wine cellar dating back to 1722. The interior is tastefully arranged with wooden barrels and old-fashioned winemaking equipment. The owner lives in the same building, and even in low season he is happy to open the *vinerija* for visitors interested in sampling and purchasing his wine, *rakija* and *prošek*.

Exploring the park

Beginning a short distance southwest of Knin (see page 227), and following the course of the River Krka almost to Skradin, the national park encompasses a steep-sided, wooded canyon and a series of seven waterfalls. The main entrance is close to **Skradinski buk**, the park's most spectacular falls, made up of a series of 17 cascades plunging over 40 m into a wide emerald-green basin, ideal for bathing. Next to the falls, a sheltered meadow, bordered by woods, offers an idyllic spot for sunbathing and picnicking. Above Skradinski buk, a series of wooden bridges and well-marked footpaths lead to the next falls, **Roški slap**, 10 km to the north. If you don't fancy the hike, it's possible to catch a second national park boat, which runs several times a day, shuttling visitors between the two falls and calling en route at the 15th-century **Visovac Samostan** (Visovac Monastery) perched on a small island in the middle of **Visovačko Jezero** (Visovac Lake).

The coast and the islands » *pp228-232.*

The tiny islands of Zlarin and Prvić are just a short ferry ride away from Šibenik and Vodice, making a restful escape from urban life. Both are car-free and offer crystal clear water for swimming.

Zlarin → *Phone code: 022. Colour map 3, B4. Population: 729.*

A 30-minute ferry ride from Šibenik, this tiny island is roughly 6 km long and 2 km wide. The sole settlement, also called Zlarin, is built around a deep bay, with a palm-lined seafront promenade overlooked by old stone houses and an 18th-century baroque parish church. During the Middle Ages, Zlarin was owned by the Šibenik chapter, and for six centuries, the islanders lived from one trade alone: collecting coral.

Prvić → *Phone code: 022. Colour map 3, B4. Population: 390.*

Ten minutes by boat from Vodice, Prvić has two settlements, Prvić Luka and Šepurine, and the local ferry stops at both. Šepurine, home to about 220 residents, is a pretty west-facing village, made up of traditional Dalmatian stone houses, dominated by a waterside church with a bell tower and onion dome. From Šepurine, a pleasant footpath (a 15-minute walk) leads across the island to the slightly smaller Prvić Luka, with 170 inhabitants. Luka, built around a deep southeast-facing bay, is popular with yachters and has a couple of harbourside restaurants.

Historically the islanders lived from farming (keeping sheep and goats which grazed freely on the nearby small uninhabited islands), fishing and producing olive oil and wine. Today tourism is slowly taking over, though many families still make their own wine, and if you're lucky enough to be offered some, be sure to try it: somewhere between a white and a rosé, it has a specific musky taste of rocky soil exposed to hours of endless sunshine.

Vodice → *Phone code: 022. Colour map 3, B3. Population: 9407. 11 km northwest of Šibenik.*

Vodice was once a quiet fishing village built around a small square with an 18th-century parish church. Then came along the tourist boom of the 1970s. Since then, a number of high-rise hotels have sprung up, many of the old buildings along the seafront have been converted into seasonal cafés, restaurants and pizzerias, and in summer the place is inundated with people from all over Europe. However, it has by no means lost its charm, and it's a far more cheerful place to stay than Šibenik – in fact, people from Šibenik often come here for a night out. Despite its success as a seaside resort, Vodice offers little in the way of good beaches. The coastal path north of town is lined with concrete bathing areas giving easy access to the water, though locals would sooner take a ferry to the small island of Prvić for a day on the beach. The well-equipped marina, immediately in front of the old town, is a popular port of call with sailing boats, and there are a couple of large charter companies based here. The town **tourist office** ⓘ *Ive Čače 1a, T022-443888, www.vodice.hr*, will provide more information.

Murter

→ *Phone code: 022. Colour map 3, B3. Population: 2075. 30 km northwest of Šibenik; 50 km southeast of Zadar.*

The small island of Murter is joined to the mainland by a 38-m bridge, spanning the Murter Channel at Tisno. With scanty pastures and a handful of minor settlements it's not a particularly attractive place, but it's close to the scattered islands of the Kornati archipelago, and is a popular launching pad for visits to the Kornati National Park. Confusingly, although the national park office is located in Murter Town, in the county of Šibenik, the park itself lies largely within the waters of North Dalmatia (see page 188), and thus falls under the county of Zadar.

Murter Town, known as Veliko Selo (Big Village) until 1715, dates back to the 13th century. The Murterini (people from Murter) traditionally lived from fishing the waters of the Kornati and cultivating olives, figs and vines on the closest islets. Tourism began in 1930, when the so-called Czech Villa was built in Slanica Bay 1 km away on the southwest coast, and today the same site boasts the island's most popular beach, overlooked by the modern **Hotel Colentum** complex. Through summer, the quay in Murter Town is busy with private agents, plying organized boat trips to the Kornati, usually with a fish lunch thrown in. There's a town **tourist office** ⓘ *Rudina bb, T022-434995, www.tzo-murter.hr*. **Kornati National Park office** ⓘ *Butina 2, T022-435740, www.kornati.hr*, is responsible for protecting the natural environment within the park, and provides very limited information of use to tourists.

Murter Town straggles east along the coast to merge with **Betina**, said to have been founded in the 16th century by mainland refugees seeking shelter from the Turks. Its narrow cobbled streets meander their way uphill to a 17th-century parish church, dedicated to St Francis. On the east side of the island, giving onto the Murterski Kanal (Murter Channel), the village of **Jezera** is home to a well-equipped ACI marina, and the base for a renowned summer sailing school, ANA.

While on the island, those interested in seafaring should look out for *gajete*, old-fashioned Murter fishing boats pointed at both the bow and the stern and usually painted white and blue. Today, the Murter shipyard is one of the few remaining places in Dalmatia to have kept alive the tradition of constructing wooden boats.

The best **beaches** lie southwest of Murter Town, between Uvala Slanica (Slanica Bay) and Uvala Cigrada (Cigrada Bay), and are well within walking distance. **Slanica Bay**, backed by a row of noisy beachside bars and a big hotel, is rather commercial and gets very busy. If you're in search of a more relaxed atmosphere, you're better off following Pod Raduc, a coastal road giving onto a rocky shoreline, to **Cigrada Bay**, where there's a lovely peaceful beach overlooked by a couple of discreet restaurants.

Primošten

→ *Phone code: 022. Colour map 3, C4. Population: 1761. 20 km southeast of Šibenik.*

Seen from a distance Primošten is enchanting. Just off the main coastal road, it is a cluster of old stone houses packed tightly on a small island joined to the mainland by a bridge. Closer inspection reveals a place not quite so magical as one first imagined. There's little of cultural interest here, though a couple of hours exploring the town's narrow winding streets and stopping for a bite to eat or a drink are certainly not ill spent.

Story has it that the island was settled by refugees from Bosnia, who fled to the coast after the Ottoman Turks conquered their land in the late 15th century. During the 16th century, a bridge was built, connecting the island to the mainland, and from then on the settlement became known as Primošten (from *primostiti*, meaning 'to bridge over'). The town **tourist office** ⓘ *Rudina Biskupa J Arnerica 2, T022-571111, www.tz-primosten.hr*, can provide more information.

Today Primošten is best known for *Babić*, an excellent full-bodied red **wine** produced in vineyards on the slopes of the nearby mainland. Driving along the coast you can't miss them – the stony land has been cleared into small square plots of the most amazing geometrical precision, with each unit surrounded by dry stonewalls. **Jurlinovi Dvori** ⓘ *Draga, 5 km from Primošten, T022-574106*, a wine cellar lying a short distance inland, is a complex of 16th-century farm buildings which have been carefully restored to form a small ethnological museum. There's a *konoba* where you can taste local *Babić* wine, served with black olives, cheese and smoked ham. The best **beaches** are in the nearby coves of Vela Raduča and Mala Raduča.

Knin and around

» *pp228-232. Colour map 3, B4.*

→ *Phone code: 022. Population: 15,190. 56 km northeast of Šibenik.*

On the main road and rail routes between Zagreb and Split, Knin is built around the remains of an impressive hilltop fortress. During the 1990s, the town hit the news as capital of the self-declared Serbian Autonomous Region of Krajina, and the traumatic events that followed left it all but abandoned. Today this once-prosperous industrial centre is struggling to re-establish itself, but with vacant factories, soaring unemployment and a population made up largely of refugees, it has some way to go. It's by no means geared up to tourists, but if does have a **tourist office** ⓘ *Tudjmanova 24, T022-664822, www.tz-knin.hr*, and if you're passing through and have time to spare, the fortress merits a visit.

Background

Guarding Kninska Vrata (Knin Gateway), a natural passage between the Dalmatian coast and the inland territories, Knin Fortress was built in the 10th century and was established as the seat of the early Croatian royalty. A town and parish grew up on the flat plain below, and in the 11th century, Knin became the seat of a bishop. The fortress was occupied by the Turks from 1522 to 1688, marking a watch point on the western border of the Ottoman Empire.

During the Tito years, Knin saw a period of rapid industrialization, as metal works, wood works and factories producing building materials and textiles were set up. It also became the headquarters of a large Yugoslav army base. By 1990, with a population of around 40,000, approximately 90% of the town's population were Serbs, who also held a marked majority in the surrounding inland region, known as Kninska Krajina. With the onset of animosity between Croats and Serbs in the early 1990s, the Serbs effectively cut the country in two by establishing an autonomous 'republic' (1991-1995) and blocking major transport routes between Zagreb and Dalmatia. In early August 1995, the Croatian army (with US backing) carried out *Oluja* (Operation Storm) and the resulting fall of Knin marked the collapse of the Serbian Autonomous Region of Krajina. On 26 August of the same year, the much-televised *Vlak Slobode* (Freedom Train), with a jubilant President Franjo Tudman aboard, was the first train to run from Zagreb to Split after a five-year lull. It stopped at Knin, but by this time the town was virtually deserted, tens of thousands of Serbs having fled the region. Many houses were quickly filled with Croatian refugees from Bosnia, though the present government is trying to encourage Serb families to return.

Tvrdjava (fortress)

ⓘ *T022-662151, 0700-sunset, 10Kn.*

Once the biggest in Dalmatia, the fortress is made up of impressive walls and grassy ramparts perched upon Sveti Spas, a rocky limestone hill in the centre of town. It is divided into three areas, joined together by drawbridges. The oldest and lowest part is to the north of the complex, while the middle and upper areas were constructed later, sometime during the Middle Ages. The ramparts were reinforced in the early 18th century. On 5 August 1995, following *Oluja*, the Croatian army hoisted the red and white chequerboard flag above the fortress, and the next day Tudman was on the spot to bless the Croatian victory and declare the region liberated. There is a restaurant within the walls.

Drniš

Driving between Šibenik and Knin, the main road passes through the unremarkable market town of Drniš. Some 9 km east of here, in the village of Otavice, the **Meštrović Mausoleum** ① *T022-872630, Jun-Sep Tue-Sun 0800-1200 and 1700- 2000, Oct-May Tue-Sun 1000-1400, 10Kn*, is in the childhood home of Croatia's best- known 20th-century sculptor, Ivan Meštrović (see page 338). In 1926 he designed this splendid mausoleum – a stone cube topped with a dome and an interior decorated with art nouveau-style religious reliefs – for his family. He emigrated to the US in 1942, but upon his death in 1962 his last wish was that he be buried here. Around 2000 people and 16 members of the clergy attended the funeral.

Sleeping

Šibenik and around *p222*

Accommodation in the city centre is limited (if you're arriving late arrange a place to sleep in advance). Few visitors choose to stay in Šibenik itself, with the nearby seaside resort of Vodice offering plentiful accommodation. However, most of the hotels are large, modern and impersonal. You'd be better off looking for private accommodation.

D **Jadran Hotel**, Obala Oslobodjenje 52, T022-212644, www.rivijera.hr. Located in the centre of town on the seafront promenade, just a 5-min walk from the bus station, this 57-room hotel provides smart, comfortable accommodation. Open all year.

E **The Konoba**, Andrije Kačića 8, T022-214 397, www.bbdalmatia.com. In Šibenik's old town, this B&B occupies 2 traditional stone buildings. The 5 rooms all have wooden floors and antique furniture, and 3 have en suite bathrooms. The Dutch owner prepares an excellent breakfast, and there's a roof terrace affording views out to sea.

E **Zlatna Ribica Pansion**, K Spužvara, Brodarica, T022-350695. Run by the same management as the neighbouring **Zlanta Ribica** restaurant. Offers 16 pleasant double rooms and 2 apartments. Open all year.

Private accommodation

Nik, A Šupuka 5, T022-338550, www.nik.hr. This agency will help you find private accommodation around Šibenik, including Vodice, Primošten, and the islands of Zlarin and Prvić. They also arrange excursions to the national parks of Krka and Kornati.

Krka National Park *p224*

Skradin tourist office can help you find private accommodation in town.

D **Hotel Skradinski Buk**, Burinovac bb, Skradin, T022-771771, www.skradinskibuk.hr. Opened in 2002, this is a family-run hotel in a carefully renovated old stone building in the centre of Skradin. There are 28 rooms, and a 3rd-floor terrace offering views down onto the River Krka. It stays open all year.

Zlarin *p225*

D **Hotel Koralj**, Zlarin, T022-553747. This small hotel has 20 guest rooms and a restaurant. They stay open all year, but are often pre-booked Jul-Aug.

Prvić *p225*

D **Hotel Maestral**, Prvić Luka, T022-448300, www.hotelmaestral.com. This 19th-century stone building overlooking the sea opened to provide a small, stylish hotel in 2004. The 12 rooms have exposed stonewalls, wooden floors and minimalist furniture. There's a waterside restaurant, and Wi-Fi internet. They stay open all year.

Vodice *p225*

See also Šibenik, above.

E Hotel Kristina, Šetalište M Sladoljeva 3, T022-444173, www.hotel-kristina.hr. Set in a garden with views of the sea and backed by pinewoods, this small family-run hotel is on Punta Peninsula, a 100-m walk along the coast from the centre. Open all year.

Private accommodation

Nik, Ante Poljička 2, T022-441730, www.nik.hr. Private accommodation is plentiful and of a high standard in Vodice and the surrounding area. This agency has a list of private rooms and apartments.

Murter *p226*

D Hotel Borovnik, Trg Šime Vlašića 3, Tisno. T022-439700, www.hotel-borovnik.com. In Tisno, overlooking the sea channel close to the bridge linking the island of Murter to the mainland, this 1970s building has 70 rooms, a restaurant and an outdoor pool.

D Prišnjak Lighthouse, contact **Adriatica Net**, Selska 34, Zagreb, T01-2415611, www.adriatica.net. Located on the islet of Prišnjak, just 300 m from the northwest tip of the island of Murter, this lighthouse has been tastefully renovated to provide a spacious apartment sleeping 4.

Private accommodation

The following Murter-based agencies both have a selection of Robinson Crusoe-type accommodation – simply furnished cottages with basic amenities, but no electricity or running water – on the Kornati islands: **Kornat Turist**, Hrvatskih vladara 2, T022-435854/5, www.kornatturist.hr; **Lori Tourist Agency**, Zdrače 2, T022-435631, www.tourist agency-lori.hr.

Primošten *p226*

Most of the hotels are big modern commercial establishments, situated along the mainland coast. You're far better off looking for private accommodation, which is plentiful and of a high standard.

Private accommodation

The following agencies can help you find rooms or an apartment: **Daltours**, Dalmatinska 7a, T022-571572, www.daltours. com; **Nik**, Raduča 1, T022-571200, www.nik.hr.

Knin and around *p227*

D Hotel Mihovil, Vrpolje bb, T022-664444, www.zivkovic.hr. 2 km northeast of town, on the road heading for Bosnia and Herzegovina, this hotel offers 26 basic but comfortable rooms and the only notable restaurant in the area. Open all year.

Eating

Šibenik and around *p222*

ƳƳƳ-ƳƳ Gradska Vijećnica, Trg Republike Hrvatske 1, T022-213605. Commanding a prime site, with tables on the main square opposite the cathedral, this restaurant is based in the 16th-century Venetian Town Hall. The house speciality is *paprika punjena sirom* (peppers stuffed with cheese).

ƳƳƳ-ƳƳ Uzorita, Bana Jelačića 50, T022-213660. Šibenik's best-known restaurant, dating back to 1898, is a 20-min walk northeast of the centre and specializes in seafood. The dining room is done out in traditional Dalmatian style with exposed stonewalls, beamed ceilings and heavy wooden furniture. In summer, tables spill out into a romantic courtyard.

ƳƳƳ-ƳƳ Zlatna Ribica, K Spužvara 46, Brodarica, on the coast 8 km south of Šibenik, T022-350300, www.zlatna-ribica.hr. Said by many to be the best fish restaurant in the area, the house speciality here is *punjeni oslic* (hake stuffed with spinach and olives). The summer terrace offers views across the sea to the small island of Krapanj, and there is live music on Fri and Sat night.

ƳƳ Konoba Dalmatino, Fra Nikole Ružića 2, T091-542 4808. In the old town, this tiny old fashioned eatery is a great spot for fresh fish and Dalmatian specialities such as *pršut* (prosciutto) and *sir* (cheese). It doubles as an up-market wine shop.

Ƴ Tržnica, the open-air market just above the bus station, is the best place to shop for a cheap snack, with several kiosks selling fresh *burek* (filo pastry filled with either cheese or meat).

Cafés

The seafront promenade, Obala Oslobodjenje and Obala prvoboraca, is lined with busy cafés with outdoor seating.

Krka National Park *p224*

ΨΨΨ-ΨΨ **Konoba Toni**, Trgovačka 46, Skradin, T022-771177. Specializes in traditional Dalmatian dishes such as *brudet sa purom* (fish stew with polenta) prepared over an open fire, and lamb and veal cooked under a *peka*. Guests are welcome to take a look inside the old-fashioned kitchen, to watch the food being made. Open all year.

ΨΨΨ-ΨΨ **Zlatne Školjke**, Grgura Ninskog 9, Skradin, T022-771022. Located in an old stone house with a summer terrace over looking ACI Marina, this restaurant is best known for *crni rižot* (black risotto), *špageti s plodovima mora* (spaghetti with seafood) and *riba na žaru* (barbecued fish). Open all year.

Prvič *p225*

ΨΨ **Punta**, Prvić Luka, T098-266274 (mob). This small, friendly restaurant serves up fish and seafood dishes on a terrace looking out over the bay. Open Easter to early Oct.

ΨΨ **Ribarski Dvor**, Šepurine, T022-448511. Whitewashed walls and a beamed ceiling hung with fishing nets lend a rustic atmosphere to **Ribarski Dvor**, where guests tuck into classic Dalmatian fish and meat dishes. Open early May to early Oct.

Vodice *p225*

ΨΨΨ-ΨΨ **Santa Maria Restaurant Pizzeria**, Kamila Pamukovića 9, T022-443319. Although you probably didn't come to Dalmatia to eat Mexican, this is the one place you might be tempted to do so. The interior comprises a split-level space with wooden floors and beamed ceilings, decorated with a fascinating array of traditional sailing equipment and South American folk objects. Some visitors complain that it's over-priced, but people from the surrounding area still drive for miles to sample the house specialities, paella and tortillas. Open all year.

ΨΨ **Restoran Adria**, Obala matice Hrvatska 8, T022-441543. Located on the seafront in the centre of town, this popular restuarant serves carefully presented seafood and charcoal-grilled meat dishes. There's also a good choice of desserts. Open Apr-Oct.

Murter *p226*

ΨΨ **Konoba Stari Mlin**, Trg Španjolskog Borca Dragutinina Bilica bb, Betina. With exposed stone walls and rustic wooden furniture, this typical Dalmatian *konoba* is a great place to enjoy local wine, along with a range of savoury eats, well into the early hours. Open late May to early Oct, 2000-0300.

ΨΨ **Tic Tac**, Hrokešina 5, Murter Town, T022-435230. In the Hramina quarter of town, in a narrow side street leading down to the harbour, this popular restaurant offers the standard selection of seafood pasta and risotto dishes, barbecued fish and meat, plus an unusual favourite, tuna *sushi*.

Ψ **Lantana**, Uvala Čigrada, 2 km south of Murter, T022-436028. Overlooking Čigrada Bay, this much loved wooden beach hut offers delicious cheap snacks such as *salata od hobotnice* (octopus salad) and *pohani škampi* (scampi in breadcrumbs), as well as pizza, daily through summer, 1000-2300. Tables are arranged on a series of levels, below the shade of a bamboo canopy. There's good music all day, and live concerts by the sea at night, 2300-0300.

Primošten *p226*

ΨΨΨ-ΨΨ **Restoran Dalmacija**, Put Murve 15, T022-570009. This highly regarded restaurant is located in the old town, with a lovely summer terrace surrounded by traditional stone cottages. Seafood and fish top the menu; try the delicious *fondi sa hobotnicom* (octopus fondue). Closed Dec-Mar.

ΨΨ **Šaricevi Dvori**, Šupljak bb, Primošten Burnji, 4 km from Primošten, T022-571197. Set amid fields a short distance from the coast, this romantic old stone building has been converted into an informal eatery. The menu focuses on typical Dalmatian fare such as *brodetto* (fish stew), and *hobotnica* (octopus) and *janjetina* (lamb) prepared under a *peka* (for which you need to call 1 day in advance). If you are without private transport and don't fancy the walk, call and they will pick you up. Open May-Oct.

Bars and clubs

Šibenik and around *p222*

Hacijenda, Magistrala bb, on the road between Šibenik and Vodice is the biggest nightclub for miles. Open-air, summer only.

Primošten *p226*

Aurora Club, www.auroraclub.hr, located 1 km from the old town. One of the largest discos in Dalmatia. Open mid-Jun to early Sep.

Entertainment

Šibenik and around *p222*

Cinema

Kino, Obala Oslobodjenje, next to **Hotel Jadran**, T022-212870.

Theatre

Šibensko Kazalište, Kralja Zvonimira 1, T022-213123.

Festivals and events

Šibenik and around *p222*

Jun-Jul Medunarodni dječji festival (International Children's Festival), late Jun to early Jul. Founded in 1958, this 2-week event is organized by Šibenik Theatre and features children's music, drama and puppet theatre. For more information, see www.mdf-si.org.

Activities and tours

Šibenik and around *p222*

Sailing

Marina Solaris, Hotel Solaris complex, 3 km south of town, T022-364000, www.solaris.hr. 305 berths, open all year.

Tour operators

Atlas Šibenik, Trg Republike Hrvatske 2, T022-330232, www.atlas-croatia.com. Arrange various excursions throughout the country, including day trips to the nearby national parks of Krka and Kornati.

Croatia Express, Fra Jerolim Milete 24, T022-333669, www.croatiaexpress.com. Provide public transport information and tickets for the entire country.

Nik, A Šupuka 5, T022-338550, www.nik.hr. Arrange excursions to the nearby national parks of Krka and Kornati.

Krka National Park *p224*

Sailing

ACI Marina, T022-771365, www.aci-club.hr. 153 berths, open all year. Private vessels are not allowed upstream of Skradinski Most (Skradin Bridge). Skradin Marina is a popular place for keeping wooden boats through winter, as the combination of fresh water (from the river) and seawater prevent wood from premature ageing.

Vodice *p225*

Boating

You'll find small motorboats for rent on the seafront. Expect to pay 400Kn for a full day, or 250Kn for a ½ day.

Diving

Neptune, Hotel Punta, T022-200493, www.neptune.com.hr.

Sailing

ACI Marina, T022-443086, www.aci-club.hr, icentre of town. 290 berths, open all year.

Murter *p226*

Boating

Eseker Tours, Mainova bb, Murter Town, T022-435669, www.esekertours.hr. A wide range of speedboats and motorized rubber dinghies for hire on a daily basis – ideal for those who wish to visit the Kornati islands without having to go with a tour group.

Diving

Nautilus, Branimirova 19, Betina, T022-435893, www.diving-adria.com.

Sailing

Activity Yachting, www.activityyachting.com; **Betina Marina**, Trg na moru 1, Betina, T022-434996, has 180 berths, open all year; **Hramina Marina**, Put Gradine bb, Murter Town, T022-434411, has 350 berths, open all year; **Sun Adriatic Yacht Charter Millennium**, www.say.hr.

ACI Marina, Jezera, T022-439315, www.aci-club.hr. 200 berths, open all year. The Adriatic Nautical Academy (ANA) run a sailing school here, with intensive courses at all levels for pupils from various parts of Europe. For further information, contact the administrative office in Opatija, T051-711814, www.sailing-ana.hr.

Primošten *p226*

Sailing

Kremik Marina, Splitska 24, T022-570068, has 265 berths, open all year; **Mande Charter**, T01-6692011, www.mande charter.com.

Transport

Šibenik and around *p222*

Bus

For additional information about buses to and from Šibenik, T060-368368.

Internal services include about 13 buses daily to **Zagreb** (6 hrs); 34 to **Split** (1½ hrs); 3 to Pula in **Istria** (8½ hrs) and 12 to Rijeka in **Kvarner** (6½ hrs). There are also daily international bus lines to **Ljubljana** (Slovenia), **Trieste** (Italy) and **Munich** (Germany). Buses depart several times a week for various other destinations in **Germany** and **Austria**.

Ferry

Jadrolinija, T022-213468, run a daily ferry service between **Šibenik** and **Vodice** (total 1 hr), with boats stopping at the islands of **Prvić** and **Zlarin** en route. Schedules vary from day to day and season to season.

Train

Šibenik train station, T022-333699; national rail information, T060-333444, www.hznet.hr.

Internal services include 3 trains daily to and from **Zagreb** (7½ hrs); 5 trains daily to **Knin** (1½ hrs) and 3 trains daily to **Split** (3½ hrs). Some services require a change at Perković.

Krka National Park *p224*

Bus

Buses run 5 times daily between **Šibenik** and Skradin (25 mins).

Ferry

Several travel agencies operate all-inclusive day trips to the national park, by boat, from **Šibenik** and **Vodice**.

Zlarin and Prvič *p225*

Ferry

Jadrolinija (contact Šibenik office, T022-213468, for information) run several ferries daily between **Šibenik** and **Vodice** (1 hr), with boats stopping en route at **Zlarin** (on Zlarin), and **Šepurine** and **Prvić Luka** (on Prvić).

Vodice *p225*

Bus

Frequent buses run along the coastal road between **Šibenik** and **Zadar** (20 mins).

Ferry

Jadrolinija (no Vodice office, contact Šibenik office, T022-213468, for information) run a daily ferry service between Vodice and **Šibenik** (total 1 hr), with boats stopping at the islands of **Prvić** and **Zlarin** en route.

Murter *p225*

Bus

Buses zig-zag their way across the island to pass through the various settlements. 5 buses run daily from **Šibenik** to Murter Town, passing through **Vodice** en route (45 mins).

Primošten *p226*

Bus

Frequent buses running along the coastal road between **Split** and **Šibenik** stop in the new part of Primošten, above the coast (30 mins from Šibenik, 1 hr from Split). From here, it's just a 100-m walk down to the historic centre, on the former island.

Knin *p227*

Bus

Knin bus station is next to the train station, T022-661005. 10 buses per day run between Knin and **Šibenik** (1 hr 20 mins) and 17 per day between Knin and **Zagreb** (about 5 hrs).

Train

Knin train station, T022-663722; national train information, T060-333444, www.hznet.hr.

Services includes 4 trains daily to and from **Zagreb** (5½ hrs); 5 to **Split** (2 hrs) and 5 to **Šibenik** (1½ hr, with a change at Perković).

Directory

Šibenik and around *p222*

Emergencies Ambulance: 94; Fire: 93; Police: 92. **Medical services** Bolnica (Hospital), on Stjepana Radica, a 15-min walk southeast of the centre, T022-246246 (24-hr casualty). **Pharmacies**: marked by a green cross. **Ljekarna Centrala**, Stjepana Radića 41, T022-213539, 24-hrs, non-stop. If it is not open, there will be a notice on the door saying which pharmacy to go to. **Post offices** The main post office is at Vladimira Nazora 51, a 5-min walk from the bus station. **Telephones** Post offices (see above), otherwise, you'll find phone kiosks on the seafront.

The coast south of Split

South of Split the coastline highway (Magistrala) twists and turns to follow the water's edge, affording fine views over the sea and islands to your right, and the rugged silhouette of the Dinaric Mountains to your left. A succession of coastal villages offers modest pebble beaches and rooms to rent in 1970s concrete block houses mellowed by draping vines and balconies lined with potted geraniums. ➧ *For Sleeping, Eating and other listings, see pages 237-240.*

Omiš

➧ *pp237-240. Colour map 3, C5.*

→ *Phone code: 021. Population: 15,472. On the E65 coastal road, 28 km southeast of Split.*

Where the River Cetina emerges from a dramatic gorge to meet the sea, lies Omiš. Many people pass straight through, but closer inspection reveals a pleasant market town with alleys of old stone houses and a port, overlooked by a hilltop fortress backed by the spectacular Omiška Dinara Mountains. Omiš makes an ideal base for exploring the Cetina Gorge, where various agencies organize adventure sports such as rafting, canoeing and kayaking and there are also a couple of highly regarded riverside restaurants.

Ins and outs

Frequent buses run from Split and there are connections with Makarska and Dubrovnik. Taxi boats run up and down the river from the bridge in town through summer. There's a town **tourist office** ⓘ *Trg Sv Stjepana 16, T/F021-861350, www.tz-omis.hr.* ➧ *See Transport, page 240, for further details.*

Background

Omiš's main claim to fame is having been the base of a fearsome band of medieval pirates. Thanks to the deep gorge carved out by the River Cetina, they were able to cause havoc on the Adriatic, raiding Byzantine and Venetian ships then taking refuge upriver out of sight. A water wall at the mouth of the Cetina prevented larger ships from pursuing them, and the pirates themselves used a secret route, closed by chains. The frequent plundering of local monasteries, coupled with the raid of a Crusader ship in 1221, even caused the wrath of Rome. Pope Honorius III invited the cities of Split and Dubrovnik to launch an attack on Omiš, but the pirates remained undeterred. Shortly afterwards Omiš was ordered to burn all its vessels – a contract was signed but the agreement never fulfilled. The looting continued right up until 1444, when the town was taken by Venice. The Ottoman Turks attacked Omiš unsuccessfully in 1498, but managed to capture it in 1537, and governed until 1684, when it passed back to Venice.

Sights

Built as part of the 16th-century fortification system set up by Venice against the Turks, the well-preserved little **fortress** stands on a hill 311 m above town. It's a steep pull up, but well worth it for the spectacular views.

The oldest surviving structure in town is the tiny 10th-century **Crkva Sv Petar** (Church of St Peter) ⓘ *closed, but worth viewing from the outside*, measuring just 6 m by 11 m. It is one of loveliest pre-Romanesque buildings in Dalmatia and clearly shows the influence of Byzantine style on early Croatian architecture. Its modern appearance is explained by restoration work carried out during the 1960s. It is north of town across the river, on the right bank of the Cetina, in an area known as Priko.

The River Cetina rises east of Knin (see page 227), at first running through a gentle valley of green meadows, which in turn becomes a dramatic landscape of spectacular *karst* formations, the **Cetina Gorge**. The last stretch cuts a high-sided canyon between the mountains of Mosor and Biokovo, to meet the sea at Omiš. A series of rapids makes the river ideal for rafting, canoeing and kayaking, while the sheer-faced cliffs attract free-climbing enthusiasts. Riverside restaurants serve up freshwater specialities such as trout, eels and frogs, making a welcome change from the omnipresent seafood of the coast.

There's a colourful fruit and vegetable **market** under the trees on the side of the main road, and one block away is **Knezova Kačića**, a peaceful cobbled street linking the old east and west town gates. At the east end stands the 17th-century parish church, where the annual **Dalmatian Klapa Festival** takes place.

There's a town beach just south of the centre, though it's somewhat spoilt by the nearby traffic. Altogether more relaxing beaches are found at **Duče**, 3 km west of Omiš, and at **Ruskamen**, 6 km to the southeast. Ruskamen is a lovely pebble beach backed by pines with a stretch reserved for nudists, and also claims to be the best place in the area for windsurfing.

Makarska

» *pp237-240. Colour map 3, C6.*

→ *Phone code: 021. Population: 13,716. 67 km southeast of Split, on the E65 coastal road.*

Makarska combines the qualities of an old-fashioned Dalmatian port and a modern-day tourist resort. The setting is impressive: a palm-lined seafront promenade is built around a large cove, protected from the open sea by a wooded peninsula to the southwest, and sheltered from the cold *bura* wind by the craggy limestone heights of Mount Biokovo to the northeast. Through summer it makes a perfect base for holidaying on the beaches of the so-called **Makarska Rivijera**, while keen walkers are drawn to the rugged landscapes and rural villages of **Biokovo Nature Park** during spring and autumn. Makarska is popular with SAGA – the only travel agency that continued operating in Croatia through the 1990s – but come summer it's overrun with young visitors and families from all over Europe, who are drawn by its pleasant beaches, vibrant nightlife and reasonably priced accommodation.

Ins and outs

There are about 20 buses daily from Split to Makarska and around 12 buses daily from Dubrovnik. Makarska is very small and you can easily explore the place on foot. The seafront promenade is closed to traffic, as are the cobbled streets of the old town. For further information, there's a town **tourist office** ① *Obala Kralja Tomislava 16, T021-612002, www.makarska-info.hr.* » *See Transport, page 240, for further details.*

Background

Makarska was founded as the Roman Mucurum, though the original settlement was devastated by the Goths in 548. It was next mentioned in 950 by the Byzantine Emperor, Constantine VII, in *De Administrando Imperio* (On Imperial Administration). Describing the coastal strip running from the River Cetina in the north to the River Neretva in the south, an area he referred to as *Pagania*, he noted four *castrum* (fortified towns): Berullia (Brela), Mokron (Makarska), Ostrok (Zaostrog) and Labinetza (Lapčan, present-day Gradac).

This entire territory later fell to the Ottoman Turks, who captured Makarska in 1499 and established it as a port and administrative centre. During the mid-16th century, the *emir* (local governor) ordered that the town be fortified and paintings from that time depict three towers connected by sturdy walls. Sadly, they are no longer in existence.

The Turks were pushed out in 1646, though locals did not fully recognize subsequent Venetian rule until 1681. However, under Venice the economy thrived, and the centre of Makarska gained its present-day appearance during the 18th century, when the baroque Crkva Sv Marko (Church of St Mark) was erected at the top end of Kačićeva Trg, the main square, around which wealthy local merchants built elegant town houses.

Tourism has a long tradition here. The first hotel was built in 1914, under the Austrians, and the Society for the Beautification of the Town was founded in 1922. In 1962, a terrible earthquake caused considerable damage to Makarska and the surrounding villages, but just a decade later it became a popular holiday destination. As the economy boomed, more hotels were constructed along the coast, and locals built increasingly large houses with rooms and apartments to let.

Sights

Franjevački Samostan (Franciscan Monastery) and **Muzej Malakološki** (Shell Museum) ⓘ *T021-611256, summer daily 1000-1200, 1700-1900, 10Kn*, was founded in the 16th century by monks from Bosnia, when the Ottoman Turks granted them special permission to build a religious home just outside the town walls. The original monastery was burnt down in the late 17th century, so the building's present appearance, with a lovely central cloister, dates largely from 1671. The main reason for visiting the complex is to see the **Shell Museum**, a well-presented collection of over 3000 shells from all over the world. It was initiated in 1963 by Fra Jure Radic (1920-1990), a nature-loving monk who also founded the Botanical Garden at Kotišina (see Biokovo Nature Park, below).

Veprič is a delightful sanctuary set in a cave next to a glade amid pinewoods 100 m off the coastal road, 2 km northwest of Makarska. It was founded in 1908 because it resembled the shrine at Lourdes in France. A small chapel, called **Our Lady of Lourdes**, was built in the opening to the cave, and an open-air altar erected in the meadow before it. Masses are held daily at 1500 through winter and 1700 in summer. The main pilgrimage days are 11 February, 25 March, 15 August, and 7 and 8 September.

Park Prirode Biokovo (Biokovo Nature Park)

You can hike to the park if you want; less athletic visitors can reach Sveti Jure by private transport from Makarska (31 km), taking the road for Vrgorac then swinging sharp left for the park. The **park headquarters** ⓘ *T021-616924, www.biokovo.com*, in Makarska, offers very limited assistance and you're better off contacting the Makarska-based **Biokovo Activ Holidays** ⓘ *Kralja P Krešimira IV 7B, T021-679655, www.biokovo.net*, an agency running organized tours of the mountain, both on foot or by jeep. They can also give you up-to-date information about which mountain huts are open.

Once within the park, the karst landscape becomes increasingly barren, with scanty pastures and bare limestone rocks supporting only the hardiest indigenous species such as herds of chamois goats and mouflon sheep. A number of mountain huts provide basic overnight accommodation during the hiking season. From Makar, a well-marked trail leads to the peak of **Vošac** (1440 m), which can be walked in 3½ hours, while another trail departs from Kotišina to reach the same peak in five hours. From Vošac, the terrain becomes increasingly rocky, though hardened hikers can attempt a final 1½-hour pull to the highest peak, **Sveti Jure** (1760 m). The summit is capped by a slightly disheartening radio and TV transmitter, while its namesake, the tiny stone chapel of Sv Jure, is close by, but remains closed for most of the year. However, the views are breathtaking, and on a clear day it is possible to see across the sea to Montegargano in Italy to the southwest, and inland to the hills around Sarajevo in Bosnia to the northeast. See Eating, below for **Vrata Biokova** restaurant.

Behind Makarska, a network of narrow country lanes and signed footpaths lead through vineyards and olive groves to the semi-abandoned stone hamlets of **Makar** (1 km northeast), **Veliko Brdo** (3 km north) and **Kotišina** (3 km east), each of which lie on the border of Park Prirode Biokovo. These settlements were badly damaged by the 1962 earthquake. Residents subsequently moved down to Makarska, though some families still keep weekend homes and smallholdings here.

Just above Kotišina, you'll find the enchanting **Kotišina Botanical Gardens**, an informal rockery established in 1984, displaying indigenous plant species, each marked with its Latin name. Above the gardens stands **Kaštel**, a 16th-century hide-away built into the cliff face, where locals took refuge from the Turks. Over the main entrance, note several small stone channels, intended for pouring hot oil over would-be attackers.

Makarska Rivijera

» *pp237-240. Colour map 3, C6.*

Apart from Makarska itself, none of the resorts offer much of cultural interest, though their pebble beaches, clean sea and large modern hotels cater well enough for visitors who simply want to swim and sunbathe. The 60-km strip of coast (www.makarska-riviera.hr) runs from Brela in the north to Gradac in the south. Local buses running along the coast stop in all the towns mentioned.

Brela

At Brela, 5 km up the coast from Baška Voda, a 2-km stretch of pebble beaches interspersed by rocky outcrops and small harbours is backed by agave and scented pinewoods. Most Dalmatians consider Brela to be the loveliest of all the Makarska Rivijera resorts. The town was founded in the 19th century, when families from Gornja Brela, on the lower slopes of Biokovo, moved down to the coast. Organized tourism began in 1937, when the first hotels were built along the seaside promenade, and although they have since multiplied, Brela still prides itself with being less commercial than its neighbours. It's possible to walk or bike along the coastal path all the way to Makarska, passing through Baška Voda en route. Brela **tourist office** ⓘ *Trg Alojzija Stepinca bb, T021-618455, www.brela.hr*, will provide local information.

Baška Voda

Baška Voda, 9 km northwest of Makarska, is made up of a string of large modern hotels, restaurants and pizzerias on the seafront. From here, a pleasant coastal path leads north to Brela and south to Makarska both of which are within walking or biking distance. Families from **Bast**, a pretty hillside village of slate-roofed cottages 2 km to the east, founded Baška Voda in the late 17th century, after the Ottoman Turks had left the region. The harbour dates back to 1912, and during the 1930s tourism began with the opening of the **Hotel Slavija**. There's a local **tourist office** ⓘ *Obala Sv Nikole 31, T021-620713, www.baskavoda.hr.*

Tučepi

The scattered hamlets of Gornji Tučepi – Podpeć, Čovići, Srida Sela, Šimići and Podstup – nestle on the lower slopes of Biokovo, 5 km southeast of Makarska. Their history dates back centuries, though since the 18th century they have seen a gradual process of depopulation, as families began moving down to Tučepi-Kraj, a 4-km-long sprawling resort along the coast. Like Makarska, Tučepi offers decent pebble beaches plus a series of footpaths leading up to Biokovo Nature Park. Tučepi **tourist office** ⓘ *Kraj 46, T021-623100, www.tucepi.com*, can provide local information.

Zaostrog

Some 37 km southeast of Makarska, Zaostrog, like its neighbours, grew up from an older settlement (deserted after the 1962 earthquake) located on the slopes of Biokovo. The first building on the coast was the Franciscan Monastery dating from 1468, where monks kept the Catholic faith alive during Ottoman occupation. Inside, there's a small museum and a charming cloistered courtyard. Zaostrog itself is an unspoilt village with a good pebble beach backed by pinewoods and olive groves. There's only one hotel, but locals rent rooms to visitors.

Gradac

Located 42 km southeast of Makarska, Gradac marks the end of the Rivijera. The newer part of town is just off the main coastal road, perched on a triangular peninsula jutting out to sea. There's a popular pebble beach, **Gornja Vala**, south of town, while the original settlement of Gradac, built into the hillside above the coast, has a watchtower from 1661, built to defend the area against the Turks. There's also a local **tourist office** ⓘ *Stjepana Radić 1, T021-697511, www.gradac.hr.*

Sleeping

Omiš *p233*

B Hotel Plaža, Trg Kralja Tomislava 6, T021-755206, www.hotelplaza.hr. With sea views, a 10-min walk from the old town, this hotel reopened after renovation in 2007. The 36 rooms and 5 suites are well equipped with discreet modern furnishing in shades of brown. A small Wellness Centre offers Finish sauna, Turkish bath, hydro-massage whirlpool, massage and beauty treatments.

C Hotel Villa Dvor, Mosorska cesta 13, T021-863444, www.hotel-villadvor.hr. Built into a cliff overlooking the River Cetina, this eco-friendly hotel has 23 comfortable rooms and a terrace restaurant affording fine views onto the canyon. It's approached up a steep flight of stone steps, so may be difficult for those with impaired mobility. The hotel boat shuttles guests down the river to nearby beaches.

Private accommodation

Active Holidays, Knezova Kačića bb, T/F021-863015, www.activeholidays-croatia.com. This agency can help you find private accommodation.

Makarska *p234*

C Hotel Biokovo, Obala Kralja Tomislava bb, T021-615401, www.hotelbiokovo.hr. Comprising 55 rooms and 5 apartments, this pleasant old-fashioned hotel in the centre of town was fully refurbished in 2004, and has a ground floor café and restaurant giving onto the seaside promenade. Open all year. Pets welcome.

C Hotel Porin, Marineta 2, T021-613744, www.hotel-porin.hr. This listed 19th-century building on the seafront promenade has been renovated to form a 7-room hotel. There's a ground-floor café and restaurant.

D Mihaljević Pansion, Fra Filipa Grabovca 9, T021-615070, www.motelmihaljevic.com. In the old town, this small family-run hotel offers comfortable rooms with wooden floors and balconies, plus a pleasant ground floor restaurant and an upper level terrace with sea view.

D Sv Petar Lighthouse. To book, contact **Adriatica Net**, Heinzelova 62a, Zagreb, T01-241 5611, www.adriatica.net. Built in 1884, on the peninsula of Sv Petar, at the entrance to Makarska Bay, this lighthouse has been refurbished to create an apartment sleeping 6. It's close to the main beach, just 800 m from town, and is accessed by an asphalt road.

Private accommodation

Mariva Turist Agency, Obala kralja Tomislava 15a, T021-616010, www.marivaturist.hr. Can help find private accommodation in Makarska and villages along the Makarska Rivijera.

Makarska Rivijera *p236*

A Bluesun Hotel Berulia, Brela, T021-603 599, www.bluesunhotels.com. This modern, 4-star, 199-room hotel is set amid a pine-wood, a short distance back from the beach. Facilities include an outoor pool, sauna, and a range of bars and restaurants. Guests are welcome to use the Croatia Wellness Centre and Spa at the nearby **Bluesun Hotel Soline**. Open Apr-Oct.

A **Bluesun Hotel Kaštelet**, Dračevica 35, Tučepi-Kraj, T021-601202, www.bluesunhotels.com. The 18th-century summer home of Don Klement Grubišic, a notorious local priest, has been converted to provide a 4-star hotel with 24 guest rooms and 4 suites. It's connected to the neighbouring **Bluesun Hotel Alga**, and guests are welcome to use their sports facilities.

B **Hotel Slavija**, Obala Sv Nikole 71, T021-604999, www.hoteli-baskavoda.hr. Baška Voda's oldest hotel, dating back to the 1930s, is set in a terraced garden overlooking a narrow pebble beach. Ask for a room with a balcony and sea view. Open Mar-Oct.

C **Hotel Marco Polo**, Obala 15, Gradac, T021-695060, www.hotel-marcopolo.com. This rather non-descript modern building conceals a friendly family-run hotel with 30 rooms, a Wellness Centre, and a pleasant terrace restaurant giving onto a pebble beach.

F **Restoran Pansion Jeny**, Gornji Tučepi 49, T021-623704, www.makarska.com/jeny. Located on the lower slopes of Biokova, just 3 km from Makarska and 2 km from the nature park, this unassuming modern building is home to an excellent restaurant. Local ingredients are used to create beautifully presented dishes. A sophisticated version of Dalmatian cooking, influenced by Italian and French cuisine. They also offer overnight accommodation with a hearty cooked breakfast.

Private accommodation

Ratours, Donji Ratac 24, T021-623169, www.ratours.com. Specialize in private accommodation in Tučepi, and also organize excursions to Split, Korčula and Hvar.

Eating

Omiš *p233*

Radmanove Mlinice, T021-862073. On the banks of the River Cetina, 6 km upstream from Omiš, this old watermill was once the home of the Radman family. Today it's a pleasant garden restaurant serving local *pastrva* (trout) and *janjetina* (roast lamb) at tables under the trees. Open Apr-Oct.

Restoran Kaštil Slanica, Slanica bb, T021-861783. 4 km upstream from Omiš, this riverside restaurant specializes in *Žabji kraci* (frog's legs), *jegulje* (eels) and *janjetina* (roast lamb), while the bread comes freshly baked from a *peka*. They also rent canoes on an hourly basis. Open all year.

Konoba u Našeg Marina, Knezova Kačića bb, T021-861328. In the centre of Omiš, the rough wooden furniture in this tiny *konoba* creates a rustic atmosphere. They do local wine along with platters of *sir* (cheese), *pršut* (ham) and *slane srdele* (salted sardines), and can also prepare meals under a *peka* if you request a day in advance. Open all year, 0800-1200 and 1700-2400.

Makarska *p234*

Hrpina, Trg Hrpina 2, T021-611619. This long-standing, family-run restaurant has a terrace lined with potted geraniums overlooking a small piazza just off the main square. Traditional Dalmatian dishes served Apr-Oct. Through winter it works just as a bar.

Restoran Susvid, Kačićev Trg 9, T021-612732. Looking out onto the main square, with predictable tourist prices, this restaurant serves excellent barbecued fish and carefully prepared vegetable and salad side dishes. It stays open all year.

Stari Mlin, Prvosvibanjska 43, T021-611 503. Housed in an 18th-century baroque building, a few blocks back from the seafront, **Stari Mlin** specializes in fish and seafood, plus a small selection of Thai dishes. The cavernous interior is warm and cosy through winter, while a large vine-covered terrace comes into use through summer. Closed Sun.

Vrata Biokova, Park Prirode Biokovo, T021-613902, www.vratabiokova.com. Some 15 km from Makarska and 897 m above sea level, this farmhouse restaurant specializes in typical rural cooking. Firm favourites are the lamb, veal and chicken dishes prepared under a *peka*, though for these you should call 1 day in advance. Visitors are welcome to take a look at the farm animals – horses, donkeys, sheep and goats – making this an amusing outing for children. Open May to mid-Oct.

Cafés

Café Hotel Biokovo, Obala Kralja Tomislava bb. With a spacious terrace beside the seafront promenade, this café is popular with locals and non-residents as well as people staying in the hotel.

Makarska Rivijera *p236*

¥¥ **Konoba Naše Malo Misto**, Starin Porat, Gradac, T021-697374. On the seafront, this traditional Dalmatian *konoba* specializes in fish and seafood.

¥¥ **Restaurant King**, Iza Placa 3, Baška Voda, T021-620640. This friendly little restaurant is known locally for good fresh fish and seafood. Open for dinner only.

¥¥-¥ **Konoba Feral**, Obala kneza Domagoja, Brela, T021-618909. A renovated restaurant, guests sit at rustic tables and benches on a terrace next to the beach, while the owner-cook serves up local seafood dishes such as *brodet* (fish stew) and house wine by the carafe.

¥ **Konoba Postup**, Kraj 56, Tučepi, T021-623531. With a summer terrace overlooking the marina, this friendly eatery serves up delicious *salata od hobotnice* (octopus salad) and *ribe na žaru* (barbecued fish). They also do a cut-price daily fixed menu, and a special vegetarian plate. Open all year.

Bars and clubs

Makarska *p234*

Grotta, Šetalište Sv Petra. Summer nightclub on the peninsula of Sv Petar, set in a natural cave affording views of the sea.

Entertainment

Makarska *p234*

Cinema

Ljetno Kino, Kralja Tomislava 8, T021-612 280. Open-air summer cinema in a walled garden, just off the seafront.

Festivals and events

Omiš *p233*

Jul Dalmatian Klapa Festival. A 3-week competitive *klapa* festival founded in 1967 with the aim of preserving this traditional form of harmony singing (see Background, page 343) and promoting new songs. It now attracts about 80 groups comprising over a thousand singers. Performances are held on Trg Sv Mihovila, Trg Stjepana Radica and inside the parish church. For further information contact Festival Dalmatinskih Klapa Omis, Ivana Katušića 5, T021-861015, www.fdk.hr.

Makarska *p234*

Jul-Aug Makarska Summer Festival, mid-Jul to late Aug. Features open-air concerts of *klapa*, folk music and Croatian pop bands.

Jul Sveti Jure (St George's Day), last Sat in Jul. Pilgrims walk up to the small chapel of Sv Jure on Mt Biokovo, where a special mass is held.

Activities and tours

Omiš *p233*

Adventure sports

Active Holidays doo, Knezova Kačića bb, T/F021-863015, www.active holidays-croatia com. Organize rafting, free-climbing, paragliding, windsurfing and scuba-diving in Omiš and the surrounding area.

Atlas, Nepotova 4, Split, T021-343055, www.atlas-croatia.com. Run full-day guided rafting expeditions on the River Cetina. They also organize 1-week adventure sports packages including canoeing, mountain biking, rafting, kayaking, horse riding and fishing in the Cetina Valley, Mar-Oct.

Diving

Calypso Diving, Obala Gusara bb, T021-530456, www.calypsodiving.hr.

Makarska *p234*

Diving

More-Sub, Kralja P Krešimira 43, T021-611 727, www.more-sub-makarska.hr.

Tennis

Tennis Centre Makarska, Put Cvitacke bb, T021-617044. This modern tennis centre, with 6 outdoor clay courts and 2 indoor courts, is often used for big tournaments. It's situated close to the main beach, and visitors are welcome to play here. Expect to pay 60Kn per hr.

Walking

Well-marked paths lead to several peaks on Mt Biokovo (see page 234).

Makarska Rivijera *p236*

Sailing

Marina Tučepi, Dračevice 35, Tučepi, T021-601111. Has 50 berths, open all year.

Transport

Omiš *p233*

Bus

Buses run from **Split** to Omiš every 30 mins (40 mins). Coaches from Split, heading for **Makarska** and **Dubrovnik**, also stop in Omiš.

Ferry

In summer small private boats run 6 km up the River Cetina from Omiš bridge, dropping visitors at the 2 restaurants (60Kn per person).

Makarska *p234*

Bus

Makarska bus station is on the main road above town, T021-612333. About 20 buses per day run between **Split** and Makarska (1 hr 10 mins), many of them on long-distance hauls along the coast between **Rijeka** and **Dubrovnik**.

Ferry

Jadrolinija (no Makarska office, for information contact Split office, T021-338 333) run a ferry service from Makarska to **Sumartin** (30 mins) on the eastern tip of the island of Brač, with an average 5 ferries per day in summer and 3 ferries per day in winter.

Directory

Makarska *p234*

Medical services Dom zdravlja, T021-612033. **Pharmacies**: Ljekarna, Kačićev Trg 10, T021-611 890. **Post offices** Trg 4 Svibanj bb, Mon-Fri 0800-2000, Sat 0800-1300.

Islands of Brač and Šolta

→ *Phone code: 021. Colour map 3, C5/6. Population: 8388.*

As the closest island to Split and the only island in Dalmatia with an airport, Brač has the advantage of being easily accessible but the disadvantage of having lost a degree of its island identity due to its proximity to the mainland. The island's top destination is Bol, home to the lovely beach of Zlatni Rat, presided over by Vidova Gora, the highest peak on any of the Adriatic islands. Bol is crawling with tourists during July and August, but if you manage to visit outside peak season it's still well worth it for the fantastic beach. The small coastal town of Pučišća has long been known for its quarries, which have supplied quality stone for renowned buildings such as Diocletian's Palace in Split, Liverpool Cathedral in the UK and the White House in Washington, US.

Šolta, separated from the mainland by the Splitski Kanal (Split Channel), has never been a particularly popular destination. The few Croatians who visit the island generally have some family connection here, and the only tourist development to be found is a modern holiday village, used as a children's camp through summer. However, if you have your own boat, the south side of Šolta offers steep cliffs punctured by a number of pleasant coves, perfect for putting down anchor and bathing, while Maslinica, on the western tip of the island, even warrants an overnight stop. The chief town, Grohote, lies inland, while the other major settlements line the north and west coast. ▸▸ *For Sleeping, Eating and other listings, see pages 245-247.*

Ins and outs

There are regular ferries from Split to Supetar (12 daily in summer, seven in winter). Local buses then cover the routes across the island from Supetar to Bol and Supetar to Milna, but the times vary through the year, so it's worth checking with the tourist office in advance: **Supetar tourist office** ⓘ *Porat 1, T021-630551, www.supertar.hr*; **Bol tourist office** ⓘ *Porat bolskih pomoraca bb, T021-635638, www.bol.hr*; **Milna tourist office** ⓘ *Riva bb, T/F021-636233, www.milna.hr*, which is on the seafront. ▸▸ *See Transport, page 247, for further details.*

Brač » pp245-247. Colour map 3, C5.

Background → *Phone code: 021.*

The ancient Greeks never settled in Brač, probably due to the lack of fresh water sources. The first inhabitants were Illyrians, who built hilltop forts, followed by the Slavs in the seventh century, who adapted the Illyrian's inland sites to form small isolated villages, where they lived from farming.

During the Middle Ages, pirates from Omiš subjected Brač to frequent raids, a factor that only reinforced the logic of the inland settlements. However, when Venice took over in 1420, the pirate problem was resolved and the islanders gradually began to move down to the north coast, though no towns of great cultural significance were to emerge. During the 15th century, an epidemic decimated much of the population, and many of the old villages were burnt in an attempt to stamp out disease. However, over the next 100 years, numbers were boosted by a steady influx of refugees from the mainland interior, who fled to Brač in preference to coming under Ottoman rule. Up until 1815, the island's chief administrative centre was the inland town of Nerežišca. After that date it transferred to Supetar.

The island's population peaked in 1900 at 24,408. Winemaking and the production of olive oil were the main sources of livelihood, and the first wine co-operative in Dalmatia was founded in Bol around this time. However, in the early 20th century, *phylloxera* (a disease that destroyed countless vineyards along the Adriatic) swept across the island, causing many families to abandon the land and emigrate for the Americas, notably to Chile. Farming here has never really recovered, and still today, only one-sixth of the land is used for the potentially lucrative cultivation of vines and olive groves. The tide of fortune turned once again in the 1960s, as tourism brought prosperity to Brač.

Supetar → *Phone code: 021. Colour map 3, C5. Population: 3889. 14 km from Split.*

This is the island's largest town and chief ferry port. While the bulk of foreigners pass straight through, on their way to the more prestigious resort of Bol, many families from the mainland have summer homes in Supetar itself. It's a pleasant enough place, with the old town focusing on a crescent-shaped harbour, and a decent bathing area, backed by several large hotels, west of the centre. There is little of cultural interest here, though the town cemetery is noted for its beautifully carved tombstones.

Findings such as ancient sarcophagi and traces of mosaics on St Nicholas Peninsula, where the graveyard lies, suggest that the Romans were here. However, the present settlement was not founded until the 16th century, when people from Nerežišća, 8 km inland, began to use it as their harbour. They named the place Supetar, after an old chapel dedicated to St Peter (Sveti Petar in Croatian), no longer in existence. The town's main period of development took place during the 18th and 19th centuries.

The most interesting monument here is the **cemetery**, located on the wooded cape of St Nicholas. The noted sculptor, **Ivan Rendić** (1849-1932), was from Supetar, and wealthy local families of his time commissioned him to create personalized tombs, ranging from whimsical art nouveau gravestones to more substantial Byzantine mausoleums. Strangely, the most prominent monument, the large Mausoleum of the Petrinović Family, is not by Rendić, but by Tomo Rosandić (1875-1958) from Split. During the Tito years, Supetar became a popular seaside resort and a large modern hotel complex was built on the coast, west of the centre.

Milna → *Phone code: 021. Colour map 3, C5. Population: 1100. 18 km from Supetar.*

In a deep, sheltered bay, Milna is found on the southwest corner of Brač. It's a restful fishing village with a seafront promenade built around a deep curving harbour. A centuries-old retreat for ships, due to its sheltered waters, it's still popular with sailing boats today, and offers Brač's only year-round marina for yachts. If you're travelling from Split by private boat, Milna makes an ideal first port of call on the way out to the surrounding islands.

Many a Roman galley in distress must have taken shelter in this protected bay, and for centuries shepherds from the island's interior are said to have wintered their flocks here, finding respite from the icy *bura* wind and capturing the late afternoon sun. However, the village itself only came into being in the late 16th century, when it was settled by families from the inland town of Nerežišća. People lived from fishing, sailing and winemaking, and Milna quickly grew into a prosperous little place. The late baroque **Church of Our Lady of the Annunciation** was erected in 1783, when only 500 people lived here, though the church's grandeur gives the impression of a place of considerable status. In 1806, at the time of the Napoleonic wars, Milna served as the island's capital during a brief period of Russian occupation. By the late 19th century, there were 2500 inhabitants and two shipyards, and Milna was producing a greater tonnage of ships than the far larger city of Split. Sadly, over the last 100 years, many families have emigrated and Milna has seen a rapid process of depopulation. Today there's just one medium-sized hotel and a summer apartment complex here, plus a marina and an annual sailing school organized by the Split-based **Ultra Sailing**. A pleasant coastal path leads to the main public beach, about 2 km from the centre, on the north side of the bay.

Bol and around

→ *Phone code: 021. Colour map 3, C5. Population: 1478. 35 km south of Supetar.*

On the south coast of Brač, Bol is home to Croatia's most-photographed beach, the spectacular **Zlatni Rat**. This once-idyllic little fishing village has somewhat lost its charm due to the rampant success brought upon it by its beach, but if you can visit outside peak season, it's more than worth the trip. Zlatni Rat is also Croatia's number one site for windsurfing, and with the heady heights of **Vidova Gora** mountain surging up behind the coastal strip, it's also a great place for hiking or mountain biking. A little way down the coast, **Pustinja Blaca**, an impressive 16th-century monastery built into the cliff face, can be visited by boat.

Background Traces of *villae rusticae* and early Christian sarcophagi show that there was some sort of community here back in Roman times. In fact, Bol claims to be the oldest settlement on the island, though whatever used to stand here was destroyed during a Saracen raid in the ninth century.

About 600 years later, Dominican monks set up a monastery on the small promontory overlooking the sea, and during the 17th century, as the islanders began to move down from the interior and build settlements along the coast, the present-day village came into being.

Islands of Brač & Šolta

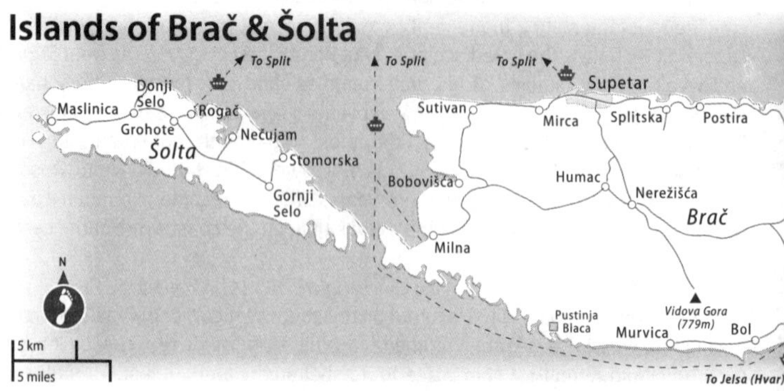

For centuries the people of Bol lived from farming, winemaking and fishing, then in 1963, tourism began. During the 1970s, a string of large hotels were built along the seaside promenade leading from the village to the beach, and Bol soon established itself as one of the country's top resorts. Today it remains a popular destination for package tours; countless agencies organize day trips to and from Bol, and along the waterfront you'll see more signs in German, English, Polish and Czech than Croatian.

Sights **Branislav Dešković Gallery** ⓘ *Porat bolskih pomoraca bb, close to the tourist office, T021-635270, Jun-Sep daily 1800-2300, Oct-May Mon-Fri 0900-1300, 10Kn*, was founded by Branislav Deškovic, a native of Brač and keen animal sculptor. It is inside a charming baroque building on the seafront. The collection concentrates on 20th-century Croatian artists who have been inspired by Dalmatia, and includes work by sculptors Ivan Rendić and Ivan Meštrović, and expressionist painter Edo Murtić.

On the eastern edge of the village, overlooking the sea, **Dominikanski Samostan** (Dominican Monastery) ⓘ *T021-778000, early May to late Sep daily 1000-1200, 1700-2000, 10Kn*, was founded in 1475. The monks keep a museum, exhibiting a vast collection of coins, notably from the ancient Greek settlements of Pharos (Stari Grad on Hvar) and Issa (Vis Town on Vis), plus amphorae, Creto-Venetian icons, and an outstanding *Madonna with Child* attributed to the Venetian Mannerist painter Tintoretto (1518-1594). The complex is set in charming gardens and it's possible to stay here overnight (see Sleeping, page 245).

Vidova Gora, the highest peak on all the Croatian islands, offers a bird's-eye picture of Zlatna Rat and Bol, plus distant views of Hvar, Vis, Pelješac Peninsula and Korčula. Through summer, a small *konoba* serves visitors *pršut* (ham), *sir* (cheese), *janjetina* (roast lamb) and local wine. It's possible to walk or bike up, though the less athletic might opt for a tour by minibus. Enquire at Bol tourist office for details.

Beaches A pleasant tree-lined promenade leads 2 km from the village of Bol to the renowned beach, **Zlatni Rat** (Golden Cape). The promenade, overlooked by the big package hotels (discreetly hidden by the trees), makes a pleasurable walk (there are no buses). An extraordinary geographical feature, it's composed of fine shingle and runs 500 m perpendicular to the coast, moving and changing its shape slightly from season to season, depending on local winds and currents. It's a perfect beach for children as the water is shallow and the seabed easy on their feet. A cluster of pines at the top end of the cape offer respite from the sun, and there's also a bar here selling cold drinks and snacks. As well as Zlatni Rat there's a stretch reserved for nudists, known as **Paklina**, just 200 m west of the cape. On the east side of Bol, there's a slightly more peaceful pebble beach next to the Dominican monastery.

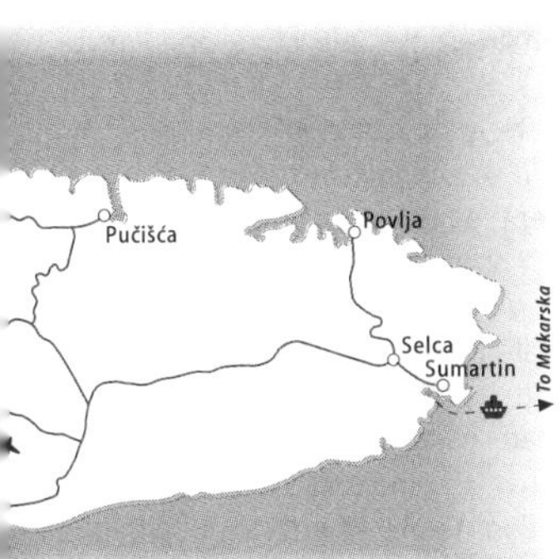

West of Bol

A pleasant 5-km walk west of Bol brings you to the coastal hamlet of **Murvica**. Just 200 m above this tiny settlement, the **Drakonjina Spilja** (Dragon's Cave) is a 20-m- long cavern, divided into four halls by a series of walls. The first hall is decorated with bizarre reliefs, carved into the stone, depicting dragons and other fabulous creatures. It's said to be the work of the monks from Blaca. The cave is kept locked, but if you ask at Bol tourist office they can arrange for someone to open it for you.

Pustinja Blaca (Blaca Hermitage) is a further 8 km west along the coast from Murvica. From here, a 2-km uphill hike brings you to this hermitage, an impressive monastery complex built into the cliffside. If you don't fancy the full hike, it's possible to reach Blaca Bay by boat from the harbour in Bol – just as the monks used to do. The hermitage was founded by monks from Poljica, on the mainland, who fled here to escape the Turks in 1550. Originally they took shelter in a cave, subsequently building the church (completed in 1588) and hermitage, and later opening a printing press and a school for children from nearby hamlets (now abandoned). The last monk to live here, Father Niko Miličević Mladi, was a keen astrologer. He set up an **observatory** in 1926 and, besides his astronomical tools, left behind a collection of old clocks. Visitors can see these, along with the old-fashioned kitchen, an armoury and a display of period furniture. Various Bol-based tour operators can arrange visits.

Šolta » *pp245-247. Colour map 3, C4/5.*

→ Phone code: 021. Population: 1500. 16 km southwest of Split.

It's a long-standing joke with little girls in Split; 'If you're naughty you'll end up marrying a man from Šolta'. There's nothing particularly horrid about the place, it's just rather desolate and slightly neglected. No great towns were ever founded here, and the *karst* landscape supports scanty pastures. Grapes, olives, figs and almonds grow well enough, but are produced in modest quantities, just enough for the local population.

In Roman times, ships would take shelter in Nečujam Bay on the north side of the island, where Emperor Diocletian had a fish farm, and when Roman Salona was sacked in the seventh century, some of the survivors took refuge on Šolta. Like most of the surrounding islands, Šolta came under Venice from 1420 to 1797, though even then it remained a sleepy backwater, with few eventful moments other than the arrival of a group of refugees from mainland Klis, following the village's capture by the Turks in 1537.

The islanders have a reputation for keeping themselves to themselves, and remain aloof from mainland politics. Traditionally Communism was well supported here, and several partisan monuments bearing the red star can still be seen, unlike on the mainland where most were demolished during the war of independence.

There are seasonal tourist offices in the villages of Rogač, Maslinica, Nečujam and Stomorska, see www.solta.hr.

Sights

The island's main port is **Rogač**, which grew up during the 18th century as the harbour to Grohote, which is 2 km inland. There's little of interest here, but local buses connect Rogač to the surrounding villages, with the timetable corresponding to incoming and outgoing boat services.

Practically in the centre of the island, **Grohote** is Šolta's chief town, and this is where you'll find services such as the post office, school, doctor's surgery and fire brigade. Most of Grohote has been rebuilt over the last three decades, though a quarter of abandoned stone houses to the south of town give a picture of how it once looked.

Some 9 km west of Rogač, perched on the western tip of the island, is **Maslinica**. It's indisputably Šolta's prettiest village – 18th-century fishermen's cottages surround three sides of a narrow bay, protected from the open sea to the west by the scattered islets of the Maslinica archipelago, creating a particularly memorable scene at sunset.

On the south side of the bay, the impressive **Dvor Conte Alberti** (Count Alberti's Castle) dates from 1708. During Tito's time it served as a hotel, but since Croatia gained independence it's one of many state properties to have been privatized. A German businessman has bought it for his own private use, with plans to open a restaurant on the ground floor.

Behind the villages, modern holiday houses are dispersed through the pinewoods to each side of the bay, and there's a decent pebble beach, **Tepli Bok**, as well as several secluded coves for bathing. Small yachts can moor up in the harbour along the seafront, and just south of Maslinica, **Uvala Šešula** is a sheltered bay offering safe overnight anchorage.

Nečujam, 7 km east of Rogač, is a deep bay backed by a modern holiday complex of 200 small whitewashed villas, set amid dense pinewoods. The focal point is a long pebble beach, and the complex encompasses tennis courts, boat rentals, a restaurant, disco and post office. It's open late May to late September, and managed by **Šoltatours** (see Sleeping, below). From mid-June to late August most of the place is taken over as a children's summer camp. Nečujam means literally 'I can't hear'. This goes back to the original Latin name, *Vallis Surda* (Deaf Cove), probably in reference to the numerous small coves that surround the bay, making communication from one point to another all but impossible.

Stomorska, 10 km east of Rogač, is a sleepy fishing village made up of 18th-century terracotta-roofed cottages, built around a small bay, with a nearby pebble beach.

Sleeping

Supetar *p241*

AL Hotel Bračka Perla, Put Vele Luke, T021-755530, www.bracka-perla.com. Looking out onto a small bay, close to the centre of Supetar, this luxurious boutique hotel is built of natural stone and centres on an outdoor pool. There are 3 rooms and 8 suites, all with wooden floors and colourful modern decor. Facilities include a small Wellness Centre and a children's playroom. Open Mar-Oct.

B Hotel Villa Adriatica, Put Vele Luka 3, T021-343806, www.villaadriatica.com. This family-run hotel is close to the main beach, and offers 24 rooms with bright, cheerful decor, plus a funky restaurant and a leafy garden with a cocktail bar and a small pool.

E Villa Britanida, T/F021-630017. This friendly 14-room hotel in a modern building is surrounded by palm trees a short distance east of the centre, close to the ferry port. There's an ample terrace with a restaurant serving typical Dalmatian seafood and meat dishes. Open all year.

Milna *p241*

Private accommodation

Several local families let out rooms and tastefully refurbished apartments; ask at Milna tourist office for details.

Bol and around *p242*

There are 3 large pricey package hotels, the **Borak**, **Elaphusa** and **Bretanide**, between the village and the beach.

B Hotel Kaštil, Frane Radića 1, T021-635995, www.kastil.hr. This old stone building overlooking the harbour offers 32 slick, minimalist-style guest rooms. It has its own restaurant, on a 1st-floor terrace above the sea, and a street level pizzeria and cocktail bar.

D Villa Giardino, Novi put 2, T021-635900. Set in lush gardens, a 5-min walk from the harbour, this cheerful family-run B&B has 5 rooms furnished with antiques. Breakfast is served in the garden and the owner, who is a sculptor, is keen to share his home-made *rajika* with guests. Open May-Oct.

F Dominican Monastery, Glavica, T021-778000. From Easter to early Oct it is possible to rent rooms and apartments in the monastery. Breakfast, lunch and dinner are also available. An extra 25% rate for a shower.

Private accommodation

Boltours, Vladimira Nazora 18, T021-635693, www.boltours.com. Can help find private accommodation as well as renting scooters, bikes and boats, and organizing scuba-diving, surfing and tennis courses.

Šolta *p244*

Private accommodation

Šoltatours, T021-338244, www.soltatours.net. Manage the holiday village of Nečujam, and can also help you find houses and apartments to rent across the island.
Split Tours, based in Split, T021-352553, www.splittours.hr. Can help find private accommodation on Šolta.

Eating

Supetar *p241*

ŸŸ **Vinotoka**, Jobova 6, T021-631341. Said by locals to be one of the best restaurants on the island, **Vinotoka** is a couple of blocks back from the bay. Fresh fish and shellfish top the menu, with most dishes prepared outside on a *roštilj* (barbecue).
ŸŸ-Ÿ **Dolac**, Ulica Petra Jakšića 8, T021-630446. Just off the bay, in the centre of town, **Dolac** offers a standard choice of meat and fish dishes. They also do a cut-price daily menu, including soup, a main course and side salad.

Milna *p241*

ŸŸ **Fontana**, Riva bb, T021-636285. The only restaurant in the village to stay open all year, **Fontana** serves up passable risotto, pasta and *frigane ligne* (fried squid) on a large summer terrace overlooking a small square, just off the seafront.

Bol and around *p242*

ŸŸ **Gušt**, Frane Radić 14, T021-635911. In an old stone building in the centre of Bol, this small restaurant offers a good range of fish and lobster dishes, as well as *janjetina* (roast lamb) and *pašticada* (beef stew). There are a few tables outside on the terrace, but you may have to queue for a seat.
ŸŸ **Konoba Tomić**, Gornji Humac bb, T021-647242. Up in the hills, 12km from Bol, on the road to Supertar, this agrotourism centre occupies an 800-year-old stone building. Everything on the menu is home-made, including the bread and the wine. House specialities include *pasta fažol* (pasta with beans) and meals prepared under a *peka*, notably lamb or octopus. Open May-Oct.
ŸŸ-Ÿ **Ribarska Kućica**, Ante Starčevića bb, T021-635033. The coastal path east of the centre leads to this informal but romantic eatery, with tables next to the sea. Fish and seafood are on offer, while pizza makes a cheaper option. Open Jun-Sep (1100-0200).

Šolta *p244*

ŸŸ-Ÿ **Konoba Saskinja**, Riva bb, Maslinica. Restaurant with a pleasant terrace overlooking the harbour. This old stone building accommodates a *konoba* serving coffee and drinks throughout the morning, and offering a standard choice of barbecued meat and fish, as well as pasta and risotto dishes, for lunch and dinner.

Entertainment

Bol and around *p242*

Varadero, Frane Radić 1. On the ground floor of **Hotel Kaštil**, close to the harbour, this bar is a popular outdoor drinking spot through summer with comfy wicker sofas and cocktails.

Activities and tours

Supetar *p241*

Diving

Kaktus, Put Plive 4, T021-630421. Based in the **Kaktus Hotel** sports complex, organizes scuba-diving courses and diving trips.

Tennis

Hotel Kaktus sports complex has 8 tennis courts and is open to non-residents.

Milna *p241*

Sailing

ACI Marina, Milna, T021-636306, www.aci-club.hr. 170 berths, open all year.

Bol and around *p242*

Hiking

Behind Bol, Vidova Gora stands 778 m high. It's possible to reach the peak following a marked footpath from the village. Be sure to wear decent walking boots and take plenty of water. Ascent 2½ hrs, descent 2 hrs.

Mountain biking

Big Blue, Podan Glavice 2, T021-635614, www.big-blue-sport.hr. Rent mountain bikes and organize biking expeditions to Vidova Gora and Blaca Hermitage, with an optional shuttle service to shorten the ride.

Tennis

Zlatni Rat (Tennis Centre), T021-635222. Close to the beach, this vast complex comprises 20 clay courts, 8 of which are floodlit. Coaching is available, and racquets and balls can be hired. The annual 1-week WTA Ladies' Open is held here, late Apr to early May.

Watersports

Big Blue, Podan Glavice 2, T/021-635614, www.big-blue-sport.hr. Organize windsurfing and diving courses. Also rents equipment.

Transport

Supetar *p241*

Air

The small airport of Brač, T021-559715, www.airport-brac.hr, is 30 km from Supetar and works summer only. Through high season there are once-weekly flights from **Amsterdam**, **Berlin**, **Frankfurt**, **London** (Heathrow), **Munich**, **Paris**, **Prague**, **Warsaw**, **Vienna**, **Zagreb** and **Zurich**.

An airport bus transports passengers to and from various destinations on the island.

Ferry

Jadrolinija, T021-631357, run a regular service from **Split**, with an average 12 ferries per day in summer and 7 ferries per day in winter (1½ hrs). Schedules vary from day to day, so you need to check times with their ticket office.

Milna *p241*

Bus

Buses from Milna to Supetar are scheduled to coincide with the ferries (30 mins). In summer, **Split Tours** run a catamaran service, departing from **Split** Mon, Wed and Fri 0900 and Sun 1815, and returning from Milna Mon, Wed and Fri 1000 and Sun 1915.

Ferry

Jadrolinija, T021-631357, run regular ferries between **Supetar** and **Split**.

Bol and around *p242*

Air

See Supetar, above, for details.

Bus

Buses from Bol to Supetar are scheduled to coincide with the ferries (50 mins).

Ferry

Jadrolinija (no Bol office, for information contact Split office, T021-338333) run a daily catamaran service from **Jelsa** on the island of Hvar to **Split**, calling at Bol en route. The boat departs from Bol at 0630 to arrive in Split at 0730, then leaves Split at 1600 to arrive in Bol at 1700. In addition, regular ferries run between the island's main port, **Supetar**, and **Split**.

Šolta *p244*

Bus

Buses connect the surrounding villages to Rogač, to correspond with incoming and outgoing boat lines.

Ferry

Jadrolinija (no Šolta office, for information contact the Split office, T021-338333) run a regular ferry service from Rogač to **Split**, with an average 5 ferries per day in summer and 3 per day in winter (1 hr). **SEM** run a daily catamaran service, designed for islanders working on the mainland, departing from Rogač at 0700 and leaving Split for the return journey at 2030 (30 mins).

Directory

Supetar *p241*

Banks There are several banks and ATMs in the town. **Medical services** Pharmacies: M Vodanoviaća 24, T021-640000. **Post offices** Vlaćica 13, Mon-Fri 0700-2000, Sat 0700-1300.

Bol and around *p242*

Banks There are several banks and ATMs in the town. **Medical services** Pharmacies: Porat Bolski Pomoraca bb, T021-635987. **Post offices** Uz Pjacu 5, Mon-Fri 0800-1400, Sat 0800-1300.

Island of Hvar

→ *Phone code: 021. Colour map 3, C5/6. Population: 8286. 68 km from east to west.*

A long, thin island, Hvar is a land of vineyards, lavender fields and old Venetian coastal villages with an altogether slower, more pleasurable way of life. The most popular and by far and away the most charming resort is Hvar Town. Close by, all grouped together on the western end of the island, are Stari Grad, Jelsa and Vrboska. The eastern end of Hvar is sparsely populated and offers little of cultural interest. If you really want to get away from it all, head for the emerald green waters and sun-scorched slopes of the south coast. ▸▸ *For Sleeping, Eating and other listings, see pages 257-262.*

Ins and outs

There are regular ferries from Split from the island's main port, Stari Grad. To get around the island, there are several buses daily between Hvar Town, Stari Grad and Jelsa. If you are staying for a while, however, it would be worth hiring a car. The area between Stari Grad and Jelsa is reasonably flat, making biking an option (mountain bikes are available for rent in Jelsa). The landscape behind Hvar Town is pretty steep though so not well suited to biking.

There's a **tourist office** ⓘ *Trg Sv Stjepana 16, T021-741059, www.hvar.hr*, in Hvar Town. ▸▸ *See Transport, pages 261, for further details.*

Background

Hvar was first settled by ancient Greeks from the Aegean island of Paros, who founded Pharos (present-day Stari Grad) in the fourth century BC. When the capital moved from Pharos in the 13th century, the new centre was named *Civitas Nova* (New Town) while Pharos became *Civitas Vetus* (Old Town), or in Croatian, Stari Grad. The name Pharos mutated to Hvar, which later came to be used for both *Civitas Nova* (present-day Hvar Town) and for the entire island.

From 1420 to 1797 Hvar came under Venice. The 15th and 16th centuries saw a degree of prosperity owed principally to shipping, which could have been greater still had the Venetians not limited the tonnage allowed to the island. During this period Hvar gave Croatian literature two prominent writers, Hanibal Lučić (1485-1553) from Hvar Town, and Petar Hektorović (1487-1572) from Stari Grad. The sons of noble families were educated in Italy, though Hvar remained an island in the true sense of the word. Regular boat connections with the mainland and surfaced roads between the island's towns and villages did not come into being until the second half of the 19th century.

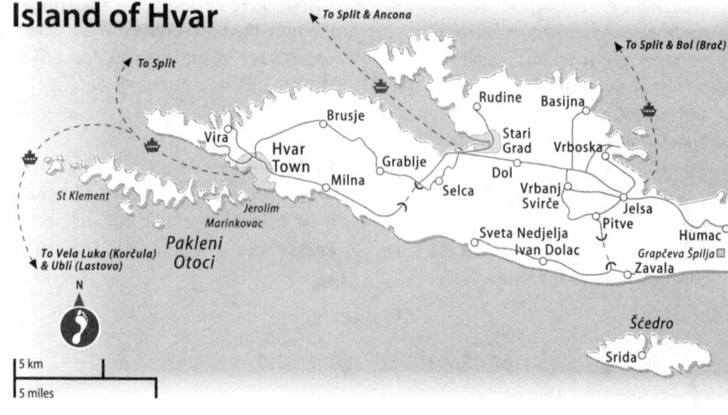

The first tourists on Hvar were Austrians, who were sent to convalesce in Hvar Town as early as 1870. One hundred years later, as part of Yugoslavia, a number of large hotel complexes were constructed just outside the old town centre along the coast, and the island became known as the Croatian Madiera.

Hvar Town

» pp257-262. Colour map 3, C5.

→ *Phone code: 021. Population: 4138. 39 km south of Split.*

Located on the southwest coast of Hvar, Hvar Town is probably Croatia's most fashionable resort after Dubrovnik. Old stone houses are built into the slopes of three hills surrounding a bay, with the highest peak crowned by a Venetian fortress, which is floodlit by night. Café life centres on the magnificent main square, giving directly onto the harbour and backed by a 16th-century cathedral. The bay is protected from the open sea to the south by the scattered **Pakleni Otoci** (Pakleni Islets), covered with dense pine forests and rimmed by rocky shores offering secluded coves for bathing. Hvar Town is a favourite retreat of the Croatian president, Stipe Mesić, and from July to late August (when it's almost unbearably crowded) various illustrious characters moor their yachts here – Goran Ivanišević, Luciano Benetton and Bernie Eccleston, to name but a few.

Background

Although people had probably lived on this site for centuries, the settlement only became a true town in 1278, when the Venetians (during a brief period of occupation) encouraged people from Pharos (present-day Stari Grad) to relocate around this southwest facing bay, which they considered a more suitable centre, as it could be better defended in the event of an attack. In the same year, the area known as Grad, north of the main square, was surrounded by protective walls, and the first public buildings were erected. Later, south of the square, the more humble quarter of Burg developed.

In 1420, the town came under Venice for a second time, and rapidly became one of the wealthiest centres in Dalmatia. The Venetians used it as port of call for trade ships travelling to and from the Orient, and also set up the headquarters of their Adriatic fleet here. Cultural life flourished, and many fine buildings were erected. However, in 1571, during the run up to the Battle of Lepanto, much of the town was devastated in a Turkish onslaught led by Uluz Ali; thus the buildings here today date almost exclusively from the late 16th century onwards.

In 1610, in an act unique for its time, an agreement was signed declaring nobles and commoners politically equal and giving people of all social classes the same right to participate in administration. From then on, for a short period, years were

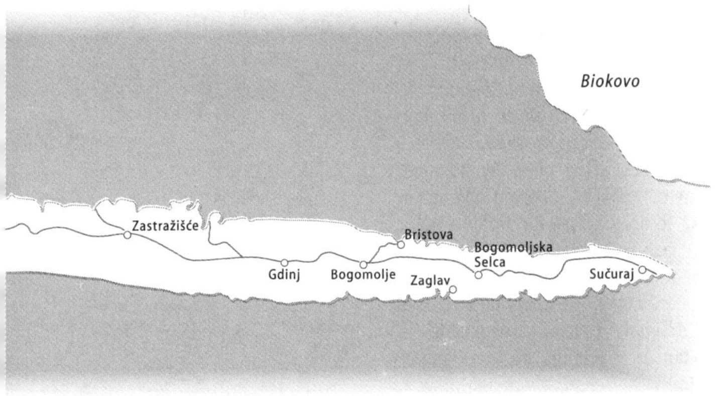

counted from that date onwards: the inscription on the entrance to the theatre bears witness to this.

Hvar Town was first promoted as a seaside and health resort when the Hygiene Society of Hvar was founded in 1868. Its main selling point was a mild climate – it receives more hours of sunshine per year than any other place on the Adriatic – and fresh sea air. Since 2006, Sunčani Hvar has refurbished and upgraded several of Hvar Town's hotels to bring them into the luxury market. They will stay open the year through, in the hope of making the resort a year round destination.

Trg Sv Stjepan (St Stephen's Square)

St Stephen's Square, the largest piazza in Dalmatia, dates back to the 13th century. The east end is backed by the cathedral, while the west end opens out onto the **Mandrac**, an enclosed harbour for small boats, which in turn gives onto the bay. The paving dates from 1780 and in the centre stands a well from 1520. Today many of the old buildings lining the square house popular cafés, restaurants and galleries at street level.

The bishopric was originally founded in Stari Grad in 1147, but relocated to Hvar Town when it took over as the political and cultural centre in the 13th century. **Katedrala Sv Stjepan** (St Stephen's Cathedral) ⓘ *Trg Sv Stjepana bb, daily 0700-1200 and 1700-1900, in summer it sometimes stays open all day*, providing a majestic backdrop to the main square, is a three- aisled basilica built in stages between the 16th and 17th centuries on the foundations of an earlier monastery, to produce a trefoil façade standing in perfect harmony with a four-storey bell tower.

The **Venetian Loža** (loggia) and **clock tower** ⓘ *Trg Sv Stjepana bb*, was reconstructed in high-Renaissance style after the former loggia was damaged during the Turkish onslaught of 1571. It was used as a café from 1868 to 1971, and then incorporated into the **Hotel Palace** to form an elegant salon. The clock tower was part of the Governor's Palace – from which the **Hotel Palace** takes its name, though the original building was destroyed in 1571 – and the clock was added in the 19th century.

On the south corner of the main square, looking onto the harbour, the **Arsenal i Kazalište** (Arsenal and Municipal Theatre) ⓘ *Trg Sv Stjepana bb, T021-741009, currently under restoration and unlikely to reopen before summer 2009*, is easily identified by its huge front arch, which allowed Venetian galleys to dock inside for repair work. It dates back to the 13th century, but was reconstructed after damage caused by the Turks in 1571. The upper floor houses the Arsenal Gallery, displaying a collection of paintings by local artists, plus the *Zvir* (Beast), a wooden prow in

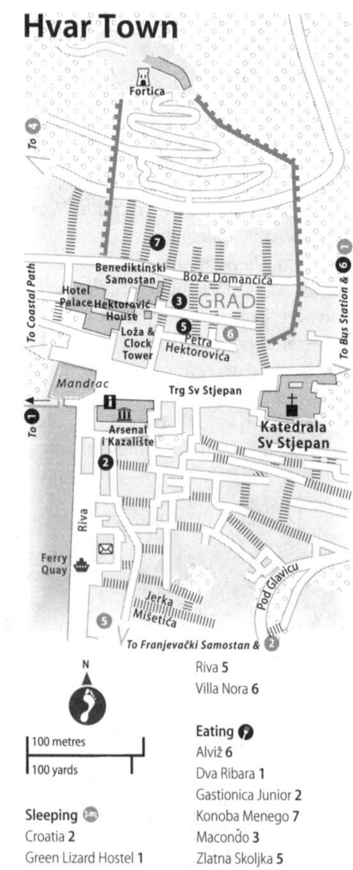

the form of a dragon, formerly mounted on the front of the town galleon, one of seven ships to represent Dalmatia at the Battle of Lepanto. Passing through the gallery you arrive at the Kazalište, which opened in 1612 and welcomed all citizens regardless of their social standing, making it one of the first institutions of its kind in Europe. An inscription on the entrance door reads *Anno secundo pacis* (The Second Year of Peace) which was 1612 in the new system of counting years, temporarily established after the agreement of 1610. The interior was refurbished in 1803, and is still used for performances today.

South of the centre

South of the centre, a pleasant seafront path leads past a series of small baroque chapels (built in 1720 by the commander of the Adriatic fleet, Marin Capello) and arrives at the **Franjevački Samostan** (Franciscan Monastery) ⓘ *T021-741 193, summer daily 1000-1200, 1700-1900, winter daily 1000-1200, 20Kn.* The main core of the complex was built between 1461 and 1471, and walled in 1545. It was damaged by the Turks in 1571, but reconstructed in 1574. The entrance is through a charming 15th-century cloister – used for classical music concerts during the summer festival – into the former refectory, now a museum. The most impressive piece on show is undoubtedly the *Last Supper*, a vast 17th-century canvas by an unknown Venetian artist, measuring 2.5 m by 8 m. The refectory opens onto a beautiful garden, with a magnificent 300-year-old cypress tree, overlooking the sea. The monastery church, **Gospa od Milosti** (Our Lady of Mercy), also dates from the 15th century and bears a relief above the main portal, *Madonna and Child*, attributed to Nicola Firentinac. Inside, set into the floor in front of the main altar, is the tombstone of the local poet Hanibal Lučić.

North of the centre

On the north side of the main square, set back from the other buildings, stands the rather eerie 15th-century **Hektorović House**. It was left unfinished after the writer's death, but the Venetian-Gothic windows are among the most beautiful examples of Venetian architecture on the island. The street leading off the square, past the house, forms several flights of stone steps, conducting one through the area known as Grad to the hilltop castle. A couple of blocks up, on the left, is the **Benediktinski Samostan** (Benedictine Convent) ⓘ *3 Ulica Nikole Karkovica, T021-741052, summer daily 0900-1100, 1600-1900, 15Kn.* Inside there's a baroque chapel and a display of lace, made by the nuns.

Above Grad, a winding footpath leads through a garden of dense Mediterranean planting, to arrive at the **Fortica** (Fortress) ⓘ *T021-741816, summer daily 0800-2400, winter by appointment, 20Kn.* A medieval castle once stood here, though the present structure was erected by the Venetians in 1557, and the ochre-coloured barracks were added by the Austrian military authorities during the 19th century. From the ramparts, you have fantastic views down onto the town and harbour, and out across the sea to the Pakleni Islets. There's a small **Amphora Collection**, consisting mainly of pieces salvaged in the 1970s from a Roman shipwreck close to the island of Palagruža, and a suitably dark and dingy **Zatvor** (Prison), accessed down a flight of steep stone steps. Up top, you'll also find a restaurant and snack bar.

Pakleni Otoci

There is a **beach** right in the town itself, although those on the islands nearby are more pleasant. The coastal path west of town leads to a south-facing bay with a good pebble beach, now unfortunately dominated by the vast modern **Hotel Amfora** complex. During the late 19th century the Austro-Hungarians set up a bathing establishment here, complete with prim changing huts and showers, but the 'Victorian' charm of the place has been somewhat spoilt by the 1970s monster behind.

You're better off taking a taxi boat (they depart regularly from the harbour through summer costing 40-60Kn) to the nearby **Pakleni Otoci**, a group of small uninhabited islands covered with pinewoods and rimmed by rocks interspersed with secluded pebble beaches. The name 'Pakleni' comes from *paklina*, meaning pine resin. The nearest island, **Jerolim**, is predominantly nudist, and has a good informal eatery with a shady terrace, serving salads and barbecued dishes daily till 1830, to coincide with the last boat back to town. The next island, **Marinkovac**, has two pleasant bays: Uvala Stipanska, overlooked by a couple of restaurants, and Ždrilica. The next and largest island, **St Klement**, is known for its particularly lush vegetation. There's an ACI marina on the north side, while a wide bay with a popular beach called Palmižana (from *spalmare*, 'to spread' in Italian – this is where wooden boats used to be pulled up out of the water and coated with pine resin) lies on the south side. Taxi boats also run from the harbour to the village of **Milna**, on the coast 6 km east of Hvar Town, where there's a decent pebble beach.

Stari Grad

» *pp257-262. Colour map 3, C5.*

→ *Phone code: 021. Population: 2187.*

This is the island's oldest settlement and chief ferry port. It's a more relaxed, slightly less swish resort than Hvar Town, with an easy-going village atmosphere. There aren't many great beaches though and little of cultural interest other than the 16th-century Hektorović House. Most of the buildings in the old part of town date from the 16th and 17th centuries – the best examples can be seen on Škor, a picturesque square enclosed by baroque houses. There is also a **tourist office** ⓘ *Nova Riva 2, T021-765763, www.stari-grad.hr.*

Background

In 385 BC, Greeks from the Aegean island of Paros founded Pharos. Their arrival was recorded later, possibly in slightly exaggerated form, by the Sicilian-born Greek historian Diodorus Siculus (90-21 BC): "This year the Parians, who had settled Pharos, allowed the previous barbarian inhabitants to remain unharmed in an exceedingly well fortified place, while they themselves founded a city by the sea and built a wall around it. Later, however, the old barbarian inhabitants of the island took offence at the presence of the Greeks and called in the Illyrians of the opposite mainland. These to a number of more than 10,000, crossed over to Pharos in many small boats, wrought havoc, and slew many Greeks. But the Governor of Lissus (Issa, present-day Vis) appointed by Dionysius sailed with a good number of *triremes* (three-banked galleys) against the light craft of the Illyrians sinking some and capturing others, and slew more than 5000 of the barbarians, while taking some 2000 captive." Little of the original Greek settlement remains today, other than the 11-m-long **Cyclop's Wall**, made up of massive stone blocks, that can be traced through some of the buildings on the south side of the bay.

During medieval times, the town continued to hold its position as the island's main centre, and a bishopric was founded here in 1147. However, when the Venetians encouraged citizens to relocate to Hvar Town in 1278, Stari Grad sunk into a period of stagnation, from which it has never really recovered.

In the early 19th century the port was expanded to facilitate the export of wine from the island, and during the 1970s, several large hotels were built on the north side of the bay, bringing Stari Grad into the package tourism market. In May 2003, a local crew from Stari Grad set sail on a 700-mile journey to the Greek island of Paros, in the hope of establishing future cultural connections with their mother town. Details about the expedition can be found at www.stari-grad-faros.hr/expedition.

Sights

Stari Grad's best-loved building is the **Tvrdjalj** (Hektorović House) ⓘ *Trg Tvrdjalj, T021-765068, Jul-Aug daily 1000-1300, 1700-2000, May-Jun and Sep-Oct daily 1000-1300, Nov- Apr by request, 10Kn*, on the south side of the bay, in the old part of town, set back about 100 m from the seafront. It originally came right up to the coast, until the front square was added in the 19th century. It's an unusual fortified residence, built by the local poet, Petar Hektorović (1487-1572) in 1520, as a home for him and his friends, and also as a place of refuge for the entire town, in the event of a Turkish invasion. Hektorović was an aristocratic landowner, who had been educated in Italy and went on to become one of Dalmatia's most prominent Renaissance poets. Much of his work celebrated the lifestyle of local fishermen and peasants – his best-known work is *Ribanje i ribarsko prigovaranje* (Fishing and Fishermen's Conversations) in which he describes a fishing trip around the neighbouring islands. Tvrdalj's centrepiece is a long rectangular fishpond, surrounded by a fine cloister, around which the living quarters, domestic area and servant quarters are arranged. On the south side of the complex, there's a walled garden where Hektorović cultivated both indigenous Mediterranean and exotic plants. The walls of the interior of Hektorović House bear many plaques, with witty and philosophical inscriptions in both Croatian and Latin.

Also on the south side of the bay, a short distance east of Tvrdalj, several blocks in from the seafront, stands the **Dominikanski Samostan** (Dominican Monastery) ⓘ *summer daily 1000-1300, 1700-2000, winter by request*. Founded in 1482, it was fortified after the Turkish attack of 1571. Inside there's a museum, with a number of ancient Greek tombstones from Pharos, plus a collection of paintings, the most notable being *Oplakivanje Krista* (The Mourning of Christ) by the 16th-century Venetian Mannerist, Jacopo Tintoretto (1512-1594). The old man in the top right corner of the painting is said to be Hektorović. The monastery church was built in 1893 on the site of a much older sanctuary and, next to the altar, set into the floor, is Hektorović's tomb.

A pleasant coastal path along the north side of the bay leads to the main **beach**, just before **Hotel Helios**. Beyond the hotel a rocky stretch of coast backed by pines also offers reasonable access to the water.

Vrboska and around

» *pp257-262. Colour map 3, C5.*

→ *Phone code: 021. Population: 526. 4 km west of Jelsa.*

This pretty fishing village is built around a long S-shaped inlet and merits a visit for its unusual fortified church and carefully laid out fishing museum. It's not a place you'd particularly choose to stay long, unless you're travelling by yacht – there's an excellent marina – or setting up a tent in the naturist camp. There's a **tourist office** ⓘ *Riva bb, T021-774137, www.vrboska.info, May-late Sep*, and out of season you can contact the tourist office in Jelsa.

Background

Vrboska's protected waters have served as a refuge for ships since Greco-Roman times. However, the town itself was not founded until the 15th century, when it became the harbour for the inland village of Vrbanj. Typical Dalmatian stone houses line each side of the narrow channel, connected by three small bridges, and to the north are several fine Renaissance and baroque *palazzi*, constructed by the local nobility. Vrboska suffered the fate of neighbouring coastal towns in 1571, when it was invaded by the

During the 1970s, a publicity stunt was launched offering visitors free hotel accommodation if it snowed (which has been known to happen); the same promise holds true today.

 Turks, in the run up to the Battle of Lepanto (see box, page 255). Through the centuries that followed, fishing became an increasingly lucrative activity, until it was usurped by tourism in the 1970s.

Sights

Located on the south side of the channel, on the hillside above the seafront, **Crkva Sv Marije** (Church of St Mary) ⓘ *Jul-Aug daily 1000-1200, 1800-2000*, is unique. Its original structure dates from the 15th century, but it was fortified in 1575, after the Turkish attack of 1571, so as to create a refuge for the townspeople, should the same thing happen again. In the apse, a tombstone laid into the floor and dated 1737 bears a chilling inscription: *Ne differas amice – hodie mihi cras tibi* (You won't be different, my friend – Me today, you tomorrow).

The 15th-century **Crkva Sv Lovrinac** (Church of St Lawrence) ⓘ *Jul-Aug daily 1000-1200, 1800-2000*, which was enlarged and took on its baroque appearance during the 17th century, is home to several invaluable works of art by Venetian masters, notably a series of three paintings above the main altar, depicting St Lawrence, St John the Baptist and St Nicholas. Experts now attribute these works to Paolo Veronese (1528-1588) though locally they were long believed to have been created by Tiziano Vecellio, better known as Titian (1485-1576).

The small but informative **Ribarski Muzej** (Fishing Museum) ⓘ *Jul-Aug daily 0930-1200, 1800-2000*, speaks of the town's long tradition of fishing. Under Venice, Vrboska began producing salted sardines for the crews of the Empire's galleons, on long-distance hauls to the Orient. Local men would go out on the open sea to fish, while the women worked from home, cleaning sardines and preserving them between layers of rock salt. The museum displays the equipment they used, amid a setting of suggestive reconstructions of how people's homes would have looked at the time.

The best beaches are on **Glavica Peninsula**, some 2 km northeast of town. Through high season, taxi boats leave from the harbour, taking visitors to and from the island of Zečevo, which is given over to nudist bathing.

Jelsa and around » *pp257-262.*

Colour map 3, C5.

→ *Phone code: 021. Population: 1798. 10 km east of Stari Grad.*

Jelsa is a lively fishing town and seaside resort, built around a natural harbour. Everyday life focuses on the 19th-century seafront promenade, lined with cheerful cafés and pizzerias, while to each side of the bay, dense pinewoods have been used to conceal a number of large hotel complexes, built during the 1970s. The town **tourist office** ⓘ *Mala Banda bb, T021-761918, www.tzjelsa.hr*, is on the seafront.

Sights

Looking onto the Hvarski Kanal (Hvar Channel) and facing Bol on the island of Brač, with distant views of Makarska and Mount Biokovo on the mainland to the northeast, Jelsa was founded in the 14th century as the port for Pitve, now a semi-abandoned village 2 km inland. There's not much of cultural interest here, but it makes a cheap option to staying in Hvar Town, and offers several decent beaches and a series of bike paths. It's also the only place on the island to have a nightclub working 12 months a year.

During the 16th century, **Trg Sv Ivana**, a square lined with Renaissance and baroque houses, many of which now accommodate cafés and shops at street level, was constructed close to the seafront. Just off the square stands the pretty miniature baroque **Crkva Sv Ivana** (Church of St John) and, inland from here, an old quarter with stone houses and winding cobbled streets is built into the hillside. The quay and

Battle of Lepanto

During the late 16th century, as the possibility of Ottoman expansion westwards became ever more real, the Holy League, an alliance of Spain, Venice, Genoa and the Papal States, massed a huge fleet on the Adriatic in the hope of halting Turkish progress. The eventual confrontation took place on 7 October 1571, in the Gulf of Lepanto, near Corfu. The league's forces, made up of 200 galleys (including seven from Dalmatia: one apiece from the towns of Zadar, Šibenik, Split, Trogir, Krk, Rab and Hvar), were well outnumbered by the Ottoman Turkish fleet, which counted over 270 ships. The battle was one of the bloodiest in naval history, with both sides losing countless vessels and thousands of men. The Holy League won, achieving their first victory over the Ottoman Empire. However, although the Ottoman navy was seriously depleted, they managed to keep their hold over much of the Balkan peninsula for the following three centuries.

In the lead up to the battle, Uluz Ali, the Ottoman Bey of Algiers, gathered a fleet of 80 galleys and staged a diversionary attack on the island of Hvar on 17 August 1571. The first settlement to be attacked was Hvar Town, after which the Turks sailed round the island and carried out similar offences on Stari Grad, Vrboska and Jelsa. Having wreaked havoc, they set sail south and joined the rest of the Ottoman fleet near Corfu.

the buildings lining the bay date from the 19th century, when the local shipping industry flourished. During the 1970s, Jelsa turned to tourism, as several large hotels were constructed along the coast to the edge of town.

West of the centre, a lovely 4-km road follows the coast, winding its way through pinewoods, to **Vrboska**, making a perfect afternoon walk or bike ride. The most central place for a swim is just west of town, where rocks and concrete bathing areas give easy access to the water. However, the best beaches are found beyond Vrboska, on **Glavica Peninsula**, and on the small island of **Zečevo**, where there's a nudist beach. Through summer, you can reach both Glavica and Zečevo by taxi boat from Jelsa harbour.

Pitve

Recorded by the ancient Greeks in the third century BC as the Illyrian settlement of *Pityeia*, Pitve, a picturesque, semi-abandoned village of old stone houses, is built into the hillside 2 km southwest of Jelsa, just before the tunnel leading to the south side of the island. Few people live here the year round, though several buildings have been tastefully renovated to make holiday houses.

Even if you don't have private transport, it's worth walking along the country road from Jelsa to eat (dinner only) at **Konoba Kod Komina**, a delightful *konoba*, with its splendid terrace surrounded by grapevines and lemon trees. Fish and meat dishes are prepared over an open fire (*komin* means fireplace) and served with home-grown vegetables, salads and excellent house wine.

East of Jelsa

A poorly maintained local road leads all the way to Sućuraj, on the eastern tip of the island. If you follow this road for 8 km, you'll see a sign to the right for **Humac**. Walk the final 400 m along a rough track, to arrive at a romantic cluster of abandoned stone houses, founded as a temporary dwelling for shepherds in the 15th and 16th centuries. No one lives here anymore, but during summer it's possible to eat at the unforgettable **Konoba Humac** (see Eating, page 258).

A 30-minute walk from Humac, **Grapčeva Špilja** ⓘ *Jun-Sep*, is a vast chamber of underground stalactites and stalagmites, with traces of human civilization from the third millennium BC. Through summer you can visit the cave with a guide. Contact Jelsa tourist office for details.

Southern Hvar

» pp257-262. Colour map 3, C4.

→ *Phone code: 021.*

Viewed from the water, much of the south coast of Hvar is made up of vertical cliffs plummeting down to the sea. However, the 8-km stretch between **Zavala** and **Sveta Nedjelja** offers a series of pebble beaches backed by steep hillsides planted with quality vineyards. Thanks to its inaccessibility – it can only be reached by boat, or through a long, narrow road tunnel running below the overlying peaks – this particular part of the island remains a world unto its own. There are no hotels and little in the way of tourist facilities, but there are a couple of good places to eat and sleep, and if you're lucky, you'll chance upon a number of idyllic coves, with stunning views out to the open sea and not a soul in sight. There is no tourist village on the south side of Hvar. The tourist office in Hvar Town can help provide information.

Background

Separated from the north side of the island by a 600-m-high plateau, the tiny coastal settlements of Zavala, Ivan Dolac and Sveta Nedelja have passed through the centuries in a state of relative isolation. In the past, families from Jelsa and the surrounding villages on the north of the island kept vineyards here, trekking over the hills by donkey during the warmer months to tend the vines and reap an annual harvest. The south-facing slopes afford the vines maximum benefit of the sun, resulting in an excellent full-bodied red, while the cooler north-facing slopes are better suited to the production of white wine.

During the 1960s, the Yugoslav army constructed a 1400-m-long tunnel through the overlying plateau, finally making year-round access possible. However, the tunnel is narrow and unlit – only one car can pass through at a time, and there is no traffic control system at either end. It is possible to pass through by motorbike, but riding a bicycle or walking are certainly not recommended.

Plans to construct a road from Dubovica, on the south coast east of Hvar Town, to Sveta Nedjelja have been in the pipeline for decades, but (thankfully) it has yet to be approved by the powers that be.

Zavala

East of the tunnel, 6 km from Jelsa, Zavala is a slightly sprawling coastal village, much of which has been constructed over the last couple of decades. It's not a particularly attractive place, but there's a decent pebble beach.

Ivan Dolac

West of the tunnel, 6 km from Jelsa, Ivan Dolac is a small stone village built into the hillside above the sea. The excellent red wine, *Ivan Dolac*, produced by Podrum Plančić, comes from here. Worth checking out is the roadside chapel from 1901, with a plaque above the door (in Croatian) reading: "In honour of the Mother of God, this church was built by Ivan Carić, the son of late Juraj. Rot and mildew have affected the grapes since 1852. There have been hard times. Root parasite has been passed down from Zadar and the grapevine is perishing. People, stop insulting God, and turn to the Blessed Virgin Mary! May God Almighty protect you from these three curses. 1901."

Podrum Plančić ⓘ *Vrbanj, T021-768030, www.plancic.com*, is a family-run wine cellar, which has been in business since 1919. It offers wine tasting and bottles for sale. Try the dry white, *Bogdanuša*, and the velvety red, *Ivan Dolac*.

Sveta Nedjelja

Some 4 km west of Ivan Dolac, nestling into the hillside below the island's highest peak, Sv Nikola (626 m), is Sveta Nedjelja. A cluster of old stone houses, making up the original village, lies 1.5 km back from the sea. In the hillside behind, the gaping entrance to a cave accommodates a small church, **Gospe Snijega** (Virgin of the Snow), founded in the 15th century by Augustinian monks who kept a retreat in the cave until 1787. Today locals live mainly from winemaking, and the name Sveta Nedjelja is now synonomous with the vineyards and wine cellars of the Plenković family. Below the village, a winding road leads through pinewoods down to the coast, where a number of holiday houses have been built (see Sleeping, page 258). There's no natural harbour, but a small marina has been constructed.

Zlatan Otok ⓘ *Sveta Nedjelja, T021-745788, www.zlatanotok.hr*, is a highly successful wine cellar best known for its red, *Zlatan Plavac*, and white, *Zlatan Otok*, which are exported as far afield as California.

Islet of Šćedro

This small island, just 3000 m from the mainland, is still more isolated. It is particularly popular with yachters due to two sheltered bays on the north side. It is visited almost exclusively by sailing boats, though in high season it's possible to get there by taxi boat from Zavala. In the larger bay, **Luka Lovišće**, you'll find a number of good summer restaurants, while the smaller bay, **Uvala Mostir**, is overlooked by the remains of a 15th-century Dominican monastery, and is also home to a pleasant informal eatery (see Eating, below). It's possible to walk right across the island, taking any one of a series of paths that run through the pinewoods, to arrive on the south coast, rimmed by rocks and a number of pleasant pebble beaches.

Sleeping

Hvar Town *p249, map p250*

LL-L **Hotel Riva**, Riva bb, Hvar, T021-750 100, www.suncanihvar.com. In an old stone building opposite the ferry quay, this hotel (formerly known as the **Slavija**) reopened in 2006 following total renovation. Now stunningly chic, the 46 rooms and 8 suites are decorated in minimalist style, in tones of grey and charcoal, with splashes of vibrant red. An amusing feature in each unit is the bathroom, which is visible from the bed through a glass wall. Out front, the **Roots Restaurant** and **B.B. Club** cocktail bar offer open-air seating on a large terrace overlooking the palm-lined waterfront. Open all year.

L **Hotel Podstine**, Pod Stine, T021-741118, www.podstine.com. Located on the coast, a 20-min walk west of the main square, this peaceful and luxurious family-run hotel has a lovely terrace restaurant by a pebble beach, backed by palms and pine trees. There are 40 rooms, each with a sea view. Open Apr-Nov.

A **Villa Nora**, Petra Hektorovića bb, T021-742498, www.villanora.eu. Occupying an elegant 14th-century Venetian *palazzo*, 1 block back from the main square, this friendly, family-run hotel opened in 2007. The 4 rooms and 5 suites are spacious and airy, with wooden floors and modern furnishing, plus extras such as a fridge, DVD player and stereo. Breakfast is cooked to order at whatever time you like, and served in the delightful Lucullus restaurant courtyard out front. Open all year.

B **Hotel Croatia**, Majerovića bb, T021-742400, www.hotelcroatia.net. This 1930s building has been converted into a small hotel set in gardens with views of the sea, a 10-min walk from the main square. There are 22 double rooms and 6 family rooms, plus a lovely terrace restaurant in the garden at the front.

E-F Green Lizard Hostel, Lučica bb, T021-742560, www.greenlizard.hr. Popular with backpackers, this new hostel offers comfortable 4-bed and 5-bed dorms, plus several double rooms. The dorms have shared showers while the rooms have private bathrooms and balconies with a sea view. Guests have the use of the kitchen and washing machine. Open Apr-Oct.

Private accommodation

Split Tours, based in Split, T021-352553, www.splittours.hr. This agency can help you find private accommodation in various towns and villages on the island of Hvar.

It's also worth checking out www.hvar.hr, for apartments to let on the island.

Stari Grad *p252*

All of Stari Grad's hotels are big, modern, commercial establishments, located on the north side of the bay. You're better off looking for private accommodation, which is plentiful and of a high standard. Ask at the tourist office for details, or check www.hvar.hr.

Vrboska and around *p253*

E Pension Darinka, Vrboska bb, T021-774 188, F021-774065. This friendly, family-run B&B offers 8 double rooms and 2 apartments in a modern building overlooking the sea channel. The same family run an adjoining restaurant with food cooked over an open fire.

Camping

Camping Nudist, T021-774034. A walled campsite giving onto the sea, with space for up to 420 guests.

Jelsa and around *p254*

Most of the hotels are modern commercial establishments outside the centre of town. You're better off looking for private accommodation, which is plentiful and of a high standard.

Globus Tours, Strossmayerova Šetalište bb, T021-761955, www.globus-tours.hr. Can help you find rooms and apartments.

Southern Hvar *p256*

E Pansion Skalinada, Zavala, T021-767019, www.skalinada-apartmani-hvar.hr. This family-run *pansion* offers 14 rooms with en suite bathrooms, minibar and balconies with sea views, as well as 4 stone cottages, a lovely terrace restaurant and a small pebble beach. They run special 1-week packages during the grape harvest and the olive picking season.

E Tamaris, Sveta Nedjelja, T021-745733, www.gmp-art-studio.com/tamaris. This is principally a restaurant (see below) but they also have a number of rooms to let. Open late May to early Oct.

Eating

Hvar Town *p249, map p250*

YYY-YY Macondo, Groda bb, T021-742850. This excellent fish restaurant is in a narrow alleyway between the main square and the fortress. In summer there are several tables outside, while the indoor space has a large open fire and is hung with discreet modern art. Start with scampi pâté, followed by a platter of mixed fried fish, and round off with a glass of home-made *orahovica* (*rakija* made from walnuts). The food and service are practically faultless, but you may have to queue for a table. Open Apr-Nov.

YYY-YY Zlatna Školjka, Petra Hektorovića 8, no phone. This 'slow food' eatery serves local specialities rarely found in restaurants, such as *kožji sir iz ulja* (goat's cheese in olive oil). There's also a good range of unusually creative dishes – try the *sotirana janjetina u kiselom umaku od aroma plodova* (lamb stew with aromatic herbs). Open Jun-Sep.

YY Dva Ribara, Fabrika 12, T021-741109. On the opposite side of the harbour from the main square, this eatery offers great views across the water to the old town, plus reasonably priced seafood.

YY Gostionica Junior, Uliča Puckog Ustanka bb, T021-741069. According to locals, this is the best place in town to eat *gregada* (fish stew with potato and onions). Run by a family of fishermen, it's a small, informal eatery with a few tables outside on a cobbled street.

Y Alviž, Dolac bb, T021-742797, www.hvar-alviz. com. This friendly family-run pizzeria occupies an old stone building behind the cathedral, opposite the bus station. The shabby-chic interior with whitewashed stone walls opens onto a lovely peaceful courtyard garden with grape vines.

Besides pizzas they also do excellent *palačink* (crêpes).

¥ **Konoba Menego**, Groda bb, T021-742036, www.menego.hr. On the steps leading up to the castle, this informal eatery and wine bar serves small platters of locally-produced Dalmatian specialties such as *kožji sir* (goat cheese), *pršut* (prosciutto) and *salata od hobotnice* (octopus salad), plus carafes of home-made wine. Typical of a *konoba*, it has exposed stonewalls, a wooden beamed ceiling and candlelit tables. Open Apr-Oct.

Stari Grad *p252*

¥¥ **Eremitaž**, Priko, no phone. Overlooking the sea on the north side of the bay, close to the main beach, this old stone building was once the quarantine, back in the days when trade ships returning from the east would stop here. The menu features typical Dalmatian fish and seafood.

¥¥ **Jurin Podrum**, Donja Kola, T021-765804. This small family-run restaurant specializes in fish and seafood, its biggest claim to fame being that King Edward and Wallace Simpson once ate here. Try the tagliatelli with scampi and mushrooms, and a carafe of the house white. In the summer, they have several tables outside. Closed for refurbishment in spring 2008 but should reopen for the summer.

Vrboska and around *p253*

¥ **Škojić**, Riva bb, T021-77424. Set in an old-fashioned courtyard garden in the centre of Vrboska, just back from the seafront, this restaurant is known for excellent pizza.

Jelsa and around *p254*

¥¥¥-¥¥ **Napoleon, Mala Banda**, T099-526 9990, www.napoleon-hvar.com. Looking out over the harbour, this friendly eatery serves up delicious Dalmatian seafood specialities – choose the *jastog* (lobster) if you want to splash out. The stone-walled dining room is decorated in naval style, with blue-and-white table linens, and outdoor tables line the water's edge.

¥¥¥-¥¥ **Taverna Arsenal**, Mala banda bb, T021-762000. The 18th-century shipyard warehouse has been refurbished to house a sophisticated restaurant, decorated with paintings of ships that were built here during the 19th century. Fish and seafood top the menu, though they also do a good steak. Open Easter to late Sep.

¥¥ **Murvica**, T021-761405. Friendly family-run restaurant serving traditional Dalmatian seafood and meat dishes. It is possible to buy bottles of the home-made wine and *rakija*, and the award-winning olive oil used in the restaurant. Open Apr-Oct.

East of Jelsa *p255*

¥¥ **Konoba Humac**, Humac, 8 km east of Jelsa, T021-768108. There's no electricity so everything is cooked as it would have been over a century ago: under a *peka* or on a *roštilj*. The bread is home-made and the cheese, salad and wine locally produced. You can't get much more authentic than this. Open daily Jun-Sep.

Southern Hvar *p256*

¥¥ **Pansion Skalinada**, Zavala, T021-767019. Serves home-made food and wine on a large summer terrace, beside a pleasant pebble beach. Open mid-May to late Sep.

¥¥ **Tamaris**, Sveta Nedjelja, T021-745733. This family-run restaurant serves up excellent fresh fish and seafood dishes, plus good local wine, on an ample stone terrace immediately above the sea. Open May-Oct.

Islet of Šćedro *p257*

¥ **Mostir**, Uvala Mostir. Run by a family from the island of Hvar, who live here most of the year. They serve fresh fish, home-grown salad and local wine at tables on a shady terrace.

Bars and clubs

Hvar Town *p249, map p250*

Carpe Diem, Riva bb, T021-717234, www.carpe-diem-hvar.com. Trendy cocktail bar with oriental furniture and a plant-filled summer terrace looking out to sea. Through peak season, when it stays open until 0300, it's so popular they have 2 bouncers outside, controlling the people waiting to get in.

Cofein, Trg Sv Stjepana bb. Overlooking the main square, this popular bar has outside tables almost the year round. Indoors, on an upper level, there's a small lounge with funky modernist armchairs. Open until 0300 in summer.

Hula Hula, on the seaside path between **Hotel Amfora** and **Hotel Podstine**. A perfect spot to watch the sunset with a drink, in a small pebble cove. Open daily Jun-Sep.

Kiva, in a narrow side street of the harbour. This tiny informal wine bar plays classic rock and alternative music. Popular with young Croatians and hard drinking sailing types, once it's full inside customers spill out onto the street. Many visitors cite it as their favourite bar on Hvar. Open Apr-Oct 2100-0300.

Entertainment

Hvar Town *p249, map p250*

Veneranda, above the coastal path west of town, set in the 16th-century Greek Orthodox Monastery of St Veneranda, www.veneranda.com.hr. The monastery was dissolved and turned into a fortified military complex by the French in 1807. It was reconstructed and arranged as an open-air theatre in 1953, with latest additions including a cocktail bar in the former church. In summer, it acts as a multi-media centre with an open-air cinema, concerts and dancing until 0500. It is the most popular nightspot on the island.

Festivals and events

Hvar Town *p249, map p250*

1 Jan International New Year Regatta.

May Dalmatia Cup International Regatta, early May. Zadar to Dubrovnik, stopping in Hvar Town en route.

Jun-Sep Hvar Summer Festival, mid-Jun to late Sep. Features various open-air cultural performances, with the main attraction being the classical music concerts held in the cloisters of a Franciscan Monastery (each evening throughout Aug at 2130, 30Kn).

Stari Grad *p252*

Jul-Aug Stari Grad Summer Festival. Features open-air theatre and music, including *klapa* performances.

Aug Faros Marathon, last weekend of Aug. An international long-distance swimming competition, 15 km from town to the end of the bay and back. First swum in the 1970s, it now attracts 50 competitors from as far afield as Russia and France.

Jelsa and around *p254*

Mar-Apr Carrying of the Holy Cross, night before Good Fri. Jelsa, Pitve, Vrisnik, Svirče, Vrbanj and Vrboska – 6 neighbouring villages – take part in an all-night procession. At 2200, a group leaves from each parish church, led by a much-honoured (and hopefully very strong) young man carrying a wooden cross. The parties pass through each of the other villages in turn, to return to their respective churches for sunrise on Good Fri morning.

Aug Fešta Vina (Wine Festival), last weekend in Aug. What used to be an authentic local celebration has turned into a bit of a tourist gimmick, but it's still a good excuse for indulging in the area's plentiful wine supply.

Activities and tours

Hvar Town *p248, map p250*

Diving

Diving Center Viking, Podstine bb, T021-742529, www.viking-diving.com.

Sailing

The official **ACI Marina** is at Palmižana, on the island of St Klement, 3.5 km from Hvar, T021-744995, www.aci-club.hr. It has 160 berths and a couple of good restaurants, and is open mid-Mar to end-Oct. However, many visitors want to be in Hvar Town itself. If you arrive in the bay by late afternoon, it is possible to moor up along the seafront, though through peak season it does get unbelievably crowded.

Vrboska and around *p253*

Sailing

ACI Marina, Vrboska, 21463 Hvar, T021-774018, www.aci-club.hr. 85 berths, open all year.

Jelsa and around *p254*

Cycling

Being quite flat, the area is ideal for cycling. A network of narrow country roads, linking nearby villages, have been called 'bike paths' by the local tourist board, though the roads are open to cars. You can rent a bike or moped from **Globus Tours**, Strossmayerova Šetalište bb, T021-761995, www.globus-tours.hr.

Diving

Divecentar Jelsa, T021-761822, www.tauchinjelsa.de.

Yoga

Suncokret, Dol, T091 7392526, www.suncokretdream.net. In Dol, just 6km from Jelsa, **Suncokret** (which means 'Sunflower') offers holistic wellness retreats combining yoga, nature walks and reiki. Guests are accommodated in cottages in the village and typical Dalmatian meals are provided. Most courses last 1-week, but visitors are also welcome to 'drop-in' for a session.

Transport

Hvar Town *p249, map p250*

Bus

Buses from **Hvar Town** to Stari Grad (35 mins) are scheduled to coincide with the ferries.

Car

If you plan to stay for more than several days it could be worth hiring a car. **Pelegrini**, T021-742743, www.pelegrini-hvar.hr; and **Luka Rent**, T021-741440, www.lukarent.com.

Ferry

Jadrolinija, T021-741132, run regular ferries to **Split** from the island's main port, **Stari Grad** (2 hrs), 20 km east of Hvar Town. **Jadrolinija** also operate a once-daily catamaran service, from Split to Ubli on the island of **Lastovo**, stopping at Hvar Town en route. It leaves Split for Lastovo in the early afternoon, then passes Hvar Town again on the return journey early the next morning, 50 mins.

Taxi

There is usually a taxi and/or minibus taxi available at the bus station in Hvar Town, T021-741888 and T021-742174.

Stari Grad *p252*

Bus

Stari Grad port is 2 km southwest of town, with a local bus laid on for all incoming and outgoing ferries.

Ferry

Jadrolinija, T021-765048, run a regular service from **Split** (2 hrs), with an average 5 ferries per day in summer and 3 in winter. Schedules vary from day to day, so you need to check times with their ticket office.

Throughout the summer, **Blue Line** ferries travelling between **Split** and **Ancona** (Italy) stop in Stari Grad a couple of times a week – check with their ticket office for the exact days.

Vrboska and around *p253*

Bus

Vrboska is linked to **Stari Grad** (15 mins) and **Jelsa** (10 mins) by local bus, which have **ferry** and **catamaran** links to the mainland (see relevant sections).

Jelsa and around *p254*

Bus

Buses from **Jelsa** to **Stari Grad** (20 mins) are scheduled to coincide with the ferries.

Ferry

Jadrolinija (no Jelsa office, for information contact Split office, T021-338333) run a daily catamaran service from Jelsa to **Split** (1½ hrs), calling at **Bol** on the island of Brač en route. The boat departs from Jelsa at 0600 to arrive in Split at 0730, then leaves Split at 1600 to return to Jelsa for 1730. In addition, regular ferries run between **Stari Grad** and **Split**.

Southern Hvar *p256*

Bus

Buses do not run through the tunnel as it is too narrow. However, during the school term, a minibus transports children to and from **Jelsa** a couple of times a day, and visitors are welcome to jump aboard if there is space. Ask at the Jelsa tourist office for details. During the school summer holiday (late Jun to early Sep) the only way to pass through the tunnel is by private transport.

Directory

Hvar Town *p249, map p250*

Banks Several banks and ATMs along the sea front and on the main square. **Medical services** Trg Sv Stjepana (main square), T021-741111, Mon- Sat, 0700-2100. **Pharmacies:** Trg Sv Stjepana, T021-741002, Mon-Sat 0800- 2030. **Post offices** Obala bb, Mon-Fri 0800-2000, Sat 0800-1300.

Stari Grad *p252*
Banks There are a couple of banks and ATMs in Hvar Town. **Medical services** Pharmacies: T021-765061 (ask here if you need a doctor). **Post offices** Ulica Braće Biancini 2, Mon-Fri 0800-1500, Sat 0800-1300.

Jelsa and around *p254*
Banks There are a couple of banks and ATMs in Hvar Town. **Medical services** Pharmacies: T021-761108 (ask here if you need a doctor). **Post offices** Strossmeyerov, Šetalište 33, Mon-Fri 0800-1400, Sat 0800-1300.

Island of Vis

→ *Phone code: 021. Colour map 3, C4. Population: 3637.*

Closed to foreigners until 1989 due to the presence of a Yugoslav naval base, Croatia's most distant inhabited island was spared the commercial brand of tourism that flourished along much of the Adriatic during the 1970s. It's now rapidly developing into a discreet but rather upmarket destination, thanks to its wild, rugged landscapes and the insight it offers into the way people once lived throughout Dalmatia. The two main settlements, Vis Town and Komiža, both lie on the coast, while there are also about a dozen semi-abandoned inland villages. There is limited holiday accommodation, but the restaurants are truly wonderful, the wines, notably the white Vugava *and the red* Viški Plavac, *are organically produced, and there are several peaceful beaches where you can soak up the sun and swim in crystal-clear waters, said to be among the cleanest in the Adriatic.* ▸▸ *For Sleeping, Eating and other listings, see pages 266-268.*

Ins and outs

Getting there After years of apparent isolation, the Croatian government subsidized a fast catamaran service to the mainland, so it's now possible for people to live in Vis and work in Split. During the summer, tourists also travel to and from the island in ever-growing numbers. ▸▸ *See Transport, pages 268, for further details.*

Getting around There are several buses daily between Vis Town and Komiža, but no service to the villages of Rukavac and Milna on the southeast coast (locals are very good about offering lifts if they see you walking, and so are Italian tourists who turn up with 4WD jeeps). There's a **tourist office** ⓘ *Šetalište Stare Isse 5, T021-717017, www.tz-vis.hr*, in Vis Town.

Background

Vis was first settled by the Greeks in the fourth century BC, when Dionysius the Elder, tyrant of Syracuse, probably attracted by the island's natural water sources, founded Issa. It soon became an independent city-state, forged its own coins and founded colonies in Lumbarda on Korčula, and Trogir on the mainland.

From the mid-15th to the late 18th century, Vis came under Venice, then spent a brief period of time during the early 19th century under the British, who saw it as an ideal base from which to confront Napoleon's Adriatic hold. In 1815 Austria took over, and fought and won the most famous sea battle of the 19th century just off the northern coast of Vis, when the Italian navy launched an offensive aimed at capturing the island. The population peaked at over 10,000 in 1910, but since then there's been a slow process of depopulation.

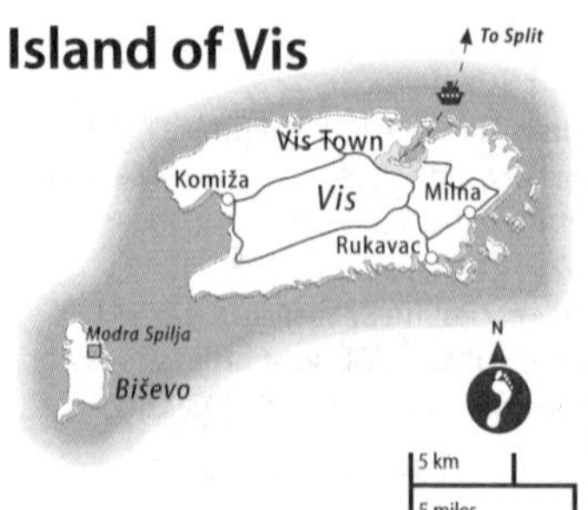

During the Second World War, Vis was occupied by Italians troops from 1941 to 1943, and many of the islander's women and children were evacuated to Egypt. In the summer of 1944 it became the head- quarters of the Partisan movement, with Marshal Tito temporarily lodging in a cave, still known as **Titova Splija** (Tito's Cave), on the south side of Hum. As of January 1944 the British also set up a naval and air base on the island, from which they supplied the Partisans, attacked German- held territories throughout Dalmatia, and also organized a meeting between Tito and the head of the royalist Yugoslav government in exile.

Vis Town » *pp266-268. Colour map 3, C4.*

→ *Phone code: 021. Population: 1960. 56 km southwest of Split.*

On the north coast of Vis, this is the island's largest town and chief port. It actually grew out of two separate settlements, so today a 3-km string of buildings, ranging from humble fishermen's cottages to noble baroque villas, hugs the large sheltered bay. To the east is **Kut**, a picturesque 16th-century residential quarter, and to the west **Luka**, where you'll find the ferry quay and tourist office, as well as another conglomeration of typical Dalmatian stone cottages and a proud **Franciscan Monastery** jutting out on a small peninsula. The entire scene is backed by craggy hills, promising the wild, unspoilt landscapes of the interior. Through summer, yachts moor up along the seafront, their crews drawn by Vis's authentic fish restaurants and fine wines.

Background

The ancient Greeks founded Issa, their first colony in Dalmatia, on the slopes above the northwest part of the bay, in 389 BC. Unfortunately there's not much left of it today, but excavations have unearthed finds now on display in the archaeological museums in both Split and Vis itself. The Romans moved in later, and built a theatre on Prirov Peninsula, the walls of which can still be traced, having been incorporated into the 16th-century Franciscan Monastery that now stands on the same spot. The present settlement developed when Luka and Kut were joined by the building of Gospa od Spilica (Church of Our Lady of Spilice) in 1512. During the centuries that followed, under Venice, several aristocratic families from the island of Hvar built summer villas here, and in the 17th century the town was fortified with four towers.

Island of Vis

From 1811 to 1814, during the Napoleonic Wars, the British took Vis as a base for their Adriatic fleet, and built two forts, St George and Wellington (both of which are now in ruins), to protect the entrance to the bay. Close by, on an islet just east of the bay, rises Hoste Lighthouse, built in 1873 and named after Captain William Hoste.

West of Kut, a small British naval cemetery, surrounded by high walls and kept locked, dates back to 1812, and pays tribute to the British who fell here, both in the Napoleonic Wars and later in the Second World War. During the Yugoslav years, when the island was closed to foreigners, exception was made for surviving British war veterans, who made an annual pilgrimage every September. A few, by now well into their 80s, still return to meet with former comrades.

Sights

Lying within the walls of a **16th-century Venetian fortress** ⓘ *Šetalište Viški Boj 12, T021-711729, Jun-Sep Tue-Sun 1000-1300, 1800-2100, Oct-May opened on request, 15Kn*, the **Gradski Muzej** (Town Museum) and **Gospina Baterija** (Our Lady's Battery) were added by the Austrians in 1842. The upper floor now houses the Archaeological Collection Issa, an enlightening display of Greek finds from Issa, including a fourth-century BC bronze head of a goddess (either Aphrodite or Arthemide, scholars have yet to decide which), plus vases and amphorae. The ground floor is devoted to the life and customs of the island: period furniture, fishing and winemaking tools are on show, and there's a section highlighting the island's role during the Second World War when Tito set up the partisan base here. In August, evening classical music concerts are held in the courtyard of the museum.

Beaches

The main beach is west of town, beyond Luka, in front of **Hotel Issa**, where it's also possible to rent motorboats. The more peaceful pebble beach of **Grandovac** is east of town, beyond Kut, behind Vila Češka, where there's a small waterside bar serving drinks, salty snacks and *palačinke* (pancakes). If you have your own transport, you could drive across the island to **Rukavac** on the southeast coast. It's a peculiar place, not so much a village as a cluster of holiday houses, built mainly by Slovenians who arrive during summer and make up the major part of a seasonal community. Here **Uvala Rukavac** (Rukavac Bay) offers a small pebble beach, while **Uvala Srebrena** (Silver Bay) is overlooked by a dramatic series of rocky ledges stepping down to the water and backed by pinewoods. Close by, the hamlet of **Milna** has a decent sand beach in **Uvala Zaglav**, accessed by a 10-minute walk along the coast. It's particularly suitable for families, as the water is shallow and the seabed smooth, making it possible for children to enjoy. There's also an excellent little restaurant, **Zoglov**, serving delicious lunchtime snacks.

Komiža

» *pp266-268. Colour map 3, C5.*

→ *Phone code: 021. Population: 1677. 18 km southwest of Vis Town.*

On the west coast of Vis, this friendly fishing village is built around a small harbour. Old stone buildings with wooden shutters and terracotta-tiled roofs line a series of narrow alleys, each of which runs down to the seafront, where locals of all generations meet for morning coffee, conduct their evening promenade and put the world to rights. Above the village, from the weather-beaten slopes of **Hum Hill**, a 13th-century monastery surveys the open waters of the Adriatic and the outlying **islet of Biševo**, home to **Modra Spilja** (Blue Cave). Through winter 20 or so wooden fishing boats animate the harbour but, come summer, elegant yachts from all parts of Europe pay call here. It's probably one of the most unspoilt places on all the islands in a fantastic setting and with excellent restaurants. There's a **tourist office** ⓘ *Riva Sv Mikule 2, T021-713455, www.tz-komiza.hr*, in the village.

Background

Although Benedictine monks from the islet of Biševo had set up a base here already in the 13th century, it was not until the 16th century that the settlement really began to develop. With a natural harbour giving onto well-stocked sea, people lived primarily from fishing, using a unique wooden boat known as a *falkuša*, tapered at both the bow and the stern, with a large triangular sail mounted diagonally to the mast. They were small but seaworthy boats, and local fishermen were known to follow shoals of sardines across the Mediterranean as far as Spain. In 1890, a sardine canning factory was set up here, the first processing plant of its sort in Dalmatia. Komiža sardines were exported to various parts of Europe, and even as far a field as Canada and the USA.

There are said to be more people originating from Komiža in San Pedro, California, than there are on the island itself.

Vis Cricket Club

The game of cricket was introduced to this distant island by British naval commander Captain William Hoste when Vis was under British protectorate (1808-1811). Hoste encouraged his men to go ashore and play cricket for recreation, and in no time at all the islanders also joined in.

The game was reintroduced to the island in 2001, primarily under the instigation of wine-producer Oliver Roki, despite the fact that the nearest club to play against was on the Greek island of Corfu.

Since then, the European Cricket Council have awarded Vis a £7000 grant to create a cricket field (which will be in Mr Roki's vineyard) and to buy equipment, and has also sponsored Manchester-based coach David Gelling to train the locals.

Their first match against foreigners took place in June 2003, when they played the Saumur Strays Cricket Club, a British team with its roots in France. The Strays meets once a year in unusual or foreign locations, and when they heard about Vis they decided to have a day there: the event was covered by Croatian TV.

A nation of natural sportsmen, by 2005 Croatia had founded three more cricket clubs, in Zagreb, Ivanić Grad and Split. Look out Yorkshire!

During the early 20th century families began emigrating to America. Some of them, accompanied by their children and grandchildren, still return to their native home each summer. The people who have remained here continue to live primarily from winemaking, seafaring and fishing (though the sardine stocks are now sadly depleted), along with the more recent addition of tourism. The local tipple is *rogoš*, a type of *rakija* flavoured with carob, which grows in abundance on the surrounding hills.

Sights

Ribarski Muzej (Fishing Museum) ⓘ *Riva bb, T021-713726, Jun-Sep daily 1700-2200, 10Kn*, is housed within Komuna, a Venetian tower erected in 1585. You can climb to the top of the tower for great views over the harbour below. The main attraction here is the last existing shipwrecked *falkuša*, built in 1925. On the first floor, a collection of fishermen's equipment, including delicately woven nets, rope knots and old sardine tins, celebrates the town's once-prosperous fishing industry. All exhibits are labelled in the Komiža dialect, which most Croatians, even Dalmatians, fail to understand.

Samostan Sv Nikola (Monastery and Church of Sv Nikola) ⓘ *closed to the public, but well worth the walk up for the view down onto town*, is perched on the hillside above town and set amid terraces of vines and olives. This fortified monastery was founded in the 13th century by Benedictine monks who fled their former abbey on the islet of Biševo, following a series of pirate raids. Each year on St Nicholas Day (6 December), the ceremonial burning of a fishing boat takes place in front of the church.

Gospa Gusarica (Church of Our Lady of the Pirates) ⓘ daily *0700-1200, 1700-1900*, overlooks the main beach, close to **Hotel Biševo**. This Renaissance building consists of three single-nave churches, each of the same size, connected by interior arches. The oldest is the middle church, dating from the 16th century, while the side churches were added during the 17th and 18th centuries.

Biševo

Modra Spilja (Blue Cave), on the east coast of the islet of Biševo, 5 km southwest of Komiža, is often compared to the Blue Cave on Capri, Italy. Some 24 m long, 12 m wide and with water 10-20 m deep, sunlight enters the cave through a submerged side entrance, passes through the water and reflects off the seabed, casting the interior in a magnificent shade of blue. Small boats ferry visitors in and out to see this natural wonder. You can visit the cave as part of an organized day trip from Komiža. Excursions are planned so you enter the cave around midday, when the light is at its best, then continue to the west side of Biševo for a few hours in **Porat Uvala** (Porat Bay), where there's a pleasant sand beach and a couple of simple restaurants. Boats depart at 0900 from the harbour and return at 1700. Enquire at Komiža tourist office for further details, expect to pay 90-180Kn per person (depending whether lunch is included).

Sleeping

Vis Town *p263*

D Hotel Paula, Petra Hektorovica 2, Kut, T/F021-711362, www.paula-hotel.htnet.hr. Hidden away in a cobbled side street, this pleasant, family-run hotel has 12 smart, modern rooms. Downstairs there's a small fish restaurant, with tables on a walled terrace. Open all year.

D Tamaris, Obala Sv Jurja 30, T021-711350. Located in the centre of town, looking over the seafront promenade, this late 19th-century building has been converted into a basic but comfortable 27-room hotel. Open all year.

Private accommodation

Split Tours Travel Agent, based in Split, T021-352553, www.splittours.hr. This agency can help you find private accommodation in Vis Town. Alternatively, check out the website www.info-vis.net.

Komiža *p264*

D Hotel Biševo, Ribarska 72, T021-713752, F021-713556, www.hotel-bisevo.com. Komiža's only hotel, the **Biševo**, is a modern structure overlooking the pebble beach west of the centre. There are 131 rooms and a small Wellness Centre. Comfortable but not particularly romantic, it tends to be invaded by tour groups.

D Palagruža Lighthouse, 70 km south of Komiža. Contact **Adriatica Net**, Heinzelova 62a, Zagreb, T01-2415611, www.adriatica.net. This lighthouse is on the small, uninhabited island of Palagruža, which makes up part of the Vis archipelago. On a hill 90 m above the sea, in the centre of the island, it dates from 1875 and has been converted into 2 apartments, each sleeping 4 people. There's a wonderful beach, but not a soul in sight, so you have to take your own provisions. Rentals are on a 1-week basis, Sat to Sat, with transfers by boat arranged from either Split or Korčula.

Private accommodation

The following Komiža-based agencies can help you find private accommodation: **Darlić and Darlić**, Riva Sv Mikule 13, T021-713760, www.darlic-travel.hr; **Srebrna Tours**, Ribarska 4, T021-713668, www.srebrnatours.hr. **Split Tours**, Split, T021-352553, www.splittours.hr. Have a list of apartments and rooms to let in Komiža.

Eating

Vis Town *p263*

ΨΨΨ-ΨΨ Villa Kaliopa, V Nazora 32, Kut, T021-711755. Close to the Town Museum, this enchanting restaurant is set in the walled garden of a Renaissance villa. The menu changes daily, depending on what fresh products are available. Dinner here is an event in itself, and worth dressing up for.

ΨΨ Konoba Vatrica, Kralja Krešimira IV 15, Kut, T021-711574. With an ample vine-covered terrace on the seafront, this restaurant gets incredibly busy in summer. Guests sit at heavy wooden tables and feast on barbecued fish and meat dishes. Open all year.

ΨΨ Roki's, Plisko Polje 7, Plisko Polje, T021-714004. Nikša Roki, one of Vis' top wine producers, hosts this small informal eatery on his vineyard in the village of Plisko Polje, on the 'old road' between Vis and Komiža. Expect authentic Dalmatian home-cooking, excellent wine, and open-air dining with outdoor tables arranged under a tree.

ΨΨ Stončica, Uvala Stončica, T021-711669. A simple fish restaurant in a beautiful

For an explanation of the sleeping and eating price codes used in this guide, see inside the front cover. Other relevant information is found in Essentials, pages 32-40.

secluded bay, several kilometres east of Vis Town. The best way to arrive here is by boat, but it's also possible to hike along a rough track from Kut. Open Jun-Sep.

Ψ **Težok**, Kralja Krešimira IV bb, Kut, T021-711271. A few doors down from **Vatrica**, this informal eatery serves up slightly cheaper 'blue fish' such as *tunj* (tuna), plus the local favourite *brodet* (fish stew) at tables with harbour views.

Ψ **Bufet Vis**, Obala Sv Jurja 32, no phone. Here you can eat as the locals do at home – a slap- up dinner of barbecued *srdele* (sardines), accompanied by fresh salad. It's opposite the ferry quay, with just half a dozen tables overlooking the sea, so you may have to queue.

Ψ **Pekara Kolderaj**, Trg Klapavica 1. A bakery selling delicious *viška pogaca*, the local version of Italian *focaccia*, filled with tomato, onion and anchovies.

Komiža *p264*

ΨΨΨ-ΨΨ **Konoba Bako**, Gundulićeva 1, T021-713742. This informal and friendly seafood restaurant is in a tiny bay with tables right up to the water's edge. The indoor dining area has rough stonewalls and a pool stocked with fresh fish and lobster, and amphorae. Open mid-Feb to mid-Nov.

ΨΨΨ-ΨΨ **Konoba Jastožera**, Gundulićeva 6, T021-713859. Opened in 2002, this restaurant is based in the former town lobster-pot house. The interior has been beautifully refurbished with tables set on wooden platforms above the water, and small boats can still enter the central space. Needless to say, the house speciality is lobster. May-Sep.

ΨΨ **Konoba Porat**, Uvala Porat, T091-100 9111, on the islet of Biševo. If you spend a day on Biševo, call here for delicious *brodet sa polentom* (fish stew with polenta). They also have a cut-price 3-course daily menu. Open early Jun to mid-Sep.

Ψ **Hajduk**, Riva 25. A small café serving delicious home-made *krafne* (doughnuts), often still warm, ideal for breakfast with a coffee overlooking the harbour.

Ψ **Pekara Kolderaj**, Trg Kralja Tomislava 1. The place to buy fresh *komižka pogača*, a flat bread filled with tomato, onion and anchovies. Open until 0200 through summer.

Ψ **Pizzeria Hum**, Riva bb, T099-673 8387. The menu here is limited to octopus salad, pizza and delicious warm tuna sandwiches. Inside there's a billiard table, making it a popular haunt for local teenagers.

Bars and clubs

Vis Town *p263*

Peronospora Blues, Obala Sv Jurja bb. A *vinerija* and gallery. Try the excellent *Plavac Mali*, a red wine produced by the owner, served with platters of ham and cheese. It's also possible to buy bottles to take home.

Komiža *p264*

There are several bars (and cafés) along the Riva, with the main concentration being at the west end on a small piazza known as **Škor**, where you can drink until the early hours.

Entertainment

Vis Town *p263*

Ljetno Kino, one the seafront promenade. Open-air cinema, open Jul-Aug. Projections start at 2115, ticket 20Kn.

Festivals and events

Komiža *p264*

Aug Ribarski Noč (Fishermen's Night), 1st Sat in Aug. Features live music, local wine and barbequed sardines on the Riva.

6 Dec Sv Nikola (St Nicholas' Day). The ceremonial burning of a fishing boat takes place at 1100 in front of St Nicholas' Church.

Shopping

Vis Town *p263*

Roki's, Obala Sv Jurja bb. A small shop selling wines produced by the Roki family. They also run **Konoba Roki**'s, preparing meals for visitors at their home at Plisko Polje, on the 'old road' between Vis and Komiža. If you don't have transport, call first and they'll come and pick you up, T021-714004 (English spoken).

Vitis Vis, Augusta Šenoa 4, set back off the Riva, next to the Ribarnica (covered fish market). A small shop selling wines and an assortment of *rakija* – *travarica*, *rogoš* and *mirta* – produced by the Lipanović family.

Komiža *p264*

Podrum Komiža, Riva 13. A warehouse selling locally produced wine and *rakija*,

including the Komiža speciality, *rogoš*.
Roki's, Ribarska 23. A small shop selling wines produced by the Roki family.

Activities and tours

Vis Town *p263*

Diving

Dodoro Diving Tours, T021-711 913, www.dodoro-diving.com. Organize ½-day diving trips for up to 12 people, as well as weekends. 5 tours with accommodation and meals.

Sailing

There is no official marina in Vis, but it is possible to moor up along the seafront in both Luka and Kut, where electricity and water supplies are available.

Komiža *p264*

Diving

Issa Diving Centre, Ribarska 91, T021-713651, www.scubadiving.hr. Offer diving courses and trips to a shipwreck and to Modra Spilja, as well as night diving. Apr-Oct.

Sailing

There is no official marina in Komiža, but it is possible to moor up along the quay at the far end of the harbour, where electricity and water supplies are available. The 3-day National Day Regatta, Split-Komiža-Split, is held each year in late May.

Tour operators

Alternatura, Hrvatskih Mučenika 2, T021-717239, www.alternatura.hr. Arrange trips around the island and adventure sports such as paragliding and sea kayaking.

Transport

Vis Town *p263*

Ferry

Jadrolinija, T021-711032, run a regular service from **Split**, with an average 3 ferries per day in summer and 2 ferries per day in winter (2½ hrs). Schedules vary, so you need to check times with their ticket office. During high season, **Split Tours** run a **catamaran** service from **Split** to Komiža.

Komiža *p264*

Bus

The island's main port is in Vis Town. From there, a bus connects incoming **ferry** and **catamaran** services to Komiža (20 mins).

Directory

Vis Town *p263*

Banks There is a bank with an ATM on the seafront. **Medical services** Dom zdravlja Vis, Poljana Svetog Duha 10, T021-711026. **Pharmacies**: Ljekarna Vis, Vukovarska 2, T021-711434. **Post offices** Obala Sv Jurja 18, Mon-Fri 0800-2000, Sat 0800-1300.

Komiža *p264*

Banks There is a bank with an ATM on the seafront. **Medical services** Dom zdravlja, T021-713122. **Pharmacies**: Ljekarna Komiža, Podšpiljska bb, T021-713445. **Post offices** Hrvatskih Mućenika bb, Mon-Fri 0800-1400, Sat 0800-1300.

South Dalmatia

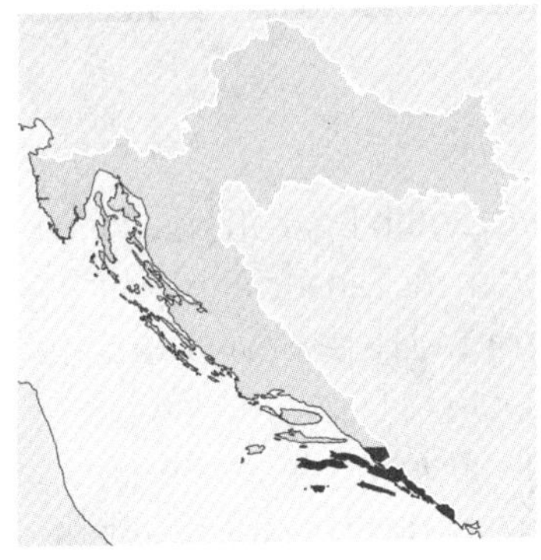

Footprint features

Introduction

The southernmost region of Croatia, South Dalmatia is a long, thin, coastal strip backed by the dramatic Dinaric Alps, which form the natural border with Bosnia and Herzegovina. Urban life centres on the former city-republic of Dubrovnik, an architect's dream contained within ancient defensive walls, facing out to sea and packed with baroque churches, elegant 17th-century town houses, well-stocked museums and open-air cafés.

A two-hour ferry ride west of the city lies the island of Mljet, one third of which is a national park, where indigenous pine forests cover the steep slopes before reaching two inter-connected saltwater lakes, one home to an island capped by a 12th-century monastery. Most visitors arrive as part of an organized day trip, so if you decide to stay the night you'll have the place (almost) to yourself. Be sure to try the lobster – Mljet's culinary specialty.

Further west still, Lastovo is one of Croatia's most remote and least visited islands, where you can escape the crowds, wallow in unspoilt nature and listen to the locals' bizarre and amusing tales of the island's history.

The region's most visited island is Korčula, with Korčula Town (often described as a smaller version of Dubrovnik) renowned for its fine cathedral and regular evening performances of the medieval *Moreška* sword dance.

The neighbouring village of Lumbarda is backed by the Grk vineyards, which in turn are criss-crossed by a network of narrow lanes: pick the right route and you'll arrive on a blissful south-facing sand beach. The easiest way to reach Korčula from Dubrovnik is to travel the length of the mountainous Pelješac Peninisula by bus. If you have time to spare, jump off at one of several roadside wine cellars, where you can sample the locally produced reds, *Dingač* and *Pelješac*, regarded by many as Croatia's most sophisticated wines.

★ Don't miss ...

1 Dubrovnik Gradske Zidine Walk a full circuit of the medieval city walls, commanding panoramic views over the city rooftops and out to sea, page 275.
2 Dubrovnik Summer Festival Attend an open-air theatrical performance or classical music concert, page 288.
3 Ston Eat fresh local oysters at a restaurant overlooking the harbour on Pelješac Peninsula, page 292.
4 Podrum Bartulovića Drink Dingač Croatia's most esteemed red wine, in this Pelješac wine cellar, page 292.
5 Koržula Town Watch a performance of the Moreška medieval sword dance, pages 296 and 297.
6 Veliko Jezero Swim in a lake surrounded by pine-covered slopes on the island of Mljet, page 310.

Dubrovnik and around

→ *Phone code: 020. Colour map 4, B3. Population: 43,770. 581 km from Zagreb, 664 km from Pula, 566 km from Rijeka and 216 km from Split.*

Backed by rugged limestone mountains and jutting out into the Adriatic Sea, Dubrovnik is one of the world's finest and best-preserved fortified cities. Its gargantuan walls and medieval fortress towers enclose the historic centre, filled with terracotta-roof town houses and monuments such as the 15th-century Rector's Palace, two monasteries with cloistered gardens and several fine baroque churches with copper domes. The old town is traversed by the main pedestrian promenade, Placa, paved with glistening white limestone and lined with open-air cafés and small boutiques. In 1979, the city became a UNESCO World Heritage Site.

Tourism has a long history here and the museums, churches, hotels and restaurants are all well geared to foreign visitors – prices are also geared to foreigners, and in Dubrovnik you should expect to pay almost double what you would anywhere else in Croatia. Today, after the lull caused by the war, Dubrovnik is once again considered one of Europe's most exclusive destinations. Cruise ships en route from Venice to the Greek islands stop here (in high season up to nine per day, which can be a bit much), several of the country's plushest and most expensive hotels can be found, and it's also a major base for charter companies hiring out yachts in South Dalmatia. ▸▸ *For Sleeping, Eating and other listings, see pages 284-291.*

Ins and outs

Getting there Through summer there are regular flights to most European capitals. The airport is at Cilipi, 21 km from the city centre. Airport buses (operated by **Atlas**) run to and from the airport, 35Kn. The new **bus station** ⓘ *Obala Pape Ivana Pavla II 44a*, is just beyond Gruž port, a 30-minute walk west of the old town. Departure information, T060-305070. There is no railway to Dubrovnik. The city port is at Gruž, 3 km west of

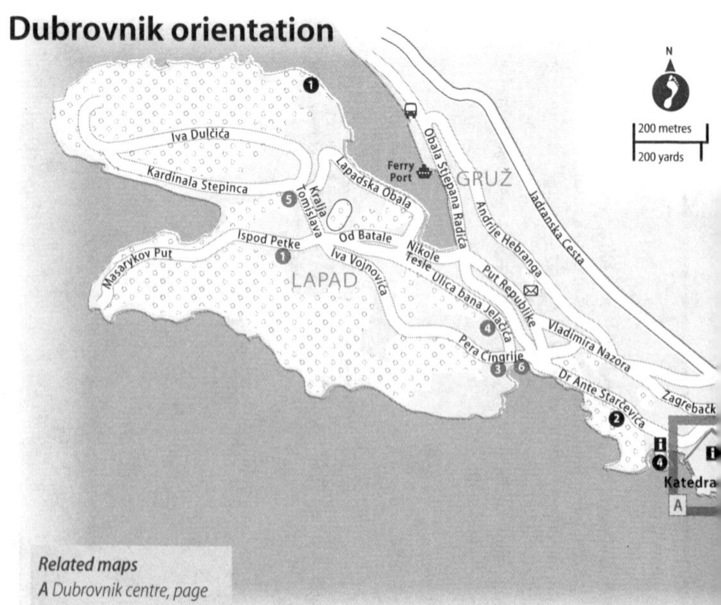

Related maps
A Dubrovnik centre, page

Arriving at night

Both the airport and bus station are perfectly safe if you arrive late at night. All incoming Croatia Airlines flights are met by an airport bus, which transports passengers to the city centre. Charter companies with incoming flights usually arrange their own bus transfers. All reputable hotels have someone on duty through the night – book ahead and let them know that you are arriving late. All ferry services to Dubrovnik arrive during the day or early evening.

the old town. **Jadrolinija** run an international ferry to Bari, in Italy, plus a twice-weekly coastal service to Rijeka, stopping at Sobra (island of Mljet), Korčula, Stari Grad (island of Hvar) and Split en route. The same company operates local ferry services tothe nearby islands of Koločep, Lopud, Šipan and Mljet. ▸▸ *See Transport, page 289, for further details.*

Getting around Dubrovnik's main sights are concentrated in the pedestrian old town, within the medieval fortifications and can easily be seen by foot. There are now two hotels inside the walls, plus several very upmarket establishments within easy walking distance of the old town, on the coastal road east of the centre. The larger, renovated, socialist-era hotels are found on Lapad Peninsula, 3 km west from the centre, and can be reached by buses No 1 and No 8 (both of which run from Pile Gate to Gruž Harbour) disembarking at Stanica Lapad.

Tourist information The new **walk-in tourist information centre** ⓘ *Široka bb, daily 0800-2000*, is within the city walls, while a **second tourist information centre** ⓘ *Dr Ante Starčevića 7, opposite the Hilton Hotel, T020-427591, www.visit dubrovnik.hr and www.tzdubrovnik.hr, daily summer 0800-2000, winter 0900-1600*, is just outside Pile Gate. In addition, there is a **tourist information centre** ⓘ *Gružka Obala bb, T020-417983, daily summer 0800-2000, winter Mon-Fri 0800-1500, Sat 0900-1400*, close to the ferry landing station. For guided tours of the city visitors should contact **Atlas** travel agency, see Activities and tours, page 289.

Best time to visit Dubrovnik is undoubtedly at its most animated between mid-July and mid-August when the **Summer Festival** is in full-swing: troupes of actors and musicians from all parts of the world arrive in town, along with a plethora of holidaymakers and cultural visitors – all great fun but it does get horribly busy and prices escalate out of all proportion. The city's churches and museums are open the year through, and during winter – when you can expect clear blue skies, mellow sunshine and an icy bite to the air – Dubrovnik can be quite enchanting. However, if you're looking to avoid the worst of the crowds but still have the possibility of sunbathing and a swim, try to visit in June or October.

Sleeping
Aquarius **1**
Bellevue **6**
R **3**
Villa Dubrovnik **2**
Youth Hostel **4**
Zagreb **5**

Eating
Orhan **4**
Orsan **1**
Tovjerna Sesame **2**

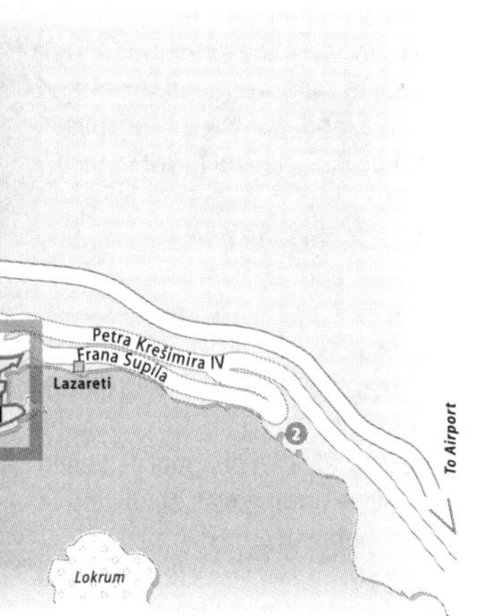

24 hours in the city

After morning coffee at an open-air café on **Placa**, begin exploring Dubrovnik by walking a complete circuit of the sturdy **city walls**, marking the perimeter of the old town and offering spectacular views over the city rooftops and out to sea.

Mid-morning visit the **Rector's Palace**, a fine Gothic-Renaissance building and home to the **City Museum**, where you can get some idea about how people lived under the Republic of Ragusa.

Afterwards, shop for a picnic at the **open-air market** on Gundulićeva Poljana, and take a taxi boat from the old port to the **Island of Lokrum**, where you can swim and enjoy a picnic lunch in the shade of the pine trees.

Return to town for late afternoon, and either check out the **Dominican Monastery** and the **city's churches**, or, if you're beginning to tire of religious art, visit the **Aquarium** and **Maritime Museum**. Round off the day's cultural sightseeing with a look in the shocking but undeniably impressive **War Photo Limited**.

If the Summer Festival is in progress, get tickets to an open-air evening concert or theatre production. For dinner, head for **Lokanda Peškarija** overlooking the old harbour and tuck into a feast of fresh seafood and local wine. Close the evening with a nightcap at the **Hard Jazz Café Trubadour**, where you may even catch a live jazz performance on the piazza. Or, during summer, go to **Eastwest** for some celebrity-spotting, cocktails and dancing into the early hours.

Background

The city was founded in the early seventh century, when the nearby Greco-Roman *Epidaurum* (present-day Cavtat, see page 283) was overrun by tribes of Avars and Slavs. Refugees fled north and took refuge on a small rocky island, which they named Laus, and later Ragusa. In the years that followed, the Slavs founded a separate settlement on the mainland hillside opposite the island, and called it Dubrovnik (from *dubrava* meaning 'oak woods'). In the 12th century the narrow channel separating Ragusa and Dubrovnik was filled in, and the two settlements became one, which was known as Ragusa until 1918.

For 450 years (1358-1808), Ragusa was a powerful independent republic, which kept its freedom by paying off potential rulers: first the Hungarian king, then, after the defeat of Hungary by the Turks at the Battle of Mohacs in 1526, the Ottoman Sultan. It owed its wealth to shipping, becoming the main outlet for silver, lead, wool and leather from the hinterland regions of Bosnia and Serbia, and carrying grain, spices, cotton and salt from Epirus (present-day northwest Greece), Syria and Egypt to Sicily, France and Spain.

As prosperity grew, so did the republic's territory, and by the late 15th century it boasted approximately 120 km of mainland coast, extending from Neum in the north to the Bay of Kotor (in present-day Montenegro) to the south. Its possessions included the island of Lastovo (as of 1252), the Pelješac Peninsula (1333) and the island of Mljet (1345). It also took the islands of Korčula, Brač and Hvar in 1414, but was forced to release them to its arch-rival, Venice, in 1417.

The republic was remarkably sophisticated for its time: the first pharmacy opened in 1317; an old people's home was founded in 1347; slave trading was abolished in 1418; and an orphanage for abandoned and illegitimate babies opened in 1432.

The chief citizen was the rector, who had to be over 50, and was elected for only a month at a time after which he could not stand for re-election for at least two years.

City under siege

In the early 1990s, when the war for independence broke out, Yugoslav forces placed the city under siege. From November 1991 to May 1992, the ancient fortifications stood up to bombardments and fortunately none of the main monuments were seriously damaged, though many of the terracotta rooftops were blasted to fragments. The international media pounced on the story, and ironically it was the plight of Dubrovnik that turned world opinion against Belgrade, even though less glamorous cities, such as Vukovar in Eastern Slavonia (see page 91), were suffering far worse devastation and bloodshed. During the second half of the 1990s, money poured in from all over world and today thanks to careful restoration work (costing an estimated US$10 million), few traces of war damage remain and Dubrovnik is once again a fashionable, high-class holiday resort.

His role was primarily symbolic, while power was held by the Grand Council (made up exclusively of members of the local nobility) and the Senate (a consultative body made up of 45 invited members over the age of 40). The Archbishop of Dubrovnik had to be a foreigner (usually an Italian), a law intended to keep politics and religion apart. Senior officers in the army and navy were members of the nobility, while the increasingly prosperous middle class were traders.

Ragusa's strength lay not in its military power, but in its diplomatic cunning. The republic remained neutral throughout the ongoing international conflicts between Christians and Muslims, and by the Pope's consent was permitted to continue trade with the Levant.

By the 16th century, Ragusa had entered its Golden Age: it had one of the world's greatest merchant fleets, with over 180 ships and 4000 sailors voyaging back and forth across the Mediterranean and the Black Sea, and consulates in over 50 foreign ports including Naples, Malta, Lisbon, Corfu, Constantinople, Tunis and Alexandria. During this period, inspired by the Italian Renaissance, the republic became the birthplace of Croatian literature, lead by local writers such as the dramatist Marin Držić (1508-1567) and the poet Ivan Gundulić (1589-1638).

In 1667, the city was hit by a severe earthquake, killing an estimated 5000 inhabitants and levelling most of the splendid Gothic and Renaissance buildings. The city walls survived the disaster and the basic urban layout remained; new buildings were erected in a rather more sober baroque style.

French troops entered the city in 1806, and in 1808 the republic lost its independence and was incorporated into Napoleon's Illyrian Provinces. In 1918 it officially became known as Dubrovnik. During the 20th century, as part of Yugoslavia, the city developed into a well-known and much-loved tourist destination. Today it is a new mecca for the rich and famous, with recent visitors including Catherine Zeta Jones and Michael Douglas. In 2007, 4.5 million people visited Dubrovnik.

Sights

Gradske Zidine (City Walls)

ⓘ *May-Sep daily 0800-1900, Oct-Apr daily 1000-1500, 50Kn. To reach the walls, climb the steps immediately to your left after passing through Pile Gate.*

The walls, as they stand today, follow a ground plan laid down in the 13th century. However, the fall of Constantinople to the Turks in 1453 sent panic waves throughout the Balkans, and Ragusa hastily appointed the renowned Renaissance architect,

 Michelozzo di Bartolomeo (1396-1472) from Florence, to further reinforce the city fortifications with towers and bastions. On average the walls are 24 m high and up to 3 m thick on the seaward side, 6 m on the inland side. The highlight of any visit to Dubrovnik has to be a walk around the city walls. To walk the full circuit, 2 km, you should allow at least an hour.

Vrata od Pila (Pile Gate)

There are two gates into the city walls – Pile Gate is to the west. The name Pile comes from the Greek *pili* meaning 'gate'. During the time of the republic, they were closed each evening at 1800 and reopened at 0600 the next morning; the keys were kept under the custody of the rector. Pile Gate, as it stands today, combines a stone bridge, a wooden drawbridge on chains, and an outer Renaissance portal from 1537 followed by a Gothic inner gate from 1460. A niche above the outer portal contains a 15th-century statue of St Blaise (the city's patron saint), while a niche above the interior gate bears a 20th-century figure of the same saint, by Ivan Meštrović. From May to October, guards in period costume stand vigilant by both gates, just as they would have done when the city was an independent republic.

Velika Onofrio Fontana (Onofrio's Greater Fountain)

ⓘ *Poljana Paska Miličevića.*

Located in the square just inside Pile Gate, this polygonal fountain was part of the city's water supply system, designed by the Neapolitan builder Onofrio de la Cava to bring water from the River Dubrovačka 20 km away. It was completed in 1444. Topped with a dome, water runs from 16 spouting masks around the sides of the fountain. Originally it would have been decorated with ornate sculptures, which were unfortunately destroyed during the earthquake of 1667.

Placa

Up until the 12th century, Placa (also known as Stradun) was a shallow sea channel, separating the island of Laus from the mainland. After it was filled in, it continued to divide the city socially for several centuries, with the nobility living in the area south of Placa, while the commoners lived on the hillside to the north. It forms the main thoroughfare through the old town, running 300 m from Pile Gate to Ploče Gate. The glistening white limestone paving dates from 1468, though the stone buildings to each side were constructed after the earthquake of 1667. While the upper levels were residential, the ground floors were used as shops, many displaying the characteristic *na koljeno* frontage (*na koljeno* translates literally to 'like a knee', which Croatians use to say were L-shaped relating here to a particular architectural feature of shop fronts, with a door and window in a single frame spanned by a semicircular arch so that the door can be kept closed and goods handed over the sills serving as counters). Still today Placa serves as the city's main public gathering place, where locals conduct their morning and evening promenades and meet at rather pricey open-air cafés.

Franjevačka Samostan (Franciscan Monastery)

ⓘ *Placa 2, T020-321410, summer daily 0900-1800, winter daily 0900-1700, 25Kn.*

The monastery complex centres on a delightful cloister from 1360 – late Romanesque arcades supported by double columns, each crowned with a set of grotesque figures, beside an internal garden filled with palms and Mediterranean shrubs. There's a small museum displaying early laboratory equipment, ceramic bowls and old medical books from the pharmacy, founded by the monks in 1318 and said to be the oldest institution of its kind in Europe.

Sinagoga (Synagogue)

ⓘ *Žudioska 5, summer Mon-Fri 1000-2000, 15Kn.*

Claiming to be the oldest surviving synagogue in the Balkans and the third oldest in Europe (after those in Prague, the Czech Republic, and Toledo, Spain), this tiny place of worship was founded in the 15th century on the second floor of a 13th-century Gothic town house. The interior was redecorated in baroque style in the 17th century, and the blue ceiling painted with stars added in the 19th.

Dubrovnik's Jewish community, first mentioned in 1352, grew in number after 1492 following the expulsion of Jews from Spain, and increased still further with a subsequent banishment from southern Italy in 1514. As of 1546, local Jews were obliged to live in a ghetto, established along today's **Žudioska** (formerly Via del Ghetto). The community peaked in 1830 with 260 members, though today there are only about 40 Jews living in the city.

Palača Sponza (Sponza Palace)

ⓘ *Luža, T020-321032, daily 1000-1600, free (ground floor only).*

At the east end of Placa, this palace was designed by Paskoje Miličević in 1522 and displays a blend of Renaissance arches on the lower level and Venetian-Gothic windows on the first floor. Through the centuries it has been used as a customs office and the city mint (Ragusa minted its own money, a convertible currency known as the *perpera*) though it now houses the state archives. The ground floor is open for temporary exhibitions, and during the **Summer Festival** concerts take place in the internal courtyard. This is one of the few buildings to survive the 1667 earthquake.

Dominikanski Samostan (Dominican Monastery)

ⓘ *Sv Dominika 4, T020-321423, summer daily 0900-1800, winter 0900-1700, 20Kn.*

Behind the Sponza Palace, in a passageway leading to Ploče Gate, the Dominican

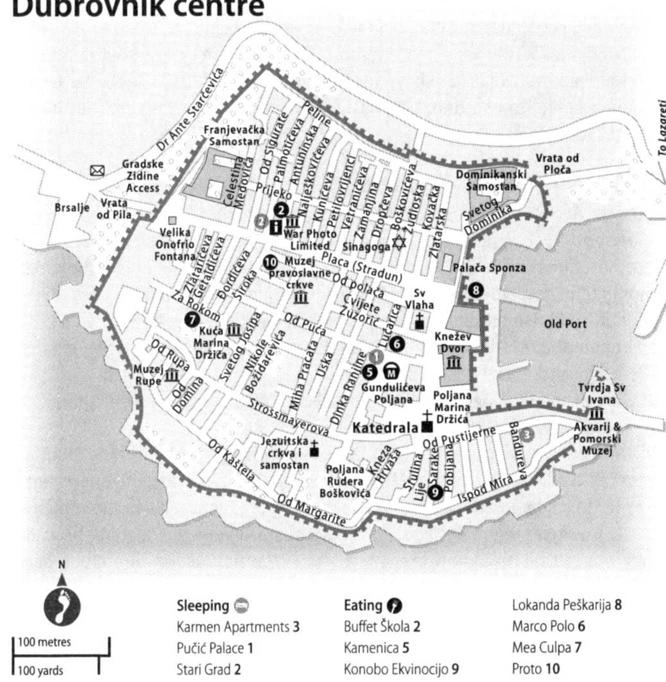

Monastery centres on a 15th-century late Gothic cloister, designed by the Florentine architect Michelozzo di Bartolomeo (1396-1472) and planted with orange trees. The east wing of the complex houses a museum exhibiting 15th- and 16th-century religious paintings by members of the Dubrovnik School – notably a triptych featuring the *Virgin and Child* by Nikola Božidarevic and a polyptych centring on the *Baptism of Christ* by Lovro Dobričević – as well as works by the city's goldsmiths and reliquaries collected by the monks through the centuries. The rather plain interior of the monastery church is worthwhile for the *Miracle of St Dominic* by Vlaho Bukovac (1855-1922), a local painter from Cavtat.

Vrata od Ploča (Ploče Gate)

The main entrance into the old town from the east, Ploče, like Pile Gate, combines a 15th-century stone bridge with a wooden drawbridge and a stone arch bearing a statue of St Blaise.

Lazareti

Just outside the walls, overlooking the sea close to Ploče Gate, this complex of brick sheds beside a central courtyard was built as a quarantine centre in the 16th century. Both land and sea travellers were obliged to check in here and stay for a period of up to 40 days before being granted permission to enter the city. Today the buildings are used by the artists' association Otok (see Bars and clubs) which organizes alternative cultural events here throughout the summer.

Crkva Svetog Vlaha (Church of St Blaise)

ⓘ *Luža, daily 0800-1200 and 1630-1900.*

Opposite the Sponza Palace, this 18th-century baroque church, built between 1705 and 1717, replaced an earlier 14th-century structure destroyed by fire following the earthquake of 1667. It is dedicated to the city's patron saint, St Blaise, and on the high altar stands a silver statue of him, holding a model of the city from the 16th century, which is paraded around town each year on 3 February, the Day of St Blaise. The stained glass windows, a feature rarely seen in churches in southern Europe, were added in the 1970s. Each year, May to June and September to October, performances of folk music and dancing are held in front of the church. They begin on Sunday at 1100.

Knežev Dvor (Rector's Palace)

ⓘ *Pred Dvorom 3, T020-321497, www.mdc.hr, summer daily 0900-1800, winter Mon-Sat 0900-1600, 35Kn.*

Behind the Church of St Blaise, this is the building where the citizen holding the one-month term as rector was obliged to reside during his time in office; he could only leave for official business and his family remained in their own home.

The original 15th-century building was damaged first by a gunpowder explosion, later by a fire and then by the 1667 earthquake, so that the structure as it stands today, with an arcaded loggia and an internal courtyard, shows a combination of late Gothic and early Renaissance styles.

In the **central courtyard** (where classical music concerts are held during the **Summer Festival**) stands a bust of Miho Pracat (1528-1607), a powerful merchant and ship owner from the nearby island of Lopud, who left his wealth to the republic for charitable purposes when he died. When the bust was erected in 1638, he became the only man to be honoured in such a way – the production of statues of local personalities was generally forbidden to prevent the cult of hero worship. Next to the courtyard are a series of large rooms where the Great Council and Senate held their meetings; over the entrance to the meeting halls a plaque reads *Obliti privatorum publica curate* (Forget private affairs, and get on with public matters).

Sveti Vlaho (St Blaise)

St Blaise, the former Bishop of Sebaste (present-day Sivas in Turkey), lost his life during a late anti-Christian campaign conducted by the Romans in AD 316 (although the Edict of Milan, officially allowing Christians the freedom to practise their religion, had been passed in AD 313, in certain parts of the Empire they were still subject to persecution for some time). As well as a spiritual leader, Blaise was a physician, who, according to legend, miraculously saved the life of a child who was choking on a fish bone. Still today, those suffering from ailments of the throat pray to St Blaise for a cure. He was made the patron saint of Dubrovnik in 972, having appeared to the rector of the cathedral in a dream, warning of an imminent Venetian attack and thus saving the city. The bearded figure of St Blaise, holding a mitre and pastoral staff, was featured on coins and seals of the republic, as well as the flag.

Upstairs, the rector's living quarters now accommodate the **Gradski Muzej** (City Museum), offering an idea of how people once lived in the Republic of Ragusa. Exhibits include paintings by Venetian and Dalmatian artists, period furniture, costumes and a curious collection of clocks, each one stopped at 1745, the hour Napoleon's men took the city on 31 January 1806, symbolizing the fall of the republic.

Gundulićeva Poljana

Each morning, Monday to Saturday, an open-air fruit and vegetable **market** sets up on Gundulićeva Poljana, west of the Rector's Palace. Come sunset, the market stalls are packed away and several restaurants put out tables in their place. In the middle of the square is a bronze statue of the Ragusan writer Ivan Gundulić (1589-1638), completed by Ivan Rendić in 1892. Gundulić is best known for his epic poem *Osman* (1626), describing the Poles' victory over the Turks, and the four sides of the stone pedestal upon which the statue is mounted are decorated with reliefs of scenes from the poem.

Katedrala (Cathedral)

ⓘ *Poljana Marina Držića, daily 0800-1200 and 1500-1730, 10Kn (Treasury).*

The original 12th-century cathedral, said to have been sponsored in part by Richard the Lionheart of England out of gratitude for having been saved from a shipwreck on the nearby island of Lokrum on his return from the Crusades in 1192, was destroyed in the 1667 earthquake. What you see today is a splendid baroque structure with three aisles and cupola, designed by Andrea Buffalini of Rome in 1671. The light but rather bare interior contains a number of paintings, notably a large polyptych above the main alter depicting *The Assumption of Our Lady*, attributed to the Venetian master, Titian (1485-1576). Adjoining the cathedral, the rich Treasury displays 138 gold and silver reliquaries, originating primarily from the East and brought to the city by the local seafarers. Pride of place is held by the skull of St Blaise in the form of a bejewelled Byzantine crown; an arm and a leg of the saint are also on show, likewise encased in elaborately decorated golden plating.

Akvarij (Aquarium)

ⓘ *Damjana Jude 2, Tvrdja Sv Ivana (St John's Fortress), T020-323978, summer daily 0900-2000, winter Tue-Sun 0900-1300, 30Kn.*

The St John's Fortress complex, behind the cathedral, guards the entrance to the old city port. At night, the port used to be closed by stretching a chain from the fortress to

Kaše, a breakwater built in the 15th century. The ground floor of the fortress now houses the aquarium, where several saltwater pools and 27 well-lit tanks display an impressive variety of Adriatic fish including ray and small sharks, and other underwater life such as octopus, sponges and urchins.

Pomorski Muzej (Maritime Museum)

ⓘ *Tvrdja Sv Ivana (St John's Fortress), Damjana Jude 2, T020-323904, www.mdc.hr, summer daily 0900-1800, winter Tue-Sun 0900-1400, 35Kn.*

Above the aquarium, on the first floor of St John's Fortress, this museum traces Dubrovnik's development into one of the world's most important sea-faring nations, with exhibits including intricately detailed model ships, as well as engine room equipment, sailors' uniforms, paintings and maps. There are also sections dedicated to the age of steam, the Second World War, and sailing and navigation techniques.

Jezuitska crkva i samostan (Jesuit Church and Monastery)

ⓘ *Poljana R Boškovića, daily 0900-1200 and 1500-1900.*

Completed in 1725, Dubrovnik's largest church was modelled on the baroque Il Gesu in Rome, which was designed by Giacomo da Vignola in the mid-16th century. To reach it, follow Uz Jezuite and climb an imposing staircase dating from 1738, often compared to Rome's Spanish Steps. Next to the church stands the Jesuit College, where many illustrious citizens, such as the mathematician and philosopher Ruder Bošković (1711-1787), were educated.

Muzej Rupe (Rupe Museum)

ⓘ *Od Rupa 3, T020-323018, www.mdc.hr, summer daily 0900-1900, winter Mon-Sat 0900-1400, 35Kn.*

The republic kept an ample supply of grain as a safe measure against siege or famine. This museum is housed in the city's main grain deposit, a vast storage space with 15 deep cisterns carved into the rock (*rupe* means 'holes') during the 16th century. The building itself is more impressive than the exhibition, which consists of an ethnological collection displaying folk costumes and local handcrafts.

Kuća Marina Držića (Marin Držić's House)

ⓘ *Široka 7, T020-323242, www.mdc.hr, summer daily 0900-1900, winter Mon-Sat 0900-1400, 20Kn.*

This memorial museum is dedicated to the life and work of the writer Marin Držić (1508-1567), whose best known script, *Dundo Maroje* (Uncle Maroje), a comedy, was performed throughout western Europe. The 40-minute audio-visual presentation (available in either Croatian or English) gives an enlightening glimpse into Ragusan society during the Renaissance.

Muzej pravoslavne crkve (Orthodox Church Museum)

ⓘ *Od Puča 8, T020-323283, summer daily 0900-1400, winter Mon-Fri 0900-1400, 10Kn.*

Next door to the Orthodox Church, built in 1877, stands the Orthodox Church Museum, with a collection of 77 religious icons, originating largely from the island of Crete and the Bay of Kotor (a short distance down the coast in Montenegro) and painted between the 15th and 19th centuries.

War Photo Limited

ⓘ *Antuninska 6, between Placa and Prijeko, T020-322166, www.warphotoltd.com. Jun-Sep daily 0900-2100; May and Oct Tue-Sat 1000-1600, Sun 1000-1400; Nov-Apr closed, 30Kn.*

This is a beautifully designed two-floor gallery dedicated to photo-journalism from war zones around the world. It has staged exhibitions from Afghanistan, Iraq, former-Yugoslavia, Israel and Palestine and is emotionally gruelling but well worth visiting.

Islet of Lokrum and other beaches

ⓘ *During the summer, regular taxi boats shuttle visitors back and forth from the old port; expect to pay 35Kn for a return ticket.*

East of the city walls, just 700 m from the old port, the small, lush island of Lokrum has some good places to swim. A **Benedictine Monastery** was founded here in 1023, and legend has it that when French authorities began closing down religious institutions in the early 19th century, local Benedictines placed a curse upon anyone who should try to possess Lokrum. A succession of subsequent owners died mysterious and horrific deaths, one being the unfortunate Archduke Maximilian von Hapsburg, who bought the island in 1859, only to be taken prisoner and shot in Mexico in 1867. Before departing, Maximilian built a **summer home** here, set amid a **Botanical Garden** filled with exotic plants and peacocks, which can still be seen today. Even now, locals remain superstitious about Lokrum, and while it is a popular bathing area during daylight hours, no one stays on the island after sunset. The best beaches are on the southwest side of the island, where there's also a small saltwater lake (usually a few degrees warmer than the sea), and beyond it an area reserved for nudists.

The main bathing area close to the old town is Eastwest Beach Club between the city walls and Lazareti, while the best bathing spot on Lapad Peninsula is **Lapad Cove,** where there's a pebble beach in a deep bay, close to **Hotel Zagreb**.

Trsteno Arboretum → *Colour map 4, B2. 24 km northwest of Dubrovnik.*

ⓘ *Trsteno, T020-751019, summer daily 0700-1900, winter daily 0800-1500, 25Kn. All buses heading north up the coast from Dubrovnik stop in Trsteno, though you should tell the driver in advance otherwise he may drive straight on (45 mins).*

The small village of Trsteno is on the main coastal road. Its 16th-century Renaissance arboretum, one of the oldest and most beautiful landscaped parks in Croatia, makes a pleasant outing the year through, though the trees and planting are at their most attractive in spring and autumn.

The 25.5-ha park, laid out in the grounds of a Renaissance villa belonging to the Gucetić family, was designed to emphasize its magnificent clifftop setting: a series of terraces tumble down to the sea, offering stunning views over Trsteno's harbour and out across the water to the Elafiti Islands, see below.

Traditionally the men of Trsteno were sailors, and wherever they went in the world they would collect seeds and saplings for the Gucetić gardens. Today, the arboretum contains pines from Japan, palms from Mexico and cypress trees from various parts of the Mediterranean, as well as pomegranate, almond and lemon trees, and exotic climbing plants such as intoxicating perfumed sweet jasmine and delicate passion flower. Pride of place is taken by a 500-year-old plane tree, with a 12 m circumference and boughs so massive that one of them has to be supported by a concrete pillar.

Behind the villa stands an ornate water garden from 1736, featuring a grotto presided over by baroque statues of Neptune and two nymphs, and a pool fed with crystal-clear water from a trickling stream.

On 2 and 3 October 1991, during the war of independence, the arboretum was shelled from the sea and part of the pinewoods was consumed by fire. However, careful restoration work has covered up the worst of the damage, and today Trsteno still evokes the sophisticated lifestyle of Renaissance Dubrovnik.

Elafiti Islands

» pp284-291. Colour map 4, B2.

→ *Phone code: 020. Population: 879.*

Regarded as one of Croatia's 'undiscovered paradises', the tiny, car-free Elafiti Islands are just a short ferry ride from Dubrovnik. The three larger islands of Koločep, Lopud and Šipan offer unspoilt nature just a short ferry ride away from the city. Pinewoods and scented shrubs such as rosemary and sage cover the island – the natural vegetation has been largely untouched, apart from on the inland area of Šipan, where there are cultivated fields of grape vines and olive trees. Being car free, the pace of life here is wonderfully slow and easy going. Through summer a number of reasonably priced no-frills fish restaurants open up on the islands, but if you plan to visit for a day's exploring out of season, be sure to pack a picnic as you're unlikely to find anything working.

Ins and outs

Getting there and around There are several ferries a day from Dubrovnik to the main islands. Cars are banned from the islands and there are no vehicles apart from a few old farm tractors on Šipan. The only way visitors can get around is on foot, but seeing as the islands are so tiny, this is hardly a problem if you don't mind walking. » *See Transport, page 289, for further details.*

Tourist information Through summer, there are small seasonal tourist offices close to the ferry landing stations on the islands of **Lopud** ⓘ *T020-759086*, and **Šipan** ⓘ *T020-758084*. Off-season, the **Dubrovnik County Tourist Board** ⓘ *T020-324999, www.visitdubrovnik.hr*, can provide basic information.

Background

The name Elafiti is said to stem from the Greek word *elafos*, meaning deer. Some scholars believe that in ancient times deer may have grazed here; others attribute the name to the shape of the islands. In 1272 the Elafiti came under the Republic of Ragusa (Dubrovnik). Initially they were governed by a rector based on Šipan, but as of 1669 the centre was relocated to Lopud, with the rector dividing his time between Lopud and Šipan, spending three months on each. During the 15th and 16th centuries, Dubrovnik aristocracy built modest summer villas and small chapels on the islands, and Franciscan monks used to gather medicinal herbs for use in the pharmacy in Dubrovnik. In 1571, in the lead up to the Battle of Lepanto (see page 255), the Ottoman Turks ransacked the Elafiti, after which a series of defence towers and fortifications were built in case of future raids. During the Tito years a couple of modern hotels were constructed, one on Koločep and one on Lopud, but there was no large-scale development.

Koločep

Lying 7 km northwest of Gruž harbour, Koločep, with a population of 174, is the smallest of the inhabited Elafiti Islands. There are two settlements: the port of **Donje Čelo** on the northwest coast and **Gornje Čelo** on the southeast side, which are linked by a pleasant footpath, shaded by pine trees. The best beach, overlooked by a large modern hotel in Donje Čelo, is of sand; there are also several secluded pebble beaches, some given over to nudism. Historically the islanders lived from diving for coral, exploiting the nearby reef of Sv Andrija.

Lopud

The island of Lopud is home to 269 residents. It's 12 km northwest of Gruž and 4.5 km long and 2 km wide. The sole village, also called Lopud, is made up of old stone houses built around the edge of a wide northwest-facing bay, with a view of Sudjuradj on Šipun across the water.

Guarding the entrance to the harbour, on the north side of the bay, stands a semi-derelict 15th-century **Franciscan monastery**. The oldest part of the building centres on an arcaded internal courtyard from 1483; during the 16th century the complex was fortified to provide a place of refuge for the entire population in the case of an attack. It has been purchased by Francesca von Hapsburg, Archduchess of Austria, who plans to restore it to its former glory, and will keep part of it for her own personal use, while opening the rest to the public.

Close by, the abandoned and roofless **Rector's Palace** is easily recognized by its fine triple Gothic windows. In stark contrast, on the south side of the bay stands the colossal **Lafodia Hotel** complex, erected in the 1980s.

From Lopud a footpath (15-minute walking time) leads across the island, passing through lush vegetation scented with sage and rosemary to **Šunj**, a south-facing cove with a generous stretch of sand beach and a couple of summer restaurants.

Šipan

Šipan, the largest of the Elafiti Islands, is 9 km long with a width of just over 2.5 km. The main settlements, **Šipanska Luka** (on the northwest coast) and **Sudjuradj** (on the southeast coast), are both built at the end of deep narrow inlets and account for a total population of 436. Šipanska Luka has a palm-lined seafront overlooked by old stone buildings and the island's only hotel – there is a decent beach a short distance from the centre. Sudjuradj is a sleepy fishing village with several small Renaissance villas and a pair of 16th-century watchtowers set back from the harbour. The two villages lie at opposite ends of **Šipansko Polje**, a fertile valley planted with olive trees and grape vines, and are connected by a 5-km asphalt road and a network of hiking paths.

Cavtat

» *pp284-291. Colour map 4, B3.*

→ *Phone code: 020. Population: 2015. 17 km southeast of Dubrovnik.*

This attractive fishing village is Croatia's southernmost seaside resort. Built around a U-shaped bay and protected by a peninsula, the old town centres on a seafront promenade lined with bars and restaurants and a row of palms. Most of the hotels are located north of town, set amid lush Mediterranean vegetation, overlooking a second bay. There is a **tourist office** ⓘ *Tiha 3, T020-479025, www.tzcavtat-konavle.hr.*

Background

Founded by ancient Greeks from Issa (on the island of Vis), the settlement was originally called Epidauros. In 228 BC, it was taken by the Romans, only to be devastated at the beginning of the seventh century by rampaging tribes of Avars and Slavs. The name Cavtat originates from *Civitas Vetus*, as Roman refugees in the newly established Ragusa (present-day Dubrovnik) used to call their former home.

The area was incorporated into the Republic of Dubrovnik during the 15th century; Cavtat was rebuilt and walled, and a rector installed to govern the town and the rural hinterland region known as Konavle. Tourism began in the early 1900s under Austro-Hungary; during the 1980s several large hotel complexes were erected and Cavtat turned into a popular package resort. For a year from October 1991, Cavtat was occupied by the JNA (Yugoslav Peoples' Army). The town suffered minimal material damage, though many houses in the villages of Konavle were looted and burnt during this period.

Housed within the 16th-century Renaissance Knežev Dvor (Rector's Palace), the **Baltazar Bogišić Collection** ① *Obala Ante Starčevića 18, T020-478556, www.mdc.hr Mon-Sat 0900-1300, 15Kn*, includes drawings by Croatian and foreign artists and an impressive canvas, *Carnival in Cavtat*, by Vlaho Bukovac. There is also a lapidarium with Roman stone pieces from the first century AD and a display of old coins, some from the Republic of Ragusa (Dubrovnik).

The birthplace of the realist painter, Vlaho Bukovac (1855-1922), has been turned into the **Vlaho Bukovac Gallery** ① *Bukovčeva bb, T020-478646, Tue-Sat 0900-1300, 1400-1700, Sun 1600-2000, 20Kn*. Bukovac spent most of his years abroad: studying in Paris, visiting England and painting portraits of various aristocrats, and later becoming a professor at the Academy of Art in Prague. However, from time to time he returned to Cavtat, and used this late 18th-century stone building as an atelier. In 1964 it was converted into a gallery displaying a collection of his paintings, drawings, furniture and mementoes.

The impressive white stone **Račić Mausoleum** ① *T020-478646, by appointment only, enquire at the Vlaho Bukovac Gallery, 5Kn*, designed by the sculptor Ivan Meštrović in 1921, stands on the highest point of the town cemetery, on Rat Peninsula. It was built in place of a 15th-century church, which was demolished after the Bishop of Dubrovnik granted that the site could be used to create a tomb for the Račićs, a family of wealthy ship owners. An octagonal structure with a cupola, it is made of white stone from the island of Brač. The entrance features a pair of art nouveau style caryatids (statues of female figures, used as columns to support the porch) and impressive bronze doors. The interior is decorated with reliefs of angels and birds in scenes symbolizing the three stages of life: birth, fate and death. Meštrović built the mausoleum to keep his promise to Marija Račić, who was rumoured to have been his lover. The bronze bell, hanging from the cupola, is inscribed with a touching epitaph, "Know the mystery of love and thou shalt solve the mystery of death and believe that life is eternal."

The best **beaches** lie in the bay east of the centre, where most of the package hotels are located, and west of town, below the gargantuan **Hotel Croatia**.

Sleeping

Dubrovnik and around *p272, map p277*
There's a lack of cheap hotels in up-market Dubrovnik. If you decide to splash out, then go for one of the top-notch places overlooking the sea, just east of the town walls. The mid-range hotels, mainly of the package variety (though some are now equipped with luxurious extras such as Wellness Centres), are on Lapad Peninsula, 3 km from the centre. However, your best bet for reasonably priced and good standard accommodation, near to town, is to rent a room or apartment through an agency. There are now 2 (rather expensive) hotels within the city walls.

LL Hotel Bellevue, Pera Cingrije 7, T020-330000, www.hotel-bellevue.hr. Built into a cliff face overlooking the sea, halfway between the old town and Lapad peninsula, this chic hotel reopened in autumn 2006 following total renovation. The 81 rooms are furnished in smart minimalist style with wooden floors, and the 12 suites also have jacuzzis. Facilities include a small beach and a luxurious Spa and Wellness Centre.

LL Pučić Palace, Ulica od Puca 1, T020-326000, www.thepucicpalace.com. In the old town, close to the open-air market, this luxurious boutique hotel is probably the most romantic place to stay in Dubrovnik, and also the most expensive. Occupying a restored 18th-century baroque palace, its 19 rooms are furnished with antiques and have extras such as Italian mosaic tiled bathrooms stocked with Bulgari toiletries. If you're going to splash out for just 1 night, this could be the place to do it. Open all year.

LL Villa Dubrovnik, V Bukovaca 6, T020-422933, www.villa-dubrovnik.hr. Due to reopen in summer 2009 following renovation, this modernist building is constructed into a cliff above a small bay and private bathing area. When work is completed it will have 56 light and airy rooms looking out to sea, 2 terrace restaurants, a stunning rooftop lounge, a pool and a Spa and Wellness Centre. A pleasant 20-min walk above the coast will bring you to the city walls, though you may prefer to use the complimentary hotel shuttle boat. Open Apr-Nov.

AL Hotel Stari Grad, Od Sigurate 4, T020-322244, www.hotelstarigrad.com. 1 of only 2 hotels within the city walls, this old stone building is close to Pile Gate, just off Placa. Inside there are 8 guest rooms furnished with reproduction antiques, and a roof terrace where breakfast is served through summer. It stays open all year.

B Hotel Aquarius, Mata Vodopića 8, on Lapad Peninsula, T020-456112, www.hotel-aquarius.net. This small, modern hotel is especially good value. It has 20 spacious rooms and 4 suites, as well as a ground floor restaurant with outdoor tables in a leafy garden. You pay a little more for a room with a balcony but it's worth it. Open Mar-Oct.

B Hotel Zagreb, Šetalište kralja Zvonimira 27, on Lapad Peninsula, 4 km from the old town, T020-438930, www.hotels-sumratin.com. Housed in a 3-storey neoclassical building erected in 1922, this hotel is set in gardens with palm trees, close to Lapad Cove and its popular pebble beach. The 24 rooms are basic but comfortable. There's a small restaurant with a terrace overlooking the promenade. Open Apr-Oct.

C Hotel R, Alberta Hallera 2, T020-333200, www.hotel-r.hr. Between the old town and Lapad Peninsula, just a 10-min walk from the Pile Gate, this modern building offers 10 rooms with en suite bathrooms, satellite TV, a/c and internet access. There's no restaurant as such, but breakfast is included in the price. Open Mar-Oct.

D Karmen Apartments, Bandureva 1, T020-323433, www.karmendu.com. For a quaint hideaway in the old town, try this delightful little guesthouse run by the Vlan Bloemen family, who also own the **Hard Jazz Café Trubador**. The 4 light and airy apartments have wooden floors, colourful painted wooden furniture and handmade bed-spreads, and offer views onto the old harbour. The entrance is down a narrow side street between the Rector's Palace and the Aquarium.

F Youth Hostel, V Sagrestana 3 (side street off Ulica bana Jelačića), T020-423241. Often filled with groups of school children, this hostel offers rooms for 4 or 6 in bunk beds. It's a 20-min walk from the new bus station, has 82 beds and stays open all year.

Private accommodation

The following agencies can help you find private accommodation: **Dubrovnik Travel**, Obala Stjepana Radića 25, T020-313555, www.dubrovniktravel.com; **Elite Travel**, Vukovarksa 17, T020-358200, www.elite.hr. Alternatively, www.dubrovnik-online.com, offers online booking in and around Dubrovnik.

Elafiti Islands *p282*

A Villa Vilina, Obala Iva Kuljevana 5, Lopud, T020-759333, www.villa-vilina.hr. Occupying a restored stone villa overlooking the sea, this boutique hotel has 14 rooms and 3 suites, a restaurant and a small outdoor pool. Open May-Oct.

B Hotel Božica, Sudjuradj 13, Šipan, T020-325400, www.hotel-bozica.com. In Sudjuradj, 5km from the port of Šipanska Luka, this hotel has 20 rooms and 4 suites, all with internet, minibar and satellite TV, and most with a balcony. There's a restaurant with a large terrace, an outdoor pool and a pier where yachts can moor.

B Hotel Šipan, Šipanska Luka, Šipan, T020-758000, www.hotel-sipan.hr. This 3-storey white building is on the edge of town, over-looking the palm-lined seafront promenade. There are 85 rooms, a bar and a restaurant. 1-day fishing trips and massage can be arranged upon request. Pets welcome. Open mid-May to mid-Oct.

C Hotel Glavović, Obala Iva Kuljevana bb, Lopud, T020-759359, www.hotel-glavovic.hr. Comfortable but with no-frills, this hotel dating back to 1927 was renovated in 2004. There are 12 rooms and 2 suites, plus a restaurant with a terrace looking out over the bay. Open May-Oct.

C La Villa, Iva Kuljevana 33, Lopud, T020-759259, www.lavilla.com.hr. In a 19th-century villa overlooking Lopud Bay, this small hotel is run by a young, friendly

Croatian couple. The 6 guest rooms have minimalist modern furniture and coloured fabrics, mosaic-tile bathrooms, and they either look out onto the open sea or the back garden's giant magnolia tree, orange trees and lavender bushes.

D **Sv Andrija Lighthouse**, Island of Sv Andrije. Contact **Adriatica Net**, Heinzelova 62a, Zagreb, T01-241 5611, www.adriatica.net. This tiny island (400 m x 80 m), 9 km west of Dubrovnik, 4 km from Koločep and 3 km from Lopud, has a rocky shoreline and is covered by sparse vegetation and pines. The lighthouse, from 1873, has been refurbished to form a 4-room apartment sleeping 8. There are no supply boats, so you need to take a week's provisions.

Cavtat *p283*

B **Hotel Villa Pattiera**, Trumbićev put 9, T020-478800, www.villa-pattiera.hr. On the seafront promenade in the centre of Cavtat, this old stone villa has been refurbished to form a delightful, family-run boutique hotel. There are 12 rooms, all with wooden floors and either a sea or garden view. Breakfast is served in the popular **Restaurant Dalmacija** on the ground floor. Open Mar-Nov.

C **Hotel Supetar**, Dr Ante Starčevića, T020-479833, www.hoteli-croatia.hr. In an old stone building 200 m from the seafront, this basic but welcoming hotel has 29 rooms, a private beach, and a restaurant and summer terrace. Pets welcome.

Private accommodation

Cavtat Tourist Office, Tiha 3, T020-479025, www.tzcavtat-konavle.hr, can help you find accommodation. Alternatively, check out the website, www.dubrovnik-online.com, for rooms and apartments available for rent.

Eating

Dubrovnik and around *p272, map p277*

TTT **Orhan**, Od Tabakarije 1, T020-414183. Just outside the city walls, with tables right by the water's edge below Lovrijenac fortress, this highly regarded restaurant offers excellent fresh fish, a romantic atmosphere and discreet service. It stays open all year.

TTT **Proto**, Široka 1, in a side street off Stradun, T020-323234. In the old town, close to the walk-in tourist information centre, **Proto** offer tables on a lovely vine-covered, upper-level, open-air terrace. The restaurant dates back to 1886 and has an excellent reputation for traditional Dalmatian seafood dishes such as oysters from nearby Ston, and barbecued meats, notably succulent steaks.

TT **Kamenica**, Gundulićeva Poljana 8, no phone. Overlooking the open-air market within the town walls, **Kamenica** is a down-to-earth eatery much loved by locals for its fresh oysters and simple seafood dishes. The platters of *girice* (small fried fish) and *pržene lignje* (fried squid) make a delicious lunchtime snack. Open all year, but closes at 2000 through winter.

TT **Konoba Ekvinocijo**, Ilije Sarake 10, T020-323633. Hidden away in the old town, close to the Aquarium, this friendly, family-run eatery serves up tasty Dalmatian dishes such as lobster soup, freshly-caught seafood and locally-produced sausages. Outdoor tables are arranged on a small terrace. Open May to mid-Oct.

TT **Lokanda Peškarija**, Na Ponti bb, overlooking the old harbour just outside the city walls, T020-324750. Offering excellent value for money and always busy, this informal seafood eatery stands next to the covered fish market. Indoors there's a split-level, candlelit dining space with exposed stonework and wooden beams, but the best tables are outside with sea views. Closed Jan-Feb.

TT **Marco Polo**, Lučarica 6, T020-323719. Located in a side street behind the Church of St Blaise, the dining room here is tiny, but through summer tables spill out onto a pretty courtyard, making it an old-time favourite of visiting actors and musicians. Seafood predominates, with *crni rižot* (black risotto in cuttlefish ink) a popular choice. Open May-Oct.

TT **Orsan**, Ivana Zajca 2, on Lapad Peninsula, T020-435933. This family-run restaurant has a pleasant, leafy terrace overlooking the small marina in Gruž Harbour. Favourite dishes are *salata od hobotnice* (octopus salad), *svježa morska riba* (fresh fish) and *rozata* (a Dubrovnik dessert similar to crème caramel).

TT **Tovjerna Sesame**, Dante Alighieria bb, in a side street off Dr Ante Starčevića, T020-412910. Just outside the city walls, close to Pile Gate, this romantic eatery is a perfect venue for a light supper over a bottle of good wine. The menu features platters of cheeses and cold meats, truffle dishes and an enticing variety of creative salads.

¥**Buffet Škola**, Antuninska ulica bb, T020-321096. In a narrow side street between Placa and Pirjeko, this family-run sandwich bar is known far beyond Dubrovnik. Sandwiches come in delicious home-made bread, filled with locally produced *sir iz ulja* (cheese in oil), *pršut* (dried ham) and tomatoes from the villages of nearby Konavle.

¥**Mea Culpa**, Za Rokom 3, T020-323430. Locally recommended for the best pizza in town. It's within the city walls, open daily until 2400, and has tables outside on the cobbled street in summer. Closed late Dec to mid-Jan.

Cafés

Placa is lined with a number of popular street cafés, all of similar ambience and somewhat inflated prices.

Gradska Kavana, the 1 establishment worth a special mention, is an old-fashioned café with an ample summer terrace looking onto Luža Sq, at the east end of Placa. It occupies the former arsenal building, where the republic's ships were built and serviced.

Elafiti Islands *p282*

¥¥**Kod Marka**, Šipanska Luka, Island of Šipan, T020-758007. Overlooking the harbour, with several tables beneath white umbrellas on the waterside terrace out front, this informal eatery serves authentic local seafood dishes such as *korčulsnska popara* (Korčula fish stew) and *rižot na lučki način* (risotto with lobster, aubergine and courgette). Be sure to try the home-made *rakija*. Open May-Nov.

¥¥**Konoba Peggy**, Narikla 22, T020-759036. Up a narrow side street above the ferry quay, this informal eatery has a pretty terrace with heavy wooden tables and benches, and fragrant lemon trees. Expect typical Dalmatian fare, notably fresh fish, which the owner cooks over an open-fire. Open Apr-Oct.

¥¥**Restoran Obala**, Obala Iva Kuljevana bb, Lopud, T020-759170. Dalmatian specialities served at tables on the seafront promenade, with fantastic sunset views across the bay. Occasional live music. Open Apr-Oct.

Cavtat *p283*

¥¥¥**Konavoski Dvori**, Ljuta, Konavle, T020-791039. Out of town, 18 km east of Cavtat. This highly regarded restaurant is beside a working watermill on the River Ljuta. It's best known for authentic regional specialities such as fresh trout, and lamb baked under a *peka*. The idyllic rural setting and waitresses dressed in traditional Konavali costume make it a popular destination for tour groups. Closed Dec.

¥¥¥-¥¥**Leut**, Trumbićev Put 11, T020-478477. In business for over 30 years, this excellent fish restaurant is in the centre of town, with a large summer terrace overlooking the seafront. The house speciality is scampi cream risotto. Closed Jan.

¥¥**Konavoski Komin**, Velji Do, Konavle, T020-479607. Out of town, 6 km northeast of Cavtat. This old stone building, with tables on a series of outdoor terraces through summer, serves traditional Dalmatian food and wine. It's possible to reach via a marked hiking path from Cavtat. Open all year.

Bars and clubs

Dubrovnik and around *p272, map p277*

Arsenal, Pred Dvorom 1, T020-321065. Overlooking the old harbour, in the arsenal, where Dubrovnik's old-fashioned galleys were once repaired, this trendy wine bar is adorned with heavy wooden furniture and red velvet curtains. Most people come here to drink fine wine, enjoy live music and dance, though it's also possible to eat here.

Buža, Od Margarite, T091-589 4936. Accessed through a small doorway in the city walls, looking out to sea, you'll find this informal bar by following the 'Cold Drinks' sign. Tables are arranged on a series of terraces set into the rocks. The drinks in question are served in plastic cups, but the mellow music and night-time candles make it many people's favourite Dubrovnik bar.

Eastwest, Frana Supila bb, T020-412220, www.ew-dubrovnik.com. In a 1970s modernist building, close to the Lazareti, during the day this chic club runs a café and a private pebble beach equipped with sun beds and umbrellas, but come early evening when the cocktail bar and restaurant are open and a party mood sets in. There's a rooftop VIP open-air lounge open till 0500, where you might spot some well-known faces from the world of sport and cinema.

Hard Jazz Café Trubadour, Bunićeva Poljana 2, T020-323476. Cosy bar filled with old furniture, candles, jazz memorabilia and signed photos of well-known people who have been here, in the old town. Occasional live jazz concerts on a small stage outside through summer. It's owned by the Van Bloemen family, who founded Londons' renowned Troubadour Café in Earl's Court in 1954, and moved to Dubrovnik in 1972.

Hemingway, Pred Dvoram bb. Near the **Trubadour**, this popular cocktail bar has tables and cushioned wicker chairs outside on the square. Mojitos are particularly good.

Labarint, Sv Dominika 2, T020-322222, www.labarint-dubrovnik.com. Opposite the Dominican Monastery, within the medieval fortifications, this smart, expensive club pulls in the 40-something crowd. The main attraction is the late night terrace bar with live music and views over the harbour, but there's also a rather sleazy black-and-red nightclub with live cabaret and occasional jazz, plus an upmarket restaurant with outdoor tables and a cosy indoor winter dining space.

Otok, Lazareti bb, T020-324633, www.the-fever.net. Alternative cultural centre, in the old town, behind the cathedral, with a late night bar and occasional exhibitions and concerts, some staged at Lazareti, see page 278, east of Ploče Gate.

Entertainment

Dubrovnik and around *p272, map p277*

Orchestra

Dubrovacki Simfoniski Orkestar (Dubrovnik Symphony Orchestra), Dr Ante Starčevića 29. Also known as the 'Festival Orchestra'.

Slavica, Dr Ante Starčevića 42, a 10-min walk west of Pile Gate, open-air summer cinema in a walled garden above the sea.

Theatre

Marin Držica Theatre, Pred Dvorom 3, T020-321419. Most performances in Croatian, apart from occasional foreign theatre groups on tour.

Festivals and events

Dubrovnik and around *p272, map p277*

3 Feb Sveti Vlaho (Feast of St Blaise) celebrates the patron saint of Dubrovnik. A ceremonial holy service is held in front of the cathedral at 1000, followed by a religious procession around town at 1130; the remains of St Blaise, in the form of relics, take pride of place. During the time of the republic, those prisoners who did not present a threat to public safety were released on this day to participate in the festivities.

Late Jun to early Jul The Libertas Film Festival, takes place each year in the old town. In 2006 guests included US actors Woody Harrelson and Owen Wilson. See www.libertasfilmfestival.com.

Jul-Aug Dubrovnik Summer Festival, mid-Jul to mid-Aug, was founded in 1950. This highly acclaimed international festival hosts drama, ballet, concerts and opera at open-air venues within the city walls. Shakespeare's *Hamlet* staged on Lovrijenac Fortress is one of the most popular performances. For information check out www.dubrovnik-festival.hr.

Cavtat *p283*

Jul-Aug Cavtat Summer Festival features an unusual mix of *klapa* concerts, see page 343, and waterpolo contests.

Shopping

Dubrovnik and around *p272, map p277*

Books

Algoritam, Placa 8, T020-322044. The best bookshop for foreign-language publications including novels, travel guides and maps.

Wine

Djardin, T020-324744, Miha Pracata 8, www.cro-art-design.com, close to the Orthodox Church. Quirky, chunky, modern jewellery made from coloured stones, and silver and gold.

Dubrovačka Kuča, Svetog Dominika bb, near Ploce Gate. T020-322092. Tastefully laid out small shop stocking the best Croatian wines, *rakija*, olive oil and truffle products. There's also a picture gallery upstairs.

Activities and tours

Dubrovnik and around *p272, map p277*

Diving

Aquarius, Mlinibb, Mlini, T098-229572, www.dubrovnik-diving.com; **Water World**, Šetalište Marka Marojiće, Mlini, T098-428088, www.diving dubrovnik.com.

Sailing

ACI Marina, Mokošica, 3 km from Gruž harbour and 6 km from the old town, T020-455020, 450 berths and open all year; **Croatia Yacht Charter**, T021-474 464, www.croatia-yacht-chater.com, a charter company based here; **TA Atlas**, Vukovarska 19, T020-442222, www.atlas-croatia.com.

Sea Kayaking

Adriatic Kayak Tours, Zrnsko Frankopanska 6, T020-312770, www.adriatickayaktours. com. Offer ½-day introductory sea-kayaking tours from Dubrovnik to the island of Lokrum, plus a 1-week itinerary kayaking around the Elafiti islands. They also arrange cycling and snorkelling trips.

Tennis

Hotels Argentina, **Splendid** and **Adriatic** all have tennis courts where non-residents are welcome to play.

Tour operators

Atlas, Vukovarska 19, T020-442222, www.atlas-croatia.com. Guided tours of the city, as well as excursions by bus to Trtsteno, Ston and the Pelješac vineyards, and by hydrofoil to the islands of Mljet or Korčula, plus yacht charters from Dubrovnik and Split.

Dubrovnik Travel, Obala Stjepana Radića 25, T020-313555, www.dubrovniktravel.com. Organize accommodation, car hire, boat hire (motorboats and yachts) and diving in the Dubrovnik area.

Generalturist, Obala Stjepana Radića 24, T020-432937, www.generalturist.com. One of the largest Croatian travel agencies, **Generalturist** specialize in tailor-made trips both with and without guides, pilgrimage tours and yacht charters.

Elafiti Islands *p282*

Sea kayaking

Adria Adventure,T020-332567, www.adriatic-sea-kayak.com. Sea kayaking tours around the Elafiti Islands, from 1 day to 1 week, food and accommodation included. It's also possible to combine kayaking, snorkelling and hiking. The company was set up by the 1998 Miss Croatia and a former member of the Croatian national waterpolo team.

Cavtat *p283*

Diving

Epidaurum Diving and Watersports Centre, Šetalište Žal bb, T020-471386, www.epidaurum-diving-cavtat.hr. Diving trips to several caves, a shipwreck and a large underwater archaeological site filled with amphorae. They can also arrange water skiing and jet-skiing.

Sailing

Adriatic Nautical Academy (ANA), run a summer sailing school in Cavtat. For further information, contact the administrative office in Opatija, T051-711814, www.sailing-ana.hr.

Transport

Dubrovnik and around *p272, map p277*

Air

Dubrovnik Airport, T020-773377 (information), T020-773328 (lost and found), www.airport-dubrovnik.hr. Airport bus service (operated by Atlas) T020-442222.

Through summer, there are regular international flights to and from **Amsterdam**, **Bari Berlin**, **Bologna Brussels**, **Catania**, **Copenhagen**, **Dusseldorf**, **Frankfurt**, **Genoa**, **Glasgow**, **Gothenburg**, **Hamburg**, **Helsinki**, **Istanbul**, **Lisbon**, **London** (Gatwick and Heathrow), **Lyon**, **Manchester**, **Munich**, **Nottingham**, **Oslo**, **Palermo**, **Paris**, **Prague**, **Rome**, **Sarajevo**, **Skopje**, **Warsaw**, **Vienna** and **Zurich**. Internal flights link Dubrovnik with **Osijek**, **Pula**, **Split** and **Zagreb**. The number of destinations and the frequency of flights are reduced in winter.

Airlines offices **Croatia Airlines**, Brsalje 9, T020-413776/7, www.croatiaairlines.hr.

Bus

For all information about buses to and from Dubrovnik, T060-305070. Left luggage costs 20Kn per item, open 0600-2100.

Internal services include 6 buses daily to **Zagreb** (10½ hrs); 12 buses to **Split** in Central Dalmatia (about 4 hrs); 5 buses daily to **Rijeka** in Kvarner (about 12 hrs); and 1 bus to **Pula** in Istria (about 14 hrs). There are also a daily buses to **Kotor** and **Budva** (Montenegro), **Sarajevo** (Bosnia and Herzegovina) and **Trieste** (Italy). Buses depart 3 times a week for **Frankfurt** (Germany).

Car

Best Buy Rent is in the city centre at V Nazora 9, T020-422043; **Budget**, T020-773290, is at the airport, www.budget.hr, and in the city centre at Obala Stjepana Radica 24, T020-418998; **Hertz**, www.hertz.hr, is at the airport, T020-771568, and in the city centre at F Supila 9, T020-425000; **Mack**, www.mack- concord.hr, is in the city centre at F Supila 3, T020-423747; **Milenium Rent**, www.milenium-rent.com, is on Lapad Peninsula at Put Iva Vojnovića 5, T020-333176.

Ferry

Jadrolinija, Stjepana Radića 40, T020-418000, run a twice-weekly overnight coastal service between **Rijeka** and Dubrovnik, stopping at **Split**, **Stari Grad** (island of Hvar), **Korčula** and **Sobra** (island of Mljet) en route. Total journey time approximately 20 hrs. **Jadrolinija** also run daily ferry services connecting Dubrovnik to the islands of **Koločep**, **Lopud** and **Šipan**, departing 3 times daily Mon-Sat and twice daily Sun, and connecting Dubrovnik to **Sobra** on the island of Mljet, departing twice daily through summer and once daily in winter (1 hr 50 mins). The island of Mljet is also served from Dubrovnik by a daily high-speed catamaran, *Nona Ana*, tickets available from **Atlantagent** (Stjepana Radića 26, T020-313355). In high season, Nona Ana continues from Mljet to Korčula (Mon and Sat only) and from Mljet to Lastovo (Tue and Thu only). In addition, Nova (Sv. Križa 3, T020-313599) run high-speed boats between Dubrovnik to Cavtat, and Dubrovnik and the Elafiti islands (Koločep, Lopud and Šipan), foot passengers only, operating Jun-Sep.

Jadrolinija run a ferry to **Bari** (Italy), departing 2 times per week throughout the summer, but just once a week through winter (8 hrs). The Italian company **Azzurra Line**, T020-313178, www.azzurraline.com, operate a similar service, Bari-Dubrovnik, Jun-Sep.

Taxi

The main taxi ranks are just outside the town gates of Pile and Ploče, at Gruž Harbour and at the bus station. **Radio Taxi Dubrovnik**, T970.

Train

As there is no railway line south of Split, Dubrovnik is not connected to the rest of the country by train.

Elafiti Islands *p282*

Ferry

Jadrolinija (contact Dubrovnik office, T020-418000 for information) run several ferries daily between Gruž harbour in **Dubrovnik** and **Luka Šipanska** (total 1¾ hrs), with boats stopping at Koločep (25 mins), Lopud (50 mins) and Sudjuradj (1 hr 10 mins) en route. Through summer (Jun-Sep), Nova (Sv Križa 3, T020-313599) run high-speed boats from Dubrovnik to the Elafiti islands (Koločep, Lopud and Šipan), foot passengers only.

Cavtat *p283*

Air

Cavtat is just 2 km from Dubrovnik airport.

Bus

The town is connected to **Dubrovnik** by an hourly bus (40 mins).

Ferry

Through summer, water taxis shuttle tourists back and forth between Cavtat and Dubrovnik (40 mins). Expect to pay 50Kn one-way. **Nova** (Sv Križa 3, T020-313599) also run high-speed boats between Dubrovnik to Cavtat (Jun-Sep).

Directory

Dubrovnik and around *p272, map p277*

Banks There are banks with ATMs on the Placa, and close to the bus station and ferry port, and inside the airport. **Consulates** Netherlands, Od Svetog Mihalja 1, T020-356141; **UK**, Buničeva Poljana 3, T020- 324597. **Emergencies** Ambulance 94; Fire 93; Police 92. **Internet** Dubrovnik Internet Club, Dr Ante Starčevića 7, T020-416703; **Netcafe**, Prijeko 21, in the old town, T020- 321025. **Medical services** General Hospital, Roka Mišetića bb, T020-431777 (24-hr casualty). **Pharmacies**: marked by a glowing green cross; **Gruž** at Gruška obala (T020- 418990) and Kod Zvonika on Stradun (T020-321133) alternate as 24-hr pharmacies. **Post offices** The main post office is at Put Republike 32, close to the bus station, Mon-Fri 0800-2100. The most central post offices are at Široka 8, in the old town, Mon-Fri 0800-1500, and Dr Ante Starčevića 2, just outside the city walls, opposite Pile Gate, Mon-Fri 0800-1500. **Telephones** It is possible to make calls from either of the above post offices, or from the blue public phone kiosks dotted round town.

Pelješac Peninsula

→ *Colour map 4, B1/B2. 46 km northwest of Dubrovnik.*

Forking out from the mainland, this long, skinny mountainous peninsula stretches almost 90 km from end to end. High above the coast, a single road runs its entire length, linking a succession of pretty hamlets and offering fine views out over the sea, with the islands of Mljet, Lastovo and Korčula clearly visible in the distance. In the past, fear of pirates meant that most settlements developed on the south-facing slopes, and it was only from the 18th century onwards that any sizeable villages grew up along the coast. Today, its relative lack of development and isolation from the mainland give Pelješac something of an island identity, and most Croatians know it purely for its red wines – Postup *and* Dingač *– which are truly excellent and can be tasted at some of the larger vineyards, which open their cellars to the public throughout the summer. However, many visitors travelling by bus between Dubrovnik and Korčula pass straight over Pelješac, missing out on its wine cellars, as well as its two most charming seaside towns, Ston and Orebić.* ▸▸ *For Sleeping, Eating and other listings, see pages 294-295.*

Ins and outs

Two buses daily, one from Korčula Town and the other from Orebić, run the length of the peninsula on their way to Dubrovnik. There is no separate local service. There is a **tourist office** ⓘ *Trg Mimbeli bb, T/F020-713718*, in Orebić and another at Ston. ▸▸ *See Transport, page 295, for further details.*

Orebić

▸▸ *pp294-295. Colour map 4, B1/C2.*

→ *Phone code: 020. Population: 1949.*

Close to the western tip of Pelješac Peninsula, Orebić is linked to Ston by a 67-km road, which runs much of its length high above the coast, passing through the local vineyards. It's become Pelješac's top resort, thanks to its fine beaches and attractive seafront. In the past, it produced many able sea captains, and when they retired they built villas here, which you can still see today, with gardens of palm, orange, lemon and almond trees. The town is protected from the cold *bura* wind by the dramatic heights of Sv Ilija Hill (961 m), whose south-facing slopes are dotted with pinewoods, cypresses and agaves. From here it's just 2 km across the Pelješki Kanal (Pelješac Channel) to the island of Korčula: the two coasts are linked by a regular ferry service, making it possible for the people of Orebić to pop over to Korčula for an evening out. For more information, visit the **tourist office** ⓘ *Trg Mimbeli bb, T020-713718, www.tz-orebic.com.*

Background

The town took the name Orebić, after a family of local sea captains, during the 16th century; before this date it had been known as Trstenica. As part of the Republic of Dubrovnik it was governed by a local rector and had very restricted dealings with neighbouring Korčula, which was at that time under Venice.

The town's greatest period of prosperity began in 1865, when locals founded their own shipping company, Associazione Marittima di Sabioncello (AMS). It had 33 impressive wooden sailing ships (each with a Biblical name from the Old Testament) and covered sea routes all the way to North America. However, it was a short-lived affair; it closed down in 1887, when steamers began replacing wind-driven ships.

Today, thanks to its pleasant climate and south-facing beaches, Orebić lives primarily from tourism. It makes a cheap alternative to the more upmarket resort of Korčula Town, with which it is connected by a frequent ferry service.

Sights

A pleasant walk up a winding road lined with cypresses brings you to the charming Gothic-Renaissance **Franjevačka Samostan** (Franciscan Monastery) ⓘ *T020-713075, summer Mon-Sat 0900-1200 and 1600-1900, Sun 1600-1900, winter upon request, 15Kn*, perched on a craggy cliff 152 m above the sea, 2 km west of Orebić. It was built in the late 15th century by Franciscan monks, who chose this site for its vista onto the sea channel and surrounding islands. At that time nearby Korčula was under Dubrovnik's arch-rival, Venice. The monks constructed a loggia and terrace, which they used as a vantage point to spy on Venetian galleys; at the first sign of trouble they would send a warning to Dubrovnik by mounted messenger. 'Friendly' ships would let out three blasts of the siren as they passed below the monastery, to which the Franciscans would reply with a peal of the church bells. Inside the monastery you can see a fine collection of religious paintings, notably the *Gospa od Angela* (Our Lady of the Angels), a Byzantine icon apparently washed up by the sea and said to protect sailors from shipwreck. There are also 20 or so votive paintings dedicated to the icon, commissioned by local seamen who survived danger on the ocean.

Set in a typical old stone villa with a courtyard garden, the small **Pomorski Muzej** (Maritime Museum) ⓘ *Trg Mimbeli 12, T020-713009, Jun-Aug daily 0900-1200, 1700-2000*, displays maps, pictures of ships and navigational equipment related to Orebić's maritime past.

Nearby **beaches** include Trstenica, a 1500-m stretch of pebble and sand beach, equipped with sunbeds, parasols, showers and a café through summer, about a 15-minute walk east of the port. There is also a nearby nudist beach called Ostupa.

The **Podrum Bartulovića** ⓘ *Prizdrina, T020-742346, Easter to late Oct 0900-1900, on road between Ston and Orebić*, is a welcoming, family-run wine cellar and shop offering wine-tasting sessions accompanied by *pršut* (ham), *sir* (cheese) and *slane srdele* (salt sardines) in a beautifully restored traditional *konoba*. If you call in advance they can arrange something more substantial than these snacks. Wine Tasting Evenings, run by the locally based **Orebić Tours** ⓘ *T020-713367, www.orebic-tours.hr*, are held here. Otherwise catch a local bus.

Alternatively, **Matuško Vina** ⓘ *Potomje, T020-742393, Jun-Sep daily 0700-2000, Oct-May daily 0700-1700*, functions purely as a shop, stocking a range of red wines from Pelješac and whites from Korčula, with tasting sessions available upon request.

Ston

» *pp294-295. Colour map 4, B2.*

→ *Phone code: 020. Population: 693. 8 km along Pelješac Peninsula and 54 km northwest of Dubrovnik.*

This fortified settlement is made up of two towns, Veli Ston and Mali Ston. It was founded when Dubrovnik took control of Pelješac in 1333, and soon became the

Pelješac wines

On Pelješac Peninsula, a single grape variety, *Plavac Mali*, produces three different red wines depending on the soil and topography of the vineyards where it is grown.

The most highly esteemed Pelješac wine, and arguably Croatia's best, is **Dingač**. This robust red has a high alcohol content (up to 15%) and is produced in very small quantities (about 200,000 bottles annually), hence the considerable prices it commands. The Dingač vineyards are located on the southwest-facing seaward slopes close to the village of Potomje and are accessed through a 400-m tunnel (before the tunnel was built, in the 1970s, the people of Potomje had to trek 20 km to reach their fields). With steep gradients of 40° to 60°, these slopes expose the vines to the country's most intense sunshine and, despite the fact that they have been terraced, they are still extremely difficult to work; everything has to be done by hand or donkey as machinery is ill adapted to such terrain. The soil is a deep red clay, and the vines grow very low and close together so as to retain humidity in an area that would otherwise be baked dry by the sun. The climatic conditions of this ecologically pristine area make spraying with pesticides unnecessary so the wine is organic.

Second comes **Postup**, another highly respectable red, which is produced on the seaward slopes southeast of Orebič. Here the terrain is less steep and the clay less red, but once again the use of chemicals is unnecessary.

Last but not least, **Plavac** is a cheaper but quite palatable red that is produced in large quantities on the flat fields of the Pelješac interior. Here the use of pesticides is inevitable, as the distance from the sea and the climate both favour the proliferation of harmful insects.

Republic's second most important centre. Lying on opposite sides of the peninsula, each with its own bay, the two towns are linked by several kilometres of well-preserved walls, effectively controlling land access onto Pelješac. Today Ston is known for oyster (February-May) and mussel (May-September) farming, and most visitors come here especially to eat at one of several excellent (but expensive) seafood restaurants. If you decide to stay overnight, there are a couple of romantic old-fashioned hotels. You can explore the area in a few hours; from Veli Ston, Mali Ston is a 15-minute walk over the hill. There's also a **seasonal tourist office** ① *Pelješki put 1, T020-754452, www.ston.hr.*

Sights

Between 1333 and 1506, under the auspices of great Dubrovnik architects such as Paskoje Miličević (who designed the Sponza Palace, see page 277), the two towns were each individually fortified and then connected by a further fortification system, to produce one of the most interesting defence structures on the Adriatic. Originally there was a total 5.5-km of **walls** observed by 40 **towers**; today, 3 km of walls and 20 towers remain.

On the south side of the peninsula, facing onto Stonski Kanal, **Veli Ston** is surrounded by walls forming an irregular pentagon, stretching from the coast up the hillside above town. Within the fortifications, Gothic and Renaissance buildings from the 14th and 15th centuries are laid out on a formal grid, and include the former Rector's Palace, the Bishop's Palace and a Franciscan Monastery. The monastery complex centres on a pretty 14th-century Gothic-Renaissance cloister and the Romanesque-Gothic church of **St Nicholas**, containing works of art such as a large painted crucifix by Blaž Jurjev Trogiranin (1412-1448) and a Gothic wooden statue of St Nicholas. There are no official opening hours, but if you telephone in advance (T020-754474) the nuns are happy to accept visitors. Below town lies an expanse of saltpans, which once covered more than 400 sq km and provided the Republic of Dubrovnik with one-third of its annual revenue.

Perched on a hilltop west of Veli Ston, the interior of the tiny pre-Romanesque church of **Sv Mihajlo** (St Michael), is decorated with 12th-century frescoes. It's kept locked, but if you ask at the tourist office they will give you the key.

The smaller twin town of **Mali Ston**, 1 km northeast of Veli Ston, on the north side of the peninsula can be reached in 15 minutes on foot, following the walls. It's a compact settlement of old stone houses laid out on a grid pattern and enclosed within rectangular ramparts, with a pleasant harbour front where you'll find several eateries serving locally grown oysters and mussels. The long narrow channel of Malostonski Zaljev, between the mainland and the peninsula, contains a mix of freshwater (from the River Neretva) and saltwater, ideal for cultivating shellfish. **Fort Koruna**, built on the hillside above town in 1347, offers great views over the channel.

The best place for swimming is **Prapratna Uvala**, where there's a pleasant pebble beach backed by olive trees, 3 km from Veli Ston.

Sleeping

Orebić *p291*

B **Grand Hotel Orebić**, Kralja Petra Krešimira IV 107, T020-798000, www.grandhotelorebic.com. Formerly known as the **Hotel Rathaneum**, this hotel reopened in May 2007 following a complete renovation. Overlooking the sea, with a small beach out front, it is a 10-min walk along the coastal path from town. The 203 rooms are smartly furnished, and most have balconies and a sea view. Facilities include a gym, and bicycles, canoes and surf boards for rent. Open Apr-Oct.

B **Hotel Indijan**, Škvar 2, T020-714555, www.hotelindijan.hr. This classy, family-run hotel which opened in 2007, overlooks the beach in the centre of Orebić. Combining traditional and modern architecture, it has 17 rooms and 2 suites, with pale-wood furniture and wooden floors. Facilities include a restaurant with a palm-lined terrace, a lounge-bar, an indoor pool and a sauna. Open all year.

Private accommodation

The following agencies can help you find rooms and apartments to rent: **Dubrovnik Travel**, Obala Stjepana Radića 25, Dubrovnik, T020-313555, www.dubrovniktravel.hr; and **Orebić Tours**, Bana Jelacica 84A, Orebić, T020-713367, www.orebic-tours.hr. Or you can check out www.dubrovnik-online.com.

Ston *p292*

B **Hotel Ostrea**, Mali Ston, T020-754556, www.ostrea.hr. This former mill has been restored to form a small luxury hotel, with 9 rooms and 1 suite, all with parquet flooring and antique furniture. Through summer, breakfast is served on a pleasant terrace. Open all year.

Eating

Orebić *p291*

Mlinica, Joza Šunja bb, T020-713886. Occupying an old mill, this popular *konoba* specializes in meals prepared under a *peka*, which need to be ordered a day in advance, though more simple dishes can be eaten without prior notice. Open for dinner only, May-Oct.

Pelješki Dvor, Obala pomoraca 28, close to the tourist office, T020-713329. Barbecued meat and seafood dishes are served all day in a sunny garden or indoors at heavy wooden tables and benches. Open Apr-Oct.

Restoran Vrgorac, Perna 24, Kućište, T020-719152. Situated 4 km west of Orebić, on the road for Vinganj, this family-run restaurant offers good home cooking and a cosy atmosphere. Favourite dishes include *brodet* (fish stew) and *punjene paprike* (stuffed peppers). Closed Dec-Jan.

Ston *p292*

Bota, Mali Ston bb, T020-754482. Occupying the 14th-century salt warehouse, this restaurant is recommended for locally grown shellfish. If you have a sweet tooth, round off with the *stonski makaruli*, a bizarre local pudding made from pasta, nuts, sugar and cinnamon baked in a pastry crust.

Kapetanova Kuća, Mali Ston, T020-754 264. This highly regarded restaurant draws connoisseurs from all over Croatia. The house speciality is fresh oysters, but there's also a good choice of seafood risotto and pasta dishes, plus fresh fish. It's run by the same family that own the nearby **Hotel Ostrea**.

Festivals and events

Ston *p292*

Jul-Aug Ston Summer Festival, late Jul to late Aug. Open-air evening music and theatre in the centre of Veli Ston, given partial coverage by Croatian television.

Activities and tours

Orebić *p291*

Diving

Adriatic, Mokalo 6, T020-714328, www.adriatic-mikulic.com, 15-min drive east of Orebić. Scuba-diving tours and tuition.

Hiking

A well-marked footpath leads from the Franciscan Monastery up to the peak of Sv Ilija (walking time 3 hrs) offering stunning views across the channel to Korčula and beyond – on a clear day it's even possible to see Italy.

Transport

Orebić *p291*

Bus

An early morning bus leaves from Orebić to **Dubrovnik** (Mon-Fri 0500, 3 hrs); if you miss it, you can still catch the bus from Korčula Town to Dubrovnik, which passes through Orebić around 0720 daily.

Ferry

Regular ferries connect Orebić to the nearby island of Korčula, 15 mins (see Transport, page 304, for details).

Ston *p292*

Bus

There are 2 buses daily from Ston to **Dubrovnik**, 1 hr 40 mins, 1 early morning and the other at midday. Likewise, 2 buses daily run the route from Ston to **Orebić**, 1 hr 20 mins, 1 early morning and the other mid-afternoon.

Island of Korčula

This long, skinny island is green and hilly, with some of the steeper north-facing slopes covered with dense pine forests. The coastline is rocky and indented, with several small coves on the south side offering secluded pebble beaches. People from the seaside towns and villages live mainly from fishing and tourism, while those from the inland settlements cultivate vineyards and olive groves to produce quality white wine and olive oil. ▸▸ *For Sleeping, Eating and other listings, see pages 301-305.*

Ins and outs

Getting there The island is connected to Split on the mainland by a once-daily catamaran service, and a once-daily ferry service, both running to Vela Luka. In addition, there are several ferries daily from Orebić on Pelješac Peninsula to Dominče (2 km from Korčula Town), and from Orebić to Korčula Town (foot passengers only). A once-daily bus service runs from Dubrovnik to Korčula Town. ▸▸ *See Transport, page 304, for further details.*

Getting around From Monday to Friday, five local buses run the length of the island, 32 km long and 8 km across at its widest point, from Korčula Town to Vela Luka, stopping at Smokvice, Čara and Blato en route.

 Tourist information The **tourist office** ⓘ *Obala Dr Franje Tudjmana bb, T020-715 701,* www.korcula.net, is housed in the 16th-century loggia on the seafront next to **Hotel Korčula,** in Korčula Town.

Background

Korčula was once covered with dense pine forest, leading the ancient Greeks to call it *Kerkyra Melaina* (Black Corfu). In fact, it had been inhabited in Neolithic times, as early as 6500 BC, as finds from Vela Spilja (Big Cave) in Vela Luka prove. The first Greeks to arrive were from Cnidos (on the Aegean coast in present-day southwest Turkey), and it seems they lived in relative peace with the local Illyrian tribes, neither attempting to conquer nor assimilate them, but sharing land rights with them, as recorded by a stone inscription from the fourth century BC found in Lumbarda.

Between the 10th and 18th centuries the island came under Venice several times, and with arch-rivals the Republic of Dubrovnik and the Ottoman Empire in close proximity, La Serenissima (see page 320) did all it could to fortify and defend its main base here, the tiny yet culturally advanced Korčula Town. During the 13th century, the legendary Venetian explorer, Marco Polo, made history with his epic journeys through the Orient. Historians are undecided as to where he originated from, but many believe he was born in Korčula Town, and an old stone building open to the public is said to have been his family home. Other attractions include a medieval sword dance (known as the *Moreška* in Korčula Town and the *Kumpanjija* in Blato), which is performed regularly through summer for tourists, plus a selection of excellent local white wines, *Grk* from Lumbarda and *Pošip* from the inland villages of Smokvica and Čara.

Finally, there is an interesting British connection. Fitzroy Maclean of Dunconnel (1911-1996), the Scottish politician, soldier, adventurer and writer, had a house in Korčula Town, the only property owned by a foreigner in former Yugoslavia. During the Second World War, as a member of the SAS, Maclean was parachuted into various parts of Dalmatia and Bosnia, and acted as Churchill's personal envoy at meetings between Tito (then head of the partisan movement) and representatives of the royalist Yugoslav government in exile, which took place on the island of Vis (see page 262), in summer 1944. Later he served as the key link between Tito and the British and American governments, levering support for the Yugoslav state. Maclean and his adventures are said to have inspired Ian Fleming's *James Bond* novels.

Korčula Town

» pp301-305. Colour map 4, inset.

→ *Phone code: 020. Population: 3126.*

On the northeast coast of the island, medieval Korčula Town is often referred to as a 'mini-Dubrovnik'. A compact cluster of terracotta-roofed houses perched graciously

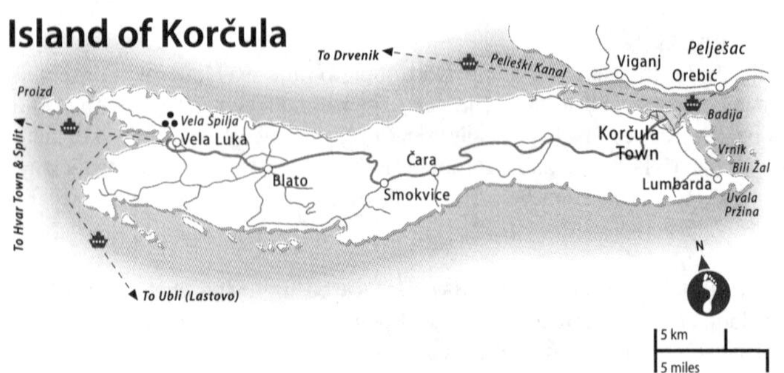

above the sea on a peninsula fortified with walls and round towers, the same elements are here, but concentrated into a far smaller space, no more than the size of a modern football stadium. The town is backed by hills covered with pinewoods, and faces onto a narrow sea channel offering views of the tall mountainous peaks of Pelješac in the distance. Large modern hotels have been built a short distance from centre, leaving the historic core as an open-air museum and making Korčula one of the most popular resorts on the islands, second only to Hvar. The main cultural attraction is the *Moreška*, a medieval sword dance performed in the old town on summer evenings.

Background

Legend has it that Korčula was founded by the Trojan hero Antenor in the 12th century BC, though there is no material evidence to back up such claims. The Venetians arrived here during the 10th century and came and went several times over the next 800 years, their final and most significant period of dominance being 1420-1797. The buildings they left behind are comparable to those in *La Serenissima* itself: Jan Morris, in *The Venetian Empire*, refers to Korčula as "one of the most Venetian of all its [Venice's] sea ports".

Korčula grew up as an extraordinarily compact settlement, built on a small but strategically important peninsula, controlling the passage of ships through the 1270-m-wide Pelješki Kanal (Pelješac Channel) between the island and the mainland. It was walled in the 13th century, further fortified during the 15th and, for defence reasons, dwellings were not permitted beyond the medieval perimeter until the 18th century. Extremely advanced for its time, a town statute was written in 1214, laying down strict rules about communal life, urban layout and human values (for example, slavery was banned). The most important period of artistic development, during the 15th and 16th centuries, bequeathed the town with many fine Gothic and Renaissance buildings, and Korčula became renowned for its skilled stone masons (notably members of the Andrijić family) and the high quality of its stone, quarried on the nearby island of Vrnik (which was also used on Diocletian's ancient Roman palace in Split, see page 201, and the sixth-century Byzantine Hagia Sofia in Constantinople). At its peak, in the early 16th century, the town accommodated around 6000 inhabitants, but the population was seriously depleted by the plague in 1529.

The first hotel opened in 1912, under Austro-Hungary, attracting European gentry and intellectuals. During the 1970s, larger hotels were constructed on the edge of town, and Korčula entered the commercial market.

Sights

Close to the main ferry quay, **Kopnena Vrata** (Land Gate) is the principal entrance to the old town. A sweeping flight of steps leads up to the 15th-century **Revelin Tower**, a crenellated quadrangular structure forming an arched gateway into the historic centre. A plaque bearing a relief of the winged Lion of St Mark, the symbol of Venice, is mounted above the arch. From here, Korčulanskog Statuta runs the length of the tiny peninsula, with narrow streets branching off at odd angles to form a herring-bone pattern, ingeniously preventing local winds from blowing through the heart of town. Through summer, the *Moreška* sword dance is performed in a walled garden to the left of the Land Gate. The old town is small and compact and can be explored in an hour or so, though you will need more time to check out the museums.

Built of warm yellow-grey stone, Korčula's much-admired Gothic-Renaissance **Katedrala Sv Marka** (Cathedral of St Mark) ⓘ *Strossmayerov Trg, summer daily*

The town claims to have been the birthplace of the great discoverer, Marco Polo; this may be true, as the Venetians recruited many sea captains from Dalmatia.

 0900-1400, 1700-2000, winter by appointment, opens out on to Strossmayerov Trg, the main square, in the heart of the old town. The Romanesque portal, by Bonino of Milano in 1412 (also responsible for the Chapel of St Domnius in Split Cathedral), is flanked by finely carved figures of Adam and Eve and topped with a statue of St Mark. The composition of the façade is completed with a central rose window. Inside, above the main altar stands a 15th-century ciborium (a canopy supported by four columns), carved by the local stonemason Marko Andrijic, who introduced the Renaissance style to the city. Beneath the ciborium, on the main altar, a 19th-century gilt sarcophagus holds the relics of St Theodore (the city's protector) brought to Korčula in 1736. Above it, the painting *St Mark with St Bartholomew and St Jerome* is an early work by the esteemed Venetian Mannerist, Tintoretto (1518-1594). In the southern nave you'll find a curious collection of cannon balls and gruesome looking weapons used against the Ottoman Turks. Above them, set in a gold frame, hangs a 13th-century icon, *Our Lady with the Child*, formerly kept in the Franciscan church on the island of Badija. When a Turkish fleet, commanded by the Algerian viceroy Uluz-Ali, attacked the town on 15 August 1571, children and the elderly prayed to the icon for divine intervention. Miraculously, a ferocious storm broke, destroying several galleys and causing others to retreat (they continued up the coast and went on to devastate Hvar instead). Also in the southern nave is an *Annunciation* attributed to Tintoretto, while in the apse, a painting above the altar depicting the *Holy Trinity* is the work of another Venetian artist, Leandro Bassano (1557-1622).

Next door to the cathedral, on the first floor of the 17th-century Renaissance-baroque Bishop's Palace, is the town treasury, **Opatska Riznica** (Abbey Treasury) ⓘ *Strossmayerov Trg, summer daily 0900-1500 and 1700-2000, winter by appointment, 15Kn*. An impressive collection of icons and religious paintings includes an outstanding polyptych *Our Lady with Saints* by Blaž Jurjev Trogiranin, a prolific Dalmatian painter, also known as Blasius Pictor (1412-1448). Other objects on display are gold and silver chalices, mass vestments (garments worn by the clergy), ancient coins and a necklace donated to Korčula by Mother Theresa, which had been given to her by the town of Calcutta when she won the Nobel Peace prize in 1979.

Opposite the cathedral, the 16th-century Renaissance Gabrielis Palace now houses the **Gradski Muzej** (Town Museum) ⓘ *T020-711420, Nov-Mar Mon-Fri 1000-1300, Apr-Jun Mon-Sat 1030-1400 and 1900-2100, Jul-Sep daily 1030-2100, Oct Mon-Sat 1030-1400, 1900-2100, 10Kn*. Exhibits include a copy of the fourth-century BC Greek *Lumbardska Psefizma* (see page 299), Roman ceramics and a section devoted to local shipbuilding. The building's interior gives some idea of how local aristocrats lived between the 16th and 17th centuries, and on the top floor the old kitchen is replete with stone pots and cookery utensils from that era.

Tucked away in a side street in the southeast part of the old town, the **Galerija Ikona** (Ikon Museum) ⓘ *Trg Svih Svetih, summer daily 1000-1300, 1800-2000, winter closed, 10Kn*, contains a display of Cretan School icons painted between the 14th and 17th centuries. They arrived in Korčula during the Candian Wars (1645-1669), when the town sent a galley to aid the Venetian fleet in its unsuccessful battle against the Turks for the possession of the Greek island of Crete.

Next to the icon gallery stands the **Crkva Svih Svetih** (Church of All Saints) ⓘ *Trg Svih Svetih, summer daily 1000-1300, 1800-2000, winter closed*. It was founded in the 13th century, making it the town's first parish church, though its present appearance dates from 300 or 400 years later. Inside, to the right of the altar is a polyptych *Our Lady the Co-redeemer* by Blaž Jurjev Trogiranin, and to the left hangs a large 15th-century Cretan crucifix, a magnificent combination of wood-engraving, painting and gilding. The coffered ceiling is decorated with biblical scenes by the Dalmatian baroque painter Tripo Kokolja (1661-1713).

Northeast of the main square, behind the cathedral, stand the modest home and watchtower of the Depolo family, **Kuća Marca Pola** (Marco Polo House) ⓘ *Jul-Aug*

Tales of the East

Tales of the exotic landscapes and highly refined lifestyles of the Orient first arrived in medieval Europe through *The Travels of Marco Polo*, a best-selling travelogue of its time, which later inspired Christopher Columbus and Vasco da Gama in their voyages of discovery.

At the age of 17, Polo (1254-1324), accompanied by his father and uncle, both of whom were Venetian merchants, travelled overland to China along the Silk Route, passing through the mountains and deserts of Persia, and then across the Gobi Desert, to arrive, three years later, at the court of the great Mongol Emperor Kublai Khan.

Polo entered the Emperor's diplomatic service, acting as his agent on missions to many parts of the Mongolian Empire for the next 17 years, visiting, or at least gaining extensive knowledge about, Siam (present-day Thailand), Japan, Java, Cochin China (now part of Vietnam), Ceylon (present-day Sri Lanka), Tibet, India and Burma (present-day Myanmar). Some 24 years after their journey began, the Polos returned to Venice, laden with jewels, gold and silk, and eager to recount the extraordinary tales of what they had seen.

In 1298, as a captain in the Venetian fleet, Marco (along with several thousand other sailors) was taken prisoner during a sea battle against the Genoese close to Lumbarda, off the island of Korčula. During a year in prison in Genoa, he dictated the memoirs of his magnificent journeys to a fellow prisoner and romantic novelist, Rusticello of Pisa.

Although the subsequent book met with commercial success, it was heavily criticized for exaggeration and whimsy, and it was only several centuries later, when future travellers to the East were able to confirm Polo's descriptions, that it was regarded as an accurate account (though to this day, the giant birds capable of carrying elephants remain something of an anomaly).

On his deathbed, Polo declared, "I have only told the half of what I saw."

daily 0900-2100, May-Jun, Sep-Oct daily 0900-1900, winter by appointment, 15Kn. Local myth has it that Marco Polo, the legendary 13th-century traveller, was born here, though the present building was constructed several hundred years after his death. However, it's an amusing enough oddity, and is also an ideal point of reference for tracking down the town's best restaurant (see Eating, page 303).

A 10-minute walk west of the centre, along the seafront, brings you to the **Memorial Collection of Maksimilijan Vanka** ① *Put Sv, Nikole bb, summer daily 0900-1200, 1800-2100, winter closed, 10Kn*, the villa-turned-museum of Maksimilijan Vanka's presenting a cross-section of his drawings and paintings and showing his development from art nouveau and expressionism through to constructivism. Vanka (Zagreb 1889-Puerto Vallorta, Mexico 1963) is an important name in modern Croatian painting. He divided his early years between Korčula and Zagreb, where he taught at the Academy of Art. In 1936 he emigrated to the United States; his best known works are the frescoes in the Church of St Nicholas, in Millvale, Pittsburgh.

The main town **beach** is east of the centre, in front of **Hotel Marco Polo**. However, it gets very busy, so you're better off visiting the tiny island of Badija or the neighbouring village of Lumbarda, see below. **Badija**, where a beautiful 14th-century Franciscan monastery has been converted into a residential sports centre (see Sleeping, page 301), is a wooded islet criss-crossed by paths leading to a series of pebble beaches, one reserved for nudists. Through summer, regular taxi boats run to the island from the main ferry harbour (15 minutes).

Lumbarda

» pp301-305. Colour map 4, inset.

→ *Phone code: 020. Population: 1221.*

At the eastern tip of the island, just 6 km southeast of Korčula Town, the tiny village of Lumbarda is best known for its idyllic sand beach and surrounding vineyards, which produce a dry white wine, *Grk*. Today, a narrow road lined with mulberry trees leads from the village through vineyards planted with *Grk* vines, which some experts consider indigenous to Dalmatia, while others, due to its name, conclude that it must have arrived here during ancient times from Greece. Whatever its origin, it grows particularly well in the area's fine reddish sandy soil.

Background

The *Lumbardska Psefizma*, a fourth-century BC inscription carved in stone, was found here. Proof of early Greek settlement on this site, it records a decree regarding land distribution, and includes the names of Greek and Illyrian families living here at the time. Today the original is in the Archaeological Museum in Zagreb, but you can see a copy at the Town Museum in Korčula, see page 298. The settlement was later abandoned, probably due to lack of defence and fear of pirates, but grew up again during the 16th century, as a village of stonecutters and seafarers who quarried and transported stone from the nearby island of Vrnik.

Beaches

There's little of cultural interest here, though the village itself is a pleasant enough place, strung around a north-facing bay, lined with fish restaurants, cafés and rooms to let. Roads through the vineyards criss-cross the eastern tip of the island, bringing you to a number of small family beaches. The island's most popular bathing spot is the south-facing sand beach of **Pržina**, backed by a fast-food kiosk and bar, 2 km south of Lumbarda. A short distance east of Lumbarda, the north-facing beach of **Bili Žal** is made up of white stones beaten smooth by the water, and overlooked by a tumble-down stone building which has been converted into a rustic restaurant. A short distance east of Bili Žal is a rocky stretch reserved for nudists.

Vela Luka

» pp301-305. Colour map 4, inset.

→ *Phone code: 020. Population: 4380.*

Located in a 7-km-long bay at the western end of Korčula, Vela Luka is the second largest settlement on all the Croatian islands, after Mali Lošinj. It's also Korčula's main port, with ferry connections to Split on the mainland and the neighbouring islands of Hvar and Lastovo. It's not a particularly attractive place and there's little of cultural interest, but it has a **tourist office** ⓘ *Ulica 41/broj 11, T020-813619, www.tzvelaluka.hr*, and it makes a good starting point for exploring the island.

Background

Built around a west-facing bay and backed by gently sloping hills, Vela Luka is often referred to as the 'oldest and youngest town on Korčula': the oldest because of prehistoric finds discovered in a nearby cave; the youngest because it only really developed from the 19th century onwards. And while Korčula Town has a somewhat aristocratic past, Dalmatians consider Vela Luka a 'town of fishermen and peasants'. During the 20th century, a couple of small factories opened up here: **Jadranka** sardine canning factory and **Greben** shipyard, both of which are still functioning. The people of Vela Luka are renowned for their fine voices, and the town has a number of *klapa* singing groups. In the 1960s, the Kalos health resort opened in Kale cove, on the north side of the bay, promoting the use of marine mud (called *liman*) for the treatment of rheumatic diseases. Vela Luka's final oddity is its system of marking streets. They are not named, but numbered: Ulica 1, Ulica 2, just like in New York, as locals point out wryly.

Sights

Kulturni Centar (Cultural Centre) ① *T020-813001, summer Mon-Sat 0900-1200, 1800-2200, winter Mon-Fri 0800-1200*, hosts contemporary art exhibitions, as well as having its own collection, including an undated work by the British sculptor Henry Moore (1898-1986). Also on display are prehistoric finds from Vela Spilja.

Located on a hillside 3 km east of town, the **Vela Spilja** (Big Cave) ① *T020-813602, www.vela-spila.hr, summer daily 1700-sunset, 10Kn*, is 53 m long and 20 m high. Finds dating back to 6500 BC, now on display in the Kulturni Centar (see above), prove that it was inhabited in Neolithic times. Klapa concerts, attended by audiences of up to 500, are sometimes held inside the cave. For further information contact the Kulturni Centar.

The main town **beach** is on the north side of the bay, in front of **Hotel Posejdon**. However, the best place for bathing is on the tiny island of Proizd, 6 km away, where you'll find lush vegetation, white-pebble beaches and clear water. There's also an informal eatery, **Restoran Proizd** in Pernana Bay, serving up a choice of seafood and grilled meats.

Blato and the south of the island

» *pp301-305. Colour map 4, inset.*

The inland town of Blato is in a fertile valley on the main road running the length of the island from Vela Luka (7 km) to Korčula Town (38 km). There is nothing on offer for tourists, but it is the economic and administrative centre of the island and the second largest town after Vela Luka. The centre is traversed by a 1-km-long avenue of lime trees, and the oldest part of town is made up of 17th- and 18th-century stone houses, many unfortunately abandoned or empty. Like many other places on the Croatian islands, Blato suffers from depopulation: while the present population stands around 3700, there are now about 15,000 people claiming to originate from Blato living in Sydney, Australia. South of town, a steep winding road (served by a sporadic bus service) leads to the south side of island, where you'll find a number of small but pleasant pebble beaches and several villages, the most popular being **Prižba** and **Prišcapac**, offering rooms to let by the sea.

If you do have to stay here for some time, it's worth taking a peek at the raised piazza, known as **Plokata**, a street back from the main road and overlooked by the 17th-century All Saints' Church. Inside, there is a chapel dedicated to Sv Vincenza (St Vincent, the town's protector), later constructed to house the bones of the saint, which were returned here by the consent of Pope Pius VI (1775-1799). Opposite the church is an open-sided loggia from 1700.

Each year on 28 April, St Vincent's Day, the *Kumpanjija* sword dance (similar to the *Moreška* in Korčula) is performed here (see box, page 302).

Sleeping

Korčula Town *p296*

AL Hotel Marco Polo, Korčula bb, T020-726 100, www.korcula-hotels.com. Korčula's most luxurious hotel, the waterside Marco Polo reopened in 2007 following total renovation. There are 94 smartly furnished rooms (most with sea views), a new outdoor pool and a luxurious Wellness Centre. Open all year.

A Hotel Korčula, Obala bb, T020-711078, www.korcula-hotels.com. Erected in 1871

Fighting feet

The *Moreška* (from *morisco*, meaning 'Moorish' in Spanish) came to Korčula via Italy in the 16th century. It originated in the 12th century in Spain, where it was inspired by the struggle of Spanish Christians against the Moors; on the East Adriatic, it was simply adapted to represent the ongoing fight of local Christians against the Turks.

Over the centuries the text, music and pattern of the dance have been altered and shortened, but the central story remains: Bula, a beautiful Muslim maiden, has been kidnapped by the Black Knight, and her sweetheart, the White Knight, comes to her rescue. The performance begins with the Black Knight (dressed in black) dragging Bula in chains, and the maiden crying out against his amorous proposals. The White Knight (confusingly, dressed in red) then arrives with his army. The two knights hurl insults at one another, then cross their swords, and the dance begins. Their armies are pulled into the confrontation, with soldiers clashing swords in pairs within a circle, to the accompaniment of a brass band. The pace of the music gradually accelerates with the black soldiers facing outwards and the circle contracting as they retreat inwards from the white army. (In the past, performers were often wounded and had to be replaced by reserves during the dance.) Finally, all the black soldiers fall to the ground, the Black Knight surrenders and the White Knight frees Bula from her chains and kisses her.

In the past, various versions of the dance were found throughout the Mediterranean, where they were probably used as much as an exercise for swordsmen as for entertainment. It also reached Northern Europe, and could well be the forerunner to English Morris dancing, where wooden poles are used instead of swords.

and originally used as a café, this building was converted into the island's first hotel in 1912. Today the only hotel in the centre, it has 20 simple but comfortable rooms, a restaurant and a glorious west-facing seafront terrace, ideal for watching the sunset. Open all year.

F **One Love Hostel**, Korčula, T020-716755, www.korculabackpacker.com. In a stone building close to the bus station, this friendly hostel opened in 2005 and scored instant success with young, fun-seeking travellers. It offers 65 beds in dorms, shared washrooms with showers, a bar and internet access.

Private accommodation

Marco Polo Tours, Biline 5, T020-715400, www.korcula.com, is an agency that can help you find accommodation. Alternatively, check out www.korcula.net.

Lumbarda *p300*

D **Hotel Lumbarda**, T020-712700, www.lumbardahotel.com. This modern hotel overlooks the sea and has 43 rooms, each with an en suite bathroom and a balcony, most with sea views. There's a small outdoor pool and a scuba-diving club. Open Jun-Sep.

Private accommodation

Private accommodation is a good option. In Orebić, **Orebić Tours**, Bana Jelačića 84A, T020-713367, www.orebic-tours.hr, can help you find private accommodation. Alternatively, check out www.korcula.net.

Vela Luka *p300*

D **Pločica Lighthouse**, Island of Polčica. Contact **Adriatica Net**, Heinzelova 62a, Zagreb, T01-2415611, www.adriatica.net. Between the islands of Korčula and Hvar, 20 km from Vela Luka, the lighthouse on this tiny island has been converted into 2 apartments, one sleeping 8, the other 6. There is no lighthouse keeper here so guests are totally alone. Scuba-diving trips can be organized upon request.

E **Hotel Dalmacija**, Obala 4/broj 21, T020-812022, www.humhotels.hr. In an old stone building overlooking the ferry quay, this 23-room hotel has a pleasant terrace bar and restaurant out front.

Private accommodation

Split Tours, based in Split, T021-352 553, www.splittours.hr, can help you find private accommodation.

Alternatively, check out the website www.korcula.net.

Eating

Korčula Town *p296*

¥¥¥-¥¥ **Adio Mare**, Svetog Roka, T020-711253. This unforgettable restaurant is in a narrow side street in the old town, close to **Marco Polo House**. It's kept the same down-to-earth menu, including *pašta-fažol* (beans and pasta), *brodet* (fish stew served with polenta) and *pašticada* (beef stewed in *prošek* and prunes, served with gnocchi), since it opened in 1974. There's an open-plan kitchen, so you can watch the cooks at work. It's outrageously popular so reservations are recommended. Open mid-Apr to early Oct, dinner only.

¥¥ **Grubinjac**, Žrnovo bb, T020-711410. In an old stone farm building, on a hill on the road between Korčula and Žrnovo, this rustic family-run eatery offers tasty local dishes and home-made wine, as well as fantastic views down onto the sea.

¥¥ **Morski Konjic**, Stari Grad 47a, T020-711642. Located in the old town, practically on the tip of the peninsula, this tiny eatery serves up delicious *punjene paprika* (stuffed peppers) and a limited range of meat and fish dishes. There are just a couple of tables inside, and 6 outside, so you may have wait for a seat. Open May-Oct, dinner only.

¥¥ **Ranč Maha**, Žrnovo, T098-494389. This small agrotourism centre occupies a stone building near the rural village of Žrnovo, and serves home-made food and wine. Open all year (weekends only during winter).

¥ **Planjak**, Plokata 19 Travnja 1914 bb, T020-711015. Friendly and totally unpretentious, **Planjak** is popular with both locals and visitors, and stays open all year. Tables are set out on a shaded terrace overlooking a small square behind the port. The menu features standard Balkan fare such as *frigane lignje* (fried squid), *ražnići* (kebabs) and *palačinke* (pancakes).

Lumbarda *p300*

¥¥ **Konoba Zure**, Lumbarda 239, T020-712008. Everything on offer at this family-run restaurant is home-made; there's no fixed menu (the choice changes from day to day) but you can look forward to delights such as octopus stew and lobster with spaghetti, and a plentiful supply of the locally produced *Grk*. Guests sit at wooden tables in a walled garden, and are offered a complimentary glass of *travarica* upon arrival. Open Apr-Dec.

Vela Luka *p300*

¥¥-¥ **Feral**, Obala 2 bb, T020-813045. This friendly, informal fish restaurant serves fresh mussels and oysters from Pelješac, as well as a choice of pasta, risotto and fish dishes. It's popular with locals, and although there's no terrace the open-sided 1st-floor dining room is light and airy and offers views over the bay. Open Jun-Sep.

¥¥-¥ **Hotel Dalmacija**, listed above, has a good restaurant.

Blato and the south of the island *p301*

¥¥ **Zlinje**, 1 street back from the main road, close to Plokata, T020-851323. From the street, an arched gateway leads to this traditional *konoba* with a flagstone floor and heavy wooden furniture. The menu features a range of barbecued meat and fish dishes, but you might come here solely to taste quality local wines: reds from Pelješac and whites from Korčula, as well as *rakija* made from carob and walnut, all of which are on sale in presentation boxes. It stays open the year through.

Bars and clubs

Korčula Town *p296*

Cocktail Bar Massimo, Šetalište Petra Kanavelića bb, T020-715073. In the old town fortifications, inside the Tiepolo Tower on the

For an explanation of the sleeping and eating price codes used in this guide, see inside the front cover. Other relevant information is found in Essentials, pages 32-40.

tip of the peninsula, this bar is famed for its splendid sunset views over the sea. May-Oct.

Festivals and events

Korčula Town *p296*

May-Oct Moreška is a traditional sword dance performed at 2100 each Mon and Thu, next to the Kopnena Vrata (Land Gate). Tickets cost 80Kn and are available from travel agencies and hotel receptions around town.

29 Jul Dan Grada (St Theodore's Day). A local holiday celebrated by mass in the cathedral and an evening performance of the *Moreška* sword dance.

Vela Luka *p300*

24 Jun Annual rowing competition, regatta in honour of St John. Competitors row from Gradine to Vela Luka (3 km). In recent years the competition has attracted about 25 boats and 2000 spectators.

Aug Summer Klapa Festival, twice weekly evening *klapa* concerts on the square in front of the 19th-century parish church, set back a short distance from the seafront.

Activities and tours

Korčula Town *p296*

Boating

Rent a Djir, Obala Hrvatskih Mornara bb, T020-711908, www.korcula-rent.com. Rent speedboats on a daily basis, as well as cars, mopeds and motorbikes.

Cycling

The surrounding area is reasonably flat and lends itself to biking – Lumbarda is just 6 km away, and there's a pleasant coastal path west of town, leading to several small bays. Bikes are available for hire from **Hotel Marco Polo**.

Sailing

ACI Marina, T020-711661, www.aci-club.hr. Located in a small cove just east of the old town, has 135 berths.

Lumbarda *p300*

Diving

MM Sub, Lumbarda T020-712288, www.mm-sub.hr.

Sailing

Neilson, www.neilson.co.uk. A British charter company with a base in Lumbarda, offers 1-week flotilla sailing, and a 2-week villa-and-flotilla combination with 1 week ashore learning the basics followed by a week aboard a boat. They can also arrange extra activities such as hiking or scuba-diving.

Vela Luka *p300*

Diving

Posejdon Croatia Divers, Hotel Posejdon, Obala 1/42, T020-812066, www.croatiadivers.com. This scuba-diving school runs courses and tours, and also rents motorized rubber dinghies on a daily basis.

Transport

Korčula Town *p296*

Bus

Korčula bus station, T020-711216.

A bus runs the length of the island to Vela Luka, 5 times daily (1½ hrs), stopping at **Smokvice**, **Cara** and **Blato** en route.

A once-daily bus service links Korčula to **Dubrovnik** (3½ hrs), with buses leaving the island at 0630 to arrive in the city around 1000, then departing at 1500 to arrive back at 1830.

Ferry

Jadrolinija, T020-715410, run a regular ferry service, winter 9 times daily, summer 14 times, from **Domince** (2 hrs 10 mins), 2 km from Korčula Town and served by a connecting bus, to **Orebić** on Pelješac Peninsula.

Mediteranska Plovidba, T020-711156, www.medplov.hr, run a passenger service from Korčula Town to **Orebić**, with 10 ferries daily through summer, 5 in winter. The same company also run a once-daily summer service from Korčula to **Drvenik** on the mainland, just south of Makarska. Their boats depart from the quay opposite **Hotel Korčula**.

In summer **G&V Line**,www.gv-line.hr, operate a high-speed catamaran called *Nona Ana*, running from Dubrovnik to Korcula (Mon and Sat only), calling at the island of Mljet en route.

Lumbarda *p300*

Bicycle

You can cycle here from **Korčula Town**, just 6 km away.

Bus
Hourly buses connect Lumbarda and **Korčula Town** (20 mins) during the summer months.

Vela Luka *p300*
Bus
Buses from Vela Luka to **Korčula Town** coincide with boat services. In addition, Mon-Fri, there are 5 buses daily to **Korčula Town**, passing through **Blato**, **Cara** and **Smokvice** en route (1½ hrs).

Ferry
Jadrolinija, T020-812015, operates a once-daily catamaran service, running from **Split** to **Ubli** on the island of Lastovo, stopping at Vela Luka en route. It departs from **Split** for **Lastovo** in the early afternoon, then passes Vela Luka again on the return journey early the following morning (1¾ hrs). The same company also runs a daily ferry service covering the same route, departing Split mid-afternoon (2 hrs 40 mins).

Island of Lastovo

➔ *Phone code: 020. Colour map 4, inset. Population: 835. 80 km southeast of Split and 80 km west of Dubrovnik.*

This is Croatia's second most isolated inhabited island (after Vis). Because of its remoteness it was chosen, like Vis, as a Yugoslav military base, and therefore closed to foreigners from 1976 to 1989. Fortunately this blocked all commercial tourist development and today it is undoubtedly one of the most unspoilt islands on the Adriatic, with dense pinewoods punctuated by meticulously cultivated farmland, an indented coastline with several sheltered bays, and only one true settlement, the charming semi-abandoned Lastovo Town, made up of old stone houses built prior to the turn of the 20th century.

Today, despite a serious problem of depopulation, life goes on. If you visit in springtime you'll see a veritable troop of elderly women (plus the occasional donkey) hard at work in the fields. Lastovo is self-sufficient in fruit and vegetables even though only 35% of potential farmland is currently under cultivation. A network of footpaths criss-cross the island, passing through fields, woods and lush vegetation scented with sage, rosemary and mint, making walking a pleasurable pursuit. The islanders will assure you that there are no poisonous snakes – according to local myth, several centuries ago a priest saw an adder here and cursed it, after which all the island's snakes threw themselves into the sea. ⏩ *For Sleeping, Eating and other listings, see pages 307-308.*

Ins and outs

A fast catamaran service to the mainland has been set up, which is subsidized by the Croatian government. Although Lastovo comes under Dubrovnik county council administration, the islanders requested a connection with Split instead, so it's now physically linked to Central Dalmatia, though it's geographically part of South Dalmatia. A sporadic bus service runs from one end of the island to the other. The **tourist office** ⓘ *T020-801018, www.lastovo-tz.net*, is opposite the bus stop on the hill above.

Lastovo Town ⏩ *See Transport, page 308, for further details.*

Background

First settled by Illyrians, the island was known to the ancient Greeks and Romans as Ladesta. Archaeological digs have unearthed fragments of ceramic vessels, proving early trade links between the Illyrians and Greeks from the island of Vis, and the remains of Roman *villae rusticae* from the first century. The first important reference to the island dates from the year 1000, when the Doge of Venice, Pietro Oreolo II, ordered the burning of the wooden houses of Lastovo, following a series of raids on Venetian merchant ships. It seems the islanders lived primarily from piracy, and with several concealed harbours ideal for hiding ships they had a perfect base However, over the next two centuries, they gave up villainous activity on the high seas and turned to the more peaceful activity of farming – the land on Lastovo is exceptionally fertile and the *polje* (fields) in the flat valley bottoms lend themselves to the cultivation of vines and olives, as well as a variety of seasonal fruit and vegetables.

In 1252 the island chose to unite with Dubrovnik, though it kept its own administration for a couple of centuries longer. The town statute, written in 1310, included a number of unusual laws: people from Hvar were banned from the island and 'foreigners' were allowed to stay for a maximum of eight days. In 1486 the Republic of Dubrovnik pressurized Lastovo into giving up its autonomy, and immediately imposed heavy taxes, compulsory military service and even built a prison. By 1602 the situation had become so bad that the islanders staged a revolt and sent an envoy to Venice, asking for assistance against the republic. Venice subsequently occupied the island in 1603, but handed it back to Dubrovnik in 1606. Lastovo's history then followed the course of the rest of the republic up until the end of the First World War, when it was awarded to Italy (along with Istria, Zadar and the islands of Cres and Lošinj). Under the Italian name of Lagosta, the economy improved and the population increased, peaking at 1940 in 1936. Many of the older islanders still speak good Italian, as it was the official language until Lastovo was reunited with the rest of Yugoslavia in 1947.

Ubli

Ubli, an insignificant cluster of modern buildings and the island's main ferry port, is on the south coast. Founded by Mussolini as a fishing village in 1936, when the island was under Italy, it was initially populated with fishermen from Istria. However, after just one year they packed up and left, so Il Duce sent a community of Italians from the island of Ponza, instead. There's nothing much to see, but from here a pleasant 3-km coastal road leads to Uvala Pasadur (Pasadur Bay), where you'll find the island's only hotel.

Lastovo Town

→ *10 km northeast of Ubli and about 1 km inland from the north coast, Lastovo Town is 86 m above sea level.*

This once wealthy community is made up of closely packed old stone houses, built into a south-facing slope, forming an amphitheatre-like space focusing on carefully tended allotment gardens in the fertile valley below. The buildings date from the 15th century onwards (before which they would have been wooden) and are noted for their unusual chimneys, strangely similar to minarets. A series of steep cobbled paths wind their way between the houses, and to the east side of town stand the 15th-century parish church of Sv Kuzme i Sv Damjana (St Cossimo and St Damian) and a pretty open-sided loggia. Above town, perched on a triangular hill known as Glavica, is Kašćel, a fortress erected by the French in 1810, now used as a meteorological station and worth the climb up for its breathtaking views.

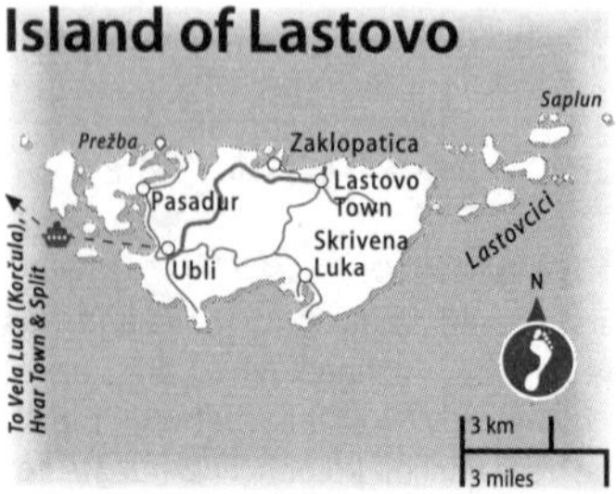

The coast

There are three north-facing bays within walking distance of town: **Lučica** (1 km), a tiny harbour made up of a dozen or

Island of Lastovo

so old stone fisherman's cottages, most of which have been restored and are now used as holiday homes; **Sv Mihovil** (1.5 km), where you'll find a large quay suitable for yachts, a summer bar and open-air disco by the water's edge, and the tiny 14th-century chapel of Sv Mihovil (St Micheal); and **Zaklopatica** (3 km), a large sheltered harbour, popular with yachters, overlooked by a string of modern summer houses and a good fish restaurant. In addition, a 7-km walk south of Lastovo Town will bring you to **Skrivena Luka**, called 'hidden bay' as it cannot be seen from the sea. A 3-km road runs the perimeter of the bay, passing a number of simple holiday cottages and a few summer restaurants, and the entrance to the bay is capped by a lighthouse, available for rent on a weekly basis (see Sleeping, below).

If you want to **swim**, the closest place to Lastovo Town is the bay of **Sv Mihovil**, where there's a large concrete quay offering easy access to the water and a rocky coastal strip shaded by pinewoods. Better still, throughout summer locals transport visitors by boat to the Lastovcici (an archipelago of over 40 islets lying northeast of Lastovo) usually stopping at the tiny uninhabited island of Saplun where there's a secluded cove with a blissful sand beach.

Sleeping

Island of Lastovo *p305*

D Hotel Solitudo, Ulava Pasadur bb, 3 km north of Ubli, T020-802100. Confusingly also known as **Hotel Ladesta**, this modern 68-room hotel is backed by pinewoods and is opposite the small island of Prežba, linked to Lastovo by a bridge. Under renovation since 2001, work has yet to be completed, though it is open to guests. Has a restaurant, bar, diving centre and a small marina. Open all year.

D Struga Lighthouse, Lastovo. Contact **Adriatica Net**, Heinzelova 62a, Zagreb, T01-2415611, www.adriatica.net. Perched 70 m above the sea, on a peninsula at the entrance into Skrivena Luka, this lighthouse dating from 1839 has been converted into 2 apartments, 1 sleeping 6, the other sleeping 4. It is about 7 km from Latsovo Town and can be reached by a rough track.

D Sušac Lighthouse, island of Sušac, 21 km west of Lastovo and 37 km south of Hva. This uninhabited island is criss-crossed by footpaths and has several pleasant bays for bathing. The lighthouse, on the edge of a steep cliff offering wonderful views, was built in 1878 and has been converted into 2 apartments, each sleeping 4. To book, contact **Adriatica Net**, Heinzelova 62a, Zagreb, T01-241 5611, www.adriatica.net.

Private accommodation

The tourist office in Lastovo Town can help find rooms and apartments to rent.

Eating

Island of Lastovo *p305*

If you opt for private accommodation outside high season you'll probably be offered the possibility of ½- or full-board, as the island's restaurants shut down for winter.

TTT-TT Konoba Triton, Zaklopatica, Ubli, T020-801161. Unanimously considered the best restaurant on the island, **Triton** is popular with yachters, who moor up directly in front of the summer terrace that has views of Zaklopatica Bay. The owner catches fresh fish daily, and has apartments to rent upstairs.

TT Konoba Bačvara, Počival bb, Lastovo Town, T020-801075. Hidden away in an old stone building in the lower part of town this traditional *konoba* serves up fresh seafood, locally produced vegetables and home-made wine, Jun-Oct.

TT Konoba Malo Lago, Uvala Pasadur bb, Ubli, T020-802100. Part of the **Hotel Solitudo** complex, this restaurant has a summer terrace overlooking Prežba. The menu features fresh fish, lobster and lamb dishes, plus local wine. Like the hotel, it stays open all year.

TT Konoba Portorus, Skrivena Luka, T020-801261. With tables set out on a

For an explanation of the sleeping and eating price codes used in this guide, see inside the front cover. Other relevant information is found in Essentials, pages 32-40.

terrace looking out over the 'hidden bay', this simple eatery attracts people with smaller boats (the water is shallow here), who can moor up outside and hop ashore for a meal.

Bars and clubs

Island of Lastovo *p305*

In the summer, a late night bar and open-air disco overlooking the sea operate in Sv Mihovil Bay, 1.5 km north of Lastovo Town.

Lounge Lizard, opposite the ferry quay, Ubli. A simple bar where locals waiting for a boat meet for early morning coffee or an evening beer.

Mamilo, Lastovo Town. The town's only bar, opposite the bus stop on the hill above town.

Festivals and events

Island of Lastovo *p305*

Feb-Mar Karneval (Carnival), Shrove Tue. Locals make a straw figurine, known as *Poklad*, who is tied to a rope and hoisted up and down the hill in the centre of town 3 times, with fireworks attached to his boots. He is put on a donkey and taken to the square in front of the parish church where he is burnt. The festivities then commence.

Activities and tours

Island of Lastovo *p305*

Diving

Paradise Diving Centre, Pasadur bb, Ubli, T020-805179, www.diving-paradise.net.

Mountain biking

It is possible to rent mountain bikes from the **Lounge Lizard** bar in Ubli, see above.

Sailing

There is a 50-berth marina in front of **Hotel Solitudo**. Yachts can also moor up along the quays in the protected bays of Skrivena Luka and Zaklopatica.

Transport

Island of Lastovo *p305*

Bus

Local These run from **Ubli** to **Lastovo Town** to coincide with incoming and outgoing boat services. During summer, early Jul to mid-Sep, they run all the way to **Skrivena Luka**.

Ferry

Jadrolinija, T020-805175, operate a once-daily catamaran service, running from **Split** on the mainland to **Ubli**, stopping at **Hvar Town** (island of Hvar) and **Vela Luka** (island of Korčula) en route. It departs from Split for Lastovo in the early afternoon, and makes the return journey very early the following morning (2¾ hrs). The same company also run a once-daily ferry service covering the same route. It departs from Split mid- afternoon to arrive in Lastovo in the evening, and makes the return journey very early the following morning (4¾ hrs). In addition, hroughout the summer **G&V Line**, www.gv-line.hr, operate a high-speed catamaran called *Nona Ana*, running from Dubrovnik to Lastovo (Tue and Thu), calling at the island of Mljet en route.

Directory

Island of Lastovo *p305*

Banks There is a bank (but no ATM) opposite the tourist office in Lastovo Town. Mon-Fri 0800-1330.

Island of Mljet

→ *Phone code: 020. Colour map 4, B1/2. Population: 1111. 27 km west of Dubrovnik, 38 km long and 3 km wide (average).*

Mljet, the southernmost of the Croatian islands, is an island of steep rocky slopes and dense pine forests. The western third is a national park and within it is one of the country's most photographed sights: a proud but lonely 12th-century monastery perched on a small island in the middle of an emerald saltwater lake. Through the passing of the centuries, Mljet has remained something of a backwater. No great towns ever grew up here, and today it is home to half a dozen small villages, linked by a single road running the length of the island. Depopulation is a serious problem; the number of people living here has halved over the last 50 years. However, each summer Mljet is rediscovered by a steady flow of nature lovers, discerning travellers and escapists – in recent years visitors include Prince Charles and Steven Spielberg. The island isn't geared towards tourism – most arrive on organized day trips from Dubrovnik, and few remain overnight – but its natural beauty and lack of commercial development make it a wonderful escape for those in search of peace and tranquillity.

▸▸ *For Sleeping, Eating and other listings, see pages 311-312.*

Ins and outs

Getting there To reach the park, if you're arriving in Sobra by ferry from Dubrovnik, take the connecting bus that runs the length of the island and drops visitors directly at the national park headquarters in Pristanište, overlooking Veliko Jezero.

▸▸ *See Transport, page 312, for further details.*

Getting around A bus runs the length of the island to coincide with incoming and outgoing ferries (from Sobra to the national park and back). There is no other service on the island. Within the park visitors can walk or rent bikes to get around.

Tourist information There's a **tourist office** ⓘ *T020-744086*, in Polače, or the National Park Office ⓘ *Pristanište 2, T020-744041, www.np-mljet.hr.*

Background

Scholars of Greek mythology have yet to identify the lost island of Ogygia, where the nymph Calypso seduced Odysseus (Latin Ulysses) on his epic journey back to Ithaca from Troy, as narrated in Homer's *Odyssey*. However, the island of Mljet may well have been home to the nymph's cave, where the Greek hero was held for seven years which passed like seven days.

What we know for certain is that Mljet was originally inhabited by Illyrian pirates, before being taken by the Romans in 35 BC, who used it as a place of exile. Their main base was present-day Polače, where they built a palace (the name Polače is derived from the Croatian *palača*, meaning palace) overlooking Uvala Polače, a deep bay offering safe anchorage to ships during storms.

In 1151, the Kings of Bosnia, who ruled the island during medieval times, gave it to Benedictine monks from Montegargano in Puglia, Italy. They built a monastery on the islet in the middle of a lake at the west end of the island, and from this safe haven exerted feudal power over the islanders, subjecting them to hefty taxes in return for religious enlightenment. As of 1345, Mljet was incorporated into the Republic of Dubrovnik, and governed by a rector who resided in the inland village of Babino Polje.

Mljet National Park

ⓘ 90Kn entry fee can be paid at any one of a number of wooden kiosks within the grounds; if you stay overnight the fee is included in the price of your accommodation.

In 1960 the western third of the island was declared a national park to protect the indigenous forest of Aleppo pines and holm oaks. Covering an area of 31 sq km, the densely forested park centres on two magnificent interconnected saltwater lakes, **Malo Jezero** (Little Lake) and **Veliko Jezero** (Big Lake). From Pristanište, national park boats shuttle visitors back and forth to **Otočić Svete Marije** (St Mary's Islet) with its charming 12th-century **Benedictine Monastery**, in the middle of Veliko Jezero. The church and cloister, now in a poor state of repair, have retained their original Apulian-Romanesque features, though much of the building was reconstructed in Renaissance style in the 16th century. The monks who lived here wielded considerable power until the monastery was dissolved when Dubrovnik fell to Napoleon in 1808. During the Tito years it was used as a hotel, but has since been returned to the Diocese of Dubrovnik, though the ground floor continues to function as a summer restaurant, with tables outside overlooking the lake. There are various rumours about foreign business tycoons wanting to buy the complex, though a sale looks unlikely.

The park is ideal for those who enjoy walking or mountain biking: a network of paths criss-cross their way through the forests, and a 9-km trail runs around the perimeter of the two lakes. Southeast of Veliko Jezero, a steep winding path leads to the highest point within the park, **Montokuc** (253 m), offering great views over Pelješac Peninsula and the island of Korčula to the north. For swimming, the best bathing areas are on **Solominji Rat**, just south of **Mali Most**, the bridge over the channel that connects the two lakes. From the bridge, you can watch the current change direction every six hours, due to the ebb and flow of the tide. **Veliko Jezero** and **Mali Jezero** offer an extended bathing season, the temperature of the water being 4°C warmer than that of the open sea.

It's possible to stay overnight within the park. The prettiest places are undoubtedly **Babine Kuće**, a cluster of old stone houses on the edge of Veliko Jezero, and **Soline**, just south of Veliko Jezero, overlooking the sea channel. However, they offer limited accommodation and if you're here in high season it's far easier to find a place in **Pomena**, where the modern **Hotel Odisej** (see below) overlooks Uvala Pomena (Pomena Bay), just a 15-minute walk from Malo Jezero. Alternatively, **Polače**, where you'll find the tourist office and the remains of a fourth-century Roman palace, has a number of rooms and apartments giving onto Uvala Polače (Polače Bay), a 45-minute walk from Pristanište. Last but not least, the inland village of **Goveđari**, on the hillside behind Veliko Jezero, was built during the late 18th century for workers on the Benedictine estates, and today several houses have been converted into holiday homes.

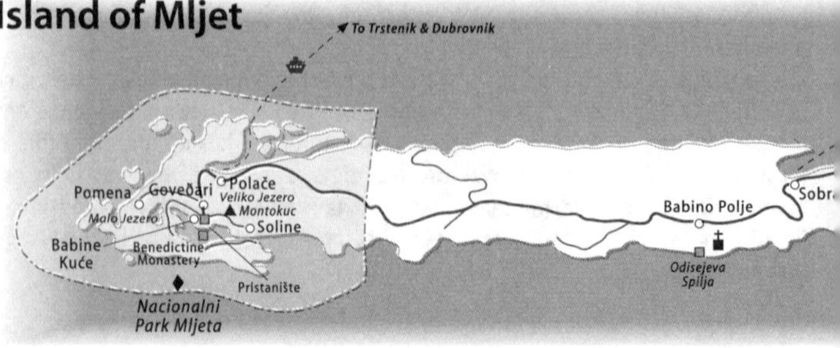

Southern and eastern Mljet

On the southeastern tip of the island **Saplunara** (from the Latin *sabalum* meaning 'sand') is a protected cove with South Dalmatia's most spectacular sand beach. Close by, in a small, scattered settlement of the same name (population 32), several families let rooms and apartments throughout the summer. There are also a handful of down-to-earth seasonal fish restaurants. A 20-minute walk from Saplunara, **Blace**, a 1-km long stretch of sand, faces south onto the open sea and backed by pines, popular with nudists.

On the south coast, below the inland village of Babino Polje, **Odisejeva Spilja** (Odysseus' Cave) is where Odysseus is said to have been held captive by the nymph Calypso. During the summer, **Hotel Odisej** in Pomena organize trips to the cave by boat.

Sleeping

Island of Mljet *p309*

Due to the lack of development, facilities are limited. There is 1 hotel, a limited selection of private accommodation and several waterside restaurants serving fresh lobster, for which the island is renowned.

C-D **Hotel Odisej**, Pomena, T020-362111, www.hotelodisej.hr. Lying within the national park, a pleasant 15-min walk from Malo Jezero, this cluster of modern white buildings, overlooking Pomena Bay, is Mljet's only hotel. The best of the 157 rooms each have a balcony, sea view, a/c, TV and minibar. Facilities include bicycles, surf boards and kayaks to rent. Open Apr-Oct.

E **Villa Mirosa**, Saplunara 26, T020-746133, www.villa-mirosa.com. Close to the lovely sandy beach of Saplunara, **Villa Mirosa** has 6 basic but comfortable rooms, all with a/c and en suite bathrooms. There's a ground floor restaurant with a lovely, shady terrace. The seafood on offer is caught by the hosts (guests are welcome to join in on fishing trips), and the olive oil, wine and rakija are all home-made. Open Jun-Sep.

E **Villa Mungos**, Sobra 65, T020-745224, www.mungos-mljet.com. Overlooking the sea in the port of Sobra, **Villa Mungos** offers 8 rooms and 2 spacious suites. There's also a restaurant serving barbecued seafood and meat dishes, and anchorage space for 5 yachts out front. Open Feb-Nov.

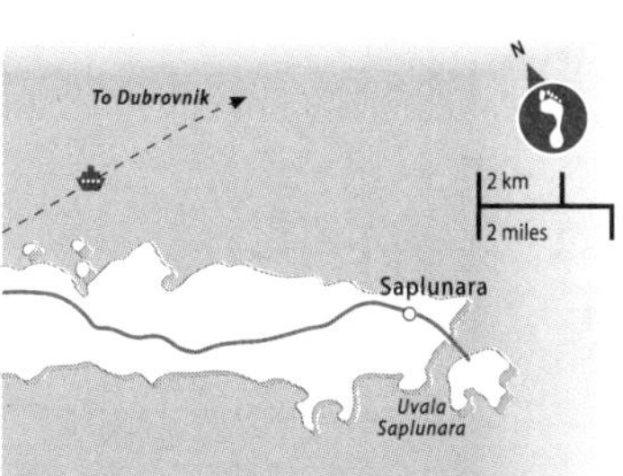

Private accommodation

For a list of private accommodation on Mljet, check out the **Croatian National Tourist Board** website, www.croatia.hr (look up 'Islands' under 'Destinations', go to 'Mljet' then click on 'Private Accommodation').

Eating

Island of Mljet *p309*

€€€ **Melita**, Otočić Sv Marije, T020-744145. Located on the islet of St Mary, in the middle of Veliko Jezero, this smart restaurant serves up a fine selection of barbecued meat and fish dishes. A restaurant boat shuttles guests back and forth from Pristanište. Open mid-Apr to late Sep.

€€€-€€ **Nine**, Pomena 6, T020-744037. Looking out over the seafront in Pomena, this restaurant is popular with the yachting fraternity, who are drawn here by its excellent lobster dishes. The live lobsters are kept in wells outside, and fished out upon request. Open mid-Apr to late Sep.

Activities and tours

Island of Mljet *p309*

Boating

Kayaks and canoes can be rented at Mali Most, the bridge between the 2 lakes. Expect to pay €2.70 per hr or €20.00 per day.

Mountain biking

Mountain bikes can be rented from **Hotel Odisej**, €2.70 per hr or €14.70 per day.

Sailing

There is a small marina in front of **Hotel Odisej** in Pomena. In addition, yachts can moor up along the quays in the protected bays of Pomena and Polače.

Transport

Island of Mljet *p309*

Jadrolinija (contact the Dubrovnik office, T020-418000, for details) run a once-daily ferry service from **Dubrovnik** (summer departure Mon-Sat 1400, Sun 2030) to **Sobra**, 2 hrs. A connecting bus then runs across the island from **Sobra** to **Pomena** (1 hr), within the national park. Jadrolinija also operate a daily ferry service from the new port of Prapratno (on Pelješac) to Sobra (45 mins).

G&V Line, www.gv-line.hr, operate a high-speed catamaran called *Nona Ana*. In summer, the service runs daily, connecting Dubrovnik to both Sobra and Polače, continuing to Korčula on Mon and Sat, and to Lastovo on Tue and Thu. In winter it runs between Dubrovnik and Sobra only. Tickets are available through the Dubrovnik-based agency **Atlantagent**, Stjepana Radića 26, T020-313355.

Atlas, Vukovarska 19, Dubrovnik, T020-442222, www.atlas-croatia.com. Organize day trips from Dubrovnik to Mljet by hydrofoil, 2 times per week, May-Oct.

Background

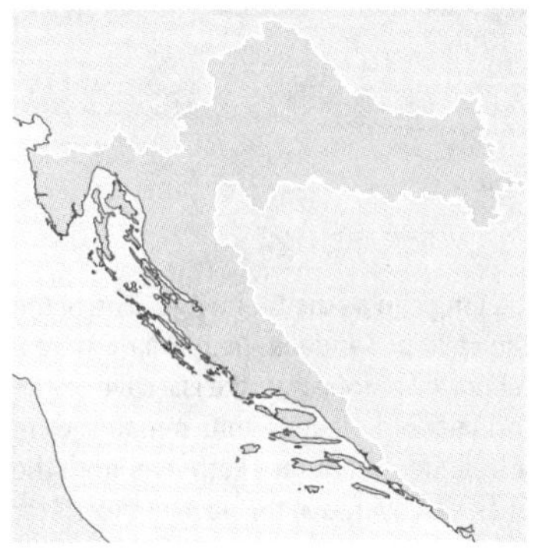

History

→ *This section was researched and written by Domagoj Mijan.*

Prehistoric times

The area that is today Croatia was inhabited as long ago as the Stone Age. One of the sites with the oldest traces of early man is the cave of Sandalja, near Pula, where a 1,000,000-year-old tooth was found. The other notable Stone Age site is a cave on the hill of Hušnjak, near Krapina, where 30,000-year-old Neanderthal remains were unearthed in the late 19th century. Traces of Neanderthal hunter-gatherers from the period preceding the last Ice Age have also been discovered in the cave of Veternica, near Zagreb, and in Vindija, near Varaždin.

During the late Stone Age, climatic and geographical factors caused a cultural division between Pannonian and Mediterranean Croatia, which were to have repercussions on the region's later history. The Adriatic coast with its hinterland up to the Dinaric Mountains came mainly under the influence of Mediterranean cultures, while the plains of northern Croatia were influenced by the Central European-Danubic cultures. Sites from this period include the cave of Grabac on the island of Hvar, where engravings of boats on fragments of a ceramic dish, dating from around 2500 BC, prove that man had already taken to the sea. At the same time, Neolithic people belonging to the Starčević culture in northern Croatia had begun building simple huts of wood and mud.

Bronze Age

The Bronze Age began here in the late fourth century BC following the arrival of the first groups of Indo-Europeans, settlers from the East who knew how to work metal. The most famous site from this period is Vučedol, near Vukovar in Eastern Slavonia, where objects such as ornamental ceramic dishes, tools and weapons have been unearthed. The best known find is the Vučedol Dove. In northern Croatia, several urn-fields (burial sites where cremated bodies were placed in an urn with a lid, which was buried in a circular pit) have been discovered. These people probably worshipped the sun, and were part of a culture that spread across Central Europe at that time.

Along the Adriatic coast and its hinterland, this period witnessed the appearance of predecessors to the Illyrian tribes of the Liburnians, Histri, Japodians and Delmati, who built simple hilltop settlements fortified with stonewalls, in the manner of the Greek acropolis. DNA analysis has proved that some families living on the islands of Brač, Hvar and Korčula today are direct descendents of these peoples. Later, people living south of the River Sava were known as Illyrians, while those north of the river were referred to as Pannonians. The Celts arrived in Slavonia in the fourth century BC, assimilated with the Pannonians and spread aspects of Celtic culture such as the potter's wheel and ironwork.

Greek colonization

The Greeks started colonizing the coast in the fourth century BC. The first settlement, Issa, was founded by inhabitants of the Greek colony of Syracuse (Sicily) on the island of Vis, and included a theatre with a capacity for 3000 spectators. Issa later became independent, and founded several more colonies such as Tragurion (Trogir), Epetion (Stobreč) and Lumbarda (on the island of Korčula). Local Illyrians traded jewellery, metalwork, glassware, salt, wine and oil with the Greeks, and thus Greek colonization induced the development of craftsmanship, the building of towns and a more sophisticated form of farming.

The arrival of the Romans

In the mid-third century BC the southern tribes united to form an Illyrian state under the leadership of the Ardedians, a people renowned for piracy. Under **King Agron** the Illyrian state encompassed South Dalmatia, part of Herzegovina, Montenegro and Albania, with its centre in Skodra (present-day Shkodar in Albania). Feeling threatened by Illyrian expansion, the Greeks called the Romans for help. In the meantime King Agron died and his place was taken by Queen Teuta, who managed the throne in the name of her under-aged son. When Roman messengers arrived to ask Teuta to curtail piracy they were promptly put to death, causing the beginning of a series of wars between the Romans and the Illyrians. After three wars fought between 229 and 167 BC, the Illyrian state was defeated and its territory turned into the Roman province of Illyricum.

The Roman *Liburnia*, which was a fast and powerful ship powered by two banks of oarsmen, was built on the original model of those used by Liburnian pirates, and the majority of sailors in the Roman military navy originated from Illyricum. Interestingly, according to Greek and Roman writers of that time, the Liburnians kept a matriarchal society.

The Illyrian tribe of the Histri was conquered in 177 BC, when the Romans took their last point of resistance, the fortified city of Nesactium (present-day Nezakcij near Pula). The Romans gradually expanded the borders of Illyricum up to the River Danube, and the territory was divided into two provinces: Pannonia and Dalmatia. The capitals of these two provinces were Poetovio (in present-day Slovenia), and Salona (near Split), which is said to have had a population of 60,000, a figure only attained by modern-day Split in the year 1960.

The first Roman settlers were traders and soldiers. Legions built military camps that soon developed into centres of Roman culture. Besides fortresses, the Roman army built roads, bridges and aqueducts, which stimulated the arrival of civilians who were attracted by the possibility of expanding trade and colonization. This lead to the development of the inland towns of Siscia (Sisak) and Sirmium (Srijemska Mitrovica), and the coastal towns of Pola (Pula), Senia (Senj), Jader (Zadar), Salona (Solin), Narona (Vid near Metković) and Epidaurum (Cavtat). The Romans built roads so as to make military intervention possible and to improve trade and communications. The two most important routes both linked Aquileus (Aquileia) in northeast Italy to Byzantium (present-day Istanbul), one passing through Emona (Ljubljana), Poetovia (Ptuj) and across Pannonia to Singidunum (Beograd) and Naissu (Niš), while the other ran south along the coast through Dalmatia and then veered east to join the Via Egnatia (Egnatian Way) through Epirus (mainland Greece).

Croatia's best preserved Roman monuments are the Arena (amphitheatre) and the Forum with the Temple of Augustus in Pula, and Diocletian's Palace in Split.

Christianity

Christianity arrived early in this part of the world. Apparently St Paul sent his disciple Titus to the area to spread the new religion, and St Paul himself was shipwrecked close to the island of Mljet. The oldest diocese in the country was probably Salona (Solin), and its founder was the martyr Venancius, who died around AD 257. The Bishop of Salona, later known as St Gaius, was elected Pope in Rome in AD 283. After the 'Edict of Milan' (which legalized Christianity) Salona became the seat of the Archbishop of Dalmatia, and its importance is testified by numerous archaeological finds on the site.

Along the coast, Christian centres also developed in Epidaurum (Cavtat), Jadera (Zadar), Parentium (Poreč) and Pola (Pula). In Pannonia the main Christian centres were Sirmium (Srijemska Mitrovica), Cibalia (Vinkovci), Mursa (Osijek) and Siscia (Sisak). Many early Christians died for their belief, with the greatest persecution taking place under Emperor Diocletian.

The end of the Roman Empire

When the Roman Empire was divided into the Eastern and Western Empires in 395 – a division that was to have far-reaching consequences for the later history of the Balkans – Dalmatia fell within the West. With the fall of the Western Empire in 476, the region became part of the Ostrogoth state of Theodoric the Great, until the Byzantine emperor Justinian I conquered the Ostrogoths in 555, and it was made a Byzantine province. During the second half of the sixth century, it was invaded by tribes of Slavs and Avars, and by 600 they had reached the most western point in their migration, Istria. They also travelled south through Dalmatia, where they demolished Salona.

According to the Byzantine Emperor and historian Constantine Porphyrogenitus, the Croats were invited to present-day Croatia by **Emperor Heraclius** (575-641) to expel the Avars. This they did, also defeating other Slavic tribes, and they soon became at the dominant force in the former Roman province of Dalmatia.

The origin of Croats

The name Hrvat (Croat) has been used by two other Slavic tribes, besides today's Croats – the so-called White Croats in Poland, who populated the area around the River Vistula, with their centre in Krakow, and the Croats of the northeast region of the Czech Republic. Other smaller groups who also called themselves Croats have been traced in Slovenia, Slovakia, Montenegro, Macedonia and even in Greece.

Many linguists believe that the name Hrvat is of Iranian origin, and that the Croats conquered the Slavs gradually but took their language, so that today Croatian belongs, without a doubt, to the Slavic group of languages. Genetic research verifies the theory that Croats came from Iran, as up to 50% of the inhabitants of the Croatian coast and the mountains that rise behind it carry these genes. Alternatively, it is possible that the Illyrians were of Iranian origin and later assimilated with the Croats.

Towns in Dalmatia

In the seventh century, citizens of Salona fled the rampaging tribes of Avras and Slavs, and took refuge within the walls of Diocletian's Palace, converting the late-Emperor's mausoleum into a cathedral. During the Middle Ages the geographical term Dalmatia narrowed, and instead of referring to the great Roman province of Dalmatia the name was applied to a few isolated islands and coastal towns populated by families of Roman descent, while the hinterland was taken by the Croats. Interestingly, all these towns, apart from Split, were built on peninsulas so they could be well defended against attack, and belonged to Byzantine theme (province) of Dalmatia. According to Constantine Porphyrogenitus this province included the coastal towns of Zadar, Trogir, Split, Dubrovnik and Kotor, and the towns of Krk, Rab and Osor on the islands. The greatest military forces of the time – the Byzantine Empire, the Franks, Arabs, Hungarians, Normans and Venetians – all fought for the control of these towns, which was essential for control over the Adriatic, and ruling the Adriatic was strategic for control of the Mediterranean, the economic, political and cultural centre of Europe in the Middle Ages. The strategic importance of these towns lay in the fact that the Eastern Adriatic boasted good sea currents and, with its indented coastline, provided shelter and safe ports essential for medieval ships.

The development of the Croatian state

The Croats were the only Slav nation fortunate enough to have settled on the culturally rich Roman Mediterranean. Very few written documents exist regarding their early years in the region, although around the year 800 we have evidence of one Duke Višeslav, whose court was based in Nin (near Zadar, in North Dalmatia).

Croatian territory covered the hinterland of the coastal towns of Zadar, Trogir and Split, but did not actually include these towns. It stretched south as far as the River

Cetina (near Omiš), and east into central and western Bosnia. To the north it included Lika and Krbava, which were governed by a *ban* (governor or viceroy) and later it also covered the province of Istria. When the Croatian rulers were at their height, Pannonia, between the River Drava and Gvozd Mountain, was part of Croatia, but during periods of weak central authority Pannonia lead a life of its own.

Trpimir, Duke of Croatia (845-864), is deemed as the founder of the dynasty that ruled the country until the end of the 11th century. He expressed a patrimonial perception of the state, considering the entire territory as his own personal property and surrounded himself with a council of hand-picked counts (*župani*), who were each responsible for a county (*županije*), to help him rule.

Trpimir's successor, **Domagoj** (864-876), built up Croatia's naval strength and came into conflict with Venice over the control of the Adriatic, which is why the Venetians called him the worst Duke of Croatia. After Domagoj, **Zdeslav** (878-879) came to power but he was assassinated and was succeeded by **Branimir** (879-882) who was loyal to the pope and obtained the first international recognition of Croatia from Pope John VIII.

At that time the 'Apostles of the Slavs', the brothers Methodius and Cyril, were requested by the Byzantine emperor to invent an alphabet that could be modified for Slavic languages and would thereby spread the Byzantine influence among these people. The papacy, worried about the strengthening of Byzantium, wanted to keep Croatia under Rome's watch.

Around the same time, an agreement known as a *tribitum pacis* was drawn up between the Byzantine emperor Basil I and the Croatian ruler, stating that Dalmatian towns would pay 710 golden coins to the Croatian ruler instead of to the head of the Dalmatian theme so as to be able to work their fields in peace. It is most likely that at the same time the Venetians also started paying tribute to the Croatian rulers so as to have safe naval passage along the Croatian coast.

Tomislav, the first Croatian king

The following century is linked with **Tomislav**'s reign (910-928). He started his rule as a *dux* (duke) but changed his title to that of *rex* (king) around 925. For his achievements in the wars against the Bulgarians, the Byzantine emperor Romanus Lacapenosus awarded him control over the Dalmatian towns and the title of 'proconsul' so he could rule them in the name of the Byzantine Empire.

During Tomislav's rule, two state-church assemblies took place in Split, one in 925 and the other in 927-928. Only a century earlier it would have been beyond imagination that a Croatian ruler should preside over a church council in the Roman city of Split. In Europe at that time, the church wielded such material wealth and political influence that rulers did not interfere directly with church matters. Croatia had its own independent bishop in Nin who had no connection with the other bishops in the Dalmatian cities. Now that Byzantine Dalmatia and coastal Croatia were united under the authority of a single ruler, bishops in Dalmatia saw a unique opportunity to spread their jurisdiction, and by doing so increase their income, which up until then depended solely on the towns. Bishop Gregory of Nin wanted to preserve the diocese of Nin, the use of Glagolitic and the Slav liturgy. But the Bishops of Dalmatia won the day, and the diocese of Nin was abolished and its jurisdiction divided between the Dalmatian dioceses.

Tomislav defeated the Hungarians and united Coastal and Pannonian Croatia. The period of Croatian history after Tomislav's death is unclear due to lack of historical sources, and the number of people living on Croatian territory at that time is uncertain. Constantine Porphyrogenitus claimed that during Tomislav's reign Croatia had an army of 100,000 infantry, 60,000 horsemen and 5000 sailors with 80 large ships and 100 smaller ships. This number is unusually high considering the size or the territory and can only be explained by the fact that all free residents (eg non-slaves) were probably seen as warriors, and thus counted as members of the army. In comparison, the Venetian fleet had only 200 ships, and the Byzantines 300, and these were said to be the strongest fleets in Europe.

Venetian claims to Dalmatia

In the year 1000, the Doge of Venice, **Peter Orseolo**, led a successful campaign to gain control over the Dalmatian coastal towns, which were subsequently forced to acknowledge Venetian rule and honour Orseolo with the title *Dux Dalmatiae*. Although these towns were later reclaimed by the Croatian crown, this was to be only the first of many attempts by Venice to take Dalmatia.

Allegiance to Rome

In 1054 the 'Great Schism', the break between Eastern and Western Christian churches, took place, and the border between the Eastern and Western Roman Empires, drawn up by Theodosius in AD 395, became the border between the Roman Catholic and Orthodox churches. The east Adriatic, bisected by this border, was of direct interest to both the pope in Rome and the patriarch in Constantinople, and the papacy was eager to keep Croatia under the Catholic wing.

During the rule of **Petar Krešimir IV** (1058-1074), two church councils met in Split, proclaiming sanctions against clergy who served sermons in the Croatian language, had beards, were married or in any other way resembled the Eastern Church. Krešimir was recognized as the King of Dalmatia and Croatia by the pope, and thus the Byzantine theme of Dalmatia was truly united with Croatia. Krešimir was not only a Byzantine official like Tomislav and Tomislav's successors, he was the absolute leader of the entire region.

The last Croatian kings

However, soon after his death a conflict blew up, provoked by the Normans, Venetians, Byzantines, Hungarians and the pope in Rome, who all hoped to gain control over Croatia and Dalmatia. The result of this was that **Zvonimir**, the former *ban* (governor or viceroy) at the time of Petar Krešimir, succeeded to the throne in 1075 and took the title King of Croatia and Dalmatia. Zvonimir was chosen thanks to the support of Pope Gregory VII, and in return he placed the country under papal sovereignty. He was linked to the Hungarian dynasty Arpadović through his wife Jelena, who was a sister of the Hungarian king Ladislas. Legend says that Zvonimir left the Croats with a curse that they would not have their own king for 1000 years.

After Zvonimir, Stjepan Trpimirović ruled for a short time, but he was too weak to put an end to difficult internal problems. This chaos was used by the Hungarian Arpadović Dynasty, with some assistance from the pope, to take control of Croatia and Dalmatia and finally fulfil their long desire to open up their land-locked territories with access to the sea. Rome favoured the Arpadovićs, and thus in 1091 the Hungarian king Ladislas came to Slavonia and claimed the right of his sister Jelena (widow of Zvonimir) to Croatia and Dalmatia. Ladislas succeeded in taking Pannonian (which from then on became known as Slavonia), and in 1094 he founded a diocese in Zagreb, but he had no luck in conquering the hills of coastal Croatia. In 1097, his successor to the throne, Koloman, defeated the last Croatian king Petar on Gvozd Mountain, which was later renamed Petrova Gora (Petar's Mountain).

In 1102, with the signing of the Pacta Conventa the heads of the 12 most powerful Croatian families recognized Koloman as their leader, and accompanied him to Biograd-na-Moru (near Zadar) where he was crowned King of Croatia and Dalmatia.

The Hungarian crown

The Hungarian Arpadović family, like the other royal dynasties that ruled Croatia, did not gain their crown through military occupation but with the approval of the

Croatian nobility. In spite of this, each royal house that ruled the country treated it as a province in their kingdom.

Croatian history from 1102 until 1991 finds the country divided into three large administrative areas that had little contact with each other – Croatia, Slavonia and Dalmatia – under foreign rulers such as the **Arpadović** Dynasty as of 1102, the **Anjou** Dynasty as of 1301, the **Hapsburgs** from 1527 and the **Karadjordjević** Dynasty from 1918. In theory this was the free choice of Croatian nobility (the people with a say in politics), but in reality it was somewhat different.

Under each foreign ruler, the Croatian nobility requested that the union should be between two equal partners, and that it should have the character of a personal or individual union. However, each dynasty, upon settling in Croatia, insisted on a real or actual union. Personal union is when both countries concerned retain autonomy in internal affairs and are linked by the persona of the ruler – the best examples of this are the countries of the Commonwealth that recognize the Queen of England as their ruler, but govern their own internal and foreign political matters. Real union is when a king has the power to make laws and the countries under him have limited local autonomy.

The Croats were misfortunate in that every time they gave their independence to foreign royalty, they then had to claim back their historical rights from them. Croatia could oppose the ruling dynasties when it still had great noble families such as the **Frankopans** and the **Subić-Zrinskis** who were powerful enough to oppose the king. But with the loss of territory upon the arrival of the Turks and the extinction of the Frankopans and the Subić-Zrinskis, and with the increase in the number of rulers in Europe (absolute monarchy), this freedom was decreased. Until the French revolution the conflict between the ruler and the nobility was a conflict between a narrow class of people, but later with the growth of a national consciousness it became a conflict between entire nations.

The change of dynasty had far-reaching consequences for Croatia. Most of the national territory – Croatia, Dalmatia, Slavonia and the county of Neretva (south of the River Cetina) – was united under the Arpadovićs, but in spite of this there were significant differences between these regions. The dualism of Croatia and Dalmatia continued, while medieval Slavonia and the county of Neretva each developed separately.

The Hungaro-Croatian alliance was positive, as the two countries would later work together to oppose the process of Germanization in the region. The Arpadović Dynasty considered themselves the heirs of the Croatian rulers in the patrimonial-feudal sense, and from the time of King Koloman onwards they were the supreme owners of the entire territory, and at the same time the direct owners of those lands that were not the legal property of free men. The special position Croatia had in this Hungaro-Croatian union was incarnated in the persona of a *ban* (governor or viceroy).

The sacking of Zadar

In 1190, Zadar, which was the largest town in Dalmatia, scored a naval victory over the Venetian fleet near Osor (island of Cres) and also fought off a subsequent attack by the blind Venetian duke Enrico Dandolo in 1194. Victory over the Venetian navy, which at that time was one of the world's leading forces, proves that Zadar was a force to be reckoned with. The French writer of Crusade chronicles, Geoffroi de Villehardouin, recorded that "there was not a bigger and richer town than Zadar". In 1202, Dandolo persuaded members of the Fourth Crusade to pay their way to the Holy land by conquering Zadar, which was one of the richest towns on the Mediterranean at that time.

Founding of the Sabor

By excessive donations of feudal estates, the king's juridical and economic power weakened. The situation climaxed at the time of **Andrew II** (1203-1235), when the feudal nobility gained certain privileges on the king's account through a charter known as the Golden Bull (1222), an agreement very similar to the English Magna Carta from 1215.

The 13th century saw the king's patrimonial power further diminished with the forming of the Sabor (parliament), where nobles would meet to discuss matters of national importance. The first meetings were held in Zagreb and attended only by nobles from Slavonia.

Also at that time, several towns in Slavonia, such as Vukovar, Virovitica, Petrinja and Samobor, which were mainly settlements of foreign craftsmen and merchants, attained autonomy. These towns were granted certain privileges by the king: they were free from the power of the local count; they could write their own laws and they practiced their own form of government.

A short history of Dalmatian communities

In 1107, five years after the rest of Croatia had done so, the coastal towns of Dalmatia recognized Koloman as their king, and in return he granted them a certain autonomy. The first town to receive a charter was Trogir, which soon became a model for those of other Dalmatian towns. According to this charter, citizens of Trogir were obliged to recognize the supreme power of the king and to give him two-thirds of all customs fees; in return they were granted autonomy in all other aspects of town life. The Hungarian kings gave greater privileges to the Dalmatian towns than to Hungarian towns as they needed them for their access to the sea.

Around this time, many towns began drawing up their own statutes: first was the statute of Korčula in 1265; then Dubrovnik in 1272; Zadar and the island of Brač in 1305; Split in 1312; Trogir in 1322 and Hvar in 1331. These statutes laid down urban planning regulations and measures to fight the plague epidemics that were rife in Europe. Consequently, each of these communities had a sewerage system and a communal watchmen, at a time when in the cities of France and England people were still throwing rubbish out of their windows onto the street. Pigs were forbidden inside the Dalmatian communities, while in western European towns they were used as watchmen. The statutes also regulated ecological problems such as the amount of fish that was caught and number of trees that were chopped. Communal matters were decided through secret votes (using small marbles), although the right to vote was confined to the local aristocracy. Juridical decisions were logical and righteous: a party that lost a case would have to pay for it, and foreigners were judged on the basis of reciprocity. In short, each town and its immediate surroundings was a community that had its own clerks, physicians, pharmacists, judges, teachers and solicitors. Even though we cannot say that life in these communities was democratic in the sense of the word today, it is clear a written statute meant a certain degree of progress.

The Anjou Dynasty

The Mongol invasion of 1241-1242 left Croatia and Hungary devastated and impoverished. It also rapidly liquidated the king's power and strengthened that of the feudal nobility and the *ban* (governor or viceroy), who substituted the king and became the political exponent of the nobles.

At the turn of the 14th century, the Hungarian Anjou Dynasty succeeded to the throne with the help of Croatia's most powerful family, the Šubićs, who had installed themselves as hereditary *bans*. Both **Carl** (1301-1342) and **Ludovic** (1342-1382) ruled without parliament, but the riots and conflicts between local noblemen left the country in a state of turmoil. Venice took advantage of the situation to gain control of the Dalmatian coastal towns of Šibenik and Trogir (1322), Split (1327) and Nin (1329).

In 1408, Ladislas of Anjou sold his rights to Zadar and its surroundings to Venice for 100,000 golden coins, and by 1420 La Serenissima had control of the entire coast from Zadar to Dubrovnik, much of which it would retain until 1797. The loss of Dalmatia severely weakened the position of Croatia.

The city-republic of Dubrovnik

The town was founded in the seventh century on a site known to the Romans as Ragusium. Dubrovnik came under the protection of the Byzantine Empire until 1205, after which it came under the Venetian Republic. Dubrovnik liberated itself from Venetian protection in 1358 and from that moment onwards its rise to glory began. Even though the town recognized the authority of the Hungaro-Croatian king, in reality it became an independent city-republic. The term republic was used for the first time in 1430. Due to the fall of the Hungaro-Croatian Kingdom and Turkish hegemony, Dubrovnik recognized the authority of the Turkish Sultan to whom it paid a fee of 12,500 golden coins.

Later the Hapsburg Dynasty became stronger and the Turks weakened, so in 1684 Dubrovnik signed a contract with the Hapsburgs, agreeing to an annual tribute of 500 golden coins, an act which revived the protection of the Hungaro-Croatian crown, whose successors were the Hapsburgs. Dubrovnik continued to pay a fee to the Turkish Sultan too. The French brought about the end of the republic in 1808, 11 years after the fall of Dubrovnik's greatest rival, Venice.

During its golden years, Dubrovnik developed diplomacy to the extent that no country before or after has ever managed. This was essential, as sitting between the mountains and the sea it was surrounded by the Ottoman Empire landwards and Venice seawards. The Dubrovnik aristocracy cherished the republic and put it above their own interests. Their motto was "With everyone nicely, with everyone carefully." They were divided between the East and the West; the secrets they discovered in the courts of the Christian rulers they would sell to the Turks, and vice versa.

In 1377, Dubrovnik was one of the first places in Europe to open an organized quarantine as protection against the plague. Following this model, other European towns founded similar quarantines. In 1570, the republic's fleet numbered 180 ships with a total capacity of 56,810 tonnes, worth almost 700,000 golden coins and, for some time, tiny Dubrovnik had the third largest merchant fleet in Europe. In the early 16th century, the city started building the biggest ships in the world at that time, with capacities of up to 2050 tonnes.

From the 16th century up until the end of the republic, merchants from Dubrovnik had their place on the London stock market. However, in the mid-16th century, with the rise in importance of the Americas, the centre of economic power in Europe shifted from the Mediterranean to the countries overlooking the Atlantic Ocean, and Dubrovnik was pushed into recession.

Ottoman expansion

Having lost Dalmatia to Venice, Croatian political life was reduced to the region of Slavonia (formerly known as Pannonia). By this time, the term Slavonia was applied further to the east, while the name Croatia was moved from Dalmatia northwards to the area between Gvozd Mountain and the River Drava.

It was at this time that the Ottoman Turks began expanding towards Croatia. The Holy Roman Emperor and King of Hungary, **Sigismund I** (1387-1437) organized a crusade against the Turks, but was defeated at the Battle of Nicopolis in 1396. It was an evil omen that signified forthcoming wars between Croatia and the Ottoman Empire that would last for centuries. Sigismund's negligence and his absence from the country brought about the disintegration of his authority. Disunited Croatian society spent all its efforts on internal conflicts and was unable to fight the Turks.

Conditions were even worse during the reigns of **Albrecht Hapsburg** (1438-1439) and **Vladislav** (1440-1444), who was also King of Poland. The more competent **Matthias Corvinus** (1458-1490), who aspired to establishing a Central Europe kingdom that would counterbalance the Turks (a role that was later played by the Hapsburg monarchy), tried unsuccessfully to enforce order in the country and protect it from the Turks.

After the fall of neighbouring Bosnia in 1463, the Croatian borderlands lay open to Turkish attack. Attempts to organize defence by setting up borderline military camps in 1435 were unsuccessful. The first defeat took place in the battle on the field of Krbava near Udbina in Lika in 1493 where the Turks achieved a great victory over the Croatian army. Constant Turkish attacks on Croatian lands brought great disruption to the country. Peoples from Serbia and Bosnia fled the Turks, seeking refuge in Croatia, and these migrations affected food production, resulting in poverty and famine. Croatia's western neighbours, namely Venice and the Hapsburgs, recognized the danger for their own countries and started worrying about how to defend Croatia in order to defend themselves. But these measures were not enough. By the end of the 15th century, conflicts between the ruling Hungaro-Croatian aristocracy culminated in the aristocracy opposing the king and the lower nobility, and the burghers opposing the clergy. In 1526, a catastrophic defeat of the Hungarian army by the Turks at the Battle of Mohacs opened the problem of electing a new king, as Louis II had somewhat ignominiously drowned in a river as he tried to escape the battle.

The arrival of the Hapsburgs

There were two aspirers to the throne: the Hungarian aristocrat Ivan Zapolja, who originated from Slavonia, and Ferdinand Hapsburg. The Croatian nobles thought that Ferdinand would give them better support against the Turks than Zapolja, so they elected him as king on 1 January 1527. But on 6 January 1527, the Slavonian nobles elected Zapolja as king, resulting in fights between the followers of the respective potential leaders. The conflict ended with the death of Zapolja in 1540. This was how **Ferdinand Hapsburg** became the leader of Croatia, Dalmatia and Slavonia, and the entire territory was absorbed into the Holy Roman Empire of the German people. At the time the Hapsburgs were the kings of Czech, Hungary, Spain, the Netherlands, Naples and they even ruled Mexico.

The Krajina

In defence of the Turks, the *Krajina* (military border) was established in the 16th century. In 1578, with the approval of Vienna, work began to build Karlovac as a nucleus of defence against the Turks – Turkish skulls were thrown into the foundation of Karlovac as a sign of the mood of the times. Other defence posts were later built to the south and east. To guard these positions, a special borderline army was formed, made up largely of Vlahi, Orthodox Serb cattle farmers who were fleeing the Turks from the east. By this time the Hapsburgs were overriding the authority of the *ban* (Croatian governor) and the *sabor* (Croatian parliament), and the *Krajina* was put under German officers who took their orders directly from Vienna and Graz.

Defending the country against the Turks

The rule of the first Hapsburgs was devoted to defending the region against the Turks. When the Turks took Klis in 1537, they effectively had control over the entire Dalmatian hinterland all the way south to the River Neretva, leaving Dalmatia divided between Venice and the Ottoman Empire. In October of the same year, the Turks defeated Ferdinand's armies at Gorjan (near Djakovo), and thus opened their way to the Croatian lands in the west. Croatia, under the authority of the *ban*, was "the remains of the remains of what it once was" (*reliquiae reliquiarum olim incliti regni Croatiae*). Ferdinand, using the excuse of installing better defence, centralized the government into his own hands in order to constitute a unified monarchy.

The Turks achieved their greatest victories at the time of Sultan Suleiman the Magnificent (ruled 1520-1566). On his campaign against Vienna, his army was detained by the Croatian *ban*, Count Nikola Zrinski, and his army at Szeged (southern Hungary). Even though Szeged was eventually conquered in 1566, Zrinski's heroic defenders aroused doubts about Turkish invincibility and also indicated the turning point that was to come. One hundred years after the disaster on Krbava field, the Turks suffered a defeat near Sisak in 1593, marking the beginning of a 13-year war against Croatia and Hungary. This war ended with a peace treaty in 1606, and was a clear symptom of the decline of Turkish power. During the first half of the 17th century, following this satisfactory peace treaty, the Croatian nobles considered that the *Krajina* (military border) had fulfilled its task, and they demanded that it should come back under the authority of the Croatian *ban*.

Re-organization of the Krajina

The *Krajina* had physically divided Croatian territory in two, which made national integration very difficult. The Emperor's Court in Vienna had two reasons not to disband the troops of the military border: on the one hand, the military border was an infinite source of cheap, well-trained and true soldiers, and, on the other hand, Vienna feared that national integration would strengthen the Croatian aristocracy. The Hapsburgs decided to train the border soldiers better, provide them with new uniforms at low cost and send them to battlefields all over Europe to serve their interests.

The Hapsburgs tighten their control

During the 200-year fight to hold back the Turks, Croatia lost not only three-quarters of its territory, but also the same proportion of its population. People either died in battle, or were captured by the Turks and taken away to be used as slaves. The survivors moved to the north and the west of the country, and even beyond its borders. The aristocracy also migrated, with the Šubić-Bribirski family, the Draškovićs, Kukuljevićs and Vranicanis all moving northwards, thus displacing the centre of the Croatian state from Coastal Croatia to Upper Croatia. The clergy, knights and military government encouraged these migrations.

Two Croatian aristocratic families in particular distinguished themselves in the wars against the Turks: the **Frankopans** and **Zrinskis**. These two families were related by blood, and also by similar political beliefs. In the 17th century, Petar Zrniski, together with a group of Hungarian aristocrats, lead a diplomatic mission to free Croatia of Hapsburg domination. But the conspiracy was soon discovered and the court in Vienna sentenced Petar Zrinski and his brother-in-law Franjo Frankopan to the guillotine. They were executed on 30 April 1671, and their extensive estates were confiscated on behalf of the court chamber, eg the Hapsburgs.

By 1718, Croatia had reclaimed all of Slavonia, a part of Srijem, Banovina, Kordun, Lika and Krbava from the Turks. These lands were immediately claimed by Vienna, even though in theory they should have been placed under the jurisdiction of the Croatian parliament and the *ban*. But the Hapsburgs did not want to strengthen Croatia, so on the pretext of having been won in war, they were placed instead under military authority, effectively becoming a constituent part of the *Krajina*. The Hapsburgs also started to give away large estates in the liberated and recently acquired Slavonia to foreign (German and Hungarian) families, such as the Odescalchis, Eltzes, Normans and Trenks, to the obvious detriment of the Croatian nobility. Therefore, the Croatian parliament started to lose its importance, and fewer and fewer noblemen participated in its meetings, attending the Hungarian parliaments instead, where they solved Hungaro-Croatian matters together with the Hungarian nobles.

Ironically, with the expulsion of the Turks, Croatia's position became even more uncomfortable, as the Hapsburgs tightened their grip on the country. By this time a sizeable Serbian population (of the Orthodox faith) were living in Croatia, and when

 Russia began to show interest in the situation, the so-called Eastern Question evolved: when the Turks finally left the Balkans, who would rule, Catholic Austria or Orthodox Russia? Later this would be one of the causes of the escalation towards the First World War.

Germanization

The Hapsburg's power gradually strengthened under **Marie Thérèse** (1740-1780) and **Joseph II** (1780-1790), and with them came a process of increased Germanization. Marie Thérèse employed centralistic rule, governing from 1764 without the parliament and issuing her own laws, pleasing Croats one moment and Hungarians the next. In 1745 she united Slavonia and Croatia under a combined administrative unit as a reward for the contribution Croatian soldiers had made to various wars the Hapsburgs were participating in. However, in 1779 she eliminated the work of the Croatian regency council, handing its affairs to the Hungarian council, effectively erasing any type of Croatian independence.

In 1784, Marie Thérèse's son, Joseph II, ordered Croatian clerics to learn the German language within a three-year period. This lead to considerable protest, as the official language in Croatia and Hungary at that time was Latin. However, the emperor went ahead with his plans and in 1786 he ordered that all administration should be carried out in German.

This decision opened a Pandora's box of national problems that eventually resulted in the fall of the monarchy. For the first time ever, the national question became the priority issue.

Hungarianization

Meanwhile, a great surprise was install for the Croatian representatives at the Hungaro-Croatian parliament in Buda (part of present-day Budapest). Instead of Joseph's decision on German being the official language, the Hungarians proposed that Hungarian should be the official language of Banska Croatia (the area of Croatia under the *ban*). However, in the upper house of parliament, where Croatian representatives had a right to veto, the proposal was declined and Latin remained the official language.

By this time the Hungarians were making claims that Slavonia was part of Hungary; indeed, a Hungarian nationalist movement was developing, which planned to establish a compact Hungarian nation all the way from the Carpathian Mountains to the Adriatic Sea.

Venetian rule in Dalmatia

By the mid-16th century, the Turks had conquered all of Dalmatia apart from the islands and the coastal cities of Zadar, Šibenik, Trogir and Split, leaving more or less the area that had been the Byzantine theme of Dalmatia in the early Middle Ages to Venice. During the Candian War (1645-1669) Venice conquered a narrow territory from Novigrad to the River Neretva together with Poljica and the Makarska coastline. Following the war against the Turks (1682-1699) in which Poland, the Hapsburgs and Russia all participated on the Venetian side, Venice extended it territories to Ravni Kotari and the towns of Knin, Sinj and Vrgorac. The Venetians applied the name Dalmatia to all these parts, including the hinterland, which had once been the centre of the Croatian kingdom. Venice, just like the Hapsburgs, declined to return territories liberated from the Turks to the Croatian aristocracy, but held onto these lands itself instead.

In 1718, the peace treaty of Požarevac awarded Venice the hinterland territory up to the Dinara Mountains, the area around Imotski, one half of the gulf of Boka Kotorska (in present-day Montenegro) and the area to each side of Dubrovnik, thus threatening the republic's 100-year independence.

However, the citizens of Dubrovnik were very skilful diplomats and, not wanting the Venetians as neighbours, they gave the area to the north around Klek (present-day Neum) and the area south around Sutorina (close to Herceg Novi in Montenegro) to the Turks, thus forming a buffer-zone between the republic and the Venetian Empire.

This was later to cause great difficulties in defining the geographical limits of Croatia. The borders of today's Croatia were drawn up according to the peace treaty in Požarevac. As Bosnia and Herzegovina remained under the Ottoman Turks until 1878, part of the territory of medieval Croatia is now western Bosnia, and the area around Neum has been awarded to Bosnia as access to the sea, thus cutting across the Croatian coast. Croatian nationalists have always resented this: during the war of the 1990s Tudjman described Croatia as a croissant-shaped country that needed a filling.

Napoleon's Illyrian Provinces

Dalmatia remained within these borders under Venetian government until the demise of Venice in 1797, when the peace treaty of Campoformio handed Dalmatia to the Hapsburgs. In this inconvenient position, the country entered the period of the French Revolution and Napoleonic Wars. In 1806, Napoleon took Dalmatia, bringing to the region a series of progressive reforms, but also imposing hefty taxes and recruiting local men to participate in his army and navy. In 1809, Napoleon united Dalmatia with parts of Slovenia and Croatia, calling the new region the Provinces Illyriennes (Illyrian Provinces), as it was believed at that time that all South Slavs (Croats and Serbs) were of Illyrian descent. During the Napoleonic Wars, the English navy defeated the French fleet near Vis, and subsequently took the island from 1811 to 1815, using it as an important strategic base on the Adriatic. After Napoleon's downfall in 1815, Dalmatia came back under the Hapsburgs.

Illyrian Movement

In 1827, the parliament in Zagreb passed a law making the Hungarian language obligatory in all secondary schools in Croatia. However, by this time new political aspirations were blossoming in Croatia, lead by the so-called Illyrian Movement, founded by **Ljudevit Gaj** (1806-1872). Gaj believed that unification of the South Slavs was the best way to oppose the increasing Germanization and Hungarianization of the region under Austro-Hungary, and aimed at doing this through a reawakening of the national consciousness, primarily through language and literature.

Besides the Illyrians, a pro-Hungarian party also existed in Croatia, made up mainly of knights, who wanted union with Hungary. Understandably, these two parties came into strong conflict. The pro-Hungarians accused the Illyrians of acting on the behalf of Russia, and the name Illyrian was thus prohibited in 1843. In its place, Gaj's movement was renamed the National Party.

The National Party rapidly gained popularity on county assemblies and as a counter-Hungarian wing in the parliament. Meanwhile, the revolutions that swept across Europe in 1848 gave further impetus to the movement. The ideas the Illyrians cherished were expressed in so-called 'Demands of the People' that were announced and accepted on 25 March 1848. These included the union of Dalmatia, Slavonia and the *Krajina* (military border), the institution of Croatian as the official language, and the foundation of a Croatian people's army.

The National Party also voted for **Josip Jelačić** as *ban* (governor), and he was instated on 4 June 1848. Croatia was now in a difficult position because the revolutionary movement in Hungary refused any possible agreement with the Croats: the Hungarian revolutionary leader, Lajos Kossuth, famously said "Where is Croatia, I do not see it on the map?" In September 1847, Jelačić thus lead his army into battle with the Hungarian revolutionaries, in the defence of both Croatia and the Hapsburgs. Not that he was protecting the empire, but rather he hoped that by so doing he would be able to procure certain favours from the Austrians.

As the situation became more complicated than had been expected, in December 1848 Emperor Ferdinand abdicated in favour of his teenage son Franz- Josef I. With the revolution in Hungary finally over (with the help of the Russian Tsar) Jelačić's dream of a 'Slavic Austria' also ended. In August 1849, the Hapsburgs returned to their old ways, with **Emperor Franz-Josef** I eliminating the new constitution he had formulated and imposing a centralistic-absolutistic regime accompanied by Germanization that eliminated all political freedom. "While the Magyars received absolutism as a punishment, the Croats got it as a reward" became a common expression at the time.

One of the National Party's demands that was eventually implemented was the integration of the *Krajina* (military border) into Croatia in 1881, which extended Croatian territory by one-third. This brought a considerable Serb population into the sphere of Croatian politics, a situation that was immediately abused by the new pro-Hungarian *ban*, **Khuen Hedervary** (1883-1903), who played off the ongoing competition between Croats and Serbs to weaken the Slav position by inciting conflicts between them. At this time there were 103 Serb representatives in the Croatian parliament, of whom 101 were pro-Hungarian.

On 16 May 1895, during a state visit by Francis Joseph, the Hungarian flag was burnt in Zagreb, reflecting a mood of discontent. Soon after that, the Croatian Peasants' Party, led by **Stjepan Radić**, entered the Croatian political scene. It represented a sizable force, as about 80% of the population were peasants at that time. All the progressive parties united themselves into one party in 1902, and the so-called Croatian Question, dealing with the destiny of Austro-Hungarian Slavs and the monarchy, came more and more to the centre of politics.

Meanwhile, in Serbia, King Alexander, of the pro-German Obrenović Dynasty, was assassinated in 1903, and substituted by Petar, of the Karadjordjević Dynasty, which was more orientated towards Russia, France and Britain. The change of dynasty brought about opposition to the Austro-Hungarian Empire within Serbia, and many Serbs in Croatia also stopped supporting Hungary, and switched their interests instead to building closer ties with the Croats.

A series of events, culminating with the assassination of the Austrian Archduke in Sarajevo (organized by a Serbian movement known as the Black Hand, without the knowledge of the Serbian king), led the entire region into the First World War (1914-1918).

The First World War

During the First World War, the centre of Croatian politics was moved outside the country with the exiled Yugoslav Committee, which represented the Yugoslavian people under the Austro-Hungarian monarchy, and aimed to unify all the South Slav countries in the Balkans into one nation.

A very important event, which somehow inspired the idea of a new South Slav nation, was an agreement between the allied forces of the Triple Entente (Britain, France and Russia) and Italy. Formulated in 1915 and known as the London Agreement, it promised a large part of the Croatian coast to Italy, provided Rome entered the war on the Allied side. Thus, in 1918, Croatia (which was on the losing side) encountered two problems: it was threatened by the Kingdom of Serbia from the east and the Kingdom of Italy from the west. Both these countries were on the winning side, and both possessed documents in which a part of Croatian territory was granted to them.

Kingdom of Serbs, Croats and Slovenes

At the end of the First World War, other European countries such as Poland, the Baltic countries, Finland and Czechoslovakia formed their own states, but this option was not open to Croatia. The Croats therefore seized the solution of forming a new South Slav country, and their neighbours, Serbs and Slovenians, agreed. After the military collapse of the monarchy on 29 October 1918, the Croatian parliament made a resolution to break all relations with Austro-Hungary and announced that Dalmatia, Croatia and Slavonia, together with the independent city-state of Rijeka, would enter a new State of Slovenians, Croats and Serbs. On 1 December 1918 this unification was officially announced in Belgrade and the new Kingdom of Serbs, Croats and Slovenes was formed. The leader of the Serbian military delegation responsible for the unification was Dušan Šimović. The only person to oppose the unification was Stjepan Radić, leader of the Croatian Peasants' Party, who said to the Croatian delegation before their journey to Belgrade, "Do not rush yourselves like geese in the fog."

The basic problem with the unification was that it was done unconditionally, leaving Croatia with little state autonomy. The unification came about not only due to the aspiration of South Slavic intellectuals from within the country, but also through the interest of France and Britain to disable German influence and the Bolshevik ideal. Meanwhile, the Treaty of Rapallo was signed in order to arrange the borders between the Kingdom of Italy and the Kingdom of Serbs, Croats and Slovenes. Istria, the islands of Cres, Lošinj, Lastovo and Palagruža, the city of Zadar and part of Slovenia were all awarded to Italy, effectively placing over 500,000 Croats and Slovenes under Italian rule.

In 1921, on St Vitus Day (28 June), parliament voted for a constitution that was centralistic, and as such could not satisfy the Croats, who were determined to keep some sort of autonomy. The Croatian Peasants' Party opposed the move and tried to obtain the support of several Western European countries, but they approved the politics of Belgrade.

Thus in 1927, the Croatian Peasant's Party, lead by Radić, together with the Independent Democratic Party, lead by **Svetozar Pribićević**, formed a political coalition named the Peasants' Democratic Coalition. Svetozar Pribićević was a Serbian politician from Croatia who initially supported Yugoslavian centralism, and was one of the people responsible for the unconditional unification, for which he had been awarded the position of Minister of Internal Affairs. However, he was later disheartened and changed his views. Realizing that there was a danger that the Serbs in Croatia might unite with the Croats, extremist politicians from Belgrade shot at members of the Croatian Peasants' Party in the parliament on 20 June 1928. Two members of the party were killed and Stjepan Radić later died of the wounds he had received.

Kingdom of Yugoslavia

King Aleksandar used the assassination to dismiss the parliament on 6 January 1929, to abolish the constitution and to set up a royal dictatorship in order "to save the people from parliamentary troubles". In the same year the king signed a law by which he changed the country's name to the Kingdom of Yugoslavia, meaning the 'Kingdom of the South Slavs', and divided the country into nine governmental regions. The use of the terms Croat, Serb and Slovene, together with their national flags, was prohibited. Exception was made for the Serbian flag, on the grounds that it was also the flag of the Serbian Orthodox Church. In 1931, the king announced the new constitution of the Kingdom of Yugoslavia, without a parliamentary vote.

The police became ever more powerful. Public demonstrators were likely to be shot, and by law the family of the deceased had to pay for the bullet. By this time, around 90% of all higher governmental official were Serbs, and out of 165 generals, 161 were Serbs and only two Croats. Out of reaction to the regime, the Bosnian-Croat **Ante Pavelić** founded the Ustaša movement, which stood for military action against the Kingdom of Yugoslavia, and was supported by extremists in Italy and Hungary. On 9 October 1934, members of this movement assassinated King Aleksandar in Marseille while on an official visit to France. After Aleksandar's death, Duke **Pavle Karadjordjević** was installed as a regent to lead the country in the name of the underage king, Peter.

Even though Duke Pavle was strongly opposed to the Germans, the kingdom was surrounded by Axis Powers, and he therefore decided to join them under reasonable conditions. In reply to a message from the American president, Franklin Roosevelt, that Yugoslavia should not approach the Germans, the duke said: “It's easy for you big nations a long way away to tell the smaller ones what to do.” Two days later, on 27 March 1941, a military putsch took place in Belgrade, organized and paid for with 100,000 pounds in gold by the British secret services.

Once the regency had been removed from power, a new government, led by General **Dušan Šimović**, was formed. Already on 6 April 1941, Germany and Italy attacked the kingdom. On 10 April, in Zagreb, the Independent State of Croatia (NDH) was proclaimed, with Ante Pavelić as leader. The Germans thought that Vlatko Maček should stand as president, but he believed that the Allied forces would eventually win and therefore refused the position.

Croatia's independence was at first met with high hopes by the majority of Croats, but when the government gave a large part of the coast to Italy, and began persecuting Serbs, Jews and Gypsies, this support suddenly vanished. The country was divided into two spheres: the south was governed by Italians, and the north by Germans.

As a reaction, the Partisan movement was founded and as the terror enforced by the Italians, Germans and the government increased, so the number of partisans increased. Even though the movement was mainly organized by Communists, members of the Croatian Peasants' Party also participated. The leader of the outlawed Communist Party, **Josip Broz**, now became the organizer of the largest anti-fascist movement in occupied Europe.

In 1943, the Zemaljsko antifašističko vijeće narodnog oslobodjenja Hrvatske (Territorial Antifascist Council for the Liberation of Croatia), or ZAVNOH, was formed. Italy capitulated on 8 September 1943, and at the following ZAVNOH assembly it was decided that both the Treaty of Rapallo from 1920 and the Treaty of Rome from 1941, through which Italy had taken possession of much of the Croatian coast, should be abolished.

Initially, the Allied forces only acknowledged the Yugoslav royal government in exile, based in London, but later the British were the first to help the partisans, having been persuaded by Winston Churchill, who even sent his son as a military agent to Tito. That was how the British established a strong military base on the island of Vis, where still today there is a British military cemetery. Vis was for some time the capital of liberated Yugoslavia and it was here, on 14 June 1944, that the first meeting between Tito and Šubašić, the representative of the Yugoslav government in exile, took place.

Since Tito was the military victor in the war, all possible agreements between the two of them were unsuccessful. At the beginning of 1945 there was a conference in Yalta in which three great leaders participated, and the well-known division of interests in a liberated Europe was agreed between Stalin and Churchill. Their interests in Yugoslavia were divided 50-50%.

Germany capitulated on 9 May 1945, bringing about the end to the Independent State of Croatia. Together with the military retreat, many pro-Ustaša civilians also tried to leave the country, frightened of possible revenge attacks. When they reached Austria, they were turned back by the British army, and regardless of whether they were soldiers or civilians, they were handed over to the partisans and killed on the field of Bleiburg.

As usual in history, when the number of war casualties comes into question, the sum of people killed varied depending on who one asks. After the Second World War the Yugoslavian government sent a report (for obtaining war reparations) to an international committee in which they stated that 1,700,000 people had been killed. But many people believe that the real number was around 1,000,000.

Estimates regarding how many people died in the infamous concentration camp of Jasenovac vary from 60,000 to 700,000.

Tito's Yugoslavia

The Federal People's Republic of Yugoslavia was proclaimed on 29 November 1945, supposedly organized as a federal and socialist country of people with equal rights. It was made up of six republics (Slovenia, Croatia, Serbia, Montenegro, Macedonia, and Bosnia and Herzegovina), and unlike the other countries of Eastern Europe, did not acknowledge Stalin as holding absolute power, as the Yugoslav partisans had liberated the country from the Germans by themselves.

This snubbing of Stalin resulted in conflict between the Soviet Informburo and the Yugoslavian Communist Party in the spring of 1948. Tito consequently broke with Stalin, and many Yugoslav Communists who supported Stalin ended up in prison.

Yugoslavia now found itself as a barrier between the Eastern and Western blocks. Placing itself midway between the Communist East and the Capitalist West, it set up the so-called self-management organizations.

By 1950 self-management had been proven a viable scheme, a third way between the free-enterprise of the West and the state planning and state economy of the Soviet Block. To put it simply, firms were managed by the workers themselves through a workers' council, which had the power to determine production, to decide on the distribution of profit and to build homes for their workers.

Post-war reconstruction was rapid and optimistic. Increased industrialization brought about mass migration from rural areas to the cities, and modern high-rise suburbs sprung up. Public health and education were well funded, and living standards rose significantly. Tourism began developing along the Adriatic coast in the 1960s, bringing with it foreign currency. All this was conducted under the ideal of 'Brotherhood and Unity', a motto Tito coined to stress the importance of holding the country together and suppressing individual nationalist aspirations.

However, the richer republics (Croatia and Slovenia) soon began to object to having to pay hefty taxes to Belgrade for investment in the less-developed parts of the country. This, plus the fact that national feelings could not be openly expressed, gradually lead to a silent discontent that culminated in the so-called 'Croatian Spring' of 1971. Those who participated in the event asked for greater autonomy for Croatia, greater cultural freedom, and for the foreign currencies received from tourism and earned by Croats working abroad to stay in the republic. Some Communist officials from Croatia of that time also participated in this movement. By the end of 1971 Tito decided that it had all gone too far and the movement was suppressed. However, some results were gained in 1973 when the Socialistic Federal Republic of Yugoslavia introduced a new constitution by which the individual republics' sovereignty was strengthened and their right to eventual independence was acknowledged.

On 4 May 1980, **Josip Broz Tito**, the persona who had held Yugoslavia together for almost four decades, died in Ljubljana. The respect he had gained abroad was illustrated by the extraordinary line up of world statesmen who attended his funeral, said to have been the largest gathering of its kind in history. Due to his policy of non-alignment and skilful manoeuvres between the East and West, Yugoslavia had gained greater importance and more loans than a country of such proportions and economic development objectively deserved. Tito left behind the proposal of a rotating presidency, whereby each republic would take a turn at leading the country for one year. But as only a charismatic persona such as Tito himself could hold so many different interests and people on one leash, future problems were in store.

Milošević rises to power

In the late 1980s, the appearance of Albanian nationalism in Kosovo gave a good excuse for the programme for a Greater Serbia. It was a continuation of the

 Serbian nationalist politics from the 19th century, which aimed to make the country the leading force in the Balkans. Having seized the presidency in Serbia, in 1988 **Slobodan Milošević** deposed the Communist leaders of Vojvodina, Kosovo and Montenegro, and in 1989 he made amendments to the Serbian constitution, thereby eliminating the autonomy of the provinces of Vojvodina and Kosovo.

The year 1989 saw the fall of the Berlin Wall and the demise of Communist regimes throughout the countries of Eastern Europe followed the disintegration of the USSR. In a way it was a case of history repeating itself, just as in 1918, when a succession of new independent countries were founded following the fall of an empire. This time, Croatia did not want to miss the opportunity.

Attempts by the Croatian economist **Ante Marković** and the Reformed Communists to save Yugoslavia seemed destined to fail from the start, mainly because of Slobodan Milošević. In spring 1990, the Croatian Democratic Union (HDZ), lead by **Franjo Tudjman**, won the elections in Croatia on a nationalist manifesto. The Assembly met for the first time on 30 May 1990, and Tudjman was elected president. However, already in August, Serbs in Knin began rebelling against the Croatian state, fearing that they would be marginalized by its nationalist agenda.

During the first months of 1991, the presidents of the six republics of Yugoslavia conducted negotiations about the governmental structure of Yugoslavia. Croatia and Slovenia wanted a confederation, while Milošević insisted on a firm federation, even though he knew it would be unacceptable to the others. In May 1991, a referendum for independence and sovereignty was held in Croatia, with 93% of those who attended voting in favour (the turn out was 82%). The Croatian parliament declared Croatia an independent state on 25 June 1991, the same day as Slovenia.

Descent into war

Already at the end of June, the Yugoslavian People's Army (JNA) was sent in to Slovenia, but fighting there lasted only several days as the country was not a target of Milošević's expansionism, having no significant Serbian minority. However, the war then transferred to Croatia, where Milošević was more than eager to defend the 600,000 strong Serbian community, who were mainly concentrated in the old *Krajina* zones. Local Serbs worked together with the JNA, who were confronted by poorly armed Croatian policemen and voluntary soldiers. Much of the former *Krajina* came under Serb control in the so-called Log Revolution (trees were felled and placed across roads to literally block access to the region), and the Republic of the Serbian Krajina was declared, effectively cutting off one-third of the country. Basically the Serbs said that if the Croats could claim independence from Belgrade, then they wanted independence from Zagreb.

Serbian TV, Milošević's main propaganda tool, predicted the resurgence of the Independent State of Croatia (NDH), spreading fear among Serbs of a return to the Second World War-style persecution. Likewise Croatian TV broadcast horrific stories of Serbian barbarianism and the evils of Communism. The seeds of ethnic hatred had been sown and it became increasingly impossible to distinguish the truth from the lies.

Since negotiations with the mediation of the European Union proved unsuccessful, the Croatian parliament broke off all relations with Yugoslavia on 8 October 1991. Also in October, the JNA and Montenegran forces placed Dubrovnik under a six-month siege, and in November, after heroic resistance by the Croats, the Serbs managed to take Vukovar in eastern Slavonia in the bloodiest and cruellest fighting the war would see.

The closing stages

Members of the EU, with much persuasion from Germany and the Vatican, recognized Croatia's independence on 15 January 1992. The JNA left Serb-occupied territories, which remained, however, in the hands of the self-proclaimed Republic of the Serbian Krajina, and in March 1992 UN peacekeepers were sent in to oversee the situation. Isolated incidents of ethnic violence continued, but all-out fighting had stopped. On 22 May 1992 Croatia became a member of the United Nations.

Under Clinton, the US began sending in American military advisors to train the Croatian army. In early May 1995, with American blessing, in the military operation Blijesak (Lightning), Croatian forces attacked a Serb-held enclave in western Slavonia. The Serbs were forced to evacuate the region, giving the Croatian army a victory and considerably reducing the Croatian territory controlled by the Serbs.

Then, in August, with the military operation Oluja (Storm), Serb-held areas of North Dalmatia, Banovina, Kordun and Lika were liberated. The fall of the Republic of the Serbian Krajina was officially announced when Croatian soldiers hoisted the red and white chequer-board flag above Knin Fortress. A mass exodus of Serbian families ensued, with most fleeing to neighbouring Bosnia and to Serbia-proper.

Through the Erdut Agreement, the area of eastern Slavonia with Vukovar and Baranja was placed under UN control, until being reintegrated into Croatian territory in January 1998.

Modern Croatia

Once hostilities were over, it was time to pick up the pieces. Despite having delivered the country its long-desired independence, Tudjman and the ruling HDZ party rapidly lost popularity. The international community accused the Croatian state of interfering with Bosnia (Tudjman had set up an embarrassing allegiance with Bosnian Croats), media manipulation, an appalling human rights record, and the failure to comply with The Hague over war crimes. During the war, Tudjman's upholding of conservative values such as the family, the church and the nation had been enough to keep many people happy.

But after several years of peace, it became apparent that the entire national economy had been undermined, and that nothing would improve until there was a complete change in policy. A new elite class had emerged – those close to the HDZ who had been awarded hefty slices of state property for their loyalty, and those who had made fast money out of black market dealings during the war. The rest of society remained impoverished, unemployment was rife, and even those who had jobs seldom saw their monthly pay cheque on time.

Ironically, in the end both Tudjman and Milošević dodged justice: Tudjman died, after a long illness, in December 1999, and Milošević in March 2006, before The Hague was able to pass sentence on either of them.

After Tudjman's death, the HDZ immediately set about trying to organize a convincing election campaign, but the Croatian public had already lost faith. At the elections in January 2000 a new centre-left six-party coalition won and former Communists **Ivica Račan** and **Stipe Mesić** were sworn in as Croatia's prime minister and president. However, early elections in November 2003 saw the HDZ back in power, the party having apparently dispelled its nationalist, authoritarian image to become a mainstream conservative movement. **Ivo Sanader** thus replaced Račan as prime minister.

The new government promised to steer the country towards the European Union and encourage national reconciliation. However, despite much-improved relations with Serbia, and the fact that the Independent Democratic Serbian Party (SDSS), which aims to facilitate the return of refugees, formed a part of Sanader's coalition government, by 2007 only 125,000 of the 250,000 displaced Croatian Serbs had returned to register in Croatia, and most of these were elderly people from rural villages, or people who had registered but were not actually living in Croatia. This slow progress is attributed to problems over property (many Serb homes were destroyed or occupied by other people during the war), unemployment and fear of discrimination.

Another major stumbling block, up until late-2005 , was Croatia's failure to hand over indicted war criminals to the Criminal Tribunal for the Former Yugoslavia (ICTY) in The Hague. The key to Croatia commencing EU accession negotiations was the capture of General Ante Gotovina (indicted for crimes during and after Operation Storm in 1995, but considered by many Croatians a national hero). In December 2005, Gotovina was arrested in Spain and handed over to The Hague. In 2005 and 2006, President Mesić of Croatia and President Tadić of Serbia exchanged official visits in a bid to improve relations between the two countries.

Sanaders's government was narrowly re-elected in November 2007. Mesić remains president, with the next presidential election due in 2010. Croatia also hopes to enter the EU in 2010.

Economy

The war and its after-effects had a devastating effect on the Croatian economy, especially in the industrial sector. Shipbuilding and maritime transport, in which former Yugoslavia held the third position in the world economy (and which were mainly concentrated along the Croatian coast), faced a sharp decline. Some 35,000 Croatian sailors now work on foreign ships.

Privatization began in earnest after the war, though it is still not complete. Most steel companies and shipyards are still under state ownership, though the financial sector has been completely privatized and 90% of banks are now owned by foreign investors.

When the Kuna was introduced as the national currency in 1994, the stability of the exchange rate Kuna-German Deutschmark was constantly maintained; now stability is monitored against the euro.

The Croatian trade deficit is constantly growing, though it is being compensated for in part by money transfers from Croats living abroad, sailors working for foreign companies, and from income from tourism: 80% of deposits in Croatian banks are in euros.

Sector by sector, the Croatian GDP is composed of agriculture and fisheries 6%, industry 27% and services 67%. In 2007 the GDP growth rate stood at 5.6% and the GDP per capita at US$ 15,500, exceeding that of many of the Eastern European countries that became EU members in 2004. The strongest Croatian companies, such as pharmaceutical company PLIVA and the food processor PODRAVKA, are present on the world market.

However, the costs of the state represent a major burden on the economy. The war and its after-effects led to a drastic rise in unemployment. In 1980 the employment rate was 5.5%, in 1989 8%; in the following years it rose as high as 22%, though by 2005 it had dropped to 14%, and by 2007 to 11.8%.

According to international economic analysts, low labour costs, a skilled work force and natural resources represent the country's top assets. The biggest potential lies in the tourism sector which, with 10 million visitors in 2006 contributed 7 billion euro to the national economy. The introduction of the euro has made Croatia more attractive to EU citizens: such clean sea cannot be found anywhere else in Europe and Croatia is probably the safest destination on the Mediterranean. Many hotels have been privatized and upgraded to offer high-class accommodation and luxurious extras such as Wellness Centres.

Croatia's greatest resource is its well-preserved natural environment. The decline of the industrial sector as a result of the war meant that an ecologically clean country became even cleaner. The high proportion of fertile land per capita gives the country the potential of producing large quantities of healthy food. Land and property prices are still lower than in most EU countries, though they have risen significantly since 2000 due to the interest shown by second-home buyers from abroad. Croatia obtains 66% of its power supply from hydroelectric power plants, and could potentially provide for its energy needs from renewable sources such as wind and sun. Drinking water is abundant and tap water is drinkable throughout the country.

Two new motorways, linking Zagreb and Split, and Zagreb and Rijeka, opened in summer 2005. In October 2007 construction work began on the new Peliješac Bridge, intended to improve connections to South Dalmatia. When completed, this 2.4 km, cable-stayed bridge will span the channel between Komarna on the mainland to Rosčica Glavica on Peliješac. If building progress runs to schedule it will open in 2011.

Culture

Architecture

Classical

The finest remaining buildings from Roman times can be seen in the cities of Pula and Split. In the former, the oldest significant monument is a first-century BC triumphal arch, known as the Arch of the Sergi. It was built to celebrate the role of three high-ranking military officers from the Sergi family at the Battle of Actium in 31 BC; upon their return home they would have led their triumphant soldiers through the arch into the walled city. Made up of a single arch flanked with slender columns with Corinthian capitals, it is ornamented with base reliefs of dolphins, a sphinx and a griffon, and an eagle struggling with a snake. Originally it would have been topped with statues of the three generals. Italian Renaissance architects Palladio and Michelangelo were obviously suitably impressed by it, as both sketched it on their travels. Close by, the present-day main square was once the forum and, of the principal public buildings that stood here, the first-century AD Temple of Augustus remains intact. Typically designed to be viewed from the front, it is elevated on a high base with steps leading up to an open portico supported by six tall columns. Located outside the former walls, Pula's best-known Roman building is the colossal first-century AD amphitheatre, which was built to host gladiator fights and could accommodate up to 22,000 spectators, making it the sixth largest surviving Roman amphitheatre in the world.

Moving south down the coast, Split grew up within the 25-m-high walls of a unique third-century palace, commissioned by Emperor Diocletian as a retirement residence. Combining the qualities of a Roman garrison and an imperial villa, this vast structure is based on a rectangular ground plan measuring 215 m by 180 m, and contains various individual monuments such as an octagonal mausoleum (now the cathedral) and a classical temple dedicated to Jupiter (now a baptistry). British and French architects and artists first acknowledged its magnificence during the 18th century when many visited it as part of the Grand Tour; it is said to have inspired the Scottish architect Robert Adam in some of his finest neoclassical projects upon his return to the UK.

Six kilometres inland from Split, the archaeological site of Salona was once the largest Roman urban centre in Croatia, with an estimated population of 60,000 in the third century AD. Sadly it was devastated in the seventh century; today only the ruins remain.

Byzantine

During the sixth century the coastal region came under Byzantium. Architecturally, the Byzantine Empire is best known for its magnificent Christian basilicas, and the most outstanding example in Croatia is Euphrasius Basilica in Poreč. Built under the rule of Emperor Justinian (AD 483-565), during the same period as Hagia Sophia in Constantinople (present-day Istanbul), this complex comprises a central atrium, with an octagonal baptistry to one side, and opposite it the basilica itself, where the central aisle focuses on a main apse decorated with splendid golden mosaics.

Pre-Romanesque

The Croats arrived in the region in the seventh century and gradually began taking on the Christian faith. Between the ninth and 11th centuries about 150 small pre-Romanesque churches, often referred to as early Croatian churches, were built, mainly along the coast. Byzantine influence is apparent in their geometric massing, though they tend towards minimum decoration, limited to finely carved stonework ornamented with plait-design motifs reminiscent of Celtic art. The most perfect example is the tiny ninth-century Holy Cross in Nin, based on the plan of a Greek cross, while the largest and most imposing is the monumental ninth-century rotonda St Donat's in Zadar, based on a circular ground plan with three semi-circular apses. You can see an excellent collection of early Croatian church stonework in the Croatian Museum of Archaeological Monuments in Split.

Romanesque

The 12th century saw the dawn of the Romanesque age, which was marked by imposing cathedrals, generally made up of triple naves with semi-circular apses, and ornate façades featuring blind arches. The most beautiful – the Cathedral of St Anastasia and the Church of St Chrysogonus – are in Zadar, though other notables examples include the Cathedral of Our Lady of the Assumption in Krk Town, the Church of St Mary the Great (which was a cathedral until 1828) in Rab Town, and the portal of the Cathedral of St Lawrence in Trogir, which was carved by the outstanding Dalmatian sculptor Master Radovan in the early 13th century. Unfortunately, Croatia's two most important Romanesque cathedrals were destroyed – the one in Zagreb by the Tartars in 1242, and the one in Dubrovnik by the 1667 earthquake (subsequently rebuilt in later styles).

Venetian Gothic

When Venice began colonizing the east Adriatic coast, it brought with it the so-called Venetian Gothic style, characterized by the pointed arch and rib vaulting. The style is apparent in 15th- and 16th-century churches and houses in Istria and Dalmatia, such as the finely carved portal of Korčula Cathedral by Bonino from Milan, and the triple pointed-arch windows of the Čipko Palace in Trogir by Andrea Aleši. It is often seen mixed with more severe Renaissance elements, most notably in the work of Juraj Dalmatinac on Šibenik Cathedral (see below), hence the term Gothic-Renaissance.

Renaissance

The Renaissance, which started in Italy, marked a revival of Roman civilization, not just in art and architecture but in an entire set of values. The movement is normally said to have dawned in Croatia in 1441, when Juraj Dalmatinac, a builder from Zadar who had trained for a short time in Venice, began work on Šibenik Cathedral. Although he did not live to see it completed, the later work was carried out by two of his pupils, Nikola Firentinac and Andrija Aleši. Dalmatinac also drew up the urban plan for Pag Town in 1443, and worked on other noted projects such as the Chapel of St Anastasius in Split Cathedral and Minčeta Fortress in Dubrovnik. You can see a 20th-century statue of Dalmatinac, by Ivan Meštrović, in front of Šibenik Cathedral.

The Renaissance continued developing along the coast, in areas not under the Turks, until the end of the 16th century. During this period many towns were fortified with defensive walls and towers, the best examples being Dubrovnik, Korčula and Hvar.

Increased wealth, plus the ideals of Renaissance philosophy, lead to the construction of more sophisticated houses, with refined details such as carved doors and window frames, balconies with balustrades, stone washbasins, decorated fireplaces and built-in cupboards. People became interested in the relationship between man and nature; houses were set in gardens with arcaded walkways, fountains and stone benches, the best examples being Tvrdalj in Stari Grad on the island of Hvar and Trsteno Arboretum near Dubrovnik, both from the 16th century.

Also worth a mention here is Lucijano Vranjanin, a Croat born near Zadar in the 15th century. He spent most of his life in Italy, where he was known as Luciano Laurana, and built several notable early-Renaissance palaces, the best known being the Ducal Palace in Urbino.

Islamic

When the Ottoman Turks moved into Slavonia they brought with them the Muslim faith. Many mosques were built, but few locals converted to Islam, so that when the Turks were finally driven out, the mosques were largely destroyed – a situation quite different to that in neighbouring Bosnia, where still today there is a sizeable Muslim population. One of the very few remaining mosques in Croatia can be seen in Đakovo, though the minaret was pulled down and it was converted into the Catholic Church of all Saints when the Turks left in 1687.

Baroque

Regarded as a symbol of Western civilization, and therefore the antithesis of Ottoman culture, the baroque style flourished in northern Croatia during the late 17th and 18th centuries. The Jesuits, who played an important part in reinforcing the Roman Catholic faith in areas threatened by the Turks, were responsible for introducing the grandiose, curvilinear baroque style to the region. As the Turks were gradually pushed out, many buildings were constructed, reconstructed or extended in baroque style.

Today, the best-preserved baroque town centre is in Varaždin – tragically Vukovar, formerly regarded as the finest baroque town in Croatia, was all but devastated during the war for independence during the 1990s. Other notable examples can be found in Osijek (the 18th-century Tvrdja complex) and in Dubrovnik (the Cathedral from 1671 and the Jesuit Church from 1725, both designed by Italian architects during reconstruction following the earthquake of 1667).

Eclectic

During the 19th century, eclectic design – the revival and reinterpretation of past styles – was popular throughout Europe. In Zagreb, the buildings of Donji Grad, constructed when the region was under Austro-Hungary, mix various elements from classical, Gothic and baroque periods. The most prolific architect in north Croatia at this time was Herman Bolle (1845-1926). Born in Koln, Germany, he participated in the construction of about 140 buildings in Croatia, including Zagreb Cathedral, Mirogoj Cemetery and the Museum of Arts and Crafts, all in Zagreb.

Vienna Secession

By the close of the 19th century, artists and architects in various parts of Europe were rebelling against the decadence of eclectic buildings and the pomp and formality of older styles, and searching instead for more pure and functional forms. In German-speaking countries this trend was known as Jugendstil, and in France as art nouveau. In 1897 in Vienna, a group of visual artists founded a movement, which became known as the Vienna Secession. The architects involved strove to give simple geometric forms to their buildings, while working in close collaboration with artists, who provided discreet, elegant details such as frescoes and mosaics. The best examples of this style in Croatia, which was still part of the Austro-Hungarian Empire at the time, are Villa Santa Maria, Villa Frappart and Villa Magnolia, all designed by the Austrian architect Carl Seidl and found in Lovran, close to Opatija. In Osijek, Europska Avenue is lined with fine Viennese Secessionist buildings by local architects.

Modernism

There are very few examples of quality modernist architecture in Croatia, though the ideals of the modern movement were held dear by the Socialist state during the second half of the 20th century. The resulting buildings are primarily high-rise apartment blocks, most of which are light and airy with large balconies, and vast hotel complexes that sprung up along the coast, which are rather impersonal but functional and comfortable.

Restoration

Croatia's wealth of historic monuments and well-preserved town centres are obviously a source of national pride and an important element in the country's tourist industry. In 1979, the historic centres of Dubrovnik and Split were designated UNESCO World Heritage Sites; Trogir and Euphrasius Basilica in Poreč followed in 1997 and in 2000 Šibenik Cathedral was added. These sites are thereby entitled to various degrees of international funding for restoration work. Careful refurbishment projects are currently underway on many other historic buildings, and most city centre damage caused by the war has been fully repaired. Visiting Dubrovnik, it is difficult to believe the city was held under a six-month siege in 1992. In addition, local people are re-evaluating the importance of folk architecture, and stone farm buildings and cottages in Dalmatia and Istria are also finally being lovingly restored and preserved for future generations. It is hoped that the growing number of foreigners buying properties along the coast will also respect the regions' traditional architecture and invest in conservation.

Art

Passing through the centuries under a series of foreign rulers, Croatia has had little opportunity to develop its own artistic movements. The rich and powerful have always been more interested in the works coming directly out of the empire they represented, be it Venice, Turkey or Austro-Hungary. Those Croats who did become successful artists were mainly educated abroad and often remained outside the country for most of their lives. However, here is brief summary of notable Croatian painters and sculptors.

Painting

The first notable Croatian movements emerged during the 15th century. In the wealthy and culturally advanced city of Dubrovnik, a group of painters inspired by Italian Gothic art and the Byzantine tradition became known as the Dubrovnik School. Unfortunately few of their works have been preserved – mainly due to the destructive earthquake of 1667 – but **Blaž Jurjev Trogiranin** (also known as Blasius Pictor) from Trogir and **Lovro Dobričević** from Kotor (present-day Montenegro) can be singled out. They produced a wealth of icons and ornate polyptychs featuring religious scenes, both for Catholic and Orthodox churches, using rich blues, greens and reds often against a golden background. Today you can see examples of Trogiranin's work in Korčula Town – a polyptych *Our Lady with Saints* in the Abbey Treasuy and a polyptych *Our Lady the Co-redeemer* in the Church of All Saints. Several outstanding pieces by Dobričević are on display in the Dominican Monastery in Dubrovnik.

In the north of the country, in Istria, a more humble school of fresco painting emerged, best represented by the works of **Vincent of Kastav** in St Mary's Church in Beram, near Pazin. Painted in 1474, this extraordinary cycle consists of 40 paintings depicting events from the life of Christ, figures of individual saints and scenes such as the *Adoration of the Kings* and the *Dance Macabre*. Full of religious symbolism it was intended as a Bible for the illiterate, being both amusing and easy to relate to, for those who could not read the scriptures. The frescoes were covered over by plaster during reconstruction in the early 18th century and only rediscovered in 1913; today their colours are muted and subtle, with shades of rusty red, ochre, blue and green.

The year 1498 saw the birth of one of Croatia's finest painters, **Julije Klović**. He grew up in Vinodol, near Rijeka, then moved to Italy where he was known as Don Giulio Clovio Croata and became one of the most important Renaissance miniaturists. He painted for the pope and the Medici family, and today has works in the Uffizi Gallery in Florence, the Louvre in Paris and the British Museum in London. While in Rome, he tutored the Cretan artist El Greco, who painted a portrait of him, now on show in the Museo di Capodimonte in Naples.

The next big name in Croatian art is the realist painter **Vlaho Bukovac** (1855-1922). Born in Cavtat, he studied in Paris and also spent some time in England, where he executed portraits of various aristocratic families, into which he was received as a friend and guest: his *Potiphar's Wife* was exhibited in the Royal Academy of London. From 1903 to 1922 he was a professor at the Academy of Art in Prague. The house were he was born in Cavtat has been turned into a gallery displaying a collection of his paintings and drawing.

Split's greatest painter is generally acknowledged to be **Emanuel Vidović** (1870-1953). He studied in Venice then moved back to Split, where he would work outdoors, making colourful sketches, then return to his studio to rework his impressions on large canvasses, often producing dark, hazy paintings with a slightly haunting atmosphere. He especially loved the neighbouring city of Trogir, and executed several painting of the interiors of the cathedrals in Split and Trogir. There are plans to open a Vidović Gallery in Split with about 70 paintings donated to the city by his family.

The one movement in painting which is unique to Croatia is the **Hlebine School**, which developed in the village of Hlebine, close to Koprivinca, in the 1930s. It evolved when Professor Krsto Hegedušić (1901-1971) met the self-taught painter **Ivan Generalić** (1914-1992) was highly impressed by his works and exhibited them as part of the Zemlja group in Zagreb and Sofia (Bulgaria). Generalić then went on to tutor a whole group of local farmers, who produced a vast range of Naïve works, typically depicting scenes from everyday rural life using bright colours painted on glass. Altogether about 200 artists make up the group, including Ivan's son Josip Generalić, Franjo Mraz and Mirko Virius. You can see their works in Koprivnica Gallery, Hlebine Art Gallery and the Croatian Naïve Art Museum in Zagreb.

A Croatian artist well known in the US is **Maximiliano Vanka** (1889-1963). Born in Zagreb, he studied at the Academy of Fine Arts, where he later became a professor of painting. He exhibited throughout Europe and obtained the Palme Academique of the French Legion of Honour. In 1936 he moved to the US, where his best-known works are the murals in the Church of St Nicholas, in Millvale, Pittsburgh, which depict traditional Catholic scenes as well as reflecting the lives and spirituality of the Croatian immigrant community. Although many of his works have remained in the US, you can see a collection of his drawings and paintings in the delightful Memorial Museum Maximilian Vanka in Korčula Town.

For many people, Croatia's most outstanding 20th-century artist is **Edo Murtić**. Born in 1921 in Velika Pisanica near Bjelovar in inland Croatia, he grew up in Zagreb where he also studied art. During the Second World War he designed posters and illustrated books connected to the Partisan liberation movement. After the war he visited New York, where he met American abstract expressionists such as Jackson Pollock, and completed a cycle of paintings called *Impressions of America*. During the 1960s and 1970s he was one of the masters of European abstract art, painting vast canvasses with mighty bold strokes and daring colours. In the 1980s his works became less abstract, featuring recognizable Mediterranean landscapes. He has paintings in the Tate Gallery in London and MOMA in New York. Sadly he died in 2005.

Sculpture

The church was the main sponsor of sculptors until the 20th century, when the state realized the powerful messages that can be put across through public works of art. Nearly all the most noted sculptors came from Dalmatia, where they worked predominantly in local stone.

The first individual artists to have been recorded in the history of Croatian sculpture were working in Romanesque style during the 13th century: **Master Radovan**, who completed the magnificent main portal of Trogir Cathedral, and **Andrea Buvina** who carved the well-preserved wooden doors to Split Cathedral.

During the 15th century, with the dawn of the Renaissance, some important artists combined the skills of architecture and sculpture, notably **Juraj Dalmatinac**, who was responsible for the 74 heads cut in stone that make up a freeze on the exterior of Šibenik Cathedral, and his pupil **Andrea Aleši**, who completed the delicately carved baptistry in the same building.

Moving forward to the 19th century, **Ivan Rendić** (1849-1932), who was born in Supetar on the island of Brač, was highly respected for the tombs and gravestones he designed for the local upper classes. He also executed several statues of prominent historic figures.

However, the country's best-known and most prolific sculptor was **Ivan Meštrović** (1883-1962). Born into a peasant family from the Dalmatian hinterland, he was sent to work with a stonecutter in Split, where he showed considerable skill and was thus sent to study at the Art Academy in Vienna, financed by a Viennese mine owner. Although he did not like his professor, he had great respect for the noted Austrian architect Otto Wagner, who also taught there, and soon became influenced by the Vienna Secession movement. In Vienna he also met Rodin, who inspired him to travel in Italy and France, and then to settle in Paris, where he became internationally renowned. He then spent several years in Rome, mixing with members of the Italian Futurist movement such as Ungaretti and de Chirico, and in 1911 he won first prize at an international exhibition in Rome, where critics hailed him as the best sculptor since the Renaissance. During the First World War he spent some time in England where he staged a one-man exhibition at London's Victoria and Albert Museum. After the First World War he returned to his homeland, taking a house in Zagreb – which is now open to the public as the Meštrović Atelier – and designing a villa in Split, today the Meštrović Gallery. However, at the beginning of the Second World War he was imprisoned by the fascist Ustaše, and it was only through intervention of his friends in Italy, including the pope, that he managed to leave the country. He spent the rest of his life in the USA, but upon his death his body was returned to Croatia where he was buried in the family mausoleum as he had requested. Today he has pieces in stone, bronze and wood on exhibition in the Tate Gallery in London and the Uffizi in Florence. In several Croatian towns you can see bronze statues of important local cultural figures, such as Grgur Ninski and Marko Marulić in Split and Juraj Dalmatinac in Šibenik, which he created as public works. In the US his best-known outdoor piece is *Indians* in Grant Park, Chicago.

During his career Meštrović took several pupils, and one of them, **Antun Augustinčić** (1900-1979) went on to have great success. Under Tito, Augustinčić became the official state artist of Yugoslavia, creating many large bronze pieces with typical socialist themes such as the Heroic Worker. His best-known work is *Peace*, on display in the gardens in front of the United Nations building in New York. In the Augustinčić Gallery, in his native town of Klanjec in Zagorje, you can see a fine display of his works.

Literature

Going back to the Middle Ages, Croatian writing consisted mainly of Church manuscripts, histories, legal codes and some poetry. It was not until the 16th and 17th centuries, despite highly unfavourable conditions of foreign occupation and ongoing battles with the Turks, that literature really began to develop, with writers publishing works in both Latin and Croatian.

Renaissance

The father of Croatian literature is generally considered to be **Marko Marulić** (1450-1524), a poet and prose writer born in the Dalmatian city of Split, which was then under Venice. You can see a 20th-century statue of him, portrayed as a thin serious man with a beard, by Ivan Meštrović on Voćni Trg in Split.

Influenced by medieval Catholic theology, Marulić believed that suffering was brought upon us by our own sins, and that real happiness could only be found through knowledge of God and the performing of good deeds. Disillusioned by local bishops, most of whom had scandalous lifestyles, Marulić became a recluse and even retreated for two years to the island of Šolta. Seeing the Ottoman onslaught as punishment, he called for repentance, and sent a dramatic letter to Pope Hadrian VI asking for help against the Turks. His best-known piece is the epic poem *Judita* from 1501, the first printed literary work in Croatian (written in the ćakavian dialect). Inspired by the biblical tale of Judith (who killed the Assyrian general Holofernes) it was a plea for the national struggle against the Turks. The message was that with God's help, they could be overcome. Another significant work by Marulić, which was read throughout Europe, was *Quinquaginta parabolae*, written in Latin and published in Venice in 1510; it was a collection of 50 allegorical stories about peasants and fishermen, each with a religious message.

Two noted writers who followed soon after Marulić were **Hanibal Lucić** (1485-1553) and **Petar Hektorović** (1487-1572), both from the island of Hvar. Lucić wrote the first secular drama in Croatian, *Robinja* (The Female Slave), while Hektorović was a poet who examined the classic Renaissance themes of nature and its beauty in most of his works, as well as the wisdom of lower classes, despite having been born into a noble family. His best-known work is *Ribarenje i ribarsko prigovaranje* (Fishing and Fishermen's Conversations) from 1556, in which he recounts the tale of a three-day fishing trip to the islands of Brač and Šolta in the company of two local fishermen. Hektorović's former home, Tvrdalj, a beautiful Renaissance residence he built in Stari Grad, is open to the public.

Another writer who took the beauty of nature as his central theme was **Petar Zoranić** (1509-1569), from Nin near Zadar, who wrote the idyllic novel *Planine* (The Mountains) in 1536, inspired by the rocky slopes of Velebit.

Around the same time, an important literary movement was developing in Dubrovnik, thanks to the number of young nobles who studied in Padua, and thus had first-hand knowledge of the Italian Renaissance. The city found its best interpreter in the dramatist Marin Držić (1508-1567) who wrote bawdy comedies about the problems of society and contemporary lifestyles, and is often regarded as the Croatian Shakespeare. His best-known work is the comedy *Dundo Maroje* (Uncle Maroje) from 1550, which was performed throughout Western Europe, and can still be seen at the Dubrovnik Summer Festival today. Držić's house in Dubrovnik has been turned into a memorial museum and is open to the public.

While the aforementioned authors were already writing in Croatian, many Croatian scholars continued to write in Latin, both at home and abroad. One of the most interesting is the inventor, philosopher and lexicographer, Faust Vrančić (1551-1617) from Šibenik. In 1595 he published the *Dictionarium quinque nobilissimorum Europae linguarum Latinae, Italicae, Germanicae, Dalmaticae et Ungaricae*, a dictionary of the 'five most noble languages', which included Latin, Italian, German, Hungarian and Croatian (or Dalmatian as it was referred to here). This was the first dictionary to include Croatian. Another work worth mentioning by Vrančić was the highly eccentric *Machinae Novae*, in which he used sketches and text (in Latin) to describe outlandish inventions including a parachute. In later life he withdrew to Rome and became a Pauline monk.

Another 17th-century intellectual concerned about the evolution of the Croatian language was the Jesuit monk **Bartol Kašić** (1575-1650) from the island of Pag, who wrote the first Croatian grammar book *Osnove ilirskog jezika* (The Basics of Illyrian language), which was published in Rome in 1604. Kašić suggested that the štokavian dialect should be the standard language.

In 1612 the first permanent public theatre in Europe opened in Hvar Town on the island of Hvar, a revolutionary idea of its time, as everyone, regardless of their social standing, was welcome to attend performances.

Baroque

The most distinguished baroque writers were from Dubrovnik, and the best known of these was the poet **Ivan Gundulić** (1589-1638). Gundulić's greatest works, clearly reflecting the city-republic's strong spirit of freedom, are the stirring epic poem *Osman*, from 1626, describing the Poles' 1621 victory over the Turks, and the play *Dubravka* from 1628. Gundulić and other Dubrovnik authors wrote in the štokavian dialect which, during the 17th century, became regarded as the accepted form of Croatian by writers throughout Dalmatia, paving the way for a uniform standard Croatian language that was to be realized in the 19th century. You can see a statue of Gundulić, by the Dalmatian sculptor Ivan Rendić, on Gundulićeva Poljana in Dubrovnik.

In the 18th century, a book that played a very important role in the awakening of the national consciousness was *Razgovor ugodni naroda slovinskoga* (A pleasant conversation of the Slav people), written in 1756 by the Franciscan monk **Andrija Kačić Miošić** (1704-1760). It was so popular that almost every house in Dalmatia had a copy and it was known affectionately as *Pismaricom* (The Song-book).

Also during the 18th century, foreign intellectuals became fascinated by the epic folk poems of inland Dalmatia, which were traditionally recited by a bard to the accompaniment of a musical instrument. The man responsible for their diffusion was **Alberto Fortis** (1741-1803), an Italian priest from Padua, whose journeys and research were financed in part by the Scotsman, John Stuart, Count of Bute, who also encouraged the study of folk songs in the British Isles. Fortis travelled through Dalmatia between 1770 and 1774, exploring the way of life of the Vlahi (inhabitants of the Dalmatian hinterland, who he referred to by their Venetian name, *Morlacchi*) collecting and studying their heroic poems, which he recorded in his internationally acclaimed *Viaggi in Dalmazia* (Travels into Dalmatia) from 1774, which was translated into English and French in 1778. Here Fortis talks about the primitive customs of the Vlahi – describing them in a rather patronizing tone as noble savages – and also mentions the tensions between them and the sophisticated urbanites of the Dalmatian coastal towns, a socio-regional divide which still exists today. He also translated the most famous Croatian ballad, *Hasanaginica* (The Wife of Asan Aga), a heroic tale of the region's ongoing battles between Christians and Turks, into Italian. This work was to have great influence on Romanticism throughout Europe, subsequently being translated into German by Goethe in 1778 and then into English by Sir Walter Scott.

Illyrian Movement

The next historical landmark for the evolution of Croatian literature was the founding of the Illyrian Movement by Ljudevit Gaj (1809-1872) from Krapina in Zagorje. Aimed at the union of South Slavs (eg Croats and Serbs) within the Austro-Hungarian federation, members of the movement believed that the Slav tongue should be acknowledged as the official language within these regions, and that it should find a uniform standard form. Gaj thus published *Kratka osnova hrvatsko slavenskoga pravopisanja* (The Basics of Croato-Slavic Orthography) in 1830, in which he proposed writing the palatals – ć, č, š and ž – according to the Czech model. Thanks to the efforts of the Illyrian Movement, a standard language based on the štokavian dialect with etymological orthography was introduced in 1836. You can see a monument of Gaj, by Ivan Rendič, on the main square in Krapina.

Literary works coming out of the Illyrian Movement were suffused with Romanticism and nationalism as can be seen in the patriotic and reflective lyrics of **Petar Preradović** (1818-1872), a soldier and poet of Serbian origin who gave his name to Trg Petra Preradovića in Zagreb, where you can see a statue of him. Here it is also worth mentioning **Antun Mihanović** (1796-1861), a poet from Klanjec in Zagorje, who wrote *Lijepa Naša*, the words to the Croatian national anthem. In northern Croatia, patriotic-romantic themes prevailed into the late 19th century, their main exponent being the poet, dramatist, journalist and critic **August Šenoa** (1838-1881).

Twentieth century

The 20th century is marked by the works of Zagreb-born **Miroslav Krleža** (1893-1981), a harsh critic of bourgeois society and forerunner of existentialism whose best-known novel is *Povratak Filipa Latinovicza* (The Return of Philip Latinowicz), which was translated into several European languages, including English. Another writer held dear to the socialist intellectuals of the Tito period was **Vladimir Nazor** (1876-1949), from Bobovišća on the island of Brač, who lived most of his life in Istria. During the Second World War, Nazor joined the Partisans at the age of 66, and his best-known work is *Veli Jože*, the story of a giant from the Istrian hill town of Motovun, who was captured by the Venetians and used as a slave.

Regarding the Yugoslav years, it is also necessary to mention **Ivo Andrić** (1892-1975) who won the 1961 Nobel Prize for Literature. He originated from Travnik in Bosnia, which was then under Austro-Hungary control, and although he officially declared himself a Serb (and lived most of his later life in Belgrade), some Croats like to include him among the ranks of Croatian literary figures – in any case, the language he was writing in at the time was Serbo-Croatian. Andrić's favourite theme was life in Bosnia under the Turks and the cultural effect of living in a region where East meets West, and he had an unrivalled skill of portraying the peculiarities of human nature through the narration of everyday situations. His two greatest novels were *Na Drini cuprija* (The Bridge on the Drina) and *Travnička hronika* (Bosnian Story), and he also wrote several collections of touching and amusing short stories.

More recently, the most highly regarded Croatian writers have been those living outside the country. Many of them, such as **Dubravka Ugresić**, author of *The Museum of Unconditional Surrender and The Culture of Lies*, were critical of the political situation and the rise in nationalism that took place in Croatia through the 1990s.

Finally, it is worth mentioning that during the second half of the 20th century, writers in Croatia and indeed in all of Eastern Europe, had a far more important role in society than those in Western Europe, and were often active in political movements, writing both for and against the state.

Language

Croatian belongs to the South Slavic branch of the Slavic group of languages – a similar language is spoken by Serbs, Montenegrins and Bosnians. While the latter three speak only the štokavian dialect, Croats speak štokavian, kajkavian and ćakavian. The names of these dialects are derived from the interrogative relative pronoun 'what', being spoken either as 'kaj', 'ća' or 'što'. Kajkavian is mainly spoken in northwest Croatia (but not in Istria), while ćakavian can be heard on all the Dalmatian islands (except Mljet) and along the Dalmatian coast near Zadar and Split. Croats in other parts of Croatia, as well as in Bosnia and Herzegovina, western parts of Vojvodina (in Serbia) and Boka Kotorska (in Montenegro) speak the štokavian dialect. Since it is the official variant taught in schools, štokavian is also spoken in kajkavian and ćakavian parts of the country.

The area where these dialects were spoken was far larger before the Turkish wars, which caused mass migrations. As a result of these population movements, today there are Croatian minorities in Burgenland (Austria), Slovakia, Moravia (Czech Republic) and the region of Molise (Italy), where the older variant of the Croatian language has been preserved.

Croatian is almost identical to Serbian, the main difference being that Croats, who are mainly Catholic, write in Latin script, while Serbs, who are predominantly Orthodox, use the Cyrillic script. Variations in grammar, spelling and pronunciation are comparable to differences between British English and American English.

During the Tito years it became normal to refer to the common language as Serbo-Croatian, though Croatian nationalists always had a problem with this, feeling their Croatian identity somehow undermined; they preferred to call the language Croato-Serbian, or even just 'Croatian'. During the war of the 1990s, Croatian nationalists tried to exaggerate the differences between Croatian and Serbian, reviving archaic expressions and even inventing new words. President Tudjman insisted the new words should be used on radio, television and in schools, but in reality relatively few are in common usage today.

Music

Croatian traditional music has a rich variety of performing styles, repertoires and instruments, reflecting the country's geographical position, turbulent history and variety of cultural spheres. Each region has its own musical style and its own characteristic instruments.

Folk music

The best-known form of Croatian traditional music is rural dance music performed by a **tambura** ensemble. A long-necked string instrument related to the Russian balalaika, the Ukrainian bandura and the Italian mandolin, the *tambura* (or *tamburica*) is considered the Croatian national folk instrument and one of the country's hallmarks. Its name originates from Turkish and it made its first appearance in Bosnia during the 14th century, when the region was part of the Ottoman Empire. Its popularity spread to other Slavic countries, including Croatia, primarily to the region of Slavonia and Baranja. Today the largest *tambura* festivals are the **Golden Strings of Slavonia** held in Požega in September and the **Croatian Tambura Music Festival** held in Osijek in May.

Other traditional instruments, which slightly lost popularity during the 20th century due to the success of the tamburica, include the **gajde** (bagpipe) also played in Slavonia; the **diplica** (a simple, ancient wind instrument) still played in Baranja;

the **trontole** (drone zither) and **cimbal** (dulcimer) played in Međimurje (notably in the Čakovec area), and the **žvegla**, **fajfa**, and **dvojnice** (all types of flute), which were once popular in Central Croatia. In the regions of Istria and Kvarner (notably on the island of Krk) traditional woodwind instruments such as the **sopile**, **mih** and **šurle** are still very popular.

In Dalmatia, special place is taken by so-called *klapa* singing; songs performed by ensembles of between five and eight vocalists, without instrumental accompaniment. *Klapa* – which in Dalmatian dialect means company or group – traditionally consists only of male voices, but nowadays many female-only and mixed ensembles have emerged, with a varying number of members. Nevertheless, its basic characteristic and distinction remain solely vocal harmony singing, only rarely discreetly and quietly accompanied by instruments. A special annual festival of amateur singers, the **Dalmatian Klapa Festival**, takes place in July in Omiš, near Split. Over the last 20 years, this festival has grown into a cultural institution of great importance and reputation.

Classical music

The first known manuscripts of church music in Coatia date back to the 11th century and some Christmas folk songs, which can be traced back to the 12th century, are still sung today. Christmas carols vary considerably from region to region, and can have a dozen different melodies.

The Glagolitic chant is a type of church music, which was first mentioned in 1177, when Pope Alexander III visited the city of Zadar. It represents a unique phenomenon in the history of European music and has three basic components: Gregorian coral, Croatian folklore and Byzantine church music. It is still preserved on some of the Croatian islands, notably during the *Za Križem* (Carrying of the Holy Cross), an all-night procession staged the night before Good Friday on the island of Hvar.

The Croatian people are very proud of having two excellent Renaissance composers: **Julije Skjavetić** (Schiavetti) and **Ivan Lukačić**, both of whom lived in Šibenik during the 16th century. Their compositions, as well as other performances of medieval, Renaissance and baroque music, are the core of the **Music Evenings** in St Donat's annual summer festival held in Zadar. The festival attracts well-known European ensembles, which also perform masterpieces from their own countries.

Having several famous opera composers makes Croatia one of only three Slavic nations (besides Czechs and Russians) who have their own national operas. The first Croatian opera *Ljubav i zloba* (Love and Malice) was composed by **Vatroslav Lisinski** in 1846. Operas composed by **Ivan Zajc** (1832-1914) and **Jakov Gotovac** (1895-1982) have been performed in concert halls throughout the world, the best known being Gotovac's *Ero s onoga svijeta* (Ero the Joker), which has been translated into nine languages and performed in about 80 countries. Renowned females opera singers from Croatia include **Milka Trnina** (1863-1941) who performed in the first *Tosca* at Covent Garden, **Maja Strozzi-Pecic** (1881-1962) and **Zinka Kunc-Milanov** (1906-1989).

Today probably the most famous Croatian musician is the pianist **Ivo Pogorelić** (born in Belgrade in 1958) who has performed with leading orchestras all over the world. Tickets for his solo performances are invariably sold out, and over the last decade he has given many charity concerts in aid of the countries of former Yugoslavia, leading UNESCO to name him an 'Ambassador of Goodwill' in 1998.

The words of the Croatian national anthem, *Lijepa naša domovino* (Our Beautiful Homeland), were written by the Croatian poet **Antun Mihanović** (1796-1861) and the music was composed by **Josip Runjanin** (1821-1878), a Serb born in Croatia. It was first sung as the national anthem at an exhibition held by the Croatian-Slavonian Economic Society in Zagreb in 1891.

Land and environment

Geography

Croatia is a boomerang-shaped country with a total surface area of 56,690 sq km, making it about three-quarters the size of Scotland. It lies on the east coast of the Adriatic and serves as the main gateway from the Mediterranean to Eastern Europe, bordering Slovenia in the northwest, Hungary in the north, Serbia in the northeast, Bosnia and Herzegovina in the east and Montenegro in the extreme south. It has 1778 km of indented mainland coastline and over a thousand islands and islets, of which only 67 are inhabited.

The territory is made of flat plains, low mountains, the mainland coast and offshore islands, and can be broken down into three regions: the Pannonian Basin, the Dinaric Mountains and the Adriatic coast.

Pannonian Basin

The gently undulating hills and expansive flat plains between the River Drava to the north (forming a natural border with Hungary), the River Danube to the east (border with Serbia) and the River Sava to the south (border with Bosnia and Herzegovina) were historically known as Pannonia, which was later renamed Slavonia. This is a region of extremely fertile agricultural land, producing wheat, corn, sugar beet and sunflowers, with lush pastures and vineyards on the hills to the north. Moving west towards Zagreb, the so-called Peri-Pannonian area is made up of low hills and pastureland suitable for livestock, which gradually gives way to industry as you approach the capital.

Dinaric Mountains

The rugged Dinaric Alps extend 640 km along the east coast of the Adriatic Sea from the Isonzo River in northeast Italy to north Albania. A narrow belt running from northwest to southeast, they mark the natural border between the west of Bosnia and Herzegovina and Croatia, and form a barrier to travel from the coast to the interior, as there are no natural passes. They are composed of limestone and dolomite, easily eroded sedimentary rocks which give rise to karst forms such as sinkholes and caves. The region is sparsely populated and supports scanty cereal production, some small orchards and vineyards, livestock breeding and dairy farming. The highest peak, also called Dinara, reaches 1831 m.

Adriatic coast

The partially submerged western slopes of the Dinaric Alps form the numerous bays, gulfs, inlets and offshore islands along the Croatian coast. The coast extends from the northwest to the southeast, following the basic extension of the Dinaric system. Between Rijeka (Kvarner) and Šibenik (Central Dalmatia), the islands run parallel to the coast, and are separated by channels, which are interlinked by straits. Southeast from here, between Split and Dubrovnik, the islands of Čiovo, Šolta, Hvar, Brač, Korčula, Vis, Lastovo and Mljet extend from the west to the east. The largest island is Krk; other sizeable islands include Cres, Brač, Hvar, Pag and Korčula. The Croatian coastal area may be further divided into the northern (Istria and Kvarner) and southern (Dalmatia) parts. The coastal areas and offshore islands grow olives, citrus fruits and vegetables.

Climate

Croatia lies halfway between the North Pole and the Equator. The Pannonian Basin displays a continental climate, the Adriatic coast a Mediterranean climate. In the Pannonia region, winter temperatures average 0°C and summer temperatures 22°C. Along the coast, winter temperatures average 2°C in the north and 9°C in the south, with summer temperatures between 24°C and 26°C respectively. The sunniest place is said to be Hvar Town, which has 2718 hours of sunshine a year (by comparison, Nice in the south of France has 2706 hours of sunshine). In the Dinaric mountains, in areas over 1500 m, winter temperatures average -6°C and summer temperatures average 18°C.

The average annual rainfall ranges between 600 mm and 3850 mm. The mountainous regions of Gorski Kotar, Biokovo and Velebit have the heaviest rainfall (3850 mm) while the lowest is found in the eastern parts of the country (600 mm).

Wildlife and vegetation

Croatia's contrasting geographic regions afford a wide variety of natural vegetation. Approximately 35% of the country is forested. The common oak predominates in the low hills on the northern edge of the Pannonian Basin, while the indigenous forests and grasslands of the eastern part have been largely felled and turned into arable land, the one exception being the wetlands of Kopaćki Rit, which have been preserved as a nature park. The Dinaric Mountains are quite barren in parts, though lower altitudes of up to 1200 m support dispersed forests of beech and fir, while individual specimens of spruce, sycamore and elm can be found in the same belt. In areas over 1200 m, the sub-alpine beech dominates. The area along the Adriatic coast and the islands are covered with sub-Mediterranean and Mediterranean vegetation. Evergreen forests of holm oak and Aleppo pine, as well as macchia, are typical of the coastal belt and the islands. Some of the islands, notably Pag and the Kornati, display typical karst features and are relatively barren, but for feather grass and sage.

There are some 380 protected animal species in Croatia, the largest and most impressive being the brown bear, the wild boar and the wolf, all of which are occasionally sighted in Risnjak, Paklenica and Plitvice national parks. The deer, wildcat and lynx are also present in Risnjak, while the otter is sometimes spotted in Plitvice. The seaward slopes of the Dinaric Mountains, notably Velebit and Biokovo, are populated by small flocks of mouflon and chamois. Large birds of prey such as Eurasion griffon vultures and peregrine vultures can be occasionally be found in seaward-facing cliffs and gorges, while wading birds such as storks and herons are seasonal visitors to the inland wetlands of Kopački Rit and Lošinjsko Polje nature parks. Various species of whales and dolphins swim in the Adriatic.

National parks

The richest and most fascinating areas of natural beauty have been designated national parks. To enter them, visitors are required to pay an entry fee, which goes towards their upkeep. Each park has an information office providing maps and a basic introduction to the area's flora and fauna. Three of the national parks (Kornati, Brijuni and Mljet) are on islands, two centre on systems of waterfalls (Plitvice and Krka) and the others are mountainous.

National park websites **Risnjak**, www.risnjak.hr; **Brijuni**, www.brijuni.hr; **Plitvice**, www.np-plitvicka-jezera.hr; **Paklenice**, www.paklenica.hr; **Krka**, www.npkrka.hr; **Kornati**, www.kornati.hr; and **Mljet**, www.np-mljet.hr.

Books

The books listed below are non-fictional and reference guides. Recommendations for Croatian fiction and poetry are under Literature, page 339.

History, politics and culture

Glenny, Misha, *The Fall of Yugoslavia* (1996) Penguin; *The Balkans: Nationalism, War and the Great Powers, 1804-1999* (2001) Penguin. Both these books give detailed and readable analysis of the history and politics of the wider Balkan region, with many relevant references to Croatia.
Judah, Tim, *The Serbs: History, Myth and the Destruction of Yugoslavia* (1997) Yale University Press. A scholarly but lively account of the last 6 centuries of Serbian history.
Morris, Jan, *The Venetian Empire* (1990) Penguin. Includes an excellent chapter about the Venetian port towns along the Croatian coast.
Silber, Laura and Little, Allan, *The Death of Yugoslavia* (1996) Penguin Group and BBC Worldwide Ltd. Based on the BBC documentary of the same name, this book gives a step-by-step account of the lead up to hostilities and the war itself.
Stavrianos, Leften Stavros, *The Balkans Since 1453* (3rd edition, 2000) New York University Press. Although written in 1958, this book gives an excellent introduction to the Ottoman Empire, tracing Balkan history from the fall of Constantinople up to the close of the Second World War.
Tanner, Marcus, *Croatia: A Nation Forged in War* (1997) Yale University Press. One of the best general accounts of Croatian history, tracing events from the arrival of the Slavs up to the 1990s.

Tito biographies

Maclean, Fitzroy, *Josip Broz Tito, a pictorial biography* (1980) McGraw-Hill, New York. Photos covering Tito's years as the leader of Yugoslavia.
Ridley, Jasper, *Tito* (1994) Constable, London. An excellent general biography, written with hindsight following the break up of Yugoslavia.

Travelogues and memoirs

Murphy, Dervla, *Through the Embers of Chaos: Balkan Journeys* (2002) John Murray. Murphy on a bike, exploring the current situation in the countries of former Yugoslavia.
West, Rebecca, *Black Lamb & Grey Falcon* (1942) Macmillan, London. Describes a journey through Yugoslavia in 1937. The first section of the book deals with the writer's experiences in Croatia at that time.

Footnotes

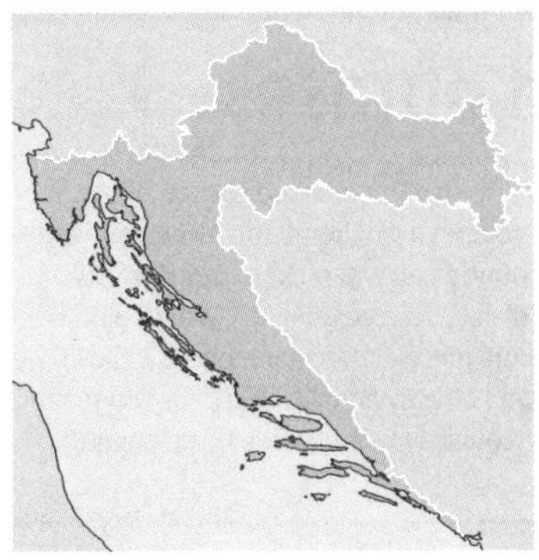

Useful words and phrases

Croatian is difficult to learn unless you already have some knowledge of another Slavic language. However, with a few basics your visit will be all the more enjoyable, and once you have spent some time in the country you will pick up more words.

Remember that each region has its own dialect. As a general rule, places along the coast use a fair smattering of Italian (or to be more precise, Venetian) terms, while in the north of the country you will hear words borrowed directly from German. For information about self-study packs, and Croatian language courses in Croatia itself, see page 45.

General pronunciation

Every letter is pronounced, so Croatian is spoken as it is written. Besides the five standard vowels (a, e, i, o, u) the letter 'r' also acts as a vowel when it appears between two consonants, or as the first letter in a word followed by a consonant so, the first syllable of the word *Hrvat* sounds like *her* in English will a rolled 'r'. There are also eight letters that are not found in the English alphabet:

Č as the *ch* in cheap
ž as the *j* in jug
Š as the *sh* in sheep
š as the *s* in leisure
Ć as the *t* in future
Đ as *d* in duke (can also be written as Dj)
Lj as the *lli* in million
Nj as the *ni* in onion

Greetings, courtesies

Hello *Bog*
Good morning *Dobro jutro*
Good afternoon *Dobar dan*
Good night *Laku noč*
Goodbye *Dovidjenja*
See you later *Vidimo se kasnije*
How are you? *Kako ste?*
Pleased to meet you *Drago mi je*
Please *Molim*
Thank you *Hvala*
Yes *Da*
No *Ne*
Excuse me *Oprostite*
I do not understand *Ne razumijem*
Please speak more slowly *Molim Vas govorite sporije*
What is your name? *Kako se zovete?*
Go away! *Odlazi!*

Basic questions

Where is_? *Gdje je_?*
How much does it cost? *Koliko košta?*
How much is it? *Koliko je ovo?*
When? *Kada?*
When does the bus leave? *Kada polazi/ kreće autobus?*
Does it take long? *Da li to dugo traje?*
When does the bus arrive? *Kada dolazi/ stiže autobus?*
Why? *Zašto?*
What for? *Zbog čega?*
What time is it? *Koliko je sati?*
How do I get to_? *Kako mogu stići do_?*

Basics

Entrance *Ulaz*
Exit *Izlaz*
Bathroom/toilet *WC* (pronounced *'vey tsey'*)
Police *Policija*
Hotel *Hotel*
Restaurant *Restoran*
Post office *Pošta*
Telephone *Telefon*
Bank *Banka*
Exchange office *Mjenjačnica*
Exchange rate *Tečaj*
Notes/coins *Papirnati novac/kovanice*
Traveller's cheques *Putni čekovi*
Cash *Gotovina*

Getting around

On the left/right *Lijevodesno*
Straight on *Ravno*
Second street on the left *Druga ulica lijevo*
To walk *Hodati*
Bus station *Autobusni kolodvor*
Railway station *Eljeznički kolodvor*
Bus *Autobus*
Train *Vlak*
Aeroplane *Avion*
First/second class *Prvi/drugi razred*
Ticket *Karta*
Ticket office *Agencija za prodaj karata*
Bus stop *Autobusna stanica*

Accommodation

Do you have a room for the night? *Imate li slobodnu sobu za noćas?*
Room *Soba*
Single/double room *Jednokrevetna soba/ dvokrevetna soba*
With private bathroom *Soba sa kupatilom*
Shower *Tuš*
Sheets *Plahte*
Blankets *Deke/pokrivači*
Pillows *Jastuci*
Toilet paper *Toaletni papir*
Key *Ključ*

Shops

Bakery *Pekara*
Book shop *Knjižara*
Butcher *Mesnica*
Cake shop *Slastičarna*
Chemist *Apoteka/ljekarna*
Fishmonger *Ribarnica*
Market *Tržnica*
Hairdresser *Frizer*
Newsagent/tobacconist *Trafika/kiosk*
Travel agent *Putnička agencija*

Sightseeing

Cathedral *Katedrala*
Church *Crkva*
Garden *Vrt*
Museum *Muzej*
Art gallery *Galerija umjetnina*
Tourist information centre *Turistički ured*
Town hall *Gradska vijećnica*
Closed for holiday *Zatvoreno zbog praznika*

Sport and activities

Beach *Plaža*
Swimming pool *Bazen*
Tennis court *Teniski teren*
Sailing boat *Jedrilica*
Diving club *Ronilački klub*
Hiking path *Pješačka staza*
Mountain refuge *Planinarski dom*

Days, months and time

Day *Dan*
Week *Tjedan*
Month *Mjesec*
Monday *Ponedjeljak*
Tuesday *Utorak*
Wednesday *Srijeda*
Thursday *Četvrtak*
Friday *Petak*
Saturday *Subota*
Sunday *Nedjelja*
January *Siječanj*
February *Veljača*
March *Ožujak*
April *Travanj*
May *Svibanj*
June *Lipanj*
July *Srpanj*
August *Kolovoz*
September *Rujan*
October *Listopad*
November *Studeni*
December *Prosinac*
At one o'clock *U jedan sat*
At half past two *U dva i trideset/ u pola* tri (North Croatia) *u dva i pol* (Dalmatia)
It's one o'clock *Jedan je sat*
It's seven o'clock *Sedam je sati*
In ten minutes *Za deset minuta*
Five hours *Pet sati*

Numbers

0 *nula*
1 *jedan*
2 *dva*
3 *tri*
4 *četiri*
5 *pet*
6 *šest*
7 *sedam*
8 *osam*
9 *devet*
10 *deset*
11 *jedanaest*
12 *dvanaest*
13 *trinaest*
14 *četrnaest*
15 *petnaest*
16 *šestnaest*
17 *sedamnaest*
18 *osamnaest*
19 *devetnaest*
20 *dvadeset*
21 *dvadeset i jedan*
22 *dvadeset i dva*
30 *trideset*
31 *trideset i jedan*
40 *četrdeset*
50 *pedeset*
60 *šezdeset*
70 *sedamdeset*
80 *osamdeset*
90 *devedeset*
100 *sto*
101 *sto i jedan*
102 *sto i dva*
200 *dvjesto*
500 *petsto*
700 *sedamsto*
900 *devetsto*
1000 *tisuću*
1001 *tisuću i jedan*

Food glossary

Eating out

Do you have a table? *Imate li stol?*
Can we have the menu? *Molim vas, moemo li dobiti jelovnik?*
Can we have the bill? *Molim vas, možemo li dobiti racun?*
Breakfast *Doručak*
Lunch *Ručak*
Dinner *Večera*
Meal *Jelo*
Drink *Piće*
Jelovnik *Menu*
Živjeli! *Cheers!*
Račun *Bill*

Snacks

Burek sa mesom Filo pastry filled with minced meat and onions
Burek sa sirom Filo pastry filled with curd cheese
Ćevapčići Meat rissoles served in pitta bread
Ribice Tiny fried fish (similar to whitebait)

Meat and meat dishes

Grah sa kobasicom Beans and sausages
Gulaš Goulash
Janjetina Whole spit-roast lamb
Kulen Salami spiced with paprika (Slavonian speciality)
Meso na žaru Barbecued meat
Miješano meso Mixed grilled meats
Odojak Whole spit-roast suckling pig
Pasticada Beef stewed in wine (Dalmatian speciality)
Piletina Chicken
Pršut Smoked ham (Istrian and Dalmatian speciality)
Punjene paprike Stuffed peppers (with meat)
Purica z mlincima i štrukle Roast turkey with savoury pastry (Zagorje speciality)
Ramsteak Rump steak
Ražnjići Kebabs (normally pork)
Sarma Cabbage leaves stuffed with meat and rice

Fish and seafood

Bijela riba 'White' fish (eg mullet, bass, bream, John Dory)
Brudet Fish stew (Dalmatian speciality, with sea fish)
Crni rižot Black risotto (prepared with cuttlefish ink)
Dagnje Mussels (various names in different regions)
Fiš paprikaš Fish stew (Slavonian speciality, with freshwater fish)
Jastog Lobster
Ostrige Oysters
Plava riba 'Blue' fish (eg tuna, mackerel)
Pržene lignje Fried squid
Riba na žaru Barbecued fish
Rižot frutti di mare Seafood risotto
Rižot sa škampima Shrimp risotto
Salata od hobotnice Octopus salad
Škampi na buzaru Shrimps in garlic and white wine
Školjke na buzaru Shells in garlic and white wine
Slana srdela Salted sardines
Špageti frutti di mare Spaghetti with seafood

Side dishes

Blitva Swiss chard
Krumpir Boiled potatoes
Mješana salata Mixed salad (usually lettuce, cucumber and tomato)
Njoki Gnocchi
Pomfrit Chips
Riža Rice
Špinat Spinach
Zelena salata Green salad (lettuce)

Sweets

Baklava Layers of filo pastry and walnut, drenched in syrup
Palačinke Pancakes
Rožata Crème caramel (Dubrovnik speciality)
Sladoled Ice cream

Fruit

Breskva Peach
Jabuka Apple
Lubenica Melon
Marelica Apricot
Naranča Orange

Miscellaneous

Ajvar Relish made from aubergines and peppers
Juha Soup
Kajmak Clotted sour cream
Maslinovo ulje Olive oil
Ocat Vinegar
Papar Pepper
Paški sir Sheep's cheese from the island of Pag
Sol Salt
Štrukli Baked cheese dumplings (Zagorje speciality)
Tartufi Truffles (Istrian speciality)

Drinks

Bijelo vino White wine
Crno vino Red wine
Gazirana mineralna voda Sparkling mineral water
Negazirana mineralna voda Still mineral water
Pivo Beer
Rakija Spirit
Tamno pivo Stout (dark beer)
Travarica Spirit flavoured with herbs
Voda Water

Index

S/Š

T

Acknowledgements

Jane would like to thank all those who helped with the research for this book, especially Želika Dubravica and Renata Janeković from the Croatia National Tourist Board; Vjenceslav Vlahov in Zagreb; Đurđa Somođi, Rudi Grula and Gordon Vrbanec in Čakovec; Vesna Jovičić in Pula; Radmila Paliska in Labin; Gordana Perić in Zadar; Ivana Rakić in Lastovo; Nila and Gordan and Tri Volta in Split; Goga at Stari Mlin in Makarska; Katerina Vignjević of the Kvarner Region TIC; Alen Karambaić on the island of Krk; Sandra Bandera in Rijeka; and Natali Mravić in Rab Town. A special mention goes to Dejan Dobrota for agreeing to embark on many impromptu journeys, by bus, ferry, bicycle and sailing boat. Jane would also like to thank the team at Footprint.

Thanks are also due to the special contributors: Domagoj Mijan, who wrote the History section and Goran Vuletić, who translated it; Sanja Kuvačić, who wrote the Music section, and Dr Charlie Easmon for adapting the Health section.

Croatia

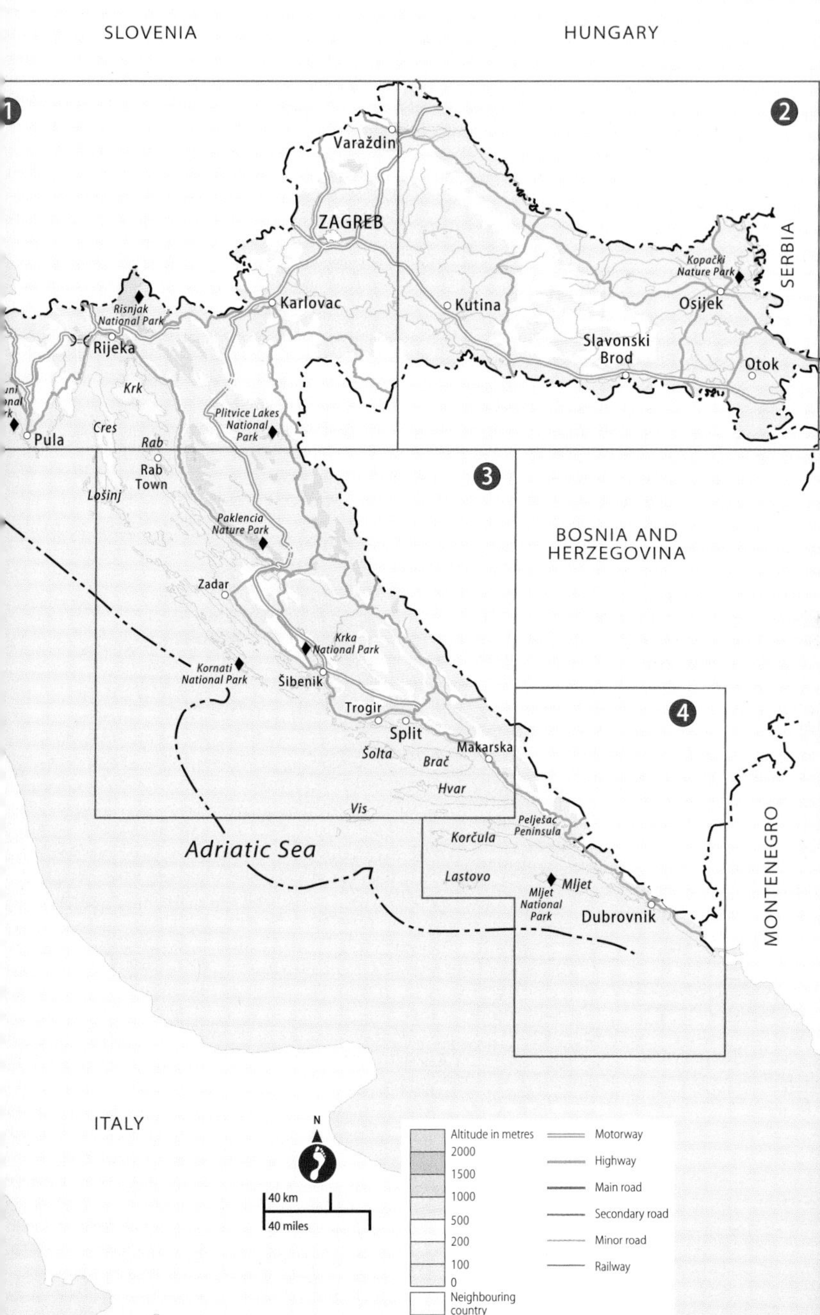

SLOVENIA
HUNGARY
1
2
3
4
Varaždin
ZAGREB
Risnjak National Park
Karlovac
Kopački Nature Park
SERBIA
Osijek
Kutina
Rijeka
Slavonski Brod
Otok
Krk
Plitvice Lakes National Park
Cres
Pula
Rab
Rab Town
Lošinj
Paklencia Nature Park
BOSNIA AND HERZEGOVINA
Zadar
Krka National Park
Kornati National Park
Šibenik
Trogir
Split
Makarska
Šolta
Brač
Hvar
Vis
Pelješac Peninsula
Korčula
Adriatic Sea
Lastovo
Mljet
Mljet National Park
Dubrovnik
MONTENEGRO
ITALY
N
40 km
40 miles
Altitude in metres
2000
1500
1000
500
200
100
0
Neighbouring country
Motorway
Highway
Main road
Secondary road
Minor road
Railway

Map 1
N
10 km
10 miles
A
B
C
1
2
3
SLOVENIA
Babno Polje
Milanev Vrh
Čabar
Skodovnik
Parg
Tršće
Smrekova Draga
Mali Lug
Gerovo
Kraj
Risnjak Nature Park
Lizidraga
Risnjak (528m)
Kuželj
Crni Lug
Delnice
Platak
Mrzia vodica
Lokve
Ravna
Omladinsko jezero
Savudrija
Marija Krasu
Brič
Momian
Umag
Buje
Šterna
Čepic
Zrenj
Buzet
Brest
Vodice
Dane
Šapjane
Rupa
Lipa
Vele Mune
Klana
Žejane
Škalinica
Mačelji
Lanišće
Roč
Brtonigla
Oprtalj
Istarske Toplice
Hum
Dolenja Vaz
Jurdani
Matulji
Kastav
Dražice
Viskcvo
Cavle
Lovrecica
Grožnjan
Livade
Novigrad
Nova Vas
Vižinada
Motovun
Draguć
Lupuglav
Vranja
Opatija
Volovsko
Sušak
Rijeka
Skrijevo
Baka
Krasica
Sunger
Vrata
Fužine
Praputnjak
Lanterna
Tar
Labinci
Kaldir
Karojba
Kašćerga
Cerovlje
Borut
Boljun
Lovran
Kostrena
Bakarac
Križišće
Lič
Bencani
Višnjan
Trviž
Pazin
Paz
Lovanska Draga
Medveja
D Kraj
Kraljevica
Kosinožići
Poreč
Baderna
Lindar
Gologorica
Šušnjevica
Mošćenička Draga
Voz
Drivenik
Ravno
Jadranovo
Tribalj
Žbanda
Gračišće
Wošcanice
Omišalj
Manesterj
Dračevac
Lovrec Paz
Rovin
Kršan
Brseó
Brestova
Crikvenica
Funtana
Sv Kring
Katarina
Nedešćina
Njivice
Čižići
Selce
Bribir
Vrsar
Flengi
Sv Ivenec
Pjomin
Porozina
Sv Vid Miholjice
Dobrinj
Šilo
Novi Vinodolsk
Limski kanal
Barzt
Žminj
Martinski
Beli
Kras
Klenovica
Valalta
Rovinjsko Sela
Kanfanar
Labin
Milohnići
Garica
Žrnovica
Rovinj
Krmed
Svetvinčenat
Rasa
Rabac
Dragozetići
Krk
Vrbnik
Kornić
Režanci
Barban
Črni
Bale
Juršići
Ravni
Valbiska
Krk Town
Punat
Draga Baščanska
Barbariga
Marčana
Diminići
Rakalj
Merag
Baška
Vodnjan
Krnica
Koromačno
Kvarner
Stara Baška
Galižana
Fažana
Brijuni National Park
Brijuni
Loborika
Cres
Kavran
Valtura
Valun
Orlec
Pula
Šišan
Kvarneri
Veruda
Pomer
Ližnjan
Vrana
Lopar
Rab
Medulin
Martšćica
Premantura
Štivan
Belej
Kampor
Rab Town
Ustrine
Sibinj
Senj
Sveti Ju
Lukovo
Kiada
Starigrad

Sv Martin
Štrigova
Mursko Središće
Železna Gora
Macinec
Cestica
Nedelišće
G Vratno
Petrijanec
Sračinec
Vinica
Varaždin
Donja Voča
G Ladanje
Vidovec
Kuršane
Trakošćan
Cvetlin
Matuševec
Novaki
Trnovec
Macelj
Bednja
Jerovec
Tužno
Črešnjevo
A
Dobovec
N Glubovec
Lepoglava
Ivanec
Belentinec
Hum n Sutli
Đurmanec
Radoboj
Petrova Gora
Kam Gorica
Desinić
Pregrad
Krapina
Kuzminec
Belec
Budinšćina
Benkovo
Vel Ves
Miljana
Hum Breznički
Sudovec
Orehovica
Sela
Krap Toplice
Mače
Zlatar
Tigovišće
Sveti Križ
Švaljkovec
Kumrovec
Klanjec
Poznanovec
Zlat Bistrica
Konjšćina
Zabok
Bedenica
Dubrovčan
Kraljevec
Banšćica
Marija Bistrica
Ratakovo
Stubičke Toplice
Komin
St Ivan Zelina
Hrastje
Dubravica
Stub Slatina
D Stubica
Luka
Jakovlje
Moravce
Krečaves
Rakovac
Pušća
Sljeme (1,033m)
D Zelina
Krkač
Dobova
G Laduč
D Bistra
Belovar
Sveta Helene
Jesenice
Brdovec
Medvednica Nature Park
Čučerje
Lonjica
Stojdraga
Bregana
Zaprešić
Ivanec
Dubrava
Soblinec
Poljana
Žumberak I Sambobar Nature Park
Grdanjc
Strmec Sam
Podsused
ZAGREB
Sesvete
Brckovljani
Samobor
Kraljevec
Dugo Selo
Kupčina
Zumb
Nedjelja
Kurestinec
Rude
Jasrušje
Kalji
Botinec
Sasi
Stupnik
Sošice
Mičevec
Rugvica
Tupčina
Horvat
Vel Gorica
Bukevja
Kostanjevac
Klinča Sela
Kuriloveo
Ivanić Grad
Jastrebarsko
Kupinečki Kaljevec
Vukovina
Petrovina
D Dragonožec
Drnek
Vjvodina
Cvetković
Mraclin
B
Topolje
Krašić
Novaki Petr
M Buna
Guci
Bratina
Dubranec
Buševec
Jurovski Brod
Vrh
Vukojevac
Zorkovac
Pisarovina
Kozjaća
Ribnik
Budrovci Draganički
G Pokupje
Jamn Kiselica
Kravarsko
Fišćetke
Benčetici
D Kupčina
Dužica
Žirčica
Zadoborje
D Pokupje
Letovanić
Lazinja
Odra
Netretić
G Stative
Luka
D Stative
Bansj Kovačevac
Žažina
Sela
Vukova Gorica
D Prilišće
Karlovac
Rečica
Pokupsko
Vratečko
Skakavac
Trepča
Sisak
Mrzlo Polje
Kamensko
Slatina
M Gorica
Jarče Polje
G Bučica
Bosanci
Cerovac
Brest
Petrinja
Pracno
Mocile
Zdihovo
Duga Resa
Vukmanički
Šišinec
Belavići
D Sjenicak
Moscenica
Bosiljevo
Stankovac
Zvečaj
Tušilović
Hrastovica
Marinbrod
Graberje
Madzari
Generalski Stol
Slavsko Polje
Blinja
Trošmarija
Krnjak
Gvozd
Glina
Jabukovac
Budačka Rijeka
Voljnić
Mateško Selo
Kolarić
Peter Ogulinski
Perjasica
Kraljevčani
Topusko
Šibine
Komogovin
Potok
Gornji Poloj
Maja
Ogulin
Zagorje
Miholjska
Perna
Zdenac
Tounj
Dragotina
Donji Poloj
Krstinja
Staro Selo
Žnidovac
M Gradac
Skočići
Kestenovac
Jagrovac
Lovča
Oštarije
Obljaj
Maljevac
Skradnik
Map 2
Hrvatski Blagaj
Klokoc
Josipdol
Brezovo Polje
Krakar
Cetin Grad
Drežnica
Modruš
Cerovnik
D Žirovac
Gvozdansko
Divuša
Nikšić
G Kremen
Cetinski Varoš
Latin
Unčani
Fodbitoraj
D Ladevac
Komesarac
Rutevac
Don Javoranj
Lokva
Slunj
Plaški
D Futjan
C
Jezero i dio
Ljubina
Jezerane
Crnec
Dvor
Stajnica
Broćanac
Križpolje
Kotarani
Lučane
Lič Jasenica
Rakovica
Lipice
Brinja
Saborsko
Kuselj
Drežnik Grad
Brlog
Smoljanac
Vaganac
Kompolje
Poljapak
Plitvice Lakes National Park
BOSNIA AND HERZEGOVINA
Plitvice
Ličko Petrovo Selo
Jezerce
Zalužnica
Rudopolje
Otočac
Prijeboj
Vrhovine
Čovići
Plitvički Ljeskovac
Sinac
G Babin Rotok
Kuterevo
4
5
Map 3
6
Ličko Lešće
Koreničica Kapela
Rudinka
Ramljani
Klanac
Vrelo
Korenica

Map 2
Peklenica
Štrukovec
Domašinec
Selo Rok
Čakovec
Hodošan
Pribislavec
Goričan
Mala Subatica
Sv Juraj u Trnju
Donji Kraljevec
Kotoriba
Pušćine
Donja Dubrava
Šemovec
Prelog
Hrzenica
Legrad
Sv Đurđ
Vrbanovec
Ludbreg
Slanje
Đelekovec
Kunovec
Leskovac Topl
Bolfan
Drnje
Rasinja
Subotica
Peteranec
Ljubešćica
Apatovac
Prkos
Hlebine
Gola
Koprivnica
Reka
Ždala
Vel Mučna
Koprivnički Bregi
Repaš
Sokotovec
Vukovec
D Glogovnica
Glogovac
Molve
Sv Helena
Jagnjedovec
Severovnci
N Virje
Carevdar
Novigrad Podravski
Ferdinandovac
Križevci
D Mosti
Virje
Đurđevac
Brodić
Sveti Petar Čvrstec
Šemovci
Kalinovac
Zrinski Topolovac
Rakitnica
Hampovica
Kloštar Podravski
M Raven
Kladare
Sveti Ivan Žabno
Diklenica
Suha Katalena
Pitomača
Tkalec
Rovišće
Kupinovac
Kozarevac
St Gradac
Terezino Polje
Gradec
Cugovec
Predavac
V Trojstvo
Sandrovac
Sedlarica
Bušetina
N Gradac
Haganj
Bolč
Tomaš
Nova Kapela
Rušani
Farkačevac
Gudovac
Ždralovi
Prespa
Vukosavljevica
Lozan
Brezovica
Lukač
V Korenova
Severin
Špišić Bukovica
Budakovac
Dubrava
Gradina
Virovitica
Kapanj
Vaška
Sišćan
Štefanje
Vel Pisanica
Milanovac
Suhopolje
Sopje
Mostari
Ivanska
Cerina
Drjanovac
V Peratovica
Rezovac
Borova
Pčelić
Vagovina
Budanica
Babinac
Vel Grđevac
Suhopolska
Berek
Dapci
Čazrna
V Barna
Lončarica
Jasenaš
Cabuna
Šimljanica
D Miklouš
Pivnica Slavonska
Sladojevci
Graberje
Grubišno Polje
G Prnjarovec
G Garešnica
Herceghovac
V Zdenci
Đulovac
Hum Voćinski
N Bukovica
Slatina
Kompator
Podgarić
Končanica
D Vrijeska
Katoličko Selišće
Brestovac Daruvarski
Koreničani
Vocin
Čeralije
V Pasijan
Bokane
G Jelenska
Kraj Kutinica
Daruvar
Okol
Garešnica
Đunčići
Potok
Popovača
Katoličke Čaire
Dežanovac
G Borki
Slatin-Drenovac
Stružec
Trojeglava
Doljani Podborski
D Gračenica
Kaniška Iva
Uljanik
Osekovo
Repušnica
Novo Autunovac
Badljevina
Galdovo
Poljana Pakračka
Španovica
Bučje
V Svinjiško
Topolovac
Kutina
Gojlo
Kukunjevac
Velika
Gaj
Prekopakra
Dragović
Radovanci
Kaptol
Prelošćica
Međuric
Kamensko
Biškupci
Gušće
Banova Jaruga
Pakrac
Toranj
Gradusa Pos
Kratečko
Orljavac
Lipik
Trenkovo
Lonjsko Polje Nature Park
Pasikovci
Bobovac
Lonja
Lipovljani
D Čaglić
Sloboština
Sunja
Strmac
Fodvrsko
Skenderovci
Treštanovci
Novska
Strmen
Vadro Polje
Bijela Stijena
Baničevac
Kostreski Saški
Širinci
Oblakovac
Brestovac
Požega
Krapje
Bročice
Trnakovac
Slovinci
Šagovina Cerničke
Graboštani
Jasenovac
Cernik
Pleternica
Okučani
Medari
Drenov Bok
Vrbovljani
Nova Gradiska
Selište
Mlaka
Dubovac Okučanski
Rešetari
St Petrovo Selo
Brenovac
Slabinja
Hrvatska Dubica
Hrvatska Kesteinica
Greðani Okučanski
Vrbova
Nova Kapela
Map 1
N Varoš
Sičice
Vrbje
Lovčić
St Gradiška
Mačkovac
Štivica
Batrina
Brodski Stupnic
Orubica
Davor
Slav Kobač
A
B
C
BOSNIA AND HERZEGOVINA
1
2
3

HUNGARY
SERBIA
A
B
C
4
5
6
N
10 km
10 miles
Osijek
Vukovar
Vinkovci
Đakovo
Slavonski Brod
Županja
Otok
Borovo
Beli Manastir
Valpovo
D Miholjac
Darda
Bilje
Kopački Nature Park
Kopačevo
Batina
Dali
Erdut
Ilok
Našica
Dobroševica
Udvar
Topolje
Kneževo
Draž
Zmajevac
Branjin Vrh
Suza
Kneževi Vinogradi
Zlatna Greda
Lug
Vardarac
Čeminac
N Čeminac
Grabovac
Švajcernica
Josipovac
Petrijevci
Bizovac
Belišće
Nard
Bolman
Baranjsko-Petrovo Selo
Čepin
Sarvaš
Aljmaš
Ovačara
Ivanovac
Antunovac
Ernestinova
Klisa
Vera
Trpinja
Bobota
Laslovo
Korog
Pačetin
Markušica
Tordinci
Bršadin
Ostrovo
Gaboš
Jarmina
Nuštar
Petrovci
Sotin
Negoslavci
Opatovac
Šarengrad
Bapska
Tovarnik
Orolik
Stari Jankovci
Mirkovci
Slakovci
Komletinci
Privlaka
Cerna
Andrijaševci
Rokovci
Gradište
Babina Greda
Podgrađe
Apševci
Lipovac
Bošnjaci
Podgajci Posavski
Soljani
Rajevo Selo
Drenovci
Gunja
Račinovci
St Mikanovci
Budrovci
Strizivojna
Vrpolje
Gundinci
V Kopanica
Sredanci
Garčin
Oprisavci
Kuti Trnjanski
Donja Peprrina
D Andrijevci
Trnjani
Podvinsko
Bukovlje
Klokočevl
Podcrkavlje
Trnava
Kondrić
Selci Đakovačka
Satnica Đakovačka
Viškovci
Koševac
Semeljci
Kesinci
Koritna
Široke Polje
Hrastin
Vuka
Vladislavci
Cepinski Martinci
Gorjani
Budimci
Lavanjska Varoš
Ruševo
Podgorač
Gradac
Lug Suboticki
Vučkovac
Koška
Harkanovci
Breznica Našicka
Markova Našički
Jelisavac
D Motičina
Đurđenovac
Klokočevci
Bokšić
Benicanci
Sljivoševci
Magadenovac
Marijanci
Čmkovci
Miholjačk Poreč
Kapelna
Rakitovica
Svali Đurad
Donje
Vilijevo

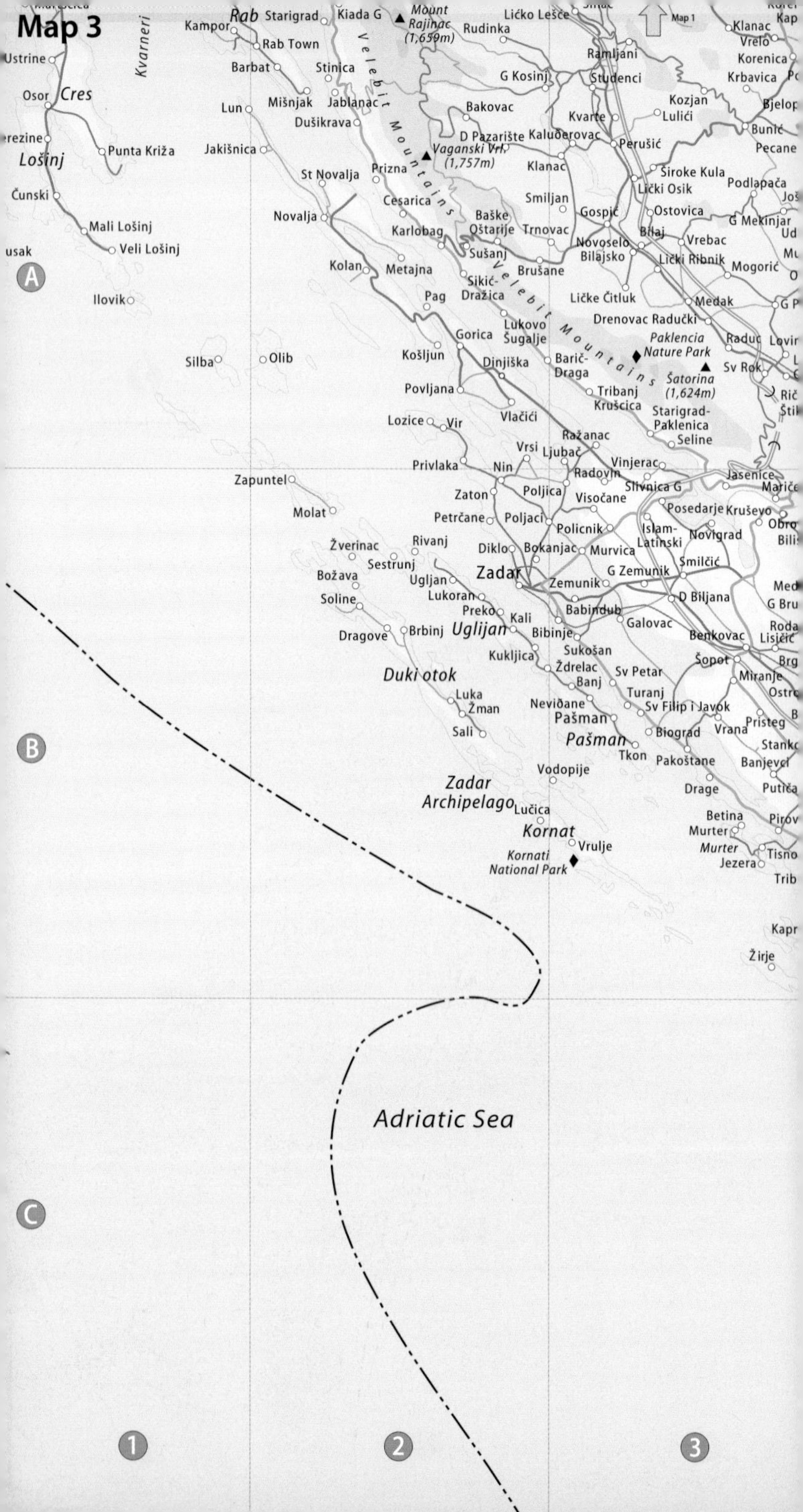

Map 3
Map 1
Kvarneri
Ustrine
Osor
Cres
Lošinj
Punta Križa
Čunski
Mali Lošinj
Veli Lošinj
Ilovik
Rab
Kampor
Starigrad
Rab Town
Barbat
Lun
Mišnjak
Jakišnica
Stinica
Jablanac
Dušikrava
Kiada G
Mount Rajinac (1,659m)
Velebit Mountains
Vaganski Vrh (1,757m)
Rudinka
Ličko Lešće
G Kosinj
Bakovac
D Pazarište
Kaluđerovac
Kvarte
Ramljani
Studenci
Perušić
Kozjan
Lulići
Klanac
Vrelo
Korenica
Krbavica
Bunić
Pecane
Široke Kula
Lički Osik
Podlapača
Ostovica
G Mekinjar
Smiljan
Gospić
Bilaj
Vrebac
Lički Ribnik
Mogorić
Novoselo Bilajsko
St Novalja
Prizna
Cesarica
Novalja
Karlobag
Baške Oštarije
Trnovac
Sušanj
Brušane
Kolan
Metajna
Pag
Sikić-Dražica
Ličke Čitluk
Medak
Drenovac Radučki
Lukovo Šugalje
Gorica
Košljun
Paklencia Nature Park
Raduč
Lovin
Sv Rok
Šatorina (1,624m)
Silba
Olib
Dinjiška
Barič-Draga
Povljana
Tribanj Kruščica
Starigrad-Paklenica
Seline
Vlačići
Lozice
Vir
Ražanac
Vrsi
Ljubač
Vinjerac
Privlaka
Nin
Radovin
Jasenice
Maslenica
Zapuntel
Slivnica G
Zaton
Poljica
Visočane
Molat
Posedarje
Kruševo
Petrčane
Poljaci
Policnik
Islam-Latinski
Novigrad
Rivanj
Žverinac
Sestrunj
Diklo
Bokanjac
Murvica
Smilčić
Božava
Zadar
G Zemunik
Ugljan
Zemunik
D Biljana
Soline
Lukoran
Preko
Babindub
Kali
Galovac
Dragove
Brbinj
Uglijan
Bibinje
Benkovac
Lisičić
Kukljica
Sukošan
Šopot
Dugi otok
Ždrelac
Sv Petar
Banj
Miranje
Turanj
Luka
Žman
Neviđane
Sv Filip i Jakov
Vrana
Pristeg
Pašman
Sali
Biograd
Pašman
Tkon
Pakoštane
Banjevci
Vodopije
Zadar Archipelago
Drage
Lučica
Betina
Kornat
Murter
Vrulje
Murter
Tisno
Kornati National Park
Jezera
Žirje
Adriatic Sea
A
B
C
1
2
3

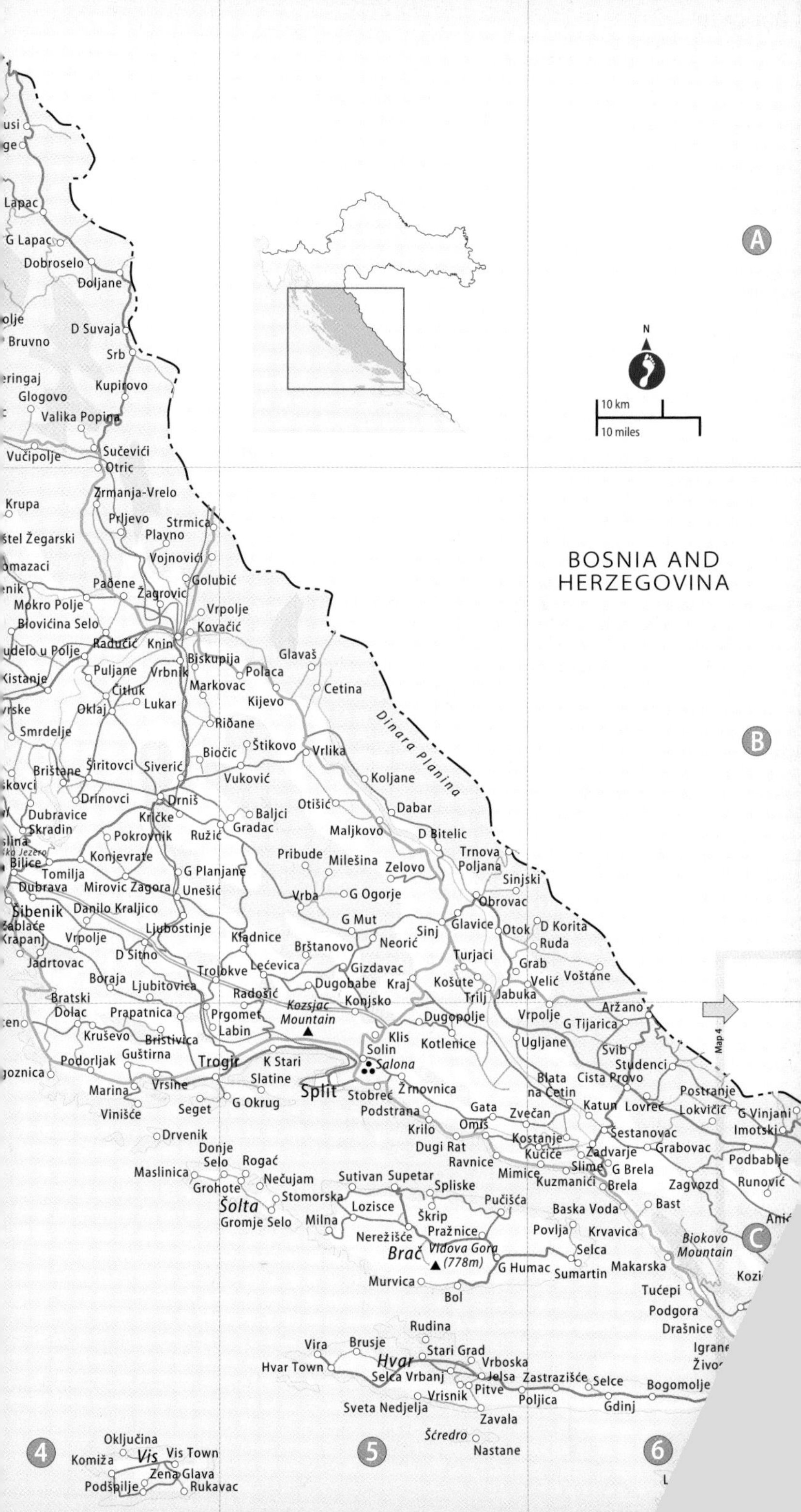

BOSNIA AND HERZEGOVINA
A
B
C
4
5
6
N
10 km
10 miles
Map 4
Dinara Planina
Kozsjac Mountain
Biokovo Mountain
Vidova Gora (778m)
Lapac
G Lapac
Dobroselo
Đoljane
Bruvno
D Suvaja
Srb
Kupirovo
Glogovo
Valika Popina
Vučipolje
Sučevići
Otric
Zrmanja-Vrelo
Krupa
Prljevo
Strmica
Plavno
Vojnovići
Golubić
Pađene
Žagrovic
Mokro Polje
Vrpolje
Kovačić
Biovićina Selo
Raduĉić
Knin
Biskupija
Polaca
Glavaš
Puljane
Vrbnik
Markovac
Čitluk
Lukar
Kijevo
Cetina
Oklaj
Riđane
Smrdelje
Biočic
Štikovo
Vrlika
Brištane
Širitovci
Siverić
Vuković
Koljane
Drinovci
Drniš
Otišić
Dabar
Dubravice
Kričke
Baljci
Skradin
Pokrovnik
Ružić
Gradac
Maljkovo
D Bitelic
Konjevrate
Pribude
Milešina
Zelovo
Trnova Poljana
Bilice
Tomilja
G Planjane
Sinjski
Dubrava
Mirovic Zagora
Unešić
Vrba
G Ogorje
Obrovac
Šibenik
Danilo Kraljico
G Mut
Sinj
Glavice
Otok
D Korita
Žablaće
Ljubostinje
Neorić
Ruda
Krapanj
Vrpolje
Kladnice
Brštanovo
Turjaci
D Sitno
Grab
Jadrtovac
Trolokve
Lećevica
Gizdavac
Voštane
Boraja
Ljubitovica
Dugobabe
Kraj
Košute
Velić
Bratski Dolac
Radošić
Konjsko
Trilj
Jabuka
Aržano
Prapatnica
Prgomet
Dugopolje
Vrpolje
G Tijarica
Kruševo
Labin
Klis
Bristivica
Solin
Kotlenice
Ugljane
Svib
Guštirna
Salona
Studenci
Podorljak
Trogir
K Stari
Blata na Cetin
Cista Provo
Marina
Vrsine
Slatine
Split
Žrnovnica
Postranje
Stobreć
Lokvičić
Vinišće
Seget
G Okrug
Podstrana
Gata
Zvečan
Katun
Lovreć
G Vinjani
Krilo
Omiš
Imotski
Drvenik
Dugi Rat
Kostanje
Šestanovac
Donje Selo
Kučiće
Zadvarje
Grabovac
Rogać
Ravnice
Mimice
Slime
G Brela
Podbablje
Maslinica
Nečujam
Sutivan
Supetar
Kuzmanići
Brela
Zagvozd
Runović
Grohote
Spliske
Stomorska
Pučišća
Bast
Šolta
Lozisce
Baska Voda
Gromje Selo
Milna
Škrip
Povlja
Krvavica
Pražnice
Nerežišće
Selca
Brač
G Humac
Sumartin
Makarska
Murvica
Bol
Tućepi
Podgora
Drašnice
Rudina
Vira
Brusje
Stari Grad
Hvar
Vrboska
Hvar Town
Selca
Vrbanj
Jelsa
Zastrazišće
Selce
Pitve
Bogomolje
Vrisnik
Poljica
Gdinj
Sveta Nedjelja
Zavala
Šćredro
Nastane
Oključina
Komiža
Vis
Vis Town
Zena Glava
Podšpilje
Rukavac

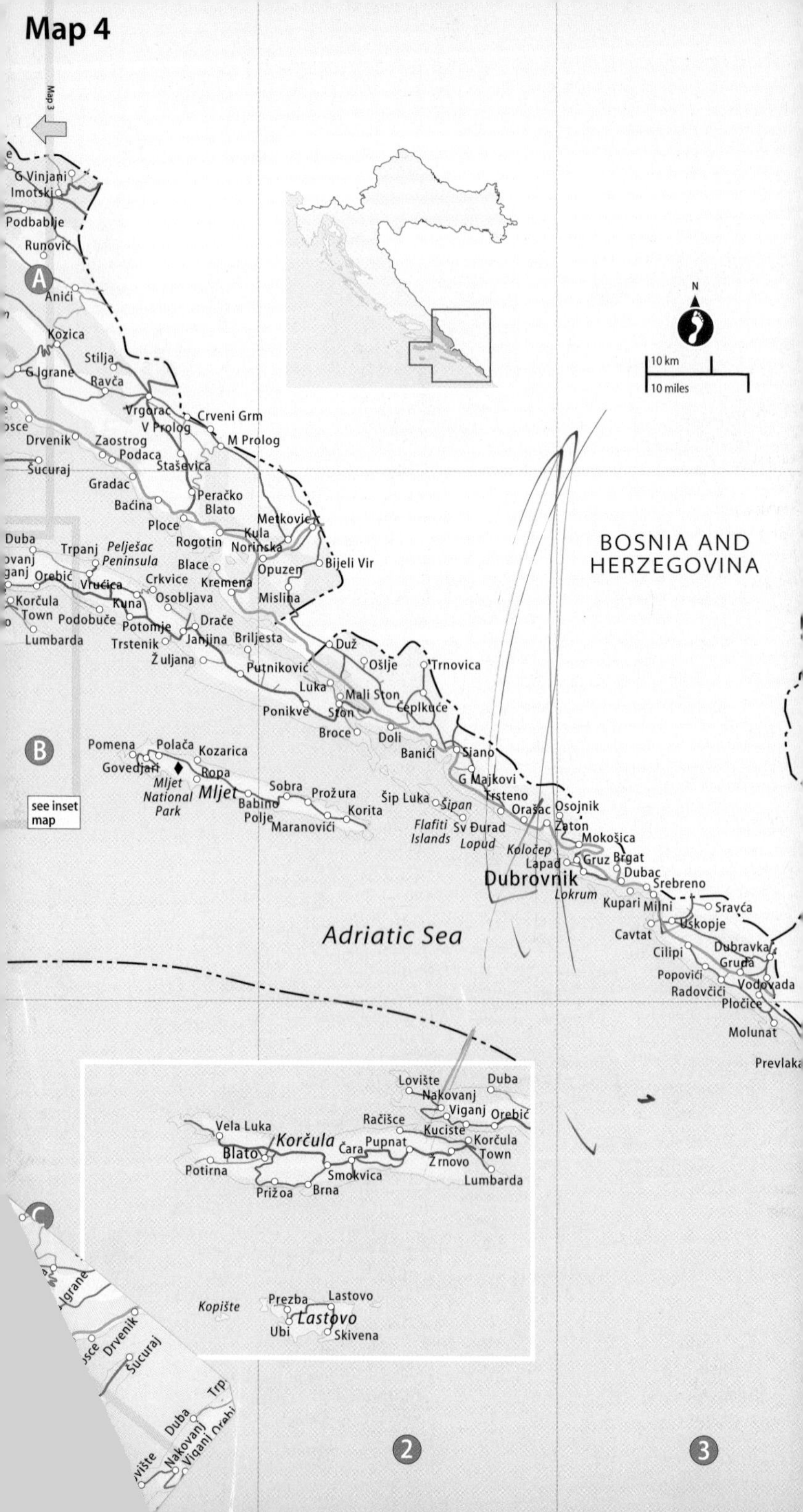
Map 4
Map 3
G Vinjani
Imotski
Podbablje
Runović
A
Anići
Kozica
Stilja
G Igrane
Ravča
Vrgorac
V Prolog
Crveni Grm
M Prolog
Drvenik
Zaostrog
Podaca
Staševica
Šucuraj
Gradac
Peračko
Blato
Baćina
Ploce
Metković
Kula
Norinska
Rogotin
Duba
Trpanj
Pelješac
Peninsula
Blace
Opuzen
Bijeli Vir
Orebić
Vrućica
Crkvice
Kremena
Korčula
Town
Kuna
Osobljava
Mislina
Podobuče
Potomje
Drače
Lumbarda
Trstenik
Janjina
Briljesta
Duž
Žuljana
Putniković
Ošlje
Trnovica
Luka
Mali Ston
Čeplkuće
Ponikve
Ston
Broce
Doli
Banići
Siano
B
Pomena
Polača
Kozarica
Govedjari
Ropa
Mljet
National
Park
Mljet
Sobra
Prožura
see inset
map
Babino
Polje
Korita
Maranovići
Šip Luka
Šipan
Flafiti
Islands
Sv Đurad
Lopud
G Majkovi
Trsteno
Orašac
Osojnik
Zaton
Mokošica
Koločep
Lapad
Gruz
Brgat
Dubac
Dubrovnik
Lokrum
Srebreno
Kupari
Milni
Sravća
Uskopje
Cavtat
Adriatic Sea
Cilipi
Dubravka
Gruda
Popovići
Radovčići
Vodovada
Pločice
Molunat
Prevlaka
BOSNIA AND
HERZEGOVINA
N
10 km
10 miles
Lovište
Duba
Nakovanj
Viganj
Orebić
Vela Luka
Račišce
Kuciste
Korčula
Korčula
Town
Blato
Čara
Pupnat
Žrnovo
Potirna
Smokvica
Lumbarda
Prižoa
Brna
C
Kopište
Prezba
Lastovo
Lastovo
Ubi
Skivena
2
3